The Correspondence of
Jonathan Swift

JONATHAN SWIFT

From the portrait by Jervas in the National Portrait Gallery

The Correspondence of
Jonathan Swift

EDITED BY

HAROLD WILLIAMS

VOLUME III

1724–1731

OXFORD
AT THE CLARENDON PRESS

Oxford University Press, Ely House, London W. 1
GLASGOW NEW YORK TORONTO MELBOURNE WELLINGTON
CAPE TOWN SALISBURY IBADAN NAIROBI LUSAKA ADDIS ABABA
BOMBAY CALCUTTA MADRAS KARACHI LAHORE DACCA
KUALA LUMPUR HONG KONG

FIRST PUBLISHED 1963
REPRINTED, WITH CORRECTIONS, 1965

PRINTED IN GREAT BRITAIN

CONTENTS

VOLUME III

VOLUME IV

VOLUME V

LIST OF LETTERS

Correspondents	*Date*	*Place*	*Original source*	*Printed source or transcript*	*Page*
S. to Charles Ford	29 Dec. 1724	Dublin	Rothschild		45
S. to Charles Ford	31 Dec. 1724	,,	Rothschild		45
S. to Thomas Staunton	5 Jan. 1725	,,	B.M. Add. 38671		47
S. to Knightley Chetwode	18 Jan. 1725	,,		Forster copy	48
S. to Knightley Chetwode	30 Jan. 1725	,,		Forster copy	49
S. to Knightley Chetwode	20 Feb. 1725	,,		Forster copy	50
S. to Charles Ford	1 Mar. 1725	,,	Rothschild		52
S. to Charles Ford	11 Mar. 1725	,,	Rothschild		52
S. to Mrs. Pratt	18 Mar. 1725	,,	Harvard College Library		53
S. to James Stopford	(?) Apr. 1725	,,		Forster copy	56
S. to Lord Carteret	17 Apr. 1725	,,	Tickell Papers		57
S. to Knightley Chetwode	(?) April 1725	,,		Forster copy	58
S. to Rev. Stafford Lightburne	22 Apr. 1725	Quilca		*Kilkenny Archaeological Society Journal*	59
S. to Knightley Chetwode	27 May 1725	,,		Forster copy	60
S. to Rev. James Stopford	19 June 1725	,,		Forster copy	62
S. to Rev. Thomas Sheridan	25 June 1725	,,		Dodsley *Miscellanies* 1745	63
S. to — Sheridan	26 June 1725	,,	Library, Armagh		65
S. to Rev. Thomas Sheridan	28 June 1725	,,		Dodsley *Miscellanies* 1745	66
S. to Rev. Thomas Sheridan	29 June 1725	,,	National Library, Dublin		68
S. to Lord Carteret	3 July 1725	,,		Dodsley *Miscellanies* 1745	70
S. to Archdeacon Walls	9 July 1725	,,	Rothschild		72
S. to Rev. John Worrall	9 July 1725	,,		Hawkesworth 1766	74
S. to Knightley Chetwode	19 July 1725	,,		Forster copy	75
S. to Thomas Tickell	19 July 1725	,,		Tickell Letter-Book No. 2	76
S. to Pope	19 July 1725	,,		Longleat xiii (Harleian transcript)	78
S. to — Sheridan	22 July 1725	,,	Library, Armagh		79
S. to Rev. Anthony Raymond	23 July 1725	,,		*Dublin Magazine* 1762	80
Viscount Bolingbroke to S.	24 July 1725	London	B.M. Add. 4805		81
E. of Oxford to S.	26 July 1725	London		Deane Swift 1768	83

Correspondents	*Date*	*Place*	*Original source*	*Printed source or transcript*	*Page*
S. to Rev. Thomas Wallis	8 Apr. 1727	Dublin		Duncombe 1772	205
'Richard Sympson' to Benjamin Motte	27 Apr. 1727	Twickenham	Morgan Library		206
S. to Rev. Thomas Sheridan	13 May 1727	London		Dodsley *Miscellanies* 1745	206
S. to E. of Oxford	13 May 1727	Whitehall	Portland MSS. Harley Papers		208
S. to E. of Oxford	18 May 1727	Twickenham	Portland MSS. Harley Papers		209
S. to Archbishop King	18 May 1727	,,		Deane Swift 1768	209
Viscount Bolingbroke to S.	18 May 1727	Dawley	B.M. Add. 4805		211
Archbishop King to S.	3 June 1727	Dublin		T.C.D. Letter-Book	212
Viscount Bolingbroke to S.	6 June 1727	Dawley	B.M. Add. 4805		212
Viscount Bolingbroke to S.	11 June 1727	,,	B.M. Add. 4805		213
Voltaire to S.	16 June 1727	London	B.M. Add. 4805		214
Viscount Bolingbroke to S.	17 June 1727	Twickenham	B.M. Add. 4805		215
Viscount Bolingbroke to S.	(?) 20 June 1727	Cranford	B.M. Add. 4805		216
L'Abbé Des Fontaines to S.	4 July [o.s. 23 June] 1727	Paris	B.M. Add. 4805		217
S. to Rev. Thomas Sheridan	24 June 1727	London		Dodsley *Miscellanies* 1745	218
S. to Mrs. Howard	June 1727	(?) London	B.M. Add. 22625		220
S. to Rev. Thomas Sheridan	1 July 1727	Twickenham		Dodsley *Miscellanies* 1745	220
S. to Mrs. Howard	9 July 1727	,,	B.M. Add. 22625		223
Viscount Bolingbroke to S.	(?) July 1727	(?) Dawley	B.M. Add. 4805		224
Andrew Ramsay to S.	1 Aug. [o.s. 21 July] 1727	Paris	B.M. Add. 4805		225
S. to L'Abbé Des Fontaines	July 1727	(?) Twickenham	B.M. Add. 4805		225
S. to Mrs. Drelincourt	7 Aug. 1727	Twickenham	National Library of Scotland		227
S. to Rev. Thomas Sheridan	12 Aug. 1727	,,		Dodsley *Miscellanies* 1745	228
S. to Mrs. Howard	14 Aug. 1727	,,	B.M. Add. 22625		230
Mrs. Howard to S.	16 Aug. 1727	Richmond	B.M. Add. 4805		231

Correspondents	Date	Place	Original source	Printed source or transcript	Page
S. to Knightley Chetwode	15 Mar. 1729	Dublin		Forster copy	317
William Flower to S.	18 Mar. 1729	Ashbrook		Deane Swift 1768	318
S. to Charles Ford	18 Mar. 1729	Dublin	Rothschild		320
John Gay to S.	18 Mar. 1729	London	B.M. Add. 4805		322
John Arbuthnot to S.	19 Mar. 1729	,,	B.M. Add 4805		325
Quaker's letter to S.	29 Mar. 1729	Philadelphia	Forster No. 563		327
Lady Johnson to S.	30 Mar. 1729	—		Deane Swift 1768	327
S. to Viscount Bolingbroke and Pope	5 Apr. 1729	Dublin		Faulkner 1741	328
Andrew Ramsay to S.	10 Apr. 1729	London	B.M. Add. 4805		331
John Arbuthnot to S.	8 May 1729	,,	B.M. Add. 4805		332
S. to Knightley Chetwode	17 May 1729	Dublin		Forster copy	333
S. to E. of Burlington	22 May 1729	,,		Elrington Ball	334
S. to Lady Catherine Jones	22 May 1729	,,		Elrington Ball	335
S. to Countess of Holderness	22 May 1729	,,		Elrington Ball	336
John Arbuthnot to S.	9 June 1729	London	B.M. Add. 4805		337
Lady Catherine Jones to S.	11 June 1729	Chelsea	B.M. Add. 4805		338
S. to Knightley Chetwode	9 Aug. 1729	Market Hill		Forster copy	339
S. to Pope	11 Aug. 1729	,,		Faulkner 1741	340
S. to Knightley Chetwode	30 Aug. 1729	,,		Forster copy	342
S. to Rev. James Stopford	30 Aug. 1729	,,		Forster transcript	344
Knightley Chetwode to S.	10 Sept. 1729	Woodbrooke		Forster copy	344
Viscount Bolingbroke to S.	30 [o.s. 19] Aug. 1729	Aix-la-Chapelle	B.M. Add. 4805		347
Pope to S.	9 Oct. 1729	Twickenham		Faulkner 1741	351
Knightley Chetwode to S.	25 Oct. 1729	(?) Woodbrooke		Forster copy	352
S. to Viscount Bolingbroke	11 Oct. 1729	Dublin		Longleat xiii, f. 123	353
S. to Pope	31 Oct. 1729	,,		Faulkner 1741	355
John Gay to S.	9 Nov. 1729	Middleton Stoney	B.M. Add. 4806		356
Viscount Bolingbroke to S.	19 Nov. 1729	(?) Dawley		Longleat xiii, f. 124	358
S. to John Gay	20 Nov. 1729	Dublin		Longleat xiii, ff. 125–6	359
Pope to S.	28 Nov. 1729	Twickenham		Faulkner 1741	362
S. to Robert Percival	11 Dec. 1729	Dublin	B.M. Add. 38671		365

Correspondents	*Date*	*Place*	*Original source*	*Printed source or transcript*	*Page*
Gay and Duchess of Queensberry to S.	8 Nov. 1730	Amesbury	B.M. Add. 4806		414
S. to John Gay	10 Nov. 1730	Dublin		Longleat xiii (Harleian transcript)	416
S. to E. of Chesterfield	10 Nov. 1730	,,		Deane Swift 1765	419
S. to John Gay and Duchess of Queensberry	19 Nov. 1730	,,		Longleat xiii (Harleian transcript)	420
S. to Mrs. Howard	21 Nov. 1730	,,	B.M. Add. 22625		422
S. to Mrs. Caesar	3 Dec. 1730	,,	T. Cottrell-Dormer		425
E. of Chesterfield to S.	15 Dec. [o.s. 4] 1730	Hague	B.M. Add. 4806		426
Gay and Duchess of Queensberry to S.	6 Dec. 1730	Amesbury	B.M. Add. 4806		427
Lady Elizabeth Germain to S.	24 Dec. 1730	(?) London	B.M. Add. 4806		429
S. to Mrs. Whiteway	28 Dec. 1730	Dublin		Deane Swift 1768	431
S. to E. of Chesterfield	5 Jan. 1731	,,		Deane Swift 1765	431
S. to Samuel Gerrard	6 Jan. 1731	,,		Scott 1814	433
S. to Pope	15 Jan. 1731	,,		Longleat (Portland Papers)	434
Viscount Bolingbroke to S.	(?) 17 Jan. 1731	Dawley		Faulkner 1741	437
William Pulteney to S.	9 Feb. 1731	London	B.M. Add. 4806		438
S. to Mrs. Barber	23 Feb. 1731	Dublin	Rothschild		439
Lady Elizabeth Germain to S.	23 Feb. 1731	London	B.M. Add. 4806		441
Knightley Chetwode to S.	Feb. 1731	Dublin		Forster copy	442
S. to Gay and Duchess of Queensberry	13 Mar. 1731	,,		Longleat xiii (Harleian transcript)	443
John Gay to S.	20 Mar. 1731	London	B.M. Add. 4806		446
Viscount Bolingbroke and Pope to S.	20 Mar. 1731	,,		Longleat xiii (Harleian transcript)	448
John Gay and Duchess of Queensberry to S.	11 Apr. 1731	Amesbury	B.M. Add. 4806		450
S. to Rev. John Blanchford	16 Apr. 1731	Dublin		Scott 1814	452
Lord Bathurst to S.	19 Apr. 1731	Ritchings	B.M. Add. 4806		453
S. to Pope	20 Apr. 1731	Dublin		Longleat xiii (Harleian transcript)	456
John Gay to S.	27 Apr. 1731	Amesbury	B.M. Add. 4806		459
S. to Knightley Chetwode	8 May 1731	Dublin		Forster copy	461

Correspondents	Date	Place	Original source	Printed source or transcript	Page
S. to Lady Worsley	11 May 1731	Dublin	Rothschild		463
Knightley Chetwode to S.	May 1731	Woodbrooke		Forster copy	465
S. to Rev. Philip Chamberlain	20 May 1731	Dublin	W. R. Le Fanu		468
Lady Elizabeth Germain to S.	5 June 1731	London	B.M. Add. 4806		470
S. to Gay and the Duchess of Queensberry	29 June 1731	Dublin		Longleat xiii (Harleian transcript)	470
S. to Lord Bathurst	17 July 1731	,,		Forster transcript	473
Duchess of Queensberry and Gay to S.	18 July 1731	Amesbury	B.M. Add. 4806		476
S. to Pope	20 July 1731	Dublin		Forster 549	478
S. to Thomas Tickell	20 July 1731	,,	Tickell Papers		481
S. to Countess of Suffolk	27 July 1731	,,	B.M. Add. 22625		482
Viscount Bolingbroke to S.	2 Aug. 1731	Dawley	B.M. Add. 4806		485
S. to Thomas Tickell	Aug. 1731	Dublin	Tickell Papers		491
S. to Gay and Duchess of Queensberry	28 Aug. 1731	Powerscourt		Longleat xiii (Harleian transcript)	492
S. to Mrs. Pilkington	6 Sept. 1731	Dublin		Mrs. Pilkington's *Memoirs*	495
Mrs. Pilkington to S.	6 Sept. 1731	,,		Mrs. Pilkington's *Memoirs*	496
Lady Elizabeth Germain to S.	7 Sept. 1731	Drayton	B.M. Add. 4806		496
Countess of Suffolk to S.	25 Sept. 1731	Hampton Court	B.M. Add. 4806		498
S. to Countess of Suffolk	26 Oct. 1731	Dublin	B.M. Add. 22625		499
Gay and Duke and Duchess of Queensberry to S.	1 Nov. 1731	Amesbury	B.M. Add. 4806		502
Lady Elizabeth Germain to S.	4 Nov. 1731	London	B.M. Add. 4806		504
S. to Gay and Duke and Duchess of Queensberry	1 Dec. 1731	Dublin		Longleat xiii (Harleian transcript)	505
John Gay and Pope to S.	1 Dec. 1731	London		Faulkner 1741	508
S. to Mrs. Fenton	28 Dec. 1731	Dublin	W. R. Le Fanu		511

Forster copy

Swift to Knightley Chetwode

Thursday morning [January 9, 1723–24].
Nine o'clock.

Sir,

I had not your letter till I returned home,[1] and if I had I could not have known what to do. I think you should have attended the Bishop,[2] and pressed him to what I desired in my letter;[3] for I could not speak more urgently nor am able to say much more with him than what I wrote. Mr. Bernard[4] is a favourite of the times, and might have credit with the Attorney General[5] to agree that the thing should be granted, but he lies still, and only leaves you to do that which he can better do himself. I would do six times more than you desire even for a perfect stranger, if he were in distress; but I have turned the matter a thousand times in my thoughts in vain. I believe your wisest friends will think as I do, that the best way will be to move the Secretary in that manner he likes best.[6] I am this moment going to prayers and so remain yours &c.

Forster copy

Swift to Knightley Chetwode

Thursday [January 9, 1723–24].

Sir,

I see nothing wrong in the petition[7] if your friends are satisfied in relation to that part where you mention the differences you have with gentlemen in the country, but others can advise you in that better. I spoke with the Bishop of C[logher] and Dr. Coghill as much as I could think of the other day,[8] and the latter particularly who said he would do all he could, and said it heartily, as did the other. I went abroad yesterday directly from church, and to-day is

[1] Chetwode's letter referred evidently to the last from Swift, who had been again at Quilca during the Christmas vacation, accompanied by Stella and Rebecca Dingley. Cf. Sheridan's poem 'To the Dean of St Patricks' (*Poems*, p. 1039) which belongs to this visit. The original in Sheridan's autograph is in the Huntington Library. [2] i.e. King. [3] To 'soften the Judges'.

[4] Francis Bernard, see ii. 452. [5] John Rogerson.

[6] Presumably to bribe Hopkins, the Duke of Grafton's secretary, with a suitable present. [7] Evidently Chetwode had sent a reply on the same day.

[8] Swift had probably asked them to bring influence to bear on Archbishop King in favour of Chetwode.

the busiest day I have in the year,[1] so that I have hardly time to write this or to think. To-morrow will be likewise a day of business; however, if it be for your service, I will to-morrow at ten find an hour to talk with you. I wish you good success and am &c.

Endorsed: Upon no great business.

Forster copy

Swift to Knightley Chetwode

January 19, 1723–24.

Sir,

I endeavoured once or twice without success to see the Bishop; he was so taken up with the delegates. But it is no great matter. I met an intimate friend of his yesterday, a considerable, who told me, that the Bishop took your affairs to heart, and would attend the Lord Lieutenant with your petition, and take the Solicitor-General[2] with him, and the person who told me these was equally concerned for you, and as I believe he would see the Bishop before me, I pressed him again. He said the Lord Lieutenant he believed went to [Conolly's[3]] yesterday, but would return in a day or two.

I am so much out of order that I could not go to church, and shall have a mixed company with me to-night, so that I cannot encourage you to be among them. I am &c.

Address: To Knightley Chetwode, Esq.

Rothschild

Swift to Charles Ford

Dublin. Jany 19th 1723–4

I had yours with the inclosed from my Sister O—[4] sent me to the Country, which we left last week,[5] and since have been too much

[1] The visitation of his cathedral mentioned specifically in his letter to Ford, 19 Jan. 1723–4.

[2] The Solicitor-General at this time was Thomas Marlay, who had been appointed to that office in 1720. He became Chief Justice of the King's Bench in 1741. It is interesting to note that after Vanessa's death her house at Celbridge became his country residence. See, further, Ball, *Judges in Ireland*, ii. 201.

[3] The name has been copied 'Pearsby' (Birkbeck Hill, p. 139), but ought without doubt to be 'Conolly'. William Conolly, Speaker of the Irish House of Commons, a self-made man, acquired great wealth and political influence. The Duke of Grafton, of whom Conolly was a chief adviser, was often a guest at his residence at Castletown, co. Kildare. For a character-sketch of him see Swift's letter to Gay, 28 Aug. 1731.

[4] The Duchess of Ormonde's letter of 9 Dec. 1723.

[5] To Quilca.

imployed in my Visitation[1] &c. I am now ill of a Cold and therefore at leisure to write; It is a Town Cold got but yesterday, for in the Country we know no such Thing, among good Fare, warm Rooms, and Mirth: all of us well in going residing and returning, without any Accident or other offence than abundance of Dirt and Wit.—So from not finding a Creature here to converse with, you are of a sudden grown so nice, that you cannot bear the Company at the Opera to be fewer than usuall.—I declare I can by no means blame your Choice of living where you do. Cæsar was perhaps in the right, when he said he would rather be the first man in some scurvy Village, than the second in Rome, but it is an infamous Case indeed to be neglected in Dublin when a man may converse with the best Company in London. This Misfortune you are able to fly from, but I am condemned to it for my Life. I am very much pleased and proud of the Kind Remembrance of Ld Ashburnham,[2] Masham, and Mr Bromley, and I beg you will tell them so in the manner you like best. Ld Mans—s Life or Death do not much affect me.[3] The Toryes here have the same wishes and Opinion with relation to Ld Bol—. I am heartily sorry for poor Doctor Arthbuthnot.[4] I think there does not live a better Man. I desire you will present my humble Service to him as well as Mr Pope and Gay if they are come to Town.—M^rs^ J— was much better in the Country,[5] and is at present not so ill as usuall. We had onely some little slight Verses on the Birth-day.[6] Once a year is too much and my Friends will wish me dead to save them Trouble.—In answer to your Important Question, I do assert that in eight days since my Return there have been 6 Deanry Dinners but no Patridge;[7] onely at my Visitation there was a Pheasant. But I design to retrench, and my Wine is so bad, that yesterday I returnd a Hogshead, and two more in Bottles about

[1] Of his cathedral. Referred to previously in his letter to Chetwode of 9 Jan. 1723-4.

[2] The third Lord Ashburnham, created Earl of Ashburnham in 1730; his first wife was a daughter of the Duchess of Ormonde.

[3] Lord Mansell died 10 Dec. 1723.

[4] See Arbuthnot's letter to Swift of 7 Nov. 1723 *ad fin.*

[5] Stella had benefited by her long summer visit to Woodpark in 1723.

[6] His own birthday, 30 Nov. Swift had established the custom by his birthday verses to Stella, 13 Mar. 1719, and subsequent years (*Poems*, pp. 720 ff.). For Swift's birthday verses to Ford, 31 Jan. 1722-3, see *Poems*, pp. 309-15.

[7] Had Ford suggested that there would be partridge? Has this any allusion to the Bickerstaff-Partridge pamphlets?

four days ago. Sheridan is still the same, I mean in the Sense that Weathercocks are still the same. My garlick keeps me from Deafness, and so you know the State of all Things of moment here.—I desire you will present my most humble Respects to my Sister:[1] I will answer her Letter when I think she will require it, but not soon for fear of tiring her, pray tell her This. What can have become of Dean Fairfax's[2] Widow?

Last Night I received the Pacquet franckt *Osborn*. I suppose it is Ld Caemarthen.[3] I was at a Loss about one of the Letters,[4] at first, but after found it was to you, and that you are a Traytor into the Bargain: else how should he know any Thing of Stella or of Horses. Tis hard that Folks in France will not let us in Ireland be quiet. I would have him and you know that I hate Yahoos of both Sexes, and that Stella and Madame de Villette are onely tolerable at best, for want of Houyhnhnms.—I presume the Verses[5] miscarryed four years ago, for I never heard of them till now. He has paraphrased onely the first Part of the Epistle, and wanders in the rest to shew himself an Esprit fort,[6] and I believe that Part of his Poem if it were printed would make his Court to the present People. But his Idea's I hope were borrowed from the Scene he is in, for it seems onely calculated to Popery; But I believe free-thinking is neither Whig nor Tory. There are a great many good Lines, but I think the whole might be more correct. There have been late doings in Parlm^{t} here, which would make much noise if they had passed among You. The Consequence of G. Rochforts missing his Election[7] have sett the two Houses at Variance, and embroyld the Government with a Vengeance. But I look on things here with the same View as I would on Boys at Span-farthing, and you look on them as something less.

[1] The Duchess of Ormonde.

[2] Charles Fairfax, Dean of Down, see ii. 444. He died 27 July 1723.

[3] Peregrine Hyde Osborne, Marquess of Carmarthen; succeeded his father as third Duke of Leeds in 1729.

[4] From Bolingbroke to Ford, dated 25 Dec. 1723. Sent by mistake to Swift. It is printed in the *Letters of Swift to Ford*, ed. Nichol Smith, pp. 238–9.

[5] Bolingbroke's paraphrase of Horace's *Epistle*, i. 1. In his letter to Swift of 25 [O.S. 14] Dec. 1723 he refers to the long epistle in metre sent about four years ago which he had difficulty in finding. Nineteen lines of the paraphrase are in his letter to Swift of 17 [O.S. 6] Mar. 1719.

[6] In his lost letter to Bolingbroke of June 1724 Swift evidently wrote to the same effect, for Bolingbroke in his reply of 12 [O.S. 1] Sept. has a long passage on the term *esprit fort*.

[7] As M.P. for Westmeath. Perhaps 'is to' is omitted after 'Election'.

My greatest want here is of somebody qualifyed to censure and correct what I write, I know not above two or three whose Judgment I would value, and they are lazy, negligent, and without any Opinion of my Abilityes. I have left the Country of Horses, and am in the flying Island, where I shall not stay long, and my two last Journyes will be soon over;[1] so that if you come here this Summer you will find me returnd—adieu—

Address: To Charles Ford Esqr, at | his Lodgings at the blue | Perewig in Pell-mell | London

Postmarks: Dublin *and* 27 IA

Rothschild

Swift to Charles Ford

Dublin. Feb. 13th 1723–4

I had yours of Janry 28th. I think you and I do not correspond on an equall Foot, for I who am reach[2] pay nothing for your Letters, which are good for something, you who are poor pay something for my Letters which are good for nothing. However when I write to Ld B— I would be glad you would tell me how I might direct them to a Member of either House, for then I shall save you a Summ worth Saving. You are mistaken in our Cub; Bad ways, abundance of Dirt and wit, ill Lodgings, worse meat, and good wine contribute to our Health. Mrs J— returns to her old rate for want of Steel, walking, Country Air, Don Carlos,[3] and Pontack.—I can not tell whether I shall see you in the Spring, for I am afraid our Farthings[4] will not pass in and we are daily threatned with them. If they pass, they will bring you English men with Irish Estates, hither with a Vengeance. Aliquisque malo fuit usus in illo.[5]—The Letter to you is

[1] An important allusion to *Gulliver's Travels*, proving that the Fourth Part, the 'Voyage to the Houyhnhnms', was written by 1723, and that the Third Part, the 'Voyage to Laputa', though it incorporates earlier portions, belongs in the main to 1724.

[2] A phonetic spelling or a slip.

[3] Charles Ford.

[4] This is the first reference in Swift's correspondence to Wood's halfpence. The first Drapier's letter was written in Feb. 1723–4. Two thousand copies were distributed in March. See *Drapier's Letters*, ed. Herbert Davis, pp. lxx, lxxxi–lxxxii.

[5] Ovid, *Metam.* ii. 332; repeated by Swift in his letter to Ford of 2 Apr.

separate, if it be to you as I suppose.[1] He thanks you for the few Lines added by you to the Letter I sent him, raillyes me upon my Southern Journey, says, and swears it is no Pun, That Stella fixed my Course, talks of the Houyhnhnms as if he were acquainted with him,[2] and in that shows you as a most finished Traitor, for which you make very indifferent Excuses. He says he knows nothing of returning: if permitted he will, otherwise resolves to retire to his Hermitage and ends with 3 Latin Lines of Cleanthes: I know not whence he got them.[3] I shall see the rest when I see you. Why will they not give poor Gay an Employment. Tis a wofull Case to be under the necessity of writing a Play for Bread when perhaps a Mans Genius is not at that time disposed.[4] I am sure it is an ill way of making a good Poet,—anxie[ta]te carens animus facit, omnis acerbi impatiens[5]—and if Philips hath as many Friends he may get a thousand Pound too.[6] My poor Friend Arthbuthnot I heartily pity, and would purchase his Health with the half of my Kingdom. I am not assez endurcy to bear the account of the Dragon's Condition, quantum distabat ab illo.[7]—I do not understand as Raillery what you say upon the Court of the Musical Academy.[8] I believe it concerns you nearer at present than Politicks, for these are desperate, but the other was your old Inclination, and is neither Whig nor Tory.—L[d]

[1] The letter of 25 Dec. from Bolingbroke. See previous letter. The accuracy of the description shows that Swift had not yet passed it on to Ford. The 'Southern Journey' is *Gulliver's Travels*.

[2] A mistake for 'them'. Bolingbroke could have heard of the Houyhnhnms only from Ford.

[3] Either directly from Seneca, *Ep.* XVIII. iv (107), or more probably from Cudworth's *Intellectual System*, 1678, p. 432. A copy of this work was at one time in Swift's library. The Latin lines are Seneca's, from the *Hymn to Zeus* of Cleanthes.

[4] Gay's tragedy, *The Captives*, had just been produced at Drury Lane.

[5] Juvenal, *Sat.* vii. 57.

[6] Gay had made £1,000 by his collected *Poems*, two volumes quarto, 1720. Hugh Boulter was made Archbishop of Armagh in Aug. 1724, and in Nov. took Philips with him to Ireland as secretary. Philips may have contemplated a collected edition of his writings.

[7] Lord Oxford had been in failing health. He died 21 May. 'Quantum mutatus ab illo', *Aeneid*, ii. 274.

[8] The Court of Directors of the Royal Academy of Music, which was formed for the performance of Handel's operas, had its first season in 1720; see Burney, *History of Music*, 1789, iv. 258 ff. The previous letter shows that Ford had been attending these performances. The satirical passage on music in the 'Voyage to Laputa', chap. ii, was written about this time.

Peterborows Gallantry[1] is exactly of a Size with the whole Tenor of his Life, onely in complyance to his Age he seeks to make a Noise without the Fatigue of travelling, though he will be less[2] able to perform his present Journy than any of his past. He neither moves my Joy Pity nor Sorrow. I apply to Him what Garth said to me of Ld Wharton; A fine Gentleman I vow to God, but he wants Probity. Our Fools here are repining like yours upon the K. of Spains Action,[3] and I judged as you do, onely I call Devotion what you wicked Laymen call Stupidity.—I hope Ld Caermarthen[s] Son is well, and then I care not whom he marryes.[4] L^dy^ M— had not the Kindness to write to me, and I am mortifyed at it, considering what a Letter I wrote to her,[5] pray tell My L^d^ this. I never received Mr Fairfax's Letter, nor know which of the Brothers writt.[6] I send a Person to get the Box,[7] if it be mended you must pay him; if not, you are desired to get it mended, unless you think it an unwholesom Office, because one Man dyed in it. Your People are well, but Mrs Ford had lately a great Cold—Adieu. If the Box be to be mended, the Manner and fancy are left to You.

Address: To Charles Ford Esqr, | at the blue Perewig in | Pell-mell | London
Postmarks: Dublin *and* 24 FE

4805 *Lady Masham to Swift*

[February 1723–4]

Dear Sr

Tis impossible for you to imagine with what satisfaction I receiv'd your kind letter,[8] and tho I had been soe long without hearing from you I cou'd never impute it to want of friendship in one whose

[1] In punishing Senesino, the leading tenor, for insulting Anastasia Robinson. He was forced to confess on his knees that she was a paragon of virtue and beauty.

[2] 'less' after 'worse' obliterated.

[3] Philip V of Spain abdicated on 14 Jan. 1724 in favour of his eldest son Louis.

[4] Cf. the previous letter. Carmarthen's first wife, Elizabeth, daughter of the Earl of Oxford, had died in childbed in 1713, leaving a son who succeeded his father as fourth Duke of Leeds. Carmarthen married for the third time in 1725.

[5] Lady Masham's reply, the following letter, was received seven days later.

[6] See previous letter, p. 4, n. 2.

[7] Stella's snuff-box, as Swift's next letter to Ford, 2 Apr., shows.

[8] It was probably Arbuthnot's letter of Nov. 1723 which had induced Swift to write to Lady Masham, apparently the first letter he had addressed to her since 1714. This letter is lost. She took longer to reply than he expected. See his letter to Ford, 13 Feb.

goodness to me has allway's been abundantly more then I cou'd deserve; I had writt often to you but haveing noe safe conveyance chose rather to enquire after your health and welfare of some people that cou'd give me an account of it; and I doe assure you from the bottom of my heart there is not a person living I have a greater friendship for then your self and shall have to the end of my life; indeed now I can show it only in expressions but I flatter my self you believe e'm sincere; I long to see you att my retir'd habittation[1] where you will meet with a most heartty wellcome and faithfull friends and none more soe then her who is yr | most Affectionate | humble servant | H[2] Masham

My lord children Brother & sister are yr humble servants

Address: To | The Reverend Dr Swift | Dean of St Patricks | at his House in | Dublin

Endorsed by Swift: Rx Feb. | 20th 1723–4 *and again with the same date, and again,* Ldy Masham

Postmark injured.

The letter is headed in another hand: 'Lady Masham to Dr Swift | Endorsed Feb. 20 1723/4'

Forster 543

Swift to Bishop Stearne

My Lord [28 February 1723–4]

If you do not appoint to morrow,[3] Monday, Tuesday, Wednesday, or Thursday to dine at the Deanry with the odd Clubb of the Walls and Ladyes;[4] I believe there may be a Mutiny; therefore pray fix the Matter for your own Sake I am Y^r^ Lordships | most dutifull | Jonath Swift

Deanry-house | Feb^r^ 28th 1723–4

Address: To | the Right Reverend | the Lord Bishop of Clogher
Endorsed by Stearne(?): Feb. 28. 1723–4.

[1] Lady Masham evidently had difficulty with the spelling of 'habitation'. She refers to the manor of Langley, near Slough, which her husband bought from Sir Edward Seymour in 1714, and sold in 1738 (about four years after the death of his wife) to Charles, second Duke of Marlborough.

[2] The letter certainly reads as an 'H'. Hawkesworth has 'H'; but Lady Masham's Christian name was Abigail.

[3] Swift was writing on Friday.

[4] Archdeacon and Mrs. Walls, Stella and Rebecca Dingley. Swift was carrying his thoughts back to gatherings at least fifteen years old. See his letter to Walls of 9 Nov. 1708 *ad fin.* Ball prints 'lodges' for 'Ladyes'.

Rothschild

Swift to Charles Ford

Dublin. Apr. 2d 1724

Before I could find time to answer your Letter, I fell into a cruell Disorder that kept me in Torture for a Week, and confined me 2 more to my Chamber, but I am now rid of it, onely left very weak, the Learned call it the Hæmorrhoides internæ which with the attendance of Strangury, loss of Blood, water-gruel and no sleep require more of the Stoick than I am Master of, to support it. You are a Stranger to sickness and not a judge pour nous autres maladifs. These frequent Disorders are the onely discouragement from venturing so far as England from the Smoak of my Chimney. Mrs J— rejoyces at her Snuffbox, but thinks as I do that it is sufficiently dear, especially when there is onely a new Bottom, wherein however we hope you are mistaken because the old Bottom had a single Fly studded on it, but the lid was raised and inlayd all over; and you see nothing how it is now. Pray buy a little wooden Box lined, to put it in, and when we hear of somebody coming over, (for you we do not expect) they shall be desired to call on you for it, and pay you, which I believe will be reasonable, for it will keep you two days longer. Mrs J— is grown a Walker. She read that part of your Letter with the Drs Advice, but is[1] not yet resumed Steel. I came just now from a Commission with the Chancellor[2] ArchBp Dublin &c. I spoke very severely to the knaves about the Farthings. I told them the Baseness and pusilanimity when they and others were sent for by the Lt[3] upon that Subject[4] they all talked as much against the Thing as I. but People are more in fear than ever. I do not know whether I told you that I sent out a small Pamphlet under the Name of a Draper,[5] laying the whole Vilany open, and advising People what to do; about 2000 of them have been dispersd by Gentlemen in severall Parts of the Country, but one can promise nothing from

[1] Perhaps Swift intended 'has'. The slips in this letter suggest that he had not well recovered from his recent disorder.

[2] Viscount Midleton.

[3] Duke of Grafton, Lord-Lieutenant.

[4] Syntax defective.

[5] The first Drapier's letter. *A Letter to the Shop-Keepers, Tradesmen, Farmers, and Common-People of Ireland, Concerning the Brass Half-pence Coined by Mr. Woods . . . By M. B. Drapier.*

such Wretches as the Irish People. if this Destructive business brings you over, aliquisque malo fuit usus in illo. In spight of your way of refining, I am ever out of humor when I leave a Place where I am easy to go to a more disagreeable one; and if I were in Jayl I would not be set at Liberty for a Week if I could. A little Business comes in my Head. There are about thirty of Priors Poems (or somewhat more) that the Subscribers will not call for, neither can I get People to take them even for a single Guinnea.[1] I have been tired and vexed enough with this Matter and I fear Ld Harley and Mr Drift[2] may think I have been negligent; but I believe you will be my Witness to the contrary. I beg you will tell Mr Drift this, or Ld Harley if you see him; and desire to know what I must do. I have about 14 or 15 Guinneas to remitt, but God knows whether I shall get any more. I will return the remaining Copyes if they think fit, and let the Subscribers be hanged, and the few Guinneas shall be remitted when they please. I think I offered them to you, but did not blame you from[3] excusing your charging your self with them. Pray set this Matter right, you know what Ireland is.—It is said the L^t^ stays here purely to keep as long in as he can.[4] Bolton[5] has got a better Bishoprick and is succeeded by a poor [har]mless obscure Creature of Conollyes,[6] but they say an honest good natured Man. My humble service to Dr Arbuthnot Mr Pope and Gay. I sometimes think,[7] D. Wharton intends to take my Advice of fancying to have Virtue. I remember Mrs Bracegirdle got more by acting that Part than any of the more abandoned Playhouse females, there is a sort of a Contrast in it. I saw a long printed Speech of his, and intend to borrow it when I can.[8] I never had Mr Gay's works;[9] but thank him

[1] Subscriptions for Prior's volume.

[2] Prior's secretary. Harley was Prior's principal executor.

[3] Query 'for'.

[4] Grafton received official confirmation that he was succeeded as Lord-Lieutenant by Carteret on 9 Apr. and left Dublin on 8 May.

[5] Theophilus Bolton, transferred to Bishopric of Elphin. The 'obscure creature' was Arthur Price, Dean of Ferns.

[6] William Conolly, Speaker of the Irish Parliament.

[7] Manuscript—'I am sometimes think'.

[8] The Duke of Wharton spoke in favour of Atterbury in the House of Lords on 22 May 1723, on the third reading of the Bill of Pains and Penalties. The third edition of the speech was advertised in Feb. 1724. It was afterwards added to editions of *The True Briton*.

[9] 'Why have not I your works?' wrote Swift to Gay, 8 Jan. 1722–3, expecting a presentation copy.

kindly however. I saw your Family in good health 2 days ago. There are good Lodgings in Dawson Street, since you are turned out of your old ones.—I shall have finished my Travells very soon if I have Health, Leisure, and humor. Robin Copes[1] Lady and Family are come to Town to Live, and Mr Cope is soon expected. He will serve for one Night to you in a Week. I see Corbet[2] often, and I believe he will prove ad unguem factus homo.[3] You are too good a prophet about Ld Bol— for we hear nothing of his beeing recalled. Pray bring over with you a printed List of the House of Lords, for I long mightily to see the Names of so many new ones in this happy Reign. L^{dy} Granard dyed yesterday, which will add 400^{ll} a year to Ld Forbes.[4] Three Fools have lately dyed and made wise wills, the B^{p} of Meath,[5] your Cousin Ld Newton,[6] and Sr J^{on} Rawden.[7]

Address: To Charles Ford Esqr.

Deane Swift 1765

Swift to Lord Carteret

April 28, 1724[8]

My Lord,

Many of the principle persons in this kingdom, distinguished for their loyalty to his present Majesty,[9] hearing that I had the honour

[1] Robert Cope of Loughgall and his family.

[2] Francis Corbet, Prebendary of St. Patrick's, Swift's successor (after Maturin) as Dean, 1746. He was one of Stella's executors.

[3] Horace, *Sat.* I. v. 32.

[4] Viscount Forbes, son of the Earl of Granard, whom he succeeded as third Earl in 1734.

[5] John Evans, Bishop of Meath, Swift's enemy, died 2 Mar. 1723–4. He bequeathed his property in England, Wales, and Ireland for the benefit of the poorer clergy of the respective countries.

[6] Theophilus Butler, Lord Newtown-Butler, died 11 Mar. 1723–4. He bequeathed '£13 per annum to be distributed in bread at five shillings each week' to the poor of St. Ann's parish, Dublin.

[7] Sir John Rawdon, of Moira, third baronet, died 2 Feb. His will disappeared in the destruction of the Irish Record Office, and no copy of it is in the possession of the Commissioners of Charitable Donations and Bequests.

[*For notes 8, 9 see overleaf.*

to be known to your Excellency, have for some time pressed me very earnestly, since you were declared Lord-Lieutenant of this kingdom, to represent to your Excellency the apprehensions they are under concerning Mr. Wood's patent for coining halfpence to pass in Ireland. Your Excellency knows the unanimous sentiments of the parliament here upon that matter: And, upon enquiry, you will find that there is not one person of any rank or party, in this whole kingdom, who does not look upon that patent as the most ruinous project that ever was contrived against any nation. Neither is it doubted, that when your Excellency shall be thoroughly informed, your justice and compassion for an injured people will force you to employ your credit for their relief.

I have made bold to send you enclosed two small tracts on this subject; one written (as it is supposed) by the Earl of Abercorn;[1] the other is entitled to a Weaver, and suited to the vulgar, but thought to be the work of a better hand.[2]

I hope your Excellency will forgive an old humble servant, and

[1] The pamphlet may have been *The True State of the Case Between The Kingdom of Ireland of the One Part, and of Mr. William Wood Of the Other Part. By a Protestant of Ireland*, 1724. Cf. Davis, *Drapier's Letters*, pp. xxvii, 355.

[2] Swift's first Drapier's Letter.

---

[8] Swift is known to have been in Quilca in Jan. 1724; and he may have been there again in April, for *The Blunders, Deficiencies, and Misfortunes of Quilca* (*Prose Works*, ed. Temple Scott, vii. 73) is dated 'April 20, 1724'. It is, however, very probable that this piece was antedated by twelve months, and that *The Blunders* should really be assigned to 1725, when Swift was at Quilca from April to October engaged in completing *Gulliver's Travels*. See *Poems*, pp. 1034–5.

[9] As early as 22 Aug. 1723 Grafton wrote a confidential letter in his own hand to Walpole expressing his concern at the general consternation aroused by Wood's patent. William Nicholson, Bishop of Derry, wrote in almost stronger terms against the patent to the Archbishop of Canterbury. Swift used no exaggerated language in telling the new Lord-Lieutenant that not only the common people but 'many of the principal persons' of the country were alarmed by the feared effects of Wood's coinage. In Sept. 1723 the Irish House of Commons resolved to present an address to the King setting forth their objections to the patent. At the same time the Lords were more emphatic. See further the Introduction to Herbert Davis's edition of the *Drapier's Letters*. On learning that Lord Carteret had been appointed to supersede Grafton as Lord-Lieutenant Swift, who had learned to know and esteem him from earlier days (*Journal*, pp. 153, 200, 484), wrote to him this letter. Carteret, who took office in Ireland during the height of the turmoil excited by Wood's halfpence, acted with a wisdom which won Swift's sincere regard, as is shown in his correspondence, several poems, and his prose *Vindication of Lord Carteret*. Cf. *Poems*, p. 382.

one who always loved and esteemed you, for interfering in matters out of his province; which he would never have done, if many of the greatest persons here had not, by their importunity, drawn him out of his retirement, to venture giving you a little trouble, in hopes to save their country from utter destruction, for which the memory of your government will be blessed by posterity.

I hope to have the honour of seeing your Excellency here, and do promise neither to be a frequent visiter, nor troublesome solicitor; but ever, with the greatest respect, *&c.*

Address: To His Excellency the Lord Carteret, | Lord-Lieutenant of Ireland.

Deane Swift 1765

Swift to Lord Carteret

June 9th, 1724.[1]

My Lord,

It is above a month since I took the boldness of writing to your Excellency,[2] upon a subject wherein the welfare of this kingdom is highly concerned.

I writ at the desire of several considerable persons here, who could not be ignorant that I had the honour of being well known to you.

I could have wished your Excellency had condescended so far, as to let one of your under-clerks have signified to me that a letter was received.

I have long been out of the world, but have not forgotten what used to pass among those I lived with, while I was in it: And I can

[1] Swift had just returned to Dublin from the installation of Henry Downes as Bishop of Meath in succession to Evans, who had died three months before. Downes was translated from Killala, a bishopric to which he had been appointed directly from England; and like Evans he was strongly of the English interest. Nevertheless, Swift impressed him favourably by his friendliness and civility, and unexpectedly, for he was well aware of the cross-purposes which marked the relationship between Evans and the Dean of St. Patrick's. It was probably on this occasion that Swift offered Downes the use of his house at Laracor until his own could be built. According to the younger Sheridan's *Life of Swift*, 1784, pp. 402–5, it was at this time that his father wrote 'A true and Faithful Inventory of the Goods belonging to Dr. Swift, Vicar of Lara Cor', in opposition to Swift's verses on Quilca. But Sheridan's verses seem to have no direct relationship to those of Swift. See *Poems*, pp. 1034–5, 1044–5.

[2] The previous letter, that of 28 Apr.

say, that during the experience of many years, and many changes in affairs, your Excellency, and one more, who is not worthy to be compared to you, are the only great persons that ever refused to answer a letter from me, without regard to business, party, or greatness; and, if I had not a peculiar esteem for your personal qualities, I should think myself to be acting a very inferior part in making this complaint.

I never was so humble, as to be vain upon my acquaintance with men in power, and always rather chose to avoid it when I was not called. Neither were their power or titles sufficient, without merit, to make me cultivate them; of which I have witnesses enough left, after all the havoc made among them by accidents of time, or by changes of persons, measures, and opinions.

I know not how your own conceptions of yourself may alter, by every new high station; but mine must continue the same, or alter for the worse.

I often told a great Minister,[1] whom you well know, that I valued him for being the same man through all the progress of power and place. I expected the like in your Lordship; and still hope that I shall be the only person who will ever find it otherwise.

I pray God to direct your Excellency in all your good undertakings, and especially in your government of this kingdom. I shall trouble you no more; but remain, with great respect, | my Lord, Your Excellency's | Most obedient, and | Most humble servant.

Rothschild

Swift to Charles Ford

Dublin. Jun. 16th 1724

I suppose you will contrive to send the other side, when you can. My Booby of an Agent who went to London, had a large Pacquet for you, and because you were out of Town brought it back, thô it was directed to the Coco-tree, and ordered to be left there, and by his not seeing you, Mrs Johnson is deferred from having the Pleasure of her Snuff-box. I am kept from my usuall summer travelling, by building a Wall,[2] which will ruin both my Health and Fortune, as

[1] i.e. Oxford.

[2] The wall enclosed 'Naboth's Vineyard', a piece of ground to the south of

well as humor; If one piece of news be true, we shall soon have you in Ireland, for I was told for certain by a Physician, that the Dutchess of Mountague[1] is coming here to drink some waters, which are very good for her Disorder, whatever it is. If that will not do the Business, the Halfpence must, for we daily expect them. We have got here a Poet for a Secretary, one Mr Tickell, born and famous since I left the World.[2] We have mutually visited, but neither of us at home; however I have dined with him at a third Place, and he is a Wit of as odd a Countenance[3] as I have seen. I am now writing at the L^dys^ —— Lodgings where Mrs Penny[4] is on a Visit, they are all well, and she tells me Mrs Ford writes to you to night. I would be glad to know a little what sort of Man Ld Carteret is grown. I writ to him about the Halfpence, at the desire of some principall Persons here, and he had not the Civility to answer me; so I writ a second time in such a Manner as he deserved, as severely and reproachfully as could consist with any good Manners.[5] I would know likewise whether poor Ld Oxford's Death[6] were attended with any Particulars. His Son is eased of a Burden, which however he could easily bear, and I am sure would have been glad to do it longer. Sheridan pursues Tisdal with Ballads and Verses, and there is one very good, called the Cobler to Jet Black.[7]—Sheridan has received your Letter, and is

the Deanery which Swift developed as a garden. He claimed the wall to be the best in Ireland. Cf. Mrs. Pilkington's *Memoirs*, i. 77–79.

[1] Lady Mary Churchill, Marlborough's youngest daughter, married to the Duke of Montagu.

[2] Thomas Tickell had been under-secretary to Addison while he was Secretary of State. It may be that Carteret then became acquainted with him. He appointed him his secretary 16 Apr. 1724. Tickell landed in Ireland, a country to which he was a stranger (*Letters to and from William Nicolson*, Archbishop of Cashel, ii. 574), on 1 June and took charge of the office in Dublin Castle. Carteret recommended him to the Lords Justices who, on 6 June, appointed him Chief Secretary. For Tickell's years in Ireland, his marriage to an Irish lady, and his burial in Glasnevin church see *Thomas Tickell*, by R. E. Tickell, pp. 93–135, 156–68.

[3] Kneller's portrait of Tickell in Queen's College, Oxford, does not give him an 'odd' countenance. See the frontispiece to R. E. Tickell's biography.

[4] Ford's sister Penelope.

[5] See Swift to Carteret 28 Apr. and 9 June. Writing from London Carteret answered with tact and friendliness on 20 June.

[6] On 21 May.

[7] Copies of the folio broadside—*A Letter from a Cobler in Patrick's-Street to Jet Black. Printed in the Year 1724*—will be found in the Bradshaw Collection, University Library, Cambridge, and in the Gilbert Collection, Dublin.

exceedingly pleased with your remembring him.—I conclude you often see Madame de V—[1] and I hope you will remember to give me her Character. I dined t'other day in Company with Mr James Forth,[2] and raillyed him on his changing of his Name, but he insists upon it, that it is a Mistake, and offers such Arguments as have almost shaken me, and I calld Mrs Penny, and she defends the Cause not very well. I doubt your Summer Journyes do you little good, considering your Companion; and that you lose just as much by raking as you gain by Exercise. The Ladyes[3] sigh after Wood-park like the flesh-pots of Ægypt, and come every hott afternoon to the Deanry as to a Country-house.—I score the other side as so much written to you, for you so little know or value Things Places or Persons here that I can have nothing to fill a Letter with making Dawson-Street,[4] Grafton Street,[5] or the Deanry the Scene; neither have I your last Letter about me,—so that if you desired to know any thing I cannot satisfy you. My humble Service to Dr Arbuthnot Mr Lewis, Mr Pope Mr Gay—adieu.

Address: To Charles Ford Esqr, to be | left at the Cocoa Tree in | Pell-mell | London

Postmarks: Dublin *and* 24 IV

4805

Lord Carteret to Swift

Arlington street. June 20th 1724.

Sir

To begin by confessing my selfe in the wrong will I hope be some proof to You, that none of the stations wch I have gone thro' have hitherto had the effects upon me wch You apprehend; If a months silence has been turn'd to my disadvantage in Yr esteem, it has at least had this good effect, that I am convinced by the kindness of yr reproaches, as well as by the goodness of yr advice that You still retain some part of yr former friendship for me, of wch I am the more

[1] Lady Bolingbroke.

[2] Ford's cousin, of Redwood, King's County, then M.P. for Philipstown. Perhaps the change which he denied was from Forth to Ford.

[3] Stella and Rebecca Dingley.

[4] The residence of Ford's mother and sister.

[5] Perhaps the residence of Stella and Rebecca Dingley.

confident from the agreable freedome wth wch you express yr selfe, & I shall not forfeit my pretensions to the continuance of it, by doing any thing that shall give you occasion to thinke that I am insensible of it; but to come to the point, Yr first letter is dated the 28th May[1] Yr second the 9th June, by the date of this you will see that the interval of silence, may be accounted for, by a few excursions wch I have made into the Country, I desire You will put the most favorable sense. The principal affaire You mention is under examination, & till that is over, I am not inform'd sufficiently to make any other judgement of the matter, than that wch I am naturally led to make, by the general aversion wch appears to it in the whole nation. I hope the nation will not suffer by my being in this great Station, & if I can contribute to its prosperity, I shall thinke it the honour & happyness of my life. I desire You to believe what I say, & particularly when I profess my selfe to be wth great truth Sr | Your most Obedient and | most humble servant

Endorsed by Swift: Ld Lt Carteret | June 20th 1724

Deane Swift 1765

Swift to Lord Carteret

July 9th, 1724.

My Lord,

I humbly claim the privilege of an inferior, to be the last writer; yet, with great acknowledgments for your condescension in answering my letters, I cannot but complain of you for putting me in the wrong. I am in the circumstances of a waiting-woman, who told her lady, that nothing vexed her more than to be caught in a lie. But, what is worse, I have discovered in myself somewhat of the bully; and that, after all my rattling you have brought me down to be as humble as the most distant attender at your levee. It is well your

[1] Carteret wrote 'May' for 'April', followed by Hawkesworth and early editors. Scott, 1814, changed to the correct month without remark, as did Ball. It seems evident that Carteret, when writing, was under the impression that Swift's second letter followed the other within eleven days instead of forty-two. He speaks also of his own 'months silence'. On the assumption that Swift's second letter followed the first at so short an interval Carteret might well have attributed to him undue impatience. On the contrary he writes with forbearing courtesy.

Excellency's talents are in few hands; for, if it were otherwise, we who pretend to be free speakers in quality of philosophers, should be utterly cured of our forwardness; at least, I am afraid there will be an end of mine, with regard to your Excellency. Yet, my Lord, I am ten years older than I was when I had the honour to see you last, and consequently ten times more testy. Therefore I foretel, that you who could so easily conquer so captious a person, and of so little consequence, will quickly subdue this whole kingdom to love and reverence you. I am, with the greatest respect, | My Lord, *&c.*

Portland MSS.

Swift to the Earl of Oxford

Dublin, 9 July 1724.

My Lord.[1]

Although I had for two years past enured my self to expect the Death of My Lord Your Father, from the frequent Accounts I received of the bad Condition of his Health, yet the News of it struck me so sensibly that I had not Spirit enough to condole with Your Lordship as I ought to have done, for so great a Loss to the World and to Your self. It is true indeed, you no longer wanted his Care and Tenderness, nor his Example to incite you to Virtue; but His Friendship and Conversation You will ever want, because they are Qualityes so rare in the World, and in which he so much excelled all others. It hath pleased me in the midst of my Grief to hear that he preserved the Greatness and calmness and Intrepidity of his mind to his last Minutes; For it was fitt that such a Life should terminate with equall lustre to the whole progress of it.

I must now beg leave to apply to Your Lordship's Justice. He was often pleased to promise me His Picture,[2] But his Troubles, and Sickness, and want of Opportunity, and my Absence prevented him. I do therefore humbly insist, that Your Lordship will please to discharge what I almost look upon as a Legacy.

I would entreat another and much greater Favor of Your Lordship, that at your Leisure hours you would please to inspect among Your Father's Papers, whether there be any Memorials that may be

[1] The first Earl of Oxford had died on 21 May, and was succeeded by his son Edward, hitherto styled Lord Harley.

[2] See ii. 468.

of use towards writing his Life, which I have some times mentioned to him, and often thought on when I little expected to survive him. I have formerly gathered severall Hints, but want many Materialls especially of his more early Times, which might be easily supplyed. And such a Work most properly belongs to me, who loved and respected him above all Men, and had the Honor to know him better than any other of my Level did.

I humbly beg Your Lordship's Pardon for so long a Letter upon so mournfull an Occasion, and expect your Justice to believe that I am and shall ever be, with the greatest Respect | My Lord | Your Lordships most obedient | most obliged and most | humble Servt | Jonath Swift

I desire to present | my most humble Respects | to My Lady Oxford.

Dublin. Jul. 9th | 1724

Tickell Letter-Book No. 2

Swift to Thomas Tickell

Deanery House *July* 11. 1724.

Sir,[1]

I shall wait on you at the time and place you appoint, although it is hard that you last comers and lodgers should invite us old house-keepers, which I would have you to know I am, and can bring you half-a-dozen men in gowns to depose it. I shall therefore attend you only on this condition, that you will be ready to fix a day for dining at the deanery with Lord Forbes[2] and Mr. Sheridan,[3] because the latter has been heard to boast that you will condescend to suffer him. | I am, with great respect | Sir | Your most obedient humble servant | Jonath. Swift.

[1] Printed from Tickell's Letter-Book, No. 2. Cf. *Thomas Tickell*, R. E. Tickell, pp. 98–99. Scott obtained the Tickell letters from family papers, and published them with an acknowledgement, dated 'Abbotsford, 1 June 1824', that he owed them to 'the liberality and kindness of Major Tickell'.

[2] Lord George Forbes, 1685–1765, son of the second Earl of Granard, distinguished himself as a naval commander and diplomatist (*D.N.B.*).

[3] The names of Sheridan and Tickell were destined to be more closely associated in a future generation. Their grandsons married the sisters Linley, well known for their portraits by Gainsborough.

Faulkner 1762

Swift to Archbishop King

Dublin, 14 July 1724.

My Lord,[1]

Your Grace will have received before this comes to your Hands, an Account of the Primate's Death, who died Yesterday, at twelve o'Clock at Noon.[2] He had left off spitting for about ten Days before, and the Want of that is thought to have been the immediate cause of his Death, although he eat heartily until the two last Days. He has left the Bishop of *Kildare*,[3] and his steward, Mr. *Morgan*, his Executors, who were both out of Town; but I suppose are sent for. Some who formerly belonged to him, think he has left 40,000*l.*; others report that he died poor.[4]

The Vogue is, that your Grace will succeed him, if you please; but I am too great a Stranger to your present Situation at Court to know what to judge. But, if there were Virtue enough, I could wish your Grace would accept the Offer, if it should be made you. Because I would have your Name left to Posterity among the Primates; and, because, entering into a new Station, is entering, after a sort on a new Lease of Life; and, because, it might be hoped, that your Grace would be advised with about a Successor; and because that Diocese would require your Grace's Ability and Spirit to reform it; and, because,—but I should never be at an End if I were to number up the Reasons why I would have your Grace in the highest Station the Crown can give you.

I found all the Papers in the Cabinet relating to Dr. Steevens's Hospital,[5] and, therefore, I brought them home to the Deanery.

[1] Swift was writing from Dublin to the Archbishop who was then in the country on one of his triennial visitations.

[2] Primate Lindsay's health had been failing for the past five years.

[3] Welbore Ellis had been Bishop of Kildare since Sept. 1705. His sympathy was with fellow bishops of the English interest; but his friendship with the Primate remained unbroken (Bishop Nicolson's *Letters*, ii. 502).

[4] There is no proof in his will of great wealth. He bequeathed to the economy fund of Armagh Cathedral £1,000, and to a former organist an annuity of £30 a year in order that he might teach 'the young charity boys how to chant'.

[5] Richard Steevens, 1653–1710, practising as a physician in Dublin amassed a considerable fortune. This he left to his sister Grizell to be vested in trustees for the building of a hospital, which was completed in 1733. Swift was one of its earliest governors.

opened the Cabinet in the presence of Mr. Bouhereau,[1] and saw one Paper which proved a Bank Note for 500 *l.* The Greatness of the Sum startled me, but I found it belonged to the same Hospital. I was in Pain because Workmen were in the Room and about the House. I therefore went this Morning to St. *Sepulchre's*,[2] and, in the presence of Mrs. Green,[3] I took away the Note, and have it secured in my Cabinet, leaving her my Receipt for it, and am very proud to find that a Scrip under my Hand will pass for 500*l.* I wish your Grace a good Journey to the Establishment of your Health; and am, with the greatest Respect, my Lord, | Your Grace's most dutiful, | And most humble Servant, | Jon. Swift.

Dublin, July 14, 1724.

Forster copy

Swift to Knightley Chetwode

Dublin, 14 July 1724.

Sir,[4]

I had yours of June 27th and have been hindered by a great variety of silly business and vexation from answering you. I am over head and ears in mortar, and with a number of the greatest rogues in Ireland which is a proud word.[5] But besides I am at an uncertainty what to say to you on the affair you mention; what new reason you may have, or discoveries you have made of foul play I cannot but be a stranger to. All I know is, that anyone who talked of your prosecution while you were here, unanimously condemned it as villainous

[1] The Rev. John Bouhereau was assistant librarian at Marsh's Library and chaplain of a church recently built at Ringsend. His father, also in Holy orders, was a French refugee. Cf. 'Elias Bouhéreau of La Rochelle', by the Rev. Newport White, in *Proceedings of the Royal Irish Academy*, xxvii, c. 126.

[2] The ancient palace of the Archbishops of Dublin near St. Patrick's Cathedral.

[3] Her husband had for many years acted as secretary to the Archbishop.

[4] The proceedings against Chetwode had been dropped by the government. Writing on 14 Apr. to the Duke of Grafton, the Duke of Newcastle says that he had laid a petition from Chetwode before the King, and that His Majesty, for reasons given by Grafton, had signified his pleasure that Chetwode's prosecution should be abandoned (Departmental Correspondence in P.R.O. of Ireland). —Ball.

[5] Swift alludes to Naboth's Vineyard.

and unjust, which hath made me think that it would be better to lie in oblivion, for my reason of agreeing formerly that an account of it would be useful, went only on the supposition, that you would be tried &c. But I protest I am no fit adviser in this matter, and therefore I would entreat you to consult other friends, as I would do if it were my own case. If you are advised to go on and pursue that advice, by drawing up the account, pray do it in folio, with the margin as wide as the writing, and I shall add, alter, or correct according to my best judgement, and though you may not be advised to publish it, yet it may be some amusement in wet winter evenings.

I hope you found your plantations answer what you expected. You will hear that the Primate died yesterday at twelve o'clock, which will set the expecting clergy all in a motion; and they say that Levinge, the Chief Justice, died about the same hour.[1] but whether the Primate's death swallows up the other I cannot tell, for either it is false or not regarded; perhaps I shall know before this is closed. Lord Oxford died like a great man, received visits to the last, and then two minutes before his death, turned from his friends, closed his own eyes, and expired. Mr. Stopford is returned from his travels, the same person he went, only more experience. He is in all regards the most valuable young man of this kingdom.[2] I am ever &c.

Levinge is dead.

Address: To Knightley Chetwode, Esq. at Woodbrooke, near Mountmellick.

Elrington Ball's Transcript[3]

Archbishop King to Swift

Carlow, July 20, 1724.

Dear Dean,

I had the satisfaction of yours of the 14th inst., and it gave me great pleasure to find you remembered me so kindly in my absence. I had

[1] Sir Richard Levinge, an Englishman, descended from a Derbyshire family, went to Ireland as Solicitor-General in 1690. He was knighted in 1692, and in 1704 was created a baronet. In 1720 he became Lord Chief Justice of the Common Pleas. His correspondence was privately printed in 1877. See Ball, *Judges in Ireland*, ii. 195–6, and *D.N.B.*

[2] The Rev. James Stopford, a step-brother of Chetwode's wife, subsequently became Bishop of Cloyne. He was fond of travelling. Swift corresponded with him; but his estimate of his abilities was not fulfilled.

[3] The original copy in Trinity College is not now available.

return of my gout three days after I left Dublin, and I have gone through the offices of confirmation and visitation in a very lame manner. I am still in pain but must go on if possible.

How the primacy will be disposed of I cannot guess, but considering how many years the late Primate was dying I am apt to think it was long ago determined who should be his successor, for I understand that is the method taken by this Ministry to determine on supposition that such or such die who shall succeed.[1] I have been importuned by my friends to apply for myself,[2] but having never asked anything I cannot now begin to do so, when I have so near a prospect of leaving the station in which I am another way. However, I have writ to several, who I believe will have an interest in the disposal of preferments, apprising them of what moment a proper person in this place will be to his Majesty's service, etc., and entreating their good offices towards procuring such an one.[3] How this will be construed, I am not much concerned, but let it take its chance.

I cannot yet hear what will the late Primate has made. Pray, if you can learn, inform me. You speak of his dying worth forty thousand pounds, people here make it fifty thousand pounds, but I am persuaded it can be nothing like either of these sums, though I believe he died rich.

I am glad you take to heart the affairs of Dr. Steevens's Hospital. We shall be in great difficulty to finish it.[4] I wish, however, we could

[1] Hugh Boulter, 1672–1742, at this time Bishop of Bristol and Dean of Christchurch, was appointed to the primacy within a few days by royal letter dated 31 Aug. In November he arrived in Ireland accompanied by Ambrose Philips as his secretary. He soon gained a powerful ascendancy, promoting English interests and subjecting Roman Catholics to penal legislation. He was not favourably received by Archbishop King, who hoped for the primacy himself; and Swift had no regard for him. See 'Ay and No', *Poems*, pp. 841–3. See also *Portland MSS*. vii. 381. Philips gathered his letters in two volumes, Oxford, 1769–70. They were published also in Dublin, 1770, by 'George Faulkner and James Williams'.

[2] Chiefly by Marmaduke Coghill and Speaker Conolly. By 'another way' King refers to the possibility of an early demise. He died within five years.

[3] It was clear that King would not have refused the primacy if it had been offered him. No friend likely to have been in his favour and of help was forgotten. Among them were the Archbishop of Canterbury, the Bishop of London, Lord Carteret, the Duke of Grafton, Lord Harcourt, and Sir Peter King, Chief Justice of the Common Pleas.

[4] Owing to generous assistance from Dr. Steevens's sister and others the building was completed. See p. 20, n. 5.

settle a constitution for it, since I believe, if that were once done, it might be a means to procure some money for it. If trusting you with a bill of five hundred pounds make you very proud, if it had been for fifty thousand pounds, I assure you I would have thought it very secure in your hands, but the worst of it is that the money is all drawn out of the banker's hands, and the note must be given up as soon as my notes are returned to me.

I have neither time nor inclination to writing, and have had more of it since I left Dublin than is agreeable either with my health or circumstances. I find a sort of damp on my pen when I write because I must write, and therefore you will excuse me, though you neither find life nor substance in this, since it is only meant to assure you that I am with true affection and sincere respect, Reverend Sir, | Your most humble servant, | W. D.

Dean Swift.

Tickell Letter-Book No. 2

Swift to Thomas Tickell

Dublin, 3 August 1724.

Sr

I should have waited on you before now if [I] had not been tormented with an old Vexatious Disorder of a Deafness and noise in my Ears[1] which has returned after having left me about 2 years, and makes mc insupportable to others and my self.

I now make bold to trouble you on an affair which goes very near my Heart. Mr Proby Surgeon generall my old Friend,[2] and most generally beloved of any Man in this Kingdom lyes under a great Misfortune at present. His Eldest son a Cap^tn^ in Lord Tirawly's Regiment hath been accused at Gallaway, for discovering an Inclination to Popery, and severall Affidavits have been made against Him.

[1] Swift suffered from a prolonged attack of deafness during the summer of 1724. Delany addressed to him verses in sympathy, to which Swift replied in verse. —*Poems*, pp. 365–7.

[2] Thomas Proby, Chirurgeon-General in Ireland, won his reputation as a young man. In his *Short Character of Wharton* Swift described him as a person 'universally esteemed'. He was one of the founders of Steevens's hospital. His wife, one of Stella's friends, mentioned several times in the *Journal*, was a notable collector of coins and china.

The young Man desires nothing but a fair Tryal—The Accusation is generally judged Malicious and false.[1] But that concerns you not. He is to be tryed in a few days, but the Matter must first go before the Lords Justices. Mr Proby being utterly unknown to you, desires the Favor to wait upon you either this afternoon or Evening,[2] or early to morrow morning. He does not intend this as a Solliciter for his Son, he has too much Discretion, but because the Business will first come before the L^ds^ Justices. He thinks it will be proper for him to wait on you, and say or ask what is convenient, and thought that my Recommendation will facilatate his Access. Therefore pray S^r^ mistake me not. I am not at all making you an Advocate, but only desiring that he may not see you wholly as a Stranger.

You will please to signify by one of your Servants what Hour will permit Mr Proby to attend you | I am with great Respect | S^r^ your obedient | humble Ser^t^ | Jonath Swift

Deanry-House | Aug. 3^d^ 1724

Endorsed: 3 Aug. 1724 | Dean Swift | proby's son.

4805

Lord Carteret to Swift

Arlington street. Aug. 4th | 1724.

S^r^

The[3] claim to be the last writer is what I can never allow, that is the priviledge of ill writers; & I am resolved to give You compleat satisfaction by leaving it with You whether I shall be that last writer or not; Methinks I see you throw this letter upon Yr table in the height of spleen because it may have interrupted some of Yr more agreable thoughts, but then in return You may have the comfort of not answering it, & so convince my Ld Leu^nt^ that You value him less now than You did ten years ago. I dont know but this might become a free speaker & a Philosopher. Whatever You may thinke of

[1] The charges may have been well founded. Ball quotes the following passage from Proby's will: 'I leave to my graceless son Thomas Proby one shilling and no more, he having already had from me more than a child's portion; it being my interest to debar and exclude him from having any part of my real or personal estate for his gross hypocrisy, apostasy and disobedience.'

[2] 'Evening' scored out in the manuscript.

[3] The] Your *Hawkesworth*, *Ball*.

it I shall not be testy, but endeavour to shew that I am not altogether insensible of the Genius, wch has outshone most of this age, & when You will display it again can convince us that its Lustre & strength are still the same. Once more I commit myselfe to Yr censure & am S^r with great respect. | Y^r most affectionate | humble servant. | Carteret.

Endorsed by Swift: Ld Lt Carteret | Aug. 4th 1724

4805

Viscount Bolingbroke to Swift

12 September [o.s. 1] 1724.

It is neither sickness, nor journeys, nor ill-humour, nor Age, nor Vexation, nor Stupidity, which has hinder'd me from answering sooner your letter of the month of June,[1] but a very prudent Consideration, and one of the greatest strains of pollicy I ever exercis'd in my life. Should I answer you in a month, you might think yr Self oblig'd to answer me in Six, and scar'd att the sore fatigue of writing twice a-year to an absent friend, you might, for ought either you or I can tell, stop short, and not write att all. now this would disappoint all my projects, for, to confess the truth, I have been drawing you in these several years, & by my past success I begin to hope that in about ten more, I may establish a right of hearing from you once a quarter. the gout neither clears my head nor warms my imagination, & I am asham'd to own to you how near the truth I kept in the description of what pass'd by my bed side on the reading of yr letter. the Scene was really such as I painted it, and the company was much better than you seem to think it. when I who pass a great part, very much the greatest, of my life alone, sally forth into the world, I am very far from expecting to improve myself by the conversation I find there, & still further from caring one jot what passes there. in short I am no longer the Bubble you knew me, and therefore when I mingle in Society it is purely for my amusement. if Mankind divert me, and I defy them to give me yr distemper the Spleen, it is all I expect to ask of them. by this sincere confession you may perceive that yr great Masters of Reason are not for my turn. their thorow base benumbs my facultys. I seek the fiddle or the flute. some thing

[1] Evidently a reply to Bolingbroke's letter of 25 Dec. o.s. 14, 1723.

to raise or some thing to calm my Spirits agreably. gay imagination runs away wth him, & who has wit enuff to be half mad, nor him who attones for a scanty imagination by an ample fund of oddnesses & singularity. if good sense & real knowledg prevail a little too much in any character, I desire there may be att least some latent ridicule, which may be call'd forth upon occasion, & render the person a tollerable Companion. By this sketch you may judge of my acquaintance. the dead friends wth whom I pass my time you know. the living ones are of the same sort, and therefore few.

I pass over that paragraph of yr letter which is a kind of an Elegy on a departed Minister,[1] & I promise you solemnly neither to mention him, nor think of him more, till I come to do him justice in an History of the first twenty years of this Century, which I believe I shall write if I live three or four years longer. But I must take a little more notice of the paragraph wch follows. the verses I sent you are very bad, because they are not very good. mediocribus esse poetis non di, non homines &c.[2] I did not send them to be admir'd, and you would do them too much honour if you criticiz'd them. Pope took the best party, for he said not one word to me about them. all I desire of you is to consider them as a proof that you have never been out of my thoughts, tho you have been so long out of my Sight, and if I remember you upon paper for the future it shall be in prose. I must on this occasion set you right as to an opinion which I should be very sorry to have you entertain concerning me. the term Esprit fort, in English free thinker, is according to my observation, usually apply'd to Men whom I look upon to be the Pests of Society, because their endeavours are directed to losen the bands of it, & to take att least one curb out of the mouth of that wild Beast Man when it would be well if he was check'd by half a score others. nay they go further. Reveal'd Religion is a lofty & pompous structure erected close to the humble & plain building of Natural Religion. some have objected to you, who are the Architects et les Concierges, we want that word in English, of the former, to you who built, or att least repair the house, & who shew the rooms, that to strengthen some parts of yr own building, you shake & even sap the foundations of the other, and between you and I, Mr Dean, this charge may be justify'd in several instances. But still your intention is not to demolish. whereas the Esprit fort, or the free thinker, is so set upon pulling down yr house about yr Ears, that if he was let alone, he

[1] i.e. Oxford.

[2] Hor. *Ars Poetica*, 372.

would destroy the other for being so near it, & mingle both in one common mine. I therefore not only disown, but detest this character. if indeed by Esprit fort, or free thinker, you only mean a Man who makes a free use of his Reason, who searches after truth wth out passion, or prejudice, & adheres inviolably to it, you mean a wise & honest Man, and such an one as I labour to be. the faculty of distinguishing between right & wrong, true & false, which we call Reason or common Sence, which is given to Every Man by our bountiful Creator, and wch most Men lose by neglect, is the light of the mind, and ought to guide all the operations of it. to abandon this rule, & to guide our thoughts by any other, is full as absurd as it would be if you should put out yr eyes, and borrow even the best Staff, that ever was in the family of the Staffs,[1] when you set out upon one of yr dirty journeys. such free thinkers as these, I am sure you cannot even in yr apostolical capacity disapprove. for since the truth of the divine Revelation of Christianity is as evident, as matters of fact, on the belief of which so much depends, ought to be, agreably to all our ideas of justice, those free thinkers must needs be Christians on the best foundation, on that which St Paul himself establish'd, I think it was St Paul, omnia probate, quod bonum est tenete.

But you have a further Security from these free thinkers, I do not say a better, & it is this. the persons I am describing think for them selves, and to them selves. should they unhappily not be convinc'd by yr arguments, yet they will certainly think it their duty not to disturb the peace of the world by opposing you. the peace & happyness of mankind is the great aim of these free thinkers, & therefore as those among them who remain incredulous, will not oppose you, so those, whom Reason enlighten'd by Grace has made Believers, may be sorry, & may express their sorrow, as I have done, to see Religion perverted to purposes so contrary to her true intention, & first design. can a good Christian behold of the meek & humble Jesus exercising an insolent & cruel usurpation over their Brethren, or the Messengers of peace & good news setting all Mankind together by the Ears, or that Religion, wch breathes charity & universal benevolence, spilling more blood, upon Reflexion & by System, than the

[1] Part of *The Tatler*, no. 35, alluding to the 'famous Family of Staffs' has, with little likelihood, been attributed to Swift (*Prose Works*, ed. Temple Scott, ix. 11). A reference therein contained recalls an account of the Staff family in *The Tatler*, no. 11, which was written by Heneage Twisden.

most barbarous Heathen ever did in the heat of action, and fury of conquest can he behold all this wth an holy indignation, and not be criminal? nay when he turns his eyes from these tragical scenes & considers the ordinary tenour of things; do you not think he will be shock'd to observe metaphysicks substituted to Theory, & Ceremony to the practice of Morality?

I make no doubt but you are by this time abundantly convinc'd of my orthodoxy, & that you will name me no more in the same breath with Spinosa, whose System of one infinite substance I despise and abhor, as I have a right to do, because I am able to shew why I despise & abhor it.

You desire me to return home, & you promise me in that case to come to London loaden with yr Travells.[1] I am sorry to tell you that London is in my apprehension as little likely as Dublin to be our place of rendez vous. the Reasons for this apprehension I pass over, but I cannot agree to what you advance wth the air of a Maxim. that Exil is the greatest punishment to Men of Virtue, because Virtue consists in loving our Country. Examine the Nature of this Love, from whence it arises, how it is nourish'd, what the bounds & measures of it are, & after that you will discover how far it is Virtue, & where it becomes simplicity, prejudice, folly & even Enthusiasm. a virtuous Man in exile may properly enuff be stil'd unhappy. you remember the Reason wch Brutus gave, because wherever he goes he carrys his virtue wth him.[2] there is a certain bulky volume wch grows daily, and the title of wch must, I think be Noctes gallicae. there you may perhaps one time or other see a Dissertation upon this Subject, & to return you threatning for threatning you shall be forc'd to read it out tho' you yawn from the first to the last page.

The word Ireland was struck out of the paper you mention. that is to satisfy yr curiosity, and to kindle it anew, Ile tell you, that this anecdote, wch I know not how you came by, is neither the only one, nor the most considerable one of the same kind. the person you are so inquisitive about[3] returns into England att the end of October. she has so great a mind to see you that I am not sure she will not

[1] The idea of going to London with the completed manuscript of *Gulliver's Travels* was evidently already in Swift's mind. He carried it into effect two years later.

[2] Brutus to Cicero: 'Neque usquam exsul esse possum, dum servire et pati contumelias pejus odero malis omnibus aliis.'

[3] His wife, the Marquise de Villette.

undertake a journey to Dublin. there is not so far from London to Dublin as from Spain to Padua, & you are as well worth seeing as Livy. But I would much rather you would leave the humid climate, and the dull company, in which, according to yr account a Man might grow old between twenty & thirty. Set yr foot on the continent. I dare promise that you will, in a fortnight, have gone back the ten years you lament so much, & be return'd to that age att which I left you. with what pleasure should I hear you inter vina fugam Stellae moerere protervae? Adieu.

Endorsed by Swift: Sep^{tr} 12th 1724 | Ld Bolingbrook | Answ^{d} Dec^{r}

Rothschild[1]

Swift to Lord Carteret

Dublin, 4 September 1724.

My Lord.

Being ten years old[er] than when I had the Honor to see Your Excellency last, by consequence if I am subject to any Aylments, they are now ten times worse. And so it happened, for I have been a Month pestered with the Return of an old Disorder, Deafness and Noise in my Ears; of great Consequence to the world: so I had not Spirit to perform the common Offices of Life, much less, to write to Your Excellency, and least of all to answer so obliging and condescending a Letter as that I received from You. But, these ugly ten Years have a worse Consequence, that they utterly destroy my Title to the good Opinion You are pleased to express of me as an Amuser of the Publick and of my self. To have preserved that Talent, I ought in Prudence as I grew older, to have removed into a better Clymat instead of being sunk for Life in a worse. I imagine France would be proper for me now, and Italy ten years hence. However I am not so bad as the World would make me. For, since I left England, such a parcel of Trash hath been there fathered upon me,[2]

[1] From the library of Gawdy Hall, Harleston, Norfolk. Sold by order of Major E. Knatchbull-Hughessen, at Hodgson's, 24 Nov. 1938, Lot 148. Now Lord Rothschild's library 2290. The letter, as first printed by Deane Swift in 1765, was obviously copied from a draft which was dated 3 Sept.; and there are many variants. For Deane Swift's text, followed by Ball, see Appendix.

[2] See ii. 421.

that nothing but the good Judgment of my Friends could hinder them from thinking me to be grown the greatest Dunce alive.

There is a Gentleman of this Kingdom just gone for England, it is Doct^{r} George Berkeley, Dean of Derry, the best Preferment among us, being above 1100^{ll} a year.[1] He takes the Bath in his way to London, where he will of course attend Your Excellency, and I suppose be presented by His Friend My Lord Burlington.[2] And because I believe you will chuse some idle Minutes to read this Letter, perhaps you may not be ill entertained with an Account of the Man and his Errand. He was a Fellow in the University here, and going young to England about 13 years ago, he there became the Founder of a Sect called the Immaterialists, by the force of a very curious Book[3] which he had written upon that Subject. Doct^{r} Smalridge[4] and many other eminent Persons were his Proselytes. I sent him at that Time Secretary and Chaplain with My Ld Peterborow to Sicily, and upon His Lordship's Return, Doct^{r} Berkeley spent above seven Years in travelling over many Parts of Europe, but chiefly thro every Corner of Italy; and Sicily and other Islands.[5] Upon his last coming to Ireld he was by the Duke of Grafton's Favor made Dean of Derry. Your Excellency will be frighted when I tell you all this is but an Introduction; for you are now to know his Errand to England. He is an absolute Philosopher with Respect to Money Titles or Power; and for three years past hath been struck with a Notion of founding an University at Bermudas by a Charter from the Crown, and Contributions of those whom he can persuade to them. He hath seduced severall of the hopefullest young Clergymen and Scholers here, many of them well provided for, and all of them in the fairest Way of Preferm^{t}. But in Engld his Conquests are greater, and I doubt will spread very far this Winter. He shewed me a little Tract,[6] which he designs to publish, and there Your Excel-

[1] In Feb. 1721–2 Berkeley had been appointed to the Deanery of Dromore. In May 1724 he was moved to the much richer Deanery of Derry.

[2] Swift is said to have introduced Berkeley to Lord Burlington (Delany, *Observations*, p. 27).

[3] *A Treatise Concerning the Principles of Human Knowledge* was published in 1710.

[4] Smalridge had died in 1719.

[5] Berkeley went abroad towards the end of 1713; returned to England in 1714; in 1716 again went abroad, as tutor to the son of Bishop Ashe; travelled extensively in Italy and Sicily; and returned to London in 1721.

[6] *A Proposal for the better Supplying of Churches in our Foreign Plantations,*

lency will see his whole Scheme, of a Life Academicophilosophicall (I shall make You remember what You were) of a College founded for Indian Scholars and Missionaryes; where he most exorbitantly proposeth a whole hundred Pounds a year for himself; 40^{ll} for a Fellow, and 10^{ll} for a Student. His Heart will break if his Deanry be not soon taken from Him, and left to Your Excellency's disposal. I tryed to discourage Him by urging the Coldness of Courts and Ministers who will interpret all this visionary or impossible; But all in vain: And therefore I do humbly entreat your Excellency either to use such Persuasions as will keep one of the first Men in this Kingdom for Virtue and Learning, quiet at home, or assist him by Your Credit to compass his Romantick Design, which however is very noble and generous, directly proper for a great Person of your excellent Education and Accomplishments to encourage.[1]

I must now in all Humility entreat one Favor of you as Lord Lieutenant. Mr Proby Surgeon generall of the Army here, layd out the greatest Part of his Fortune to buy a Captainship for his eldest Son.[2] The young Man was lately accused of discovering a Disposition to Papacy while he quartered at Gallway. The Report of the Court marshall is transmitted to Your Excellency;[3] but what it is, is not known onely hoped to be favourable; because it was the universall Opinion at the Hearing, that the Accusation was false and malicious, and the Arch Bp of Tuam in whose Diocese Gallway is, upon a strict Enquiry hath delivered it to be so. But all this is not to be understood to be of the least Weight with Your Excellency; any more than that the Father is the most universally beloved and esteemed of any man I ever knew of his Rank. All I entreat is, that you will please to hear the Opinion of others who may speak in the young Man's favor, and perhaps will tell you that, as Party is not in the Case, so you cannot do any Personal Thing more acceptable to

and for Converting the Savage Americans to Christianity. The tract, in twenty-four pages octavo, was first published by H. Woodfall, under the date 1724.

[1] By Vanessa's will, executed on 1 May 1723, Berkeley was a chief beneficiary, and he was at this time possessed of some means for his 'Romantick Design'. Vanessa died in June 1723.

[2] See p. 24.

[3] The court found that the evidence was not sufficient to prove the charge against Captain Proby, but that on account of the 'many indiscretions which he showed on that occasion', and several things which he had done at other times unworthy of His Majesty's service, he should be required to dispose of his commission (Miscellaneous Papers, 9 Dec. 1724, in P.R.O. of Ireland).—Ball.

the People of Ireld than by exercising Justice with some Lenity towards Mr Proby and his Family. I beg your Excellency will remember my Request to be onely that you would hear others, and not think me so very weak as to imagine I could hope or intend to give the least Turn to your Mind: And therefore what I have said may be pardonable in every Respect but that of taking up your Time.

I have no other Excuse for the length of this Letter but a faithfull Promise never to be guilty of the like Fault a second Time. | I am with the greatest Respect | My Lord | Your Excellency's most obedient | and most humble Servant | Jonath Swift

Dublin. Sept^{br} 4th | 1724

Endorsed: Dr Swift.

Tickell Letter-Book No. 2.

Swift to Thomas Tickell

4 September 1724

S^{r}[1]

I desire you will please to send the inclosed[2] I beg y^{r} Pardon for so often troubling you, but I owed His Excellency a Lett^{r}. I am pretty well eased of my troublous disorder intend[3] to wait on you soon, and hope you will make some Appointm^{t} with those you like best, that we may meet at the Deanry— | I am S^{r} | Y^{r} most obedient | humble Ser^{t} | J:, Swift

Deanry-house | Sep^{t} 4th. 1724

Endorsed: Deanery House 4 Sept. | 1724 | Dr Swift | R.

Deane Swift 1768

George Rochfort to Swift

9 September 1724.

Dear Sir,[4]

I find myself stand in need of the advice I bestowed on you t'other night, and therefore if you have got rid of your cold, I would

[1] A hastily written note in a larger hand than customary.

[2] The preceding letter to Carteret.

[3] Written above 'long', which is scored out. [*For note 4 see overleaf.*

prescribe a small jaunt to *Belcamp*[1] this morning. If you find yourself thus disposed, I will wait for you here in my boots: the weather may perhaps look gloomy at the deanery; but I can assure you it is a fine day in this parish,[2] where we set up for as good tastes as our neighbours: to convince you of mine, I send you this invitation. I am, dear Sir, your much obliged and obedient servant, | George Rochfort.

Wednesday morning | Sept. 9, 1725.

Forster copy

Swift to Knightley Chetwode

[September, 1724]

Sir,

I have been above 7 weeks ill of my old Deafness and am but just recovered. Your Carrier has behaved himself very honourably, because you took care to seal the cords. Your Bergamot Pears are excellent, and the Orange Bergamots much better than those about this town. Your Apples are very fair and good of their kind, and your Peaches and Nectarines as good as we could expect from the year, but it is too great a journey for such nice fruit, and they are apt to take the taste of the moss.[3] Your cherry brandy I depend on the goodness of, but would not suffer it to be tasted till another time. I could find Fault with nothing but your Paper, which was so perfumed that the company with me could not bear it.

There is a Drapier very popular, but what is that to me? If Wood

[1] The home of the Grattans, a few miles from Dublin.

[2] The Rochforts' Dublin house was in the parish of St. Mary.

[3] Sir William Temple in his *Gardens of Epicurus* wrote with authority upon gardens and particularly upon the cultivation of fruits. Swift's mind may have been travelling back to the early years at Moor Park.

---

[4] This letter, as first printed by Deane Swift in 1768, was dated 1725, and this date was followed by subsequent editors, until Ball pointed out that 9 Sept. 1725 was a Thursday, and that Swift was not in Dublin at the time. The true date may be accepted as 1724.

be disappointed it is all we desire.[1] Lord Carteret is coming suddenly over.[2] I am, |

Yours, &c.

Address: To Knightley Chetwode, Esq.
Endorsed: Only with thanks for a present I sent him from Woodbrooke; September 22, 1724.

Forster copy

Swift to Knightley Chetwode

Dublin, October, 1724.

Sir,

I received your longer letter, and afterwards your shorter by Mr. Jackman.[3] I am now relapsed into my old disease of deafness, which so confounds my head, that I am ill qualified for writing or thinking. I sent your letter sealed to Mr. Stopford.[4] He never showed me any letter of yours, nor talked of anything relating to you above once in his life, and that was some years ago, and of so little consequence that I have forgot it, and therefore I sent your letter sealed to him by a common messenger only under the inspection of a discreet servant. I have lived in good friendship with him, but not in such an intimacy as to interfere in his business of any sort, and I am sure I should not be fond of it unless I could be of service.

As to what you mention of my proposal at the Deanery, as far as a confused head will give me leave to think, I was always of opinion that those who are sure they cannot live well together, could not do a better thing than to part. But the quantum of your allowance must be measured by your income and other circumstances. I am of

[1] Popular feeling against Wood's coinage was now at its height. See *The Drapier's Letters*, ed. H. Davis, 1935; and *Poems*, pp. 329–54.

[2] Walpole and the English Ministers attributed the rising agitation against Wood's coinage to the weakness of the Duke of Grafton coupled with secret opposition of the Irish Lords Justices. Grafton was superseded by Lord Carteret, who landed on 22 Oct.

[3] Land agent in the north of Ireland who was in business relationship with Chetwode. As this letter shows Chetwode contemplated separation from his wife. Swift was clearly ill at ease at being consulted in so delicate an affair.

[4] James Stopford, a fellow of Trinity, Dublin, was a half-brother of Mrs. Chetwode. Chetwode may naturally have suspected that he would take her part against him.

opinion that this might be best done by knowing fairly, what the person herself would think the lowest that would be sufficient for what you propose, and the conditions of the place to reside in, wherein if you disapprove, you have liberty to refuse, and in this Mr. Stopford's mediation would be most convenient. I desire you will give some allowance to his grief and trouble in this matter. I solemnly protest he hath not mentioned one syllable of this to me, and if he should begin, I think I would interrupt him. It is a hard thing to convince others of our opinion, and I need not tell you how far a brother may be led by his affections. I am likewise of opinion that such a thing as parting, if it be agreed on, may be done without noise, as if it were only going to visit a friend, and the absence may continue by degrees, and little notice taken.

As to the affair of your son,[1] I cannot imagine why Mr. Stopford hath not answered your letter. I do believe there is somewhat in that business of his amour, an affair begun in much youth and kept up perhaps more out of decency and truth than prudence, but he is too wise to think of proceeding further before he gets into some settlement, which may not probably be in several years, and I prefer him as a tutor absolutely before any of his age or standing at least.[2] The discipline in Oxford is more remiss than here, and since you design he shall live in this kingdom, where Mr. Jackman tells me you are preparing so fine a habitation for him, I think it better to habituate him to the country where he must pass his life, especially since many chargeable accidents have happened to you, besides your building, which will press parsimony upon you, and 50^{ll} a year will maintain your Son a Commoner,[3] on which conditions you will place him, if you intend he shall be good for something.

You will allow for this confused paper for I have the noise of seven watermills in my ears and expect to continue so above a month, but this sudden return hath quite discouraged me. I mope at

[1] The affair was the entry of Chetwode's second son Valentine into Trinity. He matriculated 24 Nov. 1725 at the age of seventeen (*Alum. Dub.*, p. 149).

[2] Swift evidently surmised that this hesitancy was due to the necessity, on marriage, of resigning his fellowship. Ultimately he married his own cousin, a sister of James, first Earl of Courtown.

[3] *Recte* pensioner. Swift confuses the designations by which Oxford undergraduates were distinguished with those in use at Dublin. In the latter University the undergraduates are divided into three classes, sizars, pensioners, and fellow commoners, and in a subsequent letter Swift urges Chetwode not to enter his son amongst the last.—Ball.

home, and can bear no company but trebles and counter-tenors. | I am ever &c.

Your Perfumed Paper hath been ready to give me an apoplexy; either leave off these refinements or we will send you to live on a mountain in Connaught.

Address: To Knightley Chetwode, Esq., at Woodbrooke, near Portarlington: send to Mountmellick.

Endorsed: About H. C.[1] the Method of Parting, quantum of Allowance, Stopford and other materiall difficulties.

Tickell Papers

Swift to Thomas Tickell

Deanery House, 24 October 1724.

S^r^

I did not design to attend my Lord Lieutenant till his Hurry of Visits and Ceremony were over, But I fear it will be long before I can have that Honor, for I am so cruelly persecuted with the Return of my Deafness that I am fit for nothing but to moap in my Chamber.[2] I therefore humbly entreat your Favor to present my most humble Duty to His Excellency,—and to let him know the unlucky Cause that hinders me from waiting on him, which I apprehend will yet continue some Weeks, I have already had but too much Cause to complain of a Disorder which hath so long deprived me of the Happyness of your Company:

I conclude you are now a busy man, and therefore shall only add that I am ever with great Esteem S^{r} | Your most obedient | humble Servt | J: Swift

Deanry-house | Oct^{br} 24th | 1724

[1] Hester Chetwode.

[2] Swift's time was not wholly spent in moping in his chamber. Lord Carteret was greeted on his arrival with the fourth and greatest *Drapier's Letter* addressed *To the Whole People of Ireland.* It is dated 13 Oct. and was published 22 Oct. Carteret's own marked copy is among the State Papers 63, vol. 384, in the P.R.O.

Portland MSS.

The Earl of Oxford to Swift

Wimpole, 2 November 1724

Good Mr. Dean,

There has nothing of late given me so much real trouble and uneasiness as my having so long deferred writing to you to make my acknowledgments for your most kind and obliging letter,[1] and to assure you that I took every part of your letter in the manner you would wish me to do. I must say that amidst my trouble, grief and concern, it gave me a secret pleasure to find that I was thought of by you, and what was a great addition, that you still retained the same thoughts and sentiments of my dear father, and that you had not laid aside the design you once entertained of transmitting his name and story to posterity. I did indeed delay writing some time because I was in great hopes I should have been able to have given you a much more satisfactory account than I am even now able to do, notwithstanding the search I have made in answer to the question you asked, if he had left any memoirs behind him, I suppose you mean in relation to himself. I have not at present found any among his papers in town; this with some other affairs drew the time into the length it is, but if I have the satisfaction to hear from you again, as I hope I shall, I will be more punctual in my returns for I will allow nobody to value and esteem you more than I do.

There is certainly a very great number of materials for a history, a vast collection of letters and other papers, [and] a great deal may be supplied elsewhere, but give me leave to say that if you do not come into England nothing can be done; it will not be possible to do anything to purpose without this view. There would be nobody more welcome to me than yourself: you should live in your own way, and do just what was most agreeable to you. I have houses enough, you shall take your choice; I must with earnestness repeat it to you again that I beg you will think of this matter seriously.

As to what you mention of the picture, I have often heard my father say that he did design to sit for you, but did not; I shall certainly take care that you shall have a picture and a good one. Pray let me know what size you would have it of; if you design it should fit any particular place, you must send me the exact measure of the place.

[1] Of 9 July 1724.

Your sister[1] as you used to call her is much your servant. She has been at the Bath for some time; she is better than when she went. I suppose you hear sometimes from our friend Mr. Pope. He has taken another voyage into Homerland[2] as Gay calls it; I wish he may make an advantageous voyage of it. I doubt you will say that since I was so long before I began to write, that now I have begun I do not know when to end, I will therefore tell you that I am, with great truth, Sir, |

Your most obedient, humble servant,
O.

I desire your acceptance of a ring, a small remembrance of my father. How shall I send it to you?

Longleat xiii[3]

Swift to the Earl of Oxford

27 November 1724.

My Lord.

I am very happy in the Honor of Your Lordship's Remembrance,[4] and the many Marks I have had of your Favor: neither was I at all uneasy at Your Lordship's delaying to let me hear from you, because I learnt from others that you and my Lady were in good Health, and I knew your Silence did not proceed from any Change in your good Disposition towards me . . I never knew any Person more hardly drawn to write Letters of no Consequence, than My late Lord your Father; It was very seldom I got a scrip from him, and yet I never lost the least Ground in his Favor and Kindness,

What I had intended in relation to my late Lord Oxford was both some Memoirs of His Life and Ministry and likewise to make him have a great Part in a History which I writ in England,[5] and which His Lordship and the rest of the Ministers had read, but by some Accidents was not printed, and I propose to make in it severall Alterations and Additions.

I have many years frequently resolved to go for England, but was

[1] i.e. Lady Oxford.

[2] The translation of the Odyssey.

[3] This autograph letter is transcribed from the Longleat Volume xiii, ff. 51–52.

[4] The preceding letter.

[5] *The Four Last Years of the Queen.*

discouraged by considering what[1] a scene I must expect to find by the Death and Exil[2] of My Friends, and a thousand other disgusting Circumstances; And after all, to return back again into this enslaved Country to which I am condemned during Existence, (for I cannot call it Life) would be a Mortification hard to support.

However that kind Invitation Your Lordship hath pleased to give, will I hope raise up my Spirits: But there is another Inconvenience from which I ensure your Lordship for fourty years to come, and then you must look to your self, I mean the want of Health. I have the Honor to be afflicted with the same Disease with Your Lordships Father, frequent Fits of Deafness,[3] and at present I labor under one which hath confined me two Months, and hath worn out my Patience, fearing I shall never recover it; In such a Case, I must confine my self to my Deanry-House and Garden, converse onely with treble and Counter-tenor Voices, and turn a Speculative Monk: I should not have troubled your Lordship with relating my own Infirmityes, if they were not an Excuse for not immediately obeying your Lordships commands to attend you.

I return you my most humble Thanks for your Promise of My late Lord Oxford's Picture, but that alone will hardly serve your Turn, if ever I have the Honor to see you again. In the mean time, since Your Lordship pleases to ask me the Question, I desire it may be a three quarter Length, I mean below the Knees.[4]

I must be so bold to return my most humble Respects to my Lady Oxford, and my sincerest thanks for the Honor of being remembered by Her Ladyship.

My unconversable Disorder hath hindred me from seeing my old Friend the Lord Lieutenant, from whom[5] I never received since his Arrival, any more than one day Message.[6] He hath half frighten[d] the

[1] After 'what' an 'I' is scratched out and 'a' written above the line.

[2] 'Exil', *sic.*

[3] There is no allusion to Oxford's suffering from this complaint in the *Journal to Stella.* In his letter to Swift of Nov. 1723 Arbuthnot mentions that Oxford was 'a little deaf'. Deafness appears to have developed late. Cf. *Portland Manuscripts*, vii. 344–5.

[4] The portrait was ultimately received, and in Swift's will bequeathed to Pope. It is there described as 'in miniature, drawn by Zince'.

[5] 'whom' written above the line.

[6] Lord Carteret reached Dublin on 22 Oct. 1724. His instructions were to calm the people and to introduce Wood's coinage at least as far as was safely possible. On the very day of his arrival Swift's fourth and most famous *Letter . . . By M. B. Drapier* was selling the streets of Dublin. Carteret was aware of the

People here out of their Understandings. . There is a Fellow in London, one Wood, who got a Patent for coyning Halfpence for this Kingdom, which hath so terrifyed us, that if it were not for some Pamphlets against these Halfpence, we must have submitted. Against these Pamphlets the Lieutenant hath put out a Proclamation: and is acting the most unpopular Part I ever knew, though I warned him against it, by a Letter before he came over;[1] and thought by his Answer, that he would have taken my Opinions. This is just of as much Consequence to your Lordship, as the news of a Skirmish between two petty States in Greece was to Alexander[2] while he was conquering Persia, But even a Knot of Beggars, are of Importance among themselves.

I doubt Mr Popes Voyage into Homer-Land, will bring more Profit than Reputation, and I wish his Fortunes could afford him to employ his own Genius. I have been told this voyage is to supply what he lost by a former into the South-sea.

I have tired your Lordship and will abruptly conclude[3] by professing my self with the truest, and greatest Respect, | Your Lordships most | obedient and most obliged | Servt Jonath Swift.

I shall desire a Gentleman to
attend Your Lordship, for the Ring.
which I value more than if it were
from the greatest Prince in Europe.

Dublin. Novr 27th 1724

Rothschild

Swift to Charles Ford

Dublin. Novr 27th 1724

I wonder how You expect I can write Letters, when I am deaf and have been so these 2 Months, and am afraid I shall never recover,

difficulties he faced in an attempt to secure acceptance of Wood's patent. Nevertheless, he issued a proclamation offering a reward for the discovery of the author of the *Letter to the Whole People of Ireland*, although he was warned of the futility of the measure. Furthermore, his regard for Swift would prompt him to hope the proclamation ineffective. He therefore turned to find a victim in Harding, Swift's printer.

[1] In his letter of 28 Apr. 1724.

[2] 'was to Alexander' written above the line.

[3] 'with' after 'conclude' is scored out.

and yet I hear more things than ever, For this whole Town is taken up with a Monster they call the Draper, who like a Duns is endeavouring to keep you and the like of you in England; But the L^{d} L^{t} swears you shall come back and live at home, if Woods Halfpence can bring you. I am infinitely obligd to Madame de V. pray tell her I am informed that she is the most agreable conversation in the World, and to be with her and not to hear her must be the greatest Mortification. I gave Ld Oxford no Encouragement that I remember that I would come over, I have at last received a Letter from him, for he is as bad at writing as his Father.[1] He is very kind and has promised me his Father's Picture; and (by the Way) has a Ring for me, which I desire you will be so kind as to get from him, and send it by the first Person you know, who comes hither. I hear severall Packets have been directed to you of the Drapers last Letter,[2] against which the Ld Lieuten^{t} hath published a Proclamation, but that they have all miscarryed, and it seems Manly[3] hath orders to open all Letters where he supposes any Pamphlets against Wood are inclosed.—I have not seen the L^{t} since he came over being hindred by my Disorder nor ever received from him any more than one cold Compliment.[4] It seems he suspects (without Reason) that I am privy to the Draper's Pamphlets.

Friend L— for ought I know hath done a wise Thing, if the Woman (I know her) be so rich as to maintain him and her self better than he could do it without her, and I suppose all women are

[1] In his first letter (9 July) to Edward Harley as second Earl of Oxford, Swift said nothing about a visit to England, but spoke of the first Earl's papers and asked for his portrait. In his reply (2 Nov.) Oxford said that Swift would have to come to England if he was to see the papers, promised the portrait, and desired the acceptance of a ring.

[2] The fourth (see p. 37). Carteret's proclamation offering a reward of £300 for the discovery of the author was issued on 27 Oct.

[3] Isaac Manley, Postmaster.

[4] Swift received no reply to his letter to Carteret of 3 Sept. On 24 Oct. he wrote to Tickell explaining that his health prevented him waiting on Carteret, and perhaps the 'one cold compliment' was the official reply, which is not extant. This passage discredits the anecdote (Sheridan's *Life*, 1784, pp. 246–7) of Swift's encounter with Carteret on the day after the proclamation was issued. Deane Swift, *Essay*, 1752, pp. 269–70, without naming an exact date, tells the same story and claims that he had the account from Swift himself 'about three or four and twenty years ago'. The story, in whatever form accepted, must belong to the middle of Jan. 1725 when Swift first met Carteret. He refers to that meeting as having taken place 'the other day' in his letter to Chetwode of 18 Jan. 1724–5.

now pretty equal to him as a Shepherd.[1]—I desire you will let me know what Person I shall direct to, when I send you a Letter with one inclosed to Don Carlos.[2]—For I am in some pain to answer his, because it differs a little in the manner from those I used to receive. —I am glad you have made some Summer Rambles, which I have been diverted from at the Charge of 400^{ll} in building a Wall,[3] and [to] that want of Exercise I impute my present Ailment.—No we have had no great Rains, give the Devil his due. The Ladyes bear me company in my Illness, I can hear nothing but Trebbles. I have put Mrs Johnson into a Consumption by squalling to me, they desire their humble Service.

The grand Jury has been dissolved for refusing to present a Paper against Wood;[4] a Second was called who are more stubborn. The Government and Judges are all at their Witts end—The dissolving the Jury is reckoned a very illegall arbitrary Thing. I have not been out of doors these three Months, but go to morrow about 4 miles off,[5] to try new Air for a few days.

Address: To Charles Ford Esqr— | to be left at the Coco-Tree | in the Pel-mel | London

Postmark: 7 DE

Forster copy

Swift to Knightley Chetwode

Dublin, 19 December 1724.

Sir,

The fault of my eyes, the confusion of my deafness, and giddiness of my head have made me commit a great blunder. I am just come

[1] Erasmus Lewis, aged fifty-four, had married a widow, Mrs. Anne Bateman, on 1 Oct.

[2] Ford.

[3] The wall surrounding Naboth's Vineyard.

[4] The Grand Jury refused on 21 Nov. to present *Seasonable Advice to the Grand Jury* concerning the bill against Harding, the printer of the Letters, and was thereupon dissolved by Chief Justice Whitshed. The second Grand Jury proved not only stubborn but aggressive, and on 28 Nov. made a presentment condemning the patent (*Drapier's Letters*, ed. H. Davis, pp. xlviii–lvi). We may assume that the presentment was ready when Swift thus expressed his satisfaction to Ford.

[5] Probably to the Grattans at Belcamp. The 'few days' extended to three weeks.

from the country where I was about three weeks in hopes to recover my health; thither your last letter was sent me,[1] with the two enclosed, Mr. Stopford's to you and yours to him. In reading them, I mistook and thought yours to him had been only a copy of what you had already sent to him, so I burned them both as containing things between yourselves, but I preserved yours to me, to answer it, and now reading it again since my return, I find my unlucky error, which I hope you will excuse on account of my many infirmities in body and mind.

I very much approve of putting your son under Mr. Stopford's care, and I am confident you need not apprehend his leaving the College for some years, or if he should, care may be taken to put the young lad into good hands, particularly under Mr. King.[2] I am utterly against his being a gentleman commoner on other regards besides the expense: and I believe fifty pounds a year, which is no small sum to a builder, will maintain him very well a creditable pensioner. I have not seen the Lieutenant yet, being not in a condition to converse with anybody, for want of better ears, and better health. I suppose you do not want correspondents who send you the papers current of late in prose and verses on Wood, Juries, the Drapier, etc.[3] I think there is now a sort of calm, except a very few of the lowest Grub-street, but there have been at least a dozen worth reading. And I hope you approve of the Grand Jury's proceedings, and hardly thought such a spirit could ever rise over this whole kingdom. I am, &c.

Address: To Knightley Chetwode Esq. at his House at Woodbrooke, near Mountmellick.

Endorsed: About James Stopford, and placing my son Vall:[4] under his care in College of Dublin.

[1] A reply, no doubt, to Swift's last letter, see p. 35.

[2] Chetwode's son entered Trinity College under this fellow, the Rev. James King, who was one of those associated with Berkeley in his Bermuda scheme.—Ball.

[3] Some conception of the quantity of literature circulated relative to Wood's coinage may be gathered from *The Drapier's Letters*, ed. H. Davis, pp. 352–83.

[4] Valentine.

Rothschild

Swift to Charles Ford

29 December 1724.

I write to you in this Manner to save Postage to the Person concerned. He is a Clergyman marryed to a near Relation of mine;[1] He is heir to one Capt. Lightburn, a famous man in the County of Meath, whom your Father knew very well, for he was a famous man in his Generation, and was called the God of Trim.[2] He marryed my Cousin in hast before her Relations could settle Matters; He has had a long Suit about the Fortune,[3] and has been used like a Dog: I was Referee for him, but by some Accidents the Reference would not stand. The suit has cost him double the Fortune, and his Estate instead of being disencumbered is a good deal more in debt. He now has an Appeal before the House of L^ds^; and I desire you will do him the usuall Favors on these Occasions, by engaging such Lords as you know, to be there, with a good Inclination, and where I have any Credit, to add my Name; do this, and oblige y^rs^ ever—

Decr 29th 1724 | Engage friend Lewis[4]

Address: To | The Reverend | M^r^: Lightburn.[5]

Rothschild

Swift to Charles Ford

Dublin. Decr 31st 1724

The Letter on the other side[6] was by severall Interruptions stopped till this day and it was not till yesterday I received yours of the

[1] The Rev. Stafford Lightburne, Swift's curate at Laracor, married Hannah, daughter of Willoughby Swift, the Dean's cousin.

[2] Stafford Lightburne, of Staffordstown, co. Meath, died 1697, was for many years Portrieve of Trim, and latterly Member of Parliament. See *The Irish Builder* for 15 Aug. 1888, p. 213.

[3] His wife's fortune had been entrusted by her father to his stepbrother Deane (father of the biographer), and her father's creditors tried to seize it. Writing to Lightburne, 22 Apr. 1725, Swift congratulates Lightburne on the 'good success' of his litigation in this affair. See further B.M. Add. MS. 36148, f. 1.

[4] Erasmus Lewis.

[5] But the letter is written to Ford.

[6] Torn off; the letter here printed is on a half-sheet.

10th—I desire to make my most humble Acknolidgments to M. d. V.[1] for her Receit, which I will certainly make use of, because I think there is more Virtue in her Influence, than in the Medicine it self, and if it succeeds, I shall have the double Pleasure of seeing and hearing her. I find she has often promised to write to me, and I am confident that would be the best Remedy she could prescribe. I congratulate with her upon her Victory over that abominable Rascall, Decker,[2] and I am glad she had so much occasionall Money to lose. The Drapier is not the only Poet, for there are severall Writers in his Praise about as good as himself, I will send some a Post or two hence.[3] This Day is come out a fifth[4] Letter from the Drapier inscribd to Ld Molesworth, but how to send it you I know not, for although I should direct it to Ld Barrymore,[5] it would probably be opened here by Manly the Postmaster, who either by his own Pragmaticallness or the Orders of the Government opens all Pamphletable Letters, and I know nobody that goes from hence. —I am somewhat better of my Deafness, but not in a Condition to go beyond the Deanry Garden, to which I have been confined four Months,[6] and refuse all People who have not hearable Voices. Ld Carteret sent me one cold Compliment in answer to one from me, but since I have had no Commerce with him, I intend to see him when I can hear him. He has shewn more Abilityes than any one I ever knew in his Station. I suppose Ld Suffolks Works[7] sell very well, and I should be as glad to see them as you would be to see

[1] Lady Bolingbroke.

[2] Sir Matthew Decker, London merchant, a director of the East India Company, created Baronet July 1716. He had been entrusted with £50,000 of Mme de Villette's money, and as she had become Lady Bolingbroke he refused to give it up on the ground that he might be made answerable for it by Parliament. Ultimately it was arranged that Lady Bolingbroke should pay £11,000 to Lady Walsingham, daughter of the Duchess of Kendal. See Coxe, *Memoirs of Walpole*, ii. 328, 331, 345.

[3] A copy of the original print of Swift's *Prometheus* is preserved with Swift's letters to Ford. It was probably published some time in November. See *Poems*, pp. 343–7.

[4] 'fifth' written over 'fourth' crossed out. The letter is dated *From my Shop in St. Francis-Street, Dec. 14. 1724*, but as Swift's mention shows it did not appear until 31 Dec.

[5] James, fourth Earl of Barrymore.

[6] Swift ignores his recent visit of three weeks to a place within four miles of Dublin.

[7] *Miscellanies in Prose and Verse, By a Person of Quality*, dated 1725, by Edward Howard, Earl of Suffolk.

those of the Draper. How a mischief could that Parson Sr Robert Sutton[1] get 8000^ll^ a year. I suppose he is about 70 years old.—The Ladyes are just as you left them, but those who see Mrs Johnson seldom, say she grows leaner, she eats about 2 ounces a week, and even drinks less than she did. Sheridan writes Ballads, and Dr Delany grave[2] Poems.—Pray get me my Ring from Lord Oxford;—I writ to him lately.[3]—You must present my humble Service to Mr Lewis Dr Arbuthnott Mr Pope and Mr Gay.—And pray does Lewis continue to like his Match, and could he not have drunk wine enough without his Wife? adieu. Your Family are all well, which I hear though I cannot go to see them.

Address: To Charles Ford Esqr | to be left at the Coco-Tree in the Pell-mell | London
Postmarks: Dublin *and* 6 IA

B.M. Add. MS. 38671

Swift to Thomas Staunton

Dear Tom [5 January 1725]

The inclosed I received from my Manager Robt Proudfoot,[4] and what he says was the same I always suspected: You will please with

[1] Sir Robert Sutton, 1671–1746, was the grandson of Henry, younger brother of the first Lord Lexington. He matriculated at Oxford as a member of Trinity College in 1688, and graduated B.A. in 1692. 'He was educated for the Church, and took deacon's orders. In 1695 he proceeded to Vienna in the joint capacity of Chaplain and Secretary to the second Lord Lexington; on whose recall, in 1697, he was appointed Resident Minister' (*Lexington Papers*, ed. H. Manners Sutton, 1851, p. 4). Thereafter he was Minister at Constantinople and at Paris (1720), and at the time of this letter was M.P. for Nottingham. He was knighted in 1701, and in 1725 was made one of the first members of the revived Order of the Bath. On 10 Dec. 1724 he married Judith, widow of the third Earl of Sunderland, and daughter and coheiress of Benjamin Tichborne. Announcements of the marriage are to be found in London newspapers, e.g. the *Post Man* of 10–12 Dec. 1724, and in Boyer's *Political State*, Dec. 1724, p. 601.

[2] 'grave' written over 'serious' obliterated.

[3] In his letter to Oxford of 27 Nov. Swift said that a gentleman would attend on him for the ring. His Lordship's belated reply of 26 July 1725 reminded Swift that he had no knowledge of the gentleman or where he lived.

[4] Proudfoot had been employed by Swift to conduct business affairs for nine or ten years. See letters to Archdeacon Walls, 27, 30 Dec. 1716; and Thomas Staunton appears to have served in a like capacity, especially about the business of the cathedral.

Your usuall Kindness to act when you think convenient | I am ever yrs. J S.

Deanry-house | Jan[y] 5th 1725

My humble Service to your Family

Address: To Thomas Staunton Esq[r] | at his House on Usher's | Key

Forster copy

Swift to Knightley Chetwode

Dublin, 18 January 1724–25

Sir,

I answer your two letters with the first opportunity of the post. I have already often told you my opinion,[1] and after much reflection, what I think it will be most prudent for you to do. I see nothing new in the case, but some displeasing circumstances which you mention, and which I look upon as probable consequences of that situation you are in. What I would do in such a case I have told you more than once; I would give that person such an allowance as was suitable to my ability, to live at a distance, where no noise would be made. As to the violences you apprehend you may be drawn to, I think nothing could be more unhappy so that would be *vous mettre dans votre tort*; which a wise man would certainly avoid. I do not wonder that you should see a neglect of domestic care when all reconciliation is supposed impossible, everybody is encouraged or discouraged by *Motives*, and the meanest servant will not act his part if he be convinced that it will be impossible ever to please his master. I am sure I have been more than once very particular in my opinion upon this affair, and have supposed any other friend to be in the same case. There are many good towns at a great distance from you, where people may board reasonably, and have the advantage of a church and a neighbourhood.

But what allowance you are content to give must depend upon what you are able. I think such a thing may be continued without making much noise, and the person may be a good while absent as upon health or visits, till the thing grows out of observation or dis-

[1] Swift refers to the proposed separation between Chetwode and his wife. As this letter further indicates he regarded Chetwode as a difficult man with whom to be associated.

course. I entirely approve of your choice of a tutor for your son, and he will consult cheapness as well as other circumstances.[1]

I have been out of order about five months and am just getting out of a cold when my deafness was mending. Sending you papers by the post would be a great expense, and sometimes the post-master kept them. But if any carrier plied between you and us, they might be sent by bundles. They say Cadogan is to lose some of his employments,[2] and I am told, that next packet will tell us of several changes. I was the other day well enough to see the Lord Lieutenant, and the town has a thousand foolish stories of what passed between us; which indeed was nothing but old friendship without a word of politics. I am, &c.

Address: To Knightley Chetwode Esq., at Woodbroke, near Mountmellick.
Endorsed: With advice about H. C.[3] and how to manage our separation and per Residence.

Forster copy

Swift to Knightley Chetwode

30 January 1724–25.

Sir,

Your letter come this moment to my hand,[4] and the messenger waits and returns to-morrow. You describe yourself as in a very uneasy way as to Birr.[5] I know it not, but I believe it will be hard to find any place without some objections. To be permitted to live among relations will have a fair face, and be looked on as generous and good-natured, and therefore I think you should comply, neither do I apprehend any consequences from the person if the rest of the family be discreet, and you say nothing against that. I think it would be well if you had some companions in your house with whom to converse, or else the spleen will get the better, at least in long winter

[1] Cf. Swift to Chetwode 19 Dec.

[2] On the death of the Duke of Marlborough, June 1722, Cadogan succeeded to the posts of Commander-in-Chief and Master-General of the Ordnance.

[3] Hester Chetwode.

[4] Probably an answer to the preceding letter.

[5] Birr, a town in the King's county owned by the Earl of Rosse, and later generally known as Parsonstown, seems to have been suggested as a place of residence for Mrs. Chetwode.

evenings, when you cannot be among your workmen nor always amuse yourself with reading.

We have had no new thing of any value since the second letter from nobody, as they call it; the author of those two letters is said to be a Lord's eldest son.[1] The Drapier's five letters, and those two, and five or six copies of verses are all that I know of, and those I suppose you have had. The talk now returns fresh that the Lord Lieutenant will soon leave us, and the Duke of Newcastle[2] succeed, and that Horace Walpole will be Secretary of State.[3] I am, &c.[4]

Address: To Knightley Chetwode Esq.
Endorsed: A little before H. C. and I parted.

Forster copy

Swift to Knightley Chetwode

Dublin, 20 February 1724–25

I extracted the articles you sent me, and I sent them to Mr. Stopford,[5] and this morning he showed me a letter he intends for you to-night, which I think shows he is ready to do all in his power: that of contracting debts he will give bonds for; the others you cannot well expect more than his word, and you have the remedy in your power, so I hope no difficulty will remain. I am very glad you

[1] The reference is to two letters addressed to Chief Justice Whitshed on the illegality of his discharge of the Grand Jury—*A Letter from a Friend To the Right Honourable* — — —, signed N. N. and dated 'Dec the First 1724'; and *A Second Letter from A Friend To the Right Honourable* — — —, also signed N. N. and dated 'Jan. 4, 1724/5:'. They exhibit more legal knowledge than it is probable Swift possessed, and may have been written, though doubtfully, by Rob Lindsay, an eminent lawyer (*Drapier's Letters*, ed. Davis, pp. 272–86, 368–9).

[2] The Duke of Newcastle had been transferred from the office of Chamberlain to that of Secretary of State when Carteret was appointed Lord-Lieutenant.

[3] Sir Robert Walpole's younger brother, afterwards created Baron Walpole, was then Envoy-extraordinary at Paris.

[4] In the Woodbrooke transcript this letter is misplaced, following upon that of 2 June 1723. On the opposite blank page this note appears: 'This letter misplaced in transcribing it should *follow* those of *1724* instead of following them. E. W. C.' The initials stand for Edward Wilmot Chetwode, Forster's friend. The letter transcript is not in his hand.

[5] This and the preceding letter relate to Chetwode's separation from his wife.

are putting off your land, and I hope you will contract things into as narrow a circle as can consist with your ease, since your son and other children will now be an addition to your annual charge.

As soon as it is heard that I have been with folks in power, they get twenty stories about the town of what has passed, but very little truth. An English paper in print related a passage of two lines writ on a card, and the answer, of which story four parts in five is false. The answer was writ by Sir W. Fownes. The real account is a trifle, and not worth the time to relate. Thus much for that passage in your letter.[1]

As to company, I think you must endeavour to cotton with the neighbouring clergy and squires. The days are lengthening and you will have a long summer to prepare yourself for winter. You should pass a month now and then with some county friends, and play at whist for sixpence. I just steal this time to write that you may have my opinions at the same time with Mr. Stopford's letter. I do think by all means he and you should be as well together as the situation of things will admit, for he has a most universal good reputation; I think above any young man in the kingdom. I am, |

Your most obedient, &c., |

J. S.

Address: To Knightley Chetwode, Esq., at Woodbrooke, near Mountmellick.
Endorsed: About James Stopford's security to indemnify me for debts of H. C.'s[2] contracting.

[1] A letter from G. Malcolm to the Hon. John Molesworth 1725? (*H.M.C., Report on MSS. in Various Collections*, viii. 386) attributes to Swift two lines said to have been written on a card, and left in a window of Dublin Castle, when he had been kept waiting by Lord Carteret.

My very good Lord, it's a very hard task
To wait so long and have nothing to ask.

Carteret's reply is given as:

My very good Dean, there's few come here
But have something to ask or something to fear.

Nichols in a note to the 'Biographical Anecdotes' prefixed to his *Supplement to Dr. Swift's Works*, 1779, prints the couplets in a slightly different form. The two were doubtless penned in Jan. 1725 when Swift first waited on Carteret. It appears, furthermore, that the reply was not by Carteret but, as here stated, by Sir William Fownes, father of Swift's friend Mrs. Cope. See *Poems*, p. 368.

[2] Hester Chetwode.

Rothschild

Swift to Charles Ford

Mar. 1. 1724–5

I thought to have writt you a longer Letter and sent you more Papers, but I have not been able to procure them, and the Bearer Mr Williamson[1] (who is the Goldsmith I employ) coming to sudden on me, as just going to Sea, hath shortned my Letter. Mrs Johnson is as usuall, unless rather worse, for she eats now but a mouthfull a day. I wish she would go to London.

Your Family in Dawson Street are well; I dined with them lately. I will write to you soon more at large. Pray return Mr Gay thanks for my Book[2] when You see him. I have read it all over, and find some Additions that I like much especially the Geneology of the Shoe boy—Farewell.

Address: To Charles Ford Esqr

Rothschild

Swift to Charles Ford

Dublin. Mar. 11th 1724–5

I have been resolving for some time past to go to England about the End of this month, and have lately communicated my Intention to five or six Friends, who are all dissuading me with the greatest Violence, and desire that I would at least defer it till next Year. Their Reasons I do not all approve; because I know very well[3] how apt the People of Ireland are to think that their little Affairs are regarded in England. They would have it that what has been lately written about the Drapier has given great Offence on your side, that the private Malice of the Projector and those who were examined in his Behalf might tempt them to some violent Action of Revenge, and that M^r^ W—[4] thinks himself personally offended, and that somebody[5] for whose Advantage that Project was contrived would

[1] Thomas Williamson, died 1741. Vicars, *Prerogative Wills*.

[2] Gay's *Poems on Several Occasions*, 1720, which he had at last received. See Harold Williams, *Dean Swift's Library*, pp. 8, 73. The genealogy of the Shoe boy was added in this edition of *Trivia*, ii. 99–220.

[3] 'very well' written over 'were' crossed out.

[4] Walpole.

[5] The Duchess of Kendal; 'somebody' is written after 'the S.' crossed out.

use all means to prosecute whoever has opposed it, which may end in Messengers heads, Accusations, Imprisonments &c. Now in my own Mind I am quite of another Opinion. I do not think the thing is of Weight enough for a Ministry to trouble themselves about, and as for the Malice of mean paltry Rascals it may be avoyded by common Care. There was a Time when in England some great Friends looked on me as in Danger, and used to warn me against Night walking &c.; but I thought it was a shame to be afraid of such Accidents and looked as if a man affected to be thought of Importance. Neither do I find that Assassinations are things in fashion at present; and in my Opinion a Secretary of State is a much more terrible animal, when he has a mind to be malicious. Our Friend in Grafton Street[1] swears it is a Fatality upon me. In order to their Satisfaction I desire to know your Opinion, whether I may be in any Danger of being teazed at Whitehall, or have Searches for Papers &c. for as to private malice, I very little apprehend it. Pray write me your Thoughts as soon as you can, that I may take my Measures.

Our Friend with the weak Stomach eats less than ever,[2] and I am in pain about her, and would fain persuade her to go for England, but she will not. Your People are well, I dined with them very lately—

Y^{r}-

Address: To Charles Ford Esqr | to be left at the Coco-tree | in Pell-mell | London
Postmarks: Dublin *and* 19 MR

Harvard College Library[3]

Swift to Mrs. Pratt

[18 March 1724–5]

Madam,[4]

Mrs Fitzmaurice[5] did the unkindest thing she could imagine. She sends an open Note by a Servant (for she was too much a Prude to

[1] Compare the mention of Grafton Street in Swift's letter to Ford of 16 June 1724 *ad fin.* Can 'Our Friend' be Stella? There appears to be no evidence of where she resided in Dublin after 1721, when she was not at the Deanery. Mrs. Dingley lived at one time in Grafton Street after Stella's death, at the house of Mrs. Ridgeway, daughter of Mrs. Brent, the supervisor of Swift's household.

[2] Stella.

[*For notes 3, 4, 5 see overleaf.*

write me a Letter) desiring that the Dean of St Patrick's should enquire for one Howard Master of a Ship who had brought over a Screen to him the s^{d} Dean from Mrs Prat. Away I ran to the Custom-house, where they told me the Ship was expected every day; but the God of Winds in confederacy with Mrs Fitzmaurice, to teaze me, kept the Ship at least a Month longer, and left me miserable, in a State of Impatience between Hope and Fear, worse than a Lady who is in pain that her Cloaths will not be ready against the Birthday: I will not move Your good Nature by representing how many restless Days and Nights I have passed, with what Dreams my sleep hath been disturbed, Where I sometimes saw the Ship sinking, my Screen floating in the Sea, and the Mermaids strugling which of them should get it for her own Appartment. At last Mr Medlycott[1] whose Heart inclines him to pity the distressed gave me Notice of it's safe Arrival; He interposed his Authority, and over-ruling the tedious Forms of the Custom-house, sent my Screen to the Deanry, where it was immediatly opened on Tuesday the 16th instant, three minutes seven seconds after four a Clock in the afternoon, the day being fair, but somewhat windy, the Sun in Aries, and the Moon within thirty nine hours, eight seconds and a half of being full; All which I find by consulting Ptolemy, to be fortunate Incidents prognosticating, that with due Care my Screen will escape the Mops of the House mayd, and the greasy hands of the Footmen.

At the opening of the Screen just after dinner, some Company of

[1] Thomas Medlycott, one of the Commissioners of the Revenue in Ireland.

---

[3] The original of the major part of this letter, as here used, is preserved in the Harvard Library, and in this form it was printed by Deane Swift in 1765. Over twenty years earlier, however, in *A New Miscellany in Prose and Verse . . . London: Printed for T. Read, . . . 1742*, this letter, ascribed to Swift, was printed with the addition of the postscript and seven detached sentences, 'I sometimes dine', to 'upon her Return'. In this form the letter was printed by Nichols in his *Supplement*, 1779. The additional sentences, independently of the letter, are to be found in Swift's autograph in Lord Rothschild's Library, No. 2291. In this fragment there are two additional sentences, the one beginning 'Lady Kerry' the other, 'Two famous Men'. This additional part of the letter is here printed from the Rothschild manuscript.

[4] Provost Pratt's sister-in law, the wife of Captain John Pratt, was a daughter of Sir John Brookes, and connected with Lady Kerry, subsequently mentioned, by the marriage of her sister to Lord Kerry's brother. See *Journal*, 13 Dec. 1710, and note.

[5] Mrs. Pratt's sister, the wife of Lieut.-Col. William Fitzmaurice.

both Sexes were present: The Ladyes were full of Malice, and the Men, of Envy, while I remained very affectedly calm. But all agreed, that nothing shewd a better Judgment than to know how to make a proper Present and that no Present could be more judiciously chosen. For, no Man in this Kingdom wanted a Screen as much as my self, and besides, I had left the World, it was very kind to send the World to me.[1] However, one of the Ladyes affirmed, that your Gift was an open Reflection upon my Age, that she had made the same Present some time ago to her Grandfather, and that she could not imagine how any of her Sex would send a Screen to a Gentleman without a Design to insinuate that he was absolutely un homme sans consequence. For my own Part I confess I never expected to be sheltered by the World, when I have been so long endeavoring to shelter my self from it.—

See how ill you bestow your Favor, where you meet with nothing but Complaints and Reproaches instead of Acknowledgments for thinking, in the midst of Courts and Diversions upon an absent and insignificant Man buried in Obscurity. But I know it is as hard to give Thanks, as to take them, therefore I shall say no more than that I receive your acceptable Present just as I am sure you desire you should. Though I cannot sit under my own Vine or my own Fig-tree yet I will sit under my own Screen and bless the Giver; but I cannot promise it will add one Jot to the Love and Esteem I have for You, because it is impossible for me to be more than I have always been, and shall ever continue | Madam | Your most obedient and | oblidged Servant | Jonath Swift.

I just observd that the two Celestiall Maps are placed at the Bottom within two Inches of the Ground, which is the most fashionable Circumstance in the whole Work.

I sometimes dine in third Places with Your Stoick Mr Prat and find he continues in Health, but of late very busy and a Courtier.

I desire to present My most humble Service to my Lady Savil.[2] Lady Kerry is happy in her Lad's compa[ny] a hundred Miles off.

[1] As the postscript shows the screen was covered with maps.

[2] Mrs. Pratt's daughter, married to Sir George Savile, Bt., of Rufford, Nottinghamshire. Their only son, George, 1726–84, was a distinguished parliamentarian (*D.N.B.*).

Two famous Men dyed tother day, Jos[eph] and Jacob Pepper. [M^r] Fitsmorice dines temperately at a Tavern, and sometimes with Clergymen for want of better Company, but I do not hear his Bills are very frequent from Liscence.

Mr Medlycott dines with me every Sunday, and goes to Church like any thing.

Mrs Fitsmorice is left desolate: I reckoned but fifteen Ladyes and five Gentlemen tother Night in her Play-room, and I condoled with her upon it. 'tis thought she will fall out with My Lady Carteret for drawing away her Company, but at present they are very great, as I find by consulting them both.

I think you are acquainted with Lady Worseley,[1] if so, tell her how angry I am at her coming to Ireland, as I expected, and was told she was actually landed, whereupon being confined at that Time by a Deafness, I writ her a most cavalier Letter, which being brought back I tore in a Rage—

Miss Carteret[2] is every day get[ting] new Magazines of Arms to destroy all England upon her Return.

Forster No. 555

Swift to James Stopford

[? April 1725]

Dear Jim,[3]

I blundered this morning when I read your lett^r for I understood you had been ill and was well again. but here the Lodges[4] tell me you are in an Ague, and what is worse have no Creature to take care of you, for God sake have some understanding Body about you, and do not rely on a College Bedmaker. The Money is ready as I told you; & Mrs Johnson desires to know your Directions upon it.[5] | I am ever your S^t

Friday: past one

Address: To the Rev. Mr. Stopford, at his Lodgings in the College.

[1] Lady Carteret's mother.

[2] The reference is to Carteret's youngest daughter, then aged nine, to whom Philips addressed 'namby-pamby' verses.

[3] Probably written in or near Apr. 1725.

[4] Stella and Mrs. Dingley.

[5] Evidently the money Stella lent to him.

Tickell Papers

Swift to Lord Carteret

[Deanery-house, 17 April 1725]

My Lord[1]

I have been so long afflicted with a Deafness, and at present with a Giddyness in my Head (both old Distempers to me) that I have not been able to attend Your Excellency and my Lady Carteret as my Inclination and Duty oblige me; and I am now hasting into the Country to try what Exercise and better Air will do towards my Recovery.[2] Not knowing how long I may be absent, nor how soon you may think fit to leave the Kingdom, I take this Occasion of returning Your Excellency and My Lady Carteret my most humble Acknowledgements for Your great Civilityes to me, which I wish it were in my Power to deserve.[3]

I have only one humble Request to make Your Excellency which I had in my Heart ever since You were nominated Lord Lieutenant, and it is in favour of Mr Sheridan.[4] I beg You will take Your Time for bestowing him some Church-Preferment to the value of 140^ll^ a year. He is agreed on all Hands to have done more publick Service by many Degrees in the Education of Youth than any five of his Vocation, and hath much more Learning than usually falls to the

[1] Swift's autograph letter is written on a sheet folded to quarto size. The letter is written on pp. 1 and 2. P. 3 is blank. The endorsement of receipt appears on p. 4.

[2] Swift was on the point of starting for Quilca, which had been lent to him by Sheridan. Stella and Rebecca Dingley accompanied him. In a letter dated 24 Apr. Bishop Nicolson writes: 'At an adjournment of the City Sessions about ten days ago, Dr. Swift was made a freeman, though the honour was denied him on a former motion made to that purpose whilst their worthy Recorder the Attorney General was present, and one of the prints of this day gives the following remarkable account of the gentleman: "This week the Reverend Dean Swift regrettedly left this city, and is not expected home till towards the first of August."' (Archbishop Wake's Correspondence).

[3] Early meetings with Carteret were of a business and formal nature. Any social meeting with Lady Carteret probably did not take place till later in the year. See his verses addressed to her, *An Apology to the Lady Carteret* (*Poems*, pp. 374–80) in which the reference to her visit to Naboth's Vineyard, ll. 88, 126, 138, suggest that the event took place in the autumn rather than in the spring. Swift had made the acquaintance of Lady Carteret, as Miss Worsley, before her marriage in 1710.

[4] Carteret had not been long in Ireland before making Sheridan's acquaintance. He was appointed one of his chaplains.

share of those who profess to teaching, being perfectly skilled in the Greek as well as the Latin Tongue, and well acquainted with all the antient Writers in Poetry, Philosophy and History. His greatest Fault is a Wife and seven Children, for which there is no excuse but that a Wife is thought necessary to a Schoolmaster. His Constitution is so weak, that in a few Years he must give up his Business, and probably must starve without some Preferment, for which he is an ill Solliciter: My Lord Bishop of Elphin[1] hath promised to recommend this Request to Your Excellency, and I hope you will please to believe that it proceeds in me wholly from Justice and Humanity, for he is neither a Dependant nor Relation of mine, but my Plea for him is Tua me Virtus ubi fecit amicum. | I humbly take my leave, and remain | with the utmost Respect, | My Lord | Your Excellencyes | Most dutifull and most | obedient Serv[t] | Jonath Swift

Deanry-house
Ap[r] 17th 1725

Endorsed: Deanry-house 17 Ap. 1725 | Dean Swift to my Ld Lt. | R. 20

Forster copy

Swift to Knightley Chetwode

Thursday, nine at night.[2]

Sir,

You are to understand that I design to stay out a night being no very active rider, and it is very possible that may be inconvenient to you. I know not what to say, nor how far your civility carries you beyond your ease. In that case I should be under much constraint; but if the journey be what you are inclined to, and that you think that Mr. Archdeacon Walls and me worth riding so far with, I will continue to have your mare[3] ready saddled for myself between six and seven to-morrow morning at the Deanery House, which the Archdeacon tells me is directly in the way. I am, Sir, | Your most obedient humble servant, | J. Swift.

[1] Bolton after a short tenure of the bishopric of Clonfert, had been translated to Elphin just a year before. Though Swift regarded him previously as 'born to be my tormentor' (letter to Cope, 9 Oct. 1722) Bolton had joined Archbishop King in the Privy Council in opposing the proclamation against the Drapier.

[2] The date is difficult to conjecture. The earlier part of 1725 is possible.

[3] Swift's friend had evidently supplied him with a mount.

Kilkenny Archaeological Society Journal

Swift to the Rev. Stafford Lightburne

Quilca, Apr 22d, 1725.

Sr[1]

Your letter was sent hither to me;[2] I have been so ill with a Giddyness and Deafness, that I thought it best to retire into the Country where I am now in a wild Place belonging to Mr Sheridan 7 miles from Kells. I am very glad of your good success in England, for I always believed you had justice on your side; at the same Time I am grieved at the Difficultyes your Adversaryes Family must be under by their own wrong Proceedings, and should be more so if that Puppy who is heir[3] had not so behaved himself as to forfeit all Regard or Pity. Mr Worrall has the remaining Bonds of Laracor, &c., and a Power from me to receive the money, which I much want, having ruined myself by building a wall,[4] which is as bad as a Lawsuit. I desire Mr Proudfoot[5] may with his Paymts give the names of every Tenant and the summs they payd, and take Receits from Mr Worrall. Present my service to my Cozen. I hope this Journey has contributed to her Health as well as her Fortune. | I am yr most humble Servt | J. Swift.

The Postman tells me, that a letter directed to me at Mr Latimer's at Kells, and put into the By–Bag at Trim will be sent to me, so that if you have any Occasion to write, you may take that way. I have desired Mr Wallis[6] to appear for me at the Visitation.

Address: To the Reverend Mr Lightburn, | At his House in Trim.

[1] This letter was submitted at a meeting of the Kilkenny Archaeologica Society by its Chairman, Dr. Gregg, the then Bishop of Cork, Cloyne, and Ross. The owner of the manuscript was present. The letter was subsequently printed in the *Journal* of the Society, Fourth Series, vol. 5, p. 264. By permission of the same owner the letter was again printed from the original, *Notes and Queries*, vii. 4, p. 364, 5 Nov. 1887. In this printing variants are patent misreadings, with one exception.

[2] Lightburne served as Swift's curate at Laracor from 1722 to 1733.

[3] Incorrectly printed 'here' in the Archaeological Society's *Journal*. Correctly printed in *Notes and Queries*.

[4] The wall round Naboth's Vineyard.

[5] Swift's agent at Laracor.

[6] See ii. 387.

Forster copy

Swift to Knightley Chetwode

[27 May 1725.]

Sir,

The place I am in is 8 miles from the post, so it may be some days before I have convenience of sending this.[1] I have recovered my hearing for some time, at least recovered it so as not to be troublesome to those I converse with, but I shall never be famous for acuteness in that sense, and am in daily dread of relapses; against which I prepare my mind as well as I can, and I have too good a reason to do so, for my eyes will not suffer me to read small prints, nor anything by candlelight, and if I grow blind, as well as deaf, I must needs become very grave, and wise, and insignificant. The weather has been so unfavourable, and continues so, that I have not been able to ride above once, and have been forced for amusement to set Irish fellows to work, and to oversee them. I live in a cabin and in a very wild country; yet there are some agreeablenesses in it, or at least I fancy so, and am levelling mountains and raising stones,[2] and fencing against inconveniencies of a scanty lodging, want of victuals, and a thievish race of people.[3]

I detest the world because I am growing wholly unfit for it, and could be only happy by never coming near Dublin, nor hearing from it, or anything that passes in the public. I am sorry your enemies are so restless to torment you, and truly against the opinion of philosophers I think, next to health a man's fortune is the tenderest point. For life is a trifle, and reputation is supplied by innocence, but the ruin of a man's fortune makes him a slave, which is infinitely worse than loss of life or credit, when a man hath not deserved either; and I repent nothing so much, as my own want of worldly wisdom, in squandering all I had saved on a cursed wall;[4] although I had your example to warn me, since I had often ventured to rally you for your buildings, which have hindred you from that

[1] This letter, as Ball observes, was evidently evoked by a reply from Chetwode (missing) to Swift's letter of 20 Feb.

[2] Improvements to Sheridan's house at Quilca upon which Swift engaged himself.

[3] It was here during the summer of 1725 that Swift composed the lines 'To Quilca, a Country House in no very good Repair'. See *Poems*, pp. 1034–5.

[4] The wall surrounding Naboth's Vineyard.

command of money you might otherwise have had. I have been told that lenders of money abound, not from the riches of the kingdom, but by the want of trade, but whether chattels be good security I cannot tell. I dare say Mr. Lightburne will be able to take up what he wants, upon the security of land, by the judgement of the House of Lords; and I reckon he is almost a lawyer, and would make a very good solicitor.

I can give you no encouragement to go out of your way for a visit to this dismal place; where we have hardly room to turn ourselves, and where we send five miles round for a lean sheep. I never thought I could battle with so many inconveniencies, and make use of so many Irish expedients, much less could I invite any friend to share in them; and we are eight miles from Kells, the nearest habitable place. These is the state of affairs here. But I should be glad to know you had taken some method to lump your debts. I could have wished Mr. Stopford had let me know his intentions of travelling with Graham.[1] I know not the conditions he goes on, and there is but one reason why I should approve of such a ramble. I know all young travellers are eager to travel again, but I doubt whether he consults his preferment, or whether he will be able to do any good to *un enfant gaté*, as Graham is. Pray desire him to write to me. I had rather your son might have the advantage of his care, than of his chambers. I received no prints. I know not whether we have a new King, or the old; much less anything of Barber. I did not receive any packet from you. I am, |

Ever yours, &c.

The six months are over, so the discoverer of the Drapier will not get the three hundred pounds as I am told.[2] I hope the Parliament will do as they ought, in that matter, which is the only public thing, I have in my mind.[3] I hope you like Dr. Delany's country place,[4]

[1] The Right Hon. William Graham, a pupil of Sheridan and Stopford, who later married a daughter of Lord Lansdown. See further Swift's letter to him of 26 Apr. 1737.

[2] The reward for the discovery of the Drapier was only offered for that period.

[3] What Swift wanted was an inquiry into the circumstances of the grant to Wood, a request which the government could hardly regard with equanimity.

[4] Delville, a villa built by Delany and Dr. Helsham at Glasnevin to the north of Dublin, for which Swift invented the name of Heldeville from the names of the two owners. Dr. Helsham soon relinquished his interest, and the name became Delville. A description of the house and its gardens, as they appeared in 1744,

and am glad to find you among such acquaintances, especially such a person as he.

Address: To Knightley Chetwode, Esq.

Forster No. 555

Swift to the Rev. James Stopford

June 19th 1725.

Dear Jim.

I have several Reasons to be glad & sorry for your Intention to travel again,[1] I have one to be glad which I will leave you to guess.[2] I doubt you will have but little satisfaction in your Companion, for I fear he is incapable of being good for anything, but the more is your merit if you can make him so. He can bear no Authority over him, and without it he will come to nothing but be a Beaux or a Squire. However, you will glut yourself with travelling, and if you be wise you will be rich, at least out of debt, for which last, Mrs Johnson, like all usurers, is sorry.

I am sure I can safely say every thing that a human Creature can deserve in your recommendation, if any of my Friends be alive, and unchanged when you return to London. But I know none of the Court, I wish you might see Ld Carteret before you go, I would write to him to receive you favourably if you think fit: a Mr Tickell may present you. My Lord will be always a man of great consequence. I know not whether it would be convenient to you to see Ld Bolingbroke. I have been so long out of the world that I have lost all my forein Acquaintances. Perhaps in Paris they may ask after Monsir Swift. If Monsieur Giraldi[3] be alive in Florence, you will make him my Compliments, or if the Marquis de Monteleon[4] be in

will be found in the *Correspondence* of Mrs. Delany, ed. Lady Llanover, 1861, ii. 308, 314. See also Ball's *History of County Dublin*, part vi, 129–33.

[1] Doubtless Stopford had received Swift's message contained in the preceding letter to Chetwode.

[2] It appears from a subsequent sentence that Swift was glad because Stopford would now be in a position to repay Stella money which she had lent him.

[3] Secretary to the Duke of Tuscany. See Swift's letter to him in French, 25 Feb. 1714–15.

[4] The Marquis de Monteleon was in the service of the King of Spain (*Journal*, p. 585).

any Ambassy, when you go, he will be kind to any one that knew me, he is an Italian. Or young Davenant,[1] if he be yet a Minister abroad, or the Count de Gillingberg,[2] if he has not lost his Head, may perhaps be an Ambassad^r^ somewhere in your way. If he be I would be glad to know where to write to him, upon an Affair wherein he promised to inform me.

I have no Advice to give you as to your Conduct, for you want none, but to look to your Health, and make as many Acquaintances among Englishmen of Consequence as you can. I pray God protect you & I shall be ever with the most entire affection | Y^rs^, &c

I desire you will command Mr Ford in London, to carry you to Dr Arbuthnett, Mr Pope & Mr Gay, & to recommend you as he would a Friend that He & I esteem & love as much as possible, or I will write to them if you desire it: but do not carry your × × with you.

Address: To the Reverend Mr Stopford | at his Chambers | in Trinity College | Dublin.

Dodsley Miscellanies 1745, x. 77

Swift to the Rev. Thomas Sheridan

[*June*] 25, 1725.[3]

I have a Packet of Letters, which I intended to send by *Molly* who hath been stopped three Days by the bad Weather; but now I

[1] See Charles Davenant to Swift, 3 Nov. 1713, and note. The reference is to the son, Henry Molins Davenant.

[2] Charles, Count Gyllenborg, 1670–1746, was Swedish Ambassador in London 1710–16, during which time Swift made his acquaintance. He was implicated in a Jacobite plot in Jan. 1716–17, and expelled the kingdom in Aug. 1717. He afterwards held high offices in his own country. Less than three years later Swift dedicated to him his *Abstract of the History of England* (*Prose Works*, ed. Temple Scott, x. 193–268), which he previously intended to dedicate to Charles XII. After that monarch's death in 1718 he transferred the dedication to Gyllenborg, a curious choice in either instance.

[3] Editors before Ball dated this letter 25 Jan. We know Swift to have stayed at Sheridan's small country house at Quilca, co. Cavan, from Apr. to Oct. in 1725, when he was engaged in completing *Gulliver's Travels*. The letter clearly belongs to that summer visit; and June 1725 may be accepted as the true date. See *Poems*, p. 1034.

will send them by the Post To-morrow to *Kells*, and inclos'd to Mr. *Tickell* there is one to you, and one to James Stopford.[1]

I can do no Work in this terrible Weather, which hath put us all seventy times out of Patience. I have been deaf nine Days, and am now pretty well recovered again.

Pray desire Mr. *Staunton* and *Worrall* to continue giving themselves some Trouble with Mr. *Pratt*; but let it succeed or not, I hope I shall be easy.[2]

Mrs. *Johnson* swears it will rain till *Michaelmas*. She is so pleased with her Pick-ax,[3] that she wears it fastened to her Girdle on her left Side, in Balance with her Watch. The Lake is strangely overflown, and we are desperate about Turf, being forced to buy it three Miles off: And Mrs. Johnson (God help her) gives you many a Curse. Your Mason is come, but cannot yet work about your Garden. Neither can I agree with him about the great Wall. For the rest, *vide* the Letter you will have on Monday, if Mr. *Tickell* uses you well.

The news of this Country is, that the Maid you sent down, *John Farelly's* Sister, is married; but the Portion and Settlement are yet a Secret. The Cows here never give milk on *Midsummer-Eve*.

You would wonder what carking and caring there is among us for small Beer and lean Mutton, and starved Lamb, and stopping Gaps, and driving Cattle from the Corn. In that we are all-to-be-Din-gloyed.

The Lady's Room smoaks; the Rain drops from the Skies into the Kitchen; our Servants eat and drink like the Devil, and pray for Rain, which entertains them at Cards and Sleep, which are much lighter than Spades, Sledges, and Crows. Their Maxim is:

Eat like a Turk,
Sleep like a Dormouse;
Be last at Work,
At Victuals foremost.

[1] Probably the preceding letter.

[2] Captain John Pratt, Deputy Vice-Treasurer of Ireland, to whom Swift had given money to invest, was in difficulties owing to financial defalcations alleged to involve a deficiency of £100,000. In June, on failing to find security, he was committed to prison (Bishop Nicholson's *Letters*, ii. 605). In Dec. 1727 debate on the 'publick Accounts of the Nation' was resumed (*Journals of the House of Lords of Ireland*, iii. 18, 19, 39).

[3] In *Temple Bar*, lxvi. 568, Miss Frances Power Cobbe gave an account of this pickaxe then in the possession of her family.

Which is all at present; hoping you and your good Family are well, as we, &c. are all at this present Writing, *&c.*

Robin has just carried out a Load of Bread and cold Meat for Breakfast; this is their way; but now a Cloud hangs over them, for fear it should hold up, and the Clouds blow off.

I write on till *Molly* comes in for the Letter. O, what a Draggle Tail will she be before she gets to *Dublin*! I wish she may not happen to fall upon her Back by the Way.

I affirm against *Aristotle*, that Cold and Rain congregate Homogenes, for they gather together you and your Crew, at Whist, Punch, and Claret. Happy Weather for Mrs. [*Mac*],[1] *Betty*, and *Stopfords*, and all true Lovers of Cards and Laziness.

The Blessings of a Country Life

Far from our Debtors,
No Dublin *Letters,*
Not seen by our Betters.

The Plagues of a Country Life

A Companion with News,
A great want of Shoes;
Eat lean Meat, or chuse;
A Church without Pews,
Our Horses astray,
No Straw, Oats, or Hay;
December in May,
Our Boys run away,
All Servants at play.

Molly *sends for the Letter.*

The Library, Armagh

Swift to —— Sheridan

[Quilca, 26 June 1725]

S[r]

I have got two Surveys from Mr. Sheridan of his lands here, but both very imperfect; If you please to send me a Surveyor, and let me

[1] Mrs. MacFadden, Sheridan's mother-in-law.

know what I am to give him, for surveying the land in Parcels, I shall employ him, and if the Weath[r] mends I shall want y[r] Advice; I hope the Surveyor you send, will not be too great a man to lodge in a Barn, for you know the condition we are in. I desire my humble Service to Mr Fitzherbert and his Lady. I am yr humble | ser[t] |

Jonath. Swift

Quilca June 26th
1725

Address: To Mr Sheridan at Shercock.[1]

Dodsley Miscellanies 1745, x. 81

Swift to the Rev. Thomas Sheridan

Quilca, 28 June, 1725.

You run out of your time so merrily, that you are forced to anticipate it, like a young Heir that spends his Fortune faster than it comes in; for your letter is dated to-morrow, *June* 29. and God knows when it was writ, or what *Saturday* you mean;[2] but I suppose it is the next, and therefore your own Mare and Dr. *S*— Horse or Mare, or some other Horse or Mare, with your own Mare aforesaid, shall set out on *Wednesday* next, which will be *June* 30. and so they will have two Nights Rest, if you begin your Journey on *Saturday*. You are an unlucky Devil, to get a Living the furthest in the Kingdom from *Quilca*. If it be worth two hundred Pound a Year. My Lord Lieutenant hath but barely kept his Word,[3] for the other Fifty must go in a Curate and Visitation Charges, and Poxes, Proxies I mean. If you are under the Bishop of *Cork*, he is a capricious Gentleman; but you must flatter him monstrously upon his Learning and his Writings; that you have read his Book against *Toland*[4] a hundred

[1] The recipient of this letter would appear to have been in the employment of William Fitzherbert of Shercock, in the county of Cavan. He was possibly a relation of Swift's friend.—Ball.

[2] Sheridan had been presented by Carteret to the living of Rincurran, co. Cork. His letters of presentation bear date 2 July, and his institution took place on the 19th of that month.—Ball.

[3] The living of Rincurran had been vacant for some months, and perhaps Swift had it in mind when writing to Carteret, 17 Apr. 1725.

[4] John Toland's *Christianity not Mysterious*, published in London in two

Times, and his Sermons (if he has printed any) have been always your Model, &c. Be not disappointed if your Living does not answer the Sum: Get Letters of Recommendation to the Bishop and Principal Clergy, and to your Neighbouring Parson or Parsons particularly. I often advised you to get some knowledge of Tythes and Church-livings. You must learn the Extent of your Parish, the general Quantity of Arable Land and Pasture in your Parish, the common Rate of Tythes for an Acre of the several Sorts of Corn, and of Fleeces and Lambs, and to see whether you have any Glebe; pray act like a Man of this World. I doubt being so far off, you must not let your Living as I do, to the several Farmers, but to one Man: But by all means do not let it for more than one Year, till you are surely apprized of the real Worth; and even then never let it for above three. Pray take my Advice for once, and be very busy, while you are there. It is one good Circumstance that you got such a Living in a convenient Time, and just when Tythes are fit to be Let; only Wool and Lamb are due in Spring, or perhaps belong to the late Incumbent. You may learn all on the Spot, and your Neighbouring Parsons may be very useful, if they please, but do not let them be your Tenants: Advise with Archdeacon *Walls*, but do not follow him in all Things. Take care of the principal 'Squire or 'Squires, they will all tell you the worst of your Living; so will the Proctors and Tythe-Jobbers; but you will pick out Truth from among them. Pray shew yourself a Man of Abilities. After all I am but a weak Brother my-self; perhaps some Clergy in *Dublin*, who know that Country, will further inform you. Mr. *Townshend* of *Cork* will do you any good Offices on my Account, without any Letter.—Take the Oaths heartily to the Powers that be, and remember that Party was not made for depending Puppies.[1] I forgot one principal Thing, to take care of going regularly thro' all the Forms of Oaths and Inductions, for the least wrong Step will put you to the Trouble of repassing your Patent, or voiding your Living.—

editions in 1696, aroused a storm of controversy. Early in 1697 Toland found it prudent to retire to Ireland. Peter Browne, prompted by Narcissus Marsh, here attacked Toland in *A Letter in answer to a Book intitled Christianity not Mysterious*, a work which won him fame. In 1699 he became Provost of Trinity; and in 1710 he was promoted Bishop of Cork. Whimsical in some characteristics Browne was; but his great ability was generally recognized.

[1] Ball reads this to mean that Swift suspected Sheridan to entertain Jacobite leanings.

National Library, Dublin

Swift to the Rev. Thomas Sheridan

Quilca. Jun. 29th 1725[1]

I writ to you yesterday, and said as many things as I could then think on, and gave it to a Boy of Kells who brought me yours. It is strange that I and Stella and Mrs Macfadden[2] should light on the same thought, to advise you to make a great Appearance of temperance. while you are abroad. But Mrs Johnson & I go furthr and say you must needs observe all grave Forms for the want of which both you and I have suffered. On the supposal that you are under the Bp of Cork I send you a Lettr inclosed to him, which I desire you will seal. Mrs Johnson put me in mind to caution you not to drink or pledge any Health in his Company, for you know his weak side in that Matter.[3] I hope Mr Tickel has not complimented you with what Fees are due to him for your Patent; I wish you would say to him (if he refuses them) that I told you it was Mr Addison's Maxim here to excuse nobody, for, says he, I may have 40 Friends, whose Fees may be 2 Guinnees a piece, then I lose 80 Guinnees, and my Friends save but 2 a piece.

I must tell you Dan Jackson ruined his Living by hudling over the first year, and then hoping to mend it the next; Therefore pray take all the Care you can to enquire into the value and set it at the best rate to substantial People.

I know not whethr you are under the Bp of Cork or no, if not you may burn the Letter.

I must desire that you will not think of enlarging yr Expenses no not for some years to come, much less at present, but rather retrench them. You might have layn desolate[4] till Antichrist came for any thing you could have got from those you used to treat, neithr let me hear of one rag of bettr Cloaths for yr Wife or Brats, but rather plainer than ever. This is positively Stella's Advice as well as mine. She says, now you need not be ashamed to be thought poor.

[1] This letter is printed from a draft in Swift's hand in the National Library of Ireland. The first five paragraphs were first printed in Dodsley's *Miscellanies*, 1745, x. 84–87 and in Faulkner, *Works*, 1746, viii. 395–8. The manuscript draft then continues with seven disjointed sentences, followed by two paragraphs, which have been struck out.

[2] Sheridan's mother-in-law.

[3] As previously mentioned Browne, Bishop of Cork, condemned the drinking of healths to the dead as a profane practice.

[4] desolate] *MS.*, *Dodsley*, *Faulkner* destitute] *Nichols*, *Scott*, *Ball.*

We compute you can not be less than 30 days absent, and pray do not employ yr Time in lolling a bed till noon to read Homer, but mind yr Business effectually, and we think you ought to have no breaking up this August but affect to adhere to yr School closer than ever; because you will find, that your ill willers will give out you are now going to quit yr School since you have got Prefermt &c[1]

Pray send me a large Bundle of Exercises, bad as well as good, for I want something to read.

I would have you carry down 3 or 4 Sermons and preach every Sunday at yr Church and be very devout—

I sent you in my Last a Bill of 20ll on Mr Worrall, I hope you have received it.

Pray rememr to leave the Pamphlet with Worrall, and give him Directions, unless you have settld it already some othr way. You knew it must come out just when the Palmt meets.[2]

Keep these Letters when I advise you about yr Living till you have taken Advice

Keep very regular Hours for the sake of yr Health, and Credit, and wherever you lye a Night within 20 miles of yr Livings, be sure call the Family that evening [to] Prayers.

I desire you will wet no Commission with yr old Crew nor with any but those who befriend you; as Mr Tickel &c.

[*The following two paragraphs are struck out:*]

Neal understands he is to go with you, and I am clearly of opinion he should, because he will be carefull of you, and besides I find he understands Tythes, and can pick out every thing among his Countrymen.

Jan. 29.

Dr Sheridan dined here to day, and says the Fole he bought for you is come, and is but 3 years old, and not fit for you in January, he says your Heart was set upon her. but he has only given Earnest, and if she does not mend he will not buy her. So Neal rides his own Horse to attend you. Pray write to me before you go.

[*Below this paragraph, doubtfully by Swift, in large letters is written:*]

seal the Bp of Corks Letter, and that to Mr Townsend,

1 From this point the draft breaks into disconnected sentences.

2 The *Humble Address to both Houses of Parliament* (*Drapier's Letters*, ed. Davis, pp. 143–72).

Dodsley Miscellanies 1745, x. 57

Swift to Lord Carteret

3 July 1725

My Lord![1]

I am obliged to return your Excellency my most humble Thanks for your Favour to Mr. *Sheridan*, because when I recommended him to you,[2] I received a very gracious Answer, and yet I am sensible, that your chief Motive to make some Provision for him was, what became a great and good Person, your distinguishing him as a man of Learning, and one who deserved Encouragement on Account of his great Diligence and success in a most laborious and difficult Employment.

Since your Excellency hath had an opportunity so early in your Government of gratifying your *English* Dependents by a Bishoprick and the best Deanery in the Kingdom,[3] I cannot but hope that the Clergy of *Ireland* will have their Share in your Patronage. There is hardly a Gentleman in the Nation, who hath not a near Alliance with some of that Body; and most of them have Sons, usually breed one[4] to the Church; although they have been of late Years much discouraged and discontented, by seeing Strangers to the Country almost perpetually taken into the greatest Ecclesiastical Preferments, and too often, under Governors very different from your Excellency, the Choice of Persons was not to be accounted for either to Prudence or Justice.

The Misfortune of having Bishops perpetually from *England*, as it must needs quench the Spirit of Emulation among us to excel in Learning and the Study of Divinity, so it produces another Great Discouragement, that those Prelates usually draw after them Colonies of Sons, Nephews, Cousins, or old College-Companions, to whom they bestow the best Preferments in their Gift; and thus the young Men sent into the Church from the University here, have no better prospect than to be Curates, or small Country-Vicars, for Life.

[1] First printed in Dodsley's *Miscellanies*, 1745, x. 57–61, and Faulkner, *Works*, 1746, viii. 369–72.

[2] In his letter of 17 Apr. 1725.

[3] Carteret brought with him to Ireland 'three chaplains from Oxford'. To one of them, William Burscough, he had given the only bishopric which had fallen vacant, that of Limerick, and to another, William Cotterell, afterwards Bishop of Ferns, the deanery of Raphoe.—Ball.

[4] one] *Dodsley*, *Faulkner* one of them *Ball.*

It will become so excellent a Governor as you, a little to moderate this great Partiality; wherein as you will act with Justice and Reason, so you will gain the Thanks and Prayers of the whole Nation, and take away one great Cause of universal Discontent: For I believe your Excellency will agree, that there is not another Kingdom in *Europe*, where the Natives (even those descended from the Conquerors) have been treated as if they were almost unqualify'd for any Employment either in Church of State.

Your Excellency, when I had the Honour to attend you, was pleased to let me name some Clergymen, who are generally understood by their Brethren, to be the most distinguished for their Learning and Piety. I remember the Persons were Dr. *Delany*, Dr. *Ward*, of the *North*, Mr. *Echlin*, Mr. *Synge* of *Dublin*, and Mr. *Corbett*.[1] They were named by me without any Regard to Friendship, having little Commerce with most of them, but only to the universal Character they bear: This was the Method I always took with my Lord *Oxford*, at his own Command, who was pleas'd to believe that I would not be sway'd by any private Affections, and confess'd I never deceived him, for I always dealt openly when I offered any Thing in behalf of a Friend, which was but seldom, because, in that case, I made use of the common Method at Court, to sollicit by another.

I shall say nothing of the young Men among the Clergy, of whom the three hopefullest are said to be Mr. Stopford, Mr. King, and Mr. Dobbs,[2] all Fellows of the College, of whom I am only acquainted with the first. But these are not likely to be great Expectors under your Excellency's Administration, according to the usual Period of Governors here.

If I have dealt honestly in Representing such Persons among the Clergy, as are generally allowed to have the most Merit; I think I have done you a Service, and I am sure I have made you a great Compliment, by distinguishing you from most great Men I have

[1] Of these Synge became Bishop of Ferns and Leighlin, Delany became Dean of Down, Francis Corbett became a successor of Swift as Dean of St. Patrick's (1747–75, *Fasti Eccl. Hib.* ii. 105), John Echlin, whom Swift, according to Delany, consulted on matters relative his choir, became Vicar-General of Tuam in 1734 (*Fasti Eccl. Hib.* iv. 40; *Memoirs of the Echlin Family*, p. 69; *Poems*, p. 955). Only Ward, who was then a prebendary of Derry, failed to obtain further promotion.

[2] James Stopford became Bishop of Cloyne in 1753, and died six years later. King and Dobbs retired from academic life on College livings.

known these thirty Years past, whom I have always observed to act as if they never received a true Character, nor had any Value for the Best, and consequently dispensed their Favours without the least Regard to Abilities or Virtue. And this Defect I have often found among those from whom I least expected it.

That your Excellency may long live a Blessing and Ornament to your Country by pursuing, as you have hitherto done, the Steps of Honour and Virtue, is the most earnest Wishd Prayer of, | My Lord, | Your Excellency's most obedient | and most humble Servant |

Jonath. Swift.

July 3, 1725.

Rothschild[1]

Swift to Archdeacon Walls

Quilca. July. 9th 1725

Sr[2]

I thank God we have found some good Effect of our Country Life. Mrs Johnson is generally much better, and I after a short return of deafness recovered in ten Days, and in spight of the Weather which is worse than ever was heard of, we make a shift to walk, and use Exercise, and yr hopes of seeing us in Toun were wrong; for we determined, happen what could happen, to stay here till the season of the year, and not the bad Weathr should drive us to Dublin. However you are in the right to defer your Ramble, for it is a different thing to stay where one is, and to take long Journeyes for Pleasure in bad Weathr.

What you say of Sheridan is right: He might be blind, or deaf as I am, and besides the Reputation of a School-master is very

[1] Lord Rothschild's library 2281 (46).

[2] From 17 Sept. 1713 to 19 Aug. 1717, a period of four years, forty-two letters, including two undated, written by Swift to Walls, have survived. We may conclude that, during this time, Walls preserved with care all the letters he received from Swift, however unimportant. In addition we have two letters written from London in 1708, one from Trim in 1713, and one from Quilca in 1725. Possibly in these intervening periods Walls received no letters from Swift. On the whole it may be judged probable that in these gaps letters, if any, were infrequent, and thus escaped preservation.

precarious, and he has not been so well used by His Friends as he might expect.[1]

You judge truly that we do not enquire after News; all our Sollicitude is about weath[r], and we are weary of vexing to see it so bad.—I am glad they think of any Men born in this Kingdom, (begging y[r] Pardon) to be a Bishop;[2] but we never object against those bred in our University; so your Heart may be at rest.[3]

I have not been wholly negligent of that odd Prefermt of Raphoe any more than of the Bishoprick;[4] but I know not what good it may do: for I can onely represent.

I find there is some Expedient found out relating to my Business with M[r] Pratt, and that I shall not be wholly undone.[5] I have Witnesses enough, that I behaved my self with sufficient Temper in that Matter, neither was I in Raptures, to find I had saved something out of that Shipwreck, by which the Publick would have been greatr Losers than I. What I had I came honestly by, and if it should please God to disappoint me of doing publick Service with it, I must submitt, and he will not lay the Defect to my Charge.

As to the Paper You gave me to peruse, I read it often, and told you my Judgmt of it, and what I desired should be corrected. D[r] Delany if you know him, could shew you what is to be altered. The chief Things are mistakes in measure, and the little mechanicall Parts of Poetry, which are easily sett right; and then I think it will be very seasonable at this Time, or rather about the Parlmt's meeting.

The Ladyes present their Service to You & M[rs] Walls, and I heartily to her, M[rs] Dingly lately answerd y[r] Lett[r].

I am evr Y[r] most etc

Address: To the Reverend, M[r] | Archdeacon Walls, at his | House in Queen-street | Dublin

Later endorsement: D[r] Swift | July 9th 1725

[1] Ball believes the allusion is to the part some of Sheridan's friends are said to have played when, on Swift's request, Primate Lindsay offered him the mastership of Armagh School. Sheridan accepted the advice of so-called friends that he was likely to do better in Dublin, and declined the Primate's offer. In course of time these very men weakened his position by setting up another school in opposition to that of Sheridan. Sheridan, *Life of Swift*, pp. 374–8.

[2] Carteret presented Henry Maule, an Irishman, to the next bishopric which fell vacant, that of Cloyne.

[3] A reference to the fact that, although an Englishman, Walls had been educated in Trinity College, Dublin.

[4] See p. 70.

[5] See p. 64, n. 2.

Hawkesworth 1766

Swift to the Rev. John Worrall

Quilca, 9 July, 1725.

I have received your letter, and thank you heartily for it. I know not any body, except yourself, who would have been at so much trouble to assist me,[1] and who could have so good success, which I take as kindly as if you had saved me from utter ruin. Although I have witnesses that I acted with indifferency enough, when I was sure I was not worth a groat, beside my goods. There appears to be; only one hundred pounds remaining, according to my account, (except this last quarter) and if I lose it, it is a trifle in comparison of what you have recovered for me. I think Mr. *Pratt* hath acted very generously, and like a true friend, as I always took him to be and I have likewise good witnesses to swear, that I was more concerned at his misfortunes than my own. And so repeating my thanks to you, but not able to express them as I ought, I shall say no more on this subject, only that you may inquire where the money may be safely put out at six pounds *per cent.* I beg pardon that I did not compute the interest of Sir *William Fownes's* money, which reduces what is due to me about fifty-nine pounds. All of consequence is my note to him for one hundred pounds.

I gave over all hopes of my hay,[2] as much as I did of my money; for I reckoned the weather had ruined it; but your good management can conquer the weather. But *Charles Grattan*,[3] the critic, says the cocks are too large, considering the bad weather, and that there is danger they may heat. You know best.

Mrs. *Johnson* says you are an ill manager; for you have lost me above three hundred apples, and only saved me twelve hundred pounds.

Do not tell me of difficulties how to keep the —— from the wall-fruit. You have got so ill a reputation by getting my money, that I can take no excuse; and I will have the thing effectually done, though it should cost me ten groats. Pray let the ground be levelled as you please, as it must likewise be new dunged as good husbandry requires; friend *Ellis* will assist you.

[1] In respect of a bill for twenty pounds and the publication of the *Address to both Houses of Parliament*.

[2] This paragraph evidently refers to the care of Naboth's Vineyard.

[3] Master of Portora School.

I am quite undone by the knavery of *Sheriff* and *White*,[1] and all you have done for me with Mr. *Pratt* signifies nothing, if I must lose ten pounds.

I had your letter about Mr. *Johnson's* money, and she thanks you for your care; and says, considering her poverty, you have done as much for her as for me. But I thought my letter to you was enough, without a letter of attorney; for all money matters I am the greatest cully alive.

Little good may do you with your favourable weather; we have had but five good days these twelve weeks.

The ladies are pretty well; but Mrs. *Johnson*, after a fortnight's great amendment, had yesterday a very bad day; she is now much better. They both present their humble service to Mrs. *Worrall*, and so do I, and am every yours, *&c.*

Jo. who brings you this,[2] desired me to lend him twenty pounds, which I very prudently refused; but said, if he would leave the worth of it in soap and candles in the Deanry House, Mrs. *Brent* viewing them, I would empower you, as I do hereby, to pay him twenty pounds, and place it to my account. Jonath. Swift.

Pray desire Mrs. *Brent* to have ready a hogshead of bottles packed up as usual, of the same wine with the last she sent, and the next carrier shall have orders to call for it.

Let Mrs. *Brent* take out what candles or soap are necessary for the ladies, and only as much as will empty two of the boxes, that *Jo.* may have them; I mean out of those boxes which he is to leave at the Deanry for my security for the twenty pounds, which he is to receive from you.[3]

Forster copy

Swift to Knightley Chetwode

19 July 1725.

Sir,

I had yours of the 10th and your former of early date.[4] Can you imagine there is anything in this scene to furnish a letter? I came

[1] Ellis, Sheriff, and White are unidentified.

[2] Joe Beaumont must again temporarily have recovered his reason.

[3] Ball fails to print the last two paragraphs as a postscript.

[4] A reply to Swift's letter of 27 May.

here for no other purpose but to forget and to be forgotten. I detest all news, or knowledge of how the world passes. I am again with a fit of deafness. The weather is so bad and continues so beyond any example in memory, that I cannot have the benefit of riding and I am forced to walk perpetually in a great-coat to preserve me from cold and wet, while I amuse myself with employing and inspecting labourers digging up and breaking stones, building dry walls, and cutting through bogs, and when I cannot stir out, reading some easy trash merely to divert me. But if the weather does not mend, I doubt I shall change my habitation to some more remote and comfortable place, and there stay till the Parliament is over, unless it sits very late.[1]

I send this directed as the former, not knowing how to do better, but I wonder how you can continue in that dirty town. I am told there is very little fruit in the kingdom, and that I have but twenty apples where I expected five hundred. I hear Sale expected Harrison's whole estate, and is much disappointed.[2] Harrison's life and death were of a piece, and are an instance added to millions how ridiculous a creature is man. You agree with all my friends in complaining I do not write to them, yet this goes so far, that my averseness from it in this place has made me neglect even to write on affairs of great consequence to myself. I am, Your most obedient, &c.

Address: To Knightley Chetwode, Esq.

Tickell Papers

Swift to Thomas Tickell

July. 19th 1725

Sr

Your whole Behaviour with Relation to myself ever since I had the Honor to be known to you, hath tended maliciously to hinder me from writing or speaking any thing that could deserve to be read or heard. I can no sooner hint my Desire of a Favor to a Friend, but you immediatly grant it, on purpose to load me so as to put it out

[1] The session actually lasted from September to March.

[2] It appear from the will of Francis Harrison of the City of Dublin, who had numerous relations, that his friend John Sale was left in the position of a trustee without remuneration. As the will had been made ten years it may be concluded that Harrison was a knave and Sale a fool.—Ball.

of my Power to express my Gratitude, & against your Conscience you put Compliments upon the Letters I write when the Subject is onely to beg a Favor, or purpose to make me write worse or not at all for the future. I remember some faint Stroaks of this unjust Proceeding in my self when I had [a] little Credit in the World, but in no Comparison with yours, which have filled up the Measure of Iniquity.

I have often thought it a monstrous Folly in us who tyed this Kingdom, to have any Friendship with vous autres who are Birds of Passage,[1] while we are sure to be forsaken like young Wenches who are seduced by Soldiers that quarter among them for a few Months. Therefore I prudently resolved to make no other Use of you than for my present Satisfaction, by improving my self from y^r Conversation, or making use of your Interest to the Advantage of my Friends. But when you leave us, I will for my own Quiet[2] send as few Sighs after you as I can. For when Gods used to come down to Earth to converse with Females, it was true Judgment in the Lady who chose rather to marry an earthly Love than Apollo who would be always gambling to Heaven, and besides would be young when she was old.

And to shew I am serious in my Resolutions, I now entreat another good Office from you in Behalf of a young Gentleman Mr James Stopford, a Fellow of the Colledge. He is a man of Birth and Fortune, but the latter a little engaged by travailling; and having now a Strong Temptation to travail again with great Advantage as governor to a young Person,[3] he desires the Honor of being admitted to My Lord Lieutenant by your means, with no other view but the Credit that such a Reception would give him, onely whispering me, (as all Men have base Ends) that he foresees His Excellency, being about his own Age, will be always of so great Consequence in England, as many years hence he may find his Account in His Lordship['s] Protection and Countenance. He is reckoned the best Scholar of his Age among us, and abounds in every amicable Quality without any Circumstance to detract from them, except one, which I hope his Travells will put an end to, and that is Love.

In the Letter directed to Dr Delany, there is one to Mr Stopford,

[1] This was an apt suggestion that Tickell was likely to receive promotion in England. He remained, however, secretary in Dublin Castle until his death fifteen years later.

[2] In the manuscript followed by 'I will' scored out.

[3] See Swift to Chetwode, 27 May. The young man's name was Graham.

who is soon expected in Town, and therein I let him know, what I write to you, and direct him to attend you, for which I humbly desire Pardon, as well as for the trouble of sending the Packet to Dr Delany, and for teazing you with so long a Letter, which I will conclude with the Sincerest Profession of being ever with great Respect | Your most obedient and obliged | Servant | J: Swift.

The Ladyes present their most humble
Service and Thanks to you for your Remembrance,
Mrs Johnson has blunted her Pick axe[1] with work.

Endorsed on p. 4: 19 July, 1725 | Dr Swift

Longleat xiii (Harleian transcripts)

Swift to Alexander Pope

July 19th 1725

Sir,—The Young Gentleman Mr Stopford who delivers you this you will use with all goodness, if you love me; Si me amas ut ames, et ut ego te amo et amabo (Vide Tull. Epist. nescio ubi).[2] He has had his Tour of Traveles, and yet out of egerness to Travell again, he goes Governor to a Rich lad in such a manner as to grow rich enough himself to put his Estate out of Debt, yet after all he is no better nor worse then an Irish Parson born in London, without any Preferment, only Fellow of the University here, and a little foolish Land, but excepting these abatements he is such a Youth as you could wish, with abundance of Greek and other Learning, and modesty and good nature, and an humble admirer of Poetry and you, without any pretensions to the muses at least as he asserts. You will do him all the good offices you can because (tho an Englishman) he well deserves them, and I would not have him leave London without the Prividge of boasting that he is known to you. I must require you like wise to introduce him to Dr Arbuthnett Mr Gay, and others whom you will think fit.

I am so full (quod ad me attinet) of grand designs that I believe I shall never bring them to pass but to your Comfort (grandia loqui-

[1] See p. 64, n. 3.

[2] Sherburn suggests that Swift may have had vaguely in mind such passages as the beginning of Cicero to Atticus, xvi. 10. This transcript shows a few corrections in Oxford's hand.

mur) they are all in prose. I would have seen you many times if a Cursed Deafness did not Sease me every 2 or 3 Months, and then I am frighted to think what I should do in London while my Friends are all either banished or attained[1] or beggars, or retired But I will venture all if I live and you must in that Case get me two or three Harridan Ladys that will be content to nurse and talk loud to me while I am deaf. Say nothing of my being eleven years older then when we parted, Lord Oxford the young writ me word that you were again embarqued to Homers land (as he called it)[2] Are you Rich and Healthy Det vitam detopes &c.[3] Reputation you will take care to encrease though you have too much in Conscience for any Neighbor of yours to thrive while he lives by you.

Our Lord Oxford used to curse the Occasions that put you on Translations, and if he and the Qu— had lived you should have entirely followed your own Genius built and planted much, and writ only when you had a mind, pray come and show your self in Ireland and live some Months in the Deanry. you say right and yet I have heard as wild propositions. I have empowered Mr Stopford to tell you all my Story how I live; how I do nothing, how I grow old, what a Sorry life I lead, how I have not the Spleen &c. &c. &c.

I am ever | Your obedient Servant | J. Swift.

The Library, Armagh

Swift to —— Sheridan

Quilca Jul 22nd 1725

Sr

Mrs Johnson desires me to present her humble service and thanks to you. She is resolved to keep the horse upon tryall, altho we all, and our servants find he hath a terrible Hitch in his Pace, which is all the fault we can at present discover, and if Mrs Johnson can any way support that Hitch in riding some miles, she will content herself rather than want riding for which she chiefly came into the country; but if she finds his Gate too uneasy to bear, she will since

[1] Probably for 'attainted'.

[2] Oxford to Swift, 2 Nov. 1724 *ad fin.* The translation of the *Odyssey*.

[3] Horace, *Ep.* I. xviii, 112. On f. 103 of the Portland Papers transcript of this letter a modern hand has inserted the full Latin passage together with Francis's translation.—Sherburn.

you say the Bargain is not struck with the Owner, make bold to send the Horse back; but is as much obliged to you, as if the matter had wholly succeeded to her wish.

This she has desired me to say with her humble service.

I am S^r^ | Your most humble | Ser^t^ | Jonath. Swift

Address: To Mr Sheridan[1] at Shercock.

The Dublin Magazine 1762

Swift to the Rev. Anthony Raymond

July 23, 1725.[2]

Sir,

Your son brought me this minute a letter from Mrs. Raymond, with a printed copy of part of your preliminary, and letting me know the good success you have had with your sick brother, who, as I understand, cannot live many weeks.

You will forgive me if I am in much pain concerning your management at this juncture. I hope, no consideration, no scheme, will hinder you, immediately upon possessing your legacy, to pay all your debts, by transmitting bills over hither to some trusty friends; and so, at once, set yourself in credit and reputation, and easy in your fortune.[3] This great opportunity seems to be put into your hands by the extraordinary mercy of God; and if you misuse it, you will be for ever culpable in the light both of him and man. And pray, let not present affluence incite you to increase present expences, but make you more thrifty; which advice is the more

[1] Not Swift's friend, but probably a relation. Cf. the earlier letter addressed to him 26 June.

[2] Although Anthony Raymond and Swift maintained a constant friendship no letter passing between them has survived except this, which was overlooked by Ball. It was printed on p. 452 of Part I for the year 1762 of the *Dublin Magazine*. My attention was called to it by Professor D. Nichol Smith. This is without doubt a genuine letter written by Swift. The style, the allusions, the reproof of extravagance are all in keeping. In Swift's early lists of letters only two are entered as addressed to Raymond and three as received from him. These cannot be traced.

[3] Raymond is often mentioned in the *Journal to Stella*. On 7 June 1711 Swift wrote of him that 'in money matters he is the last man I would depend on'; but despite his vanity and improvidence he succeeded in retaining Swift's friendship.

seasonable, because you have been very expensive, even upon vain hopes that ruined you. In the name of God, when you have done your business there, in relation to your brother's legacies after he shall die, return home, and amuse not yourself with your history till you come hither. You are too hasty in your premises. All other writers finish their works, or, at least, the greatest part of them, before they talk of publishing a subscription; whereas you have done nothing but making loose collections, and the whole work of compiling is yet to begin.[1] I can only say, you act extremely wrong; but it would be tedious to argue it a letter. Besides I have not time; for your son is to return to-day, I have no room for him in Mr. Sheridan's cabin, where I have been these three months for my health.

Aristotle was not author of the book *de Mundo*[2] as you mention in your preliminary. Therefore, you should say, *ascribed to Aristotle*. I am your most obedient | humble servant, | J. Swift.

4805

Viscount Bolingbroke to Swift

London July the 24th 1725

Mr Ford will tell you how I do and what I do.[3] tir'd with suspense, the only insupportable misfortune of life, I desir'd, after nine years of autumnal promises and vernal expenses, a decision, and very little car'd what that decision was, provided it left me at liberty to settle abroad, or put me on a foot of living agreably att home. the wisdom of yr Nation has thought fit, instead of granting so reasonable a request, to pass an act, which fixing my fortune unalterably to this country, fixes my person here also, & those who had the least a mind to see me in England have made it impossible for me to live anywhere else. here I am then, two thirds restor'd. my person safe, unless I meet hereafter with harder treatm^{t} than even

[1] Shortly before his death in 1726 Raymond issued a prospectus of 'A History of Ireland'; but the work was never published.

[2] Swift was right in dismissing *De Mundo* as a spurious work.

[3] In spite of opposition an Act was passed in 1725 permitting the return of Bolingbroke together with the restoration of his estates. A gift of £11,000 to the Duchess of Kendal is said to have served a good purpose. Walpole, however, insisted on his exclusion from the House of Lords.

that of Sr Walter Rauleigh; and my Estate, wth all the other property I have acquir'd, or may acquire, secur'd to me. But the attainder is kept carefully & prudently in force, least so corrupt a member should come again into the House of Lords, and his bad leavan should sower that sweet untainted mass. thus much I thought I might say about my private affairs to an old friend without diverting him too long from his labours to promote the advantage of the church and state of Ireland, or from his travels into those Countrys of Giants & Pigmeys from whence he imports a cargo I value att an higher rate than that of the richest Galeon.[1] Ford brought the Dean of Derry[2] to see me. unfortunately for me I was then out of town, and the journey of the former into Ireland will perhaps defer for some time my making acquaintance wth the other, which I am sorry for. I would not by any means lose the opportunity of knowing a Man who can espouse in good earnest the Systeme of Father Malebranche,[3] and who is fond of going a Missionary into the W: Indies. my zeal for the propagation of the Gospel will hardly carry me so far, but my Spleen against Europe has more than once made me think of buying the Dominion of Bermuda, and spending the remainder of my days as far as possible from those people wth whom I have past the first & greater part of my Life. health and every other natural comfort of life is to be had there better than here. as to imaginary & artificial pleasures we are Philosophers enough to despise them what say you? will you leave yr Hibernian flock to some other shepherd, and transplant y^r^ self wth me into the middle of the Atlantick ocean? we will form a society, more reasonable, & more useful than that of Dr Berkley's Colledge, and I promise you solemnly, as Supreme Magistrate, not to suffer the currency of Wood's halfpence, nay the Coyner of them shall be hang'd if he presumes to set his foot on our Island.

let me hear how you are, and what you do, and if you really have any latent kindness still att the bottom of yr heart for me, say something very kind to me, for I do not dislike being cajol'd. if your heart tells you nothing, say nothing, that I may take the hint, and wean myself from you by degrees. whether I shall compass it or no God knows, but surely this is the properest place in the world to renounce

[1] Swift had evidently communicated to friends in England some outline of *Gulliver's Travels*.

[2] i.e. Berkeley.

[3] Nicolas Malebranche, 1638–1715, French philosopher, psychologist, and mystic. The story that argument with Berkeley induced his death is without foundation. Berkeley was in England from Aug. 1714 till 1716.

freindship in, or forget obligations. Mr Ford says he will be with us again by the beginning of the winter. yr star[1] will probably hinder you from taking the same journey. Adieu dear Dean, I had something more to say to you almost as important as what I have said already, but company comes in upon me, & releives you.

Endorsed by Swift: Ld Bolingbroke July 24 | 1725

Deane Swift 1768

The Earl of Oxford to Swift

Dover-street, July 26, 1725

Rev. Sir,

Mr. *Clayton* going to *Ireland*,[2] I take the opportunity of writing to you, in the first place to tell you, that I am ready to make good my promise which I made of sending you a picture of my father. The painter has done his part, so that the picture is now ready, but I do not know how to send it to you safe: you did tell me a gentleman should call, but where he lives, or who he is, I know not.[3] I am very desirous you should have it, because it has been so long coming; and I am very ambitious of doing any thing that may in the least be agreeable to you. You had heard of this sooner, but I have been for three months out of town; I made a long progress, even beyond *Edinburgh* fifty miles.

I inquire of you sometimes of Dean *Berkeley*: I was sorry to hear that you were troubled with that melancholy distemper, the want of hearing, although in some cases it is good; but one would have it in one's power to hear or not hear, as it suited best with one's inclinations.

I am also sorry that there is no mention made of any design of your coming into *England*. I long much for it, and do flatter myself with the thoughts of seeing you under my roof, where you shall exert more authority than I will allow to belong to any bishops made since [the Hanoverian succession].[4] Do not lay aside all

[1] Stella.

[2] Perhaps a relation of Dr. Robert Clayton, Fellow of Trinity College in 1717; and successively Bishop of Killala, Cork, and Clogher. His writings exposed him to the charge of heresy. See further *D.N.B.*

[3] Cf. Swift to Oxford, 27 Nov. 1724 *ad fin.*

[4] Deane Swift cautiously fills this space with a ——.

thoughts of coming over; change of air may do you good as well as the voyage. I thank God your sister is very well, considering the way she is in; I hope in two months, or thereabouts, she will be much better: she presents her humble service to you. *Peggy*[1] is very well.

Pope is well I suppose; he is rambling about the country. I have the pleasure of seeing a picture which is very like you every day, and is as good a picture as ever *Jervas* painted.[2] I am, Sir, your most obedient humble servant and brother | Oxford.

Forster copy, F. 44. E. S

Swift to the Earl of Oxford

14 August 1725

My Lord.[3] Your Lordship['s] Letter was sent to me where I now am, and have been for four months in a little obscure Irish Cabbin about fourty miles from Dublin, whither I fled to avoyd Company in frequent Returns of Deafness, which hath been my onely Hindrance from waiting upon your Lordship's Father and your self for severall Years past. For while I am thus incommoded I must be content to live among those whom I can govern, and make them comply with my Infirmityes. But still I hope this cause will not always continue, and that I shall once [more] have the Honor and Happyness of seeing the worthy Son of him from whom I received so many Obligations, and who was pleased to love and distinguish me in a very uncommon way. Although I could rather wish, that the Times were such as would send you hither to visit me, at least the Kingdom I am in.

I must humbly thank your Lordship for your Present of my Lord your Father's Picture, but more for your favourable Expressions in giving it me. I did tell your Lordship that a Gentleman should attend you to receive the Ring which you said you had for me, which was not done, either by your Absence, or his. But I never intended that your Lordship should be put upon the Trouble of sending to

[1] Oxford's daughter, the future Duchess of Portland.

[2] The identity of this Jervas portrait is in doubt. See Sir Frederick Falkiner's essay, *Prose Works*, ed. Temple Scott, xii. 12 ff., and *Portland MSS*. v. 638.

[3] The original of this letter was sold (Croker sale), 6 May 1853, to Pilkington for £14. Not traced further. It is here printed from a copy in the Forster Collection, Red Box, F. 44. E. 2.

him. The Person is Mr Ford, whom you may remember to have been employed as Writer of the Gazette, a very worthy Gentleman of a considerable Fortune here, and long in confinement upon his first Return from France.[1] Either he, or Mr Charleton,[2] a Person well known and Chaplain to my Lord [Somers][3] will wait on you both for the Picture and Ring.

Your Lordship judgeth rightly, that in some Cases it is a Happyness not to hear, and in this Country where Faction hath been so outrageous above anything in England, a wise or quiet man would gladly have his Ears stopt much longer than open. But a silly Accident of Brass Money hath more united them than it ever could have been imagined. I am glad your Lordship is pleased to countenance the Dean of Derry Dr Berkeley; He is a true Philosopher and an excellent Scholar, but of very visionary Virtue and is endeavouring to quit a thousand Pounds a Year for a hundred at Bermudas.

Pray God Almighty preserve my Lady Oxford, particularly in her present Circumstance, and grant that the Consequence may be such a Succession to your Lordship as may make you both happy and prove a Blessing to the Nation.

I hope the Picture of me in your House is the same which Mr Jervas drew in Ireland, and carryed over, because it is more like me by severall year than another he drew in London. It is placed where my Heart would most desire to have it, although it be an Honor which in spite of my Pride will make me vain.

May God Almighty long preserve your Lordship and family and continue to bless you in Reward of your many excellent Virtues.

I am and shall be ever with the greatest Respect and Gratitude, My Lord | Your Lordships most obedient | and most obliged Servant | Jonath Swift

August 14th 1725

I sometimes see my old Friend Lord Carteret, who uses me with

[1] Official evidence of Ford's arrest is not forthcoming. In addition, however, to this allusion by Swift his confinement is implied in a letter written to Ford by the Duc de la Force, 2 Feb. 1716. See *Letters to Ford*, p. xvi, and footnote.

[2] The Duchess of Ormonde's chaplain.

[3] In the Forster copy the name is 'Somers', but it is hardly possible that Somers, who had died ten years before, had so pronounced a Tory as Charleton as his chaplain. In his reply, 30 Aug., Oxford refers to Charleton as Lord Arran's chaplain.

old Kindness, and at my Request gave a small Preferment in the Church to one of my Friends.

I have a Print of my Lord your Father, and under it this motto

— Veteres actus *primam* juventam Prosequar? ad Sese mentem *praesentia* ducunt[1]

I will not tell your Lordship what other Picture I desire, for I have a Lawful Title to that you have given me.

Address: To the Right Honorable the | Earl of Oxford, in Dover Street | London

Rothschild

Swift to Charles Ford

Aug. 14th. 1725.

I have now been four Months at our Friends country Cabbin,[2] with our two Lady Friends. The younger[3] is better in Strength, tho often in her old Disorders, but she desires me to tell you that your nice Stomach must not be turned if you see her with a Tetter in her Chin, which she resents in a manner very unbecoming her good Sense, and the Philosophy which I hoped I had taught her. We shall not return till towards October. I am seldom without a Fitt of Deafness every Month, they come oftner, but I think do not last so long, but what new methods they will take I know not; and so much for personal Matters.

I remember when you expected to be undone in all your ready money by Stratford.[4] I was in fifty times more danger by the utter Undoing of Mr Pratt of the Treasury, whose Fall hath made a great Noise here. He owed me all and something more than all I had in the World; and was put up in Prison (where he still continues) for above 70 Thousand Pounds debt to the Crown; yet he had so much honor, that while he was in Prison, he gave a Gentleman whom I empowerd,

[1] Thus in the copy. Quoted by Swift in a letter to the first Earl, 11 Oct. 1722.

[2] Quilca. Swift's stay extended from about 20 Apr. to the end of Sept.

[3] Stella, who was younger than Rebecca Dingley.

[4] Francis Stratford and Swift were together at the grammar school of Kilkenny. He is frequently mentioned in the *Journal*. He was a Hamburg merchant and became a director of the South Sea Company in Sept. 1711. Within a few months, Jan. 1711–12, he suffered a severe financial collapse (*Journal*, pp. 462–3).

Substantiall Bills for all he owed me except about 100[ll], which he seemed a little to dispute, and was onely Interest. Thus I have miraculously escaped being perfectly worth nothing.

I had a Letter yesterday from the Earl of Oxford,[1] telling me that he had his Fathers Picture ready for me. And I remember he desired I would get somebody to call for a Ring which was to be a Memorial of His Father; and I desired you to do that Favor for me; but his or your or both being out of Town prevented it. For my Lord says nobody called for it. I had a leter lately from Mr Charleton the Earl of Arran's Chaplain, he is known enough, and I suppose not unknown to you. I have just now answered it, and desired him that if you were out of Town, he would perform this Commission to Ld Oxford; if he be in Town, I entreat you would see him, and so to concert Matters, that I may have the Picture and Ring, and that both may be lodged with You, the Ring sent me by some private Hand; and the Picture kept till it can be sent conveniently. I suppose it may go by long Sea; or as you please.

I know not why, but I am sorry your money holds out so well and yet I could not have seen you this Summer: for the Place we are in is not a Place for you. I am as busy here as if I were upon Land of my own. I have got Sheridan a small Living[2] from Ld Carteret: but it proves smaller than his Excellency or I intended it.

I have finished my Travells, and I am now transcribing them; they are admirable Things, and will wonderfully mend the World.[3]

Mrs Johnson desires to know whether there be any Agreement between the Weather on your side and ours. In four Months we have had two odd fair days, and 13 more, and all the rest foul from the 20th of April to the Hour I am writing.

Pray say something of Ld Bolingbroke, where he is, and what he does; he has told me he had his Picture for me,[4] and I would have you mention it to him, and get it for me; but I am desirous to know

[1] Oxford's letter of 26 July, delayed in transit by Swift's absence from Dublin.

[2] Rincurran. In value about £200.

[3] This statement gives the date of the conclusion of the rough draft of *Gulliver's Travels*, and is evidence of Swift's care in composition; for he set himself at once to transcribe the whole work.

[4] In the final paragraph of his letter of Aug. 1723 Bolingbroke wrote: 'This is the picture of an old friend, . . . which he will send you, if you continue still to desire it.' Swift would appear to have asked for it in his lost letter of 29 Sept. 1721. In his reply of 1 Jan. 1722 [O.S. 21 Dec. 1721] Bolingbroke promised to send it from Paris.

his present Scituation, and where he intends to live,[1] and where is Madame de Villette, and why she does not write to me. For you know my Priviledge, that Ladyes are always to make the first Advances to me.

Pray tell my Ld Masham, (with my most humble Service) that my Lady often promised me her Picture.

My humble Service to Mr Pope and Mr Gay—

Address: To Charles Ford Esqr; to be | left at the Coco-tree in Pell-mell | London

Postmarks: Kells *and* 23 AV

Rothschild

Swift to Charles Ford

Quilca. Aug. 16th 1725

Our Method about Letters here, is this, Every Saterday we send 8 miles[2] to Kells for Vittells, the Messenger carryes thither what Letters we write, and brings back whatever Letters are sent us to Kells. Thus our Letters often lye at Kells a week, and we are very indifferent, or rather vexed when we see any Letter come to us, unless from particular Friends. Thus it happened that the Messenger of Saterday last carryed a Letter to Kells directed to you in London, and brought one from you dated at Dublin. If your coming be sufficiently known, perhaps the Post master may send it to you, or if the Packet be not gone, you may send a servant for it, rather than let it have two Voyages by Sea.[3] The Letter you gave Sheridan for me, is in ill Hands, for I hear nothing of his coming down to Quilca, and if he does, it is great Odds he will leave it behind, or lose it, or forget to[4] give it me. I find you have been a better Manager than usuall, by making your Money hold out almost two years, unless you have mangé votre bled en herbe; and in that Case you will be punished with a longer Stay in Ireland. I hope you will, or rather your Friends will have one Advantage by our Absence, that it

[1] Bolingbroke was settling at Dawley, near Uxbridge.

[2] Irish miles.

[3] The postmark shows that the letter of Saturday, 14 Aug., went by London.

[4] 'to' repeated in the manuscript.

will force you to cotton a little better with the Country and the People; for upon your old System it will be impossible for you to live in it without Spleen. No men in Dublin go to Taverns who are worth sitting with, and to ask others, is just to desire them to throw away half a Crown for bad wine, (which they can ill spare,) when they know where to get good, for nothing, and among Company where they can amuse themselves with Play or trifling; and this you must do, or get you gone back to England. For we know it is not Love that sends you to us, and that nothing keeps you here an hour but Joyntures and old Leases.

The Razors will be a great Treasure to me, for want of good ones I pass one hour in eight and fourty very miserably.

In my Letter to you I desired your Assistance in getting the Ring and Picture from Ld Oxford, but fearing you might be out of Town, (though not in Ireland) I writt the same Post to Mr Charleton from whom I lately had a Letter; since I knew not what else to do. But if Mr Lewis[1] will take that Trouble, it will be much better.

Our Scheme was to stay till Michaelmas, but our Return must depend upon our Health. Mrs Johnson is much better and walks three or four Irish Miles a day over Bogs and mountain. But I have generally every month a Return of my Deafness, though the Fits do not last so long as usuall. But I have some Reasons not to be in Dublin till the Parliament here has sate a good while. Neither am I willing to see Mr Prat while he is in Prison. I believe I shall not lose above 100^{ll} Interest by him. But I despaired of every Penny, and yet I have legall Witness that I was a great Philosopher in that Matter.

We live here among a Million of wants, and where ever[y] body is a Thief. I am amusing my self in the Quality of Bayliff to Sheridan, among Bogs and Rocks, overseeing and ranting at Irish Laborers, reading Books twice over for want of fresh ones, and fairly correcting and transcribing my Travells, for the Publick. Any thing rather than the Complaint of being Deaf in Dublin.

I hope to see you well settled in a Kind of Acquaintance, and tallying with the usuall way of Life, else it had been better you had contrived to pass the Summer here, and kept London for Winter. This is an Irish Holyday when our Scoundrels will not work, else perhaps my Letter would have been shorter.

[1] Oxford entrusted the picture and the ring to Erasmus Lewis. See his Lordship's letter of 20 Aug. 1725.

My most humble Service to the Ladyes where you Live. Adieu. The Ladyes here assure me they are your humble Servants.

Address: To Charles Ford Esqr, at | Mrs Ford's House in Dawson Street | Dublin.
Postmarks: Kells *and* 20 AU[1]

Rothschild

Swift to Charles Ford

Quilca. Aug. 27th. 1725

I send you inclosed Letter to My Ld Bolingbroke, because I suppose you know where to direct to him, and in what Style;[2] If in his old One of L^{d} I suppose it will be under cover. I writt to you a Post or two ago. Mr Sheridan seems to hope you will not be so unsociable as formerly, but Ld Bol. writes that you promise to return about the Beginning of Winter,[3] and if so, I know not who would go over the Threshold to see You.

We are all as usuall—neither well nor ill, except Mrs Dingley who can do every thing but walk.

Address: To Charles Ford Esqr
No postmark.

Hawkesworth 1766

Swift to the Rev. John Worrall

Quilca. Aug. 27. 1725.

I was heartily sorry to hear you had got the gout, being a disease you have so little pretence to; for you have been all your life a great walker, and a little drinker. Although it be no matter how you got your disease, since it was not by your vices; yet I do not love to think I was an instrument, by leading you a walk of eight or nine miles, where your pride to shew your activity in leaping down a ditch, hurt your foot in such a manner, as to end in your present disease.[4]

[1] The Dublin postmark.

[2] Swift's letter is lost. It was written in answer to Bolingbroke's of 24 July.

[3] In his letter to Swift of 24 July. But Ford appears to have been in Dublin in Mar. 1726.

[4] Worrall had no doubt been on a visit to Quilca; and, as appears later on, John Grattan had also been there.

I have not yet heard of Mr. *Webb*, and if he should come here, I can do nothing with him; for I shall not take my own judgment, but leave it to some able lawyer to judge and recommend the security; for now it is time for me to learn some worldly wisdom.

I thank you for the purchase you have made of *Bristow* beer; it will soon pay for itself, by saving me many a bottle of wine, but I am afraid it is not good for your gout.

My deafness has left me above three weeks, and therefore I expect a visit from it soon; and it is somewhat less vexatious here in the country, because none are about me but those who are used to it.

Mrs. *Worrall's* observation is like herself; she is an absolute corrupted city lady, and does not know the pleasures of the country, even of this place, with all its millions of inconveniencies. But Mrs. *Dingley* is of her opinion, and would rather live in a *Dublin* cellar, than a country palace.

I would fain have a shed thrown up in the farthest corner of *Naboth's* vineyard, toward the lower end of *Sheba's* garden, till I can find leisure and courage to build a better in the center of the field. Can it be done?

The weather continues as foul as if there had not been a day of rain in the summer, and it will have some very ill effect on the kingdom.

I gave *Jack Grattan* the papers corrected, and I think half spoiled, by the cowardly caution of him and others.[1] He promised to transcribe them time enough, and my desire is they may be ready to be published upon the first day the Parliament meets.[2] I hope you will contrive it among you, that it may be sent unknown (as usual) to some printer, with proper directions. I had lately a letter without a name, telling me that I have got a sop to hold my tongue, and that it is determined we must have that grievance, *&c.* forced on us.

My intention is to return about the beginning of *October*, if my occasions do not hinder me. Before that time it will be seen how the Parliament will act. They who talk with me think they will be slaves as usual, and led where the government pleases.

My humble service to Mrs. *Worrall.* The ladies present theirs to you both. | J. Swift.

[1] The address to both Houses of Parliament.

[2] The Irish Parliament met on 7 Sept.

Deane Swift 1768

The Earl of Oxford to Swift

Dover-street, Aug. 30, 1725

Rev. Sir,

I received the favour of your letter;[1] I am vexed that the trifle of the ring should not have reached you; I found where the fault lay; I hope you will soon receive both the picture and the ring safe: I have ordered tham to the care of *Erasmus Lewis*, Esq; our old friend, and he is a punctual man, and is well acquainted with Mr. *Ford*, and my lord *Arran's* chaplain, Mr. Charleton; so I hope this method will not fail that I have now taken. I would not be wanting in the least trifle, by which I might shew the value and esteem I have, and always must and will have for you.

The picture I have of you is the same which Mr. *Jarvis* drew of you in *Ireland*, and it is very like you, and is a very good picture; and though Mr. *Jarvis* is honoured with the place of his majesty's painter, he cannot paint a picture I shall so much value as I do that of the dean of *St. Patrick*'s.

My old fellow collegiate has done so right a thing as to prefer one of your recommendation.[2] I am, Sir, your most obedient humble servant, | Oxford.

My wife sends her compliments to you; she is as well as can be expected.

Hawkesworth 1766

Swift to the Rev. John Worrall

Quilca, Aug. 31, 1725.

I have yours of the 28th.[3] I am still to acknowledge and thank you for the care of my little affairs, I hope I shall not want the silver; for I hope to be in town by the beginning of *October*, unless extreme good weather shall invite me to continue.

[1] Of 14 Aug.

[2] Lord Carteret was at Christ Church, Oxford, at the same time as Lord Oxford.

[3] A reply to Swift's letter of the 27th.

Since *Wood*'s patent is cancelled,[1] it will by no means be convenient to have the paper printed, as I suppose you, and *Jack Grattan*, and *Sherridan* will agree; therefore, if it be with the printer, I would have it taken back, and the press broke, and let her[2] be satisfied. The work is done, and there is no more need of the Drapier. Mrs. *Johnson* does not understand what you mean by her stamped linen, and remembers nothing of it; but supposes it is some jest.

The ladies are well; all our services to Mrs. *Worrall.* Mrs *Dingley* at last discovered the meaning of the stamped linen, which makes that part of my letter needless.

Pray pay *Jo. Beaumont* four pounds for a horse I bought from him, and place it to my account. | J. S.

When *Jo.* brings you a piece of linen of twenty-four yards, pray put my name upon it, and pay him six pounds, eight shillings.

Dodsley Miscellanies 1745, x. 87

Swift to the Rev. Thomas Sheridan

Quilca, Sept, 11, 1725.

If you are indeed a discarded Courtier, you have reason to complain, but none at all to wonder;[3] you are too young[4] for many Experiences to fall in your way, yet you have read enough to make you know the Nature of Man. It is safer for a Man's Interest to blaspheme God, than to be of a Party out of Power, or even to be thought so. And since the last was the Case, how could you imagine that all Mouths would not be open when you were received, and in

[1] The cancellation of the patent was announced by Carteret to the Irish Parliament when it met on 7 Sept. It is evident that this came as no news.

[2] Harding died in prison on 19 Apr. 1725 and was now represented by his widow.

[3] Hardly had Sheridan been instituted into the living of Rincurran when he gave offence by preaching on 1 Aug., the anniversary of the accession of the House of Hanover, a sermon from the text, 'Sufficient unto the day is the evil thereof'. Lord Carteret was informed of the fact, and as, in any event, Sheridan came of a family known for its Jacobite leanings, he was struck off the list of chaplains. Differing versions of the origin of the catastrophe will be found in the account given by Sheridan's son (*Life*, p. 381) and by Swift in his *Vindication of Lord Carteret* (*Prose Works*, ed. Temple Scott, vii. 241–3).

[4] Born in 1687 Sheridan was now thirty-eight.

some manner prefer'd by the Government, tho' in a poor way? I tell you there is hardly a Whig in *Ireland* who would allow a Potato and Butter-milk to a reputed Tory. Neither is there any thing in your Countrymen upon this Article more than what is common in all other Nations, only *quoad magis & minus*. Too much Avertency is not your Talent, or else you had fled from that Text, as from a Rock. For as *Don Quixote* said to *Sancho*, what business had you to speak of a Halter, in a Family where one of it was hanged?[1] And your Innocence is a Protection, that wise Men are asham'd to rely on, further than with God. It is indeed against Common Sense to think, that you should chuse such a Time, when you had received a Favour from the Lord Lieutenant, and had reason to expect more, to discover your Disloyalty in the Pulpit. But what will that avail? Therefore sit down and be quiet, and mind your Business as you should do, and contract your Friendships, and expect no more from Man than such an Animal is capable of, and you will every day find my Description of Yahoes more resembling.[2] You should think and deal with every Man as a Villain, without calling him so, or flying from him, or valuing him less. This is an old true Lesson. You believe, every one will acquit you of any Regard to temporal Interest, and how came you to claim an Exception from all Mankind? I believe you value your temporal Interest as much as any body, but you have not the Arts of pursuing it. You are mistaken. Domestick Evils are no more within a Man than others; and he who cannot bear up against the first, will sink under the second, and in my Conscience I believe this is your Case; for being of a weak Constitution, in an Employment precarious and tiresome, loaden with Children, *cum uxore neque leni neque commoda*, a Man of intent and abstracted thinking, enslav'd by Mathematicks, and Complaint of the World, this new Weight of Party Malice hath struck you down, like a Feather on a Horse's Back, already loaden as far as he is able to bear. You ought to change the Apostle's Expression, and say, I will strive to learn in whatever State, *&c*.[3]

I will hear none of your Visions; you shall live at *Quilca* but three Fortnights and a Month in a Year; perhaps not so much. You shall

[1] 'No se ha de mentar la Soga en casa del ahorcado.'

[2] Sheridan had evidently read *Gulliver's Travels*, or Swift had read portions to him.

[3] 'I have learned, in whatsoever state I am, therewith to be content'—Phil. iv. 11.

make no Entertainments but what are necessary to your Interests; for your true Friends would rather see you over a Piece of Mutton and a Bottle once a Quarter. You shall be merry at the Expense of others; you shall take care of your Health, and go early to bed, and not read late at Night; and laugh with all Men, without trusting any; and then a Fig for the Contrivers of Ruin, who now have no further Thoughts than to stop your Progress, which perhaps they may not compass unless I am deceiv'd more than usual. All this you will do, *si mihi credis*, and not dream of printing your Sermon, which is a Project abounding with Objections unanswerable, and with which I could fill this Letter. You say nothing of having preach'd before the Lord Lieutenant, nor whether he is altered towards you;[1] for you speak nothing but Generals. You think all the World hath now nothing to do but to pull Mr. *Sheridan* down, whereas it is nothing but a Slap in your turn, and away. Lord *Oxford* said once to me on an occasion; These Fools, because they hear a Noise about their Ears of their own making, think the whole World is full of it—When I come to Town, we will change all this Scene, and act like Men of the World. Grow rich and you will have no Enemies. Go sometimes to the Castle, keep fast Mr. Tickell and Balaguer;[2] frequent those on the right Side, Friends to the present Powers; drop those who are loud on the wrong Party, because they know they can suffer nothing by it.

1741

Alexander Pope to Swift

Sept. 14, 1725.

I need not tell you, with what real delight I should have done any thing you desired, and in particular any good offices in my power towards the bearer of your Letter,[3] who is this day gone for France. Perhaps it is with Poets as with Prophets, they are so much better liked in another country than their own, that your Gentleman, upon arriving in England, lost his curiosity concerning me. However, had he tried, he had found me his friend; I mean he had found me yours.

[1] According to Sheridan's son (*Life*, p. 379) Carteret was pleased with his father 'as a companion often inviting him to his private parties', and sometimes stealing out from the Castle to 'pass the evenings at Sheridan's with Swift'.

[2] Evidently Carteret's secretary or some other personal attendant.

[3] Stopford.

I am disappointed at not knowing better a man whom you esteem, and comfort my self only with having got a Letter from you, with which (after all) I sit down a gainer; since to my great pleasure it confirms my hope of once more seeing you. After so many dispersions, and so many divisions, two or three of us may yet be gathered together; not to plot, not to contrive silly schemes of ambition, or to vex our own or others hearts with busy vanities (such as perhaps at one time of life or other take their Tour in every man) but to divert our selves, and the world too if it pleases; or at worst, to laugh at others as innocently and as unhurtfully as at ourselves. Your Travels I hear much of; my own I promise you shall never more be in a strange land, but a diligent, I hope useful, investigation of my own Territories.[1] I mean no more Translations, but something domestic, fit for my own country, and for my own time.

If you come to us I'll find you elderly Ladies enough that can halloo, and two that can nurse, and they are too old and feeble to make too much noise; as you will guess when I tell you they are my own mother, and my own nurse.[2] I can also help you to a Lady who is as deaf, though not so old as your self;[3] you'll be pleas'd with one another, I'll engage, though you don' hear one another: you'll converse like spirits by intuition. What you'll most wonder at is, she is considerable at Court, yet no Party-woman, and lives in Court, yet would be easy and make you easy.

One of those you mention (and I dare say always will remember) Dr. Arbuthnot, is at this time ill of a very dangerous distemper, an imposthume in the bowels; which is broke, but the event is very uncertain. Whatever that be (he bids me tell you, and I write this by him) he lives or dies your faithful friend; and one reason he has to desire a little longer life, is the wish to see you once more.

He is gay enough in this circumstance to tell you, he would give you (if he could) such advice as might cure your deafness, but he would not advise you, if you were cured, to quit the pretence of it; because you may by that means hear as much as you will, and answer as little as you please. Believe me | Yours &c.

[1] Warburton, *Works*, 1751, ix. 51—'The Essay on Man'. Sherburn comments: 'If Warburton is right, this is the earliest mention of Pope's philosophical project'.

[2] Pope's nurse, Mary Beach, died two months later. About the same time his mother was seriously ill.

[3] Mrs. Howard, now a neighbour of Pope at Marble Hill. In middle life she began to grow deaf. At this time she was about forty-four.

Tickell's Letter-book No. 2

Swift to Thomas Tickell

[18 September 1725]

Sr

You Court People have found out the way of vexing me in all my Privacy and Monkish Manner of living. Here is Mr Sheridan perpetually teazing me with Complaints directly in the Style I have often met among State Letters, of Loss of Favor by Misrepresentation and Envy and Malice, and Secret Enemyes and the rest of that Jargon.[1] I have had Share of it my self, and so I believe have you and may have more in the Course of your Fortune. The worst Evil is, that when ill Opinions are instilled into great Men, they never think it worth their while to be undeceived, and so a little Man is ruined without the least Tincture of Guilt. And therefore the last Time I was in the World, I refused to deal with a chief Minister, till he promised me upon his Honor never to be influenced by any ill Story of me, till he told it me plainly, and heard my Defence,[2] after which if I cleared my self, it should pass for nothing, and he kept his Word, and I was never once in Pain. I was the Person who recommended Mr Sheridan. But the Bp of Elphin[3] took upon him to do it in form, and give it a Sanction and was seconded by two other Bishops all principled according to your Heart's Desire, and therefore His Excellency hath nothing to answer for. I do believe Mr Sheridan hath been formerly reckoned Tory and no otherwise than hundreds among yr Favorites, who perhaps grew Converts with more Zeal Noise and Cunning, but with less Decency. And I hope a Man may be a Convert without being a Renegade; and however the Practice is contrary, I know which of them I should most favor. It is most infallible by all Sorts of Reasons that Mr Sheridan is altogether innocent in that Accusation of Preaching, but as he is a Creature without Cunning, so he hath not overmuch Advertency. His Books, his Mathematicks, the Pressures of his Fortunes, his

[1] Cf. Swift's letter to Sheridan of 11 Sept.

[2] See Swift's account to Stella of his words with Harley, 3 Apr. 1711 (*Journal*, i. 230): 'I warned him . . . that I expected every great minister, who honoured me with his acquaintance, if he heard or saw any thing to my disadvantage, would let me know it in plain words, and not put me in pain to guess by the change or coldness of his countenance or behaviour; . . . He took all right.'

[3] i.e. Theophilus Bolton.

Laborious Calling and some naturall Disposition or Indisposition give him an egarement d'esprit as you cannot but observe. But he hath other good Qualityes enough, to make up that Defect, Truth, Candor, good Nature, pleasantness of Humor, and very good Learning, and it was upon these Regards I was bold to recommend him, because I thought it was for the generall good that he should have some Encouragement to go on with his Drudgery. But if it be determined that Part must lay her Talons upon him, there is no more to be said. My Lord Lieutenant hath too many great Affairs to allow Time for examining into every little Business, and yet it is hard that even a Beggar should suffer who is wholly innocent: I heard K. W^m^ say that if the People of Ireland could be believed in what they said of each other, there was not an honest Man in the Kingdom. And if Mr Sheridan guesses right of the Person who is his chief Accuser,[1] there is no Man who is not Altogether drunk and mad with Party would value the Accusation. If by the Clutter made upon this Occasion, it should be thought most proper for Mr Sheridan not to appear about the Castle at this Juncture, I believe he will content him self, but not that he should lose any Degree of Favor with his Excellency; and if this be the case, I hope you will so order, that My Lord will condescend to signify so much to Him — For I know too well how often Princes themselves are obliged to act against their Judgment amidst the Rage of Factions. Upon the whole, the good Treatment you have given me hath produced an ill Effect, encouraging me to further Requests, that you will endeavor to make Mr Sheridan easy. None but Converts are afraid of shewing Favor to those who ly under Suspicion in Point of Principles, and that was Mr Addison's Argument in openly continuing his Friendship to me to the very Hour of his Death. And y^r^ Case is the same, and the same I shall expect from you in a proper Degree both towards Mr Sheridan and my self.

Whether you are in Parliam^t^ or no,[2] I am sensible you are too

[1] The allusion is to Richard Tighe, long known to Swift but hitherto ignored by him (*Journal*, i. 71, 158, 268). He was, however, a person of some influence in Ireland; and under George I was named of the Privy Council. He was reported to have carried to Lord Carteret the story of Sheridan's unfortunate sermon. Thereafter Swift pursued him with verse lampoons. See *Poems*, pp. 772–82 and *passim*.

[2] Tickell did not occupy a seat in the Irish Parliament, but his predecessor, Joshua Dawson, had been a member, and there was thus precedent for one holding his office doing so.

busy at this time to bear such an Interruption as I have given you, and yet I have not said half what I Mind. My Excuse is, that I have Title to your Favor, as you were Mr Addison's Friend, and in the most honorable Part his Heir, and if he had thought of you coming to this Kingdom, he would have bequeathed me to you. | I am ever with true Esteem and Respect | Your most obedient, and | most humble Servant | Jonathan Swift

Septb 18th | 1725

Endorsed: 18 Sept. 1725 | Dr Swift

Dodsley Miscellanies 1745, x. 91

Swift to the Rev. Thomas Sheridan

Quilca. Sept. 19. 1725.

We have prevailed with *Neal*, in spight of his Harvest, to carry up Miss,[1] with your Directions; and it is high time, for she was run almost wild, though we have something civiliz'd her since she came among us. You are too short in Circumstances. I did not hear you was forbid preaching.[2] Have you seen my Lord? Who forbid you to preach? Are you no longer Chaplain? Do you never go to the Castle? Are you certain of the accuser, that it is Tigh?[3] Do you think my Lord acts thus, because he fears it would breed ill Humour if he should openly favour one who is looked on as a different Party? I think that is too mean for him. I do not much disapprove your Letter, but I think it a wrong Method; pray read over the inclosed[4] twice, and if you do not dislike it, let it be sent (not by a Servant of yours, nor from you) to Mr. *Tickell*. There the Case is stated as well as I could do it in Generals, for want of knowing Particulars. When I come to Town, I shall see the Lord Lieutenant, and be as free with him as possible. In the mean time, I believe it may keep cold; however advise with Mr. *Tickell* and Mr. *Balaguer*. I should fancy that the Bishop of *Limerick*[5] could easily satisfy his Excellency, (and that my Lord Lieutenant believes no more of your Guilt than I, and therefore it can be nothing but to satisfy the Noise of Party at this

1 Presumably one of Sheridan's daughters.
2 Before Carteret.
3 See previous letter and note.
4 The preceding letter.
5 William Burscough, Carteret's late chaplain

Juncture, that he acts as he does; and if so (as I am confident it is) the Effect will cease with the Cause. But without doubt, Tigh and others have dinned the Words Tory and Jacobite into his Excellency's Ears, and therefore your Text, *&c.* was only made use of as an Opportunity.

Upon the whole Matter you are no Loser, but at least have got something.[1] Therefore be not like him who hanged himself, because going into a Gaming-House and winning Ten thousand Pounds, he lost Five Thousand of it, and came away with only half his Winnings. When my Lord is in *London* we may clear a Way to him to do you another Job, and you are young enough to wait.

We set out to *Dublin* on *Monday* the 5th[2] of *October*, and hope to sup at the Deanry the next Night, where you will come to us if you are not already engaged.

I am grown a bad Bailiff towards the End of my Service. Your Hay is well brought in, and better stack'd than usual. All here are well.

I know not what you mean by my having some Sport soon, I hope it is no Sport that will vex me.

Pray do not forget to seal the inclos'd before you send it.

I send you back your Letter to the Lord Lieutenant.

Dodsley Miscellanies 1745, x. 94

Swift to the Rev. Thomas Sheridan

Quilca, Sep. 25, 1725

Your Confusion hindred you from giving any rational Account of your Distress, till this last Letter,[3] and therein you are imperfect enough. However, with much ado, we have now a tolerable Understanding how things stand. We had a Paper sent inclos'd, subscrib'd

[1] The allusion is to an act of generosity on the part of Archdeacon Russell of Cork in whose church Sheridan had preached his sermon. According to Sheridan's son (*Life*, pp. 383–4) the Archdeacon considered himself 'however accidentally' as instrumental in ruining Sheridan's hopes, whom he saw 'loaded with a numerous offspring, upon a precarious income', whereas he was himself a man of property 'without any family'. He therefore made over to Sheridan by deed of gift the manor of Drumlane in co. Cavan, worth £250 a year.

[2] The reading of all editors before Ball. If Swift was right in stating the day of the week it should be '4th of October'.

[3] A missing reply to the preceding letter.

by Mr. *Ford*, as we suppose; it is in Print, and we all approve it, and this I suppose is the Sport I was to expect.[1] I do think it is agreed, that All Animals fight with the Weapons natural to them (which is a new and wise Remark out of my own Head) and the Devil take that Animal, who will not offend his Enemy, when he is provoked, with his proper Weapon; and though your old dull Horse little values the Blows I give him with the Butt-end of my Stick, yet I strike on and make him wince in Spight of his Dulness; and he shall not fail of them while I am here; and I hope you will do so too to the Beast who has kick'd against you, and try how far his Insensibility will protect him, and you shall have Help, and he will be vexed, for so I found your Horse this Day, though he would not move the faster. I will kill that Flea or Louse which bites me, though I get no Honour by it.

Laudari ab iis quos omnes laudant, is a Maxim, and the contrary is equally true. Thank you for the Offer of your Mare, and how a pox could we come without her? They pull'd off her's and your Horse's Shoes for fear of being rode, and then they rode them without Shoes, and so I was forc'd to shoe them again. All the Fellows here would be T—'s, if they were but Privy-Counsellors. You will never be at ease for your Friend's Horses or your own, till you have wall'd in a Park of twenty Acres, which I would have done next Spring.

You say not a Word of the Letter I sent you for Mr. *Tickell*, whether you sent it him or no; and yet it was very material that I should know it. The two Devils of Inadvertency and Forgetfulness have got fast hold on you. I think you need not quit his and *Balaguer's* Company for the Reasons I mentioned in that Letter, because they are above Suspicions, as *Whiggissimi* and *Unsuspectissimi*. When the Lord Lieutenant goes for *England*, I have a Method to set you right with him, I hope, as I will tell you when I come to Town, if I do not *Sheridan* it, I mean forget it.

I did a *Sheridanism*; I told you I had lost your Letter inclos'd, which you intended to Lord *Carteret*, and yet I have it safe here.[2]

[1] Presumably some of the lampoons on Tighe.
[2] Not forthcoming.

Longleat xiii (Harleian transcripts)[1]

Swift to Alexander Pope

Sep. 29. 1725

⌜Sir,—I cannot guess the Reason of Mr Stopfords management[2] but impute it at a venture either to hast or bashfullness, in the latter of which he is excessive to a fault, although he had already gone the Tour of Italy and France, to harden him: perhaps this second Journey and for a longer time may amend him. He treated you just as he did Lord Carteret, to whom I recommended him. My letter you saw to Lord Bolingb.[3] has shown you the Situation I am in, and the Company I keep: If I do not forget some of the Contents. But⌝ I am now returning to the noble Scene of Dublin in to the Grande Monde, for fearing of burying my parts to Signalise my self among Curates and Vicars, and correct all Corruption crept in relating to the weight of Bread and Butter through those Dominions where I govern.[4] I have employd my time (besides ditching) in finishing correcting, amending, and Transcribing my Travells, in four parts Compleat newly Augmented, and intended for the press when the world shall deserve them, or rather when a Printer shall be found brave enough to venture his Eares, I like your Schemes[3] of our meeting after Distresses and dispertions but the chief end I propose to my self in all my labors is to vex the world rather then divert it, and if I could compass that designe without hurting my own person or Fortune I would be the most Indefatigable writer you have ever seen without

[1] Printed by Pope, 1740–2, with omissions here placed in half-brackets. Here the Harleian transcript is textually important. The scribe (who writes *guest* for *guess*, *tracked* for *treated*, and *fearing* for *fear* in the first part of the letter) is not too competent. His instructions evidently were to leave blank spaces wherever Swift's hand was illegible, and the whole letter was proof-read by Lord Oxford himself, in whose hand more than a score of words are corrected or added. Important also is the address, which is added in his hand, since the presence of an address almost certainly shows that his lordship was proof-reading against the original letter and not from any 'copy' prepared by Pope, who discarded addresses. These facts, so clear in this letter, apply presumably to most or all of the Harleian transcripts. This Longleat text seems closer to the original letter than the printed texts of Pope's day, which are based on another transcript now lost.—This important textual note I owe to Professor Sherburn, ii. 324.

[2] See Pope to Swift, 14 Sept.

[3] A reply to Lord Bolingbroke's letter of 24 July. Missing.

[4] The Liberties of St. Patrick's Cathedral.

reading[1] I am exceedingly pleased that you have done with Translations Lord Treasurer Oxford often lamented that a rascaly World should lay you under a Necessity of Misemploying your Genius for so long a time. But since you will now be so much better employd when you think of the World give it one lash the more at my Request. I have ever hated all Nations professions and Communityes and all my love is towards individualls for instance I hate the tribe of Lawyers, but I love Councellor such a one, Judge such a one for so with Physicians (I will not Speak of my own Trade) Soldiers, English, Scotch, French; and the rest but principally I hate and detest that animal called man, although I hartily love John, Peter, Thomas and so forth. this is the system upon which I have governed my self many years (but do not tell) and so I shall go on till I have done with them I have got Materials Towards a Treatis proving the falsity of that Definition *animal rationale*; and to show it should be only *rationis capax*. Upon this great foundation of Misanthropy (though not Timons manner) The whole building of my Travells is erected: And I never will have peace of mind till all honest men are of my Opinion: by Consequence you are to embrace it immediatly and procure that all who deserve my Esteem may do so too. The matter is so clear that it will admit little dispute. nay I will hold a hundred pounds that you and I agree in the Point.

I did not know your Odyssey was finished being yet in the Country, which I shall leave in three days I shall thank you kindly for the Present but shall like it three fourths the less from the mixture you mention of another hand,[2] however I am glad you saved yourself so much drudgery—I have been long told by Mr Ford of your great Atchivements in building and planting and especially of your Subterranean Passage to your Garden whereby you turned a blunder into a beauty which is a Piece of Ars Poetica

I have almost done with Harridans and shall soon become old enough to fall in love with Girls of Fourteen. The Lady whom you describe to live at Court, to be deaf and no party Woman, I take to be Mythology but know not how to moralize it. She cannot be Mercy, for mercy is neither deaf nor lives at Court Justice is blind

[1] It is difficult to know what Swift means. He was far from being 'without reading'. Does he refer to the past or the future?

[2] of another hand] of other hands *Pope 1740–42*. William Broome and Elijah Fenton were the 'other hands' who helped Pope with the translation of the *Odyssey*.

and perhaps deaf but neither is she a Court Lady. Fortune is both blind and deaf and a Court Lady, but then she is a most Damnable party Woman, and will never make me easy as you promise. It must be riches which Answers all your description; I am glad she visites you but my voice is so weak that I doubt she will never hear me.

Mr Lewis sent me an Account of Dr Arbuthnett's Illness which is a very sensible Affliction to me, who by living so long out of the World have lost that hardness of Heart contracted by years and generall Conversation. I am daily loosing Friends, and neither seeking nor getting others. O, if the World had but a dozen Arbuthnetts in it I would burn my Travells but however he is not without Fault. There is a passage in Bede highly commending the Piety and learning of the Irish in that Age, where after abundance of praises he overthrows them all by lamenting that, Alas, they kept Easter at a wrong time of the Year.[1] So our Doctor has every Quality and virtue that can make a man amiable or usefull, but alas he hath a sort of Slouch in his Walk. I pray god protect him for he is an excellant Christian tho not a Catholick and as fit a man either to dy or Live as ever I knew.

I hear nothing of our Friend Gay, but I find the Court keeps him at hard Meat I advised him to come over here with a Lord Lieutenant. ⌜Mr Tickell is in a very good Office I have not seen Philips, tho' formerly we were so intimate He has got nothing, and by what I can find will get nothing though⌝ he writes little Flams (as Lord Leicester call'd those sort of Verses) on Miss Carteret[2] and others. it is remarkable and deserves recording that a Dublin Blacksmith a great poet hath imitated his manner in a Poem to the same Miss. Philips is a Complainer, and on this Occasion I told Lord Carteret that Complainers never Succeed at Court though Railers do.

Are you altogether a Country Gentleman that I must Address to you out of London to the Hazard of your losing this pretious Letter, which I will now Conclude although so much Paper is left. I have an ill name and therefore shall not Subscribe it. but you will guess

[1] In England the celebration of Easter was practically settled by the adoption of the Roman usage at the Council of Whitby in 664. The older cycle persisted for some time in the Celtic Church. Bede, *Hist. Eccl.* iii. 3.

[2] Boulter, when he became Archbishop of Armagh, brought Ambrose Philips with him as secretary in Nov. 1724. Here Philips developed the 'namby-pamby' type of verse associated with his name. The 'flam' called 'A Poem to the Hon. Miss Carteret' appeared in London during the summer of this year.

it comes from one who esteems and loves you about half as much as you deserve. I mean as much as he can

I am in great concern at which I am just told is in some News Paper[1] that Lord Bolingbroke is much hurt by a fall in Hunting I am glad he has so much youth and Viger left of which he hath not been thrifty but I wonder he has no more Discretion.

Address [added in Oxford's hand]: For mr pope at his House | at Twickenham near | Hampton Court | by London.
Endorsement: Dean Swift's Letter | to Mr. Pope. Sepr 29. 1725,

Forster F. 44. E. 2

Swift to the Earl of Oxford

[1 October 1725]

My Lord[2]—I have given your Lordship too much Trouble, and you are infinitely too condescending;[3] But you will please to consider that it is upon a matter of great Concern to me, I had a Letter from Mr Lewis[4] at the same time with the last from Your Lordship, wherein He tells me he hath received the Picture and Ring, and I have put him in the Way of sending them to me. I here repeat my most humble Thanks to your Lordship for this and all your Favors.

I doubt not but the hearty Prayers of all good men are added to mine for the Health and Success of My Lady Oxford, and that I shall soon hear of a Son born, worthy of both your Ancestors. Or if it should prove the other Sex, yet God be praised, you both have Youth and Time and Health enough before you.

I am glad to hear of your Lordship's manner of Life, spent in Study, in domestick Entertainment, in conversation with Men of Wit, Virtue and Learning, and in encouraging their Studyes. In all which I doubt you ly too justly under the Censure of Singularity, at least in England, for my Lord Carteret seems to imitate you here as far as Party will suffer him, to which he lately sacrificed the best

[1] some News Paper] some of the news papers *Pope 1740–42*.

[2] The original of this letter was sold, with other Croker papers, at Sotheby's on 6 May 1858, and bought by 'Holloway' for £2. 16*s*. o*d*. A copy was made, now in the Forster Collection, Red Box, 44. E. 2. The letter is here printed from that transcript.

[3] See Oxford's letter of 30 Aug. 1725.

[4] See previous letter.

Grecian[1] among us, and ordered him upon a false malicious Information to be struck out of the List of his Chaplains, the same to whom he gave a Church Living at my Recommendation. My Lord your Father was never capable of such an Action, he could not endure to have Men of Wit or Learning to be his Enemyes, nor do I remember he had any of either.

I beg to present my most humble Respects to My Lady Oxford, with the highest Acknowledgments of her Favor in pleasing to remember me; and with my heartfelt Prayer for your Lordship and Family, remain with the greatest Respect and Gratitude | My Lord | your Lordship's most obedient | and most obliged Servant | Jonath Swift

October 1st
1725

Longleat xiii (Harleian transcripts)

Alexander Pope to Swift

Twitenham, near Hampton Court | Octr 15: 1725.[2]

I am wonderfully pleas'd with the suddenness of your kind answer. It makes me hope you are coming towards us, and that you incline ⌜more and more⌝ toward your old friends in proportion as you draw nearer to them; in short, that you are getting into Our Vortex. Here is one, who was once a powerful Planet. ⌜Lord Bol.⌝[3] who has now (after long experience of all that comes of shining) learn'd to be content with returning to his First point, without the thought or ambition of shining at all. Here is another,[4] who thinks one of the greatest Glories of his Father was to have distinguish'd and Lov'd you, and who loves you hereditarily. Here is Arbuthnot, ⌜yet living,⌝ recover'd from the jaws of death, and more pleas'd with the hope of seeing you again, than of reviving a world he has long despis'd every part of, but what is made up of a few men like yourself. He

[1] i.e. Sheridan.

[2] This letter follows the Longleat (Harleian) transcript. Printed by Pope in 1741, and in all his editions thereafter. The omissions in the printed texts are marked by half-brackets. Ball follows Elwin, vii. 56–60.

[3] Pope's texts omit the name, but Curll, 1741, added it in a footnote.

[4] Lord Oxford.

goes abroad again, and is more chearful than even Health can make a man, for he has a good Conscience into the bargain (which is the most *Catholick* of all Remedies, tho not the most *Universal*) I knew it would be a pleasure to you to hear this; and in truth, that made me write so soon to you.

I'm sorry poor Philips[1] is not promoted in this age; for certainly if his reward be of the next, he is of all Poets the most miserable. I'm also sorry for another reason; if they don't promote him they'l spoil a very good conclusion of one of my Satyrs,[2] where having endeavour'd to correct the Taste of the town in wit and Criticisme, I end thus.

> But what avails to lay down rules for Sense?
> In ——'s[3] Reign these fruitless lines were writ,
> When Ambrose Philips was preferr'd for wit!

Our friend Gay is used, as the friends of Tories are by Whigs, (and generally by Tories too) Because he had Humour, he was suppos'd to have dealt with Dr Swift; in like manner as when any one had Learning formerly, he was thought to have dealt with the Devil. He puts his whole trust at Court, in that Lady whom I describ'd to you, and whom you take to be an allegorical Creature of fancy. I wish she really were *Riches* for His sake; tho as for yours, I question whether (if you knew her) you would change her for the other?

Lord Bol. had not the least harm by his fall, I wish he had no more by his other Fall —⌜Our⌝ Lord Oxford had none by his[4]—But Lord B. is the most *Improv'd Mind* since you saw him, that ever was without shifting into a new body or being Paullo minus ab angelis. I have often imagined to myself, that if ever All of us met again, after so many Varieties and Changes, after so much of the Old world, and of the Old man in each of us, had been alter'd; ⌜after there has been a New Heaven, and a New Earth, in our Minds, and bodies,⌝ that Scarce a single thought of the one any more than a single atome of the other, remains just the same: I've fancy'd, I say, that we shou'd meet like the Righteous in the Millennium, quite in peace, divested

[1] The name is marked by asterisks in the Faulkner edition, and by dashes in the lines below.

[2] In *The Dunciad*, 1728, the line about Philips below came near the end of the poem, iii. 274. In the text of 1743 it became iii. 326.

[3] George's.

[4] The allusion is to the loss by Bolingbroke and the retention by Oxford of a seat in the House of Lords.

of all our former passions, smiling at all our own designs,[1] and content to enjoy the Kingdome of the Just in Tranquillity. But I find you would rather be employ'd as an Avenging Angel of wrath, to break your Vial of Indignation over the heads of the wretched pityful creatures of this World; nay would make them *Eat your Book*, which you have made as bitter a pill for them as possible.

I won't tell you what designes I have in my head (besides writing a Set of Maximes in opposition to all Rochefoucaults Principles)[2] till I see you here, face to face. Then you shall have no reason to complain of me, for want of a Generous disdain of this World, or of the loss of my ears,[3] in yours and Their service.

Lord Oxford (whom I have now the third time mentioned in this letter, and he deserves to be always mention'd, in every thing that is addrest to you, or comes from you) Expects you. That ought to be enough to bring you hither; tis vastly a better reason, than if the *Nation Expected* you. For I really enter as fully as you can desire, into your Principle, of Love of Individuals: And I think the way to have a Publick Spirit, is first to have a Private one: For who the devil can believe any man can care for a hundred thousand people, who never cared for One? No ill humoured man can ever be a Patriot, any more than a Friend.

I designed to have left the following page for Dr. Arbuthnot to fill, but he is so touch'd with the period in yours to me concerning him, that he intends to answer it by a whole letter. He too is busy about a book,[4] which I guess he'll tell you of. So adieu—what remains worth telling you? Dean Berkley is well, and happy in the prosecution of his Scheme.[5] Lords Oxford and Bol. in health. Arbuthnot's recover'd, Duke Disney so also from the gates of death; Sir W. Wyndham better. Lord Bathurst well, and a Preserver of ancient Honour and ancient Friendship. The rest, if they were d—d, what is it to a Protestant Priest, who has nothing to do with the Dead? I answer for my own part as a Papist, I would not pray them out of Purgatory.

[1] at all our own designs] at our past designs *Faulkner edition*.

[2] In his reply to Pope, 26 Nov. 1725, Swift affirmed Rochefoucauld to be his favourite author, 'because I found my whole character in him'—a misleading characterization of himself.

[3] World . . . ears] World, tho' I have not lost my ears *Pope 1740–42*.

[4] *Tables of Ancient Coins, Weights, and Measures*, published by Jacob Tonson in 1727.

[5] For a college in the Bermudas.

My name is as bad an one as yours, and hated by all bad Poets from Hopkins and Sternhold[1] to Gildon and Cibber. The first pray'd against me ⌜join'd⌝ with the *Turk*;[2] and a Modern Imitatour of theirs (whom I leave you to find out) has added the *Christian* to 'em with proper definitions of each, in this manner,

The Pope's the Whore of Babylon,
 The Turk he is a Jew
The Christian is *an Infidel*
 That sitteth in a Pew.[3]

⌜My paper is without the Doctors help.⌝

Endorsement (in Oxford's hand): Mr. Pope. to Dr Swift | Oct. 15. 1725.

4805

John Arbuthnot to Swift

London: Octbr 17 | 1725

Dear Sir

I have the vanity to think, that a few freinds have a reall Concern for me & are uneasy, when I am in distress, in Consequence of which I ought to communicate with them the joy of my recovery. I did not want a most kind paragraph in your letter to Mr Pope[4] to convince me that yow are of the number, & I know that I give you a sensible pleasure in telling yow that I think my self at this time allmost perfectly recover'd of a most unusual & dangerous distemper, an imposthume in the Bowels, such a one, that had it been in the hands of a chirurgeon, in an outward & fleshy part, I should not have been well these three months. Duke Desny our old Friend is in a fair way to recover of such another; ther have been severall of them occasiond as I reckon by the cold & wett season. people have told me of new impostures (as they call'd them) every day. poor Sir William

[1] Writers of the metrical versions of the Psalms.

[2] The allusion is to a prayer at the end of the metrical Psalms: 'From Pope and Turk defend us, Lord'—Croker.

[3] The stanza comes from 'The Monster of Ragusa', printed in *Poems on Several Occasions* (1717), and later in other publications. See Norman Ault, *Pope's Own Miscellany*, pp. xlvi and 92. See also *Twickenham Pope. Minor Poems*, ed. Ault, p. 418.

[4] 29 Sept. 1725.

Wyndham is an imposture.[1] I hope the Bath, wher he is going will do him good. The hopes of seeing once more the Dean of St patricks revives my spirits, I can not help imagining some of our old club mett together like Mariners after a Storm. for gods sake don't tantalize your freinds, any more. I can prove by twenty unanswerable arguments that it is absolutely necessary, that yow should come over to England, that it would be committing the greatest absurdity that ever was not to do it the next approaching Winter. I beleive indeed it is just possible to save your soul w^t^out it & thats all. As for your Book, (of which I have framd to my self, such an idea, that I am persuaded ther is no doing any good upon mankind without it) I will sett the letters my self rather than that it should not be publish'd. but before yow putt the finishing hand to it it is really necessary to be acquainted wth some new improvements of mankind that have appeared of late and are dayly appearing. Mankind has an inexhaustible source of invention in the way of folly, & madness. I have only one fear, that when yow come over yow will be so much cuveted & taken up by the Ministry, that unless your freind's meett you at their tables, they will have none of Your company: this is really no joke; I am quite in earnest. Your deafness is so necessary a thing, that I allmost begin to think it is an affectation. I remember yow usd to reckon dinners. I know of near half a years dinner's where you are allready bespoke. It is worth your while to come to see our old freind Lewis who is wiser than ever he was the best of husbands.[2] I am sure I can say from my own experience, that he is the best of freind's. he was so to me when he had little hope I should ever live to thank him. Yow must acquaint me before yow take [your] jurney, that we may provide a convenient Lodging for yow amongst your Freinds. I am call'd away this moment, & have only time to add that I long to see yow, & am most sincerely, Dr Sir Your most faithfull humble serv^t^ | Jo: Arbuthnott.

Address: To | The Reverend the | Dean of S^t^ patricks | Dublin | Ireland
Postmark: BB.
Endorsed by Swift: Dr Arbuthnot | Octr 17th 1725 *and a second time*

[1] See previous letter.

[2] Erasmus Lewis married at the age of fifty-four. He lived near Arbuthnot.

Portland MSS.

The Earl of Oxford to Swift

Dover Street, 19 October 1725.

Reverend Sir,

I hope you will excuse these few lines for once, when I tell you that yesterday morning, I thank God, my wife was safely delivered of a son,[1] and both mother and child are as well as can be expected. I fancy this will not be disagreeable news to the Dean of St. Patrick's, except he be very much altered, which I believe not. I will not trouble you with any more, but to tell you that I am, with great respect, Sir. | Your most obedient servant, | Oxford.

Huntington Library

Swift to the Earl of Oxford

26 October 1725.

My Lord.[2]

I have now for fifteen years been reciving continuall Favors from My Lord your Father, from your self, and from My Lady Oxford; but none of them fit to compare with that of Your Lordship's last Letter, which came yesterday to my Hands, and yet upon second and third thinking, I begin to Doubt whether it were any thing more than strict Justice, for I should highly resent your making it the least Question whether any Thing that concerns your Lordship did not equally affect me. I do therefore hope that if I live any reasonable Time your Lordship will do me the same Justice on the like Occasion, again and again, and again.

I was[3] yesterday to see the Ld Lieutenant and my Lady Carteret; both of them received the good News of My Lady Oxford's Delivery with great Satisfaction, and His Excellency commanded me in a very particular manner to tell your Lordship that no Friend you have partakes more in your good Successes than himself.

[1] On the 18th of that month Lady Oxford gave birth to a son who died four days later.

[2] The original of this letter was sold at Sotheby's, 6 May 1858 (Croker sale), to Knight for £2. It is now in the Huntington Library, HM 24016. There is a transcript in the Forster Collection.

[3] was] went *Ball.*

Mr Clayton was in such hast to return to England on my coming to Toun, that I had but one half-hour with him. I doubt this Kingdom will make but a poor Addition to your Collection of Coyns. Severall small Silver ones have been sometimes found, but they are onely of some Saxon Kings; which I suppose are no Rarityes. The Copper ones are not above three or four hundred Years old, with the names on them of the Cityes where they were coyned, as Drogheda, Waterford, and the like. For any before the Conquest in Henry the 2^ds time, I know nothing. To enquire will cost no Labor, nor money to purchase. And whatever can be got, shall be sent to y^r Lordship, which you may through[1] away when you please. . If you knew Sr And^r Fountain who was here with Ld Pembroke, he can tell your Lordship more than any body.[2]

I pray God allmighty to bless y^r Lordship and Family, and to preserve this important Addition to it.

I am ever with the greatest Respect and Gratitude |

My Lord |

Dublin. | Your Lordships most obedient |

Oct^br 26th 1725 and most obliged humble Servant |

Jonathan Swift. .

Tickell's Letter-book No. 2

Swift to Thomas Tickell

[Deanery House, 12 November 1725]

S^r

I have got slowly out of a feaverish Disorder, that hath confined me these ten days. I shall dine to morrow at home, after a sort en famille with the two Ladyes my Nurses., and if you please to be a

[1] 'through', *sic* in manuscript.

[2] Swift had no doubt been told by Clayton of Oxford's desire to procure rare coins. In addition to augmenting the collection of manuscripts with which the name of Harley is associated, the second Earl of Oxford made a large collection of coins, which, together with his library of printed books, was dispersed after his death. Swift was evidently not well versed even in the limited numismatology of his day, and would have regarded with amazement the vast number of coins struck in Ireland now to be seen in the National Museum, Dublin. They date from the time of the Scandinavian settlements, and include reproductions of the coins of some of the Saxon kings. Copper coins of so early a date as Swift mentions are unknown.—Ball.

fourth, I shall take Care that no unacceptable fifth be of the Company: And pray let me know to night or to morrow morning. for, as to Sunday I look on you as a Guest when you please[1] | I am | Y^r most $obed^t$ | J. Swift

Deanry-House | Novr 12 1725

Nichols 1801, xix

Swift to the Rev. James Stopford

Wretched Dublin, in miserable Ireland,
Nov. 26, 1725.

Dear Jim,

I had your kind letter from Paris, dated Nov. 14, N.S. I am angry with you for being so short, unless you are resolved not to rob your journal book. What have *vous autres voyageurs* to do but write and ramble? Your picture of K.C.I. will be a great present whenever I shall receive it, which I reckon will be about the time of your return from Italy; for my Lord Oxford's picture was two months coming from London.[2]

Mr. Pope is very angry with you, and says you look on him as a

[1] Swift was writing on Friday. It was customary with him to be at home to his friends on Sundays. A relic which dates from one of these social gatherings has come down among the Tickell papers: it is a draft for the inscription to be engraved on the chalice which Swift presented to Goodrich church, in memory of his grandfather, who was incumbent in the time of Charles I, and died in 1658. Tickell entered the draft in his Letter Book, no. 2, with the date 1725.

Thomas Swift hujus
Ecclesiae Rector, notus in
Historiis ob ea quae fecit
et passus estpro Carolo primo
ex hoc Calice aegrotantibus
propinavit. eundem Calicem
Jonath: Swift S. T. D. Decan.
Sanctae Patricis Dublin Thomae
ex filio Nepos huic Ecclesiae in
perpetuum dedicat 1725

See further *Thomas Tickell*, R. E. Tickell, 1931, pp. 112–13.

[2] In his will (*Prose Works*, ed. Temple Scott, xi. 412–13) Swift bequeathed to James Stopford, the donor, 'my picture of King Charles the First, drawn by Vandyck'.

prophet, who is never esteemed in his own country, and he lays all the blame upon you, but will be pacified if you see him when you come back.[1] Your other correspondents tell me, that Mr. G[raham] beside his clothes, lost 200*l.* in money, which to me you slur over. I like your Indian's answers well; but I suppose the Queen[2] was astonished if she was told, contrary to her notions, that the great people were treated and maintained by the poor. Mrs. Johnson denies you to be a slave, and says you are much more so in quality of a governor; as all good princes are slaves to their subjects. I think you are justly dealt with: You travelled with liberty to work your slavery, and now you travel with slavery to work your liberty. The point of honour will not be so great, but you have equal opportunities to inform yourself and satisfy your curiosity. The happier you were abroad in your first travels, the more miserable you were at your return; and now the case will be directly contrary. I have been confined a fortnight with a little feverish disorder, and the consequences of it, but now am as usual, with tolerable health.

As to intelligence, here is the House of Commons, with a little remains of the nation's spirit against Wood's coin, are opposing the Court in their unreasonable demands of money to satisfy the wanton and pretended debts of the Crown, and all party but that of Court and Country seem to be laid asleep.[3] I have said and writ to the Lieutenant what I thought was right, and so have my betters; but all *surdis auribus*. This is enough for such a hermit as I to tell you of public matters. Your friends are all well, and you have not been long enough absent for any material accident to fall out. Here is a great rumour of the King's being dead, or dying at Hanover, which has not the least effect on any passion in me. Dr. Delany is a most perfect courtier; Sheridan full of his own affairs and the baseness of the world; Dr. Helsham *à son aise* at home or abroad; the Dean of St. Patrick's sitting like a toad in a corner of his great house, with a perfect hatred of all public actions and persons. You are desired to bring over a few of the testons, and what a'ye call (Julio's, I think) of Parma, Florence, and Rome, which some people would be glad

[1] Stopford delivered to Pope Swift's letter of 14 Sept. 1725.

[2] Perhaps the consort of some Indian ruler whom Stopford saw in London or Paris.

[3] The Country had on the 15th of that month defeated the Court, by a majority of 111 to 83, on a question as to the sufficiency of the hereditary revenue and existing duties to meet the changes of the establishment and the national debt.—Ball.

of for curiosities, and will give you other money for them.[1] If you are rich enough to buy any good copies of pictures by great hands, I desire when you would buy two to buy three, and the third shall be taken off your hands, with thanks, and all accidents be answered by the buyer. The people of Ireland have just found out that their fathers, sons, and brothers, are not made bishops, judges, or officers civil or military, and begin to think it should be otherwise; but the government go on as if there were not a human creature in the kingdom fit for anything but giving money.[2] Your brother paid the money to the lady;[3]—What would you have more? This is a time of no events. Not a robbery or murder to be had, for want of which and poetry the hawkers are starving. Take care of your health, and come home by Switzerland; from whence travel blindfold till you get here, which is the only way to make Ireland tolerable. I am told the Provost has absolutely given away all your pupils. Pray God give you grace to be hated by him and all such beasts while you live.[4] I excused your bashfulness to the Lieutenant, who said he observed and understood it, and liked you the better. He could govern a wiser nation better, but fools are fit to deal with fools;[5] and he seems to mistake our calibre, and treats *de haut en bas*, and gives no sugar plums. Our Dean Maule and Dr. Tisdall have taken upon them the care of the Church, and make wise speeches of what they will amend in St. Andrew's vestry every week to a crew of parsons of their own kind and importance.[6] The Primate and the

[1] The julio was a silver coin struck by Pope Julius II (1503–13); the teston a name denoting in the first instance a fifteenth-century Italian coin bearing a portrait—applied later to French and Italian coins without a portrait. In English 'tester' became a slang term for sixpence.

[2] Since the accession of George I crown patronage in Ireland was directed to fostering the supremacy of the English interest. Boulter, Archbishop of Armagh 1724 to his death in 1742, used his powerful influence to further this practice in all departments of administration, whether in Church or State.

[3] To Stella. See Swift to Stopford, 19 June 1725.

[4] Richard Baldwin succeeded Benjamin Pratt as Provost of Trinity in 1717. A strong Whig he entertained a natural antipathy to Swift. See Craik, *Life of Swift*, i. 20 n.

[5] Delany, *Observations*, p. 24, cites an occasion when Swift, overcome in argument with Carteret, exclaimed: 'What the vengeance brought you amongst us, get you gone, get you gone; pray God Almighty send us our boobies back again.'

[6] The appearance of the Tory Tisdall in concert with Henry Maule is difficult to explain; although it should be remembered that Maule was an Irishman.

Earl of Cavan[1] govern the House of Lords.[1] The A.B.D.[2] attacked the same in the Castle for giving a good living to a certain animal called a [Waltham] Black,[3] which the other excused, alleging he was preferred to it by Lord Townshend. It is a cant word for a deer stealer. This fellow was leader of a gang, and had the honour of hanging half a dozen of his fellows in quality of informer, which was his merit.[4] If you cannot match me that in Italy, step to Muscovy, and from thence to the Hottentots. I am just going out of town for two days, else I would have filled my paper with more nothings. Pray God bless you, and send you safe back to this place, which it is a shame for any man of worth to call his home.

Longleat xiii (Harleian Transcripts)

Swift to Alexander Pope

⌜Dublin⌝ Novr 26, 1725

Sir,—I should sooner have acknoledged yours[5] if a Feaverish Disorder and the Relick of it, had not disabled me for a fortnight, I now begin to make excuses, because I hope I am pretty near seeing you, and therefore I would cultivate an Acquaintance, because if you do not know me when we meet you need only keep one of my Letters, and compare it with my Face, for my Face and Letters are Counterparts of my heart, I fear I have not expressed

[1] Richard (Lambart) fourth Earl of Cavan saw military service in Spain, the West Indies, and Portugal. He took his seat in the House of Lords in 1703. He died 13 Mar. 1741–2. By marriage he was related to Sir Richard Steele.

[2] Archbishop of Dublin.

[3] The name has been previously printed 'Walsh', but the allusion is to famous deer-stealers, who had lately raided the Forest of Waltham in Essex, of which Epping Forest is a survival, and had given occasion for an enactment, known as the Black Act, conferring special powers in dealing with their offence.—Ball.

[4] Although there is reason to doubt whether he admitted the truth of the allegation, Boulter before long found that the conduct of his nominee brought scandal on religion as well as disrepute on himself. The transaction is an extraordinary instance of the extent to which the ecclesiastic was subordinated to the statesman in Boulter. Without apparently further knowledge of the man than a recommendation from Lord Townshend, Boulter not only presented him to a living in his gift, but also bestowed on him priest's orders (Mant, *Hist. of the Church of Ireland*, ii. 443–5; Leslie's *Armagh Clergy*, p. 122).—Ball.

[5] 15 Oct.

that right, but I mean well, and I hate blotts; I look in your Letter, and in my Conscience you say the same thing, but in a better manner. Pray tell my Lord Bolingbroke that I wish he were banished again, for then I should hear from him, when he was full of Philosophy, and Talked de contemptu mundi. My Lord Oxford was so extremely kind as to write to me immediatly an Account of his Sons Birth, which I immediatly acknowledged, but before my Letter could reach him I wished it in the Sea[1] I hope I was more afflicted then his Lordship—Hard that Parsons and Beggars should be overrun with Bratts while so great and good a Family wants an Heir to continue it. I have received his Fathers Picture but I lament (Sub Sigillo confessionis) that it is not so true a Resemblance as I could wish⌜; I had a very kind Letter from Dr. Arbuthnot;[2] but I will not trouble him with an Answer. this is no Excuse for I would rather write then not. I will answer him when I see him; in the mean time you shall do it for me. Tis enough that I know he is in health and loves me;—⌝ Drown the World, I am not content with despising it, but I would anger it if I could with safety. I wish there were an Hospital built for it's despisers, where one might act with safety and it need not be a large Building, only I would have it well endowed.—Mr Philips[3] is fort chancellant whether he shall turn Parson or no. But all employments here are engaged or in Reversion. Cast Wits, east-Beaus and cast Beaux have a proper Sanctuary in the Church. Yet we think it a Severe Judgment that a fine Gentleman, and so much a finer for hating Eclesiasticks should be a domestick humble Retainer to an Irish Prelate. He is neither Secretary nor Gentleman usher yet serves in both Capacities. He hath published several reasons why he never came to see me, but the best is that I have not waited on his Lord. We have had a Poem sent from London in Imitation of his on Miss Carteret.[4] It is on Miss Harvey of a day old, and we say and think it is yours. I wish it were not, because I am against Monopolyes.—You might have spared me a few more lines of your Satyr but I hope in a few Months to see it all. ⌜I would have the Preferment Just enough to save your lines, let it be ever so low, for your sake we will allow it to be Preferment—Mr Ford hath explained to me your Allegoricall Lady. She is our Friend

[1] In the interval Swift had heard of the death of Oxford's infant son.

[2] 17 Oct.

[3] Mr Philips] P.** *Faulkner Edition.*

[4] The poem was Henry Carey's *Namby Pamby.*

Gays Steward.[1] He would better find his account in dealing with the Devil then with me, who have not one Friend at Court—⌉ To hear Boys like you talk of Millimums and Tranquility I am older by thirty years. Lord Bol— by Twenty and you but by Ten then when we last were together and we should differ more then ever. You coquetting a Maid of Honour. My Lord looking on to see how the Gamesters play and I railing at you both. I desire you and all my Friends will take a special care that my Affection[2] to the World may not be imputed to my Age, for I have Credible witnesses ready to depose that it hath never varyed from the Twenty First to the f—ty[3] eighth year of my Life, (pray fill that Blank Charitably) I tell you after all that I do not hate Mankind, it is vous autres who hate them because you would have them reasonable Animals, and are Angry for being disappointed. I have always rejected that Definition and made another of my own. I am no more angry with ——[4] Then I was with the Kite that last week flew away with one of my Chickins and yet I was pleas'd when one of my Servants Shot him two days after, This I say, because you are so hardy as to tell me of your Intentions to write Maxims in Opposition to Rochfoucault who is my Favorite because I found my whole character in him, however I will read him again because it is possible I may have since undergone some alterations—Take care the bad poets do not outwit you, as they have served the good ones in every Age, whom they have provoked to transmit their Names to posterity. Mævius is as well known as Virgil, and Gildon will be as well known as you if his name gets into your Verses; and as to the difference between good and bad Fame is a perfect Trifle⌈—I guess your Modern Imitator, and desire to be a Sub-imitator tho' I must bestow 4 lines upon one Sect

The Heathen doth believe in Christ
And doth all Christians hate
For never was Informer he
Nor Minister of State.[5]

[1] The reference is probably to Mrs. Howard, or it may be to Gay's patroness the Duchess of Queensberry. Cf. Pope to Swift, 14 Dec. *ad fin.*

[2] Affection] disaffection *Faulkner edition.* In the manuscript someone has written the prefix 'dis' in pencil between the lines.

[3] Swift was approaching his fifty-eighth birthday. Curll mistakenly fills in the blank as 'forty'.

[4] The blank should be filled in as 'Walpole'. Curll makes it '*Philips*'.

[5] Cf. the end of Pope's letter to Swift of 19 Oct.

But this on Second thought is not of a Piece with yours, because it is a Commendation; for which⌉ I ask a Thousand pardons, and so I leave you for this time, and will write again without concerning my self whither you write or no . . . I am ever——

⌈My Service to the Dr our Friend Gay & Mr Lewis &c.⌉

Longleat xiii (Harleian Transcripts)

Pope and Bolingbroke to Swift

Decr the 14th 1725[1]

⌈You say you don't much care whether I write to you or not, and therefore I don't much care if I do. But whereas you tell me You'l write whether I do or not; I take it as kindly as I do many an other favour you have had the kindness to do for me, whether I deserv'd it or not. I shall however begin to fancy I do deserve it, because I find my own heart so prodigiously pleas'd with it. . . . Let me tell you⌉[2] I am the better acquainted with you for a long Absence, as men are with themselves for a long affliction: Absence does but hold off a Friend, to make one see him the truer. I am infinitely more pleas'd to hear you are coming near us, than at anything you seem to think in my favour, (an opinion which perhaps has been aggrandized by the distance, or dulness of Ireland, as objects look larger thro' a Medium of Foggs.) And yet I am infinitely pleas'd with that too: For Praise is like Ambergrize; a little unexpected Whiff of it (such as I meet with in your letter) is the most agreeable thing in the world; but when a whole lump of it is thrust to your nose, it is a Stink, and strikes you down. However, like the verses on Miss Harvey as well as you will, I'm never the better for it, for they are none of mine. But I am much the happier for finding (a better thing than our *Witts*) our *Judgments* jump, in the notion of entirely passing all Scriblers by in silence: To vindicate ones self against such nasty Slanders, is much as wise, as it was in your Countryman when people said he was besh— to show the contrary by showing his A— so let Gildon and Philips rest in peace. What Virgil had to do with

[1] All Pope's earliest texts and Faulkner wrongly date this letter 10 Dec. 1725. Those passages which did not appear in the early texts are here contained within half brackets.

[2] As printed in 1737–42 the letter begins 'I find myself better acquainted. . .'.

Mævius, that he shou'd wear him upon his Sleeve to all eternity, I don't know? but I think a bright author should put an end to Slanders only as the Sun does to Stinks; by shining out, exhale 'em to nothing. I've been the longer upon this, that I might prepare you for the Reception both you and your works might possibly meet in England. We your true acquaintance, will look upon you as a good man, and love you; Others will look upon you as a Witt, and hate you: so you know the worst, unless you are as vindicative as Virgil or the foresaid Hibernian.

I wish as warmly as you, for the Hospital to lodge the *Despisers of the world* in, only I fear it would be fill'd wholly like Chelsea with Maim'd Soldiers, and such as had been dis-abled in *its* Service. And I wou'd rather have those that out of such generous principles as you and I, despise it, Fly in its face, than Retire from it. Not that I have much Anger against the Great, my Spleen is at the little rogues of it: It would vexe one more to be knockt o' the Head by a Pisspot, than by a Thunderbolt. As to great Oppressors (as you say) they are like Kites or Eagles, one expects mischief from them: But to be Squirted to death (as poor Wycherley[1] said to me on his deathbed) by *Potecaries Prentices*, by the under Strappers of Under Secretaries, to Secretaries, who were no Secretaries—this would provoke as dull a dog as Ph—s[2] himself.

But I beg your pardon, I'm tame agen, at your advice. I was but like the Madman, who on a sudden clapt his hand to his Sword of Lath, and cry'd, *Death to all my Enemies*! when another came behind him and stopt his wrath, by saying, *Hold! I can tell you a way worth twenty on't: Let your Enemies alone, and they will dye of themselves.*

So much for Enemies, now for friends. Lewis thinks all this very Indiscreet: the Dr not so; he loves mischief the best of any Good natured man in England. Lord B. is above triffling, he is grown a great Divine. Jervas and his Don Quixot are both finish'd[3] Gay is writing Tales for Prince William:[4] I suppose Philips will take this very ill, for two reasons; one, that he thinks all childish things belong

[1] This remark suggests that Pope's friendship, with interruptions, continued to the end of Wycherley's life—1716.

[2] Philips.

[3] Jervas's translation of *Don Quixote* was not published till 1742, after his death (1739). Pope's phrasing is ambiguous, but he probably means that the translation would do Jervas more harm than good.

[4] The *Fables*, published in 1727, are subscribed as 'Invented for his Amusement' and dedicated to 'William Duke of Cumberland'.

to him; and the other, because he'l take it ill to be taught, that one may write things to a Child, without being childish.—What have I more to add? but that Lord Oxford, the best man in the world, desires earnestly to see you: and that many others who you do not think the worst, will be gratify'd by it: none more be assured, than | Your very affectionate faithfull Servant | A. Pope.

⌜What is become of Mr Ford. I'm glad to hear of his name: but tell him from me, he does not know a *Maid* of Honour from a *Woman* of Honour (by what you write of Gay's Steward) I am much his Servant.⌝

⌜Lord Be—[1] ⌜I am so far from being above triffling that I wish with all my heart I had nothing else to do. But I need not take any pains to convince you that Pope advances a meer Slander; his manner of proving is like that of an Irish man whose life and death were lately Transmitted to Posterity by that great Historiographer Paul Lorraine.[2] I did not rob the witness, said your Countryman, for by my Shawl I did put my hand into his left pocket, and seize him by the left arm, not by the right.⌝ Pope and you are very great wits, and I think very indifferent Philosophers, if you dispise the world as much as you pretend, and perhaps believe you would not be so angry with it, the founder of your Sect.[3] that noble original whom you think it so great an Honour to resemble was a Slave to the worst part of the world, to the Court, and all his big words were the Language of a Slighted Lover who desired nothing so much as a reconciliation, and fear'd nothing so much as a rupture. I believe the world has us'd me as scurvily as most people, and yet I could never find in my heart to be throly angry with the Simple false capricious thing. I should blush alike to be discover'd fond of the world or piqu'd at it. Your Definition of Animal ⌜capax⌝ Rationis instead of the Common one Animal Rationale, will not bear examination. define but Reason, and you will see why your distinction is no

[1] 'Lord Be' is added in the margin to indicate that this part of the letter was written by Bolingbroke. Ball, following Elwin, prints it as a separate letter.

[2] Paul Lorraine, an ordinary of Newgate, was accustomed to publish accounts and print dying speeches of criminals whom he attended to the gallows.

[3] In the transcript 'Seneca' appears as a note in Oxford's hand; and later as a footnote by Pope, 1741–2. The true reference in this passage is, however, to Rochefoucauld. Apart from the fact, as Ball points out, that Seneca had not been mentioned in Swift's letter and Rochefoucauld had, the context shows that Bolingbroke's reference is to the latter.

better than that of the Pontiffe Cotta between mala Ratio and bona Ratio.[1] But enough of this. make us a visit and I'le subscribe to any side of these important Questions which you please. We differ less than you imagine perhaps when you wish me banish'd again. But I am not less true to you and to Philosophy in England than I was in France.

To the Reverend Dr Swift

Endorsement (in Oxford's hand): Mr Pope to Dean Swift Dec. 14. 1725

Nichols 1801, xix

Swift to Viscount Palmerston

Dublin, Jan. 1, 1725–6.

My Lord,[2]

I am desired by one Mr. Curtis,[3] a clergyman of this town to write to your Lordship upon an affair he has much at heart, and wherein he has been very unjustly and injuriously treated. I do now call to mind what I hear your Lordship has written hither, that you were pleased many years ago, at my recommendation, to give Dr. Elwood a grant of a chamber in the College, which is at your disposal. For I had then some credit with your Lordship, which I am told I have now lost, although I am ignorant of the reason. I shall therefore only inform your Lordship in one point. When you gave that grant, it was understood to continue during Dr. Elwood's continuance in the College; but, he growing to be a Senior Fellow, and requiring more conveniences, by changing one room, and purchasing another, got

[1] See Cicero, *De Natura Deorum*, iii. 28.

[2] This letter was addressed to Sir William Temple's eldest nephew, the second but first surviving son of Sir John Temple, Solicitor-General, Attorney-General, and Speaker of the Irish House of Commons. On 12 Mar. 1722–3 he was created Baron Temple of Mount Temple, co. Sligo, and Viscount Palmerston of Palmerston, co. Dublin. He died at Chelsea 10 June 1757. Since the correspondence with Lady Giffard in 1709 in which she accused Swift of publishing the third part of Temple's *Memoirs* from unfaithful copy, friendly intercourse with the Temple family had ceased; and the abrupt tone of this letter almost suggests that Swift sought a ground of quarrel with Palmerston.

[3] William Curtis matriculated at Trinity College, Dublin, in 1710. He was appointed a minor canon of St. Patrick's 18 Mar. 1728–9. He resigned in 1731; and in 1735 became Archdeacon of Ferns.

into a more convenient apartment, and therefore those who now derive under the doctor, have, during the doctor's life, the same property as if they derived under your Lordship; just as if one of your tenants should let his holding to another, during the term of his lease, and take a more convenient farm. This is directly the case, and must convince your Lordship immediately; for, Mr. Curtis paid for the chamber, either to the doctor, or to those who derived under him, and till the doctor dies, or leaves the College, the grant is good.[1]

I will say nothing of Mr. Curtis's character, because the affair is a matter of short plain justice; and, besides, because I would not willingly do the young man an injury, as I happened to do to another whom I recommended to your Lordship merely for your own service, and whom you afterward rejected, expressing your reason for doing so, that I had recommended him, by which you lost the very person of the whole kingdom who by his honesty and abilities could have been most useful to you in your offices here. But these are some of the refinements among you great men, which are above my low understanding. And whatever your Lordship thinks of me, I shall still remain | Your Lordship's most obedient | and most humble servant, | Jonath. Swift.

Address: To the Right Honourable the Lord Palmerston at his House in St. James's Square, London.

Nichols 1801, xix

Viscount Palmerston to Swift

Jan. 15, 1725–6.

Mr. Dean,

I should not give myself the trouble to answer your polite letter, were I as unconcerned about character and reputation as some are. The principles of justice I hope I have learned from those, who always treated you in another manner than you do me, even without reason.

[1] Writing to John Temple, 15 June 1706, Swift asked him to use his influence with his brother Henry (later Lord Palmerston) to confirm on John Elwood, a fellow of Trinity College, the grant of a room which was vested in him. The grant was approved. Elwood now desiring more spacious quarters Swift here proposes to Palmerston that Curtis's occupation of Elwood's former room be confirmed.

You charge me with injury and injustice done Mr. Curtis; he is still in his chamber, till he is turned out, none is done him, and he is satisfied with my proceedings, and the issue I have put it on. Your interest with me, (which if ever lost, such letters will not regain), procured Dr. Elwood the use of that chamber, not the power to job it. Your parallel case of landlord and tenant will not hold, without Dr. Elwood has a writing under my hand; if he has, I will fulfil it to a tittle; if not, he is as a tenant at will, and when he quits, I am at liberty to dispose of the premises again.

Whoever told you Mr. Staunton was dismissed, because you recommended him, told you a most notorious falsehood; he is the young man I suppose you mean. The true reason was, his demand of a large additional salary, more than he had before my time; so he left the office, and was not turned out.

My desire is to be in charity with all men; could I say as much of you, you had sooner inquired into this matter, or if you had any regard to a family you owe so much to; but I fear you hugged the false report to cancel all feelings of gratitude that must ever glow in a generous breast, and to justify what you had declared, that no regard to the family was any restraint to you. These refinements are past my low understanding, and can only be comprehended by you great wits.

I always thought in you I had a friend in Ireland, but find myself mistaken. I am sorry for it; my comfort is, it is none of my fault. If you had taken anything amiss, you might have known the truth from me. I shall always be as ready to ask pardon when I have offended, as to justify myself when I have not. I am, Sir, | Your very humble servant.

Nichols 1801, xix

Swift to Viscount Palmerston

Jan. 29, 1725–6.

My Lord,[1]

I desire you will give yourself the last trouble I shall ever put you to, ⌈I mean of reading this letter.⌉ I do entirely acquit you of any

[1] This reply by Swift to Palmerston's letter of 15 Jan. has survived (in print) in two forms—in a draft and as the posted letter. It was printed from the draft

injury or injustice done to Mr. Curtis, and if you had read that passage ⌜relating to his bad usage⌝ a second time, you could not possibly have so ill understood me. The injury and injustice he[1] received were from those who claimed a title to his chambers, took, away his key, reviled and threatened to beat him, with a great deal more of the like brutal[2] conduct. Whereupon at his request I laid the case before you, as it appeared to me. And it would have been very strange if, on account of a trifle, and of a person for whom I have no concern, further than as he was employed by me on the character he bears of piety and learning, I should charge you with injury and injustice to him, when I knew from himself, and Mr. Reading,[3] that you were not answerable for either.

As you state the case of tenant at will, it is certain no law can compel you; but to say the truth, I then had not law in my thoughts.

Now, if what I writ of injury and injustice were wholly applied in plain terms to one or two of the College here, whose names were below my remembrance, you will consider how I could deserve an answer in every line, full of foul invectives, open reproaches, jesting flirts, and contumelious terms, and what title you have to give me such ⌜contumelious⌝ treatment ⌜who never did you the least injury, or received the least obligation from you.⌝ I own myself indebted to Sir William Temple, for recommending me to the late King, although without success, and for his choice of me to take care of his posthumous writings. But, I hope you will not charge my living in his family as an obligation, for I was educated to little purpose, if I retired to his house, on any other motives than the benefit of his conversation and advice, and the opportunity of pursuing my studies. For, being born to no fortune, I was at his death as far to seek as ever, and perhaps you will allow that I was of some use to

by Faulkner, 1746, viii. 373–6. In this form it was reprinted by Nichols, 1801, *Works*, xii. 175–8. The draft was endorsed 'An Answer to Lord Palmerston's civil polite Letter'. Before the publication of his complete set of the *Works* Nichols was favoured 'by the present Lord Palmerston with the loan of the original', that is to say the letter which was posted. The letter is here printed from Nichols, xix. 41–44, when he was in possession of the original letter, now missing. There are differences between the draft and the original, although of little consequence. The words contained within half-brackets do not appear in the draft.

[1] he] the young man *Draft*.

[2] brutal] monstrous *Draft*.

[3] Daniel Reading. See Swift to John Temple, 15 June 1706.

him. This I will venture to say, that in the time when I had some little credit I did fifty times more for fifty people, from whom I never received the least service or assistance. Yet I should not be pleased to hear a relation of mine reproaching them for ingratitude, although many of them well deserve it; for, thanks to party, I have met in both kingdoms with ingratitude enough.

If I have been ill informed ⌜in what you mention of Mr. Staunton,⌝ you have not been much better, that I declared no regard to the family (as you express it) was a restraint to me. I never had the least occasion to use any such words. The last time I saw you in London was the last intercourse I ever had with the family. But having always trusted to my own innocence, I shall not be inquisitive to know my accusers.

When I mentioned my loss of interest with you I did it with concern, but I had no resentment, because I supposed it only to arise from different sentiments in publick matters.

My Lord, if my letter were polite, it was against my intentions, and I desire your pardon for it; if I have wit, I will keep it to show when I am angry, which at present I am not; because, though nothing can excuse those intemperate words your pen has let fall, yet I shall give allowance to a hasty person, hurried on by a mistake beyond all rules of decency. If a first Minister of State had used me as you have done, he should have heard from me in another style, because in that case retaliating would be thought a mark of courage: But as your Lordship is not in a situation to do me good, nor, I am sure, of a disposition to do me mischief, so I should lose the merit of being bold, because I could incur no danger, ⌜if I gave myself a liberty which your ill usage seemed to demand.⌝ In this point alone we are exactly equal, but in wit and politeness I am ready to yield to you, as much as I do in titles and estate.

I have found out one secret, that although you call me a great wit, you do not think me so, otherwise you would have been too cautious to have writ me such a letter.

You conclude with saying you are ready to ask pardon where you have offended. Of this I acquit you, because I have not taken the offence, but whether you will acquit yourself must be left to your conscience and honour.

I have formerly upon occasion been your humble servant in Ireland, and should not refuse to be so still; but you have so useful and excellent a friend in Mr. Reading, that you need no other, and I hope my good opinion of him will not lessen yours. I am, my Lord, | Your most humble servant, | Jonath. Swift.

Address: To the Right Honourable the Lord Palmerston, at his House in St. James's Square, London.
Endorsed by Lord Palmerston: Not answered.

4805

John Arbuthnot to Swift

Tuesday [5 April 1726].[1]

Dear Sir[2]

I have been at Your lodgings this morning, but yow was out early: Her Royal Highness[3] begs the honor of a visit from yow on Thursday night next at seven a clock. Yow are to be attended by | Dr Sir | Your most faithfull humble | servant Jo: Arbuthnott.

I hope yow will not engage your self at that hour;[4] but I shall see yow before that time.

Tuesday 3 a'clock

Address: To | The Reverend the | Dean of S^t patrick
Endorsed by Swift: Dr Arb- | ab^t Princess *and* Dr Arbuthnot | to me in London | 1726 *and* Dr Arbuthnot | 1726

[1] Underneath 'Tuesday 3 o'clock' Swift has written 'Ap^r 5'. Ball conjectures the following Tuesday, the 12th. But there is no reason in this instance to question Swift's date.

[2] Swift had crossed to England early in March, and taking the road through Oxford had arrived about the middle of that month in London, where he took up his abode in lodgings 'in Bury Street, next door to the Royal Chair'. There he was joined by Pope, who, writing on the 22nd, says that he had spent two days with him, and had found him in perfect health and spirits 'the joy of all here who know him as he was eleven years ago'. During the next fortnight, as Pope's letters show, Swift was taken by Dr. Arbuthnot 'a course through the town with Lord Chesterfield, Mr. Pulteney, &c.', stayed with Lord Bolingbroke at his newly acquired residence, Dawley, near Uxbridge, and visited Pope at Twickenham. Cf. *Portland MSS*. vii. 431.

[3] The Princess of Wales.

[4] It may be inferred from these words that this was not the first attempt which Arbuthnot had made to bring Swift to Leicester House. In Letters written some years later Swift says that the Princess sent for him nine or eleven times before he obeyed her command.—Ball.

Tickell Papers

Swift to Thomas Tickell

[London] April 16th 1726.

Sr[1]

Though I am to desire a Favor of you, yet I was glad it gave me an Opportunity of paying you my Respects. I am here now a Month, picking up the Remnant of my old Acquaintance, and descending to take new ones. Your People are very civil to me, and I meet a thousand times better Usage from them than from that Denomination in Ireland.[2] This night I saw the wild Boy, whose arrivall here hath been the subject of half our Talk this fortnight He is in the Keeping of Dr Arthbuthnot,[3] but the King and Court were so entertained with him, that the Princess could not get him till now.[4] I can hardly think him wild in the Sense they report[5] him. Mr Arundel[6] is made Surveyor of the Works, which I suppose you will hear before you read this.

I hope I am to give you Joy, & I am sure I wish it you.[7] The Reason I trouble you with the inclosed, is because it contains a Bill of Lading for a Picture I have from France,[8] & am afraid it

[1] This letter was first printed by Scott, 1814, xix. 363, from whom Ball takes his text. The original is preserved among the Tickell papers, and the letter is here printed from the original manuscript. See also R. E. Tickell, *Thomas Tickell*, pp. 117–18.

[2] It is known that before this letter was written Swift, with some friends, had dined with Walpole. In a letter from Boulter, addressed to the Duke of Newcastle, 10 Feb. 1725–6, the Archbishop, having learned that Swift shortly designed for England, expressed the hope that 'some eye were had to what he shall be attempting on your side of the water' (*Boulter's Letters*, i. 51). It has been supposed that Swift desired to make his peace with Walpole and further his own interests. It is more probable, however, that the invitation came from Walpole, who, we know, soon realized that he made no progress.

[3] *Sic.*

[4] The 'Wild Boy' was found in 1725 in the woods of Hameln walking on hands and feet, and feeding on roots and grass. He was brought to England, and, for a time, committed to the care of Arbuthnot. The boy was in fact a speechless idiot. Some description of him, with fanciful additions, is given in *It cannot Rain but it Pours*, 1726, which was probably, in part at least, written by Arbuthnot. See G. A. Aitken, *Life and Works of Arbuthnot*, pp. 471–4.

[5] This is the correct reading. Scott and Ball have 'respect'.

[6] Richard Arundel was M.P. for Knaresborough.

[7] Tickell was married on St. George's Day, Saturday, 23 Apr. 1726, to Clotilda Eustace. By this marriage he became a considerable landowner in co. Kildare.

[8] The picture sent to him by Stopford.

might miscarry. You will please to send one of your Servants to the Person it is direct^{ed} to, and accept my Excuses. | I am with true Respect |Sr Your most obedient |humble Servt | J: Swift

Ap^{r} 16th 1726

Address: To Thomas Tickell Esq. | at the Castle of | Dublin |Ireland
Postmark: AP
Endorsed: London 16 Apr. 1726 | Dean of St Patrick's | A^{d} 10 May

Hawkesworth 1766

Swift to the Rev. John Worrall

London, April 16, 1726.

The ladies have told you all my adventures, and I hear you are ruining me with dung.[1] I have writ several times to the ladies, and shall soon do so again. I send you inclosed the bill of lading for a picture that has lain long at sea; you will be so kind to get it out of the custom-house. Mr. *Medlycott*[2] will make it easy, if there should be any difficulties. My humble service to Mrs. *Worrall*, and the ladies and all my friends. I thank God I am in pretty good health. I have now company with me; I can say no more. I hope you are all well.

I got no voice at *Oxford*; but am endeavouring for one here.[3]

Forster copy

Swift to Knightley Chetwode

London, April 19, 1726.

Sir.

I have the favour of your letter to the 7th instant.[4] As to the poem you mention, I know several copies of it have been given about, and

[1] For Naboth's Vineyard. See Swift to Worrall, 12 July 1725.

[2] As one of the Commissioners in Ireland Medlycott could assist in getting the picture sent from France by Stopford through the Customs.

[3] For a vacancy in the Cathedral choir.

[4] In the missing letter of 7 Apr. Chetwode had evidently warned Swift that copies of 'Cadenus and Vanessa' were being shown about in manuscript. The poem was written for Vanessa and not intended for publication. Swift's

[the] Lord Lieutenant told me he had one. It was written at Windsor near fourteen years ago, and dated. It was a task performed on a frolic among some ladies, and she it was addressed to died some time ago in Dublin, and on her death the copy [was] shown by her executor.[1] I am very indifferent what is done with it, for printing cannot make it more common than it is;[2] and for my own part, I forget what is in it, but believe it to be only a cavalier business, and they who will not give allowances may choose, and if they intend it maliciously, they will be disappointed, for it was what I expected, long before I left Ireland.

Therefore what you advise me, about printing it myself is impossible, for I never saw it since I writ it. Neither if I had, would I use shifts or arts, let people think of me as they please. Neither do I believe the gravest character is answerable for a private humorsome thing, which, by an accident inevitable, and the baseness of particular malice, is made public. I have borne a great deal more; and those who will like me less, upon seeing me capable of having writ such a trifle so many years ago, may think as they please, neither is it agreeable to me to be troubled with such accounts, when there is no remedy, and only gives me the ungrateful task of reflecting on the baseness of mankind which I knew sufficiently before.

I know not your reasons for coming hither.[3] Mine were only to see some old friends before my death, and some other little affairs, that related to my former course of life here. But I design to return by the end of summer. I should be glad to be settled here, but the inconvenience and charge of only being a passenger, is not so easy as an indifferent home, and the stir people make with me gives me neither pride nor pleasure.. I have said enough and remain, Sir, |

Yours, &c.

Address: To Knightley Chetwode, Esq.

Endorsed: Dr. Swift, from London, in answer to a letter I wrote him concerning Cadenus and Vanessa. Sent by hand.

statement that it was 'written at Windsor near fourteen years ago' would carry the date of composition back to 1712. During his stay at Windsor in 1712 he was occupied with the laborious composition of his *History of the Four Last Years of the Queen*, and it is unlikely that any part of 'Cadenus and Vanessa' was then written. On this whole subject see further *Poems*, ii. 683–6.

[1] Berkeley's co-executor and beneficiary under Vanessa's will, Robert Marshall.

[2] The poem was published in Dublin, London, and Edinburgh in 1726.

[3] Evidently Chetwode had thrown out a hint of joining Swift in London.

4806

The Earl of Peterborough to Swift

Saturday evening [23 April 1726]

S[r]

one of your Irish Heroes that from the extreamity of Our English Land, came to destroy the wicked brazen project,[1] desires to meet you a munday next at Parsons green.[2] if you are not ingaged I will send my Coach for you.

S[r] Robert Wallpoole any morning except Tuesday & Thursday which are his publick dayes, about nine in the morning will be glad to see you att his London house,[3] a munday if I see you I will give you a further account | your affectionate Servt | Peterborow

Saturday Evening

Address: For Doc[t] Swift att his Lodging in Berry Street.
Endorsed by Swift: E of Peterborow—1726 | in sumr *and* L[d] Peterb.—

Nichols Supplement 1779

Swift to the Earl of Peterborough

April 28, 1726.

My Lord,

Your Lordship having, at my request, obtained for me an hour from Sir *Robert Walpole*, I accordingly attended him yesterday at eight o'clock in the morning, and had somewhat more than an hour's conversation with him. Your Lordship was this day pleased to inquire what passed between that great Minister and me, to which I gave you some general answers, from whence you said you could comprehend little or nothing.

I had no other design in desiring to see Sir *Robert Walpole*, than to represent the affairs of *Ireland* to him in a true light, not only

[1] i.e. Lord Carteret.

[2] Peterborough's residence near London.

[3] As will be afterwards seen this was a reply to a request from Swift himself. The fact that Peterborough sought an interview for him tends to discount an assertion that after the dinner at Chelsea Walpole told Peterborough that he could place no reliance on any profession which Swift might make, as in a letter to Arbuthnot which had been opened in the post Swift had mentioned his intention of deluding him by flattery.—Ball.

without any view to myself, but to any party whatsoever: and, because I understood the affairs of that kingdom tolerably well, and observed the representations he had received were such as I could not agree to, my principal design was to set him right, not only for the service of *Ireland*, but likewise of *England*, and of his own administration.

I failed very much in my design; for, I saw, he had conceived opinions from the examples and practices of the present and some former governors, which I could not reconcile to the notions I had of liberty, a possession always understood by the *British* nation to be the inheritance of a human creature.[1]

Sir *Robert Walpole* was pleased to enlarge very much upon the subject of Ireland, in a manner so alien from what I conceived to be rights and privileges of a subject of *England*, that I did not think proper to debate the matter with him so much as I otherwise might, because I found it would be in vain. I shall, therefore, without entering into dispute, make bold to mention to your Lordship some few grievances of that kingdom, as it consisteth of a people, who, beside a natural right of enjoying the privileges of subjects, have also a claim of merit from their extraordinary loyalty to the present King and his Family.

First, That all persons born in *Ireland* are called and treated as *Irishmen*, although their fathers and grandfathers were born in *England*; and their predecessors having been conquerors of *Ireland*, it is humbly conceived they ought to be on as good a foot as any subjects of *Britain*, according to the practice of all other nations, and particularly of the *Greeks* and *Romans*.

Secondly, That they are denied the natural liberty of exporting their manufactures to any country which is not engaged in a war with *England*.

Thirdly, That whereas there is a University in *Ireland*, founded by

[1] Many rumours spread abroad of Swift's purpose in desiring to see Walpole —that he sought preferment for himself by conciliating the Prime Minister, that he was offered an English benefice at a price. This letter effectively disposes of baseless gossip. Swift sought advantages for Ireland by stressing the administrative, economic, and commercial injustices under which the country laboured. He admits that he did not debate these matters at length because he realized that it would be in vain; but in this letter he sets out in full, for Walpole's benefit, the grievances which lay near his heart, and asks that the paper may be handed on for him to read. Craik, *Life*, ii. 110–17, has an admirable summary of the whole matter.

Queen *Elizabeth*, where youth are instructed with a much stricter discipline than either in *Oxford* or *Cambridge*, it lieth under the greatest discouragements, by filling all the principal employments, civil and ecclesiastical, with persons from *England*, who have neither interest, property, acquaintance, nor alliance, in that kingdom; contrary to the practice of all other States in *Europe* which are governed by viceroys, at least what hath never been used without the utmost discontents of the people.

Fourthly, That several of the bishops sent over to *Ireland*, having been clergymen of obscure condition, and without other distinction than that of chaplains to the governors, do frequently invite over their old acquaintance or kindred, to whom they bestow the best preferments in their gift. The like may be said of the judges, who take with them one or two dependents, to whom they give their countenance, and who, consequently, without other merit, grow immediately into the chief business of their courts. The same practice is followed by all others in civil employments, if they have a cousin, a valet, or footman, in their family, born in *England*.

Fifthly, That all civil employments, grantable in reversion, are given to persons who reside in *England*.

The people of *Ireland*, who are certainly the most loyal subjects in the world, cannot but conceive that most of these hardships have been the consequence of some unfortunate representations (at least) in former times; and the whole body of the gentry feel the effects in a very sensible part, being utterly destitute of all means to make provision for their younger sons, either in the Church, the law, the revenue, or, of late, in the army: and, in the desperate condition of trade, it is equally vain to think of making them merchants. All they have left is, at the expiration of leases, to rack their tenants; which they have done to such a degree, that there is not one farmer in a hundred through the kingdom who can afford shoes or stockings to his children, or to eat flesh, or drink anything better than sour milk or water, twice in a year; so that the whole country, except the *Scotch* plantation in the north, is a scene of misery and desolation, hardly to be matched on this side *Lapland*.

The rents of *Ireland* are computed to be about a million and a half, whereof one half million at least is spent by lords and gentlemen residing in *England*, and by some other articles too long to mention.

About three hundred thousand pounds more are returned thither on other accounts: and, upon the whole, those who are the best versed in that kind of knowledge, agree, that *England* gaineth annually by *Ireland* a million at least, which even I could make appear beyond all doubt.

But, as this mighty profit would probably increase, with tolerable treatment, to half a million more; so it must of necessity sink, under the hardships that kingdom lieth at present.

And whereas Sir *Robert Walpole* was pleased to take notice how little the King gets by *Ireland*, it ought, perhaps, to be considered, that the revenues and taxes, I think, amount to above four hundred thousand pounds a year; and reckoning the riches of *Ireland*, compared with *England*, to be as one to twelve, the King's revenues there would be equal to more than five millions here; which, considering the bad payment of rents, from such miserable creatures as most of the tenants in *Ireland* are, will be allowed to be as much as such a kingdom can bear.

The current coin of *Ireland* is reckoned, at most, but five hundred thousand pounds; so that above four-fifths are paid every year into the exchequer.

I think it manifest, that whatever circumstances can possibly contribute to make a country poor and despicable, are all united with respect to *Ireland*. The nation controled by laws to which they do not consent, disowned by their brethren and countrymen, refused the liberty not only of trading with their own manufactures but even their native commodities, forced to seek for justice many hundred miles by sea and land, rendered in a manner incapable of serving their King and country in any employment of honour, trust, or profit; and all this without the least demerit: while the governors sent over thither can possibly have no affection to the people, further than what is instilled into them by their own justice and love of mankind (which do not always operate); and whatever they please to represent hither is never called in question.

Whether the representatives of such a people, thus distressed and laid in the dust, when they meet in a Parliament, can do the public business with that chearfulness which might be expected from free-born subjects, would be a question in any other country, except that unfortunate island, the *English* inhabitants whereof have given more and greater examples of their loyalty and dutifulness than can be shown in any other part of the world.

What part of these grievances may be thought proper to be redressed by so wise and great a minister as Sir *Robert Walpole*, he perhaps will please to consider; especially because they have been all brought upon that kingdom since the Revolution, which, however, is a blessing annually celebrated there with the greatest zeal and sincerity.

I most humbly entreat your Lordship to give this paper to Sir *Robert Walpole*, and desire him to read it, which he may do in a few minutes. I am, with the greatest respect, my Lord, | Your Lordship's, | Most obedient humble servant | Jon. Swift.

Tickell's Letter-book No. 2

Thomas Tickell to Swift

Dublin Castle 10 *May* 1726

Sir,[1]

The first opening of Miss Eustace's eyes the morning after our marriage, was to read your letter, for the good wishes of which we both return you our sincere thanks. The ceremonies and visits that follow a wedding have too long prevented me from paying you my acknowledgments, and begging the continuance of your letters. When you can find a leisure from the importunities of the Whigs on the English side of the water, do not forget one on this, who always told you our Friends by courting you would convince the world of their good taste, and regard to their own pleasure.

We fancy by the new spirit of pleasantry which appears in London, and some instances of the same which at last are become publick, here, that

tibi, cum fluctus subter labere Sicanos,
Doris amara suam non intermisceat undam.[2]

If it be true that an Account of imaginary Travels is left in some Friend's hands in Dublin, I should think it a great distinction to be

[1] This letter, printed for the first time by R. E. Tickell in *Thomas Tickell*, 1931, pp. 119–20, was an answer to Swift's letter from London of 16 Apr., received by Tickell on the day after his wedding in Dublin, 22 Apr. 1726, to Clotilda, daughter of Sir Maurice Eustace. The letter is here printed from a draft in Tickell's hand in his Letter-book, no. 2.

[2] Virgil, *Ecl.* x. 4–5. Tickell is playing with the idea that the fountain of inspiration is not to lose its purity when it flows into salt waters of the open sea.

allowed a sight of them, before I should have a right, which the author could not prevent, of reading them in print.

I have called twice at the Deanery about one a clock, but have been told both times that noncompos-stella was not stirring. I design however to try my fortune again and shall carry a fair Lady with me to facilitate my approaches. | I am &c.

Endorsed: 10 *May* 1726 | Copy of my Letter to Dr. Swift

Portland MSS. Harley Letters

Swift and Pope to the Earl of Oxford

3 *July* 1726[1]

My Lord[2]—Mr Pope by writing first hath limited me to what space you see.[3] He prescribes all our Visits without our knoledge, and Mr Gay and I find our selves often engaged for three or four days to come, and we neither of us dare dispute his Pleasure; Accordingly this morning we go to Ld Bathurst,[4] on Tuesday Company is to dine here,[5] however I will certainly attend Your Lordship towards the End of the Week. It is too true to my sorrow, that I have not many Weeks to stay in England, and besides I have some Business that will keep me severall Days in my Journey. I confess I squandred away these four months, as People do their Lives, in neglecting their chief Business, which in me was to see and discourse with Your Lordship as often as I could, wherein however I am not so faulty as unfortunate, by Your Long Absence. I am with the greatest Respect | My Lord, Your Lordships most | obedient humble Servt | Jonath. Swift

[1] In May 1726 Swift went to stay with Pope at Twickenham. Later they were joined by Gay. They paid a visit to Lord Bathurst. It may also be that during this summer Pope took Swift to former haunts in Windsor Forest. Gay's popular ballad *Molly Mog* was probably written in July or August (*Gay's Poetical Works*, ed. G. C. Faber, p. 188).

[2] Lord Oxford seems to have been in the country during the earlier part of Swift's visit to England. It is doubtful whether they had yet met.

[3] The allusion is to the postscript.

[4] Bathurst was probably then at his other country house, Richings Park, near Colnbrook.—Ball.

[5] Swift was writing on Sunday.

Twitenham. Jul. 3d | 1726.

[Swift writes at the top of the leaf: Pope's note follows below:]

My Lord—Indeed you are very unreasonable. I never knew you so before. You say you will quarrel with me if I keep the Dean here, & let nobody see him. Pray what hinders you? *Here we are to be seen*, is the Motto over my house, but it is so written that none but such as are worthy & Enlightend can understand it. Pray show that you do any day after Thursday.

Address [in Pope's hand]: To the Right Honorable | the Earl of Oxford, in Dover-street.

Tickell Papers

Swift to Thomas Tickell

London. Jul 7th 1726[1]

Sr

I have led so restless, and visiting, and travelling, and vexations a Life since I had the Honor of your Letter,[2] that I never had humor enough to acknowledge it thô I conveyed it wrapped up safely in my Pocket. You are now so old a marryed Man that I shall not congratulate with you, but pray God you may long congratulate with your self, and that your Scituation will make you a tolerable Irishman, at least till you can make the Lady a good English-woman, which—however, I hope will be late. I cannot complain of any want of Civility in Your Friends the Whigs, and I will tell you freely that most of them agree with me in quarrelling about the same Things. I have lived these two Months past for the most part in the Country, either at Twitenham with Mr Pope, or rambling with him and Mr Gay for a Fortnight together. Yesterday My Lord Boling-broke and Mr Congreve made up five at Dinner at Twitenham. I have been very little more than a Witness of any Pleasantryes you may have seen from London I am in no sedentary way for Specula-tions of any Kind, neither do I find them so ready to occurr at this late Time of my Life. The Thing you mention which no Friend would publish was written fourteen Years ago at Windsor,[3] and shews how indiscreet it is to leave any one Master of what cannot

[1] Swift dated this letter 7 July, and that date was accepted by Tickell in his endorsement; but the London postmark indicates the day before.

[2] Tickell's letter of 10 May.

[3] *Cadenus and Vanessa.*

without the least Consequence be shewn to the World. Folly malice, Negligence, and the Incontinence in Keeping Secrets (for which we want a Word), ought to caution men to Keep the Key of their Cabinets.

As to what you mention of an imaginary Treatise,[1] I can onely answer that I have a great Quantity Paper some where or other of which none would please you, partly because they are very uncorrect, but chiefly because they wholly disagree with your Notions of Persons and Things. Neither do I believe it would be possible for you to find out my Treasures of Waste Papers without searching nine Houses and then sending to me for the Key.

I find the Ladyes make the Deanry their Villa. I have been told that Mrs Jonson's Health has given her Friends bad Apprehensions and I have heard but twice from them; but their Secretary Dr Sheridan just tells me she is much better, to my great Satisfaction. I wonder how you could expect to see her in a Morning, which I her oldest Acquaintance have not done these dozen Years, except once or twice in a Journy. I desire to present my most humble Service to Mrs Tickell. I shall return in a few Days to Twitenham and there continue till August, at the Latter end of which Month I propose to wait on you at the Castle of Dublin for I am weary of being among Ministers whom I cannot govern, who are all Rank Toryes in Government, and worse than Whigs in Church: whereas I was the first Man who taught and practiced the direct contrary Principle. | I am S^r^ | with sincere Respect | Your most obedient | humble Servant | Jonath Swift

Address: To Thomas Tickell Esq. | at the Castle of | Dublin | Ireld.
Postmark: 6 IY
Endorsed in Tickell's hand: London 7 July, 1726 | Dr Swift

Dodsley Miscellanies 1745, x. 96

Swift to the Rev. Thomas Sheridan

London, July 8, 1726

Good Doctor,[2]

I have had two Months of great Uneasiness at the ill Account of Mrs. *Johnson's* Health, and, as it is usual fear'd the Worst that was

[1] *Gulliver's Travels.*

[2] Dublin University had just conferred the degree of D.D. on Sheridan.

possible, and doubted all the good Accounts that were sent me. I pray God her Danger may warn her to be less Wilful, and more ready to fall into those Measures that her Friends and Physicians advise her to. I had a Letter two Days ago from Archdeacon *Walls*, dated six Days before yours, wherein he giveth me a better Account than you do, and therefore I apprehend she hath not mended since; and yet he says he *can honestly tell me she is now much better*. Pray thank the Archdeacon, and tell him you are to have a Share in this Letter; and therefore I will save him the Trouble of another. Tell him also, that I never asked for my 1000*l*., which he hears I have got, tho' I mentioned it to the Princess the last Time I saw her; but I bid her tell *W*—, I scorned to ask him for it,[1] but blot out this passage, and mention it to no one, except the Ladies, because I know Mrs. *J—n* would be pleased with it, and I will not write to them till I hear from them; therefore this Letter is theirs as well as yours. The Archdeacon further says, that Mrs. *J*—has not tasted Claret for several Months, but once at his House. This I dislike. I cannot tell who is the fourth of your Friends, unless it be yourself: I am sorry for your new laborious Studies, but the best of it is they will *not* be your own another Day. I thank you for your new Style, and most useful Quotations. I am only concerned, that although you get the Grace of the House, you will never get the Grace of the Town, but die plain *Sheridan*, or *Tom* at most, because it is a Syllable shorter than Doctor. However, I will give it you at Length in the Superscription, and People will so wonder how the News could come and return so quick to and from *England*, especially if the Wind be fair when the Packet goes over; and let me warn you to be very careful in sending for your Letters two Days after the Commencement. You lost one Post by my being out of Town; for I came hither To-day, and shall stay three or four upon some Business, and then go back to Mr. *Pope's*, and there continue till *August*, and then come to Town till I begin my Journey to *Ireland*, which I propose the Middle of *August*. My old Servant *Archy*[2] is here ruined and starving, and has pursued me and wrote me a Letter, but I have refused to see him. Our Friend at the Castle[3] writ to me two Months ago, to have a sight of those Papers, &c. of which I brought away a Copy. I have answered him, that whatever Papers I have are convey'd

[1] The reference is to the £1,000 which Swift had been promised towards his expenses upon installation as Dean of St. Patrick's.

[2] Swift's groom.

[3] Tickell.

from one Place to another through nine or ten Hands, and that I have the Key. If he should mention any thing of Papers in general, either to you or the Ladies, and that you can bring it in, I would have you and them to confirm the same Story, and laugh at my Humour in it, &c.

My Service to Dr. *Delany*, Dr. *Helsham*, the *Grattans*, and *Jacksons*. There is not so despised a Creature here as your Friend with the soft Verses on Children.[1] I heartily pity him.—This is the first time I was ever weary of *England*, and longed to be in *Ireland*, but it is because go I must; for I do not love *Ireland* better, nor *England*, as *England*, worse; in short, you all live in a wretched, dirty Dog-hole and Prison, but it is a Place good enough to die in. I can tell you one Thing, that I have had the fairest Offer made me of a Settlement here that one can imagine, which if I were ten Years younger I would gladly accept, within twelve Miles of *London*, and in the midst of my Friends. But I am too old for new Schemes, and especially such as would bridle me in my Freedoms and Liberalities.[2] But so it is, that I must be forced to get home partly by Stealth and partly by Force. I have indeed one Temptation for this Winter, much stronger, which is of a fine House and Garden, and Park, and Wine-Cellar in *France*, to pass away the Winter in,[3] and if Mrs. *J—n*[4] were not so out of Order I would certainly accept of it; and I wish she could go to *Montpellier* at the same time. You see I am grown Visionary, and therefore it is time to have done. Adieu.

4805

Swift to the Rev. John Worrall

Twitenham. Jul. 15th 1726

I wish you would send me a common Bill in Form upon any Bankes for 100*ll*, and I will wait for it and in the mean time borrow where I can.

[1] Ambrose Philips.

[2] This passage can, but improbably, be interpreted to mean that Swift had received an offer from Walpole for a settlement in England; but his letter to Peterborough, 28 Apr., can hardly be reconciled with this supposition. Whatever the offer may have been we may presume it to have come from a private patron.

[3] An invitation to pass the winter at the seat of Bolingbroke's wife near Nogent-sur-Seine.

[4] Stella.

What you tell me of M^rs^ J—[1] I have long expected with great Oppression and Heavyness of Heart We have been perfect Friends these 35 Years. Upon my Advice they both came to Ireld and have been ever since my constant Companions, and the Remaind^r^ of my Life will be a very melancholy Scene when one of them is gone whom I most esteemed upon the Score of every good Quality that can possibly recommend a human Creature. I have these 2 Months seen through M^rs^ D's[2] Disguises, and indeed ever since I left you my Heart hath been so sunk, that I have not been the same Man, nor ever shall be again, but drag on a wretched Life till it shall please God to call me away. I must tell you as a Friend, that if you have Reason to believe M^rs^ J— cannot hold out till my Return, I would not think of coming to Ireld, and in that Case, I would expect of you on the Beginning of Sep^tr^ to renew my Licence for another half year, which time I will spend in some Retirement far from London till I can be in a Disposition of appearing after an Accident that must be so fatal to my Quiet. I wish it could be brought about that she make her Will, her Intentions are to leave the Interest of all her Fortune to her Moth^r^ and Sister during their Lives, and afterwards to Dr Stephens's Hospital, to purchase Lands for such Uses there as she Designs.[3] Think how I am disposed while I write this, and forgive the Inconsistencies. I would not for the Universe be present at Such a Tryal of seeing her depart. She will be among Friends that upon her own Account and great worth will tend her with all possible Care, where I should be a Trouble to her and the greatest Torment to my self. In case the Matter should be desperate I would have you advise if they come to Town, that they should be lodged in some Airy healthy Part, and not in the Deanery, which besides you cannot but be a very improper Thing for that House to breath her last in. This I leave to your Discretion, and I conjure you to burn this Lett^r^ immediatly without telling the Contents of it to any Person alive.[4] Pray write to me every Week, that I may know what Steps to take, For I am determind not to go to Ireld to find her just dead or dying—Nothing but Extremity could make me so familiar with those terrible Words applyed to such a dear Friend. Let her Know I have bought her a repeating gold Watch for her Ease in winter Nights. I designed to have surprised

[1] i.e. Stella.

[2] i.e. Dingley's.

[3] With reference to Dr. Steevens's Hospital see Swift's letter to Archbishop King, 14 July 1724.

[4] Worrall failed to carry out this instruction.

her with it, but now I would have her know it, that she may see how my Thoughts were always to make her easy—I am of Opinion that there is not a greater Folly than to contract too great and intimate a Friendship, which must always leave the Survivor miserable—On the back of Brereton's Note there was written the Account of M^rs^ J—s Sickness. Pray in yr next avoyd that mistake and leave the back side blank—When you have read this Lett twice and retayn what I desire, pray burn it and let all I have said ly onely in yr own[1] Breast —Pray write every week. I have (till I know further.) fixed on Aug. 15^t^ to set out to Ireld I shall continue or alter my Measures according to yr Letters.—Adieu.

Direct yr Letters still to Mrs Rice &c

Pray tell Mr Dobbs[2] of the College that I received his Lett^r^ but cannot possibly answer it, which I certainly would if I had materialls

As to what you say about Promotion you will find it was given immediately to Maul[3] (as I am told) and I assure you I had no Offers, nor would accept them my behavior to those in Power hath been directly contrary sin[ce] I came here—

I had rather have good news from you than Canterbury, tho it were given me upon my own Terms

Address: To the Reverend Mr Worrall | at his House in big Sheep-street[4] | Dublin | Ireld

Portland MSS. Harley Papers

Swift to the Earl of Oxford

18 July 1726.

My Lord[5]

I have taken some time to think of what I was saying to your Lordship, relating to My Lord Your Father's Papers. My stay in

[1] Own] *om. Ball.*

[2] Richard Dobbs, a fellow of Trinity, who became Rector of Lisburn (*Alumni Dub.*, p. 233).

[3] The allusion is to the bishopric of Cloyne just vacant by the death of Charles Crow who had there been seated since 1702. Henry Maule, an Irishman, was appointed in his place by Lord Carteret.

[4] A street near St. Patrick's Cathedral and the Castle. Later known as Ship Street.

[5] This letter is among the Miscellaneous Papers, 1725–40, of the Portland Manuscripts, First Deposit, List I, in the British Museum.

England will be now so short, and the Work of looking into these Papers so long, that (being engaged in some little Affairs of my own) it will be impossible that the time remaining will suffice.[1] What I could wish is that Mr Thomas[2] and his Brother would be at the Pains of separating those papers which were written since that great Change of Ministry, and the Steps preceding to it, from those others which refer only to the Time when my Lord was Secretary of State, and if your Lordship would trust them with me in Ireland, I would engage either to bring them back my self, or in case of Accidents, to send them by such a sure Hand as your self shall approve of.

Your Lordship will please to consider this Proposal, and when I come to Town I will do myself the Honor to discourse with you further upon it. I am with great Respect, | My Lord Your Lordship's most obedient | and most humble Servant | Jonath. Swift

Twitenham | July 18th 1726

Since you go out of Toun the End of this Week, Mr Pope hopes you will please to remember your promise by the beginning of the next, to see him here. I hope my Lady Oxford and Lady Marget are in good Health.

Address: To the Right Honorable | the Earl of Oxford in | Dover-street | London

Nichols 1801

Swift to the Rev. James Stopford

Twitenham, near London,
July 20, 1726.

Dear Jim,

I had a letter from you three months ago, with an account of a fine picture you had sent me, which is now safe in Ireland, for which I heartily thank you; and Robert Arbuthnot[3] swears it is an original.

[1] Swift had met Oxford since writing to him on the third. In a letter written to Pope on the previous day Oxford asks him to tell Swift that he would not willingly miss 'a moment of his conversation that he could allow me' (Sherburn, ii. 381).

[2] Secretary to the first Earl of Oxford. Swift was anxious to make use of the papers for his historical writings.

[3] A younger brother of Swift's friend. He was out at Killiecrankie, escaped to France, became a banker at Rouen, helpful in transactions for Jacobite refugees.

I did not answer you because I was told you were in motion. I had yours of July 12, N.S. yesterday; and since you are fixed at Paris, I venture to send you this, though Robert Arbuthnot be here. He has lately married a lady among us of L.900 a year,[1] and I think will soon go to France; but I have chiefly lived about two months with Mr. Pope, since the town grew empty. I shall leave him the beginning of August, and so settle my affairs to be in Ireland by the end of that month, for my license of half a year will be then out. I came here to see my old friends, and upon some business I had with two of them, which, however, proves to be of little consequence.[2] The people in power have been civil enough to me; many of them have visited me. I was not able to withstand seeing the Princess, because she had commanded, that whenever I came hither, as the news said I intended, that I should wait on her. I was latterly twice with the chief Minister; the first time by invitation, and the second at my desire for an hour, wherein we differed in every point. But all this made a great noise, and soon got to Ireland, from whence upon the late death of the Bishop of Cloyne,[3] it was said I was offered to succeed, and I received many letters upon it, but there was nothing of truth, for I was neither offered, nor would have received, except upon conditions which would never be granted. For I absolutely broke with the first Minister, and have never seen him since, and I lately complained of him to the Princess, because I knew she would tell him. I am, besides, all to pieces with the Lord-Lieutenant, whom I treated very roughly, and absolutely refused to dine with him.[4] So that, dear Jim, you see how little I shall be able to assist

[1] 'About the same time [17 July] Mrs. Duke of Bentley in Suffolk was married to Mr. Arbuthnot, a banker in France' (Boyer, *Pol. State*, xxii. 100). She died in 1729.

[2] We may presume the two friends to be Lord Oxford and Pope, to consult the former about his father's papers, the latter about the manuscript of *Gulliver's Travels*. At this stage it is improbable that Erasmus Lewis had been drawn into conference about *Gulliver*.

[3] See Swift to Worrall, 15 July 1726 *ad fin*.

[4] It may be that Swift had fallen out with Carteret because the government had refused to grant Delany a dispensation to hold the parish of St. John's in Dublin with his fellowship. Boulter, writing to the Duke of Newcastle, 11 Nov. 1725, resists the proposal, and not without reason: 'I was always against persons holding any tolerable preferments with their fellowships, as being a hindrance to succession in Colleges, and excluding some or other, that may want help in their education' (*Boulter's Letters*, i. 42–43). Delany was also a strong Tory, and this would not commend him.

you with the great ones here, unless some change of ministry should happen. Yet when a new governor goes over, it is hard if I cannot be some way instrumental. I have given strict charge to Mr. Pope to receive you with all kindness and distinction. He is perfectly well received by all the people in power, and he loves to do good; and there can hardly go over a governor to whom he may not, by himself or friends, strongly recommend you.

I fear I shall have more than ordinary reasons to wish you a near neighbour to me in Ireland; and that your company will be more necessary than ever, when I tell you that I never was in so great a dejection of spirits. For I lately received a letter from Mr. Worrall, that one of the two oldest and dearest friends I have in the world is in so desperate a condition of health, as makes me expect every post to hear of her death. It is the younger of the two, with whom I have lived in the greatest friendship for thirty-three years.[1] I know you will share in my trouble, because there were few persons whom I believe you more esteemed. For my part, as I value life very little, so the poor casual remains of it, after such a loss, would be a burden that I must heartily beg God Almighty to enable me to bear; and I think there is not a greater folly than that of entering into too strict and particular a friendship, with the loss of which a man must be absolutely miserable; but especially at an age when it is too late to engage in a new friendship. Besides, this was a person of my own rearing and instructing, from childhood, who excelled in every good quality that can possibly accomplish a human creature.—They have hitherto writ me deceiving letters, but Mr. Worrall has been so just and prudent as to tell me the truth; which, however racking, is better than to be struck on the sudden.—Dear Jim, pardon me, I know not what I am saying; but believe me that violent friendship is much more lasting, and as much engaging, as violent love. Adieu.

If this accident should happen before I set out, I believe I shall

[1] Writing of Stella to Worrall, 15 July 1726, Swift says, 'We have been perfect friends these thirty-five years', and now he puts the duration of their friendship at thirty-three years. This would make 1691 or 1693 the date of their first meeting. But it is almost certain they met when Swift first went to reside with Temple in the spring of 1689. Writing *On the Death of Mrs. Johnson* (*Prose Works*, ed. Temple Scott, xi. 127) he says, 'I knew her from six years old'. But in 1687, so far as we know, Swift was still resident as a student in Dublin. Despite his natural attention to detail he was always unreliable when speaking of years and dates. The exact date of Stella's birth was 13 Mar. 1680–1.

stay this winter in England; where it will be at least easier to find some repose, than upon the spot.

If I were your adviser, I would say one thing against my own interest, that if you must leave your College, for the reason you hint at,[1] I think it would be better to live in England on your own estate, and the addition of one thousand pounds, and trust to industry and friends, and distinction here, than pass your days in that odious country, and among that odious people. You can live in a thrifty moderate way, and thrift is decent here; and you cannot but distinguish yourself. You have the advantage to be a native of London; here you will be a freeman, and in Ireland a slave. Here your competitors will be strangers; there every rascal, your contemporary, will get over your head by the merit of party.—Farewell again; though my head is now disturbed, yet I have had these thoughts about you long ago.

4805

Viscount Bolingbroke to the three Yahoos of Twickenham

23 July 1726.

Jonathan, Alexander, John, most excellent Triumvirs of Parnassus, tho' you are probably very indifferent where I am, or what I am doing, yet I resolve to beleive the contrary. I perswade myself that you have sent att least fifteen times in this fort night to Dawley farm, and that you are extreamly mortify'd att my long silence. to releive you therefore from this great anxiety of mind, I can do no less than write a few lines to you, and I please myself beforehand with the vast pleasure which this Epistle must needs give you. that I may add to this pleasure, & give you further proofs of my benificent temper, I will likewise inform you that I shall be in yr neighbourhood again by the end of next week, by which time I hope that Jonathan's imagination of business will be succeeded by some imagination more becoming a Professour divine science La Baga-

[1] The possibility of Stopford's marriage.

telle. Adieu Jonathan, Alexander, John. mirth be with you. from the Banks of the Severne[1] July the 23d. 1726.

Address: To the three Yahoos of | Twittenham
Endorsed by Swift: Ld Bolingbroke | — — 1726 July 23 *and again* Ld Bolingb

Dodsley Miscellanies 1745, x. 100

Swift to the Rev. Thomas Sheridan

July 27, 1726.

I have yours just now of the 19th, and the Account you give me, is nothing but what I have some Time expected with the utmost Agonies; and there is one Aggravation of Constraint, that where I am forc'd to put on an easy Countenance. It was at this Time the best Office your Friendship could do, not to deceive me. I was violently bent all last Year, as I believe you remember, that she should go to *Montpellier*, or *Bath*, or *Tunbridge*. I entreated, if there was no Amendment, they might both come to *London*. But there was a Fatality, although I indeed think her Stamina could not last much longer, when I saw she could take no Nourishment. I look upon this to be the greatest Event that can ever happen to me, but all my Preparations will not suffice to make me bear it like a Philosopher, nor altogether like a Christian. There hath been the most intimate Friendship between us from her Childhood, and the greatest Merit on her Side that ever was in one human Creature towards another. —Nay if I were now near her, I would not see her; I could not behave myself tolerably, and should redouble her Sorrow.—Judge in what a Temper of Mind I write this.—The very time I am writing, I conclude the fairest Soul in the World hath left its Body.—Confusion! that I am this Moment call'd down to a Visitor, when I am in the Country, and not in my Power to deny myself.—I have passed a very constrained Hour, and now return to say I know not what: I have been long weary of the World, and shall for my small Remainder of Years be weary of Life, having for ever lost that Conversation, which could only make it tolerable.—I fear while you are reading this, you will be shedding Tears at her Funeral; she loved you well, and a great Share of the little Merit I have with you, is owing to her Sollicitations. | I writ to you about a Week ago.

[1] Bolingbroke was apparently on a visit to Lord Bathurst.

Portland MSS. Harley Papers

Swift to the Earl of Oxford

[July 1726?][1]

My Lord.

I had a note from Mr Thomas, telling me you had got a Hurt in Your Hand. I hope it is but a trifle, & pray let your Servant tell mine so. How is it possible for me to obey young Mr Neddy Harley's's[2] request? I can as easily leap over the Moon as write verses in two or three days upon Demand. had the time been much longer I would not have suffered any body to depend upon me for such a Thing; though I might have promised to do my Endeavor. Neither is my head free or breath or humor good enough for such Amusements: I am | My Lord | Your Lordship's | most obedient | humble Servant and | brother | J. Swift

Sunday | morning

Harvard University

Swift to Alexander Pope

[1 August 1726][3]

There have been strange Alterations in the Scheme.—made by Lord Peterb and Dr Arbuthnot, and my Lord said he would give you notice of it. The Opera and some other Affairs have altered

[1] This brief letter, addressed to the second Earl of Oxford, is now among the Welbeck papers deposited in the British Museum—Portland Papers: F. 11. c. The date may with probability be conjectured as July 1726, for Swift asks that his Lordship's servant will speak to his own. The accident to Oxford's hand therefore must have taken place during Swift's visit to England in 1726 or 1727.

[2] The eldest son of Edward Harley, auditor of the imprest. In 1741 he succeeded his cousin as third Earl of Oxford.

[3] The original of this letter, once in the possession of Locker-Lampson, is now at Harvard. Ball, iii. 447, took his text from a copy in the Forster collection, 555; and presumed that it was probably written in June 1727. Professor Sherburn, with greater probability, suggests 1 Aug. 1726, basing his date on the assumption that Lord Peterborough was planning a dinner in Swift's honour, but had changed its date to Wednesday 3 Aug. Swift's letter to Pope, 4 Aug. 1726, written the day after the dinner, shows that Pope was too ill to be present, and that Swift was deeply concerned, especially as he was shortly leaving for Ireland. See Sherburn, v. 6.

their measures; of which I suppose you will here, and I think Wednesday is the day fixed unless they vary again. I am in confusion and will leave the Matter so; I am weary of the Town, and of little Business left in it. So that the kind Lodging in your Heart must be large indeed if it holds me; mine cannot hold the esteem and Friendship I have to you I am ever &c

Monday morn, past 9

Address: To Alexander Pope Esqr
Endorsements: from Dr. Swift | a King a Scarecrow of Straw, yet protects the corn.—a fine Lady is like a Cat, when young the most gamesome & lively of all creatures, when old the most melancholy.

Faulkner 1741

Swift to Alexander Pope

4 [August] 1726[1]

I had rather live in forty Islands than under the frequent disquiets of hearing you are out of order. I always apprehend it most after a great dinner; for the least Transgression of yours, if it be only two bits and one sup more than your stint, is a great debauch; for which you certainly pay more than those sots who are carried dead drunk to bed. My Lord Peterborow spoiled every body's dinner, but especially mine, with telling us that you were detained by sickness. Pray let me have three lines under any Hand or pothook that will give me a better account of your health; which concerns me more than others, because I love and esteem you for reasons that most others have little to do with, and would be the same although you had never touched a pen, further than with writing to me.

I am gathering up my luggage, and preparing for my journey: I will endeavour to think of you as little as I can, and when I write to you, I will strive not to think of you; this I intend in return to your kindness; and further, I know no body has dealt with me so cruelly as you, the consequences of which usage I fear will last as long as my life, for so long shall I be (in spite of my heart) entirely Yours.

[1] Faulkner and early Pope editions assign this letter to 4 May, but, as Swift was preparing to depart for Ireland, the date must be Aug. At this time he had come to stay with Gay in his lodgings at Whitehall.

4806

The Duchess of Hamilton to Swift

[? 1726]

Dear Dean[1]

When we were together last I remember we spoke of a certain stanza w[ch] yu suspected me parent of by reason there were some things in it yu was sure I wou'd have said twelve years ago, if this be a rule I'm certain yu are not Dean Swift, for twelve years ago y[r] promis'd lett[r] had not been so long in coming to me, all I can say is I wish yu had been twelve years ago w[t] I wish yu now, and that yu were now w[t] yu was twelve years ago to yr real friend & | hum[ble] servant | E Hamilton: |

Wednesday

Address: To | The Reverend Dean Swift
Endorsed by Swift: Duchs Hamilton

Forster copy

Swift to the Rev. James Stopford

London, August 6th 1726[2]

I had your Lett[r] to-day,[3] and take this opportunity by my Friend M[r] Rawlinson[4] to acknowledge it: You act very generously in your Consern for our dear Friend, of whom I had some hopes a week ago, but they are now again dashed, and I expect to hear the worst every day, for which I am preparing myself as well as I can.

[1] Swift appears to have had no correspondence with the Duchess of Hamilton after his retirement to Ireland upon the death of Queen Anne, and the 'twelve years' four times repeated by the Duchess may be accepted as correct. This letter was, therefore, probably written in or about 1726.

[2] Transcript in the Forster collection.

[3] An answer to Swift's letter of 20 July.

[4] William Rollinson, a wine merchant, settled in Oxfordshire, where he died, *c.* 1774, at about the age of ninety-four. He was a friend of Bolingbroke, Pope, and Gay. Pope left him £5 to buy a ring, 'or any other memorial'. He is mentioned by Gay in 'Mr. Pope's Welcome from Greece', stanza xx. For further biographical details see a note by Dr. E. St. John Brooks in *The Times Literary Supplement*, 16 Sept. 1944, p. 456. His first wife died in 1730, and he married as his second wife the widow of the fourth Earl of Winchelsea.

Mr Rawlinson will be ready to do you all the Civilitys he can. He is a very worthy Person a Friend to me and all my Friends, a Gentleman of a good Education and Family, but suffering somewhat by Party hath for several years past fallen into the Wine trade, & absolutely recovered his affairs. He will tell you that Mr Pope and Mr Gay will be ready to receive you with open Arms, & introduce you into the best Company; I have told them that Modesty was your only Fault, & may it ever be your Fault, tho' in a less Degree.

I think in Prudence you are in the right to differ from me and rather chuse a Certainty than the contrary, at least under your Circumstances. I do not see why a Man of Honor may not be any where in a healthy Climate with a tolerable Fortune, & an easy domestick Companion, especially in a bad World, where every thing that relates to the publick must displease, & therefore the farther one is from it the better, and at your Age it is easy to reconcile one self to new Scenes. This is all I can say in my present Situation. I determined to leave Town on the 12th[1] instant, on my Journey to Ireland, where I expect to find a very melancholy Reception. Pray God bless you, and believe me to be ever | Yours &c.

Address: A Monsieur Stopfert chez Monsr Robert Arbuthnett Banquier à Paris.

4805

Swift to the Rev. John Worrall

Londn Aug. 6th 1726

At the time that I had your Letter,[2] with the Bill (for which I thank you) I received anothr from Dr Sheridan,[3] both full of the melancholy Account of our Friend. The Doctor advises me to go over at the Time I intended, which I now design to do, and to sett out on Monday the 15th from hence. However, if any Accident should happen to me that you do not find me come over on the 1st of Sept, I would have you renew my Licence, from the 2d of Septr, which will be the Day that my half year will be out: And since

[1] The Forster copy gives '12th'. Swift set out for Ireland on the 15th. Cf. the succeeding letter addressed to Worrall.

[2] The letter with a money bill requested by Swift on 15 July.

[3] The letter acknowledged by Swift on 27 July.

it is not likely that you can answer this, so as to reach me before I leave London, I desire you will write to me, directed to Mrs Kenah in Chester, where I design to set up, and shall hardly be there in less than a fortnight from this Time and if I should then hear our Friend was no more, I might probably be absent a Month or two in some Parts of Darbyshire or Wales; However, you need not renew the Licence till the 1st of Decem^er^, and, if I come not, I will write to you from Chester. This unhappy Affair is the greatest Tryal I ever had, and I think you are unhappy in having conversed so much with that Person under such Circumstances. Tell Dr Sheridan I had his Lett^r^, but care not to answer it, I wish you would give me yr Opinion at Chestr whether I shall come over or no. I shall be there ([1]God willing, on Thursday the 18th instant—This is enough to say in my present scituation[1] I am &c.

My humble Service and thanks to Mrs Worrall for the Care of our Friend, which I shall never forget.

Address: To the Reverend Mr | Worrall, at his House in | big Sheep-street | Dublin Ireld

Endorsed by Swift: Augt 6th 1726.

Pierpont Morgan Library

'Richard Sympson' to Benjamin Motte

London Augt 8th. 1726

Sr[2]

My Cousin Mr Lemuel Gulliver entrusted me some Years ago with a Copy of his Travels, whereof that which I here send you is

[1] The parenthesis is not closed.

[2] When Swift left Ireland early in March he carried with him the manuscript of *Gulliver's Travels*. This was, almost certainly, not in his hand, but a 'fair copy' for the printer. Although he was in England for five months in 1726 negotiations with a possible publisher, Benjamin Motte, occupied only a few days at the end of his visit, opening with this letter composed by Swift, but, for purposes of secrecy, copied out in the hand of Gay, with whom, at the time, he was lodging in London. Until recently we were dependent for our knowledge of this and the two letters next following upon *The Gentleman's Magazine*, 1855, N.S., xliv. 34–36. They had come into the possession of the Rev. Charles Bathurst Woodman, and were by him communicated to *G.M.* The originals are now in the Pierpont Morgan Library. For an account of these letters and the

about a fourth part, for I shortned them very much as you will find in my Preface to the Reader. I have shewn them to several persons of great Judgment and Distinction, who are confident they will sell very well. And although some parts of this and the following Volumes may be thought in one or two places to be a little Satyrical, yet it is agreed they will give no Offence, but in that you must Judge for your self, and take the Advice of your Friends, and if they or you be of another opinion, you may let me know it when you return these Papers, which I expect shall be in three Days at furthest. The good Report I have received of you makes me put so great a trust into your Hands, which I hope you will give me no Reason to repent, and in that Confidence I require that you will never suffer these Papers to be once out of your Sight.

As the printing these Travels will probably be of great value to you, so as a Manager for my Friend and Cousin I expect you will give a due consideration for it, because I know the Author intends the Profit for the use of poor Sea-men, and I am advised to say that two Hundred pounds is the least Summ I will receive on his account, but if it shall happen that the Sale will not answer as I expect and believe, then whatever shall be thought too much even upon your own word shall be duly repaid.

Perhaps you will think this a strange way of proceeding to a man of Trade, but since I begin with so great a trust to you, whom I never saw, I think it not hard that you should trust me as much. Therefore if after three days reading and consulting these Papers, you think it proper to stand to my agreement, you may begin to print them, and the subsequent parts shall be all sent to you one after another in less than a week, provided that immediatly upon your Resolution to print them, you do within three days deliver a Bank Bill of two hundred pounds, wrapt up so as to make a parcel to the Hand from whence you receive this, who will come in the same manner exactly at 9 a clock at night on Thursday which will be the 11th Instant.

If you do not aprove of this proposal deliver these Papers to the person who will come on thursday

If you chuse rather to send the Papers make no other Proposal

publication of *Gulliver's Travels* see H. Teerink in the *Dublin Magazine*, Jan. 1948, pp. 14–27; H. Williams, *The Text of Gulliver's Travels*, 1952, pp. 3–19. See also *Gulliver's Travels*, ed. H. Williams, 1926; and *Prose Works*, ed. H. Davis, vol. xi.

of your own but just barely write on a piece of paper that you do not accept my offer. | I am | Sr. | your humble Servant |

Richard Sympson

Address: For Mr Motte.

Pierpont Morgan Library

Benjamin Motte to 'Richard Sympson'

[11 Aug. 1726.]

[1] I return you Sr your Papers with a great many thanks and do assure you that since they have been in my custody I have faithfully deserv'd the good Opinion you exprest of my Integrity; but you were much mistaken in the Estimate you made of my Abilities, when you suppos'd me able, in Vacation time (the most dead Season of the Year) at so short notice, to deposite so considerable a Sum as 200l.—By delivering the Papers to the Bearer, I have put you entirely in the same Condition they were in before I saw 'em: but if you will trust my Promise, ⌜that the Book shall be publish'd within a Month after I receive the Copy, and if the Success will allow it, I will punctually pay the money you require in Six Months, I shall thankfully embrace the Offer. The Bearer stays for an Answer so that I can only offer a Proposal without giving a Reason.⌝

I have only to add, that before I recd your Letter, I had fixt a Journey into the Country, and wrote to some Dealers there to appoint times when I would call upon 'em: so that I shall be oblig'd to set out this day Se'nnight at farthest. therefore if you think fit to favour me with any further Correspondence, desire I may hear from you as soon as possible.

[1] This letter is a draft in Motte's hand. It was inaccurately printed in *The Gentleman's Magazine* and by Ball. As first drafted a differing passage occupied the space shown above in half brackets. This read: 'or accept any Security you can contrive or require for the payment of the money in Six Months I will comply with any Method you shall propose for that purpose. In the mean time, I shall trust to your Honour and Promise, that what shall appear more than the Success of it deserves shall be repaid; as you may depend upon a proper Acknowledgment, if the Success answers or exceeds Expectation.' Motte struck out these words and substituted those in half brackets, which he drafted on the verso of the paper. The correction appears in *G.M.* and Ball as a separate letter.

'Richard Sympson' to Benjamin Motte

13 August 1726

I would have both Volumes come out together and published by Christmas at furthest

R Sympson

Addressed: P. S. To Mr Motte
aug^t 13th 1726

Portland MSS. Harley Papers

Swift to the Earl of Oxford

[August 12, 1726][1]

My Lord,

My Things are all packt up, and in the City. I therefore beg Your Lordship will please to send by the Bearer, those Papers I gave your Lordship and my Marmora.[2] I shall sett out for Ireland on Monday next, and hope by some good Accident to see Your Lordship before I go: and whatever becomes of me, while I breath, I resolve to be with the utmost Respect and Truth | My Lord | Your most obedient | humble serv^t and Broth, | J. Swift

Friday morning.

[1] This letter, removed from Welbeck, is now in the British Museum, Portland Deposit, F. 11. c. It was printed by Ball among *Additional Letters*, vi. 238. The date is unquestionable. Swift left London on Monday, 15th. Friday, therefore, was 12 Aug.

[2] This work appears in the 1715 manuscript list of Swift's books, but not in the sale catalogue. Dr. Humphrey Prideaux's *Marmora Oxoniensia* in the 1676 folio edition cost Swift a pound. Apparently the book was returned before Swift set out for Ireland. In October of the following year (Oxford to Swift, 12 Oct. 1727) the loan of the book was asked once again for the use of a new editor, Michael Maittaire, for whom the manuscript notes by Thomas Milles enhanced the value. On this occasion the work seems never to have been returned to Swift. See further *Dean Swift's Library*, H. Williams, pp. 47–48.

Hawkesworth 1766

Swift to the Rev. John Worrall

August 13th, 1726

This is *Saturday*, and on *Monday* I set out for *Ireland*. I desired you would send me a letter to *Chester*. I suppose I shall be in *Dublin* with moderate fortune in ten or eleven days hence; for I will go by *Holihead*. I shall stay two days at *Chester*, unless I can contrive to have my box sent after me. I hope I shall be with you by the end of *August*; but however, if I am not with you by the second of *September*, which is the time that my licence is out, I desire you will get me a new one; for I would not lie at their mercy, though I know it signifies nothing. I expect to be very miserable when I come; but I shall be prepared for it. I desired you would write to me at *Chester*, which I hope you will do; and pray hinder Dr. *Sheridan* from writing to me any more. | This is all I have to say to you at present. | I am, *&c.* | J. Swift.

Faulkner 1741

Alexander Pope to Swift

Aug. 22. 1726.

Many a short sigh you cost me the day I left you, and many more you will cost me, till the day you return. I really walk'd about like a man banish'd, and when I came home, found it no home. 'Tis a sensation like that of a limb lopp'd off, one is trying every minute unawares to use it, and finds it is not. I may say you have used me more cruelly than you have done any other man; you have made it more impossible for me to live at ease without you: Habitude it self would have done that, if I had less friendship in my nature than I have. Besides my natural memory of you, you have made a local one, which presents you to me in every place I frequent: I shall never more think of Lord Cobham's, the woods of Ciceter, or the pleasing prospect of Byberry,[1] but your Idea must be joyn'd with 'em; nor

[1] On the way to Cirencester Pope had evidently taken Swift to see Lord Cobham's stately improvements at Stowe. The church at Bibury stands on a hill, overlooking the river Colne, and commanding a fine view. In his letter to Pope and Gay of 15 Oct. Swift refers to the map and pictures of that neighbourhood which he had received.

see one seat in my own garden, or one room in my own house, without a Phantome of you, sitting or walking before me. I travell'd with you to Chester, I felt the extream heat of the weather, the inns, the roads, the confinement and closeness of the uneasy coach, and wish'd a hundred times I had either a Deanery or a horse in my gift. In real truth, I have felt my soul peevish ever since with all about me, from a warm uneasy desire after you. I am gone out of myself to no purpose, and cannot catch you. *Inhiat in pedes*[1] was not more properly apply'd to a poor dog after a hare, than to me with regard to your departure. I wish I could think no more of it, but lye down and sleep till we meet again, and let that day (how far soever off it be) be the morrow. Since I cannot, may it be my amends that every thing you wish may attend you where you are, and that you may find every friend you have there in the state you wish him or her; so that your visit to us may have no other effect, than the progress of a rich man to a remote estate, which he finds greater than he expected; which knowledge only serves to make him live happier where he is, with no disagreeable prospect if ever he should chuse to remove. May this be your state till it become what I wish. But indeed I cannot express the warmth, with which I wish you all things, and my selt you. Indeed you are engraved elsewhere than on the Cups you sent me, (with so kind an inscription)[2] and I might throw them into the Thames without injury to the giver: I am not pleas'd with them, but take them very kindly too: And had I suspected any such usage from you, I should have enjoyed your company less than I really did, for at this rate I may say

Nec tecum possum vivere, nec sine te.

I will bring you over just such another present, when I go to the Deanery of St. Patrick's; which I promise you to do, if ever I am enabled to return your kindness. *Donarem Pateras*,[3] &c. Till then I'll drink (or Gay shall drink) daily healths to you, and I'll add to your inscription the old Roman Vow for years to come, VOTIS X VOTIS XX. My Mother's age gives me authority to hope it for yours.

[4]All those of your friends whom I have seen are constant in their

[1] 'Devours the scent.'

[2] They were small silver cups, and the inscription was as follows: 'Jonathan Swift Alex^{ro} Pope: Pignus amicitiae exiguum ingentis.'—Elwin.

[3] Hor. *Odes*, iv. 8. 1

[4] The last paragraph appeared in Pope's clandestine volume and in Faulkner's 1741 volume. Later it was omitted by Pope.

remembrance and good wishes to you. Only the Doctor[1] I have never been able to see since. Poor Congreve is desperately ill of the gout. Lord Bolingbroke bids me again tell you, he will take as a letter to himself, and reply to, every one that you shall write to Gay or me; so that we hope you will not be deterr'd from writing to some of us, by an imagination that all will expect it. | Yours, &c.

Faulkner 1741

Swift to Alexander Pope

[Dublin, August, 1726][2]

The first letter I writ after my landing was to Mr. Gay, but it would have been wiser to direct it to Tonson or Lintot, to whom I believe his lodgings are better known than to the runners of the Post-office. In that Letter you will find what a quick change I made in seven days from London to the Deanery, through many nations and languages unknown to the civilized world. And I have often reflected in how few hours, with a swift horse or a strong gale, a man may come among a people as unknown to him as the Antipodes. If I did not know you more by your conversation and kindness than by your letter,[3] I might be base enough to suspect, that in point of friendship you acted like some Philosopher who writ much better upon Virtue than they practised it. In answer, I can only swear, that you have taught me to dream, which I had not done in twelve years further than by inexpressible nonsense; but now I can every night distinctly see Twitenham, and the Grotto, and Dawley,[4] and Mrs. B.[5] and many other et cetera's, and it is but three nights since I beat Mrs. Pope.[6] I must needs confess, that the pleasure I

[1] i.e. Arbuthnot.

[2] The Dublin editions have the superscription, '*Dublin, Oct.* 30, 1727'. The year and the day of the month are both impossible. The gift of the silver cups belonged to 1726. In 1726 Swift was back in Dublin by 25 Aug.; and, further, the letter must almost certainly have been written a few days earlier than Elwin's '*Aug.* 30, 1726', for Pope's reply (next letter) is dated 'Sept. 3'.

[3] The preceding letter.

[4] Bolingbroke's residence.

[5] Martha Blount.

[6] Pope's mother with whom Swift played at backgammon or cards.

take in thinking on you is very much lessened by the pain I am in about your health: You pay dearly for the great talents God hath given you; and for the consequences of them in the esteem and distinction you receive from mankind, unless you can provide a tolerable stock of health; in which pursuit I cannot much commend your conduct, but rather entreat you would mend it by following the advice of my Lord Bolingbroke and your other Physicians. When you talked of Cups and Impressions, it came into my head to imitate you in quoting scripture, not to your advantage; I mean what was said to David by one of his brothers: 'I knew thy pride and the haughtiness of thy heart;' so I remember it grieved your soul to see me pay a penny more than my club at an inn, when you had maintained me three months at bed and board; for which if I had dealt with you in the Smithfield way it would have cost me a hundred pounds, for I live worse here upon more. Did you ever consider that I am for life almost twice as rich as you, and pay no rent, and drink French wine twice as cheap as you do Port, and have neither coach, chair, nor mother? As to the world, I think you ought to say to it with St. Paul, *if we have sown unto you spiritual things, is it a great thing if we shall reap your carnal things?*[1] this is more proper still if you consider the French word *spiritual*, in which sense the world ought to pay you better than they do. If you made me a present of a thousand pound, I would not allow my self to be in your debt; and if I made you a present of two, I would not allow my self to be out of it. But I have not half your pride: witness what Mr. Gay says in his letter, that I was censured for begging Presents, tho' I limited them to ten shillings, and tho' I forgave Sir R— W— a thousand pound, *multa gemens*.[2] I see no reason, (at least my friendship and vanity see none) why you should not give me a visit, when you shall happen to be disengaged: I will send a person to Chester to take care of you, and you shall be used by the best folks we have here, as well as civility and good nature can contrive; I believe local motion will be no ill physick, and I will have your coming inscribed on my Tomb, and recorded in never-dying verse.

I thank Mrs. Pope for her prayers, but I know the mystery. A person of my acquaintance who used to correspond with the last

[1] 1 Cor. ix. 11. *Spirituel* means witty.

[2] The promise, before the death of Queen Anne, that he should receive £1,000 for financial assistance on his installation as Dean of St. Patrick's.

great Duke of Tuscany,[1] shewing one of the Duke's letters to a friend, and professing great sense of his Highnesses friendship, read this passage out of the letters, *I would give one of my fingers to procure your real good.* The person to whom this was read, and who knew the Duke well, said, the meaning of *real good* was only that the other might turn a good Catholick: pray ask Mrs. Pope whether this story is applicable to her and me? I pray God bless her, for I am sure she is a good christian, and (which is almost as rare) a good woman. | Adieu.

Faulkner 1741

Alexander Pope to Swift

Sept. 3, 1726.

Yours to Mr. Gay[2] gave me greater satisfaction than that to me (tho' that gave me a great deal) for to hear you were safe at your journey's end, exceeds the account of your fatigues while in the way to it: otherwise believe me, every tittle of each is important to me, which sets any one thing before my Eyes that happens to you. I writ you a long letter, which I guess reach'd you the day after your arrival;[3] since then I had a conference with Sir ——[4] who exprest his desire of having seen you again before you left us: He said he observed a willingness in you to live among us; which I did not deny; but at the same time told him, you had no such design in your coming this time, which was meerly to see a few of those you loved: but that indeed all those wished it, and particularly Lord Peterborow and myself, who wish'd you lov'd Ireland less, had you any reason to love England more. I said nothing but what I think would induce any man to be as fond of you as I, plain Truth, (did they know either it, or you.) I can't help thinking, (when I consider the whole, short List of our friends) that none of 'em except you and I are qualified for the Mountains of Wales. The Dr. goes to Cards, Gay to Court;

[1] It has been suggested that Swift's knowledge of the Tuscan Court was through Sir Andrew Fountaine.

[2] See the first sentence of Swift's preceding letter. Is a letter to Gay missing?

[3] 25 Aug.

[4] Robert Walpole.

one loses money, one loses his time. Another of our friends labours to be unambitious, but he labours in an unwilling soil.[1] One Lady you like has too much of France to be fit for Wales:[2] Another is too much a subject to Princes and Potentates, to relish that wild Taste of liberty and poverty.[3] Mr. Congreve is too sick to bear a thin air; and she[4] that leads him too rich to enjoy any thing. Lord Peterborow can go to any climate, but never stay in any. Lord Bathurst is too great a husbandman to like barren hills, except they are his own to improve. Mr. Bethel indeed is too good and too honest to live in the world,[5] but yet it is fit, for its example, he should. We are left to ourselves in my opinion, and may live where we please, in Wales, Dublin or Bermudas:[6] And for me, I assure you I love the world so well, and it loves me so well, that I care not in what part of it I pass the rest of my days. I see no sunshine but in the face of a friend.

I had a glympse of a letter of yours lately,[7] by which I find you are (like the vulgar) apter to think well of people out of power, than of people in power; perhaps it is a mistake, but however there's something in it generous. Mr. ***[8] takes it extreme kindly, I can perceive, and he has a great mind to thank you for that good opinion, for which I believe he is only to thank his ill fortune: for if I am not in an error, he would rather be in power, than out.

To shew you how fit I am to live in the mountains, I will with great truth apply to myself an old sentence. 'Those that are in, may abide in; and those that are out, may abide out: yet to me, those that are in shall be as those that are out, and those that are out shall be as those that are in.'

I am indifferent as to all those matters, but I miss you as much as

[1] Bolingbroke.

[2] Lady Bolingbroke.

[3] Mrs. Howard.

[4] Henrietta, daughter of Marlborough, wife of Francis, Earl of Godolphin, who succeeded to the titles as second Duchess of Marlborough. She befriended Congreve. During the summer of 1726 he had suffered from a severe attack of gout.

[5] Hugh Bethel, Pope's friend and correspondent.

[6] An allusion to Berkeley's scheme.

[7] William Pulteney, 1684–1764, who played a long and active part in the political life of the country. In 1726 he finally severed his alliance with Walpole and joined Bolingbroke in the publication of *The Craftsman*. In 1742 he was created Earl of Bath.

[8] i.e. Pulteney.

I did the first day, when (with a short sigh) I parted. Wherever you are, (or on the mountains of Wales, or on the coast of Dublin,

——Tu mihi, magni superas dum saxa Timavi,
Sive oram Illyrici legis æquoris——)[1]

I am and ever shall be Yours, &c.

4805

William Pulteney to Swift

3 September 1726.

I received the favour of your kind letter at my Lord Chetwyns,[2] and tho' you had so much goodness as to forbid my answering it at that time, yet I should be inexcusable, now I have perfectly recovered my health and strength, if I did not return you my very hearty thanks for your concern for me during my illness.

Tho' our acquaintance has not been of long date, yet I think I may venture to assure you, that even among your old friends you have not many who have a juster Regard for your merit than I have; I could wish that those who are more able to serve you than I am, had the same desire of doing it, & yet methinks now I consider of it, & reflect who they are, I should be sorry if they had the merit of doing so right a thing, as well as I wish you, I would rather not have you provided for yet, than be provided for by those that I don't like. Mr Pope tells me that we shall see you in spring, when we meet again, I flatter my self we shall not part so soon, & I am in hopes you will allow me a larger share of your company than you did, all I can say to engage you to come a little oftener to my House, is to promise that you shall not have one Dish of Meat at my Table so disguised, but you shall easily know what it is, you shall have a Cup of your own for small Beer & Wine mixed together, you shall have no women at Table if you don't like them, & no Men but such as like you. I wished mightily to be in London before you left it, having something which I would willingly have communicated you that I do not think so discreet to trust to a letter, do not lett your expectation be raised, as

[1] Virgil, *Eclogues*, viii. 6–7.

Whether Timavus or th' Illyrian Coast,
Whatever Land or Sea thy Presence boast.—Dryden.

[2] Walter Chetwynd of Ingestre in Staffordshire was created a Viscount in the Irish peerage.

if it was a matter of any great consequence, it is not that tho' I should be mighty glad you knew it, & perhaps I may soon find a way of letting you do so.

Our Parliament they now say is not to meet till after X^{t} mas, The chief business of it being to give money it may be proper the Ministers should know a little before it meets how much farther they have run the nation in Debt, that they may prudently conceal or provide what they think fitt. I am told, that many among us begin to grumble that England should be obliged to support the Charge of a very expensive Warr, while all the other Powers of Europe are in Peace,[1] but I will enter no farther into Publick matters, taking it for granted that a letter directed to you, & franked by me, cannot fail of raising the Curiosity of some of our vigilant Ministers, & that they will open it, tho' we know it is not customary for them so to do. | Mrs Pulteney is very much your humble Servant | & I am, with great truth sr | Your most Obedient humble servant | Wm Pulteney.

London Septr. 3^{d} | 1726

Endorsed by Swift: Mr Pulteney | Sepr 3^{d} 1726 *and*
Wm Pulteney Eqr | Sep^{tr} 3^{d} 1726

4805

John Gay to Swift

[16 September 1726]

Since I wrote last I have been always upon the ramble; I have been in Oxfordshire with the Duke & Dutchess of Queensberry and at Petersham[2] & wheresoever they would carry me; but as they will go to Wiltshire without me on Tuesday next[3] for two or three months, I believe I shall then have finish'd my travells for this Year, & shall not go farther from London than now and then to Twickenham. I saw Mr Pope on Sunday, who hath lately escap'd a very great

[1] An Ostend Company was established by the Emperor Charles VI with the object of breaking down the monopoly of trade with India exercised by England and Holland. Despite opposition the Company prospered, and at the time Pulteney was writing it was feared this might lead to the outbreak of war. But in 1727, harassed by other difficulties, the Emperor agreed to suspend the Company for seven years with the secret understanding that it was not to be revived.

[2] Besides his seat at Amesbury in Wiltshire the Duke had residences at Ham House, at Stoney Middleton, and a London house.

[3] Gay was writing on Friday.

danger, but is very much wounded across his right hand; Coming home in the dark about a week ago alone in my Lord Bolingbroke's coach from Dawley, he was overturn'd where a bridge had been broken down near Whitton about a mile from his own house, he was thrown into the river with the glasses of the coach up, & was up to the knots of his periwig in water; The footman broke the glass to draw him out, by which he thinks he receiv'd the cut across his hand. He was afraid he should have lost the use of his little finger & the next to it; but the surgeon whom he sent for last Sunday from London to examine it, told him, that his fingers were safe, that there were two nerves cut, but no tendon. He was in very good health, & very good spirits, and the wound in a fair way of being soon heal'd. The instructions you sent me to communicate to the Doctor[1] about the Singer, I transcrib'd from your own Letter and sent to him, for at that time he was going every other day to Windsor park[2] to visit Mr Congreve who hath been extreamly ill, but is now recovered, so that I was prevented from seeing of him by going out of town myself. I din'd & sup'd on Monday last with Lord & Lady Bolingbroke at Lord Berkeley's at Cranford[3] & return'd to London with the Duke & Dutchess of Queensberry on Tuesday by two a Clock in the morning, you are remember'd always with great respect by all your acquaintance, and every one of them wishes for your return. The Lottery begins to be drawn on Monday next, but my week of attendance will be the first in October.[4] I am oblig'd to follow the Gravers to make them dispatch my plates for the Fables, for without it I find they proceed but very slowly. I take your advice in this, as I wish to do in all things, and frequently revise my work in order to finish it as well as I can. Mr Pulteney takes the Letter you sent him in the kindest manner, and I believe he is, except a few excursions, fixt in town for the winter. As for the particular affair that you want to be inform'd in,[5] we are as yet wholy in the dark, but Mr Pope will follow your instructions. Mr Lancelot[6] sent for the Spectacles you left behind you, which were deliver'd to him. Mr Jervas's sheets are sent home to him mended, finely wash'd, &

[1] i.e. Arbuthnot.

[2] The residence of Henrietta, Duchess of Marlborough.

[3] Known to Swift in former days. At this time Lord and Lady Bolingbroke appear to have been living there while Dawley was undergoing repair.

[4] Gay was one of the commissioners.

[5] Probably a reference to *Gulliver's Travels*.

[6] Second husband of Swift's cousin Patty Rolt. See *Journal*, i. 18 n.

neatly folded up.[1] I intend to see Mr Pope to morrow[2] or on Sunday. I have not seen Mrs Howard a great while, which you know must be a great mortification & self-denial, but in my case 'tis particularly unhappy that a man cannot contrive to be in two places at the same time; If I could, while you are there, one of them should be always Dublin, but after all, tis a Silly thing to be with a friend by halves, so that I will give up all thoughts of bringing this project to perfection, if you will contrive that we shall meet again soon. I am | Dear Sir | Your most oblig'd & affectionate | friend & Servant | J G.

London Sept. 16. 1726.

Address: To | The Rev. Dr Swift Dean of | St Patricks in | Dublin | Ireland
Postmark: 17 SE
Endorsed by Swift: Mr Gay | Septr 16^h 1726

4805

John Arbuthnot to Swift

[*c.* 20 September 1726]

I have been ballancing Dear sir these three days whither I should write to your first? Laying aside the superiority of your dignity, I thought a notification was due to me as well as to two others of my freinds. then I considerd that this was done in the publick newes with all the formality of Reception of a Lord Lieutenant. I reflected on the dependancy of Ireland, but said I what if my freind should dispute this? then I considerd that Letters were allwayes introduced at first from the Civiliz'd to the Barbarous Kingdom . . . in short my affection, & the pleasure of corresponding with my dear freind prevail'd, & since yow most disdainfully & Barbarously confined me to two lines a month, I was resolv'd to plague yow with twenty times that Number. Tho I think it was a sort of a Compliment to be suppos'd capable of saying any thing in two lines. The Gascoygne asked only to speak one word to the ffrench King which the King confining him to, he Brought a paper & said *signez* & not a word

1 While Swift was lodging with him Gay had borrowed linen from Jervas.

2 As noted above Gay was writing on Friday. The accident which happened to Pope must have occurred between Monday the 5th and Sunday the 11th. On the 5th he wrote to Broome (and could write), on the 11th Gay saw him in his damaged condition.—Sherburn.

more. Your negotiation with the singing man is in the hands of my daughter Nanny who I can assure yow, will neglect nothing that concerns yow. She has wrote about it. I beleive yow did not gett receipts for your subscribers,[1] which they ought to have had, however I shall Lodge the names with Mr Tonson that they may call for the books. Mr Pope has been in hazard of his life by drowning, coming Late two weeks ago from Lord Bolingbroke's in his Coach & Six a Bridge on a little River[2] being broke down they were obligd to go through the water which was not too high but the Coach was overturnd in it & the Glass being up, which he could not break nor get down, he was very near drowned; for the footman was stuck in the mud, & could hardly come in time to help him he had that common with Horace, that it was occasioned by the trunk of a tree but it was trunco Rhaeda illapsa neq; faunus fatum dextra levabat for he was wounded in the left hand,[3] but thank god without any danger but by the cutting of a Large vessel lost a great dale of blood. I have been with Mrs Howard who has had a most intolerable pain in one side of her head. I had a great dale of discourse with your freind her Royal Highness. She insisted upon your witt & good Conversation. I told her R. Highness that was not what I valu'd yow for, but for being a sincere honest man & speaking truth when others were afraid to speak it. I have been near three weeks together every day at the Duchess of Marlborough's with Mr Congreve who has been like to dye with a fever, & the gout in his stomach, but he is better, & like to do well. My Brother was like to be cast away, going to France ther was a ship lost just by him. I write this in a dull Humor, but with most sincere affection to an ungratefull man as you are that minds every bodymore than me [ ] My dear freind [ ][4]

Endorsed by Swift: Dr Arbuthnot | 1726 *and* About 20 Seper 1726

[1] Presumably subscribers to Arbuthnot's *Tables of Ancient Coins &c.*, published early in 1727 by Tonson. No list of subscribers appears in this publication.

[2] The Cran, near Whitton. See further the *Harvard Library Bulletin*, ii (1948), 121–3.

[3] Adapted from Hor. *Odes*, II. xvii. 27–30. Despite Arbuthnot's 'left' it was Pope's right hand that was injured.

[4] Part of page 2 has been torn away. A part of this page and the verso of the leaf has been used by Swift for listing the incomes of English and Irish archbishoprics and bishoprics. Canterbury and Armagh are each given at £6,000.

4805

Viscount Bolingbroke to Swift

London Sep ye 22nd 1726

A Bookseller,[1] who says he is going in a few days to Dublin, calls here, & offers to carry a letter to you. I cannot resist the temptation of writing to you, tho' I have nothing to say more by this conveyance than I should have by that of the post, tho' I have lately clubb'd with Pope to make up a most elegant Epistle to you in prose & verse, & tho' I writ the other day the first paragraph of that Cheddar letter which is preparing for you.[2] the only excuse then which I can plead for writing now is that the letter will cost you nothing. have you heard of the accident which befel poor Pope in going lately from me? A Bridg was down, the coach forc'd to go thro' the waters, the Bank Steep, an hole on one side, a block of timber on the other, the night as dark as pitch, in short he overturned, the fall was broke by the water, but the glasses were up, & he might have been drownd if one of my men had not broke a glass & pull'd him out thro the window. his right hand was Severely cut; but the surgeon thinks him in no danger of losing the use of his fingers. however he had lately had very great pains in that arm from the shoulder downwards, which might create a Suspicion that some of the glass remain'd still in the flesh. StAndré[3] says there is none. if so, these pains are owing to a cold he took in a fit of gallantry which carry'd him across the water to see Mrs Howard, who has been extremely ill, but is much better. just as I am writing I hear that Dr Arbuthnot says that Popes pains are Rheumatick, & have no relation to his wound. he suffers very much, I will endeavour to see him tomorrow. let us hear from you as often as you can afford to write. I would say something to you of myself, if I had any good thing to say, but I am much in the same way in which you left me, eternally busy about trifles, disagreeable in themselves, but render'd supportable by their end, which is to enable me to bury my Self from the world, who cannot be more tir'd of me than I am of it, in an agreeable Sepulchre. I hope to

[1] The bookseller may have been George Faulkner.

[2] A letter to which several persons contribute as several dairies do to a Cheddar cheese. See Gay to Swift, 22 Oct. 1726. The 'elegant epistle' by Pope seems not to be forthcoming.

[3] Nathanael St. André, of Swiss origin. His knowledge of German led George I to appoint him anatomist to the royal household. *D.N.B.*

bring this about by next Spring, & shall be glad to see you att my funeral. Adieu.

Endorsed by Swift: Ld Boling^b | Sep^tr 22^d 1726

4805

John Gay to Swift

[September 1726]

As We cannot enjoy any good thing without your partaking of it, Accept of the following receipt for Stewing Veal

Take a knuckle of Veal,
You may buy it, or steal,
In a few peices cut it,
In a Stewing pan put it,
Salt, pepper and mace
Must season this knuckle,
Then what's join'd to a place,[1]
With other Herbs muckle;
That which killed King Will,[2]
And what never stands still,[3]
Some sprigs of that bed[4]
Where Children are bred,
Which much you will mend, if
Both Spinnage and Endive,
And Lettuce and Beet,
With Marygold meet;
Put no water at all,
For it maketh things small:
Which, lest it should happen,
A close cover clap on;
Put this pot of [5]Wood's mettle
In a hot boiling kettle,
And there let it be,
(Mark the doctrine I teach)
About—let me see—
Thrice as long as you [6]preach
So skimming the fat off,
Say Grace with your hat off,

[1] Vulg. Salary.

[2] Suppos'd sorrell

[3] This is by Dr | Bentley thought to be | Time, or Thyme.

[4] Parsley. Vide Chamberlain.

[5] Of this composition see the Works of the Copper farthing Dean.

[6] Which we suppose to be near four hours.

O then, with what rapture
Will it fill Dean & Chapter!

In the British Museum this poem, on a small single leaf, is inserted on a stub, Add. MS. 4805. f. 126, between f. 125 and f. 127. It is doubtful whether Gay was the author. The lines were frequently transcribed by contemporaries. A transcript in the British Museum, Harley 7316, p. 418, two transcripts among papers of the Marquess of Bath (*Portland Papers*, xvii, f. 130; xviii, f. 97), a transcript formerly at Panshanger, another in the Morgan Library, New York, and a transcript in the possession of the editor, all assign the authorship to Pope. See also Norman Ault, *New Light on Pope*, pp. 225–31; and Pope's *Minor Poems* (Twickenham Edition), pp. 253–5. That the poem is Pope's can hardly admit of doubt, although, owing to the injury to his hand, it was written for him by Gay. These lines are, apparently, the only part of the 'Cheddar letter' referred to by Bolingbroke to survive. The other authors were Gay, Bolingbroke, Mrs. Howard, Pulteney, and possibly Arbuthnot.

Forster No. 555

Swift to the Rev. James Stopford

Dublin, Octr 15th. 1726

I have yours of Sep^tr^ 14th[1] and have since recvd an account of Mr Rawlinson's return to England, with good news of a good Vintage, for we are in terror of losing the Wine of two Years together, Mr Rawlinson hath been talking to my Friends very much to your Advantage, & I am confident you will find them disposed to do you all the good Offices in their Power. Pray God preserve you from being preferred on Account of any Qualification that is now in Esteem, & yet a wise Man may some times in the worst Times rise to a moderate Station without the necessity of first dipping himself over Head & Ears in the Dirt: And beginners are under no obligation of Conscience or Honor to offend the Powers that be, or refuse their Favour when it is not tacked to any scandalous Condition. I believe some Friends you may find in London will be fitter to recommend you than I, for a Chapl^n^ to the Lieutenant: The misfortune of Sheridan hath sunk my Credit & I have shown myself so little complyant to his Ex^cy^ or the Ministry, Canal: But you can attend Ld. Car^t^ with any introducee upon the Character I gave him of you. For my own part, I reckon he will never return hither: but however

[1] A reply to Swift's letter of 6 Aug.

if you can get yr. self fixed with him by some English Recommendation, it will be worth 40 Irish ones. I imagine that I shall be able to do any reasonable Job for a Friend with a new Governor. The Bishop of London I know nothing of, but Dean Berkeley does. Mrs Johnson is much recovered since I saw her first, but still very lean and low. I saw Mac[1] and all your other folks there, who are in good Health and cheerful to think you will soon return; yet I think it would be better to stay at London some time to be known. You know they have[2] made a Baby of this Kingdom a Bishop about a Month or two ago. Pray write to me as soon as you get to London. Dr Sheridan gives you his service, & says you are a Senior Fellow; which will have one Advantage to you among many other, that you will be able to command the best Benefice in your College gift. Pray God Bless and prosper you. I am, Ever entirely your

Address: To Mr. Stopford at Messieurs Alexander Forbes, and William Wright, Merchants in London

Longleat xiii Portland Papers

Swift to Alexander Pope and John Gay

15 October 1726.

I received your Map and Pictures, by the latter I could not find out the Originals, and your map is as much Caricatura of Biberry, as the others must be of I don't know who.

As for your tripartite Letter,[3] which begins with his Lordship[4] I think (Gentry) it should be Settled what foot we are upon, and how you intend we are to live together in Absence, His Ldship takes the Office of a Critick, and is in a dozen Lines acting a Critick telling me of a very indifferent Letter. Is it imagined that I must be always leaning upon one Hand while I am writing with the other, Always upon the *qui vive* and the *Slip Slop* instead of an honest

[1] Perhaps Sheridan's relation, MacFadden.

[2] Henry Maule to the Bishopric of Cloyne. He was born and educated in Ireland.

[3] The Cheddar letter. Swift seems to have thought Bolingbroke, Pope, and Gay were the only contributors.

[4] Bolingbroke.

plain Letter which onely Should contain in more words Si vales bene est and me ama ut &c I have Since writ him a much longer and a more indifferent Letter which will cost him two dosen lines at least to find fault with, and will be so much Matter for an Answer, aliquisqꝫ malo fuit usus &c However as to the writing Part, you Shall no more complain for I can mend my Hand better than my Head. But may I never think again if I think three Seconds whenever I write to the best or the worst of you. Let Builders and Ministers think till they have not a Peny left in their Pockets, or a Friend in the World. Besides I am so busy with railing at those odious Beasts you send us for all Employments, that I can think of nothing else. Breed a man a dosen year in a Coal pit, he Shall pass his time well enough among his Fellows, but Send him to Light for a few Months then down with him again; and try what a Correspondent he will be —I take you in order, the next is my Landlord at Whitehall,[1] who treats me with [such] kindness and Domesticity, that he is laying in a Double Stock of Wine. He is to return my Lord Chesterfield[2] thanks for the Honor I receive in his remembring me. He is to make Mr Stopford be received by all who deserve it in the best manner possible and to thank Mr Rawlinson &c but as for Tom the water fool[3] I think he treats me with little Respect, therefor upon Mature thoughts, I conclude it below me to return his Complement and he must polish his manners before I will do him a good Office to Mr Popes Maid.

To Speak in the Second Person, I would advise you to inquire diligently whether the Mice who eat up your Buttons were whigs or Toryes, or whether of the Court or Country Party. Plutarch tells us that Diogenes was Encouraged to Continue in the Study of Philosophy by a Mouse if this be true by parallell reasoning, you Should have enemyes at Court, and probably Mrs Howard sent those Mice to eat your Buttons, as the readyist Instruments to make you a heathen Philosopher; But if mice be like Rats who haunt onely Ships that are not in danger of Sinking, then you are Safe enough, and they may perhaps be Some of Knight Roberts Mice[5] to pay you a Visit I would be Glad to know whether your Buttons were green; if

[1] Gay had entertained Swift as his Whitehall lodgings.

[2] Letter writer. The fourth Earl. He had only recently succeeded to the title. His father died 27 Jan. 1725–6. Swift had been introduced to him by Arbuthnot.

[3] Perhaps Pope's waterman, Bowry.

[4] Sir Robert Walpole's mice.

So then they must have been pontic mice, which as Olavs Magnus[1] assures us always devours whatever is green and it never flourishes again, Upon the whole, Pliny allows them to have been always an ill omen;[2] and therefore you should be advised to prepare against it either by Averruncation or Traps, for the latter you may consult Avicen.[3]—The last Part of your Part relates to my Twitenham Host therefore I shall answer it to him you ought to give me Joy that I was not present to be overturned with you, in answer let me say, that I am ready to Stand or fall with you as long as I live, however I believe my Weight would have Saved us all if it had been rightly applyed; I am so far of your Opinion that life is good for nothing otherwise than for the Love we have to our Friends, that I think the easiest way of dying is so to Contrive Matters as not to have one Friend left in the World; and perhaps it would be no ill Amendment to add, nor an Enemy neither. I hope you jest when you Say you have lost two Fingers, and it is so bad and provoking a Jest, that if I did not love you I should wish it were true. Neither are your Hopes worth a Rush a Lawyer, a Usurer, a Physicion, a Minister a Senator, a Judge must open their Hand before they Shut it else they will go off empty handed. But other Letters tell me you have onely lost Some Blood which you can ill Spare, for you had nothing to Venture except Blood and Bones. I am mustring as I told you all the little things in verse that I think may be Safely printed,[4] but I give you despotick Power to tear as many as you please. I now turn to Mr Gay. I desire you will let me know where I am to direct to Lord B;[5] when I am disposed towards him; I desire he may onely See the most indifferent Part of this Letter, and lastly to make my Acknoledgment to Mr Poltiney[6] for his Letter, and that nothing hinders me from writing again, but the Fear that his Civilityes would engage him in a very Useless Correspondence; or if you think he did expect a Second Letter, I would readily do it, although I am ever at a loss in dealing with Persons too civil, for I have a Cloud of Witnesses with My Lord Bolingbroke at their Head to prove I never practiced or possessed Such a Talent as Civility, which Sir Wm

[1] *Gentium Septentrionalium Historiæ Breviarium*, 1652, XVIII, c. xvi.

[2] *Hist. Nat.* viii. 82.

[3] Not traceable in Avicenna's *De Animalibus*. Sherburn conjectures that Swift may be joking.

[4] For the Pope-Swift *Miscellanies* of 1727.

[5] Bolingbroke.

[6] William Pulteney.

Windham[1] knew well enough when he refused to make any Returns to what I writ to him before I left you wherein he knew me better than Mr Polteney does although what I did was a pure Effect of Friend Ship, Brotherly Love, Esteem and Concern. I have received a Box with the Spectacles but by whose Care they were conveyed I know not I onely desire that My Lord Bolingbroke may be assured the Spectacles were for two old Cozens and not for me. Mr Ford is just landed after a Months raking by the Way with Some of his Tory Lords, for want of whom he must here Sink into Spleen as he uses to do. I am going to try your Receit of the Knuckle of Veal, and I wish the measure of Ingredients may prove better than of the Verses,[2] but I want the other of a Chicken in a wooden Boul from Mrs Howard, upon which you may likewise exercise your Poetry, for the Ladys here object against both, but they Swear that a Sauce Pan cannot get into a Kettle, and therefore they resolve to change it into a deep Earthen Pot. This day I was forced to dine upon Eggs alone, that I might have time to write my Letter, This is all I have leisure to Say at present

Upon four dismal stories in the Doctor's Letter,[3]
relating to four of my Friends

Here four of you got mischances to plague you
Friend Congreve a Feaver, Friend Howard an Ague
Friend Pope overturnd by driving too fast away
And Robin at Sea had like to be cast away
But, alas, the pour Dean neither Shudders nor burns
No Sea overwhelms him, no Coach overturns
Though his Claret is bad, and he foots it on Stones
Yet he gets home at night with Health and whole Bones.

Octbr 15th 1726.

[1] Wyndham was one of the founders of the Brothers' Club, and had long known Swift. He now, in conjunction with Pulteney, led the opposition in the House of Commons.

[2] In *New Light on Pope*, p. 230, Ault gives the prose recipe.

[3] Arbuthnot to Swift, 20 Sept. 1726.

4805

John Gay to Swift

22 October 1726.

Before I say one word to you, give me leave to say something of the other Gentleman's Affair.[1] The Letter was sent, and the answer was, that every thing was finish'd, & concluded according to orders; and that it would be publickly known to be so in a very few days, so that I think there can be no occasion for his writing any more about this Affair.[1]

The Letter you wrote to Mr Pope was not receiv'd 'till eleven or twelve days after date, and the Post Office we suppose have very vigilant Officers, for they had taken care to make him pay for a double Letter. I wish I could tell you that the cutting of the tendons of two of his fingers was a joke, but it is really so. The wound is quite heal'd; his hand is still weak, and the two fingers drop downwards as I told you before, but I hope it will be very little troublesome or detrimental to him.

In Answer to our Letter of Maps, Pictures & receipts, you call it a tripartite Letter;[2] If you will examine it once again, you will find some Lines of Mrs Howard, & some of Mr Pulteney which you have not taken the least notice of. The receipt of the Veal [is] of Monsieur Davoux Mr Pulteney's Cook, and it hath been approv'd of at one of our Twickenham entertainments. The difficulty of the Saucepan, I believe you will find is owing to a negligence in perusing the manuscript, for if I remember right it is there call'd a Stew-pan. Your Earthen Vessel provided it is close stopt, I allow to be a good succedaneum. As to the boiling Chickens in a Wooden Bowle, I shall be quite asham'd to consult Mrs Howard upon your account; who thinks herself entirely neglected by you in your not writing to her, as you promis'd; However Let her take it as she will, to serve a friend I will venture to ask it of her; The Prince and his family come[3] to settle in town to morrow. That Mr Pulteney expected an answer to his Letter & would be extreamly pleas'd to hear from you is very certain, for I have heard him talk of it with expectation for above a fortnight. I have of late been very much out of order with a slight feaver, which I am not yet quite free from; it was occasion'd by a cold,

[1] The affair of *Gulliver's Travels*.

[2] See the previous letter.

[3] From Richmond, where from early in June they had spent the summer.

which my Attendance at the Guildhall improv'd.[1] I have not a friend who hath got any thing under my Administration but the Dutchess of Queensberry who hath had a benefit of a thousand pounds. Your mentioning Mr Rollison so kindly will, I know, give him much pleasure, for he always talks of you with great regard and the strongest terms of friendship; He hath of late been ill of a feaver, but is recover'd so as to go abroad to take the Air.

If the Gravers keep their word with me, I shall be able to publish my Fables soon after Christmas. The Doctor's book is entirely printed off,[2] & will be very soon publish'd. I believe you will expect that I should give you some account how I have spent my time since you left me. I have attended my distrest friend at Twickenham, & been his Emanuensis, which you know is no idle Charge, & I have read about half Virgil, & half Spenser's Fairy Queen. I still despise Court Preferments so that I lose no time upon attendance on great men, and still can find amusement enough without Quadrille, which here is the Universal Employment of Life. I thought you would be glad to hear from me, so that I determin'd not to stir out of my lodgings till I had answer'd your Letter, and I think I shall very probably hear more of the matter which I mention in the first paragraph of this Letter as soon as I go abroad, for I expect it every day. We have no news as yet of Mr Stopfort, Mr Rollinson told me he shall know of his arrival, & will send me word. Lord Bolingbroke hath been to make a visit to Sir William Wyndham; I hear he is return'd, but I have not seen him. If I had been in a better State of health, & Mrs Howard were not to come to town to morrow, I would have gone to Mr Pope's to day[3] to have din'd with him there on Monday. You ask me how to address to Lord B when you are dispos'd to write to him. If you mean Lord Burlington, he is not yet return'd from France, but is expected every day. If you mean Lord Bathurst he is in Glocestershire[4] & makes but a very short stay; so that if you direct to one of them in St James's Square, or to the other at Burlington house in Piccadilly your Letter will find them. I will make your Compliments to Lord Chesterfield

[1] As commissioner of the lottery.

[2] Arbuthnot's *Ancient Coins, Weights, and Measures*, 1727.

[3] Saturday.

[4] Gay pretends to question whether Swift in his letter of 15 Oct. was referring to Burlington or Bathurst. In his postscript he gives offhand Bolingbroke's Pall Mall address.

& Mr Pulteney, and I beg you in return to make mine to Mr Ford. Next Week I shall have a new coat & new Buttons for the Birth-day, though I dont know but a turn-coat might have been more for my advantage. | Yours most sincerely & affectionately.

Whitehall. Octr 22. 1726.

I hear that Lord Bolingbroke will be in town at his house in Pellmell next week.

B.M. Add. MS. 22625

Swift to Mrs. Howard

[October 1726.]

Madam[1]

Being perpetually teazed with the Remembrance of you by the sight of Your Ring[2] on my Finger my patience at last is at an End, and in order to be revenged I here send you a Piece of Irish Plad[3] made in Imitation of the Indian, wherein our Workmen here[4] are grown so expert, that in this kind of Stuff they are said to excel that which comes from the Indies and because our Ladyes are too proud to wear what is made at home, the Workman is forced to run a gold Thread through the middle, and sell it as Indian. But I ordered him to leave out that Circumstance, that you may be clad in Irish Stuff, and in my Livery. But I beg you will not tell any Parliemt man from whence you had this Plad, otherwise out of Malice they will make a Law to cut off all our Weavers Fingers. I must likewise tell you, to

[1] As Croker rightly observes in his *Letters of Henrietta Countess of Suffolk*, 1824, i. 209, 'Mrs. Howard's intercourse with Dean Swift forms an epoch in her history and in his'. She had been appointed bedchamber-woman to the Princess of Wales; and, accepting the advances of the Prince, became his mistress. In 1724, at the Prince's expense, she built a villa at Marble Hill, Twickenham, where she became a neighbour of Pope, who intended to introduce Swift to her; but the introduction probably took place through Arbuthnot when he carried the Dean to visit the Princess at Leicester House. The acquaintance with Mrs. Howard covered a period of about five years. Latterly, as will be seen, the relationship ceased to be cordial. For Swift's famous Character of her, seemingly composed in 1727, see *Prose Works*, ed. Temple Scott, xi. 145–50. The autograph is at Longleat, xiii, ff. 45–46.

[2] The ring was of little value. See Swift to Mrs. Howard, 21 Nov. 1730.

[3] Poplin.

[4] Ball omits 'here'.

prevent Your Pride, my Intention is to use you very scurvily; for my reall Design is that when the Princess asks you where you got that fine Night-gown, you are to say, that it is an Irish Plad sent you by the Dean of St Patrick's, who with his most humble Duty to Her Royal Highness is ready to make her another such Present, at the terrible Expence of eight shillings and three pence a Yard, if she will descend to honor Ireland with receiving and wearing it. And in Recompence, I who govern the Vulgar will take Care to have Her Royal Highness's health drank by five hundred Weavers as an Encourager of the Irish Manufactury. And I command you to, add that I am no Courtier, nor have any Thing to ask.

I hope the whole Royal Family about you is in Health. Dr Arbuthnot lately mortified me with an Account of a great Pain in your Head[1] I believe no Head that is good for any thing is long without some Disorder, at least that is the best Argument I have for any thing that is good in my own.

I pray God preserve you; and entreat you to believe that I am, with great Respect | Madam | Your most obedient and | most obliged | Servant | Jonath Swift.

Endorsed: Dr Swift

Forster copy

Swift to Knightley Chetwode

Dublin, October 24, 1726.

Sir,[2]

Since I came to Ireland to the time that I guess you went out of town, I was as you observe much in the country; partly to inure myself gradually to the air of this place, and partly to see a lady of my old acquaintance who was extremely ill. I am now going on the old way having much to do of little consequence, and taking all advantage of fair weather to keep my health by walking. I look upon you as no very warm planter who could be eighteen months absent

[1] Arbuthnot to Swift 20 Sept. 1726.

[2] Swift's letter from London to Chetwode, 19 Apr. 1726, shows that he anticipated him to follow: 'I know not your reasons for coming hither.' If he entertained them at all Chetwode had not carried out his intentions. Swift's friendship with him had obviously begun to cool, probably stimulated by Chetwode's separation from his wife.

from it, and amusing yourself in so wretched a town as this; neither can I think any man prudent who hath planting or building going on in his absence.

I believe our discoursing of friends in England would be very short, for I hardly imagine you and I can have three of the same acquaintance there, death and exile having so diminished the number; and as for occurrences, I had as little to do with them as possible, my opinions pleasing very few, and therefore the life I led there was most in the country, and seeing only those who were content to visit me, and receive my visits, without regard to party or politics. One thing I have only confirmed myself in, which I knew long ago, that it is a very idle thing for any man to go for England without great business, unless he were in a way to pass his life there, which was not my case, and if it be yours, I shall think you happy.

I am as always an utter stranger to persons and occurrences here, and therefore can entertain you with neither, but wish you success in this season of planting, and remain,|

Your most faithful, &c.

Address: To Knightley Chetwode, Esq. at his house at Woodbrooke, near Mountmellick.

4805

John Arbuthnot to Swift[1]

London, 5 November 1726.

I take it mighty kindly that a man of your high post, Dear Sir, was pleased to write me so long a letter.[2] I look upon the captain Tom[3] of a great Nation to be a much greater Man than the Governour of it.

I am sorry your commission about your singer has not been executed sooner, it is not Nanny's Fault, who has spoke severall times to Dr Pepush[4] about it, & wrote three or four letters, & received for answer that he would write for the young fellow; but still

[1] Previous editors give the date of this letter as 8 Nov. Arbuthnot, however, dated it 5 Nov., and the London postmark has the same date.

[2] Probably a reply to Arbuthnot's letter of 20 Sept.

[3] i.e. the leader of a mob.

[4] John Christopher Pepusch, 1667–1752, was born in Berlin. In 1668 he came to England. Here, recognizing the superior genius of Handel, he turned to teaching and writing upon the theory of music.

nothing is done, I will endeavour to gett his name & direction & write to him my self.

Your books shall be sent as directed; they have been printed above a month, but I cannot gett my subscribers' names.[1] I will make over all my profits to you, for the property of Gulliver's Travells, which I believe, will have as great a Run as John Bunian. Gulliver is a happy man that at his age can write such a merry work.

I made my Lord ArchBishop's compliment to her R Highness who returns his Grace her thanks, at the same time Mrs Howard Read your letter to herself. The princess immediately seizd on your plade for her own use, & has orderd the young Princesses to be clad in the same. when I had the honor to see her She was Reading Gulliver, & was just come to the passage of the Hobbling prince, which she laughed at.[1] I tell yow freely the part of the projectors is the leats Brilliant. Lewis Grumbles a little at it & says he wants the Key to it, & is dayly refining I suppose he will be able to publish like Barnevelt[2] in time I gave your service to Lady Hervey She is in a little sort of a Miff, about a Ballad that was wrote on her to the tune of Molly Mog, & sent to her in the name of a begging poet. She was bitt & wrote a letter to the Begging poet & desired him to change two double entendres, which the Authors Mr Poulteny [and] Lord Chesterfield changd to single entendres.[3] I was against that . . tho I had a hand in the first. She is not displeasd I believe, with the Ballad, but only with being Bitt.

Ther has been a comical paper about Quadrille[4] describing it in terms of a Lewd debauch among four Ladys meetting four gallants two of a Ruddy & two of a swarthy complexion talking of their A—es &c. The Ridle is carried on in pretty strong terms! it was not found out a long time, the Ladys imagining it to be [a] reall thing begann

1 'A Voyage to Lilliput', c. iv. The prince with 'a Hobble in his Gait' was an allusion to the future George II.

2 Esdras Barnivelt, the professed author of *A Key to the Lock*, which proved 'beyond all Contradiction, the dangerous Tendency of a late Poem, entitul'd, *The Rape of the Lock*, to Government and Religion', was Pope himself. It appeared in Apr. 1715. See Ault, *Prose Works of Alexander Pope*, pp. lxxiii ff., lxxxvi ff., 181–207; *Minor Poems*, ed. Ault, pp. 132–6.

3 Mary Lepell, famed as a court beauty, was married to John Hervey, afterwards Lord Hervey of Ickworth, in 1720. For *Molly Mogg*, by Gay, see *Poetical Works*, ed. Faber, pp. 188–92.

4 Presumably the reference is to Arbuthnot's 'Ballad on Quadrille', printed in *Miscellanies. The Last Volume*, 1727, pp. 197–201.

to guess who were of the party. A great Minister was for Hanging the Author. in short it was made very good sport.

Gay has had a little feaver, but is pretty well recovered, so is Mr pope we shall meet at Lord BolingBrokes on Thursday in town, at dinner, & remember yow:

Gulliver is in every body's Hands Lord Scarborow[1] who is no inventor of Storys told me that he fell in company with a Master of a ship, who told him that he was very well acquainted with Gulliver, but that the printer had Mistaken, that he livd in Wapping, & not in Rotherhith. I lent the Book to an old Gentleman, who went immediately to his Map to search for Lilly putt.

We expect War here. The city of London are all crying out for it that they shall be undone without it. Ther being now a totall stoppage of all trade.[2] I think one of the best Courses will be to Rig out a privateer for the west Indies, will yow be concernd we will build her at Bermudas, & get Mr Dean Berkley to be our Manager

I had the honor to see Lord Oxford, who askd kindly for yow, & said he would write to yow. if the project gos on for printing some papers he has promised to give copys of some things, which I beleive cannot be found else where My family thank god are pretty well as far as I know. & give you their service. My brother Robert has been very ill of a Rheumatism Wishing yow all health & happiness & not daring to write my paper on the other side I must remain | Dear Sir | Your most faithfull humble | servt Jo: Arbuthnott

London Novr 5th 1726

Address: To | the Reverend The | Dean of St patricks | Dublin
Postmarks: 5 NO *and* BB
Endorsed by Swift: Novr. 8. 1726 | Dr Arbuthnt

Faulkner 1741

Alexander Pope to Swift[3]

16 November 1726.

I have resolved to take time; and in spite of all misfortunes and demurs, which sickness, lameness, or disability of any kind can

[1] Richard Lumley, second Earl of Scarborough, succeeded to the title in 1721. He was at this time Master of the Horse to the Prince of Wales.

[2] Indignation was widespread owing to competition in the East Indies by the Ostend Company. See p. 163, n. 1. [*For note 3 see opposite.*

throw in my way, to write you (at intervals) a long letter. My two least fingers of one hand hang impediments to the others, like useless dependents, who only take up room, and never are active or assistant to our wants: I shall never be much the better for 'em—I congratulate you first upon what you call your Couzen's wonderful Book,[1] which is *publica trita manu* at present, and I prophecy will be in future the admiration of all men. That countenance with which it is received by some statesmen, is delightful; I wish I could tell you how every single man looks upon it, to observe which has been my whole diversion this fortnight. I've never been a night in London since you left me, till now for this very end, and indeed it has fully answered my expectations.

I find no considerable man very angry at the book: some indeed think it rather too bold, and too general a Satire: but none that I hear of accuse it of particular reflections (I mean no persons of consequence, or good judgment; the mob of Criticks, you know, always are desirous to apply Satire to those that they envy for being above them) so that you needed not to have been so secret upon this head. Motte[2] receiv'd the copy (he tells me) he knew not from whence, nor from whom, dropp'd at his house in the dark, from a Hackney-coach: by computing the time, I found it was after you left England, so for my part, I suspend my judgment.

I'm pleas'd with the nature and quality of your Present to the Princess. The Irish stuff[3] you sent to Mrs. H.[4] her Royal Highness laid hold of, and has made up for her own use. Are you determin'd to be National in every thing, even in your civilities? you are the greatest Politician in Europe at this rate; but as you are a rational Politician, there's no great fear of you, you will never succeed.

[1] A fictitious Richard Sympson, professing himself Gulliver's cousin, submitted secretively to Benjamin Motte the manuscript of *Gulliver's Travels.*

[2] It has been suggested that these words imply that Pope may have dropped the manuscript of *Gulliver* at Motte's door; but there is no good evidence for this. A time limitation rules out Ford, who has also been suggested. A consideration of all the evidence favours Erasmus Lewis or Gay. See *The Text of Gulliver's Travels*, Harold Williams, pp. 13–19.

[3] The Irish poplin submitted as a present by Swift.

[4] Mrs. Howard.

---

[3] In the clandestine volume, in Faulkner, 1741, vii. 71, and in other early editions, this letter, dated 16 Nov., is printed just after the letter of Gay to Swift, dated, 17 Nov. The letters are here transposed. Ball conjecturally corrects '16' to '26'. The two letters were probably one.

Another thing in which you have pleased me, was what you say to Mr. P.[1] by which it seems to me that you value no man's civility above your own dignity, or your own reason. Surely, without flattery, you are now above all parties of men, and it is high time to be so, after twenty or thirty years observation of the great world.

Nullius addictus jurare in verba magistri.[2]

I question not, many men would be of your intimacy, that you might be of their Interest: But God forbid an honest or witty man should be of any, but that of his country. They have scoundrels enough to write for their passions and their designs; let us write for truth, for honour, and for posterity. If you must needs write about Politicks at all, (but perhaps 'tis full as wise to play the fool any other way) surely it ought to be so as to preserve the dignity and integrity of your character with those times to come, which will most impartially judge of them.

I wish you had writ to Lord Peterborow, no man is more affectionate toward you. Don't fancy none but Tories are your friends; for at that rate I must be, at most, but half your friend, and sincerely I am wholly so. Adieu, write often, and come soon, for many wish you well, and all would be glad of your company.

Faulkner 1741

John Gay to Swift

Nov. 17. 1726.

About ten days ago a Book was publish'd here of the Travels of one Gulliver, which hath been the conversation of the whole town ever since: The whole impression sold in a week; and nothing is more diverting than to hear the different opinions people give of it, though all agree in liking it extreamly. 'Tis generally said that you are the Author, but I am told, the Bookseller declares he knows not from what hand it came. From the highest to the lowest it is universally read, from the Cabinet-council to the Nursery. The Politicians to a man agree, that it is free from particular reflections, but that the Satire on general societies of men is too severe. Not but we

[1] Mr. Pulteney.

[2] Hor. *Ep.* I. i. 14. Faulkner translates in a footnote: 'Sworn to no Party, to no Cause attacht.'

now and then meet with people of greater perspicuity, who are in search for particular applications in every leaf; and it is highly probable we shall have keys published to give light into Gulliver's design. Your Lord ——[1] is the person who least approves it, blaming it as a design of evil consequence to depreciate human nature, at which it cannot be wondered that he takes most offence, being himself the most accomplish'd of his species, and so losing more than any other of that praise which is due both to the dignity and virtue of a man. Your friend, my Lord Harcourt, commends it very much, though he thinks in some places the matter too far carried. The Duchess Dowager of Marlborough is in raptures at it; she says she can dream of nothing else since she read it; she declares, that she hath now found out, that her whole life hath been lost in caressing the worst part of mankind, and treating the best as her foes; and that if she knew Gulliver, tho' he had been the worst enemy she ever had, she would give up all her present acquaintance for his friendship. You may see by this, that you are not much injur'd by being suppos'd the Author of this piece. If you are, you have disoblig'd us, and two or three of your best friends, in not giving us the least hint of it while you were with us; and in particular Dr. Arbuthnot, who says it is ten thousand pitys he had not known it, he could have added such abundance of things upon every subject. Among Lady-critics, some have found out that Mr. Gulliver had a particular malice to maids of honour.[2] Those of them who frequent the Church, say, his design is impious, and that it is an insult on Providence, by depreciating the works of the Creator. Notwithstanding I am told the Princess hath read it with great pleasure. As to other Critics, they think the flying island[3] is the least entertaining; and so great an opinion the town have of the impossibility of Gulliver's writing at all below himself, that 'tis agreed that Part was not writ by the same Hand, tho' this hath its defenders too. It hath pass'd Lords and Commons, *nemine contradicente*; and the whole town, men, women, and children are quite full of it.

Perhaps I may all this time be talking to you of a Book you have never seen, and which hath not yet reach'd Ireland; if it hath not, I believe what we have said will be sufficient to recommend it to your reading, and that you order me to send it to you.

But it will be much better to come over your self, and read it here,

[1] Bolingbroke. [2] 'A Voyage to Brobdingnag', c. v.
[3] 'A Voyage to Laputa.'

where you will have the pleasure of variety of commentators, to explain the difficult passages to you.

We all rejoyce that you have fixt the precise time of your coming to be *cum hirundine prima*; which we modern naturalists pronounce, ought to be reckon'd, contrary to Pliny[1] in this northern latitude of fifty-two degrees, from the end of February, Styl·Greg.[2] at farthest. But to us your friends, the coming of such a black swallow as you, will make a summer in the worst of seasons. We are no less glad at your mention of Twickenham and Dawley; and in town you know you have a lodging at Court.

The Princess is cloath'd in Irish silk; pray give our service to the Weavers. We are strangely surpriz'd to hear that the Bells in Ireland ring without your money;[3] I hope you do not write the thing that is not.[4] We are afraid that B—[5] hath been guilty of that crime, that you (like a Houyhnhnm) have treated him as a Yahoo, and discarded him your service. I fear you do not understand these modish terms, which every creature now understands but your self.

You tell us your Wine is bad, and that the Clergy do not frequent your house, which we look upon to be tautology. The best advice we can give you is, to make them a present of your wine, and come away to better.

You fancy we envy you, but you are mistaken, we envy those you are with, for we cannot envy the man we love. Adieu.

4805[6]

Mrs. Howard to Swift

[17 November 1726]

I did not expect that the Sight of my ring wou'd produce the Effects it has. I was in such a hurry to shew Your Pl— to the P^ss^,

[1] *Nat. Hist.* x. 49.

[2] Gregorian Style.

[3] Sheridan, *Life*, pp. 260–1, gives a lengthy description of the public acclamation with which Swift was received upon his return to Dublin. Citizens in boats decorated with streamers put out to meet his ship; the bells were set ringing; and he was conducted to his house with shouts of 'Long live the Drapier'.

[4] 'A Voyage to the Houyhnhnms', c. iv.

[5] This cannot stand for Bolingbroke. Ball may be right in regarding B as a misprint for P, and the allusion to be to Swift's agent Proudfoot.

[6] There is also a draft of this letter in the British Museum, 22625, ff. 7–8. In Horace Walpole's original Book of Materials, which he started in 1759, now

that I cou'd not stay to put it into the Shape you desir'd. it pleas'd extremely, and I have orders to fitt it up according to the first design but as this is not proper for the Publick you are desir'd to send over for the same Pss use the hight of the Brobdingnag Dwarf[1] Multipli'd by 2.½. the Young Pss must be taken care off. theres must be in three shares.[2] for a short method you may draw a line of twenty foot, and upon that by two circles form an Equilateral Triangle; then measuring each side you will find the proper quantity and proper Division. if you want a more particular, or better rule; I refer you to the Academy of Lagado.[3] I am of opinion that many in this Kingdom will soon appear in your Pl—.[4] to this end, it will be highly Necessary that care be taken of disposing of the Purple, the Yellow, and the white silks.[5] and tho' the G—ns[6] are for the Pss the officers are very Vigilant, so take care they are not seiz'd. don't forget to be observant how you dispose the Colours. I shall take all particular precautions to have the money ready; and to return it the the way you Judge safest. I think it wou'd be worth Your reflecting in what manner the Chequer might be best managed.

The Pss will take care that you shall have pumps sufficient to serve you till your return to England; but thinks you can not in Comon Deciency appear in heels; and therefore advises your Keeping Close till they Arrive.[7] here is several Lilliputian Mathematicians; so that the Length of your head, or of your foot is a sufficient Measure; send it by the first oppertunity. don't forget our good friends the five Hundred Weavers. You may omitt the Gold thread. Many disputes has arrise here, whether the Big-Endian's ever differ'd in opinion about the braking of Eggs,[8] when they were either to be butter'd, or Poach'd? or whither this part of Cooking was ever known in Lilliput?

in the possession of Mr. W. S. Lewis, Farmington, Connecticut, there is a note stating that this letter was dictated by Arbuthnot.

[1] 'A Voyage to Brobdingag', c. iii. The dwarf's stature is given as 'not full thirty Foot high'. The quantity of material desired would therefore be twenty-five yards.

[2] Six and two-thirds yards each.

[3] 'A Voyage to Laputa', c. v.

[4] i.e. plaid.

[5] 'A Voyage to Lilliput', c. iii. These colours may have been thus stated by Motte in the first edition of *Gulliver* for fear of giving offence. In his copy of the work Ford corrected them to 'Blue', 'Red', 'Green', the colours of the orders of the Garter, Bath, and Thistle respectively. Faulkner, 1735, followed the alteration. See also Swift's 'Verses on the Revival of the Order of the Bath', *Poems*, ii. 388.

[6] Gowns.

[7] 'A Voyage to Lilliput', c. iv.

[8] Ibid., c. iv.

I cannot conclude without telling you that our Island is in great Joy; one of our Yahoo's having been diliver'd of a Creature, half Ram, and half Yahoo; and an other has brought forth four perfect Black Rabits.[1] may we not hope? and with some probabillity expect that in time our female Yahoo's will produce a race of Honyhnhnms. I am Sir Your most | humble Ser^{t} | Sieve Yahoo[2]

Endorsed by Swift: Mrs Howard | Nov —1726 | answered on 17th *and*
Mrs Howard | Nov. 1726

H.M.C. Report V, App. p. 296

Swift to Mrs. Greenfield

Dublin, Nov. 23, 1726.

Madam,[3]

I have had a letter by me above six weeks expecting every day to have sent it with the picture by a gentlewoman who was to go for England, but hath now put off her journey. This was the reason of your not hearing from me sooner. I have at last heard of a Chester owner, one Mr. Whittle, who hath undertaken to deliver it to you. It is the best of the several cuts that have been drawn for me, and made up as well as our workmen here can do it. I hope Mr. Greenvil and you are in health, as well as your girl, if you have not spoiled her with fondness. When you see Mrs. Kenna, pray give her my thanks for the friendly care she took of my goods which came all safe.

Address: To Mrs. Greenvil at her house in Abbey Court, Chester.

[1] An allusion to the imposture practised by Mary Tofts of Godalming.

[2] Towards the end of chapter vi of 'A Voyage to Laputa' Swift gives a long list of words conveying hidden meanings. Among them 'sieve' indicated a court lady.

[3] See H.M.C. Report V, Appendix, p. 296. The original manuscript, which was then in the possession of Lord Hatherton cannot now be traced, as I am informed by Lord Hatherton, 12 Aug. 1952. As appears by the registers of St. Oswald's, Chester, the name should be Greenfield. On 23 Sept. 1673 Abygell, daughter of Isaac Swift, merchant and churchwarden, was baptized. On 16 Dec. 1714 John Greenfield of Preston, Lancashire, gentleman, married Abigail Swift of the Abbey Court, spinster. Whether this Mrs. Greenfield, or the Cozn Abigail, mentioned by Swift in the *Journal to Stella*, 2 Sept. 1710, were in any way related to him is very questionable. Information kindly supplied by W. H. Walpley, Cooleen, co. Antrim. See further P. D. Mundy in *Notes and Queries*, cxcix (1954), 248–9, and W. H. Walpley, pp. 339–40.

B.M. Add. MS. 22625

Swift to Mrs. Howard

[Dublin Novr 27th 1726]

Madam.

When I received your Letter[1] I thought it the most unaccountable one I ever saw in my Life, and was not able to comprehend three words of it together. The Perverseness of your Lines astonished me, which tended downwards to the right on one Page, and upward in the two others. This I thought impossible to be done by any Person who did not squint with both Eyes; an Infirmity I never observed in you. However, one thing I was pleased with, that after you had writ me *down*, you repented, and writ me *up*. But I continued four days at a loss for your meaning, till a Bookseller sent me the Travells of one Cap^{tn} Gulliver, who proved a very good Explainer, although at the same time, I thought it hard to be forced to read a Book of seven hundred Pages in order to understand a Letter of fifty lines; especially since those of our Faculty are already but too much pestered with Commentators. The Stuffs you require are making, because the Weaver piques himself upon having them in perfection, but he has read Gulliver's Book, and has no Conception of what you mean by returning Money, for he is become a Proselyte of the Houyhnhnms, whose great Principle (if I rightly remember) is Benevolence. And as to my self, I am rightly affronted with such a base Proposall, that I am determined to complain of you to her Royal Highness, that you are a mercenary Yahoo fond of shining Pebbles. What have I to do with you or your Court further than to show the Esteem I have for your Person, because you happen to deserve it, and my Gratitude to Her Royall Highness, who was pleased, a little to distinguish me; which, by the way is the greatest Compliment I ever made, and may probably be the last. For I am not such a prostitute Flatterer as Gulliver; whose chief Study is to extenuate the Vices, and magnify the Virtues, of Mankind, and perpetually dins our Ears with the Praises of his Country, in the midst of Corruptions, and for that Reason alone, hath found so many readers; and probably will have a Pension, which, I suppose, was his chief design in writing: As for his Compliments to the Ladyes, I can easily forgive him as a naturall Effect of that Devotion which our Sex always ought to pay to Yours.

[1] That of 17 Nov.

You need not be in pain about the Officers searching or seising the Plads, for the Silk hath already payd duty in England, and there is no Law against exporting Silk Manufacture from hence.

I am sure the Princess and you have got the length of my foot, and S[r] R[t] Walpole says he has the length of my Head, so that you need give me the Trouble of sending you either. I shall onely tell you in generall, that I never had a long Head, and for that Reason few People have thought it worth while to get the length of my foot. I cannot answer your Queryes about Eggs buttered or poached; but I possess one Talent which admirably qualifyes me for roasting them. For, as the world with respect to Eggs is divided into Pelters and Roasters, it is my Unhappyness to be one of the latter, and consequently to be persecuted by the former. I have been five days turning over old Books to discover the meaning of those monstrous Births you mention. That of the four black Rabbits seems to threaten some dark Court Intrigue, and perhaps some change in the Administration. for the Rabbit is an undermining animal that loves to work in the dark. The Blackness denotes the Bishops, whereof some of the last you have made, are persons of such dangerous Parts and profound Abilityes. But Rabbits being cloathed in Furs may perhaps glance at the Judges. However, the Ram (by which is meant the Ministry) butting with his two horns, one against the Church, and the other against the Law, shall obtain the Victory: And whereas the Birth was a Conjunction of Ram and Yahoo, this is easily explained by the Story of Chiron Governor, or (which is the same thing) chief Ministr to Achilles and was half Man and half Brute, which, as Machiavel observes, all good Governors of Princes ought to be. But I am at the end of my Line and my Linen this is without a Cover to save money, and plain Paper because the gilt is so thin it will discover Secrets betwixt us. In a little room for words I assure you of my being with the truest respect Madam Your most obed[n] humble Serv[t]

Address: To the Honorable M[rs] | Howard at Her Royal | Highnese's House in Leicester-fields | London

Stamp: DUBLIN

Faulkner 1741

Swift to Alexander Pope

Dublin, Nov. [27] 1726[1]

I am just come from answering a Letter of Mrs. Howard's[2] writ in such mystical terms, that I should never have found out the meaning, if a Book had not been sent me called *Gulliver's Travellers*, of which you say so much in yours.[3] I read the Book over, and in the second volume observe several passages which appear to be patched and altered, and the style of a different sort (unless I am much mistaken)[3] Dr. Arbuthnot likes the Projectors least, others you tell me, the Flying island; some think it wrong to be so hard upon whole Bodies or Corporations, yet the general opinion is, that reflections on particular persons are most to be blamed: so that in these cases, I think the best method is to let censure and opinion take their course. A Bishop here said, that Book was full of improbable lies, and for his part, he hardly believed a word of it; and so much for Gulliver.

Going to England is a very good thing, if it were not attended with an ugly circumstance of returning to Ireland: It is a shame you do not persuade your Ministers to keep me on that side, if it were but by a court expedient of keeping me in prison for a plotter; but at the same time I must tell you, that such journeys very much shorten my life, for a month here is longer than six at Twickenham.

How comes friend Gay to be so tedious? another man can publish fifty-thousand Lies sooner than he can publish fifty Fables.[4]

I am just going to perform a very good office, it is to assist with the Archbishop,[5] in degrading a Parson who couples all our beggars, by which I shall make one happy man: and decide the great question of an indeleble character in favour of the principles in fashion; and this I hope you will represent to the Ministry in my favour, as a point of merit; so farewel till I return.

I am come back, and have deprived the parson, who by a law here

[1] 'Nov. 17', the date printed in early editions, must be wrong, for the first sentence refers to Swift's answer to Mrs. Howard's 'Sieve Yahoo' letter of 27 Nov. He was writing to Pope on the same day.

[2] That of 17 Nov.

[3] Here Swift refers to alterations in the text of *Gulliver* made by Motte for fear of venturing within the power of the law.

[4] Gay's *Fables* did not appear till the following March.

[5] i.e. King.

is to be hanged the next couple he marries: he declared to us that he resolved to be hanged, only he desired that when he was to go to the Gallows, the Archbishop would take off his Excommunication. Is not he a good Catholick? and yet he is but a Scotch-man. This is the only Irish event I ever troubled you with, and I think it deserves notice. Let me add, that if I were Gulliver's friend, I would desire all my acquaintance to give out that his copy was basely mangled, and abused, and added to, and blotted out by the printer; for so to me it seems, in the second volume particularly. | Adieu.

B.M. Add. MS. 22625, ff. 11–12

'*Lemuel Gulliver*' *to Mrs. Howard*

Newark[1] in Nottinghamshire. | Novr 28. 1726.

Madam

My correspondents have informed me that your Lady^p^ has done me the honor to answer severall objections that ignorance, malice, and party have made to my Travells, and bin so charitable as to justifie the fidelity and veracity of the Author. This Zeal you have shown for Truth calls for my particular thanks, and at the same time encourages me to beg you would continue your goodness to me by reconcileing me to the Maids of Honour whom they say I have most grievously offended.[2] I am so stupid as not to find out how I have disobliged them; Is there any harm in a young Ladys reading of romances? Or did I make use of an improper Engine to extinguish a fire that was kindled by a Maid of Honour?[2] And I will venture to affirm, that if ever the Young Ladies of your Court should meet with a man of as little consequence in this country, as I was in Brobdingnag, they would use him with as much contempt: But I submit my self and my cause to your better judgment, and beg leave to lay the crown of Llliput at your feet, as a small acknowledgment of your favours to my book & person[3] I found it in the corner of my wastcoat pockett into which I thrust most of the valuable furniture of the

[1] According to Richard Sympson the author of the *Travels* 'made a small Purchase of Land, with a convenient House, near Newark', to which he retired.

[2] 'A Voyage to Lilliput', c. v.

[3] Scott, *Memoirs*, 1814, p. 347, has a footnote: 'This toy is still possessed by Mrs. Howard's representatives.'

Royall apartment when the palace was on fire, and by mistake brought it with me into England, for I very honestly restored to their Majesties all their goods that I knew were in my possession; May all courtiers imitate me in that, and in my being | Madam | your admirer and obt | humble servant. | Lemuel Gulliver.

4805

The Earl of Peterborough to Swift

29 November 1726.

Sr

I was endeavouring to give an answer to yours in a new dialect which most of us are very fond of, I depended much upon a Lady who had a good Ear and a pliant Tongue, in hopes she might have taught me to draw sounds out of consonants,[1] but she being a profest friend to the Italian speech & vowels, would give me no assistance, & so I am forced to write to you in the yahoo language.

The new one in fashion is much studied, and great pains taken about the pronunciation, Every body (since a new Turn) approves of it, but the women seem most satisfied, who declare for a few words, & Horse performance, itt suffices to lett you know, that there is a Neighing Duetto appointed for the next Opera.

Strange distempers rage in the nation which your friend the Doctor[2] takes no care of, in some, the imagination is struck with the apprehension of swelling to a Giant, or dwindling to a pigmee, others expect an Oration equall to any of Cicero's from an Eloquent Barb, and some take the braying of an Asse for the Emperor's speech in favour of the Viena Alliance, the knoledge of the antient world is of no use, men have lost their Tittles, continents, & islands have gott new names just upon the appearance of a certain Book in the world, women bring forth Rabbetts,[3] and Every man, whose wife has conceived, expects an Heir with Four leggs, Itt was concluded not long agoe that such confusion could be only brought about by the black Art, and by the spells of a notorious scribbling Magitian, who was generally suspected, and was to be recommended to the mercy of the Inquisition.

[1] Ball suggests a possible reference to Anastasia Robinson whom Peterborough had married secretly four years earlier. This seems very probable.

[2] i.e. Arbuthnot.

[3] An allusion to Mary Tofts.

Inditements were upon the anvill, a charge of Sorcery preparing & Merlin's friends were afraid that the Exasperated Pettyfoggers would persuade the jury to bring in Billa vera.

For they pretended to bring in Certain proofs of his appearing in severall shapes, att one time a Drappier, att another a Wapping Surgeon, sometimes a Nardac,[1] sometimes a Reverend Divine. Nay more that he could raise the Dead, that he had brought Philosophers, Heroes, & poets in the same Caravan from the other World, & after a few questions, had sent them all to play at Quadrille in a flying Island of his own.

This was the scene not many days agoe, and burning was too good for the Wizard. But what mutations amongst the Lillyputians! the greatest Lady in the nation resolves to send a pair of shoes without heels to Capt Gulliver, she takes vi et Armis the plad from the Lady it was sent too, which is soon to appear upon her Royall person, and Now who but Capt Gulliver?

The Capt indeed has nothing more to doe but to chalk his pumps, learn to daunce upon the Rope, and I may yett live to see him a a bishop, verily, verily I believe he never was in such imminent danger of preferment. | S^r | your affectionate Tar[2]

Nov: the 29th 1726

Endorsed by Swift: E. of Peterborw | Novr 29th 1726

Faulkner 1741

Swift to Alexander Pope

December 5, 1726.

I believe the hurt in your hand affects me more than it does your self, and with reason, because I may probably be a greater loser by it. What have accidents to do with those who are neither jockeys, nor fox-hunters, nor bullies, nor drunkards? and yet a rascally Groom

[1] The highest rank in Lilliput.

[2] See *Poems*, ii. 398:

> 'Shines in all Climates like a Star;
> In Senates bold, and fierce in War,
> A Land-Commander, and a Tarr.'

shall gallop a foundred horse ten miles upon a causeway, and get home safe.

I am very much pleas'd that you approve what was sent,[1] because I remember to have heard a great man say, that nothing required more judgment than making a present; which when it is done to those of high rank, ought to be of something that is not readily got for money. You oblige me, and at the same time do me justice in what you observe as to Mr. P.[2] Besides it is too late in life for me to act otherwise, and therefore I follow a very easy road to virtue, and purchase it cheap. If you will give me leave to join us, is not your life and mine a state of power, and dependance a state of slavery? We care not three pence whether a Prince or Minister will see us or no: We are not afraid of having ill offices done us, nor are at the trouble of guarding our words for fear of giving offence. I do agree that riches are Liberty, but then we are put into the balance how long our apprenticeship is to last in acquiring them.

Since you have receiv'd the verses,[3] I most earnestly intreat you to burn those which you do not approve, and in those few where you may not dislike some parts, blot out the rest, and sometimes (altho' it may be against the laziness of your nature) be so kind to make a few corrections, if the matter will bear them. I have some few of those things I call thoughts moral and diverting; if you please I will send the best I can pick from them, to add to the new volume.[4] I have reason to chuse the method you mention of mixing the several verses, and I hope thereby among the bad Critics to be entitled to more merit than is my due.

This moment I am so happy to have a letter from my Lord Peterborow, for which I entreat you will present him with my humble respects and thanks, although he all-to-be Gullivers me by very strong insinuations. Although you dispise Riddles, I am strongly tempted to send a parcel to be printed by themselves, and make a nine-penny jobb for the Bookseller. There are some of my own, wherein I exceed mankind, *Mira Poemata!* the most solemn that were ever seen; and some writ by others, admirable indeed, but far

[1] The Irish poplin.

[2] Mr. Pulteney.

[3] For the Pope–Swift *Miscellanies*.

[4] A gathering of 'Thoughts on Various Subjects' appears at the end of vol. i of the *Miscellanies*, 1727, and another gathering at the end of vol. ii. According to Spence, *Anecdotes*, 1820, p. 158, Pope said: 'Those at the end of one volume are mine; and those in the other Dr. Swift's.' The 'Thoughts' in the first volume are Swift's.

inferior to mine, but I will not praise my self.[1] You approve that writer who laughs and makes others laugh; but why should I who hate the world, or you who do not love it, make it so happy? therefore I resolve from henceforth to handle only serious subjects, *nisi quid tu docte Trebati, Dissentis.*[2] | Yours, &c.

Swift to ———

8 December 1726.

On the 10th of June 1909 an autograph letter of Swift's to a person unknown was sold by Sotheby. The letter was bought by Messrs. B. F. Stevens, 79 Duke Street, Grosvenor Square, London, W. 1. The firm can trace the letter no farther. Ball dates the letter 28 Dec.; but Sotheby's catalogue assigns it to 8 Dec. 1726.

Forster 561

Charles Ford to Benjamin Motte

Dublin Jan. 3. 1726–7

Sir[3]

I bought here Captn Gulliver's Travels, publish'd by you, both because I heard much Talk of it, and because of a Rumor, that a Friend of mine is suspected to be the Author. I have read this Book twice over with great care, as well as great Pleasure, & am sorry to tell you that it abounds with many gross Errors of the Press, whereof I have sent you as many as I could find, with the Corrections of them as the plain Sense must lead, and I hope you will insert them when you make another Edition.

[1] See *Poems*, iii. 914–39. The riddles were not included in the miscellany volumes.

[2] Hor. *Sermones*, II. i. 79. Translated by Faulkner in a footnote: 'Unless you, and my learned Friend, differ in Opinion.'

[3] The original of this letter written by Charles Ford is in the Forster collection, 561, Victoria and Albert Museum, South Kensington. It was probably composed by Swift himself, who, immediately upon the publication of *Gulliver's Travels*, expressed strong dissatisfaction with editorial liberties taken by the printer. A list of corrections, for which see *Gulliver's Travels*, ed. H. Williams, Appendix I, follows the letter. The letter and list occupy the rectos of two folio leaves.

I have an entire Respect for the Memory of the late Queen, and am always pleas'd when others shew the same; but that Paragraph relating to her looks so very much beside the Purpose that I cannot think it to have been written by the same Author. I wish you & your Friends would consider it, and let it be left out in the next Edition. For it is plainly false in Fact, since all the World knows that the Queen during her whole Reign governed by one first Minister or other. Neither do I find the Author to be any where given to Flattery, or indeed very favourable to any Prince or Minister whatsoever.

These things I let you know out of perfect good will to the Author and yourself, and I hope you will understand me, who am | Sr your affectionate Friend & Servant | Cha: Ford.

Address: To | Mr Benjamin Motte, Bookseller | near the Temple in | London

B.M. Add. MS. 22625, ff. 13–14

Swift to Mrs. Howard

1 February 1726–7.

Madam.

I am so very nice, and my Workmen so fearful, that there is yet but one piece finished of the two, which you commanded me to send to her Royall Highness. The other was done: but the Undertaker confessing it was not to the utmost perfection, hath obtained my leave for a second attempt, in which he promiseth to do wonders; and tells me it will be ready in another Fortnight; although perhaps the humour be gone off both with the Princess and you; for such were Courts when I knew them. . I desire you will order her Royal Highness to go to Richmond as soon as she can this Summer, because she will have the Pleasure of my Neighburhood,[1] for I hope to be in London about the middle of March; and I do not love you

[1] See 'A Pastoral Dialogue', *Poems*, ii. 407–11, in which Swift represents Richmond Lodge, used as a summer residence by the Prince and Princess of Wales, and Marble Hill, occupied by Mrs. Howard, meeting 'to talk of News'—

> 'For by old Proverbs it appears,
> That Walls have Tongues, and Hedges, Ears.'

When the Prince and Princess were in residence Swift was wont, he tells us, 'To spunge a Breakfast once a Week'.

much when you are there. And I expect to find you are not altered by flattery or ill company. . I am glad to tell you now that I honor you with my Esteem, because when the Princess grows a crowned head, you shall have no more such compliments; and it is a hundred to one whether you will deserve them. Besides, it so happens that the King is too tough a person for me to value any reversion of favour after him, and so you are safe; I do not approve of your advice to bring over Pumps for my self, but will rather provide another Shoe for his Royal Highness against there shall be occasion.

I will tell you an odd Accident, that this night, while I was caressing one of my Houyhnhnms, he bit my little finger so cruelly, that I am hardly able to write, and I impute the Cause to some foreknowledge in him, that I was going to write to a Sieve Yahoo (for so you are pleased to call yourself) Pray tell Sr Robert Walpole, that if he does not use me better next Summer than he did last, I will study revenge, and it shall be *vengeance ecclesistique* . . I hope you will get your House and wine ready,[1] to which Mr Gay and I are to have free access when you are safe at Court; for as to Mr Pope, he is not worth mentioning on such Occasions. I am sorry I have no Complaints to make of her Royal Highness. therefore I think I may let you tell her that every grain of Virtue and good Sense in one of her rank considering their bad Education among Flatterers and Adorers, is worth a dozen in any inferior Person, now if what the world says be true, that she excells all other Ladyes at least a dozen times, then, multiply one dozen by the other you will find the number to be 144. If anyone can say a civiler thing let them.[2] For I think it too much from me.

I have some title to be angry with you for not commanding those who write to me to mention your remembrance, can there be any thing baser[3] than to make me the first Advance and then be inconstant? It is very hard that I must cross the Sea and ride 200 miles to reproach you in person, when at the same time I feel my self with the most entire Respect | Madam | Your most obedient and most | obliged humble ser^t | Jonath Swift

[1] The reference is to Marble Hill.

[2] them] him *Ball.*

[3] baser] more base *Ball.*

4805

Viscountess Bolingbroke to Swift

de dawley ce premier | fevrier [1726–7][1]

on m'a dit Monsieur que vous vous plaignés de n'avoir point recû de mes lettres, vous avés tort, je vous traitte come les divinités qui tiennent conte aux hom̃es de leurs intentions, il y a dix ans que j'ay celle de vous écrire; avant que davoir lhonneur de vous connoitre lidée que je me faisois de votre gravité, me retenoit depuis que jay eu celuy de voir votre Reverence je ne me suis pas trouvée assés dimagination pour l'hazarder. un certain Mr de Gulivers avoit un peu remis en mouvement cette pauvre imagination cy éteinte par l'air de Londres, et par des conversations dont je n'entend que le bruit, je voulu me saisir de ce moment pour vous ecrire mais je tombay malade et je lay toujours esté depuis trois mois. je profite donc monsieur du premier retour de ma santé de vous remercier de vos reproches dont je suis tres flattée et pour vous dire un mot de mon amy Mr Guliver, j'apprend avec une grande satisfaction, quil vient d'etre traduit en françois et come mon sejour en angleterre a beaucoup redoublé mon amitié pour mon pays et pour mes compatriottes je suis ravie quils puissent participer au plaisir, que ma fait ce bon monsieur, et profiter de ses decouvertes, je ne desespere meme pas que 12 vaisseaux que la france vient darmer ne puissent etre destinés a une embassade chés Mrs les Ouynhms[2] en ce cas je vous proposeray que nous fassions ce voyage en attendant je scay bon gré a un ouvrier de votre nation, qui pour instruire les dames les quelles comme vous scavés Monsieur font icy un grand usage de leurs éventails en a fait faire ou touttes les avantures de notre veridique voyageur sont depeintes, vous juges bien quelle part il va avoir dans leur conversation, cela fera a la verité beaucoup de tort a la pluye et au beautems qui en remplisoient une partie, et en mon particulier je serai privée des very cold et very warm qui sont les seuls mots que jentende, je conte de vous envoyer de ces

[1] Lady Bolingbroke's orthography has been followed as nearly as is possible in print.

[2] At this time a general war seemed inevitable. But the Emperor, deserted by Russia and other hoped-for allies, accepted the need for prudence. On 31 May the Austrian ambassador signed at Paris the preliminaries of peace with England, France, and Holland. The preparations of France were against the Emperor and his allies.

éventails par un de vos amis. vous vous en ferés un merite avec les dames dirlande sy tant est que vous en ayés besoin ce que je ne crois pas du moins si elles pensent comme les francoises le seigneur de dawley Mr Pope et moy sommes icy occupés a boire manger dormir ou ne rien faire priant dieu quainsy soit de vous, revenés ce printems nous revoir monsieur jattend votre retour avec impatience pour tuer le bœuf le plus pesant et le cochon le plus gras qui soit dans ma ferme l'un et l'autre seront servis en entier sur la table de votre Reverence crainte qu'elle n'accuse mon cuisinier deguisement vous brillieres parmy nous du moins autant que parmy vos chanoines et nous ne serons pas moins empressés a vous plaire. Je le disputeray a tout autre etant plus que personne du monde votre tres humble et tres obeissante servante.

Endorsed by Swift: L^{dy} Bolingbroke | Feb 1st 1726–7 *and* Lady Bolingbroke | Feb 1st | 1726–7

Forster copy

Swift to Knightley Chetwode

Dublin, February 14, 1726–7

Sir,

I should have sooner answered your letter[1] if my time had not been taken up with many impertinences, in spite of my monkish way of living, and particularly of late, with my preparing a hundred little affairs which must be dispatched before I go for England, as I intend to do in a very short time, and I believe it will be the last journey I shall ever take thither, but the omission of some matters last summer, by the absence of certain people, hath made it necessary.[2] As to Captain Gulliver, I find his book is very much censured in this kingdom which abounds in excellent judges; but in England I hear it hath made a bookseller almost rich enough to be an alderman. In my judgement I should think it hath been mangled in the press, for in some parts it doth not seem of a piece,[3] but I shall hear more when I am in England.

[1] No doubt a reply to Swift's letter of 24 Oct.

[2] Swift alludes probably to his failure to make any progress towards a memoir of the first Earl of Oxford owing to the absence of the second Earl of Oxford from London during the previous summer.—Ball.

[3] Swift refers to the liberties Motte had taken with the text of *Gulliver's Travels.*

I am glad you are got into a new part of your improvements, and I know nothing I should more desire than some spot upon which I could spend the rest of my life in improving. But I shall live and die friendless, and a sorry Dublin inhabitant, and yet I have spirit still left to keep a clatter about my little garden,[1] where I pretend to have the finest paradise stocks of their age in Ireland. But I grow so old, that I despond, and think nothing worth my care except ease and indolence, and walking to keep my health.

I can send you no news, because I never read any, nor suffer any person to inform me. I am sure whatever it is it cannot please me. The Archbishop of Dublin is just recovered after having been despaired of, and by that means hath disappointed some hopers.[2]

I am, Sir |
Your &c.

Address: To Knightley Chetwode, Esq. | at his house at Woodbrooke, near Mountmellick.

4805

Viscount Bolingbroke to Swift

Feb. the 17th 172$\frac{6}{7}$

This opportunity of writing to you I cannot neglect, tho I shall have less to say to you than I should have by another conveyance, Mr Stopford[3] being fully inform'd of all that passes in this boisterous climate of ours, & carrying with him a cargo of our weekly productions.[4] you will find anger on one side, & Rage on the other. Satire on one side, & defamation on the other. Ah! ou est Grillon?[5] you suffer much where you are, as you tell me in an old letter of yours

[1] Naboth's Vineyard.

[2] King had been seriously unwell. Boulter was disturbed by fears that in the event of his death a successor might be appointed who did not share his views.

[3] At this time Stopford was in London on his way back from the Continent to Ireland.

[4] The cargo presumably consisted, at least for the most part, of early numbers of *The Craftsman*, which was edited by Nicholas Amherst and directed by Pulteney against Walpole, who soon enlisted contributions from Bolingbroke. For the first six months it appeared twice a week. From 13 May 1727 onward the title became *The Country Journal; Or, The Craftsman.*

[5] An inaccurate recollection of Gildrig, the name applied by the King of Brobdingnag to Gulliver.

which I have before me, but you suffer with the hopes of passing next summer between Dawley and Twickenham, & these hopes, you flatter us enough to intimate, support y^r spirits.[1] Remember this solemn Renewal of y^r Engagements, Remember that tho' you are a Dean, you are not great enough to despise the reproach of breaking y^r word. y^r deafness must not be a hackney excuse to you as it was to Oxford.[2] what matter if you are deaf, what matter if you cannot hear what we say? you are not dumb, & we shall hear you, and that is enough. my wife writes to you her Self,[3] and sends you some fans just arriv'd from Lilliput, which you will dispose of to the present Stella, whoever she be. Adieu Dear friend, I cannot, in conscience, keep you any longer from enjoying Mr Stopfords conversation. I am hurrying myself here[4] that I may get a day or two for Dawley, where I hope that you will find me establish'd att y^r Return. there I propose to finish my Days in ease with out sloth, & believe I shall seldom visit London, unless it be to divert myself now [and] then with annoying fools and knaves for a month or two. once more Adieu no man loves [you] better than | yr faithful | B——

Endorsed by Swift: Lord Bolingbroke | Feb. 17th 1726–7

Faulkner 1741

Alexander Pope to Swift

17(?) February 1726–7[5]

Mr. Stopford will be the bearer of this letter, for whose acquaintance I am, among many others favours, obliged to you; and I think

[1] Hawkesworth, followed by later editors, reads, 'and these hopes, you flatter us, are enough to support your spirits'.

[2] Swift, writing to the second Earl of Oxford, 27 Nov. 1724, refers to 'your Lordship's father' as suffering from attacks of deafness.

[3] 1 Feb. 1726–7.

[4] In London.

[5] The 1740 volume, Faulkner 1741, and later editions dated this letter 8 Mar. Ball, iii. 380, was the first to draw attention to the manifest error, suggesting 18 Feb., for Gay's letter of that date (see next letter) accompanied that of Pope. But Pope's letter was presumably of an even earlier date, for it was consigned to Stopford, as bearer, in a letter of 17 Feb. See Sherburn, ii. 426. It may be that Pope did not date the letter, and that Swift endorsed it with the date of receipt, which was eventually printed as the date of writing.

the acquaintance of so valuable, ingenious, and unaffected a man, to be none of the least obligations.

Our Miscellany is now quite printed. I am prodigiously pleas'd with this joint-volume, in which methinks we look like friends, side by side, serious and merry by turns, conversing interchangeably, and walking down hand in hand to posterity; not in the stiff forms of learned Authors, flattering each other, and setting the rest of mankind at nought: but in a free, un-important, natural, easy manner; diverting others just as we diverted our selves. The third volume[1] consists of Verses, but I would chuse to print none but such as have some peculiarity, and may be distinguish'd for ours, from other writers. There 's no end of making Books, Solomon said, and above all of making Miscellanies, which all men can make. For unless there be a character in every piece, like the mark of the Elect, I should not care to be one of the Twelve-thousand signed.

You received, I hope, some commendatory verses from a Horse and a Lilliputian, to Gulliver; and an heroic Epistle of Mrs. Gulliver.[2] The Bookseller would fain have printed 'em before the second Edition of the Book, but I would not permit it without your approbation; nor do I much like them. You see how much like a Poet I write, and yet if you were with us, you'd be deep in Politicks. People are very warm, and very angry, very little to the purpose, but therefore the more warm and the more angry: *Non nostrum est, Tantas componere lites.*[3] I stay at Twitnam, without so much as reading news-papers, votes, or any other paltry pamphlets: Mr. Stopford will carry you a whole parcel of them, which are sent for your diversion, but not Imitation. For my own part, methinks, I am at Glubdubdrib[4] with none but Ancients and Spirits about me.

I am rather better than I use to be at this season, but my hand (tho' as you see, it has not lost its cunning) is frequently in very aukward sensations, rather than pain. But to convince you it is pretty well, it has done some mischief already, and just been strong enough to cut the other hand, while it was aiming to prune a fruit-tree.

[1] Volumes i and ii were published in June 1727; the next volume, entitled *The Last*, not till 7 Mar. 1727–8.

[2] It is probable that Pope was the author of all these pieces. For a lengthy discussion of the whole problem see Ault, *New Light on Pope*, pp. 231–42; and *Minor Poems*, pp. 266–81.

[3] Cf. Virgil, *Ecl.* iii. 108. 'It is not mine such Factions to compose'—Faulkner's footnote.

[4] The Island of Sorcerers—'A Voyage to Laputa', c. vii.

Lady Bolingbroke has writ you a long, lively, letter, which will attend this; She has very bad health, he very good. Lord Peterborow has writ twice to you; we fancy some letters have been intercepted, or lost by accident. About ten thousand things I want to tell you: I wish you were as impatient to hear them, for if so, you would, you must come early this spring. Adieu. Let me have a line from you. I am vext at losing Mr. Stopford as soon as I knew him: but I thank God I have known him no longer. If every man one begins to value must settle in Ireland, pray make me know no more of 'em, and I forgive you this one.

4805

John Gay to Swift

[18 February 1726–7]

Dear Sir

I believe tis now my turn to write to you, though Mr Pope hath taken all I have to say & put it in a long Letter, which is sent too by Mr Stopfort, but however I could not omit this occasion of thanking you for his acquaintance; I don't know whether I ought to thank you or no, considering I have lost him so soon; though he hath given me some hopes of seeing him again in the Summer. He will give you an account of our negotiations together, and I may now glory in my success, since I could contribute to his. We din'd together to day at the Doctor's,[1] who with me was in high delight upon an information Mr Stopfort gave us, that we are like to see you soon. My fables are printed, but I cannot get my plates finish'd, which hinders the publication. I expect nothing, & am like to get nothing. tis needless to write for Mr Stopfort can acquaint you of my Affairs more fully than I can in a letter. Mrs Howard desires me to make her Compliments, she hath been in an ill state (as to her health) all this winter, but I hope is somewhat better. I have been very much out of order myself for the most part of the winter, upon my being let blood last week, my Cough & my head ach are better. Mrs Blount always asks after you. I refus'd supping at Burlington house to night in regard to my health, & this morning I walk'd two hours in the Park. Bow'rey[2] told me this morning that Mr Pope had

[1] Arbuthnot's. [2] Pope's waterman.

a Cold, but that Mrs Pope is pretty well. The contempt of the world grows upon me, and I now begin to be richer and richer, for I find I could every morning I wake be content with less than I aim'd at the day before. I fancy in time, I shall bring my self into that state No man ever knew before me, in thinking I have enough. I really am afraid to be content with so little, lest my good friends should censure me for indolence, and the want of laudable ambition, so that it will be absolutely necessary for me to improve my fortune to content them. How solicitous is mankind to please others! Pray give my sincere service to Mr Ford. Dear S^r^ | Y^rs^ most affectionately; | JG.

Whitehall. Feb. 18th 172$\frac{6}{7}$.

Address: To | Dr Swift | Dean of St Patrick's. | Dublin.

Endorsed by Swift: Mr Gay. Rx Mar. 8. 1726–7 *and* Mr Gay | Feb. 18—1726–7.

Deane Swift 1768

'*The Prince of Lilliput*' *to* '*Stella*'

[11 March 1726–7.]

† * * ‡ *[1]

In *European* characters and *English* thus;

The high and mighty prince EGROEGO[2] born to the most puissant empire of the *East*,

Unto STELLA, the most resplendent glory of the *Western* hemisphere, sendeth health and happiness.

BRIGHTEST PRINCESS,

That invincible heroe, the MAN MOUNTAIN, fortunately arriving at our coasts some years ago, delivered us from ruin by conquering the fleets and armies of our enemies, and gave us hopes of a durable peace and happiness. But now the martial people of *Blefuscu*, encouraged from his absence, have renewed the war,[3] to revenge upon us the loss and disgrace they suffered by our valiant champion.

The fame of your superexcellent person and virtue, and the huge esteem which that great general has for you, urged us in this our second distress to sue for your favour. In order to which we have sent our able and trusty Nardac KOORBNILOB,[4] requesting, That if

[1] Here we have a parcel of characters formed at random, by way of the address in the *Lilliputian* tongue.—Deane Swift.

[2] i.e. O'George.

[3] In February Spain had begun to besiege Gibraltar.

[4] Bolingbroke.

our general does yet tread upon the terrestrial globe, you, in compassion for us, would prevail upon him to take another voyage for our deliverance.

And, lest any apprehensions of famine amongst us, should render Nardac MOUNTAIN averse to the undertaking, we signify to you, that we have stored our folds, our coops, our granaries and cellars with plenty of provision for a long supply of the wastes to be made by his capacious stomach.

And furthermore, because as we hear you are not so well as we could wish, we beg you would compleat our happiness by venturing your most valuable person along with him into our country; where, by the salubrity of our finer air and diet, you will soon recover your health and stomach.

In full assurance of your complying goodness, we have sent you some provision for your voyage, and we shall with impatience wait for your safe arrival in our kingdom. Most illustrious lady, farewel. | Prince EGROEGO.

Dated the 11th day of the 6th Moon, in the
2001 year of the *Lilliputian* aera.[1]

Alfred Morrison Catalogue

Swift to Thomas Tickell

7 April 1727.

Sir[2]

I humbly desire the Favor of you to order one of your Clerks to prepare a License for me to go to England for 6 Months. I wish it might be finished tomorrow or at least the order got, after which I

[1] In affixing a date to this letter the figures in the year have been taken to denote half, and to be intended to convey that there were only six months in the Lilliputian year.—Ball. Earlier editors date by the year, '1727', only. Scott observes: 'This seems to be an attempt at humour, compounded, probably, by the Princess of Wales, Mrs. Howard, or both, in the name of the prince, afterwards George II.'

[2] This letter was formerly in the possession of Mr. Alfred Morrison. A facsimile appears in the catalogue of his collection of manuscript letters. It passed into the possession of Mr. G. W. Panter, of Foxrock, co. Dublin, and was, on his death, sold at Sotheby's (lot 56), 15 July 1929. A copy of the letter is to be found in Tickell's hand in his Letter Book, No. 2. See *Thomas Tickell*, R. E. Tickell, pp. 128–9.

find I may set out legally. I am told the Vessel I go in will set out tomorrow or on Sunday morning.[1] I would desire that instead of England it might be expressed Partis transmarinis because it is probable my Health may force me to Aix-la Chapelle. I suppose the Bishop of Ferns's Licence, when he went to France ran in some such Style.[2]

I have been so embroyled in my private Affairs by the Knavery of Agents that I have not had Time to wait on you. I am with true respect | Sr Your most obe^t^ humble Ser^t^ | J. Swift

Deanry House | Apr. 7. 1727

Duncombe 1772

Swift to the Rev. Thomas Wallis

Dublin, *April* 8, 1727.

Sir,

I am just going for England, and must desire you to be my proxy at the bishop's visitation.[3] I find there is likewise a triennial visitation,[4] and think the enclosed may serve for both, with your wise management. The ladies are with me, being now come to live at the deanry for this summer; you have their service, and so has Mrs. Wallis, as well as mine; I reckon you are now deep in mire and mortar, and are preparing to live seven years hence. I have been plagued with the roguery of my deanry proctor, whom I have discharged. I believe I am worse for him, 600l., and his brother is not much better. I wish you had been at my elbow to advise one, for you are fitter for the world than I am. I hope to come safe back, and then to have done with England. | I am ever yours, *&c.* | J. S.

[1] Swift was writing on Friday.

[2] Josiah Hort, Bishop of Ferns, lost his voice while on his first visitation. He went abroad for its recovery, and returned 'with a voice but a very weak one' (Bishop Nicolson's *Letters*, ii. 566, 607).

[3] Swift's old rival Lambert, who was not likely to view his absence with a lenient eye, had shortly before been translated from the bishopric of Dromore to that of Meath, which had become vacant by the translation of Downes to the Bishopric of Derry. These removes were consequent on the death of Archbishop Palliser, in whose room Nicolson had been promoted from Derry to Cashel.—Ball.

[4] As in this case he had to represent his absent friend before Primate Boulter, Wallis was certainly being assigned no enviable duty.—Ball.

Pierpont Morgan Library

'Richard Sympson' to Benjamin Motte

[27 April 1727]

Mr Motte[1]

I sent this enclosed by a friend to be sent to you, to desire that you would go to the house of Erasmus Lewis Esqr in Cork-street behind Burlington house and let him know that you are come from me. for to the s^d Mr Lewis I have given full power to treat wth you concerning my Coz^n Gulliver's book and what ever he & you shall settle I will consent to so I have written to him You will see him best early in the morning

I am y^r humble ser
-vant

Apr. 27th
1727

Richd Sympson

Address: These ffor Mr. Motte, a | Bookseller, at the middle temple | gate in | ffleet-street

Endorsed on back of letter by Lewis: London. may. 4. 1727. | I am fully satisfyd. E. Lewis.

Endorsed on fold of address by Motte: Paper relating to Gulliver

Dodsley Miscellanies 1745, x. 102

Swift to the Rev. Thomas Sheridan

London, *May* 13, 1727.[2]

This goes by a private Hand, for my Writing is too much known, and my Letters have been stopt and open'd. I had yours of the

[1] Swift appears to have left Ireland on 9 Apr. in pursuance of the intention he announced to Tickell in his letter of the 7th. See p. 204. From Chester he went to Goodrich in Herefordshire to visit the old family home. Thence he continued his journey by Oxford. By Saturday, 22 Apr., he was with Pope at Twickenham. See Pope's letter of that date to Lord Oxford (Sherburn, ii. 430). It is probable that Pope prompted Swift to write this letter concluding his agreement with the bookseller. The letter and the address are in Swift's hand with a clumsy attempt at disguise.

[2] The text of this letter is printed from *Miscellanies. The Tenth Volume . . . London: Printed for R. Dodsley in Pall Mall*, 1745, pp. 102–5. The letter was next printed by Faulkner, 1746, viii. 410.

4th Inst. and it is the only one I have received out of *Ireland* since I left you. I hardly thought our Friend[1] would be in danger by a Cold; I am of Opinion she should be generally in the Country, and only now and then visit the Town:—We are here in a strange Situation; a firm, settled Resolution to assault the present Administration, and break it if possible.[2] It is certain that *W*— is Peevish and Disconcerted, stoops to the vilest Offices of hiring Scroundels to write *Billingsgate* of the lowest and most prostitute Kind, and has none but Beasts and Blockheads for his Pen-men, whom he pays in ready Guineas very liberally. I am in high Displeasue with him and his Partisans;[3] a great Man, who was very kind to me last Year, doth not take the least Notice of at the P—'s[4] Court, and there hath not been one of them to see me. I am advised by all my Friends not to go to *France*, (as I intended for two Months) for fear of their Vengeance in a Manner which they cannot execute here.—I reckon there will be a warm Winter, wherein my Comfort is, I shall have no Concern. I desire you will read this Letter to none but our two Friends, and Mr. *P*—;[5] his Cousin with the red Ribbon enquired very kindly after him.—I hear no News about your Bishops, farther than that the Lord Lieutenant stickles to have them of *Ireland*, which *W*—[6] always is averse from, but does not think it worth his Trouble to exert his Credit on such Trifles.[7] The Dispute about a War or no War still continues, and the major Part inclines to the latter, although ten Thousand Men are order'd for *Holland*.[8] But this will bring such an addition to our Debts, that it will give great Advantages against those in Power, in the next Sessions. *W*— laughs at all this, but not so heartily as he used. I have at last seen the P—s[9] twice this Week by her own Commands;

[1] i.e. Stella.

[2] The opposition was gaining weight. Bolingbroke had been admitted to an audience with the King. *The Craftsman* sustained the vigour of its attacks on Walpole.

[3] As Ball suggests it is probable that Walpole suspected Swift of inspiring attacks upon him more than was actually the case.

[4] Prince's.

[5] Pratt, the Deputy-Vice-Treasurer of Ireland.

[6] i.e. Walpole.

[7] The Archbishopric of Cashel had become vacant through the death of Nicolson a few weeks after his promotion to that see. Delay in the appointment arose. Carteret urged the translation of Theophilus Bolton from Elphin, and Boulter, who was successful, the translation of Timothy Godwin from Kilmore.

[8] To assist in resisting an expected advance on the country by the Emperor.

[9] i.e. Princess. Swift was writing on Saturday.

she retains her old Civility, and I my old Freedom; she charges me without Ceremony, to be the Author of a bad Book, though I told her how angry the Ministry were; but she assures me that both she and the P— were very well pleased with every Particular; but I disown'd the whole Affair, as you know I very well might, only gave her leave, since she lik'd the Book, to suppose what Author she pleased. —You will wonder to find me say so much of Politicks, but I keep very bad Company, who are full of nothing else.—Pray be very careful of your Charge, or I shall order my Lodgers the Bulk of their Glasses, and the Number of their Bottles.—I stole this Time to write to you, having very little to spare. I go as soon as possible to the Country, and shall rarely see this Town.

My Service to all Friends.

I desire you will send me six Setts of the Edition of the Drapiers,[1] by the first Convenience of any Friend or Acquaintance that comes hither.

Portland MSS. Harley Papers

Swift to the Earl of Oxford

Whitehall | May. 13[h] 1727

My Lord.

M[r] Pope's mother hath been much out of order for about a fortnight past, and still continues so weak, that he cannot yet think of being absent from her, I am just going down with D[r] Arbuthnot to Twitenham, and from thence shall be able to give your Lordship a better account, what time we can appoint to attend you.[2]

Here are every day new Scribbles coming out full of the meanest and most stupid scurrility against those who have dared to glance at the Ministry, by which proceeding I apprehend those in power have acted in a manner that may not be to their advantage their credit or their ease; but I am none of their Counsellors. It is said they pay well, but are a little unlucky in the choice of their advocates, whether

[1] *Fraud Detected: Or, The Hibernian Patriot*, published by Faulkner, 2 Oct. 1725. See *The Drapier's Letters*, ed. Davis, p. lxxxix.

[2] After arriving at Twickenham Swift, anxious to lose no opportunity of seeing him, notified Lord Oxford of his arrival, but Oxford was then going to Wimpole, where Swift visited him at the end of July.

for want of judgement, a failure of genius in the nation or the Sterility of other arguments in the cause than what are to be gathered among the Shoe-boys.

I wish your Lordship health and satisfaction in the country, and remain with great respect My Lord | Your Lordship's most obedient | and most humble servt | Jonath Swift

White hall | May. 13^{h} 1727

Portland MSS. Harley papers

Swift to the Earl of Oxford

[18 May 1727]

My Lord.

I had this Morning the Honor of a letter from your self to invite me to Wimpole,[1] which having read to Mr Pope, he pressed me to entreat Your Lordship to excuse me, because Mrs Pope is recovering, and he is determined to accompany me to Your Lordships as soon as his Mother is quite out of danger; and he is so kind to add that it would be uneasy to him to be left alone during her indisposition, which altogether confines him at present. Your Lordship will therefore please to leave us to shift for our selves, and we will find some means of waiting on you together, with the first opportunity, or we will give notice to my Lady Oxford as soon as we are able. I am with the greatest respect | My Lord | Your Lordship's most obedient | and most humble serv^{t} | Jonath Swift

Twitenham. | May. 18th 1727

Address: To the Right Honorable | the Earl of Oxford

Deane Swift 1768

Swift to Archbishop King

May 18th, 1727.

My Lord,

I understand, by some letters just come to my hands, that, at your Grace's visitation of the Dean and Chapter of St. Patrick's,

[1] Cf. Swift to Lord Oxford, 13 May 1727.

a proxy was insisted on from the Dean, the visitation adjourned, and a rule entered that a proxy be exhibited within a month.[1] If your Grace can find, in any of your old records or of ours, that a proxy was ever demanded for a Dean of St. Patrick's, you will have some reason to insist upon it: But, as it is a thing wholly new and unheard of, let the consequences be what they will, I shall never comply with it. I take my Chapter to be my proxy, if I want any: It is only through them that you visit me, and my sub-dean is to answer for me. I am neither civilian nor canonist: Your Grace may probably be both, with the addition of a dexterous deputy. My proceeding shall be only upon one maxim: Never to yield to an oppression, to justify which no precedent can be produced. I see very well how personal all this proceeding is; and how, from the very moment of the Queen's death, your Grace hath thought fit to take every opportunity of giving me all sorts of uneasiness, without ever giving me, in my whole life, one single mark of your favour, beyond common civilities. And, if it were not below a man of spirit to make complaints, I could date them from six and twenty years past. This hath something in it the more extraordinary, because during some years when I was thought to have credit with those in power, I employed it to the utmost for your service, with great success, where it could be most useful against many violent enemies you then had, however unjustly, by which I got more ill-will than by any other action in my life, I mean from my friends. My Lord, I have lived, and by the grace of God will die, an enemy to servitude and slavery of all kinds: And I believe, at the same time, that persons of such a disposition will be the most ready to pay obedience wherever it is due. Your Grace hath often said, you would never infringe any of our liberties. I will call back nothing of what is past: I will forget, if I can, that you mentioned to me a licence to be absent.[2] Neither my age, health, humour or fortune, qualify me for little brangles; but I will hold to the practice delivered down by my predecessors. I thought, and have been told, that I deserved better from that Church and that kingdom: I am sure I do from your Grace. And, I believe, people on

[1] The Archbishop's visitation was then a very formal function. See Swift to Deane Stearne, 17 Apr. 1710.

[2] Opposition to Wood's coinage had promoted better feeling between King and Swift. This demand for a proxy momentarily endangered their kindlier relationship. Mason, *Hist. of St. Patrick's*, p. 365, contends that Swift was in the right. Fortunately the matter was dropped.

this side will attest, that all my merits are not very old. It is a little hard, that, the occasion of my journey hither, being partly for the advantage of that kingdom, partly on account of my health, partly on business of importance to me, and partly to see my friends, I cannot enjoy the quiet of a few months, without your Grace interposing to disturb it. But, I thank God, the civilities of those in power here, who allow themselves to be my professed adversaries, make some atonement for the unkindness of others, who have so many reasons to be my friends. I have not long to live; and, therefore, if conscience were quite out of the case for me to do a base thing, I will set no unworthy examples for my successors to follow: And, therefore, repeating it again that I shall not concern myself upon the proceeding of your Lordship, I am, *&c.*

4805

Viscount Bolingbroke to Swift

May the 18th 1727

I liv'd on tuesday[1] with you and Pope, yesterday another of my friends found his way to this retreat, and I shall pass this day alone, would to God my whole life could be divided in the same manner. two thirds to friendship, one third to my self, & not a moment of it to the world.

in the Epistle, a part of which you shew'd me, mention is made of the author of three occasional Letters, a person entirely unknown.[2] I would have you insinuate there, that the only reason Walpole can have had to ascribe them to a particular Person is the authority of one of his Spies, who wriggles himself into the company of those who neither love, esteem, nor fear the Min—, that he may report, not what he hears, since no man speaks with any freedom before him, but what he guesses.

fryday morning. I was interrupted yesterday when I least expected it, & I am going to day to London, where I hear that my Wife is not very well. Let me know how Mrs Pope do's.

[1] Bolingbroke was writing on Thursday from Dawley.

[2] The reference is to the first draft of Swift's 'Letter to the Writer of the Occasional Paper', which was printed by Deane Swift in 1765. The additions suggested by Bolingbroke appear in the printed version. See *Prose Works*, vii. 375–81.

I had a hint or two more for you. but they have slipp'd out of my memory. do not forget the 60 nor the 20 guineas, nor the Min—[1] character transferr'd into the administration. adieu I am ever faithfully y^rs^ my Dear & Reverend Dean. | I embrace Pope.

Address: To the Reverend Dr Swift | Dean of St Patricks att | Mr Popes att Twickenham

Endorsed by Swift: May. 18^h^ 1727 | Ld Bolingbroke

Trinity College, Dublin, N. 3. 8, f. 199

Archbishop King to Swift

Dublin June 3^d^ 1727

Revd S^r^

I had yours without Date time or place,[2] for answ^r^ to it, I am advised that it is necessary you should appear either in person or by Proxy, If a Proxy come any time this Month it will do, writing is very uneasy to me, which is the Reason for the shortness of this from | Revd S^r^ | Your most Humble | serv^t^ & B^r^ | W: D.

To Dean Swift

Address: To Revd. Jonath Swift Dean of St. Patrick's | At the Lodgings of John Gay Esq., | In Whitehall London

4805

Viscount Bolingbroke to Swift

tuesday [6 June 1727]

I return you the papers which I have read twice over since you was here. they are extreamly well.[3] but the Craftsman has not only advertis'd the publick that he intended to turn News writer.[4] he has

[1] Minister's.

[2] Cf. Swift's letter of 18 May and the footnote on the contentious question of a proxy.

[3] The revised version of Swift's 'Letter to the Writer of the Occasional Paper'.

[4] In his letter Swift refers to the declared intention of the writer of *The Craftsman* of giving 'accounts of domestic and foreign intelligence'.

begun, & for some weeks continu'd to appear under that new character. this consideration inclines me to think that another turn might be given to the introduction, and perhaps this would naturally call for a fourth letter from the occasional writer, to account for his silence, to prosecute y^{r} argument, to state the present disputes about pollitical affairs, & in short to revive & animate the paper war.[1] when we meet next, I will explain myself better than I can do by a letter, writ in haste with mowers & Haymakers about me. adieu, let Pope share my embraces with you.

Endorsed by Swift: Ld Bolingbroke | about some Papers | 1727

4805

Viscount Bolingbroke to Swift

Sunday [11 June 1727].

You may be sure of Letters[2] from me to people who will receive you with all the honours due to so great a Traveller, & so exact an Author. I am oblig'd to stay tomorrow in the Country by some business relating to my poor farm, which I would willingly make a rich one, & for which purpose a Person is with me who comes from Suffolk on my summons. on tuesday by Seven in the evening I will certainly be in the Pallmall, & there you shall have, if you meet me, & not otherwise, both my letters & instructions which will be of use to you. raillery apart, since you do go into France, I shall be glad to talk with you before y^{r} departure, & I fancy you would not leave England without embracing the man in England who loves you best. adieu my best services attend all with you.

Address: To the Reverend | The Dean of St Patricks
Endorsed by Swift: Lord Bolingbroke | on my going to | France about June | 1727

[1] Swift's letter is incomplete. Bolingbroke may not have been altogether satisfied with it.

[2] Letters of introduction to people in France, whither Swift intended to go in a few days.

4805

Voltaire to Swift

Friday, 16 [June 1727.]

Sir,[1]

I send you here inclos'd two letters one for Mr de Morville, our Secretary of State, and the other for Mr de Maisons, both desirous and worthy of y^r acquaintance. be so Kind as to let me Know if you intend to go by Calais, or by the way of Rouen. in case you resolve to go by Rouen, I will give you some letters for a good lady who lives in her country castle just by Rouen. She will receive you as well as you deserve, there you will find two or three of my intimate friends who are yr admirers and who have learn'd english since I am in England. all will pay you all the respects and procure all the pleasures they are capable off. they will give you hundred directions for paris, and provide you with all the requisite conveniencies. vouchsafe to acquaint me with y^r resolution, I shall certainly do my best endeavours to serve you and to let my country know, that I have the inestimable honour to be one of y^r friends | I am, with the highest respect and esteem |

yr most Humble obedient | faithfull Servant Voltaire

friday 16

(*Enclosure*)

Voltaire to Comte de Morville

Monseigneur

Je me suis contenté jusqu'icy d'admirer en silence votre conduitte dans les affaires de l'europe, mais il n'est pas permis à un homme qui aime votre gloire, et qui vous est aussi tendrement attaché que je le suis de demeurer plus long temps sans vous faire ses sinceres compliments.

Je ne puis d'ailleurs me refuser l'honneur que me fait le celebre Mons Swift, de vouloir bien vous presenter une de mes lettres. Je sai que sa reputation est parvenue jusqu'à vous, et que vous avez envie de le connoitre. il fait lhonneur d'une nation que vous estimez. vous avez lu les traductions de plusieurs ouvrages qui luy sont

[1] Pope had probably introduced Swift to Voltaire, who, informed of Swift's intention of visiting France, had pleasure in providing him with letters of introduction.

attribuez. eh qui est plus capable que vous, Monseigneur, de discerner les beautez d'un original à travers la foiblesse des plus mauvaises copies. Je croi que vous ne serez pas faché de diner avec monsieur Swift, et Mr le president Henaut.[1] et je me flatte que vous regarderez comme une preuve de mon sincere attachement à votre personne la liberté que je prens de vous presenter un des hommes les plus extraordinaires que l'angleterre ait produits, et les plus capable de sentir toute letendüe de vos grandes qualitez.

Je suis pour toute ma vie avec un profond respect et un attachement remply de la plus haute estime Monseigneur | votre très humble, et très obeissant serviteur, Voltaire.

Address: a Monseigneur | monseigneur le comte de Morville | ministre et Secretaire d'Etat | a Versailles

4805

Viscount Bolingbroke to Swift

Saturday att Popes [17 June 1727][2]

I am going to London & intend to carry this letter, which Ile give you if I see you, & leave for you if I do not see you. there would not be common sense in yr going into France att this juncture, even if you intended to stay there long enough to draw the sole pleasure & profit, which I propose you should have in the acquaintance I am ready to give you there. much less ought you to think of such an unmeaning journey, when the opportunity of quitting Ireland for England is I believe fairly before you. to hanker after a Court is fit for Men with blew ribbands, pompous Titles, gorgeous Estates. it is below either you or me, one of whom never made his fortune, & the others turn'd rotten at the very moment it grew ripe.[3] But without hankering, without assuming a suppliant dependant air, you may spend in England all the time you can be absent from Ireland, &

[1] Charles-Jean-François Hénault, French dramatist and President of the Chamber of Inquests. On 11 June 1768 Horace Walpole printed at Strawberry Hill an edition of 200 copies of his tragedy *Cornélie*, *vestale*.

[2] On Thursday news had reached London of the death of George I on his way to Hanover. On that same day Swift had come from Twickenham to town. His endorsement of this letter, presumably made later, is a week at fault.

[3] Here Bolingbroke appears to reflect on his position on the death of Queen Anne. It is not to current events that he refers.

faire la guere a l'orgueil. there has not been so much inactivity as you imagine, but I cannot answer for contingences. Adieu. if you can call on me to morrow morning in yr way to church about ten aclock, you will find me just returning to Cranford[1] from the Pall mall

I shall be returnd again to London on monday evening.

Endorsed by Swift: Ld Bolingbroke | Jun. 24th 1727

4805

Viscount Bolingbroke to Swift

Cranford tuesday [20 June 1727.][2]

I have so severe a defluxion of Rhume on both my eyes that I dare hardly stir abroad. you will be ready to say, Physician cure thy self, and that is what I am about. I took away by cupping yesterday fourteen ounces of blood, and such an operation would I believe have done you more good than Steel & Bitters, waters & Drops. I wish John Gay success in his pursuit. but I think he has some quallitys which will keep him down in the world. good God! what is man? polish'd, civiliz'd, learned Man? a Liberal education fits him for Slavery, and the pains he has taken give him the noble pretension of dangling away life in an anti chamber, or of employing real tallents to serve those who have none, or, which is worse than all the rest, of making his Reason & his knowledg serve all the purposes of other mens follys and vices. you say [a] word to me about the publick, of whom I think as seldom [as][3] possible. I consider myself as a Man with some little satisfaction, & with some use, but I have no pleasure in thinking I am an Englishman, nor is it I doubt to much purpose act like one. Serpit enim Res, quæ proclivis ad perniciem, cûm semel cœpit, labitur. Plures enim discunt quemadmodum hæc fiant, quàm quemadmodum his resistantur. adieu, let me know how you do. if y^r^ Landlord is return'd my kindest services to him.

Address: To the Reverend Dr Swift | Dean of St Patricks | att Mr Popes House | att Twickenham

Endorsed by Swift: Ld Boling^e^ *and* Ld Boling^e^ | 1727

[1] Lord and Lady Bolingbroke were only in temporary residence at Cranford.

[2] The date is conjectural. The day of the week affords a guide.

[3] The paper is torn.

4805

L'Abbé Desfontaines to Swift

A Paris, le 4 Juillet [o.s. 23 June] 1727

Jai lhonneur, Monsieur, de vous envoyer la 2e édition de votre ouvrage que Jai traduit en François.[1] Je vous aurois envoïé la première, si Je n'avois pas eté obligé, pour des raisons que Je ne puis vous dire, d'inserer dans la préface un endroit, dont vous n'auriez pas eu lieu d'etre content, ce que J'ai mis assurément malgré moi. Comme le Livre s'est debité sans contradiction, ces raisons ne subsistent plus, et J'ai aussitôt supprimé cet endroit dans la 2e Edition, comme vous verréz. J'ai aussi corrigé l'endroit de Mr Carteret, sur le quel J'avois eu de faux memoires. Vous trouveréz Monsieur en beaucoup d'endroits une traduction peu fidèle, mais tout ce qui plaît en Angleterre n'a pas ici le même agrément, soit parce que les moeurs sont differentes, soit parce que les allusions et les allégories, qui sont sensibles dans un pays, ne le sont pas dans un autre: soit enfin parce que le goût des deux Nations n'est pas le même. Jai voulu donner aux François un Livre, qui fût a leur usage; voila ce qui m'a rendu Traducteur libre et peu fidèle. Jai même pris la liberté d'ajouter, selon que votre imagination echauffoit la mienne. Cest a vous seul, Monsieur, que je suis redevable de Lhonneur, que me fait cette traduction, qui a eté debitée ici avec une rapidité étonnante et donc il y a deja trois éditions. Je suis penetré, d'une si grande estime pour vous et je vous suis si obligé, qui si la suppression, que J'ai faite ne vous satisfaisait pas entierement, Je ferois volontiers encore davantage pour effacer jusqu'au souvenir de cet endroit de la Preface. au surplus, Je vous supplie, Monsieur, de vouloir bien faire attention à la Justice, que je vous ai rendüe dans la même Preface.

on se flatte, Monsieur, qu'on aura bientôt Lhonneur de vous posseder ici. Tous vos amis vous attendent avec impatience. on ne parle ici que de votre arrivée, et tout Paris souhaitte de vous voir. Ne differez pas notre satisfaction, vous verrez un Peuple qui vous estime infiniment. En attendant Je vous demande Monsieur,

[1] The first French translation of *Gulliver's Travels* appeared at The Hague in Jan. 1727 in two duodecimo volumes. The Paris edition, also in two duodecimo volumes, did not come out till April. The earlier translation was complete; the Paris edition, done by the Abbé Pierre-François Guyot Desfontaines, was an abridgement and adaptation. Cf. Swift's reply to the letter of Desfontaines.

lhonneur de votre amitié, et vous prie detre persuadé, que personne ne vous honore plus que moi et n'est avec plus de consideration et d'estime | Votre tres humble et tres | obeissant serviteur | Labbé des fontaines

Mr Arbuthnot[1] a bien voulu se charger de vous faire tenir cette Lettre avec L'*Exemplaire* que jai lhonneur de vous envoier.

Dodsley Miscellanies 1745, x. 105

Swift to the Rev. Thomas Sheridan

London, June 24, 1727.[2]

I have received your last, with the inclosed Print. I desire you will let Dr. *D*— know that I transcrib'd the Substance of his Letter, and the Translation of what was Register'd, and added a whole State of the Case,[3] and gave it to Mrs. *H—d*[4] to give to the Prince from me, and to define that as Chancellor, he would do what he thought most fit. I forgot to ask Mrs. *H—d* what was done in it, the next Time I saw her, and the Day I came to Town came the News of the K—'s Death, of which I sent Particulars the very same Day to our Friend;[5] since then we have been all in a Hurry, with Millions of Schemes. I deferr'd kissing the K— and Q—'s Hands till the third Day, when my Friends at Court chid me for deferring it so long. I have been and am so extreamly busy, that tho' I begin this Letter, I cannot finish it till next Post; for now it is the last Moment it can go, and I have much more to say. I was just ready to go to *France*, when the News of the K—'s Death arrived, and I came to Town in order to

[1] Robert Arbuthnot, the banker.

[2] The text of this letter is printed from Dodsley's *Miscellanies. The Tenth Volume*, 1745. It was reprinted in Faulkner, 1746, viii. 413.

[3] A quarrel had arisen between the senior fellows of Trinity and Provost Baldwin, who refused to elect to a junior fellowship a candidate favoured by all but one of the board. Boulter, writing to the Archbishop of Canterbury, 6 July 1727 (*Letters*, i. 145), admitted that Baldwin was exercising a power beyond that of any head of college in Oxford, but that it was little enough to prevent the college becoming 'a seminary of jacobitism'. To this Faulkner, the publisher of the Dublin edition of the *Letters*, retorts in a footnote that 'His Grace . . . was grossly imposed upon', for the University of Dublin was 'remarkable for charity, piety, religion, learning and loyalty'.

[4] Mrs. Howard.

[5] i.e. Stella.

begin my Journey. But I was desired to delay it, and I then determined it a second Time: When upon some new Incidents, I was with great Vehemence dissuaded from it by certain Persons whom I could not disobey. Thus Things stand with me. My Stomach is pretty good, but for some Days my Head has not been right, yet it is what I have been formerly us'd to. Here is a strange World, and our Friend would reproach me for my Share in it; but it shall be short, for I design soon to return into the Country. I am thinking of a Chancellor for the University, and have pitched upon one,[1] but whether he will like it, or my Word be of any Use, I know not. The Talk is now for a moderating Scheme, wherein no-body shall be used the Worse or Better for being call'd Whig or Tory, and the King hath received both with great Equality; shewing Civilities to several who are openly known to be the latter. I prevailed with Dozen that we should go in a Line to kiss the K— and Q—'s Hands. We have now done with Repining, if we shall be used well, and not baited as formerly; we all agree in it, and if Things do not mend it is not our Faults: We have made our Offers: If otherwise, we are as we were. It is agreed the Ministry will be changed, but the others will have a soft Fall; although the K— must be excessive generous if he forgives the Treatment of some People. I writ long ago my Thoughts to my Viceroy,[2] and he may proceed as he shall be advised. But if the A.B. goes on to proceed to *sub poena contemptus*, &c. I would have an appeal at proper Time, which I suppose must be to Delegates, or the Crown, I know not which. However, I will spend a hundred or two Pounds, rather than be enslav'd, or betray a Right which I do not value Three-pence, but my Successors may. My Service to all Friends; and so thinking I have said enough, I bid you farewell heartily, and long to eat your Fruit, for I dare eat none here. It hath cost me five Shillings in Victuals since I came here, and ten pounds to Servants where I have dined. I suppose my Agent in *Sheep-Street*[3] takes Care and enquires about my new Agent.

[1] The chancellorship naturally became vacant with the accession of the Prince to the throne. The successor to whom Swift alludes was Lord Scarborough.

[2] The sub-dean, to whom Swift refers Sheridan for details of the dispute with Archbishop King.

[3] i.e. Worrall.

B.M. Add. MS. 22625

Swift to Mrs. Howard

[June 1727]

Madam

The last time I had the honor to wait on you, I forgot to ask what you had done with the memoriall I gave you for his then Royal Highness as Chancellor of the University of Dublin[1]

I doubt his Majesty must act as Chancellor,[2] I mean His Vice-chancellor[3] must act the next Commencement, which will be the 7th or 8th of July, which is a Solemn time when Degrees are given, as His Secretary Mr Molyneaux knows. But, after that it is to be supposed that his Majesty will resign that Office, and unless the Prince of Wales will accept it,[4] I do believe, and am told that the Earl of Scarborough[5] would be the fittest Person on all accounts. In saying this I do not meddle out of my province, and it is a matter that should now be thought on. | I am with the greatest | respect. | Madam | Your most obedient, and | most humble Servant | Jonath Swift

Dodsley Miscellanies 1745, x. 108

Swift to the Rev. Thomas Sheridan

Twickenham, July 1, 1727.[6]

I had yours of *June* 22. You complain of not hearing from me; I never was so constant a Writer. I have writ six Times to our Friends, and as many to you. Mr. *Pope* is reading your *Persius*;[7] he is frequently sick, and so at this Time; he has read it, but you must wait

[1] Cf. previous letter. The Prince before his accession to the throne.

[2] 'or rather' struck out.

[3] Bishop Stearne then held that position.

[4] '(who I doubt is too young.)' struck through.

[5] Lord Scarborough, a favourite with the new King, might obtain benefits for the University.

[6] Printed from Dodsley's *Miscellanies. The Tenth Volume*, 1745, x. 108.

[7] Sheridan's *Satyrs of Persius* appeared in the following year printed in Dublin by George Grierson. It contains both text and translation, and was dedicated to Edward, third Viscount Mountcashell, who had been a pupil of Sheridan.

till next Letter for his Judgment. He would know whether is designed for an elegant Translation, or only to shew the Meaning; I reckon it an Explanation of a difficult Author, not only for learners, but for those also who are not expert in Latin, because he is a very dark Author: I would not have your Book printed entire, till I treat with my Bookseller here for your Advantage. There is a Word (*Concacuus*)[1] which you have not explained, nor the Reason of it. Where you are ignorant, you should confess that you are ignorant. I writ to *Stella* the day we heard the K— was dead, and the Circumstances of it. I hold you a Guinea I shall forget something. *Worrall* writ to me lately. In Answer, I desire that when the A. Bp. comes to a determination, that an Appeal be properly lodged,[2] by which I shall elude him till my Return, which will be at *Michaelmas.* I have left *London*, and stay here a Week, and then I shall go thither again; just to see the Q—, and so come back hither. Here are a thousand Schemes wherein they would have me engaged, which I embrace but coldly, because I like none of them.[3] I have been these ten Days inclining to my old Disease of Giddiness, a little Tottering; our Friend understands it, but I grow Cautious, and am something better: Cyder and Champagne and Fruit have been the Cause. But now I am very regular, and I eat enough. I took Dr. *D*—[4] Paper to the K— when he was Pr—; he and his Secretary are discontented with the Provost, but they find he has Law on his Side. The King's Death hath broke that Measure. I propos'd the Pr. of *Wales* to be Chancellor, and I believe so it will go. Pray copy out the Verses I writ to *Stella* on her collecting my Verses,[5] and send them to me, for we want some to make our Poetical Miscellany large enough, and I am not there to pick what should be added. Direct them, and all other double Papers to Lord B— in *St. James's Square*, *London.* I was in a Fright about your Verses about *Stella's* Sickness, but glad when they were a Month old.[6]

[1] There is no such word in Persius or elsewhere. Evidently an unpleasant jest in association with *concaco.*

[2] Cf. Swift to Archbishop King, 18 May 1727.

[3] Sir Spencer Compton, in common with Lord Scarborough, a close favourite of the King, was chosen to displace Walpole. His triumph lasted only a few days, for his incapacity immediately became apparent. He was induced to relinquish his station; and Walpole regained his ascendancy to the astonishment of the Opposition who were driven to devising new schemes.

[4] i.e. Delany's.

[5] *Poems*, ii. 727–32.

[6] These verses in Sheridan's hand, headed 'The humble Petition of Stella's

Desire our Friends to let me know what I should buy for them here, of any Kind. I had just now a long Letter from Mr. *Dingley*, and another from Mr. *Synge*:[1] Pray tell the latter, that I return him great Thanks, and will leave the Visiting Affair to his Discretion. But all the Lawyers in *Europe* shall never persuade me that it is in the A. Bp's Power to take or refuse my Proxy, when I have the King's Leave of Absence. If he be violent, I will appeal, and die two or three Hundred Pounds poorer, to defend the Rights of the Dean. Pray ask Mr. *Synge* whether his Fenocchio[2] be grown; it is now fit to eat here like Sellary, either with or without Oil, &c. I design to pass my Time wholly in the Country, having some Business to do, and settle, before I leave *England* for the last Time. I will send you Mr. *Pope*'s Criticisms, and my own, on your Work. Pray forget nothing of what I desire you. Pray God bless you all. If the K— had lived but ten Days longer, I should be now at *Paris*. Simpleton! the *Drapier's* should have been sent unbound, but 'tis no great Matter; two or three would have been enough. I see Mrs. *Fad*[3] but seldom, I never trouble them but when I am sent for; she expects me soon, and after that perhaps no more while I am here. I desire it may be told that I never go to Court, which I mention because of a Passage in Mrs. *D*—'s[4] Letter; she speaks mighty good things of your Kindness. I do not want that Poem to *Stella* to print it entire, but some Passages out of it, if they deserve it, to lengthen the Volume. Read all this Letter without Hesitation, and I'll give you a Pot of Ale. I intend to be with you at *Michaelmas*, barr Impossibilities.

Friends', will be found in the British Museum, Add. MS. *5017, f. 75. The lines are signed by Mr. and Mrs. Worrall, Delany, Rebecca Dingley, and Sheridan. They are dated 'June the eleventh—1727'.

[1] Edward Synge, son of the Archbishop of Tuam.

[2] Sweet or dwarf fennel.

[3] Presumably some of Sheridan's relations were in London.

[4] i.e. Dingley's.

B.M. Add. MS. 22625

Swift to Mrs. Howard

9 July 1727.

Madam.

Mr Gay by your commands as he says, shewed me a lettr to you from an unfortunate Lady, one Mrs Prat,[1] whose case I know very well, and pity very much, but I wonder she should make any mention of me, who am almost a stranger to you, further than as your goodness led you a little to distinguish me. I have often told Mrs Prat that I had not the least interest with the friend's friend of any body in power, on the contrary I had been used like a dog for a dozen years by every soul who was able to do it, and were but sweepers about a Court. I believe you will allow that I know Courts well enough to remember that a man must be got many degrees above the power of recommending himself, before he should presume to recommend another, even his nearest relation. and for my own part you may be secure that I will never venture to recommend a mouse to Mrs Cole's cat, or a shoe-cleaner to your meanest domestick. But you know too well already, how very injudicious the generall tribe of wanters are: I told Mrs Prat, that if she had friends, it was best to sollicite a Pension. But seems she hath mentioned a place. I can onely say that when I was about Courts the best Lady there had some cousen or near dependent whom she would be glad to recommend for an Employment, and therefore would hardly think of Strangers. For I take the matter thus, that a pension may possibly be got by commiseration, but great personal favor is required for an employment: There are Madam thousands in the world, who if they saw your dog Fop[2] use me[3] kindly; would, the next day in a letter tell me of the delight they heard I had in doing good; and being assured that a word of mine to you would do any thing, desire my interest to speak to you, to speak to the Speaker,[4] to speak to Sr R. Walp— to speak to the King &c. Thus wanting people are like drowning people, who lay hold of every reed or bulrush in their way.

[1] The wife of the discredited Deputy Vice-Treasurer.

[2] See Ault, *New Light on Pope*, pp. 337–50, 'Pope and his Dogs', and *Minor Poems*, pp. 366–71, 'Bounce to Fop'. The same dog is probably alluded to in the line 'Fop is the delight of a lady' in *Molly Mog*, a composite poem, in the main written by Gay (Faber, p. 188).

[3] 'may' manuscript.

[4] Sir Spencer Compton.

One place I humbly beg for my self which is in your own gift, if it be not disposed of; I mean the perquisite of all the Letters and petitions you receive, which being generally of fair, large, strong paper, I can sell at good advantage to the Ban-box and trunk-makers; and I hope will annually make a pretty comfortable penny.

I hear while I was at church Mr Pope writ to you upon the occasion of Mrs Pratts letter, but they will not shew me what is writt. Therefore I would not trust them, but resolved to justify my self, and they shall not see this.

I pray God grant you patience, and preserve your eye-sight, but confine your memory to the Service of your royall mistress and the happyness of those who are your truest friends, and give you a double portion of your own spirit to distinguish them: | I am with the truest respect | Madam | Your most obedient and | most obliged humbl Servt | Jonath Swift.

Twitenham. July 9th | 1727. Between Church and | dinner time.

4805

Viscount Bolingbroke to Swift

thursday[1] [July 1727.]

L^{d} B:[2] is so ill, & so much alone, the common fate of those who are out of power, that I have not left him one day since my return from London. Let me know how you are. Say something very kind from me to Pope, toss John Gay over the water to Richmond, if he is with you. adieu.

Address: To the Reverend Dr Swift | Dean of St Patricks att | Mr Pope's att Twickenham.

Endorsed by Swift: Ld Bolingbroke 1727 *and* Ld Boling^{e} 1727

[1] Swift's endorsement gives us the year; and the address leaves no doubt but that the letter was written in July or August (possibly in September) 1727.

[2] i.e Lord Bathurst.

4805

Andrew Ramsay to Swift

1 August [O.S. 21 July] 1727.

Reverend Sir[1]

Mr Hooke having acquainted me with what Goodness and patience, you have been pleas'd to examine a performance of mine, I take this occasion to make my acknowledgments. Nothing could flatter me more sensibly than your approbation. To acquire the Esteem of persons of your Merit, is the principal advantage I could wish for by becoming an author, and more than I could flatter my self with. I should be proud of receiving your commands, if I could be any way usefull to you in this part of the world, where I assure you, your Reputation is as well establish'd as in your own Country. I am with the utmost regard and esteem | Reverend Sir | your most humble, & most | obligd obedient servant | A R—y.

at paris August 1st N.S. | 1727

4805

Swift to L'Abbé des Fontaines

[July 1727.]

Monr Swift a L'abbé desfontaines[2]

Il y a plus d'un mois que j'ay recûe vôtre lettre du 4e de Juillet, Monsieur, mais l'exemplaire de la 2e edition de votre ouvrage ne m'a pas eté encore remis. J'ay lû la Preface de la premiere, et vous me permettrez de vous dire, que j'ay eté fort surpris d'y voir, qu'en me donnant pour Patrie un Pais dans lequel Je ne suis pas né, vous ayez trouvé a propos de m'attribuer un livre qui porte le nom de son auteur qui a eu le malheur de deplaire a quelques uns de nos Ministres, et que je n'ay jamais avoué.

[1] At the head of this letter Swift has written: 'Scotch author | in France'; and endorsed the letter: 'Chevalier AR | from Paris | Aug. 1. N.S. 1728' (*sic*). Andrew Ramsay, 1686–1743, born in Ayr, passed by way of the Netherlands to France, where in 1710 he made the acquaintance of Fénelon and entered the Roman Catholic Church. For a brief period he acted in Rome as tutor to the Pretender's sons. His famous *Les Voyages de Cyrus*, Paris, 1727, was translated into English in twenty days by Nathanael Hooke.

[2] This letter is a draft only, the writer and addressee indicated by a marginal caption.

Cette plainte, que je fais de vôtre conduite à mon egard ne m'empeche pas de vous rendre justice. Les Traducteurs donnent pour la plupart des louanges excessives aux ouvrages qu'ills traduisent, et s'imaginent peut etre que leur Reputation depend en quelque facon de celle des Auteurs qu'ills ont choisis. Mais vous avez senti vos forces, qui vous mettent au dessus de pareilles precautions. capable de corriger un mauvais livre, entreprise plus difficile, que celle d'en composer un bon, vous n'avez pas craint, de donner au public la traduction d'un ouvrage, que vous assurez etre plein de pollisoneries, de sottises, de puerilites &c. Nous convenons icy que le gout des Nations n'est pas toujours le meme. mais nous sommes portes a croire que le bon gout est le meme par tout ou il y a des gens d'esprit, de judgement et de Scavoir. si donc les livres du Sieur Gulliver ne sont calcules que pour les Isles Britanniques, ce voyageur doit passer pour un tres pitoyable Ecrivain. les memes vices, et les memes follies regnent par tout, du moins, dans tous les pays civilises de l'Europe, et l'auteur qui n'ecrit que pour une ville, une province, un Royaume, ou meme un siecle, merite si peu d'être traduit qu'il ne merite pas d'etre lû.

Les Partisans de ce Gulliver, qui ne laissent pas d'etre en fort grand nombre chez nous, soutiennent, que son Livre durera autant que notre langage, parce qu'il ne tire pas son merite de certaines modes ou manieres de penser et de parler, mais d'une suite d'observations sur les imperfections, les folies, et les vices de l'homme.

Vous jugez bien que les gens, dont je viens de vous parler n'approuvent pas fort votre critique et vous serez sans doute surpris de scavoir qu'ills regardent ce chirurgien de vaisseau comme un Auteur grave, qui ne sort jamais de son serieux, qui n'emprunte aucun fard, que ne se pique point d'avoir de l'esprit, et qui se contente de communiquer au public, dans une Narration simple et naive, les avantures qui luy sont arrivées, et les choses qu'il a vû ou entendu dire pendant ses voyages.

Quant a l'article qui regarde my Ld Carteret, sans m'informer d'ou vous tirez vos memoires, Je vous diray que vous n'avez ecrit que la moitié de la verité, et que ce Drapier, ou reel ou supposé, a sauvé l'Irlande, en ameuuant toute la nation contre un projet qui devoit enrichir au depense du public un certain nombre de particuliers.

Plusieurs accidens, qui sont arrivé m'empêcheront de faire le voyage de la France presentement, et je ne suis plus assez jeune pour me flatter de retrouver un autre occasion. Je scais, que j'y perds beaucoup, et je suis tres sensible a cette perte. l'unique consolation qui me reste, c'est de songer, que J'en supporteray mieux le pais, au quel la Fortune m'a condamné.

National Library of Scotland

Swift to Mrs. Drelincourt[1]

Twitenham. Aug. 7th 1727

Madam.[2]

Two days ago I received a Letter signed M. Earbery (if I read it right) which name it seems belongs to the person recommended by your Brother as a sufferer by the times, and desirous to help himself by the translation of an Italian book.[3] I shewed his letter to my friends here, who all agree that it is an original in it's kind, beyond what we have any where met with, being a heap of strange insolence and scurrility without the least provocation. What I desired you to tell him was, that I thought his observations were too long, and that in my opinion it would be better to enlarge his notes. When I met Miss Drelincourt[4] on the Mall I likewise said that I could not decently give publick encouragement to such a work where Mr Pope was openly reflected on by name. As for a distressed Person, and a Clergyman that hath suffered for his opinion, I should be very ready to contribute my mite, and have done it oftener than it was deserved from me. but this same Mr Earbery would be countenanced

[1] This letter was first printed by Scott, 1814, xix. 388–90, with a footnote: 'This original letter was found in the repositories of Viscountess Primrose (the Miss Drelincourt mentioned in the letter), by her executrix, Mrs. Lillias Waldie, and is now in the possession of Mrs. Smith of Kelso.'

[2] The recipient of this letter was the widow of Peter Drelincourt, Dean of Armagh, who died 7 Mar. 1721–2. He was a son of Charles Drelincourt, a minister of the French reformed church, author of *Les Consolations de l'Ame contre les Frayeurs de la Mort*, 1669. A monument to his memory by Rysbrack was erected in Armagh Cathedral by his widow.

[3] Mathias Earberry was a pamphleteer on religious and miscellaneous subjects. In 1727 he published a translation of Thomas Burnet's *De Statu Mortuorum et Resurgentium*, second edition 1728. The translation of an Italian book does not seem to have been published. He died in 1740.

[4] Daughter of the Dean of Armagh.

as *an Author*, and a *genius*, whereof I am no judge, and therefore it would be more convenient for him to apply to others who are. But I think, whoever he applyes to for encouragm^{t} he would not succeed the worse, if he thought fit to spare the method of threatning, and ill language; although I have been too long out of the world, that perhaps I may be mistaken, and that these are the[1] new arts of purchasing favor. For the same reason, let me add one thing more, that being wholly a stranger to the present way of writing, the objection I made to his Observations, may be altogether injudicious, for want of knowing the tast of the age, or of conversing with its productions. This you may please to tell the writer of the letter; and that I promise never to meddle with his liberty of understanding, although what he means is past mine. | I am with true respect | Madam | Your most obedient | humble Servant, | Jonath Swift.

My humble service to Miss Drelincourt. I assure you she makes a good figure on the Mall, and I could in conscience do no less than distinguish her.

I have desired Mr Gay to shew you the Letter writ to me by this Mr Earbury, and I have writt a word or two at the bottom, for you to read.

Address: To Mrs Drelincourt
On verso, or another piece of paper: ? for Swift . . .[2]
M^{r} E strange lettr
July 1727

Dodsley Miscellanies 1745, x. 112

Swift to the Rev. Thomas Sheridan

Twickenham, Aug. 12, 1727

I am cleverly caught, if ever Gentleman was cleverly caught; for three Days after I came to Town with Lord *Oxford* from *Cambridgeshire*,[3] which was ten Days ago, my old Deafness seized me, and

[1] 'the' above the line in the manuscript.
[2] Not in Swift's hand, and not wholly legible.
[3] For this ramble to Cambridge see Pope's letter to Fortescue, 5 Aug., Sherburn, ii. 441.

hath continued ever since with great Encrease; so that I am now Deafer than ever you knew me, and yet a little less, I think, than I was Yesterday; but which is worse, about four Days ago my Giddiness seized me, and I was so very ill, that Yesterday I took a hearty Vomit, and though I now totter, yet I think I am a Thought better; but what will be the Event, I know not; one thing I know, that these deaf Fits use to continue five or six Weeks, and I am resolved if it continues, or my Giddiness, some Days longer, I will leave this Place, and remove to *Greenwich*, or somewhere near *London*, and take my Cousin *Lancelot* to be my Nurse. Our Friends know her; it is the same with *Pat Rolt*. ⌜If my Disorder should keep me longer than my Licence of Absence lasts, I would have you get Mr. *Worral* to renew it; it will not expire till the sixth or seventh of *October*, and I resolved to begin my Journey *Sept.* 15th. Mr. *Worrall* will see by the Date of my Licence what time the new one should commence; but he hath seven Weeks yet to consider: I only speak in time⌝.[1] I am very uneasy here, because so many of our Acquaintance come to see us, and I cannot be seen; besides Mr. *Pope* is too sickly and complaisant; therefore I resolve to go somewhere else. This is a little unlucky, my Head will not bear writing long: I want to be at home, where I can turn you out, or let you in, as I think best. The K— and Q— come in two Days to our Neighbourhood,[2] and there I shall be expected, and cannot go; which however, is none of my Grievances, for I had rather be absent, and have now too good an Excuse. I believe this Giddiness is the Disorder that will at last get the better of me; but I had rather it should not be now; and I hope and believe it will not, for I am now better than Yesterday.—Since my Dinner my Giddiness is much better, and my Deafness a hair's breadth not so bad. 'Tis just as usual, worst in the Morning and at Evening. I will be very Temperate; and in the midst of Peaches, Figs, Nectarins, and Mulberries, I touch not a bit. I hope I shall however set out in the middle of *September*, as I design'd.—This is a long Letter for an ill Head: So adieu. My Service to our two Friends and all others.

[1] In 1746 (viii. 419), and in later editions, Faulkner omits the sentences within half-brackets.

[2] i.e. Richmond.

B.M. Add. MS. 22625, ff. 16–17

Swift to Mrs. Howard

14 August 1727

Madam.

I wish I were a young Lord, and you were unmarryd. I should make you the best husband in the world, for I am ten times deafer than ever you were in your life, and instead of a few pain[s] in the face, I have a good substantial giddyness and Head-ake; the best of it is, that although we might lay our heads together, You could tell me no secrets, that might not be heard five rooms distant. These disorders of mine, if they hold as long as they used to do some years ago, will last as long as my Licence of absence; which I shall not renew, and then the Queen will have the misfortune not to see me, and I shall go back with the satisfaction never to have seen her since she was Queen, but when I kist her hand; and although she were a thousand Queens, I will not lose my privilege of never seeing her but when she commands it. I told my two Landlords here that I would write you a love-letter, which, I remember you commanded me to do last year; but I would not shew it to either of them. I am the greatest Courtier and flatterer You have, because I try your good sense and tast more than all of them put together, which is the greatest compliment I could put upon you, and you have hitherto behaved your self tolerably under it; much better than your Mistress, if what a Lady told me be true, that talking with the Queen about me, Her Majesty said I was an odd sort of man, but I forgive her; for it is an odd thing in an honest man[1] to speak freely to Princes.

I will say another thing in your praise; that goodness would become you better than any Person I know, and for that very reason there is nobody I wish to be good so much as your self | I am ever with the truest respect and esteem | Madam | Your most obedient and | most humble servant | Jonath Swift

Twitenham | Aug. 14th[2] 1727.

[1] Earlier editors omit 'in an honest man'.

[2] Nichols and Scott date the letter 15 Aug. Swift first wrote '19' and then above '14'.

4805

Mrs. Howard to Swift

[16 August 1727]

I did desire you to write me a love letter but I never did desire You to talk of marrying me. I had rather you and I were dumb as well as deaf for ever then that shou'd happen; I wou'd take your giddyness, your head-ake or any other complaint you have, to resemble you in one circumstance of life. so that I insist upon your thinking your self a very happy man, at least whenever comparasion between you and I. I likewise insist upon your taking no resolution to leave England till I see you which must be here for the most disagreeable reason in the world and the most shocking. I dare not come to you. beleive nobody that talks to you of the Queen, without you are sure the Person likes both the Queen, and You. I have been a Slave twenty years without ever receiving a reason for any one thing I ever was oblig'd to do. and I have now a mind to take the pleasure once in my life of absolute power which I expect you to give me in obeying all my orders without one question why I have given them

Address: To | the Re[d] Dean Swift
Endorsed by Swift: M[rs] Howard. 1727

B.M. Add. MS. 22625, f. 17

Swift to Mrs. Howard

17 August 1727.

Madam

I will send three words in answer to your letter, although I am like a great Minister in a tottering condition. I chiefly valued my self upon my bad head and deaf ears if these be no charms for you, I must give over. I am sure I should love a cat the better for being deaf, and much more a Christian. But since my best qualityes will not move you, I am so desperate that I resolve to get rid of them as soon as possible and accordingly am putting my self into the apothecary's books, and swallowing the poisons he sends me by the Doctors orders.

As great an enemy as I am to arbitary power, I will obey your command with the utmost zeal and blindness, and when I can walk, without staggering, and hear a Musquet let off, I will have the honor of attending you, being with the truest respect Madam | Your most obedient and | most humble Servant | Jonath Swift.

Twitenham | Aug 17th 1727

4805

Mrs. Howard to Swift

[18 August 1727]

I write to you to please myself. I hear you are Melancholy because you have a bad head, and deaf ears these are two misfortunes I have labour'd under several Years; and yet was never peevish with my self or the world; have I more Philosophy and resolution then you? or am I so stupid that I don't feel the evil? is this meant in a good natur'd view? or do I mean, that I please my self when I insult over you? answer these Query's in writing if *poison* or other methods don't enable you soon to appear in person. tho' I make use of your own word poison give me leave to tell you it's nonsense, and I believe you will take more care for the time to come how you endeavour to impose upon my understanding by making no use of your own.

Address: To | the Red Dean of St Patricks
Endorsed by Swift: Mrs Howard J | 1727

B.M. Add. MS. 22625, f. 18

Swift to Mrs. Howard

19 August 1727

Madam,

About two hours before you were born, I got my Giddyness by eating a hundred golden pippins at a time, at Richmond, and when you were four years and a quarter old bating two days, having made a fine seat about twenty miles farther in Surrey where I used to read and sleep, there I got my Deafness, and these two friends have visited me, one or other, every year since, and being old acquaintance have now thought fit to come together.[1] So much for the calamityes wherein I have the honor to resemble you; and you see your sufferings are but children in comparison of mine, and yet, to shew my Philosophy I have been as cheerfull as Scarron. You boast that your disorders never made you peevish. . where is the virtue? when all the world was peevish on your account, and so took the office out of your hands. Whereas, I bore the whole load my self, nobody caring threepence what I suffered, or whether I was hanged or at ease. I tell you my Philosophy is twelve times greater than yours, for I can call Witnesses that I bear half your pains besides all my own, which are in themselves ten times greater. Thus I have most fully answered Queryes. I wish the *poison* were in my Stomach (which may be very probable considering the many Drugs I take) if I remember to have mentioned that word in my Letter, but Ladyes who have poison in their eyes, may be apt to mistake in reading— Oh, I have found it out; the Word Person I suppose was written like poison. ask friends I write to, and they will attest this mistake to be but a trifle in my way of writing, and could easily prove it if they had any of my letters to shew: I make nothing of Slily for Ilay,[2] Knights of a Share for Knights of a Shire, Monster for Minister; in writing Speaker I put an n for a p[3] and a hundred such blunders, which cannot be helped, while I have a hundred oceans rolling in my ears, into which no sense has been poured this fortnight; and therefore if I write nonsense, I can assure you it is genuine, and not borrowed.

Thus I write by your commands, and besides, I am bound in duty to be the last writer. but deaf or giddy heaving or steddy, I shall ever be, with the truest respect | Madm | Your most obedient and | most humble Servant | Jonath: Swift.

Twitenham | Aug. 19th 1727.

[1] On Swift's illness see Appendix VII.

[2] Archibald Campbell, who succeeded as third Duke of Argyll in 1743, was in 1705 appointed one of the commissioners for treating of the union. His services were recognized by his being created Earl of Islay. In the conduct of Scottish affairs he was a special confidant of Walpole.

[3] Swift thought that by his surrender to Walpole Sir Spencer Compton had sacrificed his friends.

Dodsley Miscellanies 1745, x. 114

Swift to the Rev. Thomas Sheridan

Twickenham, Aug. 29, 1727.

I have had your Letter of the 19th, and expect, before you read this, to receive another from you with the most fatal News that can ever come to me,[1] unless I should be put to Death for some ignominious Crime. I continue very ill with my Giddiness and Deafness, of which I had two Days intermission, but since worse, and I shall be perfectly content if God shall please to call me away at this Time. Here is a triple Cord of Friendship broke, which hath lasted thirty Years, twenty-four of which in *Ireland*. I beg if you have not writ to me before you get this, to tell me no Particulars, but the Event in general: My Weakness, my Age, my Friendship will bear no more. I have mentioned the Case as well as I knew it, to a Physician who is my Friend; and I find his Methods were the same, Air, and Exercise, and at last Asses-Milk. I will tell you sincerely, that if I were younger, and in Health, or in Hopes of it, I would endeavour to divert my Mind by all Methods in order to pass my Life in quiet; but I now want only three Months of Sixty. I am strongly visited with a Disease that will at last cut me off; if I should this Time escape, if not, I have but a poor Remainder, that is below any wise Man's valuing. I do not intend to return to *Ireland* so soon as I purposed; I would not be there in the very midst of Grief. I desire you will speak to Mr. *Worrall*, to get a new Licence about the beginning of *October*, when my old one, (as he will see by the Date) shall expire; but if that fatal Accident were not to happen, I am not able to travel in my present Condition. What I intend, is immediately to leave this Place, and go with my old Cousin for a Nurse about five Miles from *London*, on the other Side towards the Sea, and if I recover, I will either pass the Winter near *Salisbury-Plain*, or in *France*; and therefore I desire Mr. *Worrall* may make this Licence run like the former [To *Great-Britain* or elsewhere for Recovery of his Health].

⌜Neither my Health nor Grief will permit me to say more: Your Directions to Mr. *Lancelot*,[2] at his House in *New Bond-street*, over against the *Crown and Cushion* will reach me. Farewell.⌝[3]

[1] The death of Stella.

[2] See p. 164, n. 6. Husband of Swift's cousin Patty Rolt.

[*For note 3 see opposite*

This stroke was unexpected, and my Fears last Year were ten Times greater.

Ball, iii. 448

Swift to Martha Blount

Twickenham Garret, Thursday[1]
morning at nine—1727 (?)

Madam Patt,

You are commanded by Mr. Pope to read that part of the enclosed which relates to Mr. Gay and yourself, and to send a direct answer to your humble servant by my humble servant the bearer. Being at an end of all my shoes and stockings, I am not able to wait on you to-day, after so rainy a night and so auspicious a morning. Mrs. Pope is yours; but I with the greatest respect, Madam, | Your most obedient and devoted servant, | Jonath: Swift.

Pray do give a copy of this letter to Curll the bookseller.

Dodsley Miscellanies 1745, x. 117[2]

Swift to the Rev. Thomas Sheridan

London, *Sept*. 2, 1727.

I had yours of the 19th of *August*, which I answered the 29th, from *Twickenham*. I came to Town on the last Day of *August*, being impatient of staying there longer, where so much Company came to us while I was so Giddy and Deaf. I am now got to my Cousin *Lancelot*'s House, where I desire all Letters may be directed to me; I am still in the same Condition, or rather worse, for I walk like a

[1] The original of this letter was at one time at Mapledurham in vol. iii of the bound letters, lying in Drawer H. Vol. iii of the bound letters no longer contains the letter.

[2] This letter appeared in Dodsley's *Miscellanies. The Tenth Volume*, p. 117; and thereafter in Faulkner, 1746, viii. 422. The text is printed from Dodsley.

---

[3] The words in half-brackets do not appear in Faulkner's text, 1746, or in his later editions.

drunken Man, and am deafer than ever you knew me. If I had any tolerable Health, I would go this Moment to *Ireland*; yet I think I would not, considering the News I daily expect to hear from you. I have just received yours of *August* 24; I kept it an Hour in my Pocket, with all the Suspense of a Man who expected to hear the worst News that Fortune could give him; and at the same Time was not able to hold up my Head. These are the Perquisites of living long: The last Act of Life is always a Tragedy at best; but it is a bitter Aggravation to have one's best Friend go before one. I desired in my last, that you would not enlarge upon that Event; but tell me the bare Fact. I long knew that our dear Friend had not the *Stamina Vitae*; but my Friendship could not arm me against this Accident altho' I foresaw it. I have said enough in my last Letter, which now I suppose is with you. I know not whether it be an Addition to my Grief or no, that I am now extreamly ill; for it would have been a Reproach to me to be in perfect Health, when such a Friend is desperate. I do profess, upon my Salvation, that the distressed and desperate Condition of our Friend, makes Life so indifferent to me, who by Course of Nature have so little left, that I do not think it worth the Time to struggle; yet I should think, according to what hath been formerly, that I may happen to overcome this present Disorder; and to what Advantage? Why, to see the Loss of that Person for whose sake Life was only worth preserving. I brought both those Friends over, that we might be happy together as long as God should please; the Knot is broken, and the remaining Person, you know, has ill answered the End; and the other who is now to be lost, was all that is Valuable. You agreed with me, or you are a great Hypocrite. What have I to do in the World? I was never in such Agonies as when I received your Letter, and had it in my Pocket.—I am able to hold up my sorry Head no longer.[1]

[1] Faulkner, 1746, appends the following note to the letter: 'That ingenious Lady, for whom the Author expresseth so much Concern in the two foregoing Letters, was Stella; so often celebrated in the Author's Poems, for her fine Person, Wit, and many Virtues. Her Physician told her when she was near dying, that she was at the Bottom of the Hill, and they must endeavour to get her up again. But she plainly saw the Approaches of Death, and readily replied, That she found she would be out of Breath before she got up to the Top. She died a few Months after the Date of these Letters, on the 28th of January 1727[–8].' Faulkner also added a brief footnote which led to comments by Delany, *Observations*, pp. 54–59; and for a caustic rejoinder from Deane Swift, *Essay*, pp. 267–8.

Trinity College, Dublin, N. 3. 9

Archbishop King to Swift

[? September 1727]

Extract of an Order of the Trustees for Mrs Steeven's Charity dated at St Selpulchers Augt 22^d^ 1727—Ordered that his Grace the Lord Archbp of Dublin be desired to write to the Dean of St Patricks about the papers delivered to him by Mr Proby[1] relating to the Establishment of Dr Steevens's Hospitall.

In complyance with the above order I send the Copie I Recd this Day. the Parlement being now near and the Trustees having an intention to apply for a settlement by an act desires (*sic*) to have those papers which they conceive may be usefull to them, your assistance might likewise be of service and acceptable in particular to | Revd S^r^ | Your most humble Servt | & Brother | W D

Dr. Swift Dean of St Patricks[2]

4805

Swift to the Rev. John Worrall

London. Sepr 12th 1727

I have not writ to you this long time, nor would I now if it were not necessary. By D^r^ Sh—ns[3] frequent Letters I am every post expecting the Death of a friend with whose loss I shall have very little regard for the few years that nature may leave me. I desire to know where my two friends lodge. I gave a caution to Mrs Brent, that it might not be in domi decanus,[4] quoniam hoc minime decet, uti manifestum est, habeo enim malignos, qui sinistrè hoc interpretabuntur, si eveniet[5] (quod deus avertat) ut illic moriatur. I am in such a condition of health, that I cannot possibly travel; D^r^ Sh— to whom I write this post will be more particular, and spare my weak disordered head. Pray answer all calls of money power to Mrs Dingley, and desire her to ask it. . I can not come back at the time of

[1] See Swift to Tickell, 3 Aug. 1724.

[2] The address to Swift 'at the lodging of John Gay, Esq., in Whitehall, London', printed by Ball (iii. 418), does not now appear.

[3] Sheridan's.

[4] Decanus—*sic*.

[5] Thus in manuscript.

my Licence, I am afraid. Therefore 2 or 3d[1] before it expires which will be the beginning of Octobr (you will find by the date of the last,) take out a new one for another half year, and let the same clause be in of leave to go to great Britain or elsewhere, for recovery of health for very probably if this unfortunate event should happen of the loss of our friend (and I have no probability or hopes to expect better) I will go to France if my health will permit me, to forget my self. . I leave my whole little affairs with you. I hate to think of them. If Mr Deacon[2] or Alderman Person come to pay rent, take it on account, unless they bring you their last acquittance to direct you. But Deacon owes me 75ll and interest upon his bond.; so that you are to take care of giving him any receit in full of all accounts.

I hope you and Mrs Worrall have your health: I can hold up my head no longr. I am sincerly yrs | &c

You need not trouble your self to write, till you have business for it is uncertain where I shall be.

Address: To the Reverend Mr Worrall | at his house in big Sheep-street | Dublin | Ireld
Postmark: 12 SE
Endorsed by Swift: 7br 12th 1727

B.M. Add. MS. 22625, f. 19

Swift to Mrs. Howard

Madam, [? 14 September 1727]

This cruel disorder of deafness attended with a continual giddyness still pursues me and I have determined, since I have a home in Dublin, not inconvenient to return thither before my health and the weather grow worse. It is one comfort that I shall rid you of a worthless companion, though not an importunate one. . I am infinitely obliged to you for all your civilityes, and shall preserve a remembrance of them as long as any memory left.

I hope you will favor me so far as to present my most humble duty to the Queen and to tell her Majesty my sorrow that my disorder was

[1] '2 or 3d' above the line in manuscript.
[2] Tenant of Kilberry.

of such a nature as to make me incapable of attending her, as she was pleased to permit me. I shall pass the remainder of my life with the utmost gratitude for her Majesty's favors. I pray God restore your health and preserve it, and remove all afflictions from you. I shall be ever with the truest respect | Madam | Your most obedient | and most humble Servant |

Jonath Swift.

London Sep^{tbr} 14th | 1727.[1]

The Dublin Journal, 31 May–3 June 1729

John Wheldon to Swift

[September 1727]

Reverend Sir,

Understanding that you are at Holyhead, in order for Dublin,[2] and inform'd that you are a Lover of the Mathematicks, I make bold to trouble you with this writing. I have about 12 Months since imparted my Discourse to Dr. Dobbs,[3] Professor of Mathematicks at the College of Dublin, of finding out the Longitude by two known Stars; the same Copy I sent to the Lords of the Admiralty and the Trinity Masters,[4] and also to Dr. Halley[5] at Greenwich, and to the Commanders of Ships at Liverpool and elsewhere. I begg'd either

[1] Hawkesworth dates 'Sept. 1727'. Croker, *Letters to and from Henrietta, Countess of Suffolk*, i. 271, and Ball, iii. 419, give the day of the month as '18'. Swift wrote '14th'. On Monday, 18 Sept., Swift set out on his journey to Ireland.

[2] On the conclusion of his visit to England in 1727 Swift set out for Ireland on Monday 18 September. He reached Holyhead on Sunday the 24th where he was delayed a week by stormy weather. He employed his time in writing verses and keeping a diary in a small notebook. On the 27th he refers to a letter he had received 'from one Wheldon' who claimed to have 'found out the Longitude'. He sent back the letter with his 'answer under it'. Wheldon's letter together with Swift's answer were printed in Faulkner's *Dublin Journal*, No. 378, 31 May–3 June. I am grateful to Professor Louis A. Landa for calling my attention to this last fact. For *The Holyhead Journal* see *Prose Works*, Temple Scott, xi. 391–403.

[3] Presumably Richard Dobbs, elected Fellow of Trinity College 1724.

[4] Trinity House of Deptford, incorporated by Henry VIII, had jurisdiction over pilotage and was a general lighthouse authority.

[5] Edmund Halley (1656–1742), the famous astronomer.

Approbation or Objection, and their Reason to the contrary, and ever since, which is above three Months past, have not had a Tittle of Answer. If you are that way inclin'd, you may have a View of my Discourse. I beg Pardon for this Freedom, and remain your humble Servant:

John Wheldon.[1]

The Dublin Journal, 31 May–3 June 1729

Swift to John Wheldon

Holy. Sept. 27, 1727[2]

I understand not Mathematicks, but have been formerly troubled too much with Projectors of the Longitude to my great Mortification and some Charges by encouraging them. It is only to Mathematicians you must apply. Newton, Halley, and Keil[3] have all told me they doubted the Thing was impossible. If you can demonstrate that you have found it, there is, I hear, a course taken that you may discover it in London without being defrauded of your Invention. One of my Projectors cut his Throat, and the other was found an Imposter. This is all I can say; but am confident you would deceive others, or are deceived yourself.

Faulkner 1741

Alexander Pope to Swift

Oct. 2, 1727

It is a perfect trouble to me to write to you, and your kind letter left for me at Mr. Gay's affected me so much, that it made me like a

[1] John Wheldon has not been identified. The determination of the longitude had long exercised 'projectors'. Joseph Beaumont, Swift's friend, was deranged by researches into the problem. William Whiston (1667–1752) made several attempts to devise means for discovering the longitude, for which a substantial reward was offered by Parliament.

[2] *Sic.*

[3] John Keill (1671–1721), born in Edinburgh, gained great distinction as a mathematician and astronomer. His Savilian lectures were held in high repute.

girl. I can't tell what to say to you; I only feel that I wish you well in every circumstance of life: that 'tis almost as good to be hated, as to be loved, considering the pain it is to minds of any tender turn, to find themselves so utterly impotent to do any good, or give any ease to those who deserve most from us. I would very fain know, as soon as you recover your complaints, or any part of them. Would to God I could ease any of them, or had been able even to have alleviated any! I found I was not, and truly it grieved me. I was sorry to find you could think your self easier in any house than in mine, tho' at the same time I can allow for a tenderness in your way of thinking, even when it seem'd to want that tenderness. I can't explain my meaning, perhaps you know it: But the best way of convincing you of my indulgence, will be, if I live, to visit you in Ireland, and act there as much in my own way as you did here in yours. I will not leave your roof, if I am ill. To your bad health I fear there was added some disagreeable news from Ireland, which might occasion your so sudden departure:[1] for the last time I saw you at Hammersmith,[2] you assured me you would not leave us, unless your health grew better, this whole winter; and I don't find it did so. I never comply'd so unwillingly in my life with any friend as with you, in staying so intirely from you: nor could I have had the constancy to do it, if you had not promised that before you went, we shou'd meet, and you would send to us all to come. I have given your remembrances to those you mention in yours: we are quite sorry for you, I mean for ourselves. I hope, as you do, that we shall meet in a more durable and more satisfactory state; but the less sure I am of that, the more I would indulge it in this. We are to believe, we shall have something better than even a friend, there, but certainly here we have nothing so good.

Adieu for this time; may you find every friend you go to as pleas'd and happy, as every friend you went from is sorry and troubled. | Yours, &c.

[1] Swift had made no allusion to Pope of his anxiety about Stella; but a letter from Pope to Sheridan, 6 Sept. 1727 (Sherburn, ii. 445), shows that he knew 'a particular Friend of the Dean's' was 'upon the brink of another World'.

[2] The words 'at Hammersmith' are omitted in some early editions. It may be that Swift found Lancelot's house in New Bond Street too accessible to friends, and that this led him to remove to Hammersmith.

Faulkner 1741

Swift to Alexander Pope

Dublin, Oct. 12, 1727.

I have been long reasoning with my self upon the condition I am in, and in conclusion have thought it best to return to what fortune hath made my home; I have there a large house, and servants and conveniencies about me.[1] I may be worse than I am, and I have no where to retire. I therefore thought it best to return to Ireland, rather than go to any distant place in England. Here is my maintainance, and here my convenience. If it pleases God to restore me to my health, I shall readily make a third journey; if not, we must part as all human creatures have parted. You are the best and kindest friend in the world, and I know no body alive or dead to whom I am so much obliged; and if ever you made me angry, it was for your too much care about me. I have often wish'd that God almighty would be so easy to the weakness of mankind, as to let old friends be acquainted in another state; and if I were to write an Utopia for heaven, that would be one of my Schemes. This wildness you must allow for, because I am giddy and deaf.

I find it more convenient to be sick here, without the vexation of making my friends uneasy; yet my giddiness alone would not have done, if that unsociable comfortless deafness had not quite tired me: And I believe I should have returned from the Inn,[2] if I had not feared it was only a short intermission, and the year was late, and my licence expiring. Surely besides all other faults, I should be a very ill judge, to doubt your friendship and kindness. But it hath pleased God that you are not in a state of health, to be mortified with the care and sickness of a friend: Two sick friends never did well together; such an office is fitter for servants and humble companions, to whom it is wholly indifferent whether we give them trouble or no. The case would be quite otherwise if you were with me; you could refuse to see any body: Here is a large house where we need not hear each other if we were both sick: I have a race of orderly elderly people of both sexes at command, who are of no consequence, and have gifts proper for attending us; who can bawl when I am deaf, and tread softly when I am only giddy and would sleep.

I had another reason for my haste hither, which was changing my

[1] This letter is a reply to the preceding one.

[2] The inn in Aldersgate Street from which the Chester coach started.

Agent, the old one having terribly involved my little affairs; to which however I am grown so indifferent, that I believe I shall lose two or three hundred pounds rather than plague my self with accompts: so that I am very well qualified to be a Lord, and put into Peter Walter's[1] hands.

Pray God continue and increase Mr. Congreve's amendment, though he does not deserve it like you, having been too lavish of that health which Nature gave him.

I hope my White-hall landlord is nearer to a place than when I left him; as the Preacher said, 'the day of judgment was nearer, than ever it had been before.'

Pray God send you health, *det Salutem, det opes, animam aequam ipse tibi parabis.*[2] You see Horace wished for money, as well as health; and I would hold a crown he kept a coach; and I shall never be a friend to the Court, till you do so too. | Yours, &c.

Deane Swift 1768

The Earl of Oxford to Swift

Dover-street, Oct. 12, 1727.

Rev. Sir,[3]

I was very much concerned to hear that you were so much out of order when I went to the North; and upon my return, which was but lately, I was in hopes to have found you here, and that you would not have gone to your deanery till the *Spring*. I should be glad to hear that you are well, and have got rid of that troublesome distemper, your deafness.

I have seen *Pope* but once, and that was but for a few minutes; he was very much out of order, but I hope it only proceeded from being two days in town, and staying out a whole opera. He would

[1] An attorney, usurer, miser, agent for the Duke of Newcastle and other noblemen. He was believed to have amassed a fortune of over £200,000 by lending money at extortionate interest. He was frequently satirized by Pope and Fielding. In *Joseph Andrews* he was caricatured as Peter Pounce.

[2] Adapted from Horace, *Ep.* I. xviii. 112. 'Det vitam, det opes; aequum mi animum ipse parabo.'

[3] A draft of this letter appears in Longleat, xiii, f. 53. The earlier part of the draft, with many scorings out, was written by Oxford. The latter portion, within half-brackets, is in the hand of an amanuensis. The letter is endorsed by Oxford: 'A copy to the Dean of St Patricks. Oct. 12, 1727.'

not see the coronation,[1] although he might have seen it with little trouble.

I came last night well home, after attending and paying my duty in my rank at the coronation. I hope there will not be another till I can have the laudable excuse of Old Age not to attend; which is no ill wish to their present majesties, since *Nottingham* at fourscore could bear the fatigue very well.[2] I will not trouble you with an account of the ceremony; I do not doubt but you will have a full and true account from much better hands.

⌜I have been put in hopes that we shall see you again early in the *Spring*, which will be a very great pleasure to me.

There is a gentleman that is now putting out a new edition of the *Oxford Marmora*: I should take it as a great favour if you would be so kind to lend me your copy of that book.[3] I think there are some corrections: if you think fit to do this, Mr. *Clayton*,[4] who is in *Ireland*, will take care to bring it safe to me, and I will with great care return it to you again.

I must not conclude this without making my wife's compliments to you. I am, with true respect, Sir, your most humble servant, | Oxford.⌝

[You forgot to send me the ballad.][5]

Mr. *Clayton* will call upon you before he comes to *England*; I have written to him to that purpose.

Faulkner 1741[6]

Gay and Pope to Swift

Oct. 22, 1727

Though you went away from us so unexpectedly, and in so clandestine a manner; yet by several enquiries,[7] we have inform'd our selves of every thing that hath happen'd to you.

[1] George II was crowned on the preceding day.

[2] Daniel Finch, second Earl of Nottingham, satirized by Swift in *The Intended Speech of a Famous Orator*, 1711 (*Poems*, p. 141), was born in 1647. He had retired from public affairs for some years, and died on 1 Jan. 1729–30.

[3] For Prideaux's *Marmora Oxoniensia* see Swift to Oxford 12 Aug. 1726.

[4] A relation of Bishop Robert Clayton. On several occasions he conveyed missives between Swift and Oxford.

[5] This sentence does not appear in the draft. [*For notes 6, 7 see opposite.*

To our great joy you have told us your deafness left you at the Inn in Aldersgate-street:[1] No doubt your ears knew there was nothing worth hearing in England.

Our advices from Chester tell us, that you met Captain Lawson;[2] the Captain was a man of veracity, and set sail at the time he told you; I really wish'd you had laid hold of that opportunity, for you had then been in Ireland the next day: Besides, as it is credibly reported, the Captain had a bottle or two of excellent claret in his Cabbin. You would not then have had the plague of that little smoaky room at Holy-head; but considering it was there you lost your giddiness, we have great reason to praise smoaky rooms for the future, and prescribe them in like cases to our friends. The maid of the house writes us word, that while you were there you were busy for ten days together writing continually—and that as Wat drew nearer to Ireland, he blunder'd more and more. By a scrap of paper left in this smoaky room, it seem'd as if the Book you was writing, was a most lamentable account of your travels; and really, had there been any wine in the house, the place would have not been so irksome. We were further told, that you set out, were driven back again by a storm, and lay in the ship all night. After the next setting sail, we were in great concern about you, because the weather grew very tempestuous. When to my great joy, and surprize, I receiv'd a letter from Carlingford in Ireland, which inform'd us that after many perils you were safely landed there.[3] Had the oysters been good it would have been a comfortable refreshment after your fatigue. We compassionated you in your travels through that country of desolation and poverty in your way to Dublin, for it is a most dreadful circumstance to have lazy dull horses on a road where there are very bad or no Inns. When you carry a sample of English Apples next to Ireland, I beg you would either get them from Goodrich or

[1] See Swift's letter to Pope, 12 Oct. 1727.

[2] Lawson was the captain of the government yacht which plied constantly between Parkgate and Dublin. But Swift, eager to reach Dublin as soon as possible, pushed on to Holyhead, which he reached on Sunday, 24 Sept. Here he was detained for over a week by adverse winds. See *The Holyhead Journal*, *Prose Works*, ed. Temple Scott, xi. 391–403; *Poems*, pp. 418–24.

[3] In co. Louth, sixty miles from Dublin.

[6] Pope in his quarto and folio volumes of 1741 omitted the first three paragraphs, using the last two only, beginning with 'The Queen's family is at last settled'.

[7] Evidently the news came by letter from Sheridan.

Devonshire.[1] Pray who was the Clergyman that met you at some distance from Dublin? because we could not learn his name.[2] These are all the hints we could get of your long and dangerous journey, every step of which we shar'd your anxieties—and all that we have now left to comfort us, is to hear that you are in good health.

But why should we tell you what you know already? The Queen's family is at last settled, and in the list I was appointed Gentleman-usher to the Princess Louisa, the youngest Princess; which, upon account that I am so far advanc'd in life, I have declin'd accepting; and have endeavour'd, in the best manner I could, to make my excuses by a letter to her Majesty. So now all my expectations are vanish'd; and I have no prospect, but in depending wholly upon my self, and my own conduct. As I am us'd to disappointments I can bear them, but as I can have no more hopes, I can no more be disappointed, so that I am in a blessed condition.—You remember you were advising me to go into Newgate to finish my scenes[3] the more correctly—I now think I shall, for I have no attendance to hinder me; but my Opera is already finished. I leave the rest of this paper to Mr. Pope.

Gay is a free-man, and I writ him a long congratulatory letter upon it. Do you the same: It will mend him, and make him a better man than a Court could do. Horace might keep his coach in Augustus's time, if he pleas'd, but I won't in the time of our Augustus. My Poem[4] (which it grieves me that I dare not send you a copy of, for fear of the Curl's and Dennis's of Ireland, and still more for fear of the worst of Traytors, our friends and Admirers) my Poem, I say, will shew you what a distinguishing age we lived in? Your name is in it, with some others under a mark of such ignominy as you will not much grieve to wear in that company. Adieu, and God bless you, and give you health and spirits.

Whether you chuse Cervantes' serious air,
Or laugh and shake in Rablais' easy chair,
Or in the graver Gown instruct mankind,
Or silent, let thy morals tell thy mind.[5]

[1] Swift came from Goodrich in Herefordshire, Gay was born at Barnstaple in Devonshire.

[2] Probably Sheridan.

[3] In *The Beggar's Opera*.

[4] *The Dunciad*.

[5] In *The Dunciad* the last two lines become:

'Or praise the Court, or magnify Mankind,
Or thy griev'd Country's copper chains unbind.'

These two verses are over and above what I've said of you in the Poem. Adieu.

Portland MSS. Harley Papers

Swift to the Earl of Oxford

[17 Nov. 1727]

My Lord.

I deferred acknowledging the honor of Your Lordship's Letter[1] till I could do it by Mr Clayton, and at the same time obey your commands of sending you the book of the Arundel marbles: the value of it consists onely in the great number of amendments which were made by Doctor Mills, who it seems was very famous in that kind of literature, and I hope it will be of good use to the Gentleman who undertakes the new edition.

I must now return my most humble thanks for your Lordships great favors and civilityes to me while I was last in England. My haste hither was occasioned meerly by the despair of being under so long a disorder of giddyness and especially deafness, which made me as uneasy to my friends as to my self: and I think whoever is deaf is fit for nothing but a cloyster. God be thanked my journey relieved me from both disorders, and here I am with very little use for my ears.

I cannot find there are any old Irish Coyns, at least not of any great antiquity, but long since the Conquest by Henr 2d.[2] The Coyns found here underground are generally of the Saxon Kings, or some of the later Emperors. I shall see what can be done about an affair which Mr Clayton hath begun, relating to the late Bishop Nicolsons papers.[3] As to Letters from learned men to him, I cannot hope much. He sent me one of his Books which contained a catalogue of Writings proper for one who would write a History of Ireland wherein I found he took many things very weakly upon trust, and referred the reader to papers which I found to contain nothing at all of the matter he mentions. I shall, by the help of some Clergymen in

[1] Oxford to Swift, 12 Oct. 1727.

[2] See Swift to Oxford, 26 Oct. 1725.

[3] William Nicholson had only been translated from Derry to the Archbishopric of Cashel when he died, 14 Feb. 1726–7.

the neighborhood of the Bishops Son,[1] learn as much as I can about his Father's papers, and, if they be of any use, purchase them.

I hope Your Lordship and My Lady Oxford and Lady Marget are in good health which I humbly pray to God you all may long enjoy, with a continuance of honour and happyness. | I am with the greatest respect | My Lord | Your Lordship's most obedient | and most obliged servant | Jonath Swift

Dublin. | Novr 17th 1727

Endorsed: Dean of St Patricks | Nov. 17. Dublin. Rx | Dec. 11: 1727 by Mr Clayton

Forster copy

Swift to Knightley Chetwode

Dublin, November 23, 1727.

Sir,

I have yours of the 15th instant, wherein you tell me that upon my last leaving Ireland, you supposed I would return no more, which was probable enough, for I was nine weeks very ill in England, both of giddiness and deafness which latter being an unconversible disorder I thought it better to come to a place of my own, than be troublesome to my friends, or live in a lodging, and this hastened me over, and by a hard journey I recovered both my ailments. But if you imagined me to have any favour at Court you were much mistaken or misinformed. It is quite otherwise, at least among the Ministry. Neither did I ever go to Court, except when I was sent for and not always then. Besides my illness gave me too good an excuse the last two months.

As to politics; in England it is hard to keep out of them, and here it is a shame to be in them, unless by way of laughter and ridicule, for both which my taste is gone. I suppose there will be as much mischief as interest, folly, ambition and faction can bring about. But let those who are younger than I look to the consequences. The public is an old tattered house, but may last as long as my lease in it, and therefore like a true Irish tenant I shall consider no further.

[1] Nicolson was, even in his own day, accused of undue patronage of his relations. The best benefice in the diocese was alleged to have been bestowed on his son.

I wish I had some retirement two or three miles from this town to amuse myself, as you do, with planting much, but not as you do, for I would build very little. But I cannot think of a remote journey in such a miserable country, such a climate, and such roads, and such uncertainty of health. I would never if possible be above an hour distant from home, nor be caught by a deafness and giddiness out of my own precincts, where I can do or not do, what I please; and see or not see, whom I please. But if I had a home a hundred miles off I never would see this town again, which I believe is the most disagreeable place in Europe, at least to any but those who have been accustomed to it from their youth, and in such a case I suppose a jail might be tolerable. But my best comfort is, that I lead here the life of a monk, as I have always done; I am vexed whenever I hear a knocking at the door, especially the raps of quality, and I see none but those who come on foot. This is too much at once. I am, | Yours &c.

Address: To Knightley Chetwode, Esq., at his House at Woodbrooke, near Mountmellick.

Longleat xiii (Harleian transcript)[1]

Swift to John Gay and Alexander Pope

Dublin Novr 23d 1727.

⌜I had your double Letter[2] some time agoe, whereof the first and greatest part is of your own head, and contains a very exact account of my journey from London to this Place, wherever you got it, or whatever Familiar you dealt with. I did actually amuse my self with writing a Journal of my distresses and living at Holyhead at least when it grew dark, for then I never read. I did miss my passage from Chester, which would have saved much time weariness and money. I wanted wine for 4 days of the 8. I staid there. I did set out and was driven back, and all the other Circumstances—Carlingford, bad Horses, worse roads, and Welch apples are all true, and nothing but

[1] The parts of this letter enclosed in half-brackets were omitted by Pope in early editions, and he added to the letter sections belonging to letters from Swift dated 26 Feb. 1727–8 and 28 May 1728. See Sherburn, ii. 460, n. This transcript is in a different hand to the majority of the Harleian transcripts.

[2] The letter of Gay and Pope of 22 Oct. 1727.

the Devil could have informed you, for I kept no Company but travelled alone. Or else it must be Poetical conjuring, as Homer recites the dreams of those who were killed in their Sleep. I heard nothing of the Q—'s family Settling, nor ever hear one Syllable of News any more than at Twitenham. Remember how I detested your three half penny worth of News at Whitehall, which made me think myself in a Coffee-House.⌝

I entirely approve your refusal of that Employment, and your writing to the Q— I am perfectly confident you have a firm Enemy in the Ministry.[1] God forgive him, but not till he puts himself in a State to be forgiven. Upon reasoning with Myself, I should hope they are gone too far to discard you quite, and that they will give you something, which altho' much less than they ought will be as far as it is worth, better circumstantiated. And since you already just live, a middling help will make you just tolerable. Your lateness in Life (as you so soon call it) might be improper to begin the World with, but almost the oldest Men may hope to see Changes in a Court. A Minister is always Seventy, and you are thirty Years younger, and Cromwell himself did not begin to appear till he was older than you:——I beg you will be thrifty and learn to value a shilling, which Dr Birch[2] said was a serious thing. Get a stronger fence about your 1000ll, and throw the Inner fence into the Heap; and be advised by your Twitenham Landlord and me about an Annuity. You are most refractory honest good natured Men I ever have known. I could argue out this Paper. I am very glad your Opera is finished; and hope your friends will join the readyer to make it succeed, because you are used by others so ill

⌜Scene. Twitenham-house. Just after Dinner.⌝

I have known Courts these 36 years, and know they differ, but in some things they are extreamly constant: First, in the trite old Maxim of a Minister never forgiving those he hath injured; secondly, in the insincerityes of those who would be thought the best Friends; thirdly, in the Love of fawning, cringing and Tale bearing. Fourthly in sacrificing those whom we realy wish well, to a point of Interest or Intrigue. Fifthly, in keeping every thing worth taking for those, who can do service or disservice. ⌜I could go on to four and twentythly.

[1] Gay had been suspected, without justification, of a libel on Sir Robert Walpole. No ill-feeling was aroused, for Gay's appointment as a commissioner of the lottery was renewed without question. Cf. Elwin, vii. 106, n. 3.

[2] Perhaps Peter Birch, Archdeacon of Westminster, for whom see *D.N.B.*

But with all the partiality of my Inclination, I cannot acquit this Characterized Person; it is against my original fundamental Maxims. I durst appeal to our friend at Dawly, tho' I know more than he, because I was a Subaltern, and have even deceived him to do more for some I did not over much value, then the other who pretends to have so strong a regard for our Friend. Neither will your mutato nomine &c satisfie me unless things are monstrously changed from what you taught me. For I was led to believe that the present unexpected scituation or Confirmation of things was brought about above 2 years ago by the intervention of that Person whose Character was drawn.[1] But if it be as you say, the fate of the Princess des Ursines ought to be rememberd[2]—As to Ireland, the Air of this House is good, and of the Kingdom very good, but the best fruits fall short a little. All things to Eat and drink except very few, better then in London, except you have 4000ll a year. The ridings and coachings a hundred times better in Winter. You may find about six rational, good, civil learned Easy Companions among of the Males; fewer of the females; but many civil, hospitable, and ready to admire and Adore. About a dozen tolerable he Companions, without impertinence. No Paulteneys nor Dawleys nor Arbuthnots. A very good Apartment, good French Wine, and Port. and among the Extravagant, Hoch, Burgundy, Rackpunch &c but too dear for me. Onely I hope to have Cyder from Goodridge. If you like this Bill of Fare, and air, and Company; The sea, the Towngates, and the Door of this House are open.[3] You can have an Eighteen penny Chicken for 7 pence. I will send Dr Delany and Mr Stopfort as far as Chester to Conduct you and thus I have enterd your Chalenge. I repeated your Civilities to Dr Sheridan, who reced them as he ought, and resolves to get you all sorts of those foolish Wines your Caprices are so fond of; and has a garden 2 Miles off to amuse you with; but inconveniency is, it will have very good fruit in it. I desire you will present my most humble service to Sir Spencer Compton

[1] Mrs. Howard's character by Swift, dated 12 June 1727, will be found in *Prose Works*, xi. 147–50. The original is among the manuscripts of the Marquess of Bath, Longleat, xiii, ff. 45–46.

[2] This princess exerted influence in the court of Philip V of Spain, as, in a lesser degree, Mrs. Howard in the court of George II. In 1714 the Princess des Ursins was suddenly dismissed.

[3] For Swift's description of Sheridan's purchase of 'a rotten house' and 'a strip of ground, not being worth twenty shillings a year' at Rathfarnham, near Dublin, see *Prose Works*, ed. Temple Scott, xi. 154.

(or the Speaker if he must be so) and desire he will perform his promise of giving me 3 or 4 MarSeill's Figs, and some of his most early grapes, and do you get them put into boxes with Earth, and send them to Whitehall, and let them be kept cool and I will send for them. .—My humble Service and kind remembrance to Mrs Pope, and to Betty Blount, and to Lord Bolingbroke, Lord Bathurst, Dr Arbuthnot and Family, Mr Lewis, and Mrs Howard, who must remember my Duty to the Queen, and to all others without naming, but you are to name them in a particular manner, especially to Mr Pulteney—Adieu, God bless you.⌝

4805

John Arbuthnot to Swift

London. Novr 30 1727

I have heard Dear Sir with great pleasure of your safe arrivall & which is more of the recovery of your health; I think it will be the best expedient for me to take a Jurney. Yow will know who the enclosed comes from, & I hope yow will value mine for what it contains: I think every one of your freinds have heard from you except my self. either yow have not done me justice or your freinds have not done yow, for I have not heard from them of my name being mentiond, in any of your letters. if my curiosity wanted only to be gratifyd I dont stand in need of a Letter from your self to inform me what yow are doing, for ther are people about Court who can tell me every thing that yow do or say so that yow had best take care of your Conduct yow see of what importance you are . . how ever all quarels aside; I must ask yow if yow have any interest; or do yow think that I could have or procure any with My Lord Lieutent to advance a relation of mine one Captain Innes,[1] I think in Cōll Wilson's Regiment & now in Limerick; he is an exceeding worthy man, but has stuck long in a low post for want of freinds. pray tell me which way I shall proceed in this matter. I was yesterday with all your friends at St James's. Ther is certainly a fatality upon poor Gay. as for hopes of preferment by favour these he has laid aside,

[1] There are three officers of the name of Innes in Dalton's *Army Lists* and *George the First's Army*. No relationship with Arbuthnot is known.

he had made a pretty good bargain, that is a Smithfield one;[1] for a little place in the custom house which was to bring him in about a hundred a year. it was done as a favour to an old Man, & not at all to Gay. when every thing was concluded, the man repented, & said he would not part with his place. I have begd Gay not to buy an annuity upon my life. Ime sure I should not live a week. I long to hear of the safe arrival of Dr Delany. pray give my humble service to him.

As for newes it was wrote from Spain; to me from my Brother in France that the preliminarys were ratify'd & yet the Ministry know nothing of it nay some of them told me ⌜that the answer was rather surly.⌝[2] Lord Townsend[3] is very ill but I think by the description of his case it is not Mortal. I was with our friend; at the Back Stair's[4] yesterday & had the honor to be call'd in & prettily chid for leaving off, &c. The first part of the discourse was about Yow Mr Pope Curle & myself. my family are well, they & my Brother in France, & one that is here all give their service to yow; if yow had been so lucky as to have gone to Paris last summer yow would have health, honor, & diversion, in abundance; for Ile promise yow would have recover'd of the spleen. I shall add no more but my kindest wishes & that I am with the greatest affection & respect | Yours &c

Address: The Reverend The | Dean of St patricks | Dublin
Endorsed by Swift: Novr 30th 1727 Dr Arbuth, & Ldy Bolingbroke[5]
Postmark: 30 NO BB

Dodsley Miscellanies 1745, x. 61

Swift to Mrs. Moore

[Deanery House, 7 December 1727]

Dear Madam![6]

Though I see you seldomer than is agreable to my Inclinations, yet you have no Friend in the World that is more concerned for

[1] See *Journal*, p. 214.

[2] Words in half-brackets above the line. The negotiations with Spain were not brought to a conclusion till the following March.

[3] Lord Townshend continued in public life for another three years, and did not die till 1738.

[4] Mrs. Howard.

[5] The endorsement indicates an enclosure from Lady Bolingbroke. This is not forthcoming.

[6] Mrs. Moore was the widow of 'the handsome parson' mentioned in Swift's

any thing that can affect your Mind, your Health, or your Fortune; I have always had the highest Esteem for your Virtue, the greatest Value for your Conversation, and the truest Affection for your Person; and therefore cannot but heartily condole with you for the Loss of so amiable, and (what is more) so favourite a Child. These are the necessary Consequences of too strong Attachments, by which we are grieving ourselves with the Death of those we love, as we must one day grieve those who love us, with the Death of ourselves. For Life is a Tragedy, wherein we sit as Spectators awhile, and then act our own Part in it. Self-love, as it is the Motive to all our Actions, so it is the sole Cause of our Grief. The dear Person you lament, is by no Means an Object of Pity, either in a moral or religious Sense. Philosophy always taught Men to despise Life, as a most contemptible thing in itself, and Religion regards it only as a Preparation for a better; which you are taught, to be certain that so innocent a Person is now in Possession of; so that she is an immense Gainer, and You and her Friends the only Losers. Now, under Misfortunes of this Kind, I know no Consolation more effectual to a Reasonable Person, than to reflect rather upon what is left, than what is lost. She was neither an only Child, nor an only Daughter. You have three Children left, one of them of an Age to be Useful to his Family, and the two others as promising as can be expected from their Age;[1] so that according to the general Dispensations of God Almighty, you have small Reason to repine upon that Article of Life. And Religion will tell you, that the truest way to preserve them, is not to fix any of them too deep in your Heart; which is a Weakness God seldom leaves long unpunished: Common Observation shewing us, that such favourite Children are either spoiled by their Parent's Indulgence, or soon taken out of the World; which last is, generally speaking, the lighter Punishment of the two.

God, in his Wisdom, hath been pleased to load our declining Years with many Sufferings, with Diseases, and Decays of Nature, with the Death of many Friends, and the Ingratitude of more: Sometimes with the Loss or Diminution of our Fortunes, when our Infirmities most need them; often with Contempt from the World, and always

letter to Vanessa, 6 June 1713. He was the Hon. and Reverend John Moore, son of the third Earl of Drogheda. He died on 1 June 1716.

[1] The eldest is said to have been a son by her first marriage. By her second two children survived Mrs. Moore: John, and Mary who married in 1735 Skeffington Randal Smith.—Ball.

with Neglect from it; with the Death of our most hopeful or useful Children; with a want of Relish for all worldly Enjoyments, with a general Dislike of Persons and Things: And tho' all these are very natural Effects of encreasing Years, yet they were intended by the Author of our Being, to wean us gradually from our Fondness of Life, the nearer we approach towards the End of it. And this is the Use you are to make, in Prudence as well as in Conscience, of all the Afflictions you have hitherto undergone, as well as of those which in the Course of Nature and Providence you have Reason to expect. May God, who hath endowed you with so many Virtues, add Strength of Mind and Reliance upon his Mercy in Proportion to your present Sufferings, as well as those he may think fit to try you with through the Remainder of your Life.

I fear my present ill Disposition both of Health and Mind has made me but a sorry Comforter: However, it will shew that no Circumstance of Life can put you out of my Mind, and that I am with the truest Respect, Esteem, and Friendship, | Dear Madam, Your most obedient, | Most humble Servant, | Jonath. Swift.

Deanry-House, |
Dec. 7th, 1727.

Forster copy

Swift to Knightley Chetwode

Dublin, December 12, 1727.

Sir,

I thought to have seen your son, or to have spoken to his tutor.[1] But I am in a condition to see nobody; my old disorder of deafness being returned upon me, so that I am forced to keep at home and see no company; and this disorder seldom leaves me under two months.

I do not understand your son's fancy of leaving the University to study law under a teacher. I doubt he is weary of his studies, and wants to be in a new scene. I heard of a Fellow some years ago who followed that practice of reading law, but I believe it was to lads, who had never been at a University. I am ignorant of these schemes, and you must advise with some who are acquainted with them. I only know the old road of getting some good learning in a University,

[1] i.e. Stopford.

and when young men are well grounded, then going to the Inns of Court. This is all I can say in the matter, my head being too much confused by my present disorder. I am |

Your obedient, &c.

Address: To Knightley Chetwode, Esq. at his house at Woodbrooke, near Mountmellick.

4805

Voltaire to Swift

[14 December 1727]
in London, maidenlane
at the white peruke
Covent garden

14 december

Sir

You will be surprised in receiving an english essay from a french traveller: pray forgive an admirer of you, who ows to y^r^ writings the love he bears to y^r^ language, which has betrayd him into the rash attempt of writing in english

you will see by the advertisement that j have some designs upon you, and that j must mention you for the honour of y^r^ country, and for the improvement of mine do not forbid me to grace my relation with y^r^ name let me indulge the satisfaction of talking of you as posterity will do

In the mean time can j make bold to intreat you to make some use of y^r^ interest in ireland about some subscriptions for the henriade,[1] which is almost ready and does not come out yet for want of little help the subscriptions will be but one guinea in hand |

j am with the highest esteem and the utmost gratitude |

y^r^ most humble and most obedient |
servant voltaire

[1] The first edition of Voltaire's *La Ligue* (better known as *La Henriade*) was published clandestinely at Rouen in 1723. Other editions followed 1723–4. After a gap a spate of editions came under the new title, *La Henriade*, in 1728. At the time this letter was written Voltaire was in financial difficulties, and thus we find him asking Swift to canvass subscriptions for the projected edition. The subscription list gives evidence that Swift provided help. The handsome quarto published early in 1728 would appear to be the first edition of the *Henriade* under that title.

Forster No. 544[1]

Swift to Benjamin Motte

Dublin. Dec^{br} 28th 1727

I had yours of the 16th[2] from Mr Hyde, and desire that henceforth you will write directly to me without scrupling to load me with the Postage. My Head is so confused with the returns of my deafness to a very great degree, (which left me after a fortnight and then returned with more violence), that I am in an ill way to answer a Letter which requires some thinking. As to having Cuts in Gullivers travells; you will consider how much it will raise the price of the Book; The world glutted it self with that book at first, and now it will go off but soberly, but I suppose will not be soon worn out . . The Part[3] of the little men will bear cuts much better than the great. I have not the Book by me, but will speak by memory. Gulliver in his carriage to the Metropolis, his extinguishing [the fire].[4] The Ladyes in their Coaches driving about his table. His rising up out of his Carriage when he is fastned to his House. His drawing the Fleet. The Troop upon his Handkerchief. The Army marching between his Legs. His Hat drawn by 8 horses. Some of these seem to be the fittest to be represented, and perhaps two adventures may be sometimes put in one Print.

It is difficult to do any thing in the great men,—because Gulliver makes so diminutive a figure, and he is but one in the whole Kingdom. Among some cuts I bought in London, he is shown taken out of the Bowl of cream, but the hand that holds him hides the whole body. He would appear best, wedged in the marrow bone up to the middle, or in the Monkey's arms upon the roof, or left upon the ridge and the footman on the ladder going to relieve him or fighting with the Rats on the farmers bed, or in the spaniels mouth, which being described as a small dog, he might look as large as a Duck in one of ours; One of the best would I think be to see his Chest just falling into the Sea while three Eagles are quarelling with one another. Or the monkey hauling him out of his box.

[1] The original is in the Forster collection, no. 544. The letter was first printed in *The Gentleman's Magazine*, N.S., xliii, 150, 1855.

[2] Written above '22^{d}' scrawled out.

[3] 'Part' written above 'Book'; and 'first' scratched out.

[4] Hole in the paper.

Mr Wotton[1] the Painter, who draws Landscips and Horses, told Mr Pope and me that the Gravers did wrong in not making the big folks bear something [large][2] and enormous in their shapes, for as drawn by those gravers, they look only like common human creatures Gulliver being alone and so little, cannot make the contrast appear. The Flying Island might be drawn as large as described in the Book, and Gulliver drawing up into it, and some Fellows with Flappers. I know not what to do with the Projectors. Nor what figure the Island of Ghosts would make, or any passage related in it because I do not well remember it. The Country of Horses, I think would furnish many. Gulliver brought to be compared with the Yahoo, The Family at dinner and he waiting. The Grand Council of Horses assembled, sitting, one of them standing with a hoof extended as if he were speaking, The She-Yahoo embracing Gulliver in the River, who turns away his head in disgust. The Yahoos got into a Tree to infest him under it. The Yahoos drawing Carriages, and driven by a Horse with a whip in his hoof. I can think of no more; But Mr Gay will advise you and carry you to Mr Wotton, and some other skilfull people.

As to the poeticall Volumes of miscellanys I believe five parts in six at least are mine. Our two friends[3] you know have printed their works already, and we could expect nothing but slight loose papers. There is all the Poetry I ever writ worth printing. Mr Pope rejected some, I sent him, for I desired him [to][4] be severe as possible; and I will take his judgment. He writ to me that he intended a pleasant discourse on the Subject of Poetry should be printed before the volume[5] and says that discourse is read[y]

The paper torn.

On the verso of the torn leaf the following words appear:

not have let me suffer for my modesty, when I expected he would have done better. Others more prudent and cannot be blamed. I am as weary with writing as I fear you will be with reading. I am yr | &c

Address: To Mr Benjamin Motte, | Bookseller at the middle | Temple gate in Fleet street | London

[1] John Wootton, 1678?–1765, painter of horses and dogs. He designed the majority of the plates in the first volume of Gay's *Fables*.

[2] Hole in the paper.

[3] Pope and Gay.

[4] Hole in the paper.

[5] Pope's *ΠΕΡΙ ΒΑΘΟΥΣ Or . . . The Art of Sinking in Poetry* occupies the first part of *Miscellanies: The Last Volume*, published on 7 Mar. 1727–8.

Deane Swift 1765

Swift to Lord Carteret

January 18, 1727–8.

My Lord,[1]

I was informed, that your Excellency having referred to the University here, some regulation of his Majesty's benefaction for professors; they have, in their answer, insinuated as if they thought it best, that the several professorships should be limited to their fellows, and to be held only as they continue to be so.[2] I need not inform your Excellency, how contrary such a practice is to that of all the universities in Europe. Your Excellency well knows how many learned men of the two last ages, have been invited by princes to be professors in some art or science, for which they were renowned; and that the like rule hath been followed in Oxford and Cambridge. I hope your Excellency will shew no regard to so narrow and partial an opinion, which can only tend to mend fellowships and spoil professorships: Although I should be sorry, that any fellow should be thought incapable on that account, when otherwise qualified. And I should be glad that any person, whose education hath been in this university, should be preferred before another upon equal deservings. But that must be left to those who be your Excellency's successors, who may not always be great clerks: And I wish you could, in some measure, provide against having this benefaction made a perquisite of humour or favour. Whoever is preferred to a bishoprick, or to such a preferment as shall hinder him from residing within a certain distance of this town, should be obliged to resign his professorship.

As long as you are Governor here, I shall always expect the liberty

[1] Having been reappointed Lord-Lieutenant on 29 July 1727 Carteret returned to Ireland in November. Genuinely as he admired Carteret Swift entertained dissastisfaction with him at this time for passing over recommendations for preferment submitted to him. Delany, for example, had not received the precentorship of Christ Church Cathedral, Dublin. Another had been appointed in his place (*Portland MSS.* vii. 447). But this incident was now forgotten. Two days before this letter was written Delany had been given the chancellorship of Christ Church Cathedral.

[2] The reference is to the foundations, under the trusts of the will of Erasmus Smith, of professorships of Natural and Experimental Philosophy and Oratory and History in Dublin University. The latter chair was held by Delany, who resigned then his fellowship, and would have lost his professorship if the proposed regulations had come into force.—Ball.

of telling you my thoughts; and I hope you will consider them, until you find that I grow impertinent, or have some bias of my own.

If I had not been confined to my chamber, by the continuance of an unconversable disorder, I would have exchanged your trouble of reading for that of hearing. I am, *&c.*

I desire to present my most humble respects to my Lady Carteret.

Your friend Walpole hath lately done one of the cruellest actions I ever knew, even in a minister of state, these thirty years past; which, if the Queen hath not intelligence of, may my right hand forget it's cunning.[1]

Longleat xiii (Harleian transcript)

Alexander Pope to Swift

[? January 1727–8][2]

I have a mind to be in the Spleen and quarrel with half the accidents of my Life, they have so severally and successively hinder'd me from writing to you. First a Continuation of such very ill health that I cared not to give you such an Account as from your friendship, would have been so uneasy to you, And which almost disabled me indeed from giving it, by attacking me in that part which only qualifies one to write. Then I was advised to a Journey, which gave me as Sore an Ailment at the other end, and was no sooner crawld home, but I found my Mother at the Gates of Death, we did not for two days expect her life, and in that Day of trouble I really thought of flying to You in my anguish, if it had pleased God to have taken her from me. She is still very weak, but we think in a fair way (if there can be such a thing at her Age) of Recovery. Pray do your utmost to preserve the Friend that I shall have left, against that Loss arrives, which cannot be far off. Dr Delany gave me a pleasure which I hope was not ill grounded, in saying (since I heard from you) that your Deafness was removed.[3] The Season here is very

[1] Gay had been offered a post unworthy of a man in his station. For this indignity Swift suspected Walpole. Cf. Swift to Gay and Pope, 23 Nov. 1727.

[2] The exact date of this letter is doubtful. It is a reply to the one from Swift of 23 Nov. Undated in the Longleat transcript.

[3] Delany had been in England in 1726 or 1727 and must have then made the acquaintance of Pope.

sickly, and all honest men will be dead, or in danger, by the meeting of your House. I have not seen Lords B. B.[1] nor the Dr. nor Lewis, nor Gay, nor any body above once since you writ last; Lord Bolingbroke not these 3 Months. Naming Lewis, I should tell you that I've ten times spoken to Gay to give him the Note to send to M. and he was within this week so careless as not to have done it. I will take it my self at my next going to town, and see Mr L. write about it. The third Volume of the Miscellanies is coming out post now,[2] in which I have inserted the Treatise *περὶ βαθοῦς* I have entirely Methodized and in a manner written, it all, the Dr grew quite indolent in it, for something newer, I know not what. It will be a very Instructive piece. I want to see the Journal of your Travels from Holyhead, which Mr Sheridan seems highly delighted with. And it grieves me to the Soul that I cannot send you my Chef d'œuvre, the Poem of Dulness, which after I am dead and gone, will be printed with a large Commentary, and letterd on the back, *Pope's Dulness.* I send you however what most nearly relates to yourself, the Inscription to it, which you must consider, re-consider, criticize, hypercriticize, and consult about with Sheridan, Delany, and all the Literati of (the Kingdom I mean) to render it less unworthy of you.

Incipit Propositio
Books and the Man I sing—&c.
Inscriptio

And Thou! whose Sence, whose Humour, and whose Rage
At once can teach, delight, and lash the Age!
Whether thou chuse Cervantes' serious Air,
Or laugh and shake in Rab'lais' easy chair,
Praise Courts and Monarchs, or extoll Mankind,
Or thy griev'd Country's copper Chains unbind:
Attend, whatever Title please thine ear,
Dean, Drapier, Bickerstaff, or Gulliver.
From thy Boeotia, lo! the Fog retires;
Yet grieve not thou at what our Isle acquires:
Here Dulness reigns with mighty wings outspread,
And brings the true Saturnian Age of Lead. &c.[3]

[1] Lords Bolingbroke, Bathurst, nor Arbuthnot.

[2] See Swift to Motte, 28 Dec. 1727 *ad fin.*

[3] Pope was busying himself with *The Dunciad*, now taking shape, during the summer of 1727 when Swift was staying with him at Twickenham. The first publication of the poem was in May 1728. In subsequent editions, 1728, 1729,

John Gay's Opera[1] is just on the point of Delivery. It may be call'd (considering its Subject) a Jayl-Delivery. Mr Congreve (with whom I have commemorated you) is anxious as to its Success, and so am I; whether it succeeds or not, it will make a great noise, but whether of Claps or Hisses I know not. At worst it is in its own nature a thing which he can *lose* no reputation by, as he lays none upon it.

Mrs Patty is very grateful for your Memory of her, but not a jot the wiser for another winter; It's hard Time should wrinkle faces, and not ripen heads. But she is a very honest Woman, and deserves to be whipt. To make her wise is more than you can do, but 'tis in your power by writing to her once in your life to make her proud, which is the best Suppliment for want of wisdom.

Courts I see not, Courtiers I know not, Kings I adore not, Queens I compliment not; so am never like to be in fashion, nor in dependance. I heartily join with you in pitying our poor Lady[2] for her unhappiness, and should only pity her more, if she had more of what we call Court happiness. I've seen her very seldome. I had lately many Compliments to you from Mr Morris, &c.[3] Pray make mine to all you think worth remembering, But I will not exclude Mrs Delany, Sheridan, & Stopfort, the latter of whom treats me the most kindly by never writing to me, which proves he thinks himself, as he is, secure of my remembrance. I wish I could make Dr and Mr Sh. so uneasy by my not writing to 'em, as to bring them hither the sooner. As for yourself, you cannot be absent, go where you will. Do you but keep well and live, and if I keep well and live, we *must* meet. Adieu.

To mortify you, I acquaint you that I am a hundred pound a year richer, than when you was here; And I owe it to no Great Man. And I believe I am in as good health as you, and my Lord Oxford has given me a great Gold Cup and Salver, which quite eclypses your Silver ones.—

micat inter omnes
Harleium Sydus, quales inter ignes
Luna minores[4]

and later to the final form of 1743, the lines quoted in this letter underwent extensive revision. See *The Dunciad*, ed. James Sutherland, pp. 62–63, 270–1.

[1] *The Beggar's Opera*, first performed 29 Jan. 1727–8.

[2] Mrs. Howard.

[3] Morrice, son-in-law of Bishop Atterbury. The guarded '&c.' is used to hint the relationship and his return from abroad.

[4] Adapted from Horace, *Odes*, I. xii. 46–48.

(Send me an Inscription to grave at the bottome of it) I have also a fine seal of Plato, with which I will not seal this Letter.

Endorsements: (*by the scribe*): Verses
(*by Lord Oxford*): Mr Pope to Dean Swift.

Forster No. 545

Swift to Benjamin Motte

Dublin Feb^r^ 1727–8

S^r^[1]

Mr Jackson,[2] who gives you this goes to London upon some Business; he is a perfect Stranger, and will have need of those good Offices that Strangers want, he is an honest worthy Clergyman, and friend of mine, I therefore desire you will give him what assistance and information you can. I have been looking over my Papers to see if anything could be fo[und in the ho]use fit to add to that volume,[3] but [great] numbers of [my poems have been so impo[unded by certain Accidents that I co[uld only find those I send] here inclosed, two of which Mr Pope already [has seen. He sent back these] because they were translations which indeed they are not and therefore I suppose he did not approve them; and in such a case I would by no means have them printed; because that would be a trick fitter for those who have no regard but to profit;

I wrote to you a long letter some time ago,[4] wherein I fairly told you how that affair stood, and likewise gave you my Opinion as well as I was able, and as you desired, with relation to Gulliver.

I have been these ten weeks confine[d] by my old disorders of Deafness and giddyness by two or three relapses; though I have got a rememdy which cured me twice, but obliges me to avoyd all cold. If I have any confirmed health I may probably be in London by the end of Summer, where I shall settle matters relating to those Papers

[1] The original of this letter, Forster Collection, No. 545, is written on the recto of a folio sheet. It carries no address, and is in a damaged condition. Missing words, supplied conjecturally, are enclosed within square brackets. The letter was printed in *The Gentleman's Magazine*, N.S., xliii. 152.

[2] Probably the Rev. John Jackson, vicar of Santry.

[3] The so-called 'Last' volume, which finally appeared on 7 Mar. 1728. For a discussion of the contents of this volume see *The Text of 'Gulliver's Travels'*, H. Williams, pp. 71–74.

[4] Swift to Motte, 28 Dec. 1727.

that I have formerly spoke to you about, and some of which you have seen

I hope you . . . my Service to Mrs | . . . and I | . . . your very humble Sert | J.S.

I send you likewise a little trifle for a [prose] volume, which Ben[1] printed, but you could not find a Copy

The enclosed Verses must be shown to Mr Pope and Mr Gay [and] not published without their approbation

Faulkner 1741

Viscount Bolingbroke and Alexander Pope to Swift

[Feby. 1727–8]

Pope charges himself with this letter; he has been here two days, he is now hurrying to London, he will hurry back to Twickenham in two days more, and before the end of the week he will be, for ought I know, at Dublin. In the mean time his *Dulness*[2] grows and flourishes as if he was there already. It will indeed by a noble work: the many will stare at it, the few will smile, and all his Patrons from Bickerstaff to Gulliver will rejoice, to see themselves adorn'd in that immortal piece.

I hear that you have had some return of your illness which carried you so suddenly from us (if indeed it was your own illness which made you such haste to be at Dublin) Dear Swift take care of your health, I'll give you a receipt for it, *a la Montagne*, or which is better, *a la Bruyere. Nourisser bien votre corps; ne le fatiguer jamais: laisser rouiller l'esprit, meuble inutil, voire outil dangereux: Laisser sonner vos cloches le matin pour eveiller les chaoines, et pour faire dormir le Doyen d'un sommeil doux et profond, qui luy procure de beaux songes: Lever vous tard, et aller al' Eglise, pour vous faire payer d'avoir bien dormi et bien dejeune.* As to myself (a person about whom I concern myself very little) I must say a word or two out of complaisance to you. I am in my farm,[3] and here I shoot strong and tenacious roots: I have caught hold of the earth, (to use a Gardener's phrase) and neither my enemies nor my friends will find it an easy matter to transplant me again. Adieu, let me hear from you, at least of you: I

[1] Ben Tooke.

[2] *The Dunciad* in progress.

[3] Dawley.

love you for a thousand things, for none more than for the just esteem and love which you have for all the sons of Adam.

P.S.[1] According to Lord Bolingbroke's account I shall be at Dublin in three days. I cannot help adding a word, to desire you to expect my soul there with you by that time; but as for the jade of a body that is tack'd to it, I fear there will be no dragging it after. I assure you I have few friends here to detain me, and no powerful one at Court absolutely to forbid my journey. I am told the Gynocracy[2] are of opinion, that they want no better writers than Cibber and the British Journalist;[3] so that we may live at quiet, and apply ourselves to our more abstruse studies. The only Courtiers I know, or have the honour to call my friends, are John Gay and Mr. Bowry; the former is at present so employed in the elevated airs of his Opera, and the latter in the exaltation of his high dignity (that of her Majesty's Waterman) that I can scarce obtain a categorical answer from either to any thing I say to 'em. But the Opera succeeds extremely, to yours and my extreme satisfaction, of which he promises this post to give you a full account. I have been in a worse condition of health than ever, and think my immortality is very near out of my enjoyment: so it must be in you, and in posterity, to make me what amends you can for dying young. Adieu. While I am, I am yours. Pray love me, and take care of your self.

4805

John Gay to Swift

15 February 1727–8

I have deferr'd writing to you from time to time till I could give you an account of the Beggar's Opera. It is Acted at the Playhouse in Lincoln's Inn fields, with such success that the Playhouse hath been crouded every night; to night is the fifteenth time of Acting, and 'tis thought it will run a fortnight longer. I have order'd Motte to send the Play to you the first opportunity. I made no interest either for approbation or money nor hath any body been prest to take tickets for my Benefit, notwithstanding which, I think I shall

[1] By Pope.

[2] Queen Caroline and her ladies-in-waiting.

[3] The writer of *The British Journal* at this time may have been William Arnall or James Pitt.

make an addition to my fortune of between six and seven hundred pounds. I know this account will give you pleasure, as I have push'd through this precarious Affair without servility or flattery. As to any favours from Great men I am in the same state you left me, but I am a great deal happier as I have no expectations. The Dutchess of Queensberry hath signaliz'd her friendship to me[1] upon this occasion in such a conspicuous manner, that I hope (for her sake) you will take care to put your fork to all its proper uses, and suffer nobody for the f[uture] to put their knives in their mouths. Lord Cobham says that I should [have] printed it in Italian over against the English, that the Ladys might have understood what they read.[2] The outlandish (as they now call it) Opera hath been so thin of late that some have call'd that the Beggars Opera, & if the run continues, I fear I shall have remonstrances drawn up against me by the Royal Academy of Musick.[3] As none of us have heard from you of late every one of us are in concern about your health. I beg we may hear from you soon. By my constant attendance on this affair I have almost worried myself into an ill state of health, but I intend in five or six days to go to our Country seat at Twickenham for a little air. Mr. Pope is very seldom in town. Mrs Howard frequently asks after you & desires her compliments to you; Mr George Arbuthnot,[4] the Doctor's Brother, is married to Mrs Peggy Robinson.[5] I would write more, but as to night is for my Benefit, I am in a hurry to go out about business, | I am | Dear Sir | Your most affectionate | & obedient Servant, | J Gay.

Address: To | The Reverend Dr Swift | Dean of St Patricks in | Dublin | Ireland
Postmark: 15 FE
Endorsed by Swift: Mr Gay | Feb. 15th 1727–8 | Mr Gay. | Feb. 22d; 1727–8 | Ansd May 11th 1728
In another hand: Leskibar blanc

[1] The beautiful and famous Lady Catherine Hyde, second daughter of the Earl of Clarendon, Prior's 'Kitty', whom Swift knew as a child; but he had not seen her since her marriage in 1720 to the third Duke of Queensberry. She became the patron of Gay, the correspondent of Swift, the friend of Congreve, Prior, Pope, and other men of letters.

[2] A sarcasm on the prevailing rage for Italian opera.

[3] A society of which Handel was director.

[4] Arbuthnot's much younger brother, George. In 1714 he was a captain in a regiment of foot; but he appears to have taken part in the rising of 1715. He left the country and joined his brother Robert in France. The date of his death is uncertain.

[5] The sister of Anastasia who was secretly married to Lord Peterborough.

Longleat xiii (Harleian transcript)

Swift to John Gay

26 February 1727–8[1]

Now.—Why does not Mr Pope publish his dullness, the rogues he mawles will dy of themselves in peace, and So will his friends, and So there will be neither punishment nor reward. Pray enquire how My Lord St John does there is no mans health in Engld I am more concerned about then, his[2]—I wonder whether you begin to tast the pleasure of independancy, or whether you do not Sometimes leer upon the Court oculo retorto; Will you now think of an annuity when you are two years older, and have doubled your purchase-money? Have you dedicated your opera and got the usuall dedication-fee, of 20 guinneas. How is the Doctor, does he not chide that you never called upon him for hints. Is My Lord Bol— at the moment I am writing, a planter, a Philosopher or a writer, Is Mr Pultaney in expectation of a Son, or My Lord Bathurst of an employment, or My Lord Oxford of a new old manuscript, ask Mrs Howard whether She will take the remedy with which I twice perfectly cured my deafness, tho' I am again relapsed; and I will Send her the receit I Said Something of this to Mr Pope,[3] Does W—[4] think you intended an affront to him in your opera. Pray God he may, for he has held the longest hand at hazard that ever fell to any Sharpers Share and keepe his run when the dice are changed: Present my most humble Service to the deliverer of this letter,[5] for So he must be, and not Dr Delany; who Stole away without it; by an accedent[6]—It is

[1] This letter, although begun on the 26th, was not completed till the 29th as the following letter shows.

[2] Bolingbroke's father, raised to the peerage as Baron St. John of Battersea and Viscount St. John in 1716, despite dissolute habits, lived to his ninetieth year, dying in 1742. Evidently Swift did not desire Bolingbroke to remove from Dawley to the family seat.

[3] Probably in reply to Pope's last letter.

[4] In the Longleat transcript the 'W—' has been expanded to 'Walpole' by a nineteenth-century hand.

[5] i.e. the post.

[6] It was on the day this letter was written that Delany's resignation of his fellowship took effect. In addition to his chancellorship he was given the College living of Derryvullen in the county of Fermanagh, and, as appears from the next letter, signalized his appointment to a cure of souls by going on a visit to England.—Ball.

probable I have forgot Something of more moment than any thing here My Service to Mr Pope & all friends.—adieu—I bought your opera to day for 6 pence, a cursed print I find there is neither dedication nor preface, both which wants I approve it is in the grand goût.

B.M., Stowe MS. 755[1]

Swift to Miss Martha Blount

Dublin, Feb. 29th. 1727–8

Dear Patty,—I am told you have a mind to receive a Letter from me,[2] which is a very undecent declaration in a young Lady, and almost a confession that you have a mind to write to me; for, as to the fancy of looking on me as a man sans consequence, it is what I will never understand. I am told likewise you grow every day younger and more a fool, which is directly contrary to me, who grow wiser and older, and at this rate we shall never agree. I long to see you a London Lady where you are forcd to wear whole cloaths and visit in a chair, for which you must Starve next summer at Petersham with a mantow out at the sides; and spunge once a week at our house without ever inviting us in a whole Season to a cow-heel at home. I wish you would bring Mr Pope over with you when you come, but we will leave Mr Gay to his beggars and his operas till he is able to pay his club. How will you pass this Summer for want of a Squire to Ham-common and Walpole's lodge;[3] for, as to Richmond lodge and Marble-hill they are abandond as much as Sr Spencer Compton. And Mr Schutz's[4] coach that usd to give you so many a Set-down, is wheeled off to St James's. You must be forced to get a horse and gallop with Mrs Jansen[5] and Miss Bedier.[6] Your greatest happiness is

[1] The original of this letter, Stowe MS. 755, f. 47, has not passed through the post.

[2] Pope to Swift, Jan. 1727–8: 'It is in your power by writing to Mrs Patty once in your life to make her proud.'

[3] In Richmond Park.

[4] Augustus Schutz, a favourite of George II and a friend of Patty Blount.

[5] A daughter of Sir Theodore Janssen, born in France, he came to England in 1680, where he acquired a large fortune. He was created a baronet by Queen Anne. He became a director of the South Sea Company. On its collapse he lost £50,000, was expelled the House and committed to the Tower. See *Sir Robert Walpole*, J. H. Plumb, i. 340–1.

[6] The use of the word 'Miss' indicates a companion, a servant, or a child.

that you are out of the chiding of Mrs Howard and the Dean, but I suppose Mr Pope is so just as to pay our arears, and that you edify as much by him as by us, unless you are so happy that he now looks upon you as reprobate and a castaway, of which I think he hath given me some hints. However I would advise you to pass this Summer at Kensington where you will be near the Court, and out of his jurisdiction, where you will be teazed with no lectures of gravity and morality, and where you will have no other trouble than to get into the mercer's books, and take up a hundred pounds of your principal for quadrille. Monstrous indeed that a fine lady in the prime of life and gayety must take up with an antiquated Dean, an old Gentlewoman of fourscore,[1] and a sickly poet. I will stand by my dear Patty against the world: if Teresa[2] beats you for your good, I will buy her a fine whip for the purpose. Tell me, have you been confined to your lodging this winter for want of chair-hire.—[Do you know that this unlucky Dr Delany came last night to the Deanery, and being denyed without my knowledge is gone to England this morning, and so I must send this by the Post. I bought your opera to day for 6 pence, so small printed that it will spoyl my eyes. I ordered you to send me your edition, but now you may keep it till you get an opportunity.] Patty: I will tell you a blunder. I am writing to Mr Gay,[3] and had almost finished the letter. But by a mistake I took up this instead of it and so the six lines in a hook are all to him, and therefore you must read them to him, for I will not be at the trouble to write them over again. My greatest concern in the matter is that I am afraid I continue in love with you, which is hard after near six Months absence. I hope you have done with your rash and other little disorders, and that I shall see you a fine young healthy plump lady, and if Mr Pope chides you, threaten him that you will turn Heretick. Adieu dear Patty, and believe me to be one of your truest Friends and humblest Servants, and that since I can never live in England, my greatest happyness would be to have you and Mr Pope condemned during my life to live in Ireland, he at the Deanery, and you for reputation Sake just at next door, and I will give you eight dinners a week, and a whole half dozen of pint bottles of good french wine at your lodgings, a thing you could never expect to arrive at, and every year a suit of 14 penny stuff, that should not be worn out at the right side; and a chair costs but sixpence a jobb, and

[1] Pope's mother. [2] Her sister.
[3] The letter of 26 Feb.

you shall have catholicity as much as your please, and the catholick Dean of St Patricks, as old again as I, to your Confessor. Adieu again dear Patty—

Address: To Patty Blount

Pierpont Morgan Library

Benjamin Motte to Woodford

12 March 1727–8

Revd Sir.[1]

The Dispute with Mr Curll stands as follows.

For many years past he has made it his business to pick up straggling and imperfect Copies of Verses, which he has father'd upon Dr Swift or Mr Pope or some other name of reputation. Some of these were really written by these Gentlemen, but publish'd by him without their knowledge and against their Consent; and many Pieces were laid to their charge, which they knew nothing of, and were so worthless, that they had reason to be asham'd of them.

To vindicate their Reputation, they made a Collection of such things as were genuine, and have just now publish'd them, having before for a valuable and substantial Considerations (*sic*) made a formal Conveyance of the Copy right of them to me in May last.[2] On the publication of them I receivd the following Letter from Curll.

Mr Motte

I have carefully examin'd your New last Volume of old Miscellanies, in the Art of Sinking your Authors have printed the Project for Advancing the Stage,[3] which is my Copy. And most of the other pieces in the Volume have been by me publish'd many Years ago.

[1] This document was first printed in *The Gentleman's Magazine*, N.S., xliv (1855), 364. Sherburn, ii. 477, prints from G. M. Ball, iv. 15, notes the letter, states that the original was at one time in the possession of Mr. Sabin, but he made, apparently, no attempt to trace the original; nor does he print any text. The original has for many years been in the Pierpont Morgan Library, whence the text is here printed. The document is on two folio sheets. The letter to Woodford, the quoted Curll letter, and the legal query are in Motte's hand, as also is the heading to Woodford's opinion. The legal opinion is, presumably, in the hand of Woodford.

[2] The agreement was signed 29 Mar. 1727.

[3] As chapter xvi of *The Art of Sinking in Poetry*.

To morrow night you'll find I have in some measure undeiceiv'd the Town. And to do my self justice, will reprint whatever is *New* in this last Volume, as a just reprisal for what they have taken from me that is *Old*.

Yrs E Curll.

However Swift and Pope agree,
Nor They nor You shall bubble me.

Q. Whether in case he be in execution in the Court of King's Bench, that Court has not a power to curb him in such Enormities?

I am with grateful respect
Your oblig'd humble Servant
B Motte

Mar. 12. 1727/8

Mr Woodford's Opinion abt the Three Volumes of Miscallanies.[1]

[2]If Mr Curl be not entirely dismissed from his prosecution on criminal account but is detained by the Court of Kings Bench, no Civil process can be taken out against him unless leave from that court is first obtained to do it. If Mr Curl sends a threatning Letter or publishes an advertisement that he will do you an injurious action by publishing what is your Property care must be taken that good proof is produced that such Letter or advertisement or both were Mr Curls & Oath must be thereon made that such menacing Letter or Advertisement are from him & on such Oath made an injunction may be prayed for & obtained from the Chancery to hinder his farther proceeding.

4805

John Gay to Swift

20 March 1727–8

I am extreamly sorry that your disorder is return'd, but as you have a medicine which hath twice remov'd [it] you I hope by this time, have again found the good effects of it. I have seen Dr Delany at my Lodgings, but as I have been for a few days with Mr Pulteney at Cashioberry[3] I have not yet return'd his visit, I went with him to wait upon Lord Bathurst & Lord Bolingbroke both of whom desire

[1] Motte's hand. [2] ? Woodford's hand.

[3] William Capel, third Earl of Essex, who married the Duchess of Queensberry's elder sister, resided at Cassiobury, near Watford.

me to make you their compliments. Lady Bolingbroke was very much out of order; and with my Lord is now at Doyley;[1] she expects a letter from you. Mrs Howard would glady have the receipt you have found so much benefit by; she is happier than I have seen her ever since you left us, for she is free as to her conjugal affairs by articles of agreement.[2] The Beggar's Opera hath now been acted thirty six times, and was as full the last night, as the first, and as yet there is not the least probability of a thin audience; though there is a discourse about the town that the Directors of the Royal Academy of Musick design to sollicite against it's being play'd on the *outlandish* Opera days, as it is now call'd. On the Benefit day of one of the Actresses last week one of the players falling sick they were oblig'd to give out another play or dismiss the Audience; A Play was given out, but the people call'd out for the Beggar's Opera, & they were forc'd to play it, or the Audience would not have stayed. I have got by all this success between seven & eight hundred pounds, and Rich[3] (deducting the whole charge of the House) hath clear'd already near four thousand pounds. In about a month I am going to the Bath with the Dutchess of Marlborough and Mr Congreve; for I have no expectations of receiving any favours from the Court. The Dutchess of Queensberry is in Wiltshire, where she hath had the small pox in so favourable a way, that she had not above seven or eight in her face; she is now perfectly recover'd. There is a Mezzo-tinto Print publish'd to day of Polly,[4] the Heroine of the Beggar's Opera, who was before unknown, & is now in so high vogue, that I am in doubt, whether her fame does not surpass that of the Opera itself. I would not have talk'd so much upon this subject, or upon any thing that regards myself but to you; but as I know you interest yourself so sincerely in everything that concerns me, I believe you would have blam'd me if I had said less. Your Singer[5] owes Dr Arbuthnot some

[1] Dawley.

[2] Her husband, Charles Howard, who, three years later, became Earl of Suffolk, was not an attractive character, but he had reasonable cause for complaint.

[3] The manager of the theatre in Lincoln's Inn Fields. According to a witticism of the day the success of *The Beggar's Opera* made 'Gay rich and Rich Gay'.

[4] Lavinia Fenton, who took the part of Polly Peachum. She became mistress of the third Duke of Bolton, who, upon the death of his wife, 1751, married Lavinia.

[5] As Swift's reply, 28 Mar. 1728, explains, the reference is to William Fox, a member of Swift's choir from 1727 till his death in 1734.

money, I have forgot the sum; I think it is two Guineas; the Dr desir'd me to let you know it. I saw him last night with Mr Lewis at Sr William Wyndham's, who if he had not the Gout would have answer'd your Letter you sent him a year & a half ago; he said this to me a week since; but he is now pretty well again, & so may forget to write, for which reason, I ought to do him justice and tell you that I think him a sincere well-wisher of yours. I have not seen Mr Pope lately, but have heard that both he & Mrs Pope are very well. I intend to see him at Twickenham on sunday next. I have not drunk out of the Gutheridge Cyder yet, but I have not so much as a single pint of Port in my Cellar. I have bought two pair of Sheets against your coming to town, so that we need not send any more to Jervas upon that ac[count][1] I really miss you every day, and I would be content th[at] yo[u shoul]d have one whole window to yourself, & half [another] to have you again. | I am | Dear Sir | Yours most affectionately.

You have a half years interest due at Lady-day, & now 'tis March 20th 1727–8

Address: To | The Reverend Dr Swift | Dean of St Patrick's in | Dublin | Ireland

Endorsed by Swift: Mr Gay. Mar. 20 | 1727–8 *and* Mr Gay. Mar. 20. 1727–8 | Answd. Mar. 28th

Faulkner 1741

Alexander Pope to Swift

March 23, 1727-8.

I send you a very odd[2] thing, a paper printed in Boston in New-England, wherein you'll find a real person, a member of their Parliament, of the name of Jonathan Gulliver.[3] If the fame of that Traveller has travel'd thither, it has travel'd very quick, to have folks christen'd

[1] Gay to Swift, 16 Sept. 1726.

[2] Faulkner mistakenly reads 'old'.

[3] The Rev. Matthew Byles had enclosed in a letter to Pope, 7 Oct. 1727, a copy of *The New England Weekly Journal* for 5 June 1727. This issue of the Boston paper contained verses by Byles complimenting Pope. It also contained a mention of 'Capt. Jonath. Gulliver', who was at this time member of the General Court ('Parliament') of the province for the town of Milton. It is an interesting coincidence that in the seventeenth century settlers in the town of Milton included both Gullivers and Swifts.—Sherburn.

already by the name of the supposed Author. But if you object, that no child so lately christen'd could be arrived at years of maturity to be elected into Parliament, I reply (to solve the Riddle) that the person is an *Anabaptist*, and not christen'd till full age, which sets all right. However it be, the accident is very singular, that these two names should be united.

Mr. Gay's Opera has acted near forty days running, and will certainly continue the whole season. So he has more than a fence about his thousand pound: he'll soon be thinking of a fence about his two thousand. Shall no one of us live as we would wish each other to live? Shall he have no sure annuity, you no settlement in this side, and I no prospect of getting to you on the other? This world is made for Cæsar—as Cato said,[1] for ambitious, false, or flattering people to domineer in: Nay they would not, by their good will, leave us our very books, thoughts, or words, in quiet. I despise the world yet, I assure you, more than either Gay or you, and the Court more than all the rest of the world. As for those Scriblers for whom you apprehend I would suppress my *Dulness*, (which by the way, for the future you are to call by a more pompous name, The *Dunciad*) how much that nest of Hornets are my regard, will easily appear to you when you read the Treatise of the Bathos.

At all adventures, yours and my name shall stand linked as friends to posterity, both in verse and prose, and (as Tully calls it) in *consuetudine Studiorum*.[2] Would to God our persons could but as well, and as surely, be inseparable! I find my other Tyes dropping from me; some worn off, some torn off, others relaxing daily: My greatest, both by duty, gratitude, and humanity, Time is shaking every moment, and it now hangs but by a thread! I am many years the older, for living so much with one so old; much the more helpless, for having been so long help'd and tended by her; much the more considerate and tender, for a daily commerce with one who requir'd me justly to be both to her; and consequently the more melancholy and thoughtful; and the less fit for others, who want only in a companion or a friend, to be amused or entertained. My constitution too has had its share of decay, as well as my spirits, and I am as much in the decline at forty as you at sixty. I believe we should be fit to live together, cou'd I get a little more health, which might make me not

[1] Addison's *Cato*, v. i. 19.

[2] Ball suggests that this may be a slip for *conjunctione studiorum* (*Ep. ad Fam.* ix. 8, 1).

quite insupportable: Your Deafness wou'd agree with my Dulness; you wou'd not want me to speak when you could not hear. But God forbid you shou'd be as destitute of the social comforts of life,[1] as I must when I lose my mother; or that ever you shou'd lose your more useful acquaintance so utterly, as to turn your thoughts to such a broken reed as I am, who could so ill supply your wants. I am extremely troubled at the returns of your deafness; you cannot be too particular in the accounts of your health to me; every thing you do or say in this kind obliges me, nay delights me, to see the justice you do me in thinking me concern'd in all your concerns; so that tho' the pleasantest thing you can tell me be that you are better or easier; next to that it pleases me that you make me the person you would complain to.

As the obtaining the love of valuable men is the happiest end I know of this life, so the next felicity is to get rid of fools and scoundrels; which I can't but own to you was one part of my design in falling upon these Authors, whose incapacity is not greater than their insincerity, and of whom I have always found (if I may quote myself)

That each bad Author is as bad a Friend.

This Poem will rid me of those insects,

Cedite Romani Scriptores, cedite Graii,
Nescio quid *majus nascitur Iliade*,[2]

I mean that *my Iliad*; and I call it *Nescio quid*, which is a degree of modesty; but however if it silence these fellows, it must be something greater than any Iliad in Christendom. Adieu.

Longleat xiii (Harleian transcript)

Swift to John Gay

Dublin Mar 28th 1728

I had yours of the 20th last night As to the remedy that twice cured my deafness, I would not take it the 3d time because it made me so tender that the least cold brought on my disorder again, which

[1] This is Pope's first letter to Swift since the death of Stella, 28 Jan. 1727–8. This thought was evidently in his mind.

[2] Propertius, ii. 34, 65–66.

went of however without using it any more. This I say on Mrs Howards account, yet she shall have it if she pleases, I am now tolerable well but my fears of relapsing hang over me, and very much take down my mettle. I will write to my Lady Bolingbroke; but I would be glad first, that you would know from her whether she will have such Usquebagh as I can get, and how much, and whether the green or the yallow, (for there is no such thing as white) or will she leave all but the quantity to my discretion?[1] We have your opera for 6d and we are as full of it pro modulo nostro as London can be continuall[2] acting, and house Crammd, and the Lord Lieut.[3] severall times there, laughing his heart out I wish you had sent me a Copy as I desired to oblige an honest BookSeller, it would have done Motte[4] no hurt, for no English copy has been sold but the Dublin one has run prodigiously. I did not understand that the Scene of Locket and Peachum's quarrels was an imitation of one between Brutus and Cassius till I was told it; I wish Mackheath when he was going to be hang'd had imitated Alexdr the great when he was dying. I would have had his fellow rogues, desire his commands about a Successor, and he to answer, let it be the most worthy: &c, we hear a million of Storys about the opera, of the ancore at the Song, *That was levelled at me*,[5] when 2 great Ministers were in a Box together, and all the world staring at them I am heartily glad your opera hath mended your purse though perhaps it may Spoyl your Court I think that rich rogue Rich Should in conscience make you a present of 2 or 3 hundred Guineas. I am impatient that Such a dog by Sitting Still Should get five times more than the Author. you told me a month ago of 700ll, and have you not quite made up the Eight yet, I know not your methods. how many third days are you allowd, and how much is each day worth, and what did you get for the Copy? Pray give one to Dr Delany for me, will you desire My Lord Bolingbrok Mr Pulteney and Mr Pope to command you to buy an annuity with two thousand pounds that you may laugh at Courts. and bid Ministers kiss &c—and ten to one they will be ready to grease you when you are fat I hope your new Dutchess will treat you at the Bath, and that you will be too wise to lose your money at play: Ever preserve Some

[1] The word whisky derives from the Irish *uisge-beatha*, water of life—originally a spirit flavoured with various condiments.

[2] 'continually' all printed editions.

[3] Carteret.

[4] In the Harleian transcript the name 'Motte' is supplied in Oxford's hand.

[5] Air XXX, Act II, of *The Beggar's Opera*.

Spice of the Alderman and prepare against age and dulness and Sickness and coldness or death of friends. A whore has a ressource left that She can turn Bawd: but an old decayd Poet is a creature abandond and at mercy when he can find none. Get me likewise Polly's mezzo-tinto. Lord, how the School-boys at Westminster, and University Lads adore you at this juncture; have you made as many men laugh, as Ministers can make to weep? I am glad your Goddess-Dutchess[1] hath preserved a face which I never Saw Since it was on the shoulders of a girl. Doct Arbuthnot[2] lent Fox the Singer whome he Sent me, 5 guineas, and had his note, This note I took from the Doctr and payd him the 5 Guinneas honestly at his house in Cork Street over against my Lord Harvy's; If he lent the Fellow any other money without a note, I know nothing of it; I will excuse Sir Wm Windham the trouble of a Letter. when Ambassdors came from Troy to condol with Tiberius upon the death of his Nephew., after two years. The Emperor answered that he likewise condoled with them for the untimely death of Hector.[3] I always loved and respected Sir Wm W.[4] very much, and do so Still as much as ever and it is a return Sufficient if he pleaseth to accept the offers of my most humble Service. I have 20 Dozen of Gudridge Syder as good as yours; which cost me 8 pounds, and if you will just cross the water heither from the Bath I will give you a Bottle of it every day. I had a Letter from Jo Taylor last Post, recommending one Waghern for my Quire.[5] He must be answered by your means, that I did admit him to a half place a year ago, or more, and have recommended him to the Dean of our other Cathedrall to be taken in there But the man by his indiscretion is got So deep in debt, that I doubt he must run away back to England; as I Suppose he did from thence hither for the Same reason, This I would have Said to Mr Taylor[6] without troubling him with a Letter; neither do I know his address unless it be to Bridewell My most humble Service to Mr Pulteney, and Mrs

[1] It was rumoured that the Duchess of Queensberry was suffering from smallpox.

[2] See Gay to Swift, 20 Mar. 1727–8.

[3] 'Quin et Iliensium legatis paulo serius consolantibus . . . irridens se quoque respondet vicem eorum dolore quod egregium vicem Hectorem amisissent' (Suet. *Tib.* 52).

[4] Sir William Wyndham.

[5] John Waghorne, who had been appointed to Swift's choir in 1726, and remained a member till his death in 1733.

[6] Taylor was clerk of the Bridewell hospital.

Howard, and Mr Pope, &c, and the Doctr. I hope Dr Delany hath Shown you the Tale writ by Mrs Barbar[1] a Citizen's wife here in praise of your Fables There is Something in it hard upon Mr Congreve, which I Sent to her (for I never Saw her) to change to Dryden, but She absolutely refused. I am now descended * * * * *

But I have not yet descended So low as a halfpenny, that indeed would be an indignity[2] Tel D. Delany that our Town is full of Speculations about his Journey, and they have found outt three Ladyes for him One is Lady Rawden[3] of Irland another is a Daughter of Sir Const Phipps, and the third is a Lady who hath no name, but 600ll a year estate. These conjectures entertained this Town, till your opera drove them out So that I fear at present they are under little concern whether he gets a wife or no— The Beggers Opera hath knockt down Gulliver, I hope to see Popes Dullness knock down the Beggers Opera, but not till it hath fully done its Jobb, They have not been told how easy a thing it is to gett 800ll by two or three months writing An Aldermans you could never failing of writing two or three Such trifles every year to expose vice and make people laugh with innocency does more publick Service than all the Ministers of State from Adam to Walpol, & So adieu

4806

Lady Bolingbroke to Swift

Lady Bolingbroke to Dr Swift[4] [1728]

Mr Pope ma fait grand plaisir, monsieur, de m assurer que votre santé est bonne et de me monter dans une de vos lettres des marques de lhonneur de votre souvenir ie trouve que vous prenez fort mal

[1] Mary Barber, wife of a Dublin clothier, befriended by Swift, and encouraged by him as a poetess. See her quarto volume of *Poems on Several Occasions*, London, 1734. The poem to which Swift alludes appears on pp. 7–12 of that volume. The reference to Congreve has disappeared.

[2] An allusion to the low value of Irish coinage. The rate of exchange was continually in question (*Mist's Weekly Journal*, 13 Apr. 1728).

[3] The widow of Sir John Moira. She was a daughter of Chief Justice Levinge, and married soon after this letter was written, as her second husband, Charles Cobbe, then Bishop of Dromore, and afterwards Archbishop of Dublin.

[4] These words at the head of the letter are in Swift's hand. The date of the letter is in doubt; but that it was written in the early part of 1728 seems most probable.

votre tems d habiter votre dublin pendant que nous habitons notre dawley nous aurions eu grand soin de vous cet hiver et nous aurions haï en ensemble le genre humain autant quil vs auroi tplû car ie trouve quil n'embellit point au croitre. on a fait deux pieces de theatre en france tireé soit disant des ideés de Guliverr ie ne vous les envoye point car elles sont detestables mais cela prouve au moins que ce bon voyageur a sy bien reuissi chez nous qu'on a cru qu'en mettant seulement son nom aux plus mauvaises pieces on les rendroit recommandables au publique nostre fermiér vous embrasse il a plaint et boude de ce que vous este parti sans quil ait pu vous dire adieu et de ce quil a vu une de vos lettres ou vous ne dites pas un mot pour luy mais ie croy come les coquettes qui ce fiant a leurs charmes ne sembarasse pas de leurs torts. en effet ils vous seront pardonnés a la premiere lettre et encore plus aisement a la premiere esperance de vous revoir adieu monsieur porti vous bien et nous serons contant ie ne maviseray pas de vous mader des nouvelles de ce pays cy, je suis etrangere de plus en plus et ie ne serois tentée de me faire naturaliser que dans ceux on il pourrois vivre avec vous.

Endorsed by Swift: Lady Bolingbroke.

Hawkesworth 4805

Voltaire to Swift

[? March 1728][1]

Sir,

I sent the other day a cargo of *French* dulness to my lord lieutenant. My lady Bolingbroke has taken upon herself to send you one copy of the *Henriade*. She is desirous to do that honour to my book; and, I hope, the merit of being presented to you by her hands will be a commendation to it. However, if she has not done it already, I desire you to take one of the cargo, which is now at the lord lieutenant's. I wish you a good hearing; if you have got it, you want nothing. I have not seen Mr. *Pope* this winter; but I have seen the third volume

[1] Apparently Swift had not replied to Voltaire's letter of 14 Dec. 1727. In this undated letter Voltaire alludes to having seen the 'third volume' of Pope and Swift *Miscellanies*, which was described as *The Last*. This appeared on the 7th or 8th of March 1727–8. The above letter was therefore probably written before the end of that month. A copy of the *Henriade* appears in the sale catalogue of Swift's library, no. 536.

of the *Miscellanea*; and the more I read your works, the more I am ashamed of mine. I am, with respect, esteem, and gratitude, Sir, your most humble obedient servant, | Voltaire.

Forster No. 562[1]

John Browne to Swift

Dawson Street April the 4: 1728.

Rev^{d} S^{r}

By a Strange fatality, tho you were the only Person in the world from whome I wo^{d} conceal my being and author yet you were unacountably the only one lett into the secret of it; The ignorant poor man who was instructed by me to deliver out the little books, tho he kept the Secret from all others, yet from the Nature of the Subject, he concluded that I could have noe Interest in concealing it from you, who were soe universally known to be an Indefatiguable Promoter of the generall welfare of Ireland: but tho the accident gave me some uneasiness at first, yet when I consider your Character I cannot doubt (however slender the foundation of such a hope may be from any Meritt of my own) but y^{r} Generosity will oblige you to conceal what chance has revealed to you, and incline you to judge of me, not from the report of my Enemies, but from what I appear in the little tracts which have waited on you.

I shan't presume S^{r} to detain you with the narrative of the originall amd progress of the Parliamentory accusations and Votes against me, thô wo^{d} you doe me the honour to enquier I could easyly convince you from my own particular case, that Men have two Characters, one which is either good or bad, according to the prevailing number of their friends or Enemies. And one which never varys for

[1] John Browne of the Neale, co. Mayo, had an ironworks there. He had left Ireland on account of a prosecution against him ordered by the House of Commons, 'for contriving and maliciously carrying on a conspiracy to take away the life of John Bingham, and others'. He had been censured and ordered to be taken into the custody of the Sergeant-at-Arms. He escaped to England and gave evidence before the English Privy Council in favour of Wood's coinage, for which Swift attacked him in the third *Drapier's Letter* (*The Drapier's Letters*, Herbert Davis, pp. 48–49). See further for a full account of Browne, Davis, op. cit., pp. 226–8. In this letter he tried to assuage Swift's anger against him. On his return to Ireland Browne had assumed a patriotic character appealing for help for the people in their sufferings from famine.

Either: one which has little or noe regard to the Virtue or Vice of the Subject, and one which regards that alone, is inherent (if I may say soe) in the Subject and describes it what it really is, without regard either to friends or Enemies.

All I begg of you is to suspend your Judgemt upon it, Since all parties allow that thô I had severall summons from the Committee for Monday, and many Evidences on the Road in obedience to their Summons, yet I was tyed down by the Committee the preceding Saturday, and deprived of the benefitt of all my Evidences. Notwithstanding any thing I could urge to the contrary; this I hope I may say without injury to Mr Bingham, for sure he may be intirely innocent, and yet a Magistrate under the imediate direction of the Lord Chief Justice who takes Examinations against him, Examinations that don't even contain Matter to form an Indictment upon, may be innocent allsoe.

It shall suffice therefore to say I went from Ireland loaded with the severest Censures of the house of Comons; Injured as I thought and oppressed to the greatest Degree imaginable, robb'd of that Character which was dearer to me than life it self, and all that by an overbearing, overpowering Interest.

I sought in England for that Peace and protection which was deny'd me at home; My Publick Character followed me: My Country men avoided me, the Nature of Man is sociable: I was forced to herd with Strangers; a Prime Minister Engaged in the success of a Scheme wants noe Emissary's to spy out all that makes for him, and to fly wth what they have found to their Employer; I was unfortunately sett by those sort of Creatures; My sentiments on the state of our money Matters were industriously sifted thrô Me, and when that was done before I knew any thing of the Matter, I was served with his Majesty's summons; in a hurry I ran out of Towne and stay'd in the Country awhile, but on My return again found another summons at my lodgings, and terrifyed by the dismall Effects of power att home from Risking a second shipwreck abroad, I yielded to it, and appeared at the Cock pitt.

Tis true my appearance at the Cockpitt to those who knew me only by the Votes of the house of Comons must have looked like a designe of Revenge, and I had many and powerful Enemies who gave all My actions the worst collour, but to take the Matter impartially Sr is there no allowance to be made for a mind already broken by the dismall Effects of prevailing Power, and filled with the apprehensions of second Dangers? Is there noe allowance for a Man young in the Knowledge of the World under all these fears and misfortunes, if he has yielded to the repeated Sum̃ons of the Councill of England in which his Majesty was present, and if he was there after a long and strenuous opposition forced to tell his sentiments? forced S^r to tell his sentiments not in the manner represented to the World but in a manner the most cautious of giving room for a pretence to oppose the inclinations of our Parliament.

But alas the consequence! You S^r the defender of Ireland was soon engaged against me on that account and that fatall genius of yours in an Instant ruined my Character; but even ruin bearing as it was I blessed it; The Cause which you undertook was dear to me, and thô fame is the last thing which one would sacrifice even for his Country, yet I parted with that with pleasure, whilst you thought it necessary for the publick good soe to do. But now the End is served D^r S^r may not the man have his Mare again—[1]

Plato being tould that certain Persons aspersed his Character and represented him abroad as a very ill Man, instead of expostulating with his enemies and returning reproach for reproach, concealed himself saying, 'No matter my friends, the whole life of Plato shall give his accusers the lye.'

Could I sett before me a greater Example? Under the generall Displeasure of my country, under all the censures which the restless malice of my Enemies could devise, and under the keen Edge of the Drapiers witt the only Revenge I indulged my self in, was by a steady love for My Country, and by manifest acts of affection thereto, to be a silent reproach to the foul tongues of my Enemies.

Permitt then S^r permitt me in peace to take his great example and no longer give way to the power of My Enemies by continuing to oppress me; they have already gained their cause by you, but I must say it was not the Sword of Ajax but the Armour of Achilles which he put on, that won the day.

The cause for which you undertook my ruin, was the Cause of my Country: it was a good Cause and you shall ever find me of that side, you have carryed it and I know you will noe longer be My Enemy; But alas S^r as long as your Works subsist, where ever they be read, even unto the end of time must I be branded as a Villain?

[1] 'The man shall have his mare again and all shall be well' (*Midsummer Night's Dream*, III. ii, 463). In 1735, vol. iv of Faulkner's edition of the *Works*, Swift removed the reference to Browne.

tis a hard Sentence and yet unless the Spear of Achilles, the same instrument which gave the wound administers the remedy it must be soe.

In short S^r^ you must be a man of honour: tis not possible that Honour sho^d^ be wanting where all the distinguishing Characteristicks of it are found: I cannot doubt it; and I will therefore lett you fully into a secret which accident has given you a part of, and I am sure you will keep it.

The source of all my Misfortunes was the Vote of the house of Com̃ons: but I have laboured however as I allways shall to serve My Country, and make my self agreeable to them, and thô the misfortune of bad publick character deprived me of the private conversation of my Country men, which is the surest and best way to know our true interest; yet I flatter myself that my little Essays may be usefull, at least they may be no bad beginning, and you know it is easy to add to a Work once begun, but if the Work is known to be Mine the very Name will condemn it and render it useless to My Country.

Whatever the faults may be I have publickly applyed to you to amend them before the Bearers mistake made me determine this private application to You, and I must here say that I shall reckon it no small degree of honour, if you take that trouble upon you.[1]

In the mean time I shall begg the favour of you to keep a secrett which not other person but my Printer, my Bookseller and the Bearer knows | I am | Rev^d^ S^r^ | Y^r^ most obed^t^ Servt—

Jo: Browne

Deane Swift 1768

Martha Blount to Swift

May 7 1728.

Sir,—I am very much pleased with your letter,[2] but I should have thought myself much more obliged, had you been less sincere, and

[1] Browne afterwards obtained a seat in the Irish Parliament; and the recovery of his reputation was probably in some degree due to Swift, as he erected a monument in Swift's honour at his home in the County of Mayo. See Appendix.—Ball.

[2] Of 7 Feb. 1727–8.

not told me, I did not owe the favour entirely to your inclinations, but to an information that I had a mind to hear from you: and I mistrust you think even that as much as I deserve. If so, you really are not deserving of my repeated inquiries after you, and my constant good wishes and concern for your welfare; which merits some remembrance without the help of another. I can't say I have a great inclination to write to you, for I have no great vanity that way, at least not enough to support me above the fear of writing ill: but I would fain have you know how truly well I wish you.

I am sorry to hear no good account of your health: mine has been, since *Christmas* (at which time I had my fever and rash) neither well, nor ill enough to be taken notice of: but within these three weeks I have been sick in forms, and kept my bed for a week, and my chamber to this day.

This confinement, together with the mourning,[1] has enabled me to be very easy in my chair-hire: for a dyed black gown, and a scoured white one, have done my business very well; and they are now just fit for *Petersham*, where we talk of going in three weeks; and I am not without hopes I shall have the same squire[2] I had last year. I am very unwilling to change; and moreover I begin to fear I have no great prospect of getting any new danglers; and therefore, in order to make a tolerable figure, I shall endeavour to behave myself mighty well, that I may keep my old ones.

As a proof that I continue to be well received at *Court*, I will tell you where the royal family design to pass their *Summer*: two months at *Richmond-Lodge*, the same time at *Hampton Court*, and six weeks at *Windsor*. Mrs. *Howard* is well, and happier than ever you saw her; for her whole affair with her husband is ended to her satisfaction.[3]

Dr. *Arbuthnot* I am very angry with: he neglects me for those he thinks finer ladies. Mr *Gay*'s fame continues, but his riches are in a fair way of diminishing: he is gone to the *Bath*: I wish you were ordered there, for I believe that would carry Mr. *Pope*, who is always inclined to do more for his friends than himself. He is much out of order, and is told nothing is so likely to do him good.

My illness has prevented my writing to you sooner. If I was a favourite at *Court*, I would soon convince you that I am very sincerely your faithful friend and very humble servant, | M. B.

[1] The Court mourning for George I.

[2] Swift.

[3] See p. 269.

Faulkner 1741

Swift to Alexander Pope

Dublin, May 10, 1728.

I have with great pleasure shewn the New-England News-paper with the two names Jonathan Gulliver,[1] and I remember Mr. Fortescue sent you an account from the assizes,[2] of one Lemuel Gulliver who had a Cause there,[3] and lost it on his ill reputation of being a liar; and these are not the only observations I have made upon odd strange accidents in trifles, which in things of great importance would have been matter for Historians. Mr. Gay's Opera hath been acted here twenty times, and my Lord Lieutenant tells me it is very well perform'd; he hath seen it often, and approves it much.[4]

You give a most melancholy account of your self, and which I do not approve. I reckon that a man subject like us to bodily infirmities, should only occasionally converse with great people, notwithstanding all their good qualities, easinesses, and kindnesses. There is another race which I prefer before them, as Beef and Mutton for constant dyet before Partridges: I mean a middle kind both for understanding and fortune, who are perfectly easy, never impertinent, complying in everything, ready to do a hundred little offices that you and I may often want, who dine and sit with me five times for once that I go to them, and whom I can tell without offence, that I am otherwise engaged at present. This you cannot expect from any of those that either you or I or both are acquainted with on your side; who are only fit for our healthy seasons, and have much business of their own. God forbid I should condemn you to Ireland (*Quanquam O!*) and for England I despair; and indeed a change of affairs would come too late at my season of life, and might probably produce nothing on my behalf. You have kept Mrs. Pope longer, and have had her care beyond what from nature you could expect; not but her loss will be very sensible whenever it shall happen. I say one thing, that both summers and winters are milder here than with you; all things for life in general better for a middling fortune; you will have an absolute command of your company, with whatever obsequiousness or

[1] See Pope to Swift, 23 Mar. 1727–8.

[2] See Pope to Fortescue, 5 Aug. 1727 (Sherburn, ii. 441). Swift had probably met at Twickenham William Fortescue, then a barrister, afterwards Master of the Rolls. *D.N.B.*

[3] Refers to the Salisbury Assizes.

[4] See Swift to Gay, 28 Mar. 1728.

freedom you may expect or allow. I have an elderly housekeeper, who hath been my *Walpole* above thirty years, whenever I liv'd in this kingdom.[1] I have the command of one or two villa's near this town: You have a warm apartment in this house, and two Gardens for amusement.[2] I have said enough, yet not half. Except absence from friends, I confess freely that I have no discontent at living here; besides what arises from a silly spirit of Liberty, which as it neither sowers my drink, nor hurts my meat, nor spoils my stomach farther than in imagination, so I resolve to throw it off.

You talk of this Dunciad, but I am impatient to have it *volare per ora*[3]—there is now a vacancy for fame: the Beggars Opera hath done its task, *discedat uti conviva satur.*[4] | Adieu

Portland Manuscripts

Swift to the Earl of Oxford

11 May 1728

My Lord.

I must desire Your Lordships pardon if out of ignorance I send you medals that are perfect trash; but you have an easy remedy, to throw them out of the windows.[5] There is a very fair one of Cromwell, which for ought I know may be as common as a milled shilling; there is one of a Roman Emperor which is fair, but I know not of whom; it was given me by a Portuguise Cozen, who brought it with her from Portugall.[6] The small one seems to be a Saxon; the other two are onely Edwards, and I think very common, but perhaps you may want one to compleat a Series. That Portuguese Cozen hath likewise a very fine Gold Medallion of Titus, with a reverse of Domitian when he was Cesar; some fool (if she does not lye) offered

[1] 'Above thirty years' means that Mrs. Brent had acted as his housekeeper since Swift was Prebendary of Kilroot. She is frequently mentioned in the *Journal.* According to Nichols ('Biographical Anecdotes' prefixed to his *Supplement*, 1779) Swift's mother used to lodge with her in Dublin.

[2] The garden round the Deanery and Naboth's Vineyard.

[3] *Georgics*, iii. 9.

[4] Hor., *Sermones*, II. i. 118.

[5] Swift, as already noted (cf. letter to Oxford, 26 Oct. 1725), was an imperfectly informed numismatist.

[6] Hannah, daughter of Willoughby Swift, Lisbon merchant, by his second wife. She married the Rev. Stafford Lightburne.

her three times more than the weight of it. So I shall not meddle with it. the intrinsick value is not above 4 pounds.

I have not heard of any Coin of this Kingdom before the Conquest under Henry. 2^{d}. Those since are of no value or curiosity not above 3 or 4 hundred years old; with the Names of the Cityes; as Civitas Waterford. Civitas Dublin. Civitas Drogheda &c.

I hope My Lady Oxford and Lady Margaret are in good health, as well as Your Lordship. You and your Family have my daily prayers and good Wishes | I am with great Respect | My Lord, | Your Lordships most | obedient and most humble | Servant | Jonath Swift

Dublin—May 11th | 1728

Endorsed: The Dean of St Patricks | May: 11: 1728. Rx.–May 27: 1728

4805

John Gay to Swift

Bath, 16 May 1728

Dear S^{r}

I have been at the Bath about ten days, and Lewis who is very much your humble Servt He is here upon account of the ill-state of health of his Wife who hath as yet found very little benefit by the waters. Lord & Lady Bolingbroke are here, I think she is better than when I came here, they stay as I guess only about a fortnight longer; they both desird me to make their compliments, as does Mr Congreve, who is in a very ill state of health, but somewhat better since he came here. Mr Lewis tells me that he is promis'd to receive a hundred pounds upon your account[1] at his return to London; he having (upon request) comply'd to stay for the payment 'till that time. The two hundred pounds you left with me are in the hands of Lord Bathurst together with some money of mine, all which he will repay at Midsummer, so that we must think of some other way of employing it, and I cannot resolve what to do.

I dont know how long I shall stay here, because I am now, as I

[1] The reference is to a payment by Motte for *Gulliver's Travels.* In the following February the £100 still seems to have been outstanding (Swift to Pope, 6 Feb. 1729–30). On the little evidence we have it seems probable that Swift received £300 in all for the work, and perhaps more. See *Gulliver's Travels*, ed. Harold Williams, p. xxxi.

have been all my life at the disposal of others. I drink the waters, and am in hopes to lay in a stock of health, some of which I wish to communicate to you. Dr Delany told me you had been upon a journey, and I really fancy taking horse is as good as taking the waters. I hope you have found benefit by it.[1] The Beggar's Opera is acted here, but our Polly here hath got no fame, but the Actor's have got money. I have sent by Dr Delany[2] the Opera Polly Peachum, & Captain Macheath, I would have sent you my own head wch is now graving to make up the Gang, but it is not yet finish'd. I suppose you must have heard that I have had the honour to have had a Sermon preach'd against my works by a Court Chaplain, which I look upon as no small addition to my fame.[3] direct to me here when you write, and, and the sooner that is, the sooner you will make me happy.

Bath, May, 16 1728.

Address: To | The Revd Dr Swift Dean of St | Patrick's in | Dublin. | Ireland.
Endorsed by Swift: Mr Gay | May. 16th, 1728 *and again.*

Faulkner 1741

Swift to Alexander Pope

June 1, 1728.

I look upon my Lord Bolingbroke and us two, as a peculiar Triumvirate, who have nothing to expect, or to fear; and so far fittest to converse with one another: Only he and I are a little subject to schemes, and often upon[4] very weak appearances, and this

[1] At this time *The Intelligencer*, written by Swift and Sheridan, began to appear. The first number, by Swift, was published on 11 May. The second, by Sheridan, described an accident which occurred while two clergymen were 'travelling to the Country for their Health'. The two were Swift and Sheridan who were making a tour of the south-east part of Ireland.

[2] Who then returned to Ireland.

[3] The Court chaplain was Dr. Thomas Herring, at this time preacher at Lincoln's Inn, later, 1743, Archbishop of York, and in 1747 Archbishop of Canterbury. He preached a sermon against *The Beggar's Opera* in March 1728. In the third *Intelligencer* Swift declared his belief that Gay's play would 'probably do more Good than a thousand Sermons of so stupid, so injudicious, and so prostitute a Divine'.

[4] and often upon] and one of us (I won't say which) upon *London editions.*

you have nothing to do with. I do profess without affectation, that your kind opinion of me as a Patriot (since you call it so) is what I do not deserve; because what I do is owing to perfect rage and resentment, and the mortifying sight of slavery, folly, and baseness about me, among which I am forced to live. And I will take my oath that you have more Virtue in an hour, than I in seven years; for you despise the follies, and hate the vices of mankind, without the least ill effect on your temper; and with regard to particular men, you are inclined always rather to think the better, whereas with me it is always directly contrary. I hope however, this is not in you from a superior principle of virtue, but from your situation, which hath made all parties and interests indifferent to you, who can be under no concern about high and low-church, Whig and Tory, or who is first Minister—Your long letter was the last I received until this by Dr. Delany,[1] although you mention another since. The Dr. told me your secret about the Dunciad,[2] which does not please me, because it defers gratifying my vanity in the most tender point, and perhaps may wholly disappoint it. As to one of your enquiries, I am easy enough in great matters, but have a thousand paltry vexations in my little station, and the more contemptible, the more vexatious. There might be a Lutrin writ upon the tricks used by my Chapter to teize me. I do not converse with one creature of Station or Title, but I have a set of easy people whom I entertain when I have a mind; I have formerly described them to you, but when you come you shall have the honours of the country as much as you please, and I shall on that account make a better figure, as long as I live. Pray God preserve Mrs. Pope for your sake and ease, I love and esteem her too much to wish it for her own: If I were five and twenty, I would wish to be of her age, to be as secure as she is of a better life. Mrs. P. B.[3] has writ to me, and is one of the best Letter-writers I know; very good sense, civility and friendship, without any stiffness or constraint. The Dunciad hath taken wind here,[4] but if it had not, you are as much known here as in England, and the University lads will crowd to

[1] Not forthcoming.

[2] The secret was the preparation of a larger edition with the inscription to Swift.

[3] Patty Blount.

[4] On 18 May *The Dunciad* was published. On the title-page of the first edition appeared the imprint, 'Dublin, Printed, London Reprinted for A. Dodd, 1728'. This led to the supposition of a first edition published in Dublin. The imprint, however, was intended to mislead the public. The only Dublin edition of 1728 was published by Faulkner. See *The Dunciad*, ed. James Sutherland, pp. xvii ff.

kiss the hem of your garment. I am griev'd to hear that my Lord Bolingbroke's ill health forced him to the Bath. Tell me, is not Temperance a necessary virtue for great men, since it is the parent of Ease and Liberty? so necessary for the use and improvement of the Mind, and which philosophy allows to be the greatest felicities of life? I believe, had health been given so liberally to you, it would have been better husbanded, without shame to your parts.

Faulkner 1741

Alexander Pope to Swift

Dawley, June 28, 1728.

I now hold the pen for my Lord Bolingbroke, who is reading your Letter[1] between two Haycocks, but his attention is sometimes diverted by casting his eyes on the clouds, not in admiration of what you say, but for fear of a shower. He is pleas'd with your placing him in the Triumvirate between your self and me; tho' he says that he doubts he shall fare like Lepidus, while one of us runs away with all the power like Augustus, and another with all the pleasures like Anthony. It is upon a foresight of this, that he has fitted up his farm, and you will agree, that this scheme of retreat at least is not founded upon weak appearances. Upon his return from the Bath, all peccant humours, he finds, are purg'd out of him; and his great Temperance and Oeconomy are so signal, that the first is fit for my constitution, and the latter would enable you to lay up so much mony, as to buy a Bishoprick in England. As to the return of his health and vigour, were you here, you might enquire of his Hay-makers; but as to his temperance, I can answer that (for one whole day) we have had nothing for dinner but mutton-broth, beans and bacon, and Barn-door fowl.

Now his Lordship is run after his Cart, I have a moment left to my self to tell you, that I overheard him yesterday agree with a Painter for 200*l.* to paint his country-hall with Trophies of Rakes, spades, prongs, &c. and other ornaments merely to countenance his calling this place a Farm[2]—now turn over a new leaf—

[1] The preceding one.

[2] Pope, writing to Lord Bathurst from Dawley, 7 Nov. 1728 (Sherburn, ii. 525), alludes to 'all the Insignia and Instruments of Husbandry painted now in the Hall'.

He bids me assure you he should be sorry not to have more schemes of kindness for his friends, than of ambition for himself: There, tho' his schemes may be weak, the motives at least are strong; and he says further, if you could bear as great a fall, and decrease of your revenues, as he knows by experience he can, you wou'd not live in Ireland an hour.

The Dunciad is going to be printed in all pomp, with the inscription, which makes me proudest. It will be attended with *Proeme*, *Prologomena*, *Testimonia Scriptorum*, *Index Authorum*, and Notes *Variorum*. As to the latter, I desire you to read over the Text, and make a few in any way you like best, whether dry raillery, upon the stile and way of commenting of trivial Critics; or humorous, upon the authors in the poem; or historical, of persons, places, times; or explanatory, or collecting the parallel passages of the Ancients. Adieu. I am pretty well, my Mother not ill, Dr. Arbuthnot vext with his fever by intervals; I am afraid he declines, and we shall lose a worthy man: I am troubled about him very much. | I am, &c.

4805

John Gay to Swift

Bath, 6 July 1728

Dear Sir,

The last news I heard of you was from Mr Lancelot who was at this place with Lord Sussex,[1] who gave me hope of seeing of you, the latter end of this summer; I wish you may keep that resolution, & take the Bathe in your way to town. You in all probability will find here some or most of those you like to see. Dr Arbuthnot writ to me to day from Tunbridge where he is now for the recovery of his health, having had several relapses of a feaver, he tells me, that he is much better, since he came there, & and[2] that in August he intends to come hither. Mr Lewis will be here the beginning of August, &

[1] Talbot Yelverton, second Viscount de Longueville and sixteenth Baron Grey de Ruthyn, was created Earl of Sussex by George I. The calling of Lancelot, Patty Rolt's husband, is not known. The William Lancelot of New Bond Street, whose death on 7 Aug. is announced in *The Gentleman's Magazine* for 1743, can only doubtfully be identified with him.

[2] '& and' thus in manuscript.

I have some hopes of seeing Mr Pope too. Mr Congreve & I often talk of you, & wish you health & every good thing, but often out of self interest we wish you with us. In five or six days I set out upon an excursion to Herefordshire to Lady Scudamore's,[1] but shall return here in the beginning of August. I wish you could meet me at Guthridge.[2] The Bathe did not agree with Lady Bolingbroke, & she went from hence much worse than she came; since she came to Dawley, by her own inclination without the advice of Physicians, she hath taken to a milk diet, & she hath writ me an account of prodigious good effects both of recovery of her appetite & Spirits. The weather is extreamly hot, the place is very empty. I have an inclination to Study but the heat makes it impossible. The D. of Bolton I hear hath run away with Polly Peachum, having settled 400 a year upon her during pleasure, & upon disagreement 200*l* a year. Mr Pope is in a state of Persecution for the Dunciad, I wish to be witness of his fortitude, but he writes but seldom. 'Twould be a consolation to me to hear from you, I have heard but once from Mrs Howard these 3 months, & I think but once from Mr Pope. My Portrait Metzotinto is publish'd from Mrs Howard's painting, I wish I could contrive to send you one, but I fancy I could get a better impression at London. I have ten thousand things to talk to you (but few to write, but deferr writing to you no longer knowing you interest yourself in everything that concerns me so much that I make you happy, as you will me, if you can tell me you are in good health; Which I wish to hear every morning as soon as I wake. | I am—Dear Sr | Yrs most affectionately.

Bathe · July · 6 · 1728.

Address: To | The Reverend Dr Swift | Dean of St Patricks in | Dublin | Ireland
Postmark: 8 IY
Endorsed by Swift: July 6th 1728 | Mr Gay

[1] Frances, only daughter of Simon, fourth Lord Digby, married James, third and last Viscount Scudamore, who had died in 1716. Her country seat was at Holme Lacy on the Wye.

[2] Goodrich.

Faulkner 1741

Swift to Alexander Pope

July 16, 1728.

I have often run over the *Dunciad* in an Irish edition (I suppose full of faults) which a gentleman sent me.[1] The Notes I could wish to be very large, in what relates to the persons concerned; for I have long observed that twenty miles from London no body understands hints, initial letters, or town-facts and passages; and in a few years not even those who live in London. I would have the names of those scriblers printed indexically at the beginning or end of the Poem, with an account of their works, for the reader to refer to. I would have all the Parodies (as they are called) referred to the authors they imitate—When I began this long paper, I thought I should have filled it with setting down the several passages I had marked in the edition I had, but I find it unnecessary, so many of them falling under the same rule. After twenty times reading the whole, I never in my opinion saw so much good satire, or more good sense, in so many lines. How it passes in Dublin I know not yet; but I am sure it will be a great disadvantage to the poem, that the persons and facts will not be understood, till an explanation comes out, and a very full one. I imagine it is not to be published till towards winter, when folks begin to gather in town. Again I insist, you must have your Asterisks filled up with some real names of real Dunces.

I am now reading your preceding letter, of June 28, and find that all I have advised above is mentioned there. I would be glad to know whether the quarto edition is to come out anonymously, as published by the Commentator, with all his pomp of preface, &c. and many complaints of spurious editions?—I am thinking whether the Editor should not follow the old style of, This excellent author, &c. and refine in many places, when you meant no refinement? and into the

[1] When Swift wrote this letter he had been for more than a month the guest of Sir Arthur and Lady Acheson at Market Hill, near Armagh. Sir Arthur Acheson, the fifth baronet, was of Scottish descent. Lady Acheson's father was the Right Hon. Philip Savage, for more than twenty years Chancellor of the Exchequer in Ireland, a friend of Swift from early days (*Journal*, 12 Dec. 1710). Swift was entertained at Market Hill for long visits, the periods of which may here be noted: (1) June 1728–Feb. 1729. (2) June 1729–8 Oct. 1729. (3) end of June 1730–end of Sept. 1730.

bargain take all the load of naming the dunces, their qualities, histories, and performances?[1]

As to your self, I doubt you want a spurrer-on to exercise and to amusements; but to talk of decay at your season of life is a jest. But you are not so regular as I. You are the most temperate man God-ward, and the most intemperate your self-ward, of most I have known. I suppose Mr. Gay will return from the Bath with twenty pounds more flesh,[2] and two hundred less in money; Providence never design'd him to be above two and twenty, by his thoughtlessness and Cullibility. He hath as little foresight of age, sickness, poverty, or loss of admirers, as a girl of fifteen. By the way, I must observe, that my Lord Bolingbroke (from the effects of his kindness to me) argues most sophistically: The fall from a million to an hundred-thousand pounds is not so great, as from eight hundred pounds a year to one: Besides, he is a controller of Fortune, and Poverty dares not look a great Minister in the face, under his lowest declension. I never knew him live so great and expensively as he hath done since his return from Exile; such mortals have resources that others are not able to comprehend. But God bless You, whose great genius has not so transported you as to leave you to the courtesy of Mankind; for wealth is liberty, and liberty is a blessing fittest for a philosopher—and Gay is a slave just by two thousand pounds too little.—And Horace was of my mind,—and let my Lord contradict him if he dares—

Longleat xiii (Harleian transcript)

The Earl of Oxford to Swift

July 27. 1728

Reverend Sir,[3]—It is now compleat two Months since I receivd the favor of your letter[4] and a very great one I esteem it, and also

[1] Pope whole-heartedly adopted this pretence of commentators other than himself responsible for the notes. It led him to annotate recklessly so far as true facts were concerned.—Sherburn.

[2] Gay was of a stout and heavy build.

[3] This copy of Oxford's letter was made on the blank verso of a cover addressed: 'To | The Right Honble the Earl of | Oxford at Down Hall Essex.'—Sherburn.

[4] 11 May 1728.

some Medals which were of use to me in my Collection please to accept my thanks for them Mr Clayton has been going this six weeks which was one reason of my not writing and I think I should not give you the trouble of two letters upon the same Subject resolving to write by him when ever he went. I have heard some kind of Whisper as if the Dean of St Patricks would be in England this Winter I wish he may but it is too good news to be true I fear. Mr Pope stands by himself Athanasius Contra Mundum; there is never a Newspaper comes out but he is favord with a letter; a poem and Epigram even to a Distich from the newmorous Herd of Dunces and Blockheads that are in and about London and the Suburbs there of. I saw him the other day he is as to his health much of the Same as you left him he has at last taken a resolution of going to Bath this Season I hope it will be of Service to him my Wife and Peggy are much your humble Servants the my Wife goes this next Season to the Bath I hope it will do her good for the Badness of her Stomach I hope this will find you very well where ever it be for I hear you often make excurtions into the Country I shall be glad to hear that you are free from your Deafness you complaind of when you went out of England last.

I am Sir with true esteem | Your most Affectionate Humble | Servant | O

The medalion you mention is a | Curiosity but it is too high | prized for me.

Endorsement: A Copy of a letter | to the Dean of St Patrick's | July 27. 1728

Dodsley Miscellanies 1745, x. 119

Swift to the Rev. Thomas Sheridan

Market-Hill, *Aug.* 2, 1728.

Our Friends here,[1] as well as myself, were sadly disappointed upon hearing the Account of your Journey. No body in Town or Country, as we were informed, knew where you were; but I persuaded our Family that you were certainly in a Way of making yourself easy, and had got that Living you mentioned, and accordingly we were grieved and rejoiced at the Loss and Settlement

[1] The Achesons.

of a Friend, but it never entered into our Heads that you were bestowing forty Days in several Stages between Constable and Constable, without any real Benefit to yourself, further than of Exercise;[1] and we wished that no body should have had the Benefit of your long Absence from your School, but yourself, by a good Living, or we by your good Company: much less that the Pleasure of spighting *T*—[2] had been your great Motive. I heartily wish you were settled at *Hamilton*'s Bawn,[3] and I would be apt to advise you not to quit your Thoughts that Way, if the Matter may be brought to bear; for by a Letter I just received from the Bishop of *Cork*,[4] which was short and dry, with the stale Excuse of Pre-engagements, I doubt you can hope from him.—As to what you call my Exercise,[5] I have long quitted it, it gave me too much Constraint, and the World does not deserve it. We may keep it cold till the middle of Winter.

As to my Return there are many Speculations. I am well here, and hate Removals; my Scheme was, that you should come hither as you say, and I return with you in your Chaise. Sir *A*—, on hearing your Letter, pressed me to stay longer.[6] I am a very busy Man, such as at *Quilca*, which you will know when you come; yet I would contrive to be pres'd more to stay till *Christmas*, and then you may contrive to be here again, and take me back with you time enough for my own Visitation: And my Reason of Staying is, to be here the Planting and Pruning Time, &c. I hate *Dublin*, and love the Retirement here, and the Civility of my Hosts. This is my State and Humour upon it, and accordingly you are to manage my Scheme.

[1] A letter from Archbishop King to Sheridan, 25 July, furnishes evidence that the latter had been in Cork. The letter, conveying a stern rebuke, calls Sheridan to account for failing to appear 'when school-masters were summoned'. As a clergyman, acquainted with the rules of the Church, he was expected to set an example to other people.

[2] Tighe. The eighth and tenth numbers of *The Intelligencer* consisted largely of verse satires on Tighe by Swift—'Mad Mullinix and Timothy' and 'Tim and the Fables' (*Poems*, iii. 772–83).

[3] An anglicized form of the Irish *badhun*. See *Ulster Journal of Archaeology*, I. vi. 125; and cf. 'Hamilton's Bawn', written by Swift at Market Hill about June 1729 (*Poems*, iii. 863–73).

[4] Peter Browne.

[5] i.e. *The Intelligencer*.

[6] Cf. Swift's poem beginning:

> 'The Dean wou'd visit Market Hill
> Our Invitation was but slight.'
>
> *Poems*, iii. 859.

However I would have you keep your Vacation of *September* here; and let Mrs. *Brent* send me a dozen Guineas (half of them Half-Guineas) by you, and a Periwig, and a new riding Gown and Cassock, and whatever else I may want by a longer Absence, provided you will resolve and swear that I shall stay.

I had all Mrs. *Brent*'s Packets by Mr. *Little*. My service to Mrs. *Dingley*; I cannot say that I have more to say, than to say that I am, &c.

Dodsley Miscellanies 1745, x. 122

Swift to the Rev. Thomas Sheridan

Sept. 18, 1728

My Continuance here is owing partly to Indolence, and partly to my Hatred of *Dublin*. I am in a middling Way, between Healthy and Sick, hardly ever without a little Giddiness or Deafness, and sometimes both; So much for that. As to what you call my Lesson, I told you I would think no more of it, neither do I conceive the World deserves so much Trouble from you or me. I think the Sufferings of the Country, for want of Silver, deserves a Paper,[1] since the Remedy is so easy, and those in Power so negligent. I had some other Subjects in my Thoughts; but truly I am taken up so much with long Lampoons on a Person who owns you for a Back, that I have not Time for any Thing else; and if I do not produce one every now and then of about two Hundred Lines,[2] I am chid for my Idleness, and threaten'd with you. I desire you will step to the Deanry, speak to Mrs. *Brent*, bid her open the middle great Drawer of *Ridgeway*'s[3] 'Scrutore in my Closet, and then do you take out from thence, the History[4] in Folio, marble Cover; and two thin Folio's fairly writ. I forget the Titles, but you have read them one is an Account of the Proceedings of Lord *Oxford*'s Ministry, and the other to the same Purpose.[5] There are foul Copies of both in the same Drawer, but

[1] No. XIX of *The Intelligencer* deals with this subject.

[2] The reference is to 'My Lady's Lamentation and Complaint against the Dean', running to 226 lines. The poem is dated 28 July 1728 (*Poems*, iii. 851–8).

[3] Ridgeway had married Mrs. Brent's daughter.

[4] 'History of the Four Last Years of the Queen.'

[5] 'Memoirs relating to that Change in the Queen's Ministry' and the 'Enquiry into the Behaviour of the Queen's Last Ministry'.

do you take out the Fair-ones, not in my Hand. Let them be pack'd up, and brought hither by the Bearer. My Lady is perpetually quarrelling with Sir *Ar*— and me, and shews every Creature the Libels I have writ against her.

Mr. *Worrall* sent me the Particulars of the Havock in *Naboth*'s Vineyard.—⌜The D— burst, &c.[1]

I think Lady *Dun*'s burning[2] would be an admirable Subject to shew how hateful an Animal a human Creature is, that is known to have never done any good. The Rabble all rejoicing, &c. which they would not have done at any Misfortune to a Man known to be Charitable.

I wish you could get in with the Primate, on the Account of some Discourse about you here to-day, with *Whaley*, and *Walmsley*. *Whaley* goes to *Dublin* on *Monday* next in order for *England*. I would have you see him. I fancy you may do some Good with the Primate as to the first good vacant School, if you wheedle him, and talk a little Whiggishly.⌝

Rothschild

Swift to Charles Ford

Sept. 20th 1728.

Mr Whaley[3] the late Primat's Chaplain delivers you this. He hath an appeal before the H. of Lords for a very considerable Living, in which that abominable puppy and Poet Dean Daniel is his adversary. He is a Gentleman of great worth, and I must entreat you to desire the Lords of your Acquaintance not onely to hear the cause, but right or wrong to befriend him, although the Rascal his opposer hath nothing but party on his side. Pray get Mr Lewis and Dr Arbuthnot to speak to as many Lords as they know.

I have been here[4] with Sr Arthur Acheson these three Months, in

[1] The latter part of the letter, here inclosed within half-brackets, was not printed by Faulkner, 1746 (viii. 429) or 1762 (vii. 306), although printed by Dodsley, 1745, x. 122–4. Inundations from the flooding of a stream called the Poddle, near St. Patrick's Cathedral, often had disastrous results.

[2] The residence of Sir Patrick Dun's widow which, with its contents, was completely consumed.

[3] For Nathaniel Whaley and his appeal to the English House of Lords see the following letter addressed to the Earl of Oxford.

[4] Market Hill.

a various, but somewhat tolerable State of health, but with a family so agreable, that joyned to the happyness of being absent from Dublin, I do not much pity my self. I hope not so much as my friends do, and you particularly who think nothing tolerable five miles from London. Yet I have one great advantage that I am wholly ignorant how the world passes, and am consequently not half so much out of humor and patience with it as you. However it gives you amusement, and that with good company is enough. | I am &c

Address: To Charles Ford Esqr

Carl H. Pforzheimer[1]

Swift to the Earl of Oxford

[21 September 1728]

My Lord.

Mr Clayton sent me Your Lordship's Letter[2] to the North of this Kingdom where I have been these three months, and still continue, in the same degree with Yorkshire and where Codlins will sometimes grow ripe, provided it be a favorable season. I shall not accept your Lordship's thanks, because I have not even so much merit as the poor man who presented his Prince with a greater turnip than ordinary. If I deserve them on any account it is for having given you so many opportunityes of shewing your Generosity and goodness.

I intended to have passed this Winter in London. But my health is so uncertain with the frequent return of those two impertinent disorders giddyness and deafness, that I am forced to prefer a scurvey home where I can command people to speak as loud as I please, before the vexation of making a silly figure and tearing the Lungs of my friends.

I hear that myself and one or two more have a share in the Scurrilityes that the Dunciad hath occasioned, as a just punishment

[1] The original of this letter appeared at the Croker sale, 6 May 1858, and was sold to Tate for £12. A copy was made for the Forster Collection, now Red Box, 44. E. 2. On 17–18 Oct. 1944 it came up in the Parke-Bernet Galleries, New York, at the sale of Literary and Historical Manuscripts and Letters of the Drexel Institute of Technology. It is now in the Carl H. Pforzheimer Library, Hidden Brook Farm, Purchase, New York. By kind permission the text here is printed from the original.

[2] The letter of 27 July.

for the friendship we have for Mr Pope. These are usuall events. for almost six months ago a Pamphlet[1] was sent to me by post and to my great cost not franked, but no doubt from some special well-wisher, wherein I was handled with the like decency upon the account of a meer Trifle, onely for joyning with some great Confederates to break the present Ministry, and utterly destroy Sr R. W.[2] Whereas God knows, I was at that time quiet with Mr Pope. I cannot say better employd, but much more to my own satisfaction.

I pray God send My Lady Oxford success at the Bath, and that she may soon and long encrease the market Bills in your Lordship's Family, and take corporeal food like us mortals, which I cannot charge my memory to have ever seen her do. I desire to present my most humble service to her Ladyship, and to my Lady Marget. | I am ever with great respect | My Lord | Your Lordships most obedient | and most humble Servant | Jonath Swift.

This Letter[3] will be delivered to your Lordship by Mr Whaley, who was a fellow of Wadham in Your Lordships time and invited over hither by the late Primate Lyndsey, by whom he was preferred. He has now an Appeal before the House of Lords for a Church living of near a thousand pounds a year, of which he has been long and legally possessed; and his Adversary one Dean Daniel is the greatest Puppy and vilest Poet alive, with a very bad cause to be supported by a Party. Mr Whaley is so worthy a Person that I could not refuse his Request of recommending him to your Lordship's favor on this occasion and your Credit with the Lords of your Acquaintance to attend at the Cause, when it will be of most use.[4]

Address: To the Right Honorable | the Earl of Oxford.
Endorsed: R by Dr whaley Nov. 11. 1728. | in Dover Street

[1] The pamphlet to which reference is made is questionable.

[2] *The Dublin Intelligence* of 20 June 1727 reported a rumour, but contradicted it, that Swift had been taken into custody; and this rumour may have cropped up again from time to time.

[3] This postscript is in Swift's hand, but written with a different quill.

[4] Whaley, chaplain to Primate Lyndsay, had been given the rectory of Armagh; but the government nominated Richard Daniel (*Fasti. Eccl. Hib.* iii. 33, 228). Whaley carried an appeal to the English House of Lords; and at last won his case. See Oxford's letter to Swift, 15 July 1730.

4805

Swift to the Rev. John Worrall

Sept^{br} 28th 1728.

I had all the Letters given my[1] by my Servant, so tell Mr Brent and Dr Sheridan. and I thank you for the great care you had in the commissions I troubld you with.[2] I imagine Mrs Brent is gone into the Country but that you know where to send to her. I desire you will pay her four Pounds, and Sixteen Pounds to Mrs Dingley, and take their Receits, I beg Mrs Dingley's pardon for not remembering her debt sooner, and my humble service to her. I desire Mrs Brent to send me the best Receit she hath for making Meath, She may send me her Receit for making the strong Meath, and that for making the next strong, and the third strong. Hers was always too strong, and on that account she was so wilfull, I would suffer her to make no more. There is a vexatious thing happend about the Usquebagh for My Lord Berkeley; but I thought I had desired you to add · for Ld Bolingbroke: but there is nothing in that; for I wrote to the Earl of Berkeley to give him notice; But Mr Gavan who maryed the Daught^{r} of Mrs Kenna who keeps the Inn at Chester[3] hath just sent me a Letter informing me that the Usquebagh came to Park gate within seven miles of Chester, and that Mr Whittle the Owner of the Ship was to deliver himself, but he sent it by a man of a noted bad Character, who as Mrs Kenna supposes, kept it some time, and opend it, before he delivered it. For, immediatly upon the delivery of it Mrs Kenna sent to Park-gate to have the Usquebach brought up to Chester, but was told that the Fellow had brought it away, that he sayd, he sent it as directed, but that no doubt he must have some view of paying himself for the trouble, which made him so busy, but whether it was by changing the Usquebagh, or over rating the Charges of it, Mr Gavan cannot tell: but adds, that if I should hear of any thing amiss, I should write to Mrs Kenna his Mother, who will endeavr to make the Fellow do me justice. All this I have transcribed from Mr Gavans Letter, and I desire you will call upon his Father Mr Luke Gavan, (who is a known man in Dublin.[4] and desire him when he writes to his Son to give my Service to him

[1] Thus written by Swift. [2] See Swift to Sheridan, 18 Sept. 1728.

[3] See Swift to Mrs. Greenfield, 23 Nov. 1726.

[4] He was a merchant and shipowner and the father of seven sons.—Ball. The parathensis is not closed.

and Mrs Kenna, and let them know I will do as they direct. I am very unfortunate in this affair; but have no remedy. However I will write to Ld Bolingbroke, thô I fear I am cheatd of it all, for I do not find that the Fellow demanded any thing from Mrs Kenna, or came to her at all.—Your new fancies of making my riding Gown and Cassock, I mean Mrs Brent's fancyes do not please me at all, because they differ so much from my old one.—You are a bad packer of bad Grapes. Mrs Dingley says she cannot persuade Mrs Brent to take a vomit. . Is she not (do not tell her) an old fool. She had made me take many a one without mercy. . Pray give Mrs Worrel a thousand thanks from me for her kind present and workmanship of her fairest hands in making me two night caps.

We have a design upon Sheridan. He sent us in print a Ballad upon Ballyspelling, which he has employd all the Rimes he could find to that word; but we have found fifteen more, and employd them in abuseing his Ballad, and Ballyspelling to, I here send you a Copy, and desire you will get it printed privately, and published.[1] | I am ever yours &c.

Your Periwig maker is a cursed Rogue, the Whig he gave you is an old one with a new Call, and so long that I cannot wear it, and the curles all fallen. I just tryed it on my head, but cannot wear it.

Address: To the Reverend M^r^ | Worrall at his house in big | Sheep-street | Dublin
Postmark: Illegible

Faulkner 1741

Alexander Pope to Swift

Bath, 12 [Oct] 1728[2]

I have past six weeks in quest of health, and found it not; but I found the folly of sollicitude about it in a hundred instances; the

[1] Ballyspellan, not far from Kilkenny, has a chalybeate spring which was, in Swift's day, greatly in favour for its medicinal properties. For Sheridan's poem and Swift's reply see *Poems*, ii. 437–43. The manuscript of Swift's poem, in his hand, accompanying the letter to Worrall, is in the B.M., Add. MS. 4805, f. 181. There is now no trace of printed broadsheet or pamphlet editions of Sheridan's ballad or Swift's answer.

[2] Faulkner 1741 and Pope's editions of 1740–2 print the month of this letter as November. But Pope had left Bath before that date. A letter to Lord Bathurst of 7 Nov. is dated from Twickenham.

contrariety of opinions and practices, the inability of physicians, the blind obedience of some patients, and as blind rebellion of others. I believe at a certain time of life, men are either fools or physicians, and zealots or divines, for themselves.

It was much in my hopes that you intended us a winter's visit, but last week I repented that wish, having been alarm'd with a report of your lying ill on the road from Ireland; from which I am just relieved by an assurance that you are still at Sir Acheson's, planting and building; two things that I envy you for, besides a third, which is the society of a valuable Lady: I conclude (tho' I know nothing of it) that you quarrel with her, and abuse her every day, if she is so. I wonder I hear of no Lampoons upon her, either made by yourself, or by others because you esteem her.[1] I think it a vast pleasure that whenever two people of merit regard one another, so many scoundrels envy and are angry at them; 'tis bearing testimony to a merit they cannot reach; and if you knew the infinite content I have received of late, at the finding yours and my name constantly united in any silly scandal, I think you would go near to sing *lo Triumphe!* and to celebrate my happiness in verse; and I believe if you won't, I shall. The inscription to the Dunciad is now printed and inserted in the Poem. Do you care I should say any thing farther how much that poem is yours? since certainly without you it had never been.[2] Would to God we were together for the rest of our lives! The whole weight of Scriblers would just serve to find us amusement, and not more. I hope you are too well employed to mind them: every stick you plant, and every stone you lay, is to some purpose; but the business of such lives as theirs is but to die daily, to labour, and raise nothing. I only wish we could comfort each other under our bodily infirmities, and let those who have so great a mind to have more Wit than we, win it and wear it. Give us but ease, health, peace, and fair weather, I think it is the best wish in the world, and you know whose it was. If I lived in Ireland, I fear the wet climate would indanger more than my life, my humour, and health, I am so Atmospherical a creature—I must not omit acquainting you, that what you heard of the words spoken of you in the Drawing-Room,

[1] The Market Hill poem in mind was probably 'My Lady's Lamentation and Complaint against the Dean. July 28, 1728' (*Poems*, iii. 851–8).

[2] During his visit of 1727 Swift had no doubt encouraged Pope in the production of *The Dunciad*; but to describe much of the poem as 'yours', and to declare that without him 'it had never been' goes far beyond truth to fact.

was not true.[1] The sayings of Princes are generally as ill related as the sayings of Wits. To such reports little of our regard shou'd be given, and less of our conduct influenced by them.

Duncombe

Swift to the Rev. Thomas Wallis

Market-hill, Nov. 16, 1728.

Sir,

I am extremely obliged to you for your kind intention in the purchase you mention; but it will not answer my design, because these lands are let in leases renewable for ever, and consequently can never have the rent raised which is mortal to all estates left for ever to a public use,[2] and is contrary to a fundamental maxim of mine; and most corporations feel the smart of it.

I have been here several months to amuse me in my disorders of giddiness and deafness, of which I have frequent returns—and I shall hardly return to Dublin till Christmas.

I am truly grieved at your great loss.[3] Such misfortunes seem to break the whole scheme of man's life: and although time may lessen sorrow, yet it cannot hinder a man from feeling the want of so near a companion, nor hardly supply it with another. I wish you health and happiness, and that the pledge[4] left you may prove a comfort. I am, with great sincerity, | Your most obliged | and most humble servant, | Jonath . Swift.

[1] The reference to the words spoken has been lost.

[2] By his will, devising his fortune for the foundation of a hospital, Swift forbade his executors to purchase lands that were 'encumbered with leases for lives renewable'.

[3] The death of Mrs. Wallis.—Duncombe.

[4] A son, now a barrister at law.—Duncombe.

4805

John Gay to Swift

London Decem[r] 2. 1728.

Dear Sir.

I think this is my 4th Letter, I am sure tis the third without any answer.[1] If I had had any assurance of your health I should have been more easy. I should have writ to you upon this subject above a month ago had it not been for a report that you were upon the road in your way to England, which I fear now was without any foundation. Your money with part of my own is still in the hands of Lord Bathurst which I believe he will keep no longer, but repay upon his coming to town; when I will endeavour to dispose of it as I do of my own unless I receive your orders to the contrary. Lord and Lady Bolingbroke are in town, she hath lately been very ill, but is now somewhat better. I have had a very severe attack of a feaver which by the care of our friend D[r] Arbuthnot hath I hope now almost left me; I have been confin'd about ten days but never to my bed, so that I hope soon to get abroad about my business, which is, the care of the second part of the Beggar's Opera which is now almost ready for rehearsal. But Rich receiv'd the Duke of Grafton's commands (upon an information he was rehearsing a Play improper to be represented) not to rehearse any new Play whatever 'till his Grace hath seen it;[2] what will become of it I know not, but I am sure I have written nothing that can be legally supprest, unless the setting the vices in general in an odious light, and virtue in an amiable one may give offence. I past five or six months this year at the Bath with the Dutchess of Marlborough, and then in the view of taking care of myself, writ this peice. If it goes on, in case of success, I have taken care to make better bargains for myself, I tell you this, because I know you are so good to interest yourself so warmly in my affairs, that 'tis what you would want to know. I saw M[r] Pope on friday, who as to his health is just as you left him; his Mother, by his

[1] Only two have been preserved, 16 May, 6 July.

[2] When *Polly*, Gay's sequel to *The Beggar's Opera*, was ready for rehearsal, the Duke of Grafton, then Lord Chamberlain, instructed by the King, who was influenced by Walpole, forbade the representation. The result was that Gay netted more from the sale of published copies than he was likely to have done from the theatre. The Duchess of Marlborough gave £100 for a single copy; the Duchess of Queensberry was forbidden the Court for canvassing subscriptions.

account is much the same. Mr Lewis, who is very much your servant, (as are all I have mention'd) tells me further time is still desir'd of him about the 100*l*. Dr. Arbuthnot particularly desires his compliments, & Mrs Howard often asks after you. Prince Frederic is expected over this week.[1] I hope to go abroad in two or 3 days; I wish I could meet you either abroad or at home.

Endorsed by Swift: Mr Gay Decr 2^d 1728

B.M. Add. MS. 38671

Swift to Thomas Staunton

[Dublin, 15 December 1728]

Dear Tom.

I have feed Mr Lyndsay,[2] to look into Mr Lightburns Decree, and advise whether it would be security to lend him 800^ll upon it, and he hath not yet determined the Matter. mean time Mr Lightburn tells me he is impatient to be out of Mr Percivals debt, and you call upon him for the Interest, which he would gladly pay Principal and all. You are acting for your Clyent Percival,[3] as you ought, and I am acting to save Mr Lightburn from Ruin, he marryed the Daugh^tr of my near Relation, for whom I had great Kindness, and to whom I ow some Obligations . . and I think the poor Gentleman hath suffered enough,[4] and therefore I shall help him as far as it is safe for me. He will pay you when the Writings are finished between him and me: Which I hope will be in a very few days. | I am ev^r | Y^rs. | J Swift

Deanry-house | Decr 15th. 1728

[1] Frederick, Prince of Wales, born 1707, died 1751 before his father, leaving his son to ascend the throne as George III. The news of his arrival in England reached Dublin on the 13th.

[2] Robert Lindsay was called to the Irish bar in 1709, became counsel for the proctor of St. Patrick's Cathedral 1722, and seneschal to the cathedral 1724. In 1729 he was returned as a knight of the shire for co. Tyrone (Ball, *Judges in Ireland*, ii. 203). He was consistently on friendly terms with Swift. See further Swift to Oxford, 6 Jan. 1734–5, and note.

[3] John Percival of Knightsbrook.

[4] Litigation had been taking place between Stafford Lightburne, who had married Hannah, daughter of Willoughby Swift, concerning her fortune, which her father entrusted to his brother Deane, and which her father's creditors tried to seize (B.M. Add. MS. 36148, f. 1).

I hope your Family are | all in Health, and desire | to present my humble Service to them.

Address: To Thomas Staunton Esqr | at his House | on Usher's Key

Hawkesworth 1766

Swift to the Rev. John Worrall

Market-Hill, Jan. 4, 1728–9.

I had your long letter, and thank you heartily for your concern about my health. I continue very deaf and giddy; but however, I would certainly come to town not only for my visitation,[1] but because in these circumstances, and in winter, I had rather be at home. But it is now *Saturday* night, and that beast *Sheridan* is not yet come, although it has been thawing since *Monday*.[2] If I do not come, you know what to do. | My humble service to our friends, as usual.

Hawkesworth 1766

Swift to the Rev. John Worrall

Market-Hill, Jan. 13, 1728–9

I just received your letter, and should never have done if I returned you thanks so often as I ought for your care and kindness; both my disorders still continue: however, I desire that Mrs. *Brent* may make things ready, for my raggedness will soon force me away. I have been now ill about a month, but the family are so kind to speak loud enough for me to hear them; and my deafness is not so extream as you have known when I have fretted at your mannerly voice, and was only relieved by Mrs. *Worrall*.

[1] Swift's visitation of his cathedral seems usually to have taken place early in each year.

[2] A great quantity of snow had fallen in Dublin before Christmas, and had been followed by severe frost. Although a thaw is said to have set in at the close of the year, the *Dublin Intelligence* announces on 11 Jan. that the roads continued so bad as 'to retard the coming in of our posts'.—Ball.

I send you enclosed the fruit of my illness, to make an Intelligencer; I desire you will inclose it in a letter to Mrs. *Harding*,[1] and let your letter be in an unknown hand, and desire her to shew it to the author of the Intelligencer, and to print it if he thinks fit. There is a letter, you will find, that is to be prefixed before the verses, which letter is grounded on a report, and if that report be false, the former part of the letter will be unseasonable, but the latter will not, and therefore the Intelligencer must be desired to alter it accordingly.

It should be sent soon, to come time enough for the next Intelligencer.

Pray, in your letter to Mrs. *Harding*, desire her to make her people be more correct, and that the Intelligencer himself may look over it, for that everbody who reads those papers, are very much offended with the continual nonsense made by her printers. | I am yours, | J. Swift.

Hawkesworth 1766

Swift to the Rev. John Worrall

Market Hill, Jan. 18. 1728–9.

I have yours of the 14 instant, but you had not then received my last, in which was inclosed a paper for the Intelligencer, which I hope you have disposed of as desired. My disorder still continues the same for this fortnight past, and am neither better nor worse. However, I resolve to return on the first mending of the weather; these three last days there being as violent a storm as I have known, which still continues: we have been told my lord *Mountcashell* is dead at *Drogheda*, but I believe it to be a lie. However, he is so tender, and affects so much vigour and fatigue, that we have been in pain about him.[2]

[1] The widow of John Harding, printer of the *Drapier's Letters.* She issued the separate numbers of the *Intelligencer*, which are dated from 11 May to 2 Dec. 1728. An additional number xx, 7 May 1729, containing Swift's satirical verses 'Dean Smedley Gone to seek his Fortune' (*Poems*, ii. 454) also appeared. The verses to which Swift refers came out not as an *Intelligencer* but as a small octavo pamphlet of eight pages entitled *The Journal of a Dublin Lady* (*Poems*, ii. 443).

[2] Edward, third Viscount Mountcashel, an outstanding pupil of Sheridan. The rumour of his death was without foundation. He died in 1736.

I had a letter two days ago, which cost me six shillings and four-pence; it consisted of the probate of a will in *Leicestershire*, and of two inclosed letters, and was beyond the weight of letters franked. When I went a lad to my mother, after the revolution, she brought me acquainted with a family where there was a daughter with whom I was acquainted.[1] My prudent mother was afraid I should be in love with her; but when I went to *London*, she married an inn-keeper in *Loughborow*, in that county, by whom she had several children. The old mother died, and left all she had to her daughter aforesaid, separate from her husband. This woman (my mistress with a pox) left several children,[2] who are all dead but one daughter, *Ann* by name. This *Ann*, for it must be she, about seven years ago writ to me from *London*, to tell me she was daughter of *Betty Jones*, for that was my mistress's name, till she was married to one *Perkins*, inn-keeper, at the *George* in *Loughborow*, as I said before. The subject of the girl's letter was, that a young lady of good fortune was courted by an *Irishman*, who pretended to be barrack-master-general of *Ireland*, and desired me, as an old acquaintance of her mother, *Betty Jones*, alias *Perkins*, to enquire about this *Irishman*. I answered, that I knew him not, but supposed he was a cheat; I heard no more. But now comes a letter to me from this *Betty Jones*, alias *Perkins*, to let me know, that her daughter *Ann Giles*, married an *Irishman*, one *Giles*, and was now come over to *Ireland* to pick up some debts due to her husband, which she could not get; that the young widow (for her husband *Giles* is dead) hath a mind to settle in *Ireland*, and to desire I would lend her daughter *Giles*, three guineas, which her mother will pay me when I draw upon her in *England*, and Mrs. *Giles* writes me a letter to that purpose. She intends to take a shop, and will borrow the money from Mrs. *Brent* (whose name she hath learned) and pay me as others do. I was at first determined to desire you would, from me, make her a present of five pounds, on account of her mother and grandmother, whom my mother used to call cousin. She hath sent me an attested copy of her mother's will, which, as I told you cost me six shillings and four-pence. But I am in much doubt; for by her mother's letters, she is her heiress, and the grand-mother left *Betty Jones*, alias *Perkins*, the mother of this woman in *Dublin*, all she had, as a separate maintanance from her husband (who

[1] See vol. i, p. 3, n. 1.

[2] Notwithstanding the word 'left' a subsequent part of the letter shows that as far as Swift knew Betty Perkins was still alive.

proved a rogue) to the value of five hundred pounds. Now, I cannot conceive why she would let her only daughter and heiress come to *Ireland*, without giving her money to bear her charges here, and put her in some way. The woman's name is *Ann Giles*, she lodges at one Mrs. *Wilmot*'s, the first house in *Molesworth-court*, on the right hand, in *Fishamble-street*. I have told you this long story, to desire you will send for the woman, this *Ann Giles*, and examine her strictly, to find if she be the real daughter of *Elizabeth Jones*, alias *Perkins*, or no, and how her mother, who is so well able, came to send her in so miserable a condition to *Ireland*. The errand is so romantic, that I know not what to say to it. I would be ready to sacrifice five pounds, on old acquaintance, to help the woman; I supect her mother's letters to be counterfeit, for I remember she spells like a kitchen maid. And so I end this worthy business.

My bookseller, Mr. *Motte*, by my recommendation, dealt with Mr. *Hyde*;[1] there are some accounts between them, and Mr. Hyde is in his debt. He hath desired me to speak to Mr. *Hyde*'s executors to state the account, that Mr. *Motte* may be in a way to recover the balance. I wish you would step to Mr. *Hyde*'s house, and enquire how that matter stands, and how Mr. *Motte* is to be paid. I suppose Mr. *Hyde* died in good circumstances, and that there will be no danger of his creditors suffering by his death.

I inclose a letter to Mr. *Motte*, which you will be so kind to send to the post-office.

I desire likewise that you will make Mrs. *Brent* buy a bottle of usquebaugh, and leave it with the woman who keeps Sir *Arthur Acheson*'s house in *Capel-street*,[2] and desire her to deliver it to captain *Creichton*,[3] who lodges at the *Pyed Horse*, in *Capel-street*, and is to bring down other things to my lady *Acheson*.

My most humble service to Mrs. *Worrall*, Mrs. *Dingley*, and love to Mrs. *Brent*.

I wish you all a happy new year.

[1] Printer of the first Dublin edition of *Gulliver's Travels*. The will of 'John Hide of the city of Dublin stationer' was proved a week before the writing of this letter.

[2] A street in the northern part of Dublin, dating from the latter part of the seventeenth century when the Earl of Essex was viceroy.—Ball.

[3] The hero of the *Memoirs of Captain John Creichton* (*Prose Works*, ed. Temple Scott, xi. 165).

Faulkner 1741

Swift to Alexander Pope

[Dublin, Feb. 13, 1728[–9][1]

I lived very easily in the country: Sir Acheson[2] is a man of Sense, and a scholar, has a good voice, and my Lady a better; she is perfectly well bred, and desirous to improve her understanding, which is very good, but cultivated too much like a fine Lady. She was my pupil there, and severely chid when she read wrong;[3] with that, and walking and making twenty little amusing improvements, and writing family verses of mirth by way of libels on my Lady, my time past very well and in very great order; infinitely better than here, where I see no creature but my servants and my old Presbyterian house-keeper, denying myself to every body till I shall recover my ears.

The account of another Lord Lieutenant was only in a common news-paper,[4] when I was in the country, and if it should have happened to be true, I would have desired to have had access to him as the situation I am in requires. But this renews the grief for the death of our friend Mr. Congreve,[5] whom I loved from my youth, and who surely besides his other talents, was a very agreeable companion. He had the misfortune to squander away a very good constitution in his younger days; and I think a man of sense and merit like him, is bound in conscience to preserve his health for the sake of his friends, as well as of himself. Upon his own account I could not much desire the continuance of his life, under so much pain, and so many infirmities. Years have not yet hardened me, and I have an addition of weight on my spirits since we lost him, although I saw him so seldom; and possibly if he had lived on should never have seen him more. I do not only wish as you ask me, that I was unacquainted with any deserving person, but almost, that I never had a

[1] This is Swift's reply to Pope's letter of 12 Nov. 1728.

[2] Sir Arthur was a graduate of Trinity College. The verses 'To Dean Swift' (*Poems*, iii. 875) attributed to him are, however, clearly by Swift himself, and belong to the summer of 1729.

[3] The verses 'A Panegyrick on the Dean' (*Poems*, iii. 886), from which Ball quotes in illustration, belong to the year 1730.

[4] A rumour had spread that Carteret was to be superseded as Lord-Lieutenant by the Duke of Argyll. He remained in office, however, till the following year.

[5] As the result of an injury received from a carriage accident at Bath Congreve died in London on 19 Jan. 1728–9.

friend. Here is an ingenious good-humoured Physician,[1] a fine gentleman, an excellent scholar, easy in his fortunes, kind to every body, hath abundance of friends, entertains them often and liberally, they pass the evening with him at cards, with plenty of good meat and wine, eight or a dozen together; he loves them all, and they him; he hath twenty of these at command; if one of them dies, it is no more than poor Tom! he gets another, or takes up with the rest, and is no more moved than at the loss of his cat; he offends no body, is easy with every body—is not this the true happy man? I was describing him to my Lady Acheson, who knows him too, but she hates him mortally by my character, and will not drink his health: I would give half my fortune for the same temper, and yet I cannot say I love it, for I do not love my Lord—who is much of the Doctor's nature. I hear Mr. Gay's second Opera which you mention, is forbid, and then he will be once more fit to be advised, and reject your advice. Adieu.

Deane Swift 1765

Swift to Alexander Pope

March 6th, 1728–9.

Sir,—If I am not a good correspondent, I have bad health; and that is as good. I passed eight months in the country, with sir *Arthur* and my lady *Acheson*, and had at least half a dozen returns of my giddiness and deafness, which lasted me about three weeks a piece, and, among other inconveniencies, hindred me from visiting my chapter and punishing enormities, but did not save me the charges of a visitation-dinner. This disorder neither hinders my sleeping, nor much my walking, yet is the most mortifying malady I can suffer. I have been just a month in town, and have just got rid of it in a fortnight: and, when it is on me, I have neither spirits to write, or read, or think, or eat. But I drink as much as I like; which is a resource you cannot fly to when you are ill. And I like it as little as you: but I can bear a pint better than you can a spoonful. You were very kind in your care for Mr *Whalley*; but, I hope, you remembered, that *Daniel*[2] is a damnable poet, and consequently a public enemy to mankind. But I despise the lords decree, which is a jest upon

[1] Dr. Helsham.

[2] See Swift to Oxford, 21 Sept. 1728.

common sense: for, what did it signify to the merits of the cause, whether *George* the Old, or the Young, were on the throne?[1]

No: I intended to pass last winter in *England*, but my health said No: and I did design to live a gentleman, and, as *Sancho's* wife said, to go in my coach to court.[2] I know not whether you are in earnest to come hither in spring: if not, pray God you may never be in jest. Dr. *Delany* shall attend you at *Chester*, and your apartment is ready; and I have a most excellent chaise, and about sixteen dozen of the best cyder in the world; and you shall command the town and kingdom, and *digito monstrari*, *&c.* And, when I cannot hear, you shall have choice of the best people we can afford, to hear you, and nurses enough; and your apartment is on the sunny side.

The next paragraph strikes me dumb. You say I am to blame, if I refuse the opportunity of going with my lady *Bolingbroke* to *Aix-la-Chapelle*. I must tell you, that a foreign language is mortal to a deaf man. I must have good ears to catch up the words of so nimble a tongued race as the *French*, having been a dozen years without conversing among them. Mr. *Gay* is a scandal to all lusty young fellows with healthy countenance; and, I think, he is not intemperate in a physical sense.[3] I am told he has an asthma, which is a disease I commiserate more than deafness, because it will not leave a man quiet either sleeping or waking. I hope he does not intend to print his Opera[4] before it is acted; for I defy all your subscription to amount to 800*l.* And yet, I believe, he lost as much more for want of human prudence.

I told you some time ago, that I was dwindled to a writer of libels on the lady of the family where I lived, and upon myself; but they never went further: and my lady *Acheson* made me give her up all the foul copies, and never gave the fair ones out of her hands, or suffered them to be copied. They were sometimes shewn to intimate

[1] Nichols, 1801, xviii. 262, has a long footnote on the litigation, from which this extract is relevant: 'A doubt arising whether the writ was not abated, having been taken out in the lifetime of king George I, but not returnable till after that king's death; their lordships determined that it was abated, and therefore reversed the judgment, Feb. 26, 1728, 9.'

[2] 'If I am put to it, I'll go to Court, and set up a coach like all the world; for she who has a governor for a husband may very well have one and keep one.'

[3] Gay was at this time seriously ill as subsequent letters will show.

[4] *The Beggar's Opera* brought Gay about £800. *Polly*, as already noted, was forbidden representation, and the receipts from the sale of printed copies amounted to a much larger sum.

friends, to occasion mirth, and that was all. So that I am vexed at your thinking I had any hand in what could come to your eyes. I have some confused notion of seeing a paper called *Sir Ralph the Patriot*,[1] but am sure it was bad or indifferent; and, as to the *Lady at Quadrille*,[2] I never heard of it. Perhaps it may be the same with a paper of verses called, *The Journal of a Dublin Lady*, which I writ at Sir *Arthur Acheson's*; and, leaving out what concerned the family, I sent it to be printed in a paper which doctor *Sheridan* had engaged in, called, *The Intelligencer*, of which he made but sorry work, and then dropt it. But the verses were printed by themselves, and most horridly mangled in the press, and were very mediocre in themselves; but did well enough in the manner I mentioned, of a family-jest. I do sincerely assure you, that my frequent old disorder, and the scene where I am, and the humour I am in, and some other reasons which time hath shewn, and will shew more if I live; have lowered my small talents with a vengeance, and cooled my disposition to put them in use. I want only to be rich, for I am hard to be pleased; and, for want of riches, people grow every day less solicitious to please me. Therefore I keep humble company, who are happy to come where they can get a bottle of wine without paying for it. I give my vicar a supper, and his wife a shilling, to play with me an hour at back-gammon once a fortnight. To all people of quality, and especially of titles, I am not within; or, at least, am deaf a week or two after I am well. But, on *Sunday* evenings, it costs me six bottles of wine to people whom I cannot keep out. Pray, come over in *April*, if it be only to convince you that I tell no lies, and the journey will be certainly for your health. Mrs. *Brent*, my house-keeper, famous in print for digging out the great bottle,[3] says she will be your nurse; and the best physicians we have shall attend you without fees: although, I believe, you will have no occasion but to converse with one or two of them to make them proud.

Your letter came but last post, and you see my punctuality. I am unlucky at every thing I send to *England*. Two bottles of usquebagh

[1] Under the title of 'The Progress of Patriotism. A Tale' this poem appeared in *The Country Journal: or*, *The Craftsman* of 3 Aug. 1728, and was reprinted in *The Intelligencer*, no. xii. It was not by Swift.

[2] It seems probable that Pope by the 'Lady at Quadrille' had in mind *The Journal of a Modern Lady*.

[3] The reference is to 'Stella's Birth-Day. A great Bottle of Wine, long buried, being that Day dug up' (*Poems*, p. 740), which was first printed in *Miscellanies. The Last Volume*, 1727.

were broken. Well, my humble service to my lord *Bolingbroke*, lord *Bathurst*, lord *Masham*, and his lady my dear friend, and Mr. *Pultney*, and the doctor, and Mr. *Lewis*, and our sickly friend *Gay*, and my lady *Bolingbroke*; and very much to *Patty*, who I hope will learn to love the world less, before the world leaves off to love her. I am much concerned to hear of my lord *Peterborow* being ill. I am exceedingly his servant, and pray God recover his health. As for your courtier Mrs. *Howard*, and her Mistress, I have nothing to say, but that they have neither memory nor manners; else I should have some mark of the former from the latter, which I was promised above two years ago; but, since I made them a present, it would be mean to remind them.[1] I am told poor Mrs. *Pope* is ill: Pray God preserve her to you, or raise you up a useful as friend.

This letter is an answer to Mr. *Ford*, whose hand I mistook for yours, having not heard from him this twelve-month. There you are not to stare; and it must be lost, for it talks to you only.

Again, forgive my blunders: for, reading the letter by candle-light, and not dreaming of a letter from Mr. *Ford*, I thought it must be yours, because it talks of our friends.

The letter talks of *Gay*, and Mr. *Whalley*, and lord *Bolingbroke*, which made me conclude it must be yours: so all the answering part must go for nothing.

Deane Swift 1768

Francis Geoghegan to Swift

March 10, 1728–9.

Sir,[2]

Your time is precious, your curiosity not very small, my esteem of you very great; therefore come not within the walls of the four courts in hopes of hearing a matrimonial decree in this reign; for on *Monday*, (viz.) that is to say, the 10th of this instant *March*, 1728, his excellency Thomas Wyndham,[3] Esq; lord high-chancellor of

[1] The reference is to a medal which was promised to him by Queen Caroline before he sent her the poplin.

[2] Born in co. Westmeath, the writer of the letter was a member of the Irish Bar.

[3] Thomas Wyndham, 1681–1745, descended from a distinguished Wiltshire family, was called to the Bar in 1705. In 1724, the same year as Boulter, he went

Ireland, pronounced after your back was turned, and not with the assistance of the two chiefs, his decree in the case of *Stewart* v. *Stewart*, on *A. Powel* to this effect:[1] He said there was a full consent till such time as the draught of the settlement was sent down to Mrs. *Stewart*, to be considered by her and her friends; and after she had considered it, she shall not be at liberty to make any objections; for all the restrictions of marriage are odious in the civil law, and not favoured by the common law, especially after the age of one and twenty;[2] therefore marry they may, and let Mr. *Nutley*[3] be a lawyer for Mrs. *Rebecca Stewart*, the plaintiff, to take care of the settlement for her advantage, and let *Powel* chuse another lawyer for himself; though by the bye. Mr. *Nutley* would serve for both; and it is not necessary to inquire what *Powel* makes by his practice, although he assured the mother it amounted to one thousand four hundred pounds *per annum*.[4]

> *Ovid*, 'tis true, successfully imparts
> The rules to steal deluded virgins hearts;
> But oh! ye fair ones, pious *Nutley*'s skill
> Instructs you to elude, by magick bill,
> The laws of God, and gratify your will.

You will, I hope, excuse this liberty in one, who, to resent the indignity offered to you by *Ram*'s coachman, made him drunk soon after at *Gory*, which so much incensed the aforesaid *Ram*, that he discharged him his service,[5] and he is now so reduced, that he has

to Ireland, where he soon gained an outstanding reputation. He became Chancellor in 1726, acted as Speaker in the Irish House of Lords, and in 1731 was created Baron Wyndham of Finglas. He developed Irish sympathies and numbered Swift among his friends (Ball, *Judges in Ireland*, ii. 197–8; *D.N.B.*).

[1] This suit concerned the will of a gentleman who had died seven years before, leaving a widow and two daughters, and originated in the widow's seeking to enforce a provision that his daughter's enjoyment of his estate should be conditional on their marrying with their mother's consent (Chancery Bill, 18 June 1728). Powell, whose Christian name was Charles, a chancery official, was the prospective bridegroom.—Ball.

[2] The mother admitted that the daughter in question, who was the elder, came of age shortly after her husband's death.

[3] Richard Nutley, *Judges in Ireland*, ii. 72.

[4] According to the mother's statements Powell had for some years made yearly by his practice £1,400 to £1,500.

[5] The reference is to an incident recounted in the second number of *The Intelligencer*. This was not written by Swift.

no other way of getting his bread but by crying in this city, *Ha' you any dirt to carry out?* I am, Sir, your sincere friend and humble servant, | Francis Geoghegan.

Forster copy

Swift to Knightley Chetwode

Dublin, March 15, 1728–9.

Sir,

I had the favour of yours of the 5th instant[1] when I had not been above a fortnight recovered from a disorder of giddiness and deafness, which hardly leaves me a month together. Since my last return from England I never had but one letter from you while I was in the country,[2] and that was during a time of the same vexatious ailment, when I could neither give myself the trouble to write or to read. I shall think very unwise in such a world as this, to leave planting of trees and making walks, to come into it. I wish my fortune had thrown me anywhere rather than into this town and no town, where I have not three acquaintances, nor know any person whom I care to visit. But I must now take up with a solitary life from necessity as well as inclination, for yesterday I relapsed again, and am now so deaf that I shall not be able to dine with my Chapter on our only festival in the year, I mean St. Patrick's Day.[3]

As to any scurrilities published against me, I have no other remedy than to desire never to hear of them, and then the authors will be disappointed, at least it will be the same thing to me as if they had never been writ; for I will not imagine that any friend I esteem can value me the less upon the malice of fools and knaves, against whose republic I have always been at open war.[4] Every man is safe from evil tongues, who can be content to be obscure, and men must take

[1] Missing.

[2] Swift had apparently forgotten the letters which he had received from Chetwode during the autumn of 1727, and is referring to one sent him during the previous year.

[3] 17 Mar.

[4] Swift may have had especially in mind *Some Memoirs Of The Amours and Intrigues Of a Certain Irish Dean*, &c., published by J. Roberts, London. It was issued in two parts, and in 1728. Swift is called Polidore; Vanessa and Stella (under the name of Abigail) figure in it.

distinction as they do land, *cum onere*. I wish you happy in your retreat, and hope you will enjoy it long and am your etc.

Address: To Knightley Chetwode, Esq. at his house at Woodbrooke, near Mountmellick.

Deane Swift 1768

William Flower to Swift

Ashbrook, March 18, 1728–9.

Sir,

As I have been honoured by some of your letters, and as you are my old acquaintance,[1] though to my sorrow not intimately so, I trust you will pardon this presumption. Perhaps you will be at a loss to guess what title I have to an old acquaintance with you; but as several little accidents make indelible impressions upon the minds of school-boys, near thirty years ago, when I was one, I remember I was committed to your care from *Sheene* to *London*:[2] we took water at *Mortlake*, the commander of the little skiff was very drunk and insolent, put us ashore at *Hammersmith*, yet insisted, with very abusive language, on his fare, which you courageously refused; the mob gathering; I expected to see your gown stript off, and for want of a blanket to take a flight with you in it, but

Tum pietate gravem ac meritis si forte virum quem
Conspexere, silent, arrectisque auribus adstant:
Ille regit dictis animos, et pectora mulcet.

Virg. Æn. I. 155.[3]

By your powerful eloquence you saved your bacon and money, and we happily proceeded on our journey. But it is not an inclination purely to tell you this old story, which persuades me to write. A friend from *Dublin* lately obliged me with a very entertaining paper, entitled *The Intelligencer*, it is number 20, a posthumous work of

[1] William Flower was known to Swift through his mother, who was a niece of Sir William Temple and a sister of the first Viscount Palmerston. The family mansion in co. Kilkenny was, apparently, then called Ashbrook. It was later known as Castledurrow. On 27 Oct. 1733 Flower was created Baron Castle Durrow. He died 29 Apr. 1746.

[2] Flower's maternal grandfather, Sir John Temple, lived at Sheen for some of his latter years.

[3] Should be i. 151–3; and in the last line 'Iste' for 'Ille'.

Nestor Ironside;[1] a correspondent mentioning these papers in a letter raised my curiosity, with the specimen I had of them, to read the rest. For my part, I have buried myself in the country, and know little of the world, but what I learn from news-papers; you, who live so much in it, and from other more convincing proofs, I am satisfied are acquainted with the *Intelligencer*. I wish his zeal could promote the welfare of his poor country, but I fear his labour is in vain.

The miseries of the North, as represented, demand the utmost compassion,[2] and must soften the malice of the most bitter enemy; I hope they, whose interest it is, if they rightly considered it, to relieve those miserable wretches, will redress so publick a calamity; to which, if, as I have heard, some of the clergy, by exacting of tithes, have contributed; they deserve as great censure, as a certain dean,[3] who lends several sums without interest to his poor parishioners, has gained credit and honour by his charitable benificence. Bad men, to be sure, have crept in, and are of that sacred and learned order; the blackest of crimes, forgery, treason and blasphemy recently prove this: such should be spued out of it with utmost contempt, and punished according to their demerit with severe justice. If this allegation be true, I hope to see them censured by the *Intelligencer*, and recommend to him the words of *Jeremiah* to expatiate upon, c. x. ver. 21. c. xii. ver. 10, 11.[4] I imagine the poor widow, his printer,[5] is in danger of punishment. She suffered very cruelly for the *Drapier*'s works. I hope several contributed to ease her misfortunes on that occasion; I confess I am sorry I did not, but if you will give her a piece of gold, not in my name I beg, being unwilling to vaunt of charity, but as from a friend of yours, I shall by the first safe hand send one; in return I expect the *Drapier*'s Works entire.

[1] This was not *The Intelligencer*, no. xx, already noted, which was published in May 1729, but a disreputable production for which the editor was about to be prosecuted.

[2] Boulter, writing to the Duke of Newcastle, 13 Mar. 1728, says, 'the scarcity and dearness of provision still increases in the north; and many have eaten the oats they should have sowed their land with'.

[3] The allusion is probably to Swift.

[4] 'For the pastors are become brutish, and have not sought the Lord: therefore they shall not prosper, and all their flocks shall be scattered. . . . Many pastors have destroyed my vineyard, they have trodden my portion under foot, they have made my pleasant portion a desolate wilderness. They have made it desolate, and being desolate it mourneth unto me; the whole land is made desolate, because no man layeth it to heart.'

[5] i.e. Mrs. Harding.

I am sorry that, for the benefit of the ladies, the author[1] has not given us the *English* of

Motus doceri gaudet Ionicos
Matura virgo.[2]

Not having *Creech*'s *Horace*, a gentleman prevailed on me to attempt translating it in a couple of distichs; the science, which the compound *English* and *Greek* word signifies, little concerns a widower, but I should be glad to see it improved by good proficients in the *Ionick* jig. I own, in my little reading, I never met with this word, which puts me in mind of a passage on the *Thames*. My younger uncle, the grave Mr. *Flower*, his wife and mine, and Parson *Dingle*, one day made the tour of the city: we saw *Bedlam*, the lions, and what not, and finished with a view of that noble engine under *London* Bridge;[3] then we took water for *Whitehall*; rowed very silently to opposite the glass-house, where a dyer, his boat at anchor, was angling: poor *Jack* unfortunately asked, addressing himself to our waterman, What that man was fishing for. The wag answered very brisk, For —, Master, will you buy any? You are a man of too much humour not to be pleased with the reply. I never can think of it without a laugh; and am sure need not describe the scene to you. He is since called in our family by the name of *Jack Fisher*.

Rothschild

Swift to Charles Ford

Dublin. Mar. 18th 1728–9.

The very day I received your Letter, I relapsed into this odious Disorder of Deafness, which is constantly attended with Giddyness, although the latter is tolerable, but the first is perfectly vexatious, and truly I now compound if I can get an equall time of being well and ill. It is so long since I had any commerce with you in writing, that being no good reader in the night and your talking of L^dy^ Bolingbroke and Mr Gay I thought it had been Mr Pope's, and you happened not to name him. And I immediately writt him a long

[1] Presumably of the so-called *Intelligencer*.

[2] Horace, *Odes*, iii. 6, 21.

[3] A forcier for pumping Thames water into pipes for distribution to citizens' houses was erected in 1582. It was removed in 1822.

answer[1] till the next morning looking into you Letter I found the difference. For your saying you would come this Summer to Ireland, I easily construed that of Mr Pope, because he frequently raillyes of his intention to pay me a visit if his Mother should happen to dy. I hear your friends are well but I have not seen them for in three days after I came to Town, I fell ill, and after a short intervall of being well which I spent in long walks thinking it would continue, I grew deaf before I could wait on them. I am very well pleased with the Decree of the Lords[2] because it will at least keep Whalley a little longer in possession: but it makes me despise Law, when a decree turns upon a quirk without one Syllable relating to the merits of the Cause. We are told you are positively intended to give up Gibraltar and Minorca, wherein you will crown your good conduct.[3] We have been very well entertained with the Ds of Queensbury's Letter on her Banishment from Court.[4] I would be contented with the worst Ministry[5] in Europe to live in a Country which produces such a spirit as that Girles, and am sorry I was not acquainted with her. Pray tell Gay so when you see him, and let him tell the Dutchess. In a Kingdom where Law supports bold answers, it may be S. R. W.s Politicks, but no wise man's to provoke them, and somebody is sure to be a great Loser, and this Somebody is not the Dutchess. We have likewise the Poem in print upon the same Subject.[6] I am extreamly glad to be assured that Mr Gay will not fare the worse.[7] Let Mr Gay likewise tell the Dutchess, that I promise never to take up my Meat on a knife.[8] I was to see your friends in Dawson Street, and Mr Ford was at Cards, and she has my misfortune to be deaf, and

[1] Written 6 Mar.

[2] See p. 313. The decision of the Lords, in the case of Whaley, that, owing to the death of George I, a new writ was necessary. Judgement in favour of Whaley was not reached until 30 Apr. 1730.

[3] The question of giving up Gibraltar had been prominent since the Congress of Soissons in June 1728. Spain silently waived her claim to it in the Treaty of Seville, signed 9 Nov. 1729.

[4] See next letter, Gay to Swift.

[5] Manuscript reads 'worst and Ministry'.

[6] The 'Excellent new Ballad called A Bob for the Court', printed in *The Craftsman* of 28 Dec. 1728.

[7] As stated previously Gay made more by subscriptions to *Polly* than he was likely to have done by performances of the play.

[8] Gay, writing to Swift, 15 Feb. 1727–8, asks him to be careful to put his fork 'to all its proper uses and suffer nobody for the future to put their knives in their mouths'. See also Swift to Gay, 20 Nov. 1729, 19 Mar. 1729–30, 10 Nov. 1730. Gay's cautionary advice seems to have rankled with Swift.

Mrs Monk[1] was rooking her at two headed[2] Ombre, and she has given up her Coach, and allows poor Mrs Penny[3] onely a crown a week for chair-hire. As to what you say of writing, you are mistaken about Sr Ralph the Patriot,[4] for I believe it was writ in England; I think I saw it, but do not remember it was printed here. When I was last Summer at Sr A. Achesons, I writ little family verses, but no Copy ever went out, except some Verses called the Journal of a Dublin Lady, which I sent to make up a Paper that ran here under the name of the Intelligencer, which was scurvily kept up a while, and at last dropt.[5] The Journal was printed all into nonsense, and I believe was never heard of on your side. I assure you this disorder and my Monastick life takes off all invention, and there is not in Ireland a duller man in a gown than my self. If you come to Ireland I know what drives you hither, and what remedy will send you back; but I could wish you would cotton more with the valuable people while you are here. I do suppose no body hates and despises this kingdom more than my self, and yet when I am well I can be easy among a set of honest people who neither shine in titles nor Wit: but I do not recommend my text to You. The time may come when you will have a less relish for Variety. I wish you well, and pray walk more, and drink and eat less.—I am &c.

Address: To Charles Ford Esqr, to | be left at the Cocoa Tree in | Pell-mell | London.

Postmarks: Dublin and 27 MR

4805

John Gay to Swift

[18 March 1728–9]

Dear Sr

I have writ to you several times, and having heard nothing from you makes me fear my Letters have miscarried;[6] Mr Pope's Letter

[1] Probably the wife of Charles Monk (1678–1752) and grandmother of the first Viscount Monck.

[2] Not 'two handed'; usually played by three.

[3] Ford's sister Penelope.

[4] The poem entitled *The Progress of Patriotism*, first printed in *The Craftsman*, 3 Aug. 1728, and reprinted in *The Intelligencer*, no. xii. Not by Swift; he disclaims it in letters to Pope of 6 Mar. 1729 and 12 June 1732.

[5] *The Journal of a Dublin Lady* was printed as a separate pamphlet.

[6] During 1728 Gay had written five letters to Swift and received two in return Of any surviving this letter was the first from Gay in 1729.

hath taken off my concern in some degree, but I hope good weather will entirely re-establish you in your health. I am but just recover'd from the severest fit of sickness that ever any body had who escap'd death; I was several times given up by the Physicians and every body that attended me; and upon my recovery was judg'd to be in so ill a condition that I should be miserable for the remainder of my life, but contrary to all expectation I am perfectly recover'd, and have no remainders of the distempers that attack'd me, which were at the same time, Feaver, Asthma & Pleurasie. I am now in the Duke of Queensberry's house; and have been so ever since I left Hampstead, where I was carried at a time that it was thought I could not live a day. Since my coming to town, I have been very little abroad, the weather has been so severe: I must acquaint you, (because I know 'twill please you) that during my Sickness I had many of the kindest proofs of friendship, particularly from the Duke & Dutchess of Queensberry, who, if I had been their nearest relation and meanest friend could not have treated me with more constant attendance then, and they continue the same to me now.

You must undoubtedly have heard that the Dutchess took up my defence with the King and Queen in the cause of my Play, and that she hath been forbid the Court[1] interesting herself to increase my fortune for the publication of it without being acted; the Duke too hath given up his employment which he would have done, if the Dutchess had not met this treatment, upon account of ill usage from the Ministers; but this hasten'd him in what he had determin'd.[2] The Play is now almost printed with the Musick, words & Basses engrav'd on 31 Copper plates, wch by my friends assistance hath a probability to turn greatly to my advantage. The Dutchess of Marlborough hath given me a hundred pound for one Copy, & others have contributed very handsomely but as my account is not yet settled I cannot tell you particulars.

For writing in the cause of Virtue and against the fashionable vices, I am look'd upon at present as the most obnoxious person

[1] The public performance of Gay's *Polly* was prohibited by the Duke of Grafton, Lord Chamberlain, on 12 Dec. 1728. The Duchess of Queensberry thereupon solicited subscriptions for the play, in consequence of which she was, 27 Feb. 1729, forbidden the Court by an official letter.

[2] In a pamphlet entitled *The Female Faction or the Gay Subscribers*, published in 1729, the Duchess is described as making

'—her tender Lord her quarrel join,
And the fair honours of his post resign.'

almost in England, Mr Pulteney tells me I have got the start of him. Mr Pope tells me that I am dead and that this obnoxiousness is the reward of my inoffensiveness in my former life. I wish I had a Book ready to send you, but I believe I shall not be able to compleat the work 'till the latter end of next week. Your Money is still in Lord Bathurst's hands, but I believe I shall receive it soon; I wish to receive your orders how to dispose of it. I am impatient to finish my work, for I want the country air, not that I am ill, but to recover my strength, and I cannot leave my work till it is finish'd. While I am writing this I am [in] the room next to our dining room with sheets all round it, and two people from the Binder folding Sheets. I print the Book at my own expence in Quarto, which is to be sold for six shillings with the Musick.[1] You see I dont want industry, and I hope you will allow that I have not the worst Œconomy. Mrs Howard hath declar'd herself strongly both to the King & Queen as my advocate.[2] The Dutchess of Queensberry is allow'd to have shown more Spirit, more honour, and more goodness than was thought possible in our times; I should have added too more understanding and good sense. You see my fortune (as I hope my Virtue will.) increases by oppression. I go to no courts, I drink no wine, and am calumniated even by Ministers of State, and yet am in good Spirits. Most of the Courtiers, though otherways my friends, refuse to contribute to my undertaking, but the City, and the people of England take my part very warmly, and I am told the best of the Citizens will give me proofs of it by their contributions. I could talk to you a great deal more, but I am afraid I shall write too much for you, and for myself; I have not writ so much together since my sickness. I cannot omit telling you that Dr Arbuthnot's attendance and care of me show'd him the best of friends; Dr Hollings[3] though entirely a stranger to me was join'd with him & us'd me kindest and

[1] *Polly: An Opera. Being the Second Part of the Beggar's Opera. . . . Printed for the Author. MDCCXXIX* appeared in quarto. No other authorized edition seems to have been published in Gay's lifetime, although numerous pirated editions appeared.

[2] *The Female Faction* represents her as imitating the duchess:

> 'On chaste Calista let us cast our Eye,
> By their example thine and Wit's ally.'

[3] John Hollings (1683?–1739) was admitted a fellow of the Royal College of Surgeons in 1726. He rose to be physician-general to the army and physician-in-ordinary to the King.

most handsome manner. Mr & Mrs[1] Pulteney was greatly concern'd for me, visited me and show'd me the strongest proofs of friendship; when I see you, I will tell you of others as of Mr Pope, Mrs Blount, Mr and Mrs Rollinson,[2] Lord and Lady Bolingbroke &c I think they are all your friends & well-wishers I hope you will love them the better upon my account, but do not forget Mr Lewis nor Lord Bathurst, Sr W. Wyndham & Lord Gower,[3] and Lord Oxford among the number.

From the Duke of Queensberrys | in Burlington Gardens. | March 18. 1728/9. My service to Dr Delany & | Mr Stopfort.

Endorsed by Swift: Mr Gay. March 18 | 1728–9, *and again.*

4805

John Arbuthnot to Swift

London March 19 1728–9

This is the second or third time Dear Sir that I have wrote to yow;[4] without hearing a word of You or from you; only in general, that you were very much out of order, sometimes of your two old complaints the vertigo & deafness, which I am very sorry for. The gentleman[5] who carrys this has come better off than I did imagine, I us'd my little interest as far as it would go in his affairs. he will be able to give yow some account of your friends many of whom have been in great distress this winter, John Gay I may say with vanity owes his life under god, to the unwearied endeavours & care of your humble servant for a physician who had not been passionately his friend could not have savd him. I had besides my personal concern for him, other motives of my case he is now become a publick person a little Sacheverel, & I took the same pleasure in saving him, as Ratcliff did in preserving My Lord chief Justice Holt's wife whom he attended out of spite to the husband who wishd her dead.[6]

1 '& Mrs' written above the line, hence 'was'.

2 William Rollinson, the London wine merchant, whose acquaintance was favoured by Bolingbroke, Swift, Pope, and Gay. See *Journal*, p. 231.

3 A kinsman of the Duchess of Queensberry.

4 Some letters must be missing. The last two on record from Arbuthnot to Swift are 8 Nov. 1726, 30 Nov. 1727.

5 Nathaniel Whaley.

6 The story that Sir John Holt, 1642–1710, devoted himself incessantly to business to avoid the society of his wife, if questionable, is accepted (Campbell, *Lives of the Chief Justices*, ii. 177).

The inoffensive John Gay is now become one of the obstructions to the peace of Europe, the terror of Ministers, the chief author of the Craftsman & all the seditious pamphlets which have been published against the government.[1] he has gott several turnd out of their places, the greatest ornament of the court Banishd from it for his sake,[2] another great Lady in danger of being chasé likewise,[3] about seven or eight duchesses pushing forward like the ancient Circum Celliones[4] in the Church who shall suffer Martyrdome upon his account first, he is the darling of the city; if he should travel about the country, he would have hecatombs of Roasted oxen sacrificd to him. Since he became so conspicuous Will poultny hangs his head; to see himself so much outdone in the career of Glory. I hope he will gett a good dale of money by printing his play. but I really believe he would gett more by showing his person: and I can assure you this is the very identical John Gay whom yow formerly knew & lodgd with in Whitehall two years ago. I have been diverting my self with making an extract out of a History which will be printed in the year 1948 I wish I had your assistance to go through with it for I can assure yow it riseth to a very solemn piece of Burlesque.

As to the condition of your little club, it is not quite so desperate as you might imagine, for Mr Pope is as high in favour as I am affraid the rest are out of it. The King upon the perusal of the last edition of his Dunciad, Declard he was a very honest Man. I did not know till this moment, that I had so good an opportunity to send yow a letter & now I know it I am calld away and obligd to end with my best wishes & respects being most sincerely yours &c.

Address: To | The Reverend The | Dean of St patricks | Dublin
Endorsed by Swift: Dr Arbuthnot. | Mar. 19th 1729

[1] In the preface to *Polly* Gay wrote: 'I am accused, in general terms, of having written many disaffected libels and seditious pamphlets. As it hath ever been my utmost ambition . . . to lead a quiet and inoffensive life, I thought my innocence in this particular would never have requir'd justification.'

[2] The Duchess of Queensberry.

[3] Mrs. Howard.

[4] A fourth-century sect of African Donatists who rambled from town to town.

Forster No. 563[1]

—— *to Swift*

Philad · March · 29: 1729

Frd[2] Jona · Swift

having been often agreeably amused by thy Tale &c &c. and being now loading a small Shipp for Dublin . . . I have sent the[e] a Gammon the Product of the Wilds of America which perhaps may not be unacceptable at thy Table since it is only Designed to Lett thee Know that thy Witt and Parts are in Esteme at this Distance from place of thy Residence . . . thee need ask no Questions who this comes from since I am a Perfect Stranger to thee

Address: To Jon Swift in Dublin
Endorsed by Swift: Rx May 29 1729 | Quaker's Lett from | Philadelphia, | with a Ham
Endorsed in another hand: A Quaker's Lett | from | Philadelphia

Deane Swift 1768

Lady Johnson to Swift[3]

[30 March 1729]

Hon^d^ S^r^

I am a Huckster and Lives in *Strand Street* & has Dealings with Several familys, a saterday Night a Case of Instruments[4] was sent me in pawn by a Certain person in *Marys Street*, for two Rowls a print of Butter four Herrings and three Nagins of strong Waters, my foster brother who ply's about that End of the town tells Me he wanst saw it in your hand, fearing Hawkins's[5] whip I send it to you, and will take an Other Course to gett My Money, so I remain yours Hon^rs^ | Humble Sarv^t^ to Command | Martha Sharp.

Address: To the Revd The Dean of St. PaTricks.
Endorsed by Swift: The best letter I ever read.

[1] The original of this letter is in the Forster Collection. It was first printed by Deane Swift in 1765.

[2] i.e. 'Friend'.

[3] Lady Johnson was an aunt of Sir Arthur Acheson. Her husband, who resided at Gilford in the county of Down, had been knighted soon after the accession of George I, and had died some years before this letter was written.—Ball.

[4] It is not unlikely that this was a present of a case of instruments from Lady *Johnston* to the Dr.—Deane Swift.

[5] *Hawkins* was keeper of *Newgate*.—Deane Swift. According to Ball his malpractices subsequently led to the institution of criminal proceedings against him.

Faulkner 1741

Swift to Viscount Bolingbroke and Alexander Pope

Dublin, April 5, 1729.

I do not think it could be possible for me to hear better news than that of your getting over your scurvy suit,[1] which always hung as a dead weight on my heart; I hated it in all its circumstances, as it affected your fortune and quiet, and in a situation of life that must make it every way vexatious. And, as I am infinitely obliged to you for the justice you do me in supposing your affairs do at least concern me as much as my own; so I would never have pardoned your omitting it. But before I go on, I cannot forbear mentioning what I read last summer in a news-paper, that you were writing the history of your own Times. I suppose such a report might arise from what was not secret among your friends, of your intention to write another kind of history; which you often promised Mr. Pope and me to do:[2] I know he desires it very much, and I am sure I desire nothing more, for the honour and love I bear you, and the perfect knowledge I have of your publick virtue. My Lord, I have no other notion of Oeconomy than that it is the parent of Liberty and Ease, and I am not the only friend you have who hath chid you in his heart for the neglect of it, although not with his mouth, as I have done. For, there is a silly error in the world, even among friends otherwise very good, not to intermeddle with mens affairs in such nice matters. And, my Lord, I have made a maxim, that should be writ in letters of diamonds, That a wise man ought to have Money in his head, but not in his heart. Pray my Lord enquire whether your Prototype, my Lord Digby, after the Restoration when he was at Bristol, did not take some care of his fortune, notwithstanding that quotation I once sent you out of his speech to the H. of Commons? In my conscience, I believe fortune like other drabbs, values a man

[1] The suit concerned the first Lady Bolingbroke's property.—Ball.

[2] On 18 Sept. 1728 Swift requested Sheridan to send him from the deanery 'the history in folio, marble cover', which he was anxious, while staying with the Achesons, to revise. This was the work which appeared posthumously as *The History of the Four Last Years of the Queen*. Doubtless it was his re-reading of his own manuscript which led him to seek information from Bolingbroke about a project upon which he believed him to be engaged. Writing to Swift, 2 Aug. 1731, Bolingbroke gave him a fairly full description of the history, which, however, he did not write.

gradually less for every year he lives. I have demonstration for it; because, if I play at piquet for six-pence with a man or woman two years younger than my self, I always lose; and there is a young girl of twenty who never fails of winning my money at Back-gammon, though she is a bungler, and the game be Ecclesiastic. As to the publick, I confess nothing could cure my itch of medling with it but these frequent returns of deafness, which have hindred me from passing last winter in London; yet I cannot but consider the perfidiousness of some people who I thought when I was last there, upon a change that happened, were the most impudent in forgetting their professions that I have ever known. Pray will you please to take your pen and blot me out that political maxim from whatever book it is in; that *Res nolunt diu male administrari*; the commonness makes me not know who is the author, but sure he must be some Modern.

I am sorry for Lady Bolingbroke's ill health; but I protest I never knew a very deserving person of that sex, who had not too much reason to complain of ill health. I never wake without finding life a more insignificant thing than it was the day before: which is one great advantage I get by living in this country, where there is nothing I shall be sorry to lose; but my greatest misery is recollecting the scene of twenty years past, and then all on a sudden dropping into the present. I remember when I was a little boy, I felt a great fish at the end of my line which I drew up almost on the ground, but it dropt in, and the disappointment vexeth me to this very day, and I believe it was the type of all my future disappointments. I should be ashamed to say this to you, if you had not a spirit fitter to bear your own misfortunes, than I have to think of them. Is there patience left to reflect by what qualities wealth and greatness are got, and by what qualities they are lost? I have read my friend Congreve's verses to Lord Cobham, which end with a vile and false moral,[1] and I remember is not in Horace to Tibullus, which he imitates, 'that all times are equally virtuous and vicious' wherein he differs from all Poets, Philosophers, and Christians that ever writ. It is more probable that there may be an equal quantity of virtues always in the world, but sometimes there may be a peck of it in Asia, and hardly a thimble-full in Europe. But if there be no virtue, there is abundance of sincerity; for I will venture all I am worth, that there is not one

[1] Congreve's 'Letter to Viscount Cobham' ends with the couplet:

'Believe it, Men have ever been the same,
And all the Golden Age, is but a Dream.'

human creature in power who will not be modest enough to confess that he proceeds wholly upon a principle of Corruption. I say this because I have a scheme in spite of your notions, to govern England upon the principles of Virtue, and when the nation is ripe for it, I desire you will send for me. I have learned this by living like a Hermit, by which I am got backwards about nineteen hundred years in the Æra of the world, and begin to wonder at the wickedness of men. I dine alone upon half a dish of meat, mix water with my wine, walk ten miles a day, and read Baronius.[1] *Hic explicit Epistola ad Dom.* Bolingbroke *& incipit ad amicum Pope.*

Having finished my Letter to Aristippus,[2] I now begin to you. I was in great pain about Mrs. Pope, having heard from others that she was in a very dangerous way, which made me think it unseasonable to trouble you. I am ashamed to tell you, that when I was very young I had more desire to be famous than ever since; and fame, like all things else in this life, grows with me every day more a trifle. But you who are so much younger, although you want that health you deserve, yet your spirits are as vigorous as if your body were sounder. I hate a crowd where I have not an easy place to see and be seen. A great Library always maketh me melancholy, where the best Author is as much squeezed, and as obscure, as a Porter at a Coronation. In my own little library, I value the compilements of Grævius and Gronovius,[3] which make thirty-one volumes in folio (and were given me by my Lord Bolingbroke) more than all my books besides; because whoever comes into my closet, casts his eyes immediately upon them, and will not vouchsafe to look upon Plato or Xenophon.[4] I tell you it is almost incredible how Opinions change by the decline or decay of spirits, and I will further tell you, that all my endeavours from a boy to distinguish my self, were only for want of a great Title and Fortune, that I might be used like a Lord by those

[1] In the sale catalogue of Swift's books 'Baronii Annales Ecclesiastici in 12 vol.—Antv. 1629' appears as no. 606. They were annotated. These volumes also appear in the 1715 list of his books as costing £6.

[2] Aristippus was a favourite philosopher of Bolingbroke, mentioned several times in letters passing between him and Swift.

[3] These 'compilements' appear in the catalogue as nos. 556, 567, and 579, running to twenty-nine volumes, for three volumes were bound as one. They are not marked as annotated. They are priced at £40 in the 1715 list.

[4] There were two editions of Plato in Swift's library. That which he chiefly prized was the Estienne edition of 1578 in three folio volumes, which cost him £4. 10*s.* 0*d.* His Xenophon, no. 81, Paris, 1625, is marked as annotated.

who have an opinion of my parts; whether right or wrong, it is no great matter; and so the reputation of wit or great learning does the office of a blue riband, or of a coach and six horses. To be remembred for ever on the account of our friendship, is what would exceedingly please me, but yet I never loved to make a visit, or be seen walking with my betters, because they get all the eyes and civilities from me. I no sooner writ this than I corrected my self, and remember'd Sir Faulk Grevil's Epitaph, 'Here lies, &c. who was friend to Sir Philip Sidney.' And therefore I most heartily thank you for your desire that I would record our friendship in verse,[1] which if I can succeed in, I will never desire to write one more line in poetry while I live. You must present my humble service to Mrs. Pope, and let her know I pray for her continuance in the world, for her own reason, that she may live to take care of you.

4805

Andrew Ramsay to Swift

[London, 10 April 1729]

Sir[2]

One of the greatest pleasures I propos'd to my self in a Journey to England was that of seing you at London and it is a very sensible mortification to me to find my self disappointed in so agreeable an Expectation. It is now many years since I had the highest Esteem of your Genius and Writings, and when I was very young I found in some of them certain Ideas that prepard me for relishing those principles of universal religion, which I have since endavord to unfold in Cyrus. I could not let our Common friend M[r] Lesley[3] go back to Ireland without seizing the opportunity of acknowledging the oblidging Zeal you have pleasure to make my work esteem'd. Such marks of friendship do me a great deal of honor as well as pleasure, and I hope I have a thorough sense of them. as I have much enlargd my book, I am going to publish a new Edition by Subscription, I have given a hundred coppys of the proposals to our friend

[1] The inscription, which was his own composition, is still to be read in St. Mary's Church at Warwick: 'Fulke Greville, servant to Queen Elizabeth, councillor to King James, and friend to Sir Philip Sidney. Tropaeum Peccati.'

[2] See Ramsay's former letter, 1 Aug. [O.S. 20 July] 1727.

[3] The son of the non-juror.

and flatter my self that I may count upon the Continuation of your friendship. I am with great respect | Sir | your most oblidgd obedient humble servant | A Ramsay.

London the · 10th | of April · 1729.

Endorsed by Swift: Apr. 10. 1729 | Chevalr Ramsey

4805

John Arbuthnot to Swift

[London, 8 May 1729]

Dear Sir

I have wrote three times to Mr Dean of St patricks without receaving so much as an acknowledgment of the receipt of my Letters;[1] at the same time I hear of other Letters, which his acquaintances receave from him. I beleive I should hardly have brought my self to have wrote this were it not to serve you & a freind at the same time. I recommended one Mr Mason son of Mason Gentleman of the Queens Chappell, a Baritone Voice, for a vacancy of a Singer in your Cathedral this Letter was wrote from Bath Last September The same Mason informs me that ther is another Vacancy. therfor I renew my request.[2] I beleive you will hardly gett a better. he has a pleasant mellow voice & has sung severall times in the Kings chappell this winter, to the satisfaction of the Audience. I beg at least your Answer to this. Your freinds in town, such as I know are well Mr pope is happy again, in having his mother recoverd Mr Gay is gone to Scotland with the Duke of Queensbury. he has about twenty Law suits with booksellers, for pyrating his book.[3] The King gos soon to Hanover. These are all the news I know. I hope yow don't imagine I am so Little concernd about your health as not to desire to be informd of the state of it from your self. I have been tolerably well this winter I thank god. My Brother Robin is here & longs as

[1] Arbuthnot makes the same complaint in beginning his letter of 19 Mar.

[2] The letter from Arbuthnot to Swift of Sept. 1728 is missing. John Mason became subsequently a vicar-choral in both the Dublin Cathedrals, and held his place in them for over fifty years. He was also for part of that time a vicar-choral of Armagh Cathedral.

[3] *Polly*.

well as I to know how yow do. This with my best wishes & respects from | Dear sir | Your most faithfull humble | servant Jo: Arbuthnott.

London. May 8th | 1729

Address: To | The Reverend Dr Swift | Dean of St patricks | Ireland Dublin
Postmark: ? MA
Endorsed by Swift: Dr Arbuthnot | May . 8h 1729

Forster copy

Swift to Knightley Chetwode

Dublin, May 17, 1729.

Sir,

That I did not answer your former letter[1] was because I did not know it required any, and being seldom in a tolerable humour by the frequent returns or dreads of deafness, I am grown a very bad correspondent. As to the passage you mentioned in that former letter, and desired my opinion, I did not understand the meaning, and that letter being mislaid I cannot recollect it, though you refer to it in the last. I shall not make the usual excuses on the subject of lending money, but as I have not been master of thirty pounds for thirty days this thirty years, so I have actually borrowed several small sums for these two or three years past for board-wages to my servants and common expenses. I have within these ten days borrowed the very poor-money lodged in my hands to buy clothes for my servants, and left my note in the bag in case of my death. These pinches are not peculiar to me, but to all men in this kingdom, who live upon tithes or high rents, for as we have been on the high road to ruin these dozen years, so we have now got almost to our journey's end. And truly I do expect and am determined in a short time to pawn my little plate, or sell it, for subsistence.

I have had the same request you make me from several others, and have desired the same favour from others, without success; and I believe there are hardly three men of any figure in Ireland, whose affairs are so bad as mine, who now pay interest for a thousand pounds of other people's money which I undertook to manage, without receiving one farthing my self, but engaged seven years in a lawsuit

[1] The last letter from Chetwode to Swift which to this date survives lies more than five years in the past.

to recover it.[1] This is the fairest side of my circumstances, for they are worse than I care to think of, much less to tell, and if the universal complaints and despair of all people have not reached you, you have yet a vexation to come.[2] I am in ten times a worse state than you, having a lawsuit on which my whole fortune depends, and put to shifts for money which I thought would never fall to my lot. I have been lately amazed as well as grieved at some intimate friends, who have desired to borrow money of me, and whom I could not oblige, but rather expected the same kindness from them. Such is the condition of the kingdom, and such is mine. I am, | Yours &c.

Address: To Knightley Chetwode, Esq., at Woodbrooke, near Mountmellick.

Chapter Book of St. Patrick's Cathedral

Swift to the Earl of Burlington

Deanery House, Dublin, 22 May 1729.

My Lord,[3]

The two last times I was in England I often mentioned to your Lordship the repairing the monument of the first Earl of Cork, your ancestor, which you readily complied with, and promised to send an order to some of your managers here that it might be done.[4]

I did then likewise humbly propose to your Lordship to settle

[1] Swift refers to money invested in the South Sea stock. See his letter to Archdeacon Walls, 11 June 1714.

[2] At this time the povetry of Ireland and the sufferings of its people occupied Swift's thoughts. See *Prose Works*, ed. Davis, vol. xii *passim*. Writing to the Lord-Lieutenant he confessed that 'looking upon the kingdom's condition as absolutely desperate, I would not prescribe a dose for the dead'.

[3] This and the text of the two following letters were extracted by Ball from the Chapter Book of St. Patrick's Cathedral. These copies have disappeared, and cannot be traced.

[4] This monument, which now stands at the western end of the Cathedral, was erected early in the reign of Charles I by the first Earl of Cork in memory of his second wife. It is made of black marble and alabaster, and is very lofty and elaborate, with numerous effigies arranged in four tiers. The design was made by the Irish pursuivant of the time, who received a fee of £40, and the work was executed at a cost of £400 by a stonecutter who resided at Chapelizod, near Dublin. The monument is of historic interest, as a dispute with regard to its original situation, which was behind the communion table, helped to bring the Earl of Strafford to his doom (see Archbishop Bernard's *St. Patrick's Cathedral*, p. 47, and Litton Falkiner's *Illustrations of Irish History*, p. 378).—Ball.

some small rent on the Dean and Chapter of St. Patrick's and their successors, not exceeding five pounds a year, in trust for keeping the said monument in repair for ever, and if your Lordship should please to comply with this last request, we are of opinion that the said five pounds a year should not be a rent charge, but a small quantity of land now worth at a full rent five pounds a year, because it would always be of the same intrinsic value, whether money or land should rise or fall, and the Dean and Chapter will enter into the Chapter book the said gift as a standing record, and oblige themselves to apply the whole rent of the said land to no other use than the preservation of the said monument entire and in good order. I believe that your Lordship will agree that the Dean and Chapter can have no other design in making this request than the desire of preserving a monument which does some honour to your Lordship's family, and is an ornament to the Cathedral.

I send your Lordship a copy of the order of the Dean and Chapter, by which I am desired to write to you upon this occasion.[1] I am, with great respect, my Lord, Your Lordship's most obedient and most humble servant, | J.S.

Address: To the Right Honble. the Earl of Burlington.

Chapter Book of St. Patrick's Cathedral

Swift to Lady Catherine Jones

Deanery House, Dublin, 22 May 1729.

Madam,[2]

The monument to your Ladyship's grandfather, the Earl of Ranelagh, in the Cathedral Church of St. Patrick's, Dublin, whereof I have the honour to be Dean, being much out of repair, I am desired by an order of the Dean and Chapter, of which I send you a copy, to apply to your Ladyship that you would please to direct one of your receivers here to repair the said monument, which will do an

[1] Ordered by the aforesaid Dean and Chapter that the Dean do write to the several persons hereafter named to request their compliance for repairing and erecting monuments in the aforesaid Cathedral Church in remembrance of their ancestors, which will more fully appear by a copy of each letter herein entered.

[2] She was the third daughter of the Earl of Ranelagh, and died unmarried 12 Apr. 1740. Her father had died 5 Jan. 1711–12, when the earldom became extinct.

honour to the memory of your Ladyship's family, and be some ornament to our Cathedral without any considerable expense.[1]

Although I am a stranger to your Ladyship's person, yet I have heard much of your piety and good works, and your Ladyship will easily believe that neither the Chapter nor I can have any other view in this request than the honour of your family, whereof one was Archbishop of Dublin,[2] and the care we have of keeping our Cathedral as decently as we can. I am, with great respect, Madam, | Your Ladyship's &c | J.S.

Address: To the Right Honble. the Lady Catherine Jones.

Chapter Book of St. Patrick's Cathedral

Swift to the Countess of Holderness

Deanery House, Dublin, 22 May 1729.

Madam,[3]

I took the liberty of writing to your Ladyship some years ago upon the note of an old acquaintance, but you were not so good as to return me an answer, although my letters were altogether intended to the honour of your Ladyship's family, and particularly of that great person the Duke of Schomberg, your grandfather, whose body lies in a vault of St. Patrick's Cathedral, where I have the honour to be Dean.

The Chapter and I having reflected with much concern that the

[1] The monument is similar to that of the Earl of Cork, although of smaller dimensions, and was erected about the same time. It contains effigies of the first Viscount Ranelagh, who was Lady Catherine's great-grandfather, and of his father, who was Archbishop of Dublin. Her father was the only Earl of his line.—Ball.

[2] Archbishop Jones had been a predecessor of Swift as Dean of St. Patrick's. On a deed relating to property of the Cathedral Swift stigmatizes him as a 'rascal' for agreeing to the renewal of a lease, apparently for only two pounds a year, of lands that 'are now probably worth 150*l*. per annum'.

[3] Lady Frederica, daughter and coheir of Meinhard (Schomberg), third Duke of Schomberg, was married, 26 May 1715, to Robert (Darcy), third Earl of Holderness. He died at Bath, 20 Jan. 1721–2, aged thirty. She married as her second husband, 18 June 1724, Benjamin (Mildmay), Earl Fitzwalter, who died 29 Feb. 1756. She died 7 Aug. 1751, aged sixty-three. Owing to their physical limitations Lady Mary Wortley Montagu ridiculed the match between Lady Holderness and Mr. Mildway for being 'as curious as that between two oysters'.

remains of a general so renowned all over Europe, and so highly deserving both of England and this kingdom, shoud lie so obscurely without any monument over him, have made a formal order in full assembly, whereof I send you a copy annexed, that I should be desired to represent this matter to your Ladyship, and to request that you would be pleased to assign what moderate sum you think fit to erect a plain marble monument over his Grace. It shall be submitted to your Ladyship whether you will choose to get an epitaph drawn by some friend of your own or leave it to us. Your Ladyship may be firmly assured that the money shall be laid out with the utmost good management, because it is a matter which the Chapter and I have much at heart.

I send this letter under a cover to Sir Conyears Darcy,[1] being wholly ignorant where to address your Ladyship. I am with great respect, Madam, &c. | J.S.

Address: To the Right Honble. the Countess of Holderness now Countess Fitzwalter.[2]

4805

John Arbuthnot to Swift

[London, 9 June 1729]

Dear Sir

This is givn you by Mr Mason; whom I believe you will find answer the character I gave of him; which really was not partial; for I am not so much as acquainted with his father or him self.[3] I explaind every thing to him according to the tenor of the letter which I receaved from you some time ago and for which I most heartily thank you . . . Lett him now speak for himself I have been enquiring about a Counter tenor; but have as yet no intelligence of any.

I am really sensibly touchd with the account you give of Ireland. it is not quite so bad here but really bad enough; at the same time we are told that we are in great plenty & happiness. Your freinds whom you mention in yours are well; Mr Gay is returnd from

[1] Her first husband's brother.

[2] Mildmay was not created a Viscount till 1730 and Earl till 1735.

[3] See Arbuthnot's previous letter, 8 May.

Scotland, & has recoverd his strength by his jurney. M^r^ pope is well. he had gott an injunction in chancery against the printers who had pyrated his Dunciad; it was dissolv'd again because the printer could not prove any property, nor did the Author appear, that is not Mr Gays case for he has own'd his book.[1] Mr Poulteny gives you his service. They are all better than my self. for I am now so bad of a constant convulsion in my heart that I am like to expire sometimes.

We have no news that I know off. I am apt to beleive that in a little time this matter of the provisional treaty will be on or off The young Man waits for my [letter] I shall trouble you no more at present but remain with my best wishes & most sincere affection | Dear Sir | Your most faithfull humble Servant | Jo: Arbuthnott

My family all send you their love & service.

London · June 9th | 1729

Endorsed by Swift: Dr Arbuth | Jun. 9th 1729

4805

Lady Catherine Jones to Swift

[Chelsea, 11 June 1729]

I receved the favour of your Letter of 22d off May and own my obligation to Mr Dean for the information of the decay of my Grandfathers Monument in the Cathedral church of St Patrick's Mr French[2] the present receiver of my Fathers Estate will be some time next month in that Kindom who I have order to wait upon you for yor direction in that affair in which when he has informd me of the expence I shall immadiatly give directions to have it done agreeabl to the desier of the Dean & chapters & as well as the duty due to the

[1] Gay's judgement is reported in *The Universal Spectator* for 14 June as recently granted. Pope, less fortunate, now proceeded to persuade Lords Burlington, Bathurst, and Oxford to put their signatures to a document assigning property in *The Dunciad* to Lawton Gilliver, the publisher. The document was executed 16 Oct. 1729. On 21 Nov. Gilliver entered *The Dunciad Variorum* at Stationers' Hall (presumably in octavo: he had entered the quarto on 12 Apr.), and on 26 Nov. he issued the 'second edition' of the work in octavo.—Sherburn.

[2] Perhaps Humphrey French, who became Lord Mayor of Dublin. Swift held him in such high esteem that he contemplated writing a memoir of him. The name, however, as written by Lady Jones, might be 'Trench'.

memory of my Grandfather without adding further trouble to Mr Dean from his | Most humble and | obedient Servant |

Catherine Jones

ye 11 of Jun 1729 | Chelsea

Address: To the Reverend Dean | Swift at the deanry house | Dublin | Ireland
Readdressed: At Sr Arth: Achessons | Bar^t^ at Market Hill | in the County of Armagh | by Newry[1]
Postmark: 1 ? IV
Endorsed by Swift: Jun. 4th Ldy Catharine Jones[2]

Forster copy

Swift to Knightley Chetwode

August 9, 1729.

Sir,

Your letter of July 30th I did not receive till this day. I am near sixty miles from Dublin,[3] and have been so these ten weeks. I am heartily sorry for the two occasions of the difficulties you are under. I knew Mrs. Chetwode from her childhood, and knew her mother and sisters, and although I saw her but few times in my life, being in a different kingdom, I had an old friendship for her, without entering into differences between you, and cannot but regret her death.[4] As to Mr. Jackman I have known him many years; he was a good-natured, generous and gentlemanly person, and a long time ago, having a little money of my own, and being likewise concerned for a friend, I was inclined to trust him with the management of both, but received some hints that his affairs were even then not in a condition so as to make it safe to have any dealings of that kind with him.[5] For

[1] Early in June Swift had gone, for the second time, to stay with the Achesons.

[2] Swift's endorsement of date is at fault.

[3] Market Hill is about sixty Irish miles from Dublin.

[4] Chetwode's separation from his wife seems to have continued till her death. She was a half-sister of James Stopford. She may not have been known to Swift until after her mother married Stopford's father.

[5] As subsequently appears, Jackman had induced Chetwode to become surety for him. He was agent for a great estate in the north of Ireland near Carrickmacross, which was granted by Queen Elizabeth to the Earl of Essex, and descended from him to the first Earl Ferrers, who bequeathed it to his younger sons. As the site of Lough Fea, the Irish home of Evelyn Philip Shirley, 1812–82, the distinguished antiquary, the estate became widely known in the last century.—Ball.

these fourteen years past, he was always looked on as a gone man, for which I was sorry, because I had a personal inclination towards himself, but seldom saw him of late years, because I was only a general acquaintance, and not of intimacy enough to advise him, or meddle with his affairs, nor able to assist him. I therefore withdrew, rather than put my shoulders to a falling wall, which I had no call to do.

This day upon reading your letter I asked a gentleman just come from Dublin, who told me the report was true, of Jackman's being gone off. Now, Sir, I desire to know, how it is possible I can give you advice being no lawyer, not knowing how much you stand engaged for, nor the situation of your own affairs. I presume the other security is a responsible person, and I hope Mr. Jackman's arrears cannot be so much as to endanger your sinking under them. It is to be supposed that Mr. Shirley will give time, considering the case. I think there is a fatality in some people to embroil themselves by their good nature. I know what I would do in the like condition. It would be, upon being pressed, to be as open as possible, and to offer all in my power to give satisfaction, provided I could have the allowance of time. I know all fair creditors love free and open dealings, and that staving off by the arts of lawyers makes all things worse at the end. I will write to Mr. Stopford by the next post, in as pressing a manner as I can. He is as honest and benevolent a person as ever I knew. If it be necessary for you to retrench in your way of living, I should advise, upon supposing that you can put your affairs in some settlement here under the conduct of your son assisted by some other friends, that you should retire to some town in England in a good country and far from London, where you may live as cheap as you please, and not uncomfortably, till this present storm shall blow over. This is all I can think of after three times reading your letter. I pray God direct you. I am, | Ever &c.

Address: To Knightley Chetwode, Esq. at Woodbrooke, near Mountmellick.

Faulkner 1741

Swift to Alexander Pope

Aug. 11, 1729.

I am very sensible that in a former letter I talked very weakly of my own affairs, and of my imperfect wishes and desires, which however I find with some comfort to now daily decline, very suitable to my state of health for some months past. For my head is never perfectly free from giddiness, and especially towards night. Yet my disorder is very moderate, and I have been without a fit of deafness this half year; so I am like a horse which though off his mettle, can trot on tolerably; and this comparison puts me in mind to add that I am returned to be a rider, wherein I wish you would imitate me. As to this country, there have been three terrible years dearth of corn, and every place strowed with beggars, but dearths are common in better climates, and our evils here lie much deeper. Imagine a nation the two-thirds of whose revenues are spent out of it, and who are not permitted to trade with the other third, and where the pride of the women will not suffer them to wear their own manufactures even where they excel what come from abroad:[1] This is the true state of Ireland in a very few words. These evils operate more every day, and the kingdom is absolutely undone, as I have been telling it often in print these ten years past.

What I have said requires your forgiveness; but I had a mind for once to let you know the state of our affairs, and my reason for being more moved than perhaps becomes a Clergyman, and a piece of a philosopher: and perhaps the increase of years and disorders may hope for some allowance to complaints, especially when I may call my self a stranger in a strange land. As to poor Mrs. Pope (if she be still alive) I heartily pity you and pity her: her great piety and virtue will infallibly make her happy in a better life, and her great age hath made her fully ripe for heaven and the grave, and her best friends will most wish her eased of her labours, when she hath so many good works to follow them. The loss you will feel by the want of her care and kindness, I know very well, but she has amply done her part, as you have yours. One reason why I would have you in Ireland when you shall be at your own disposal, is that you may be master of two or three years revenues, *provisae frugis in annos copia*,[2] so as not to be pinched in the least when years increase, and perhaps your health impairs: And when this kingdom is utterly at an end, you may

[1] Swift had renewed his attack against neglect of Irish manufactures. His *Proposal for the universal Use of Irish Manufacture* appeared as a Dublin pamphlet in 1720. The *Proposal that All the Ladies and Women of Ireland should appear constantly in Irish Manufactures* (*Prose Works*, ed. Davis, xii. 119–27), though written in 1729, was first printed by Deane Swift in 1765, and reprinted by Faulkner in the same year.

[2] 'A Stock of Wine laid up for many Years'—Faulkner 1741.

support me for the few years I shall happen to live; and who knows but you may pay me exhorbitant interest for the spoonful of wine, and scraps of a chicken it will cost me to feed you? I am confident you have too much reason to complain of ingratitude; for I never yet knew any person, one tenth part so heartily disposed as you are, to do good offices to others without the least private view.

Was it a Gasconade to please me, that you said your fortune was increased 100 *l.* a year since I left you? you should have told me how.[1] Those *subsidia senectuti*[2] are extreamly desirable, if they could be got with justice, and without avarice; of which vice tho' I cannot charge myself yet nor feel any approaches towards it, yet no usurer more wishes to be richer (or rather to be surer of his rents) but I am not half so moderate as you, for I declare I cannot live easily under double to what you are satisfied with.

I hope Mr. Gay will keep his 3000 *l.* and live on the interest without decreasing the principal one penny; but I do not like your seldom seeing him: I hope he is grown more disengaged from his intentness on his own affairs, which I ever disliked, and is quite the reverse to you, unless you are a very dextrous disguiser. I desire my humble service to Lord Oxford, Bathurst, ⌜Lord B—st,⌝[3] and particularly to Mrs. B—,[4] but to no Lady at court.[5] God bless you for being a greater Dupe than I: I love that character too myself, but I want your charity. Adieu.

Forster copy

Swift to Knightley Chetwode

30 August 1729.

Sir,

I have received your letter by a man that came from Dublin with some things for me.[6] This is the first post since. I come now to answer your questions. First whether you shall marry. I answer that if it may be done with advantage to your fortune, to a person where friendship and good usage will be reciprocal, and without loss to your present children, I suppose all your friends, as I, would approve

[1] Pope to Swift, Jan. 1727–8 *ad fin.*

[2] 'Supports to Old Age.'—Faulkner 1741.

[3] Bathurst (?).

[4] Mrs. Blount. But omitted in later texts.

[5] i.e. *not* to Mrs. Howard.

[6] An answer to Swift's letter of the 9th of the month.

it. As to the affair of letter of licence, &c., I profess I am not master of it. I understand it is to be given by all the creditors before the debtor can be secure; why it is desired of you, I know not, unless as a creditor, and how you are a creditor, unless as being bound for him, I am as ignorant, and how Jackman in his condition can be able to indemnify you is as hard to conceive; I doubt his rich friends will hardly do it. This is all I can see after half blinding myself with reading your clerk's copies.

As to your leaving Ireland, doubtless your first step should be to London for a final answer from the lady. If that fails, I think you can live more conveniently in some distant southern county of England, though perhaps cheaper in France. To make a conveyance of your estate, etc., there must, I suppose, be advice of good lawyers. Mr. Stopford will be a very proper person,[1] but you judge ill in thinking on me who am so old and crazy that for several years I have refused so much as to be executor to three or four of my best and nearest friends both here and in England. I know not whether Mr. Stopford received my letter, but I will write to him again. You cannot well blame him for some tenderness to so near a relation, but I think you are a little too nice and punctilious for a man of this world, and expect more from human race than their corruptions can afford. I apprehend that whatever the debt you are engaged for shall amount to, any unsettled part of your estate will be liable to it, and it will be wise to reckon upon no assistance from Jackman, and if you shall be forced to raise money and pay interest, you must look only towards how much is left, and either retrieve by marriage or live retired in a thrifty way.

No man can advise otherwise than as he follows himself. Every farthing of any temporal fortune I have is upon the balance to be lost. The turn I take is to look on what is left, and my wisdom can reach no higher. But as you ill bear public mortifications, it will be best to retire to some other country where none will insult you on account of your living in an humbler manner. In the country of England one may live with repute, and keep the best company, for a hundred pounds a year. I can think of no more at present. I shall soon leave this place,[2] the weather being cold, and an Irish winter country is what I cannot support. I am, Sir, | Your most, &c.

Address: To Knightley Chetwode, Esq., at Woodbrooke, near Mountmellick

[1] To act as a trustee.

[2] Swift remained at Market Hill to 8 Oct.—nearly six weeks longer.

Forster No. 555

Swift to the Rev. James Stopford

Market Hill. Aug[t] 30th | 1729[1]

I have received two letters from M[r] Chetwoode upon a great distress he is under by being bound for M[r] Jackman who is withdrawn. Jackman was receiver for M[r] Shirley a son of Lord Ferrers. Upon Mr. Shirleys coming over, Jackman being in arrear went off, what the Arrear is, M[r] Chetwoode knows not. He writ twice for my advice on that & other parallell matters, & desired I would persuade you to write to him, which I would not have done, if his children did not demand some of your care, as your nephews. You know his temper, & how far you will think fit to offer in concerning yourself in his affairs. I writ to you before, but believe my letter misscarryed. I hope your health is fixed, without any dread of your late ailment returning. I know not where you are, but direct at a Venture. I intend to be soon in town. My humble services to your Lady[2] & all others about you of my acquaintance.

If you should have occasion to write, inclose to me under a cover to S[r] Arth. Acheson at Market Hill by Newry.

Address: To the Reverend M[r] James | Stopford at Collonell Butlers[3] | house in Dawson Street | Dublin

Frank: Free | Arth. Acheson

Forster copy

Knightley Chetwode to Swift

[10 September 1729.][4]

Sir,

A person of some figure and distinction, whom probably you saw every day you lived when in London,[5] came hither the morning I

[1] Printed from a copy, not the original, in the Forster Collection, no. 555.

[2] Although he had failed to obtain the best or any college living, Stopford had entered the married state, and had twelve months before resigned his fellowship. He had been subsequently appointed by Archbishop King vicar of Finglas, the parish near Dublin formerly held by Dilly Ashe and Parnell.—Ball.

[3] A son of the first Viscount Lanesborough. The Viscount's brother, Lord Newtown-Butler, had married an aunt of Stopford's wife.—Ball.

[4] This letter does not appear in Birkbeck Hill's volume.

[5] Charles Jervas.

proposed to acknowledge your favour of the 30th; so that I was compelled to lose post to hear him talk of fine pictures, distant prospects, and Elysian fields. He pressed me hard to hasten to England at least; but at last it came almost to Paul and Agrippa, for when I walked him through Versailles' labyrinth,[1] and through some of my other improvements, [and] that he had gorged himself with what he called better fruit than he eat in England or abroad, [and] flew the hawks at my partridge which in almost every field I sprang for him, he swore I was happier than if crowned, and that he would willingly quit the world, and come into my retreat. But for God's sake is it true, as he says, that your friend Lewis is married to my friend Bateman,[2] whom you so merrily described to me with a shining face as if a calf had licked it? He tells me of a lady I valued, who has ran through thirty thousand pounds in a single state, quitted our Church, gone into France, and shut herself in religion, as they term it, there. In short he gave me a full natural day to hear him relate unnatural things, and then left me at gaze like a boy who had lost his bird. He tells me Shirley, with whom I am likely to have more dealings than I like, is a worthy honest man, and married to your Lord Bathurst's sister,[3] and that your friend Ford, who he says is in Dublin, knows him, and has he believes some interest in him. I have none in Mr. Ford; you have.

But to leave his chimerical world, at least a world I have so long lived out of, as to have forgot as much of it as old Serjeant Maynard said he had of his law,[4] I return to what I can say I know and feel. I am to acquaint you that along with your letter I got one from a lady who mentions you. I am sorry for it, for she says that even Lady Acheson has not preserved you from being broke and shattered terribly, which agrees too well with what you write me in excuse for your non-compliance with what I desired from you, but I am inexpressibly troubled at what you write that every farthing of any

[1] A note appended to this letter by Edward Wilmot-Chetwode states that there used to be at Woodbrooke in a beech grove a labyrinth in imitation of that at Versailles.

[2] On 1 Oct. 1724 Erasmus Lewis married in London Anne Bateman, whose first husband had died in 1719. She was for years an invalid assiduously tended by him.

[3] Shirley's sister was married to Lord Bathurst's brother.

[4] Jeffreys's legal learning was notoriously small. Once he ventured in open court to tax Sir John Maynard with having forgotten his law, to meet the retort, 'In that case I must have forgotten more than your lordship ever knew'.

temporal fortune you have is upon the balance to be lost. I suppose you mean at Drapier's Hill;[1] take care it comes up to Cooper's. I remember a certain person talked twice or thrice to me of some money in the South Sea, and Ben Tooke said somewhat of it to me in England, but as I had no commission from you, I little noticed it more than decorum and good breeding obliged me to in regard to the Sec[retary].[2]

I received the other day a letter from brother Stopford which pleased me. He says in it he will be plain with me; and I have been so with him, upon your assuring me he was as honest, benevolent a person as you ever knew, and I have told him so. I meant to please him, for your recommendation will ever direct me in my choice of friends, and I wish you had sooner interested yourself in it. I have often reflected whether as you say I am not too punctilious for a man of this world, and expect more from human race than their corruptions can afford, for pretty near the same thing has been urged to me, by at least half a dozen of the most considerable men I ever corresponded or conversed with, of which old Duke of Buckingham and your patron Oxford were two. I aver that from them I had almost the same thing in almost the same words. But few men I really believe know as well as I do what comfort there is in lying down in a content arising from the following motives: that I cannot accuse myself of one wilful breach of honour in the whole course of my life; that the secrets, lives, and fortunes of some have been safely in my keeping; and that even the quickness of my passions by nature or acquired pride could never provoke me, even when I was assured I was laughed to scorn, to break in on my integrity in any of these points. This is a matter of solid comfort to me amidst the vexations of sundry crosses and disappointments, how ill soever I am qualified to bear public mortifications. But as you have formerly charged me with being a great refiner, and in that article compared me to a person whose principles I hate, though I admire his fine parts and other accomplishments, and whom I cannot help esteeming a Judas, though you own you love him, I must desist since I

[1] See 'Drapier's Hill' (*Poems*, iii. 873–5). In 1729 Swift purchased land from Sir Arthur Acheson with the intention of building. He soon changed his purpose. Before the end of the year (31 October) he wrote to Pope: 'The frolic is gone off, and I am only a hundred pounds the poorer.'

[2] The reference is evidently to Bolingbroke, whom Chetwode, when living abroad, must have met.

know this will not please you, and what I could say will not come within the compass of a letter.

When I was got so far I was obliged to see Lord and Lady Mountrath, who have taken a house for a year within a mile of me.[1] Before we parted I saw a nose enter, which upon inquiry I found belonged to Dan Jackson,[2] for whom his patron[3] had sent his coach. I must now acquaint you that I have received another letter from Fletcher, the schoolmaster, pressing me upon Jackman's affair. I hope you will not only excuse my troubling you on that head, but that you will in generosity and kindness to me, as your friend and servant, try to think of some expedient to extricate me out of this damned affair, since a part of your trade, if I may say so, is to save sinners, and in this I have, I allow, sinned against prudence, God and the Dean. Forgive me upon repentance, whereby I forsake this sin, steadfastly purposing to lead a new life in this article *à L'avenir*. For God's sake think of me, write to me, advise me, assist me; the rather since I freely own I am so nice that I cannot bring myself to go whither my other interests and a call requires, lest it looks like a dishonourable flight, till I have ended this affair of Jackman's now depending. I hope this will find you safe and sound in Dublin. I am ever, dear Mr. Dean, | Your faithful &c.

4805

Viscount Bolingbroke to Swift

Aix la Chapelle Aug: the 30th [O.S. 19] 1729[4]

I took a letter of yours from Pope,[5] and brought it with me to this place, that I might answer att least a part of it. I begin today, when I shall finish I know not, perhaps when I get back to my farm. the

[1] The reference is to the sixth Earl of Mountrath. He occupied a seat in the British House of Commons as well as in the Irish House of Lords.—Ball.

[2] The Rev. Daniel Jackson's large nose was a subject of jest in the circle of Swift's friends.

[3] George Rochfort.

[4] The text is here printed from Bolingbroke's original letter in the B.M. The text Pope printed in 1741 was a slightly abbreviated version of a text already shortened for Lord Oxford, now Portland Papers, Longleat xiii. The Longleat transcript was endorsed by Oxford, 'Ld Boling. to Dean | Swift Sepr 27 · 1729'.

[5] The letter of 5 Apr.

waters I have been perswaded to drink, and those which my friends drink, keep me fuddled or employed all the morning. the afternoons are spent in airings or visits, and we go to bed with the chicken.

Brussels Sep: the 27th [O.S. 16] 1729

I have brought your french acquaintance[1] thus far on her way into her own country, and considerably better in her health than she was when she went to Aix. I begin to entertain hopes that she will recover such a degree of health as may render old age Supportable. Both of us have closed the 10th Luster, and it is high time to determine how we shall play the last act of the Farce. might not my life be entituled much more properly a *What d'ye call it*[2] than a Farce? Some Comedy, a great deal of Tragedy, and the whole interspersed with Scenes of Harlequin, Scaramouch, and Doctor Baloardo,[3] the prototype of your Hero Oxf—d. I used to think sometimes formerly of old Age and of Death, enough to prepare my mind, not enough to anticipate Sorrow, to dash the joys of youth, and to be all my life a dying. I find the benefit of this practice now, & shall find it more as I proceed on my journey. little Regret when I look backwards, little apprehension when I look forwards. you complain greivously of your situation in Ireland. I could complain of mine too in England, but I will not, nay I ought not, for I find by long experience that I can be unfortunate without being unhappy. I do not approve your joyning together the *figure of living* and *the pleasure of giving*, tho' your old prating friend Montagne does something like it in one of his Rhapsody's[4] to tell you my Reasons would be to write an Essay, & I shall hardly have time to write a letter. but if you will come over, & live with Pope & me Ile shew you in an instant why those two things should not aller de pair, and that forced Retrenchments on both may be made without making us even uneasy. you know that I am too expensive, & all mankind knows that I have been cruelly plundered, and yet I feel in my mind the power of descending without anxiety two or three Stages more. in short Mr Dean if you will come to a certain farm in Middlesex, you shall find that I can live frugally without growling att the world, or being peevish with those

[1] Lady Bolingbroke.

[2] Gay's farce, *The What d'ye call it*, performed at Drury Lane, was published 19 Mar. 1715. Without a reading of the preface the play was not easily intelligible for the images are comic and the actors grave.

[3] Accepted characters of Italian comedy.

[4] *Essays*, book i, c. xxvii.

whom fortune has appointed to eat my bread, instead of appointing me to eat theirs, and yet I have naturally as little disposition to frugality as any man alive. you say you are no Philosopher, and I think you are in the right to dislike a word which is so often abused, but I am sure you like to follow Reason, not custom, which is sometimes the Reason & oftner the Caprice of others, of the Mob of the world. now to be sure of doing this, you must wear your philosophical Spectacles as constantly as the Spaniards used to wear theirs. you must make them part of your dress, and sooner part with your broad brimmed Beaver, your Gown, your Scarf, or even that emblematical vestment your Surplice, thro' this medium you will see few things to be vexed att, few persons to be angry att. ostend Oct: the 5th

and yet there will frequently be things which we ought to wish altered, and persons whom we ought to wish hanged. Since I am likely to wait here for a wind, I shall have leisure to talk with you more than you will like perhaps. if that should be so, you will never tell it me grossly, and my vanity will secure me against taking a hint. In your letter to Pope you agree that a Regard for fame becomes a man more towards his Exit than att his entrance into life, and yet you confess that the longer you live the more you grow indifferent about it. your Sentiment is true & natural, your Reasoning I am afraid is not so upon this occasion. Prudence will make us desire fame, because it gives us many real & great advantages in all the affairs of life. fame is the wise man's means, his ends are his own good & the good of Society. you Poets and orators have inverted this order, you propose fame as the End, and good, or att least great, actions as the means. you go further. you teach our Self Love to anticipate the applause which we Suppose will be pay'd by posterity to our names, and with idle notions of immortality you turn other heads besides your own. I am afraid this may have done some harm in the world.

Calais oct. the 9th. I go on from this place, whither I am come in hopes of getting to sea, which I could not do from the port of Ostend. Fame is an object which men pursue successfully by various & even contrary courses. your Doctrine leads them to look on this End as essential, & on the means as indifferent, so that Fabricius & Crassus, Cato & Cæsar pressed forward to the same goal. after all perhaps it may appear from a consideration of the Depravity of Mankind that you could do no better, nor keep up virtue in the world, without calling this passion, or this direction of Self Love in to your aid. Tacitus has crowded this excuse for you, according to his manner, into a Maxim. contemptu famæ contemni virtutes.[1] But now whether we consider fame as an useful Instrument in all the occurrences of private & publick Life, or whether we consider it as the cause of that pleasure which our Self Love is so fond of, methinks our entrance into Life, or to Speak more properly, our youth, not our old age, is the Season when we ought to desire it most, & therefore when it is most becoming to desire it with ardor. if it is useful, it is to be desired most when we have, or may hope to have a long Scene of action open before us. towards our Exit, this Scene of action is, or should be closed, and then methinks it is unbecoming to grow fonder of a thing which we have no longer occasion for. If it is pleasant the sooner we are in possession of Fame the longer we shall enjoy this pleasure. when it is acquired early in life it may tickle us on till old age; but when it is acquired late the sensation of pleasure will be more faint, and mingled with the Regret of our not having tasted it sooner.

From my farm[2] Oct the 5th o: s: I am here, I have seen Pope, & one of my first enquirys was after you. He tells me a thing I am sorry to hear. you are building it seems on a piece of Land you have acquired for that purpose in some County of Ireland.[3] tho' I have built in a part of the world which I prefer very little to that where you have been thrown & confined by our ill fortune and yours, yet I am sorry you do the same thing. I have repented a thousand times of my Resolution, and I hope you will repent of yours before it is executed. Pope tells me he has a letter of yours which I have not seen yet. I shall have that Satisfaction shortly, and shall be tempted to Scribble to you again, which is another good Reason for making this Epistle no longer than it is already. Adieu therefore my old & worthy Friend, may the physical evils of life fall as easily upon you as ever they did on any man who lived to be old; and may the moral evils which surround us, make as little impression on you, as they ought to make on one who has such superior sense to estimate things by, and so much virtue to wrap himself up in.

my Wife desires not to be forgot by you. She is faithfully your Servant, & Zealously your admirer. She will be concerned & disappointed not to find you in this Iland att her Return, which hope both She & I had been made to entertain before I went abroad.

Endorsed by Swift: Lord Boling Aug. 30 · 1729.

[1] *Annals*, iv, c. 38 *ad fin.*

[2] Dawley.

[3] 'Drapier's Hill' (*Poems*, p. 873). This information seems to have been sent in Swift's letter of 11 Aug., but to have been omitted in the printed version.

Faulkner 1741

Alexander Pope to Swift

Oct. 9, 1729.

It pleases me that you received my books at last;[1] but you have never once told me if you approve the whole, or disapprove not of some parts, of the Commentary, &c. It was my principal aim in the entire work to perpetuate the friendship between us, and to shew that the friends or the enemies of one were the friends or enemies of the other: If in any particular, any thing be stated or mention'd in a different manner from what you like, pray tell me freely, that the new Editions now coming out here, may have it rectify'd. You'll find the octavo rather more correct than the quarto, with some additions to the notes and Epigrams cast in,[2] which I wish had been encreased by your acquaintance in Ireland. I rejoyce in hearing that Drapiers-Hill is to emulate Parnassus; I fear the country about it is as much impoverished. I truly share in all that troubles you, and wish you removed from a scene of distress, which I know works your compassionate temper too strongly. But if we are not to see you here, I believe I shall once in my life see you there. You think more for me, and about me, than any friend I have, and you think better for me. Perhaps you'll not be contented, tho' I am, that the additional 100*l.* a year is only for my life? my mother is yet living, and I thank God for it: she will never be troublesome to me, if it but please God she be not so to herself: but a melancholy object it is to observe the gradual decays both of body and mind, in a person to whom one is tyed by the links of both. I can't tell whether her death itself would be so afflicting.

You are too careful of my worldly affairs; I am rich enough, and I can afford to give away 100*l.* a year. Don't be angry; I will not live to be very old. I have Revelations to the contrary. I would not crawl upon the earth without doing a little good when I have a mind to do it: I will enjoy the pleasure of what I give, by giving it, alive, and seeing another enjoy it. When I die, I should be ashamed to leave enough to build me a monument, if there were a wanting friend above ground.[3]

[1] His copies of *The Dunciad Variorum.*

[2] Not yet off the press. See Pope to Swift, 28 Nov., and Griffith, book 224.

[3] Pope had so arranged the family monument in Twickenham church that upon his death the only charge was the addition of the two words: *et sibi.*—Sherburn.

Mr. Gay assures me his 3000*l.* is kept entire and sacred; he seems to languish after a line from you, and complains tenderly. Lord Bolingbroke has told me ten times over he was going to write to you. Has he, or not? The Dr.[1] is unalterable, both in friendship and Quadrille: his wife has been very near death last week: his two brothers buried their wives within these six weeks. Gay is sixty miles off, and has been so all this summer, with the Duke and Duchess of Queensberry. He is the same man: So is every one here that you know: mankind is unamendable. *Optimus ille Qui minimus urgetur*[2]—Poor *[3] is like the rest, she cries at the thorn in her foot, but will suffer no-body to pull it out. The Court-lady[4] I have a good opinion of, yet I have treated her more negligently than you wou'd do, because you like to see the inside of a court, which I do not. I've seen her but twice. You have a desperate hand at dashing out a character by great strokes, and at the same time a delicate one at fine touches. God forbid you shou'd draw mine, if I were conscious of any guilt: But if I were conscious only of folly, God send it! for as no body can detect a great fault so well as you, no body would so well hide a small one. But after all, that Lady means to do good, and does no harm, which is a vast deal for a Courtier. I can assure you that Lord Peterborow always speaks kindly of you, and certainly has as great a mind to be your friend as any one. I must throw away my pen; it cannot, it will never tell you, what I inwardly am to you. *Quod nequeo monstrare, & sentio tantum.*

Forster copy

Knightley Chetwode to Swift

25 October 1729[5]

Sir,

The last letter I had the honour to receive from you bore date the 30th August; the post after it came to my hands I answered it, viz., on the 10th of September. As you then designed soon for Dublin, I deferred my congratulatory compliments till I should know

[1] Arbuthnot. His wife died 3 May 1730.

[2] Horace, *Sermones*, I. iii. 68–69.

[3] Martha Blount is probably meant.

[4] Mrs. Howard.

[5] This letter does not appear in Birkbeck Hill's volume.

certainly you were arrived. I hear you are there and well, which affords me great satisfaction.[1] I consulted you on two affairs I conceive of great consequence to my well-being; you advised me, and I retain a grateful sense of the favour. Will you now consent I send you two letters to read, and afford me your opinion upon them? I would not send to you upon it, without your permission. I shall ever treat you with the greatest deference and respect. I would have everybody else do the like, and if I could, I would have the nation's public thanks to you recorded for the evil you have delivered us all from. But it is easier for a man to mend his own than the faults of the public, and I conceive the public is exceedingly faulty in neglecting you. If you will favour me with the answer to my last and this letter, it will be very satisfactory and obliging to me, who am truly, | Yours, &c.

Longleat xiii (Portland Papers)

Swift to Viscount Bolingbroke

Dublin Octr 31th 1729.

I received you Lordships travelling letter of several dates, at several States, and from different Nations, Languages and Religions.[2] Neither could any thing be more obliging than your kind remembrance of me in so many places. As to your Ten Lustres, I remember when I complain'd in a letter to Prior, that I was fifty Years old, he was half angrey in jest, & answered me out of Terence, ista commemoratio est quasi exprobatio.[3] How then ought I to rattle you when I have a dozen Years more to answer for, all Monastically passed in this Country of Liberty and delight and Money and good company. I go on answering your Letter; it is you were my Hero, but the other[4] ne'er was, yet if he were, it was your own fault, who taught me to love him, and often vindicated him in the beginning of

[1] Swift had returned to Dublin on the 8th of the month, and was received with general rejoicing from the populace, the ringing of bells, bonfires, and illuminations.

[2] The letter beginning on 19 Aug. o.s.

[3] *Andria*, I. i. 17. By putting me in mind of your Favours, you in a Manner upbraid me with them.—Faulkner.

[4] Lord Oxford. This passage must have proved very unpleasing to the second Earl of Oxford.

your Ministry, from my Accusations. But I granted he had the greatest inequalitys of any Man alive, and his whole Scene was fifty times more a what d'ye call it, than Yours, for I declare yours was *Unie* and I wish you would so order it, that the wild World be as wise as I upon that Article. And Mr Pope wishes it too, and I believe there is not a more honest Man in England, even without Wit. But you regard us not. I was 47 Years old[1] when I began to think of death; and the reflections upon it now begin when I wake in the Morning, and end when I am going to Sleep. My Lord I writ to Mr Pope, and not to you. My Birth although from a Family not undistinguished in its time is many degrees inferior to Yours, all my pretensions from Persons[2] and parts infinitely so; I a Younger Son of younger Sons,[3] You born to a great Fortune. Yet I see you with all your advantages Sunk to a degree that could never have been so without them. But yet I see you as much esteemed, as much beloved, as much dreaded, & perhaps more (though it be almost impossible) than e'er you were in your highest exaltation, but I grieve (like an Alderman) not so rich. And yet, my Lord I pretend to value mony as little as You, and I will call 500 Witnesses, (if you will take Irish witnesses) to prove it. I renounce your whole Philosophy, because it is not your practice by the figure of Living, (if I used that expression to Mr Pope) I do not mean the Parade, but a Suitableness to your mind; and as for the pleasure of giving I know your Soul suffers when you are debarred of it. Can you when your own generosity and contempt of outward things, (be not offended, it is not Ecclesiastical but an Epictetian Phrase) can you, could you, come over and live with Mr Pope and Me at the Deanery when you are undone. I could almost wish the Experiment were tryed.—No—God forbid, that ever such a Scoundrel as *want* should date to approach you. But in the meantime do not brag; Retrenchments are not your Talent, but as old Weymouth said to me in your Ministry,[4] and in his Lordly Latin Philosophia verba, ignava opera[5] I wish you could learn Arithmetick, that 3 and 2 make 5, and will never make more. My

[1] The year of Queen Anne's death.

[2] Persons] person *early Pope editions.*

[3] Swift had no brothers. Ball suggests that the expression is to be read figuratively.

[4] Sir Thomas Thynne, 1640–1714. In 1682 he was created Viscount Weymouth, and also came into the possession of Longleat. Lady Carteret was a granddaughter.

[5] Philosophical Writings are idle Treatises.—Faulkner.

Philosophical Spectacles which you advise me to, will tell me that I can live on 50ll a Year (Wine excepted which my bad health forces me to) but I cannot endure that your Otium should be sine dignitate. My Lord what I would have said of Fame is meant of Fame which a Man enjoys in his Life, because I cannot be a great Lord, I would acquire what is a kind of Subsidium, I would endeavour that my betters shall seek me by the merit of something distinguishable instead of my seeking them. But the desire of enjoying it in after times is owing to the Spirit and folly of Youth: but with age we learn to know the house is so full that there is no room for above one or two at most, in an age through the whole World. My Lord I hate and love to write to you, it gives me pleasure, and kills me with Melancholy. The D— take Stupidity that it will not come to supply the want of Philosophy.

Faulkner 1741

Swift to Alexander Pope

Oct. 31, 1729.

You were so careful of sending me the Dunciad, that I have received five of them, and have pleased four friends.[1] I am one of every body who approve every part of it, Text and Comment; but am one abstracted from every body, in the happiness of being recorded your friend, while wit, and humour, and politness shall have any memorial among us. As for your octavo edition, we know nothing of it, for we have an octavo of our own, which hath sold wonderfully considering our poverty, and dulness, the consequence of it.

I writ this post to Lord B. and tell him in my letter, that with a great deal of loss for a frolick, I will fly as soon as build; I have neither years, nor spirits, nor money, nor patience for such amusements. The frolick is gone off, and I am only 100*l.* the poorer. But this kingdom is grown so excessively poor, that we wise men must think of nothing but getting a little ready money. It is thought there are not two hundred thousand pounds of species in the whole island; for we return thrice as much to our Absentees, as we get by trade, and so are all inevitably undone; which I have been telling them in

[1] This letter is an answer to Pope's letter of the 9th.

print these ten Years, to as little purpose as if it came from the pulpit. And this is enough for Irish politicks, which I only mention, because it so nearly touches my self. I must repeat what I believe I have said before, that I pity you much more than Mrs. Pope. Such a parent and friend hourly declining before your eyes is an object very unfit for your health, and duty, and tender disposition, and I pray God it may not affect you too much. I am as much satisfied that your additional 100 *l. per Annum* is for your life as if it were for ever: you have enough to leave your friends, I would not have them glad to be rid of you, and I shall take care that none but my enemies will be glad to get rid of me. You have embroiled me with Lord B— about the figure of living, and the pleasure of giving. I am under the necessity of some little paltry figure in the station I am; but I make it as little as possible. As to the other part you are base, because I thought my self as great a giver as ever was of my ability, and yet in proportion you exceed, and have kept it till now a secret even from me, when I wondred how you were able to live with your whole little revenue.

L— C— who doth his duty of a good governor in enslaving this kingdom as much as he can, talks to me of you in the manner he ought.[1]

4805

John Gay to Swift

[9 November 1729]

I have long known you to be my friend upon several occasions and particularly by your reproofs & admonitions. There is one thing which you have often put me in mind of, the overrunning you with an answer before you had spoken, you find I am not a bit the better for it, for I still write & write on without having a word of an answer. I have heard of you once by Mr. Pope. Let Mr Pope hear of you the next time by me. By this way of treating me, I mean by your not letting me know that you remember me you are very partial to me, I should have said very just to me: you seem to think that I do not want to be put in mind of you, which is very true, for I think of you very often, and as often wish to be with you. I have been in Oxfordshire

[1] In September Lord Carteret had returned to Ireland for the third time.

with the Duke of Queensberry for these three months, & have had very little correspondence with any of our Friends. I have employ'd my time in new writing a damned play, which I writ Several Years ago call'd the Wife of Bath,[1] as 'tis approv'd or disapprov'd of by my friends when I come to town I shall either have it acted or let it alone if [we]ak Brethren do not take offence at it. The ridicule turns upon Supe[rsti]tion, & I have avoided the very words Bribery & corruption. Folly indeed is a word that I have ventured to make use of, but that is a term that never gave fools offence. 'Tis a common saying that he is wise that knows himself; what hath happened of late I think is a proof that it is not limited to the wise. My Lord Bathurst is still our Cashier, when I see him I intend to settle our accounts, & repay myself the five pounds out of the two hundred that I owe you. Next week I believe I shall be in town. Not at Whitehall for those lodgings were judg'd not convenient for me & disposed of.[2] Direct to me at the Duke of Queensberrys in Burlington Gardens near Piccadilly. You have often twitted me in the teeth with hankering after the Court, in that you mistook me, for I know by experience that there is no dependance that can be sure but a dependance upon ones-self. I will take care of the little fortune I have got, I know you will take this resolution kindly; and you see my inclinations will make me write to you whether you will write to me or no. | I am | Dear Sir | Yours most sincerely & | most affectionately. J.G.

Middleton Stoney.[3] Novemr. 9. 1729.

To the Lady I live with I owe my Life & fortune. Think of her with respect, & value & esteem her as I do, & never more despise a Fork with three prongs. I wish too you would not eat from the point of your knife.[4] She hath so much goodness, virtue & generosity that if you knew her you would have a pleasure in obeying her as I do. She often wishes she had known you.

Address: To | The Revd Dr Swift Dean | of St Patrick's | Dublin | Ireland.
Endorsed by Swift: (twice)—Mr Gay. Nov. 9th 1729

[1] *The Wife of Bath*, 1713, proved a failure on the stage. The 1730 version, practically a new play, equally failed to meet with public favour.

[2] By the government on account of *Polly*.

[3] One of the Duke of Queensberry's residences.

[4] On Swift's habits with knives and forks see Gay's letter addressed to him 15 Feb. 1727–8.

Longleat xiii (Portland Papers)

Viscount Bolingbroke to Swift

Novr 19th 1729.

I find you have laid aside your Project of building in Ireland,[1] and that we shall see you in this Island Cum Zephyris,—et Hirundine prima.[2] I know not whether the love of fame increases as we advance in age. Sure I am that the force of Friendship does; I lov'd you almost twenty Years ago, I thought as well as I do now, better was beyond the power of conception, or to avoid an Equivoque, beyond the extent of my Ideas. Whether you are more obliged to me for loving you as well when I knew you less, or for loving you as well after loving you so many Years, I shall not determine. What I would say is this, whilst my mind grows daily more independant of the World, and feels less need of leaning on external objects, the Ideas of friendship return oftner, they busy me, they warm me more, is it that we grow more tender as the moment of our great separation approaches? or is it that They who are to live together in another State, (for vera amicitia non nisi inter bonos) begin to feel more strongly that Divine Sympathy which is to be the great band of their future Society? there is no one thought which sooths my mind like this. I encourage my imagination to pursue it, and am heartily afflicted when another faculty of the Intelect comes boisterously in and awakes me from so pleasing a dream, if it be a Dream. I will dwell no more on Oeconomicks than I have done in my former letter, thus much only I will say, that otium cum Dignitate is to be had with 500ll a Year as well as with 5000ll the difference will be found in the value of the Man, not in that of the Estate. I do assure you that I have never quitted the Design of Collecting, revising, improving, and extending several Materials which are still in my power; and I hope that the time of setting my self about this last[3] Work of my life is not far off. Many papers of much curiosity and importance are lost, and some of them in a manner which would surprize and anger you. However I should be able to convey severall great Truths to Posterity, so clearly and so Authentically, that the Burnets and the Oldmixons of another Age, might rail, but should

[1] Drapier's Hill.

[2] Horace, *Ep.* i. 7, 13. With the soft Zeyphrs and the first Swallow.—Faulkner.

[3] The scribe omitted 'last', which was supplied above the line by Oxford (?).

not be able to deceive. Adieu my friend, I have taken up more of this paper than belongs to me, since Pope is to write to you; no matter, for upon recolection the rules of proportion are not broken; He will say as much to you in one Page, as I have said in three. Bid him talk to you of the Work he is about.[1] I hope in good earnest; it is a fine one: it will be in his hands an Original. His sole complaint is, that he finds it too easy in the execution. This flatters his laziness, it flatters my Judgment, who always thought that, (universal as his Talents are) this is eminently and peculiarly his, above all the Writers I know living or dead; I do not Except Horace. | Adieu.

Endorsed by Oxford: Dr. Swift to Ld Bolin | Ld Bolin to Dr Swift.—

Longleat xiii (Portland papers)

Swift to John Gay

Dublin Nov. 20. 1729.

In Answer to your kind Reproaches of the 9th Instant I declare myself to have not received above 2 letters from you at most since I left England. I have every Letter by me that you writ since I first knew you. Although neither those nor of some other Friends are in such Order as I have long intended them.[2] But one thing you are to consider, because it is an old compact, that when I write to you or Mr Pope I write to both, and if you are such a Vagabond and absent as not to see your Friends above on[ce] a Quarter, who is to blame? Who could write to you on Scotland[3]? Yet I am glad you were in a Country nine times worse than this, wherein I speak very favourably of the Soil, the Climate, and the Language; but you were among a brave People, and Defenders of their Liberty, which outbalances all our advantages of Nature. Here I will define Ireland a Region of good eating and drinking, of tolerable Company, where a Man from England may sojourn some years with Pleasure, make a Fortune, and

[1] Pope's continuation of this letter, mentioned here by Bolingbroke, is letter XLIV of Pope's publication (Pope to Swift, 28 Nov. 1729) of 1741, and this letter of Bolingbroke XLIII. The assumption is that Pope left over writing his letter for nine days.

[2] Sherburn suggests that this remark, which Pope doubtless saw, may have served to heighten his anxiety to retrieve his own letters to Swift from their casual deposit. It was at this time that he was having the Harleian transcripts made.

[3] Where earlier in the year Gay had been (Arbuthnot to Swift, 8 May 1729).

then return home, with the spoyls he has got by doing us all the Mischeif he can, and by that make a Merit at Court. Pray tell Mr Pope what a wise thing he has done. He gave my Lord Allen's Lady a Commission to buy him here a Bed of Irish Stuff.[1] Like a right Englishman he did not imagine any Nation of human Creatures were deprived of sending their own Goods abroad. But we cannot send an Inch of wrought Woollen to any foreign Place without the Penalty of 500ll and forfeiture of the Stuff, and the English sea publicans[2] grumble if we carry our own Nightgowns, unless they be old. Lady Allen used all endeavours, but found it impossible and I told her she was a fool to attempt it. But if he will come over he shall lye in one of mine. I have heard of the Wife of Bath, I think in Shakespear,[3] if you wrote one it is out of my head. I had not the Cant word *Damned* in my head; but if it were acted and *Damned* & printed I should not be your Councellour to new lick it. I wonder you will doubt of your Genius.

The world is wider to a Poet than to any other Man, and new follyes and Vices will never be wanting any more than new fashions. Je donne au diable the wrong Notion that *Matter* is exhausted. For as Poets in their Greek Name are called Creators, so in one circumstance they resemble the great Creator by having an infinity of Space to work in. Mr Pope hath been teazed ten times to pay your 5 Guineas, and in his last letter he says it is done. But you say otherwise. However I do not understand Lord Bathurst to be my Casheer, but my Cully and Creditor upon Interest; else you are a bad Manager, and our Money had better been in the Funds. I assure you I will give Lord Cartaret a note on him for nine guineas, which his

[1] Joshua, second Viscount Allen, was alleged to have been tricked into a marriage with a Miss Du Pass, whom he refused for some time to acknowledge as his wife; until, on the death of a brother, she came into a fortune, when he became as eager to prove the marriage. In 1725 the corporation of Dublin voted Swift the freedom of the city, and on 16 Jan. 1729–30 it was resolved to present it to him in a gold box. According to Marmaduke Coghill an 'arrogant inscription' for the box was drafted by Delany, upon which Lord Allen took up the mayor and aldermen 'very roundly and wondred how they coud complain of Poverty, when they were so lavish as to give a gold box to a man . . . wrote a libell on the King Queen & the Government' (B.M. Add. MS. 21122, f. 114). Swift retorted in an *Advertisement* to the mayor and the aldermen (*Prose Works*, ed. Temple Scott, vii. 167–76). Thereafter he attacked Lord Allen unsparingly (*Poems*, 475, 494, iii. 795, 799, 836).

[2] In Swift's time the word publican was commonly used of a tax collector.

[3] Presumably a jesting remark.

Excellency hath squeez'd from many of us for a Jobb to Buckley the Gazetteer, who in conjunction with a Jacobite Parson is publishing a most monstrous unreasonable Edition of Thuanus.[1] I understand the Parson is only to be paid as a Corrector of the Press, but Buckley is to have all the Profit. The Parson's name is Cart. I wish you would occasionally inquire into this Matter, for the Subscribers on your side are many and glorious. I cannot be angry enough with My Lord Burlington. I sent him an Order of the Chapter of St Patrick's desiring the Dean would write to his Lordship about his Ancestor's Monument in my Cathedrall.[2] The Gentlemen are all Persons of Dignity and Consequence, of Birth and Fortune, not like those of your hedge Chapters in England; and it became him to send an answer to such a Body on an Occasion where onely the Honor of his Family is concerned. I desir'd in England that he would order the Monument to be repair'd, which may be done for 50ll and that he would bestow a bit of Land not exceeding 5ll a year to repair it for ever; which I would have ordered to be enter'd in our records in the most solemn manner. This he promised me. I believe the Dean and Chapter are worth in Preferments and real Estates above ten thousand pounds a year, they being 25 and the Dean, and he cannot imagine they whould cheat his Posterity to get about 3*s.* 6*d.* a man. Pray tell him this in the securest Manner, and charge it all upon me, and so let the Monument perish.

So, they have taken away your Lodgings.[3] This is a Sample of Walpole's Magnanimity. When Princes have a private quarrel with the Subjects, they have always the worst of the Lay.—You have sent us over such a Cargo of violent Colds, that [the] well are not sufficient to tend the Sick, nor have we servants left to deliver our Orders. I apprehend myself to be this moment seized, for I have coughed more these three minutes past, than I have done in as many years.

I wish for her own sake that I had known the Dutchess of Q.[4] because I should be a more impartial Judge than you: But it was her own fault, because she never made me any advances. However as to

[1] Swift's copy of Thuanus is an earlier edition. It appears in the sale catalogue as no. 599. 'Thuani Historiae suae Temporis cum Continuatione in 4 vol. Aurel. 1626'. It was marked as annotated by Swift; and it appears in the 1715 list of his books. From 1722 to 1733 Dr. Richard Mead (*D.N.B.*) provided the means for a new edition in seven folio volumes. Buckley was the chief editor.

[2] Cf. Swift to Lord Burlington, 22 May 1729.

[3] The result of his printing *Polly*.

[4] Duchess of Queensberry.

you, I think the Obligation lyes on her Side, by giving her an Opportunity of acting so generous and honourable a Part, and so well becoming her Dignity & Spirit. Pray tell her Grace that the fault was in Mr Pope's Poetical forks, and not in my want of manners; and that I will rob Neptune of his Trident rather than commit such Solecism in good breeding again; and that when I return to England I will see her at the tenth Message, which is one fewer than what I had from another of her Sex.[1] With my humble respects to her Grace, I beg she will be your Guardian, take care to have your money well put out, and not suffer you to run in debt or encroach on the Principal. And so, God continue to you the felicity of thriving by the Displeasure of Courts and Ministreyes; and to your Goddess, many disgraces that may equally redound to her honour with the last. My most humble Service to my Lord Peterborow, Lord Oxford, Lord Boling—Lord Masham, Lord Bathurst, Mr Pulteney, the Doctor, Mr Pope and Mr Lewis. Alass poor Alderman Barber I doubt he hath left me Nothing.[2]

Faulkner 1741

Alexander Pope to Swift

Nov. 28, 1729.

This letter (like all mine) will be a Rhapsody; it is many years ago since I wrote as a Wit. How many occurrences or informations must one omit, if one determin'd to say nothing that one could not say prettily? I lately receiv'd from the widow of one dead correspondent, and the father of another,[3] several of my own letters of about fifteen or twenty years old; and it was not unentertaining to my self to observe, how and by what degrees I ceas'd to be a witty writer; as either my experience grew on the one hand, or my affection to my correspondents on the other. Now as I love you better than most I have ever met with in the world, and esteem you too the more the longer I

[1] The Queen.

[2] The death of John Barber was mistakenly announced in the *Dublin Intelligence* of 22 Nov.

[3] Thought to be letters to Edward Blount of Blagdon and those to Lord Digby's son Robert; but there must be some doubt: the letters Pope printed as to Blount may not have been in most cases sent to Blount.—Sherburn.

have compar'd you with the rest of the world; so inevitably I write to you more negligently, that is more openly, and what all but such as love another will call writing worse. I smile to think how Curl would be bit, were our Epistles to fall into his hands, and how gloriously they would fall short of every ingenious reader's expectations?

You can't imagine what a vanity it is to me, to have something to rebuke you for in the way of Oeconomy? I love the man that builds a house *subito ingenio*,[1] and makes a wall for a horse; then cries, 'We wise men must think of nothing but getting ready money'. I am glad you approve my annuity; all we have in this world is no more than an annuity, as to our own enjoyment: But I will encrease your regard for my wisdom, and tell you, that this annuity includes also the life of another, whose concern ought to be as near me as my own, and with whom my whole prospects ought to finish. I throw my javelin of Hope no farther, *Cur brevi fortes jaculamur ævo*—&c.[2]

The second (as it is called, but indeed the eighth) edition of the Dunciad, with some additional notes and epigrams, shall be sent you if I know any opportunity; If they reprint it with you, let them by all means follow that octavo edition—The Drapier's letters are again printed here, very laudably as to paper, print, &c. for you know I disapprove Irish politicks (as my Commentator tells you) being a strong and jealous subject of England. The Lady you mention,[3] you ought not to complain of for not acknowledging your present; she having just now receiv'd a much richer present from Mr. Knight of the S. Sea; and you are sensible she cannot ever return it, to one in the condition of an out-law: it's certain as he can never expect any favour, his motive must be wholly dis-interested.[4] Will not this reflection make you blush? Your continual deplorings of Ireland, make me wish, you were here long enough to forget those scenes that so afflict you: I am only in fear if you were, you would grow such a patriot here too, as not to be quite at ease, for your love of old

[1] With a start of Genius.—Faulkner.

[2] Horace, *Odes*, II. xvi. 17.

'Why do we dart, with eager Strife,
At Things beyond the Mark of Life?'—Faulkner.

[3] The Queen. She was not mentioned in Swift's letter, 31 Oct. Robert Knight, cashier of the South Sea Company, when brought up for examination before a committee of the House of Commons, realized his danger, and, first destroying or taking with him as much incriminating evidence as he could, fled the country Any gift from him to the Queen must have been in the nature of a bribe.

[4] Pope writes ironically.

England. It is very possible, your journey, in the time I compute, might exactly tally with my intended one to you; and if you must soon again go back, you would not be un-attended. For the poor woman decays perceptibly every week; and the winter may too probably put an end to a very long, and a very irreproachable, life. My constant attendance on her does indeed affect my mind very much, and lessen extremely my desires of long life; since I see the best that can come of it is a miserable benediction at most: so that I look upon myself to be many years older in two years since you saw me: The natural imbecillity of my body, joyn'd now to this acquired old age of the mind, makes me at least as old as you, and we are the fitter to crawl down the hill together; I only desire I may be able to keep pace with you. My first friendship at sixteen, was contracted with a man of seventy, and I found him not grave enough or consistent enough for me, tho' we lived well to his death. I speak of old Mr. Wycherley; some letters of whom (by the by) and of mine, the Booksellers have got and printed not without the concurrence of a noble friend of mine and yours,[1] I don't much approve of it; tho' there is nothing for me to be asham'd of, because I will not be asham'd of any thing I do not do myself, or of any thing that is not immoral but merely dull (as for instance, if they printed this letter I am now writing, which they easily may, if the underlings at the Post-office please to take a copy of it.) I admire on this consideration, your sending your last to me quite open, without a seal, wafer, or any closure whatever, manifesting the utter openness of the writer. I would do the same by this, but fear it would look like affectation to send two letters so together.—I will fully represent to our friend (and I doubt not it will touch his heart) what you so feelingly set forth as to the badness of your Burgundy,[2] &c. He is an extreme honest man, and indeed ought to be so, considering how very indiscreet and unreserved he is: But I do not approve this part of his character, and will never join with him in any of his idlenesses in the way of wit. You know my maxim to keep clear of all offence, as I am clear of all interest in either party. I was once displeas'd before at you, for complaining to Mr.**[3] of my not having a pension, and am so again at

[1] Lord Oxford, here referred to, could not have acted the part attributed to him, as a copy of Pope's correspondence was not in his possession at the time Wycherley's correspondence was published.

[2] As appears later the wine was Hermitage sent to Swift by Robert Arbuthnot.

[3] The name Dodington occurs in Pope's clandestine volume. Faulkner and

your naming it to a certain Lord.[1] I have given some proofs in the course of my whole life, (from the time when I was in the friendship of Lord Bolingbroke and Mr. Craggs even to this, when I am civilly treated by Sir R. Walpole) that I never thought myself so warm in any Party's cause as to deserve their money; and therefore would never have accepted it; but give me leave to tell you, that of all mankind the two persons I would least have accepted any favour from, are those very two, to whom you have unluckily spoken of it. I desire you to take off any impressions which that dialogue may have left on his Lordship's mind, as if I ever had any thought of being beholden to him, or any other, in that way. And yet you know I am no enemy to the present constitution; I believe, as sincere a well-wisher to it, nay even to the church establish'd, as any minister in, or out of employment, whatever; or any Bishop of England or Ireland. Yet am I of the Religion of Erasmus, a Catholick; so I live; so I shall die; and hope one day to meet you, Bishop Atterbury, the younger Craggs, Dr. Garth, Dean Berkly, and Mr. Hutchenson,[2] in that place, To which God of his infinite mercy bring us, and every body!

Lord B's[3] answer to your letter I have just receiv'd, and join it to this pacquet. The work he speaks of with such abundant partiality, is a system of Ethics in the Horatian way.

B.M. Add. MS. 38671

Swift to Robert Percival

[11 December 1729]

S[r][4]

M[r] Daniel Griffin tells me you will pay me no Tythes but stop them on account of an Island, which I held from your Father for

the London reprintings use an asterisk or two for the name. It seems first to have reappeared in Elwin's text. Swift appears to have met with Dodington while staying with Pope. When Swift parted from his friends and set out for Ireland on 18 Sept. 1727 he carried with him a small notebook, which he used for keeping a diary and writing verses. This little book is now in the Forster Collection. On the inside of the cover is written in Swift's hand: 'This book I stole from | the Right Hon[rble] George Dodington | Esq[r] one of the Lords of the Treasury | June 1727 | But the scribblings are all | my own' (*Poems*, ii. 418).

[1] Lord Carteret.

[2] John Hutchinson, author of *Moses's Principia*.

[3] i.e. Bolingbroke's. [*For note 4 see overleaf.*

two Shill pr annum, and payd him constantly till his Death. I believe he has been dead about 12 years, and I have not been in possession of it these seven years at least, and you have stopt at least four or five year's tyths on that account. This odd way of dealing among you folks of great estates in Land and money, although I have been used to, I cannot well reconcile myself with, especially when you never give me above a quarter value for your tythes, on which account alone you should not brangle with me. It is strange that Clergymen have more trouble with one or two squires and meet with more injustice from them than with fifty farmers. If your Tenants payd your Rents as you pay your Tyths, you would have cause to complain terribly. By my computation you value that Island at fourty pounds an Acre. and would make me pay the same rate seven years after I gave it up. This is what I can not well afford, though I am with great truth your, | most obedient | humble Servant | Jonath Swift. Deanry-house | Decbr 11th 1729

Address: To Robert Percival Esqr

B.M. Add. MS. 38671

Swift to Robert Percival[1]

Dublin. Jan. 3d 1729–30

Sr

Seeing your frank on the outside, and the[2] address in the same hand, it was obvious who was the writer, and before I opened it, a worthy friend being with me, I told him the subject[3] of the difference between us: That your Tythes being generally worth 5 or 6ll a year, and by the terror of your[4] Squireship frighting my Agent, to take what you graciously thought fit to give, you wronged me of half my due every year . . That having held from your father an Island worth three pence a year, which I planted, and payd two Shillings annually

[1] Deane Swift, by whom this letter was first printed, 1765, superscribed it 'To a certain ESQUIRE'. [2] the] your *D.S.*
[3] subject] contents *D.S.* [4] your] om. *D.S.*

[4] The recipient of this letter was the eldest son of John Percival, Swift's former neighbour at Knightsbrook in the parish of Laracor, who had died in 1718. The son had succeeded his father as M.P. for Trim. In business relationship he seems to have been as objectionable as his father.

for, and being out of possession of the s^d Island seven or eight years, there could not possibly be above 4^s due to you; for which you have thought fit[1] to stop 3 or 4 years of Tyth at your own rate of 2^ll–5^s a year (as I remember) and still continue to stop it, on pretence that the s^d Island was not surrendered to you in form; although you have cutt down more Plantations of Willow and Abeilles than would purchase a dozen such Islands. I told my friend, that this talent of Squires formerly[2] prevayled very much in the County of Meath; that as to your self, from the badness of your Education[3] against all my advice and endeavors, and from the cast of your Nature, as well as another circumstance which I shall not mention, I expected nothing from you that became a Gentleman. That I had expostulated this scurvy matter very gently with you, that I conceived this letter was an answer: that from the prerogative of a good estate[4] the practice of lording over a few Irish wretches, and from the naturall want of better thinking, I was sure your answer would be extremely rude and stupid, full of very bad language in all senses: That a Bear in a wilderness will as soon fix on a Philosopher as on a Cotteger; and a Man wholly voyd of education, judgment, or distinction of person has no regard in his insolence but to the passion of fear; and how heartily I wished, that to make you shew your humility, your quarrell had been rather with a Captain of Dragoons than the Dean of St Patricks.

All this happened before my opening your Letter; which being read, my friend told me I was an ill guesser . . That you affirm you despise me onely as a Clergy-man, by your own Confession: And that you had good[5] reason, because Clergymen pretend to learning, wherein you value your self as what you are an utter Stranger to.

I took some pains in providing and advising about your Education, but since you have made so ill use of my rules; I cannot deny according to your own Principles that your usage of me is just . . You are wholly out of my danger; the weapons I use will do you no hurt, and to that which would keep a nicer man in aw, you are insensible. A needle against a stone wall can make no impression. Your faculty lyes in making bargains: stick to that; leave your Children a better estate than your father left you; as he left you

[1] fit] proper *D.S.* [2] formerly] om. *D.S.*
[3] Percival does not appear to have been a graduate of any university.
[4] Deane Swift adds the words 'however gotten'.
[5] good] om. *D.S.*

much more than your Grandfather left him. Your father and you are much wiser than I, who gave amongst you fifty years purchase for land, for which I am not to see one farthing. This was intended as an Encouragement for a Clergyman to reside among you, whenever any of your posterity shall be able to distinguish a Man from a Beast. One thing I desire you will be set right in; I do not despise All Squires. It is true I despise the bulk of them.[1] But, pray take notice, that a Squire must have some merit before I shall honor him with my contempt. For, I do not despise a Fly, a Maggot, or a Mite.

If you send me an answer to this, I shall not read it, but open it before company, and in their presence burn it; for no other reason but the detestation of bad spelling, no grammar, and that pertness which proceeds from ignorance and an invincible want of tast.

I have ordered a Copy of this Letter to be taken[2] with an intention to print it, as a mark of my esteem for you; which however perhaps I shall not pursue; For I could willingly excuse our two names from standing in the same paper, since I am confident you have as little desire of Fame, as I have to give it you.

I wish many happy new years to you and your family and am with truth | Your friend and humble Servt | J: Swift.

Let me add something serious; that, as it is held an imprudent thing to provoke valour, so I confess it was imprudent in me to provoke rudeness: which, as it was my own standing rule never to do except in cases where I had power to punish it, so my error proceeded from a better opinion of you than you have thought fit to make good . . for with every fault in your Nature, your education, and your understanding, I never imagined you so utterly devoyd of knowing some little distinction between persons.

Address: To Robert Percival Esqr | at Knightsbrook near | Trim | County of Meath

Endorsed above the address: S^{r} pray return | the Cover of this Letter— | Cha Nuttall

[1] Hawkesworth, 1767, prints as letter CCCCX a characterization of an Irish squire without explanation of why he treats it as a letter. He definitely attributes it to Swift 'but when or to whom written is uncertain'. On the whole it reads as if written by Swift. See *Prose Works*, ed. Temple Scott, xi. 191–4.

[2] The nature of the variants between the posted letter in the British Museum and Deane Swift's version suggests that he was printing from the copy.

Longleat xiii (Portland papers)

Swift to Alexander Pope

Dublin Feb. 6th 1729

There are three Citizens wives in this town;[1] one of them whose name is Grierson, a Scotch Booksellers wife, She is a very good Latin and Greek Scholar, and hath lately published a fine Edition of Tacitus, with a Latin Dedication to the Lord Lieutenant and she writes *carmina Anglicana non contemnenda*. The second is one Mrs Barber, wife to a Wollen Draper, who is our chief Poetess, and upon the whole hath no ill Genius. I fancy I have mentioned her to you formerly. The last is the bearer hereof, and the wife of a Surly rich husband who checks her vein; whereas Mrs Grierson, is only well to pass, and Mrs Barber as it becomes the chief Poetess is but poor. The bearer's name is *Sikins*. She has a very good tast of Poetry, hath read much, and as I hear hath writ one or two things with applause, which I never saw, except about six lines she sent me unknown, with a piece of Sturgeon, some Years ago on my birth day. Can you shew such a Triumfeminate in London? They are all three great Friends and Favourites of Dr Delany, and at his desire, as well as from my own inclination, I give her this Passport to have the honor and happyness of seeing you, because She hath already seen the Estrich, which is the only rarity at present in this Town,[2] and her ambition is to boast of having been well received by you, upon her return; and I do not see how you can well refuse to gratify her, for if a Christian will be an Estrich, and the only Estrich in a Kingdom he must suffer himself to be seen, and what is worse, without money.

I writ this day to Mr Lewis to settle that Scrub affair with M—.[3]

[1] The first of these three, Constantia, 1706?–33, was married to George Grierson, a Dublin printer. Born in humble circumstances her love of learning was encouraged by her father, and her scholarly attainments in a short life were remarkable. Her *Terence* appeared in 1727, and in 1730 came her notable edition of *Tacitus*. Only the first volume of the latter reached the sale room, no. 638, at the disposal of Swift's library. Mrs. Mary Barber, 1690?–1757, an indifferent versifier, was generously patronized by Swift. In his poem 'On Psyche', 1731?, Swift celebrated the domestic skill of Mrs. Sican (*Poems*, ii. 579–80). In a subsequent letter to Pope, 2 May 1730, Swift admitted that she was no poet.

[2] The *Dublin Intelligence* for 28 Oct. 1729 records the presence of an ostrich in Dublin, 'as is supposed for a show'.

[3] The allusion is to payments to Swift for *Gulliver* and to Pope for the *Miscellanies*.

It is now at an end, and I have all the money or receipts for it, except 20. which is in Mr Lewis's hands; so that I have come off better than you.

I am enquiring an opportunity to send you four Bottles of Usquebagh. Pray God bless Mrs Pope. I despair of seeing her in this World, and I believe the most pious person alive would be glad to share with her in the next.

You will see 18 lines relating to your self,[1] in the most whimsical paper that ever was writ, and which was never intended for the publick.

I do not call this a letter, for I know I long owe you one, for I protest you must allow for the Clymate, and for my disposition from the sad prospect of affairs here, and the prostitute Slavery of the Representers of this wretched Country

I have not been deaf these 10 Months but my head is an ill Second to my feet in the night

To Alexander Pope Esq

Forster copy

Swift to Knightley Chetwode

Dublin, February 12, 1729–30.

Sir,

I did not come to town till October, and I solemnly protest that I writ to you since I came, with the opinion I was able to give on the affairs you consulted me about;[2] indeed I grow every day an ill retainer of memory even in my own affairs, and consequently much more of other peoples, especially where I can be of little or no service. I find you are a great intelligencer, and charge me at a venture with twenty things which never came into my head. It is true I have amused myself sometimes both formerly and of late, and have

[1] Lines 71–88 of Swift's *Libel on Doctor Delany and a Certain Great Lord* (*Poems*, ii. 482–3). The story that Pope deserted his villa to escape a visit from the Queen is fictitious. See Yale edition of *Horace Walpole's Correspondence*, ix. 305 n. 8.

[2] Presumably Swift had in mind the letter he wrote to Chetwode on 30 Aug. 1729.

suffered from it by indiscretion of people. But I believe that matter is at an end, for I would see all the little rascals of Ireland hanged rather than give them any pleasure at the expense of disgusting one judicious friend.

I have seen Mr Jackman twice in the Green,[1] and therfore suppose there hath been some expedient found for an interval of liberty, but I cannot learn the state of his affairs. As to changing your single life, it is impossible to advise without knowing all circumstances both of you and the person. Archbishop Sheldon[2] advised a young Lord to be sure to get money with a wife, because he would then be at least possessed of one good thing. For the rest, you are the only judge of person, temper and understanding. And those who have been married may form juster ideas of that estate than I can pretend to do. I am, Sir, | Your most obedient, &c.

Address: To Knightley Chetwode, Esq. at Woodbrooke, near Mountmellick.

4805

Lord Bathurst to Swift

[12 February 1729-30]

Dear Dean

I have this moment recd a letter from yu,[3] but it is the first I can call a letter ; the other scraps were only to direct me to convey the corresponce[4] to others, & I thought I answer'd them best by obeying yr com̃ands;[5] but now yu have deign'd to send me one in form with a proper beginning & ending I will not wait even for a post day but have taken pen & ink im̃ediately to tell you how much I think my self obligd to you and how sincerely I am—well I might end her if I would but I can't part with yu so soon, & I must lett yu know that as to yr money affairs tho' I have pay'd off John Gay I still keep yr

[1] St. Stephen's Green in Dublin.

[2] Gilbert Sheldon, 1598–1677; elected Archbishop of Canterbury 1663.

[3] Allen Bathurst, 1685–1775, who was raised to the peerage as Baron Bathurst, 1 Jan. 1711–12, as one of Queen Anne's twelve new peers. He was a member of the Brothers' Club and a lifelong friend of Swift and Pope; but it was only with this letter that an active correspondence with Swift began. He played a part in public life during four reigns.

[4] Thus in the manuscript.

[5] com̃ands] demands *Ball.*

200ll for wch I have giv'n him a Note, I have pay'd him interest to this time for it wch he must acc^t to y^u for.[1] Now y^u must imagine that a Man who has nine Children to feed can't long afford *alienos pascere nummos* but I have 4 or 5 that are very fit for the table, I only wait for the Lord Mayors day to dispose of the largest, & I shall be sure of getting off the youngest whenever a certain great man makes another entertainment at Chelsea.[2] now y^u see tho' I am y^r Debtor I am not without my proper ways & means to raise a supply answerable to y^r demand. I must own to y^u that I shou'd not have thought of this method of raising money but that y^u seem'd to point it out to me, for just at the time that scheme came out wch pretended to be calculated only for Ireland;[3] y^u gave me a hint in one of y^r Envelopes (Anglice covers) that y^u wisht I might provide for my numerous family, & in this last y^u harp upon the same string. I did im̃ediately propose it to Lady Bathurst as y^r advice, particularly for her last boy wch was born the Plumpest finest thing that cou'd be seen; but she fell in a Passion & bid me send y^u word that she wou'd not follow y^r direction, but that she wou'd breed him up to be a Parson & he shou'd live upon the fat of the Land, or a Lawyer & then instead of being eat himself he shou'd devour others. y^u know women in Passion never mind w^t they say, but as she is a very reasonable woman I have almost brought her over to y^r opinion now, & having convinst her that as matters stood we cou'd not possibly maintain all the 9 she does begin to think it reasonable the youngest shou'd raise fortunes for the Eldest. and upon that foot a man may perform family duty with more courage & zeal, for if he shou'd happen to get twins the selling of one might provide for the other. or if by any accident whilst his wife lies in, with one child he shou'd get a second upon the body of a second woman, he might dispose of the fattest of the two & that wou'd help to breed up the other. The more I think upon this scheme the more reasonable it appears to me, & it ought by no means to be confin'd to Ireland, for in all probability we shall in a very little time be altogether as poor here as y^u are there; I beleive indeed we shall carry it further, & not confine our luxury only to

[1] Gay to Swift, 9 Nov. 1729: 'My Lord Bathurst is still our cashier.'

[2] In the previous summer Walpole gave a sumptuous banquet to the Queen and royal family at his Chelsea house.

[3] Swift's *Modest Proposal For preventing the Children of Poor People From being a Burthen to their Parents, and For making them Beneficial to the Publick* (*Prose Works*, ed. Davis, pp. 109–18) was published in the preceding October.

the eating of Children, for I happen'd to peep the other day into a large assembly[1] not far from Westminster Hall, & I found them roasting a great fat fellow;[2] for my own part I had not the least inclination to a slice of him, but if I guessed right, 4 in 5 of the Company had a devilish mind to be at him. Well adieu y^{u} begin now to wish I had ended when I might have done it so conveniently.

12th feb. 1729/30

Endorsed by Swift: Ld Bathurst | Febr. 12. 1729–30 and Ld Bathurst | Rx. Feb. 1729

Longleat xiii (Harleian transcript)

Swift to Alexander Pope

Dublin Feb. 26. 1729.

My memory is so bad, that I cannot tell whether I answered a Letter from you, and another from Lord Bolin— that I received in Jan. last.[3] I have read them so often, that I should think I answered them, and yet I cannot recall one particular of what I said to either of you. I find you have been a writer of Letters almost from your infancy, and by your own confession had Schemes even then of Epistolary fame. Montaigne says that if he could have excelled in any kind of writing, it would have been in Letters;[4] but I doubt they would not have been naturally, for it is plain that all Pliny's Letters were written with a view of publishing, and I accuse Voiture himself of the same crime, although he be an Author I am fond of. They cease to be Letters when they become a a jeu d'esprit.

I am innocent of half your reproaches on the Subject of O'economy. It is true I did some years ago at a great expence build a Wall to enclose a Field for horses,[5] being tired with the knavery of Grooms who foundered all my horses, and hindred me from the only remedy against encreasing ill health: But the house is no more than a Plan, and shall never be more, for Sublata causa tollitur effectus. I wish

[1] The House of Commons.

[2] Walpole.

[3] This letter answers that from Pope of 28 Nov., and, presumably, that of 19 Nov. from Bolingbroke. No letter from Bolingbroke which Swift might have received in January is known.

[4] *Essays*, i, xxxix.

[5] Naboth's Vineyard.

these were the worst parts of my management; for I am in danger of losing every groat I have in the World by having put my whole fortune no less than 1600l. into ill hands upon the advice of a Lawyer and a friend. I have absolutely got clear of M—[1] and have all the money in my hands, or paid to Mr L—.[2] I believe he is poor, or too great an undertaker, and rich only in the worst kind of Stock.—I have not seen the new 8°. Dunciad nor do I believe they will reprint it here: The Kingdom cannot afford it. I think you have had some correspondence with my Lady Allin. Her Lord hath shewn an odd instance of his Madness. He hath for some years professed a particular Friendship for me; but a peny paper having been lately printed called a Libel on D.D. and a certain great Lord, meaning as it suppos'd Dr Delany and the Lord Lieutenant This same Allin about a fortnight ago, at the Privy Council, the Lord Mayor being sent for, accused me for the Author, and reproached the City for their resolution of[3] giving me my freedom in a Goldbox, calling me a Jacobite Libeller &c.[4] and hath now brought the same affair into the H. of Lords, that the Printer &c may be prosecuted. And there is a circumstance in this Affair, that when it is over, may be worth your hearing. There is not much in the paper, and they say it was printed in London before we had it. I have done with Court Ladyes and their Mistress: yet I think to write a moral letter to our half discarded friend.[5] I suppose it was purposely intended as a Slur, what was in some of the prints, that she was to be preferr'd to the place of Maid of Honour. I allow the great disinterestedness of the other, which is fully acknowledged by the most Loyal Whigs among us—I have some Usquebagh, ready to be sent to you on the first opportunity. These happen so seldom that I am out of patience, there are but four quart bottles, for the lightness of carriage from Chester: but since they were pack'd up I am advised to send them by long sea, and directed to Lord Bathurst, because a Lords name will give them a Sanction. But this I have mentioned to his Lordship, and may you, that he may not be at a loss. My coming to England depends on two things the settlement of my health, and of my little affairs. The times are so miserable I can get in no Money, and among us Clergy here, all go to wreck in absence: for although Tythes be of

[1] Motte. [2] Lewis

[3] The scribe omitted 'their resolution of'. Supplied above the line by Oxford.

[4] See Swift to Gay, 20 Nov. 1729 and footnote.

[5] Mrs. Howard.

Divine institution they are of diabolical execution: and God knows how long my Law Suit may last for my 1600ll. As much as I love you, to establish your health I would load you (not from myself) with half a Score Years. Yet on condition not to abate one grain of your Genius. For, (a mischief on it) I find neither prose[1] nor Rime will come to me as it used, but that is not the worst, for I am daily harder to please, and less care taken whether I am pleas'd or not I dine alone, or only with my House keeper. I go to my Closet immediately after dinner there sit till eleven and then to bed. The best company here grows hardly tolerable, and those[2] who were formerly tolerable, are now insupportable. This is my life five nights in Seven. Yet my Eyes are hurt with reading by candle-light, so that I am forced to write and burn whatever comes into my head. If I sent my last letter without a Seal it was an honest pure blunder, of which I make fifty every day, and what encreases them, is my fear of encreasing them. I'll hold a crown that in revising[3] this letter I shall be forced to make thirty verbal corrections. Yet I hope to mend a little, being cured of Irish Politicks by despair: and I have ordered in my will that my body shall be buried at Holy-head with an Epitaph whereof this is a part.[4]

As to my Hermitage misfortune,[5] it is a very afflicting trifle, whereof your abstemiousship is no judge: but I am very serious in telling you, that I expect the Doctor will this very Summer make his Brother give me ample satisfaction. I suppose he is rich else it would not be contemptible if he got the Custom of several Persons here who liked my first Hermitage so well (which was sent by Robin Arbuthnot) that they resolved to send for Cargoes if I succeeded in my Second, and I tell you, that good wine is 90 per Cent in living in Ireland, but in you, I sing to the deaf: I will refer it to our friend Gay, who hath writ to me lately, and you must promise my answer. I have not writ to Lord Burlington, but will soon with a vengeance, unless you prevent it—Sure, I answered your last before, about what you say of Doddington &c. I would not be so nice about poking in a sore eye as in doing any thing wrong in so tender a point neither am I guilty in the least: but the Lieutenant knows himself and hath

[1] The scribe wrote 'gross'. Corrected above the line to 'prose'.
[2] 'and those' above the line.
[3] The scribe wrote 'receiving'. Corrected above the line to 'revising'.
[4] The Epitaph is omitted.
[5] Pope, writing to Swift, 28 Nov. 1729, thought it was burgundy.

often known from me your Spirit in this matter. I hope your Ethick System is towards the umbilicum[1] I will write to Lord Bol— My most humble service to him and Lord Masham Lord Oxford, Mr Pulteney, and Dr Mr Lewis. I will write to Lord Bath—t from whom I received a very kind letter.

4805

John Gay to Swift

[London, 3 March 1729–30]

I find you are determin'd not to write to me according to our old stipulation. Had I not been every post for some time in expectation to have heard from you I should have wrote to you before to have let you know the present state of your affairs, for I would not have you think me capable of neglecting yours whatever you think of me as to my own. I have receivd 21l–13–4 interest from Lord Bathurst, for your 200l from October 1727 to Xmas 1729 two years and two months at 5l p Cent. Lord Bathurst gave me a note for your 200l again, & to allow interest for the same dated January 15 1729/30. If you would have me dispose of your money any other way, I shall obey your orders; Let me know what I shall do with this interest money I have receiv'd. What I have done for you I did for myself, which will be always the way of my forwarding any thing for you. My old vamp'd Play got me no money, for it had no success. I am going very soon into Wiltshire with the D of Queensberry with intention to stay there all the winter; since I had that severe fit of sickness. I find my health requires it, for I cannot bear the town as I could formerly. I hope another Summer's Air & exercise will reinstate me. I continue to drink nothing but water, so that you cannot require any Poetry from me; I have been very seldom abroad since I came to town, & not once at Court; this is no restraint upon me, for I am grown old enough to wish for retirement. I saw Mr Pope a day or two ago in good Spirits, & with good wishes for you, for we always talk of you; the Doctor does the same. I have left off all great folks but our own family; perhaps you will think all great folks little enough to leave off us in our present situation. I dont hate

[1] That is, towards a conclusion. The word 'umbilicum' defeated the scribe, who left a blank which was filled in by Oxford.

the world but I laugh at it; for none but fools can be in earnest about a trifle. | I am Dear Sir | Yours most affectionately.

London. March 3. 1729/30.

direct to me at the D. of Q. in Burlington Gardens.

Address: To | The Revd Dr Swift Dean | of St. Patricks in | Dublin | Ireland.
Endorsed by Swift: March 3d 1729–30 | Mr Gay | About money in | Lord Bathursts hands
Mr. Gay. Mar 3d · 1729 | Answerd. Mar. 19—
Lord Bathurst | Feb 12 1729–301[1]

Faulkner 1741

Alexander Pope to Swift

[4 March 1729–30][2]
April 14, 1730

This is a letter extraordinary, to do and say nothing, but to recommend to you, (as a Clergy-man, and a charitable one,) a pious and a good work, and for a good and an honest man: Moreover he is above seventy, and poor, which you might think included in the word honest. I shall think it a kindness done myself if you can propagate Mr. Westley's subscription for his Commentary on Job,[3] among your Divines (Bishops excepted, of whom there is no hope) and among such as are believers, or readers, of scripture. Even the curious may find something to please them, if they scorn to be edified. It has been the labour of eight years of this learned man's life; I call him what he is, a learned man, and I engage you will approve his prose more than you formerly could his poetry. Lord Bolingbroke is a favourer of it, and allows you to do your best to serve an old

[1] The last endorsement is Swift's reminder of Lord Bathurst's letter of 12 Feb. (see pp. 371–3), which also dealt with money affairs.

[2] Sherburn assumes, credibly, that the original letter was undated, and that when Pope edited it for printing, 1740, he guessed its date as 14 Apr. It is, fairly obviously, a sort of covering letter sent with that from Lord Oxford to Swift, which is dated 4 Mar. In printing Pope joined his letter, unusually brief, to that of Bolingbroke to Swift, 9 Apr. 1730, giving the two letters the date of 14 Apr. See also Faulkner, 1741, pp. 152–5.

[3] The Rev. Samuel Wesley (1662–1735) was father of the famous John Wesley, founder of Methodism. The father wrote copious verse, including a life of Christ, 'an Heroic Poem', in ten books. His later life was devoted to an exhaustive commentary on Job, which appeared posthumously.

Tory, and a sufferer for the Church of England, tho' you are a Whig, as I am.

We have here some verses in your name, which I am angry at. Sure you wou'd not use me so ill as to flatter me? I therefore think it is some other weak Irishman.[1]

Longleat xiii (Portland papers)

The Earl of Oxford to Swift

Dover Street March 4. 1729–30

Good Master Dean

It is now above a whole year and six Months since I have had the favor and pleasure of a Line from your own self,[2] and I have not troubled you with any from my self, the answer that you would naturaly make is very obvious, why do you then trouble me now? I reply it is to join with my Friend Mr Pope in recommending the Person in the enclosed proposal to your favor and protection[3] & to entreat that you would be so good as to promote his interest, I have not sent any of his Receipts but will when you will please to let me know what number you can dispose of, I believe that your Bishops have more Learning at least would be thought to have more than our Bench here can pretend to so I hope they will all subscribe; The Person concerned is a worthy honest Man and by this work of his he is in hopes to get free of the Load which has hung upon him some years, this debt of his is not owing to any Folly or extravagance of his but to the Calamity of his House being twice burnt which he was obliged to rebuild and having but small preferment in the Church and a large Family of Children he has not been able to extricate himself out of the difficulties these accidents have brought upon him, Three sons he has bred up at Westminster, and they are excellent Scholars the eldest has been one of the Ushers in Westminster school since the year 1714.[4]

[1] The reference is to the *Libel on Doctor Delany*. Pope had not received Swift's last two letters, 6 and 26 Feb.

[2] 21 Sept. 1728.

[3] i.e. Samuel Wesley.

[4] Samuel Wesley, 1691–1739, the younger, John Wesley's eldest brother, was a friend of Atterbury and out of sympathy with his brother's views. He was head-usher of Westminster School, and later, 1733–9, master of Blundell's School.

He is a man in years yet Hearty and able to study many hours in a day. This in short is the Case of an Honest, Poor, worthy Clergyman and I hope you will take him under your Protection, I cannot pretend that any recommendation should have any weight with you but as it is joined to and under the wing of Mr Pope.

I took hold of this opportunity to write to you to let you know you had such an humble servant in being, that often remembers you and wishes to see you in this Island, my Family I thank God is well, my Daughter had last summer the small-Pox realy, and in the natural way, and she is not markt at all, my Wife and Daughter desire that you will accept of their humble services, and say that they want much to see you here.

I obeyed your Commands and did Mr Whaley all the little service I was capable of, it was little enough that was in my power God knows, he comes again before us soon after Easter, He seems to be in great hopes. I wish they may be well founded.

I think it is now time to release you, which I will not do till I have told you I may say repeat to you that I have a House for you or House-room come when you please, and you shall do what you please provided you come soon. I am with true respect and esteem | Your most obliged and most | humble Servant | Oxford

Your Ld L. would do well | to encourage this poor Man | He deserves it better than Bukley.[1]

Endorsed on verso of leaf: Copy of a Letter to The | Revd Dean Swift | March 4 1729/30

Longleat xiii (Portland papers)

Swift to John Gay

Dublin Mar. 19. 1729.

I deny it:[2] I do write to you according to the old Stipulation, for when you kept your old Company, when I writ to one I writ to all. But I am ready to enter into a new Bargain, since you are got into a new world, and will answer all your Letters. You are first to present

[1] Samuel Buckley, Gazetteer and publisher of Mead's *History of Thuanus*.

[2] The reference is to the stipulation to correspond faithfully. See Gay to Swift, 3 Mar. 1729–30.

my most humble respects to the Dutchess of Queensberry, and let her know that I never dine without thinking of her, although it be with some difficulty that I can obey her, when I happen to dine with Forks that have but two prongs, and the Sawce is not very consistent; and I desire she will order Lady Charlotte Hyde[1] to read before me when I go next to my Lord Clarendon's; for when I saw her last she behaved herself like a young Sempstress, or a Country Parson's Daughter. You must likewise tell her Grace that she is a general Toast among all honest Folks here, and particularly at the Deanery even in the face of my Whig subjects. I will leave my money in Lord Bathurst's Hands, and the Management of it (for want of better) in Yours. But I hope you have paid yourself the five Guinneas; and pray keep the Interest Money in a bag, wrapt up and sealed by itself, for fear of your own fingers under your Carelessness and necessityes. I pay an Annuity of 15ll per Ann: in Surrey,[2] and shall soon send you a direction for part of it, And besides My Lord Lieutenant hath forced me against my will to pay nine Guinneas for the New Edition of Thuanus which I know to be a jobb for Buckley,[3] and I shall put the Payment on you or Mr Lewis, who likewise hath some money of mine in his Hand. And now I have learnt a way of making my Friends write, it is but letting them keep my money, for till then I never had a line from Mr Lewis, nor hardly from you. Mr Pope talks of you as a perfect Stranger. But the different pursuits and manners and Interests of Life as fortune hath pleased to dispose them, will never suffer those to live together, who by their Inclinations ought never part. I hope when you are rich enough, you will have some little oeconomy of your own, either in Town or Country, and be able to give your friend a pint of Port and a bit of mutton; for the domestick Season of Life will come on. We are taught to hope here, that Events may happen in no long time, which may give the Court another face with reguard to you as well as all wellwishers to their Country. But I hope you will be wise enough after you have got your bit to do decently off. I had never much hopes of your Vampt Play, although Mr Pope seem'd to have, and although it were ever so good: But you should have done like the Parsons, and changed your Text, I mean the title and the Names of

[1] Daughter of Henry, second Earl of Rochester. A subsequent sentence shows that Swift was not quite certain of the relationship.

[2] The payment was probably to his sister.

[3] See footnote to previous letter.

the Persons. After all it was an Effect of Idleness, for you are in the Prime of Life when Invention and Judgement go together. I wish you had 100ll a year more, for Horses. I ride and walk whenever good Weather invites, and am reputed the best Walker in this Town and five Miles round. I writ lately to Mr Pope, I wish you had a little Villakin in his Neighborwood; but you are yet too Volatile, and a Lady and Coach and Six Horses would carry you to Japan.[1] I complain to you as I did to Mr Pope of the Doctor's Roan[2] Brother, who sent me 150 Bottles of Hermitage, that by the time they got into my Cellar cost me 27ll and in less than a year all turned sowr; tho' what I had formerly from his Brother Robin was not fit to drink till two years, and grew better at seven, as a few left, yet shew. For this I expect satisfaction. The Dissappointment is five times more than the loss. But what care you for this, who have left off drinking Wine; and would not now think it hard if Mr Pope should tell us towards the bottom of a pint; Gentlemen I will leave you to your wine. And by the way, this is an ill encouragement for me to come among you, if my Health and buissiness would permit. Mr Pope's Usquebagh is, I hope, at sea, and directed to my Lord Bathurst. Tell his Lordship I will write to him soon with one enclosed to my Lord Bolingbroke, whose address I do not well know and wish you would tell me. My humble service to the Doctor; with other Acquaintance of mine you see I know not, except Mr Pulteney, whose humble servant I shall ever be, in all Fortunes, and he is another of our Stock-Healths. I Know not your Duke but love him for his Spirit. In my Conscience I forget-whether your Dutchess be daughter of my Mistress Rochester,[3] or no. Pray venture on Horseback when you are in Wiltshire, there is very cold riding if you are near Salisbury. Adieu, and God preserve you.

[1] As printed by Pope the letter finished at this point.

[2] For Rouen where Robert Arbuthnot had offices as well as in Paris.

[3] Henry Hyde, second Earl of Rochester, married Jane, daughter of Sir William Leveson Gower by whom he had two daughters famous for their beauty, Jane, afterwards Countess of Essex, and Catherine, afterwards Duchess of Queensberry. Cf. *Journal*, 1 Oct. 1710, and note.

Faulkner 1741

Swift to Viscount Bolingbroke

Dublin, March 21, 1729–30.[1]

You tell me you have not quitted the design of collecting, writing, &c.[2] This is the answer of every sinner who defers his repentance. I wish Mr. Pope were as great an urger as I, who long for nothing more than to see truth under your hands, laying all detraction in the dust—I find my self disposed every year, or rather every month, to be more angry and revengeful; and my rage is so ignoble, that it descends even to resent the folly and baseness of the enslaved people among whom I live. I knew an old Lord in Leicestershire who amused himself with mending pitchforks and spades for his Tenants *gratis*:[3] Yet I have higher ideas left, if I were nearer to objects on which I might employ them; and contemning my private fortune, would gladly cross the channel and stand by, while my betters were driving the Boar out of the garden, if there be any probable expectation of such an endeavour. When I was of your age I often thought of death, but now after a dozen years more, it is never out of my mind, and terrifies me less. I conclude that providence hath ordered our fears to decrease with our spirits; and yet I love *la bagatelle* better than ever: For finding it troublesome to read at night, and the company here growing tasteless, I am always writing bad prose, or worse verses, either of rage or raillery, whereof some few escape to give offence, or mirth, and the rest are burnt.

They print some Irish trash in London, and charge it on me, which you will clear me of to my friends, for all are spurious except one paper,[4] for which Mr. Pope very lately chid me. I remember your Lordship us'd to say, that a few good speakers would in time carry any point that was right; and that the common method of a majority, by calling, To the question, would never hold long when reason was on the other side. Whether politicks do not change like gaming by

[1] Pope placed this Letter as if it were written in 1729 and Faulkner, 1741, pp. 118–22, follows this error, but the allusion to the *Libel on Dr. Delany* shows that it must belong to 1730.

[2] Cf. Swift to Bolingbroke, 19 Nov. 1729.

[3] Ball suggests that the allusion is probably to the second Viscount Carrington of Burford, whose seat, Ashby Folville, was near the parish in Leicestershire of which Swift's uncle was vicar. Lord Carrington died in 1701 at the age of eighty.

[4] *A Libel on Doctor Delany and a Certain Great Lord.*

the invention of new tricks, I am ignorant? But, I believe in your time you would never, as a Minister, have suffered an Act to pass through the H. of C—'s,[1] only because you were sure of a majority in the H. of Lords to throw it out; because it would be unpopular, and consequently a loss of reputation. Yet this we are told hath been the case in the qualification-bill relating to Pensioners.[2] It should seem to me, that Corruption, like avarice, hath no bounds. I had opportunities to know the proceedings of your ministry better than any other man of my rank; and having not much to do, I have often compared it with this sixteen years of a profound peace all over Europe, and we running seven millions in debt. I am forced to play at small game, to set the beasts here a madding, meerly for want of better game, *Tentanda via est qua me quoque possim &c.*[3]—The D— take those politicks, where a Dunce might govern for a dozen years together. I will come in person to England, if I am provoked, and send for the Dictator from the plough. I disdain to say, *O mihi praeteritos*[4]—but *cruda deo viridisque Senectus.*[5] Pray my Lord how are the gardens? have you taken down the mount, and removed the yew hedges? Have you not bad weather for the spring-corn? Hath Mr. Pope gone farther in his Ethic Poems? and is the headland sown with wheat? and what says Polybius? and how does my Lord St. John?[6] which last question is very material to me, because I love Burgundy, and riding between Twickenham and Dawley.—I built a wall five years ago, and when the masons played the knaves, nothing delighted me so much as to stand by while my servants threw down what was amiss:[7] I have likewise seen a Monkey overthrow all the dishes and plates in a kitchen, merely for the pleasure of seeing them tumble and hearing the clatter they made in their fall. I wish you would invite me to such another entertainment; but you think as I ought to think, that it is time for me to have done with the world, and so I would if I could get into a better before I was called into the best, and not die here in a rage, like a poisoned rat in a hole. I wonder you are not ashamed to let me pine away in this kingdom while you are out of power.

[1] House of Commons.

[2] The object of this bill was to make previous legislation effective in preventing the election to the House of Commons of persons in receipt of pensions from the Crown.—Ball.

[3] Virgil, *Georgic*, iii. 8.

[4] *Aeneid*, viii. 560.

[5] *Aeneid*, vi. 304.

[6] Bolingbroke's father.

[7] See Swift to Chetwode, 14 July 1724.

I come from looking over the *Melange* above-written, and declare it to be a true copy of my present disposition, which must needs please you, since nothing was ever more displeasing to myself. I desire you to present my most humble respects to my Lady.

4805

John Gay to Swift

[31 March 1730]

Dear Sir.

I expect in about a fortnight to set out for Wiltshire, & am as impatient as you seem to be to have me to get on horseback;[1] I thought proper to give you this intelligence because Mr Lewis told me last sunday that he was in a day or two to set out for the Bath, so that very soon you are like to have neither of your Cashiers in town. Continue to direct to me at this House, the Letters will be sent to me wherever I am. My Ambition at present is levell'd to the same point that you direct me to, for I am every day building Villakins, and have given over that of Castles. If I were to undertake it in my present circumstance, I should in the most thrifty Scheme soon be straiten'd, & I hate to be in debt, for I cannot bear to pawn five pounds worth of my liberty to a Taylor or a Butcher; I grant you this is not having the true spirit of modern Nobility, but tis hard to cure the prejudice of education. I have made your compliments to Mr P who is very much your humble servant. I have not seen the Doctor, & am not like to see his Roan Brother[2] very often for he is gone to China. Mr Pope told me he had acquainted the Doctor with the misfortune of the Sour Hermitage, My Lord Oxford told me He at present could match yours & from the same person. The Doctor was touch'd with your disappointment & hath promis'd to represent this affair to his Brother at his return from China. I assure you too for all your gibes, that I wish you heartily good wine though I can drink none myself. When Lord Bolingbroke is in town he lodges at Mr Chetwynd's[3] in Dover Street, I do not know how to direct to him

[1] To ride to Amesbury, the Duke of Queensberry's residence in Wiltshire.

[2] Robert Arbuthnot.

[3] Viscount Chetwynd, created 1717, was succeeded by his eldest brother in 1736 by special remainder in the patent of creation. He had been a Lord of the Admiralty 1717–27.

in the Country. I have been extreamly taken up of late in settling a Steward's Account. I am endeavouring to do all the justice & service I can for a friend, so I am sure you will think I am well employ'd. Upon this occassion I now & then have seen Jo Taylor,[1] who says he hath a demand upon you for Rent, you having taken his house in the Country, & he being determin'd not to let it to any body else; and he thinks it but reasonable that you should either come & live in it or pay your rent. I neither ride nor walk but I design to do both this month & become a laudable practitioner. The Dutchess wishes she had seen you & thinks you were in the wrong to hide yourself and peep through the window that day she came to Mr Popes. The Duke too is oblig'd to you for your good opinion & is your humble servant. If I were to write, I am afraid I should again incurr the displeasure of my superiors, for I cannot for my life think so well of them as they themselves think they deserve. If you have a very great mind to please the Dutchess and at the same time to please me, I wish you would write a Letter to her to send to her Brother Lord Cornbury[2] to advise him in his travells, for she says she would take your advice rather than mine, and she remembers that you told her in the Park that you lov'd & honour'd her family.[3] You always insisted upon a Lady's making advances to you; I do not know whether you will think this declaration sufficient. Then too when you were in England she writ a Letter to you, & I have been often blam'd since for not delivering it. The day the Pension Bill was thrown out of the House of Lords Lord Bathurst spoke with great applause. I have not time to go to Mr Pope's; in a day or two very probably I shall see him & acquaint him about the Usquebagh. I will not embezzle your interest money though by looking upon accounts I see how money may be embezzled; as to my being engag'd in an affair of this kind, I say nothing for myself, but that I will not do all I can, for the rest I leave Jo Taylor to speak for me. today I dine with Alderman Barber the present Sheriff feast in the city. Does not Chartres[4] misfortunes grieve you, for that great man is like to save his life and lose some of his money, a very hard case!

[1] Clerk of the Bridewell Hospital.

[2] Henry Hyde, Viscount Cornbury, and Baron Hyde, 1710–53, a friend of Bolingbroke and Pope.

[3] This must have been when she was a child.

[4] Col. Charteris was then in confinement, convicted at the Old Bailey for rape, but after a short imprisonment and some confiscations he was pardoned by the King.

I am just now come from the Alderman's feast, who had a very fine dinner & a very fine Appearance of Company. The post is just going away.

March · 31 · 1730.

Address: To the Reverend | Dr Swift Dean of S^t^ | Patrick's in Dublin | Ireland.
Postmark: ? MR
Endorsed by Swift: Mr Gay. Mar^h^ 31 | 1730

Longleat xiii (Portland Papers)

Alexander Pope and Viscount Bolingbroke to Swift

[9 April 1730]

I have received two or three Letters of one kind or other from you,[1] and answer'd them either jointly or seperately as I could. I also saw a Letter[2] of one Mrs Sykins, but mist the sight of the Lady by an accident. She came from London one night, sent yours to my house about 7. it raining very hard, I sent word I would be at home all the next day at her Service. The next morning it raining still, I sent my Servant by nine, to ask at what hour I should send a Chariot for her, and she was gone 2 hours before, back to London: So she has seen no greater monster, yet, than the Estrich. I don't wonder, if people from all parts should flock to see me, after the Picture lately drawn of me by a very peculiar Painter in Ireland,[3] who has made the finest Show-Board of me, in the World: I forgive that Painter, tho' there may be others who do not, and tho he flatters my Virtue, which is a Greater Sin sure than to flatter one's Vanity. —I am pleased to see however your partiality, and 'tis for that reason I've kept some of your Letters and some of those of my other friends. These if I put together in a Volume, (for my own secret satisfaction, in reviewing a Life, past in Innocent amusements &

[1] This letter replies to that of Swift dated 26 Feb. In the Harleian transcript the date is pencilled in by a modern hand. It may be accepted as near the truth. Pope's part of the letter was first printed by Elwin, vii. 191. Bolingbroke's part Pope printed as a postscript to the brief letter, Pope to Swift, printed by Sherburn, and here [4 Mar. 1729–30]. Faulkner, 1741, pp. 152–5.

[2] The letter of introduction with which Swift had furnished Mrs. Sican, 6 Feb. 1729–30.

[3] The lines in *A Libel on Doctor Delany and a Certain Great Lord* eulogizing Pope.

Studies, not without the good will of worthy and ingenious Men) do not therefore say, I aim at Epistolary Fame: I never had any Fame less in my head; but the Fame I most covet indeed, is that, which must be deriv'd to me from my Friendships.

I am truly and heartily concern'd at the Prospect of so great a Loss as you mention, in your fortune, which I wish you had not told me, since I can't contribute to help it by any remedy. For God's sake acquaint me if you come off well. I shall be thoroughly uneasy till I know the Event. If there be any Virtue in England I would try to stir it up in your behalf, but it dwells not with Power: it is got into so narrow a Circle that 'tis hard, very hard, to know where to look for it. Among your Friends I have been seeking it, and have hopes, there, some Occasion may arise, which will not be neglected, to invite you to us once again. I don't dislike your writing a Moral Letter to a Courtier, provided you inclose it to me, but the Slur you mention in the News was not level'd at her,[1] but at a poor Maid of Honour. As to your writing to Lord Burl. I would by no means have you, 'twill tend to no good, and only anger, not amend. You are both of you Positive men.—I shew'd Arbuthnot the passage in two of your letters about the bad wines: his answer I doubt not will be fully Satisfactory to you. He own'd the Wines were execrable, for (sayd he) so were all the wines my Brother had at that time. And to make you amends he thinks highly reasonable, which (sayd he) My Brother will surely do as soon as he returns from China, whither he set out some three Weeks since. In the meantime if the Dean will step and see my Brother at his house in China I'm sure he will make him welcome to the best wine the Country affords—

—what can a Man desire more?

You make me smile at appealing to Gay, rather than to me, for pitying any Distress in a friend, but particularly this of your bad wine: Do not you know he has wholly abstain'd from wine almost these two years? and I drink nothing else. I am really heartily vext at this piece of ill luck, and wish you would come and revenge it upon our good wines here, rather than follow the Doctor's direction to China. If your Lawsuit (Quod Deus bene vertat) can be finish'd, why not? You'l see here more of what you like, or less of what you hate, at least. I am in hope your health is tolerable, and

[1] Not levelled, that is, against Mrs. Howard. Pope's attempt to prevent Swift from being offensive to Mrs. Howard and Lord Burlington is interesting. —Sherburn.

cannot be worse in a better Clime (for so I believe ours is, in respect to Deafness, as the Air is rather clearer.)

Dr Whalley[1] has given me his Cases again, upon a Rehearing and you may be confident I will do him whatever Service I can. I lately saw your Cosen Lancelot,[2] who is a man extreamly affectionated to you, and to me. Every man here asks of you, Lord Oxford lately wrote to you in behalf of a very valuable Clergyman's Father's Book.[3] I wish you could promote it, but expect little from poor Ireland, by your accounts of it. The best thing it affords is what you have sent me, its Usquebagh, but we hear nothing, yet, of it: nor by what Ship it comes.

[4]I did not take the pen out of Pope's hands I protest to you, but since He will not fill the Remainder of the Page, I think I may without offence. I seek no Epistolary fame, but am a good deal pleased to think that it will be known hereafter that you and I lived in the most friendly intimacy together.—Pliny writ his letters for the Publick, so did Seneca, so did Balzac, Voiture &c. Tully did not, and therefore these give us more pleasure than any which have come down to us from Antiquity, when we read them, we pry into a Secret which was intended to be kept from us, that is a pleasure. We see Cato, and Brutus, and Pompey and others, such as they really were, and not such as the gaping Multitude of their own Age took them to be, or as Historians and Poets have represented them to ours, that is another pleasure. I remember to have seen a Procession at Aix la Chappelle, wherein an Image of Charlemagne is carried on the Shoulders of a Man, who is hid by the long Robe of the Imperial Saint, follow him into the Vestry, you see the Bearer Slip from under the Robe, and the Gigantick figure dwindles into an image of the ordinary Size, and is set among other lumber.—I agree much with Pope, that our Climate is rather better than that you are in, and perhaps your publick Spirit would be less grieved, or oftener comforted, here than there. Come to us therefore on a Visit at least, it will not be the fault of several persons here if you do not come to live with us. But great good will and little power produce such slow and feeble effects as can be acceptable to Heaven alone and heavenly Men.—

[1] Cf. Oxford to Swift, 4 Mar. 1729–30.
[2] Patty Rolt's second husband.
[3] Samuel Wesley's book on Job.
[4] Here Bolingbroke begins to write.

I know you will be angry with me, if I say nothing to you of a poor Woman,[1] who is still on the other side of the Water in a most languishing State of health, if She regains Strength enough to come over, and She is better within a few Weeks, I shall nurse her in this Farm with all the care and tenderness possible, if she does not, I must pay her the last dutys of friendship wherever she is, tho' I break thro' the whole plan of life which I have formed in my mind. Adieu.

I am most faithfully and affectionately yours.[2]

Deane Swift 1765

Swift to Lord Carteret

[April 1730][3]

My Lord,

I told your Excellency that you were to run on my errands. My Lord Burlington hath a very fine monument of his ancestorr the Earl of Cork, in my cathedral, which your Excellency hath seen. I and the chapter have written to him in a body to have it repaired, and I in person have desired he would do it.[4] And I desired likewise, that he would settle a parcel of land, worth five pounds a year, (not an annuity) to keep it always in repair. He said he would do any thing to oblige me; but he was afraid that, in future times, the five pounds a year would be misapplied, and secured by the dean and chapter to their own use. I answered, that a dean and twenty-four members of so great a chapter, who, in livings, estates, *&c.* had about 4000*l.* a year amongst them, would hardly divide four shillings amongst them to cheat his posterity; and that we could have no view but to consult the honour of his family.[5] I therefore command your

[1] Lady Bolingbroke.

[2] Faulkner, 1741, adds the signature 'B' to this part of the letter. Sherburn adds an interesting note: 'The footnotes in this edition, not reprinted in the London editions, together with the "B" seem to the present editor evidence that Swift himself edited the letter from Faulkner's texts.'

[3] Deane Swift has a footnote to the first printing of this letter: 'This letter is not dated, but endorsed "To Lord Lieutenant Carteret before his going off." ' Carteret left Ireland finally on 20 Apr.

[4] 22 May 1729; and he wrote to Lady Holderness on the same date.

[5] Swift, writing to Gay, 20 Nov. 1729, estimated the endowment of the Dean and Chapter at more than £10,000 a year.

Excellency to lay this before him, and the affront he hath put upon us, in not answering a letter written to him by the dean and chapter in a body.

The great Duke of Schomberg is buried under the altar in my cathedral. My Lady Holderness is my old acquaintance, and I writ to her about a small sum, to make a monument for her grandfather. I writ to her myself; and also, there was a letter from the Dean and Chapter to desire she would order a monument to be raised for him in my cathedral. It seems Mildmay, now Lord F[itzwalter], her husband, is a covetous fellow; or, whatever is the matter, we have had no answer. I desire you will tell Lord F[itzwalter] that if he will not send fifty pounds to make a monument for the old Duke, I and the chapter will erect a small one of ourselves for ten pounds, wherein it shall be expressed, That the posterity of the Duke, naming particularly Lady Holderness and Mr. Mildmay, not having the generosity to erect a monument, we have done it of ourselves. And if, for an excuse, they pretend they will send for his body, let them know it is mine; and rather than send it, I will take up the bones, and make of it a skeleton, and put it in my registry-office, to be a memorial of their baseness to all posterity. This I expect your Excellency will tell Mr. Mildmay, or, as you now call him, Lord Fitzwalter: And I expect likewise, that he will let Sir Conyers Darcy know how ill I take his neglect in this matter; although, to do him justice, he averred that Mildmay was so avaricious a wretch, that he would let his own father be buried without a coffin to save charges.

I expect likewise, that if you are acquainted with your successor,[1] you will let him know how impartial I was in giving you characters of clergymen, without regard to party; and what weight you laid on them: And that having but one clergyman who had any relation to me, I let him pass unpreferred:[2] And lastly, that you will let your said successor know, that you lament the having done nothing for Mr. Robert Grattan; and give him such a recommendation, that he may have something to mend his fortune.[3]

These are matters I leave in charge to your Excellency: And I

[1] These words are evidence that Carteret was not expected to return.

[2] Presumably his cousin the Rev. Stafford Lightburne.

[3] Robert Grattan was appointed that year to a more valuable prebend in St. Patrick's Cathedral than he had hitherto held and resigned St. Bride's. He appears to have been in no want of money, as he retired a few years later from clerical life and adopted the role of a country gentleman at Belcamp.—Ball.

desire that I, who have done with courts, may not be used like a courtier. For, as I was a courtier when you were a school-boy, I know all your arts. And so God bless you, and all your family, my old friends: And remember, I expect you shall not dare to be a courtier to me. I am, *&c.*

Endorsed by Swift: To Lord Lieutenant Carteret before his going off.—Deane Swift.

Deane Swift 1765

Swift to Lady Worsley

April 19th, 1730

Madam,[1]

My Lady Carteret (if you know such a Lady) commands me to pursue my own inclination; which is, to honour myself with writing you a letter; and thereby endeavouring to preserve myself in your memory, in spite of an acquaintance of more years, than in regard to my own reputation, as a young gentleman, I care to recollect. I forgot whether I had not some reasons to be angry with your Ladyship, when I was last in England. I hope to see you very soon the youngest great-grandmother in Europe: and fifteen years hence (which I shall have nothing to do with) you will be at the amusement of 'Rise up daughter,' *&c.* You are to answer this letter, and to inform me of your health and humour; and, whether you like your daughter better or worse, after having so long conversed with the Irish world, and so little with me. Tell me what are your amusements at present; cards, court, books, visiting, or fondling (I humbly beg you Ladyship's pardon, but it is between ourselves) your grandchildren? My Lady Carteret hath been the best Queen we have known in Ireland these many years; yet is she mortally hated by all the young girls, because (and it is your fault) she is handsomer than all of them together. Pray, do not insult poor Ireland on this occasion, for it would have been exactly the same thing in London. And therefore I shall advise the K—g, when I go next to England, to send no more of her sort, (if such another can be found) for fear of turning all his loyal female-subjects here against him.

How is our old friend Mrs. Barton? (I forget her new name). I

[1] During his last visits to England, 1726–7, Swift renewed his acquaintance with Lady Carteret's mother. She had refrained from crossing to Ireland to visit her daughter.

saw her three years ago, at court, almost dwindled to an echo, and hardly knew her;[1] while your eyes dazzled me as much as when I first met them: Which, considering myself, is a greater compliment than you are aware of. I wish you may have grace to find it.

My Lady Carteret hath made me a present, which I take to be malicious, with a design to stand in your place.[2] Therefore I would have you to provide against it by another, and something of your own work, as hers is. For you know, I always expect advances and presents from Ladies. Neither was I ever deceived in this last article by any of your sex but the Q—n, whom I taxed three years ago with a present of ten pounds value. Upon taking my leave, she said, she intended a medal for me, but it was not finished. I afterwards sent her, on her own commands, about five and thirty pounds worth of silk, for herself and the Princesses; but never received the medal to this day. Therefore, I will trust your sex no more. You are to present my most humble service to my old friend Sir Robert Worsley. I hope my friend Harry is well, and fattening in the sun, and continuing a batchelor, to enrich the poor Worsley family.[3]

I command you to believe me to be, with the greatest truth and respect, *&c.*

B.M., Portland Papers[4]

Swift to the Earl of Oxford

Dublin · Apr · 28th 1730.

My Lord.

I had the Honor of Your Lordships letter dated the 4th of March last; and I deserved my Acknowledging it thus long to see what success I could have in recommending Mr Wesley's book. I have fewest acquaintance in this kingdom of any man who is condemned to live in it. I am hated mortally by every creature in power, and by

[1] Catherine Barton, Miss Long's companion and niece of Sir Isaac Newton (see *Journal*, i. 17 n.) married John Conduitt who succeeded Newton as Master of the Mint. Despite Swift's words she appears to have retained her vigour.

[2] A subsequent letter shows that the present was a tea-caddy.

[3] Her brother-in-law, Henry Worsley, previously envoy to Portugal, Governor of Barbadoes 1722 to 1728.

[4] Portland Papers, First Deposit in B.M., List 1 of Miscellaneous Papers, 1725–40, 714 A.

all their followers. The Author's name is utterly unknown here except by some who read verses and have chanced to read some where he is distinguished as an unfortunate medler in Poetry. I gave the Proposalls to a Clergyman who knows more of his tribe than I do; but such is the Poverty, the indifference, the ignorance and the pride of people among us, that he hath not got me one Subscriber. Therefore I fear it will all terminate in my desiring Mr Pope to subscribe for me. That I do not trouble Your Lordship with my Letters, is the greatest mark I can give you of my respect. It is not possible for any person in this Kingdom to be either of use or entertainment, and particularly to Your Lordship, who are wholly a stranger as well to the people as to the concerns of so wretched a Scene. And I am almost in the same case; I do not visit one Lord either temporal or spirituall, nor am acquainted with above three squires, and half a dozen Parsons. If my own little affairs, I mean the whole small fortune I have, had not been embroyled by Law, and yet in peril of being entirely lost; I believe I should have ventured this summer to have waited on Your Lordship, and quartered once more on my good friend Mr Pope; for although my health is uncertain I am still an excellent walker and a tolerable rider. But I have other difficultyes besides my private affairs to detain me: No offence to Your Lordship, I am not very fond of the publick Scituation. I see nails that I thought might be pulled out, now more strongly riveted than ever. I heartily congratulate with Your Lordship, and my Lady Oxford for Lady Margarets good success in coming out so happily from a disease so ruinous to Ladyes as the small pox, and without being obliged to the Turkish manner of inoculating . . I hope my Lady Oxford eats more than she did when I was a witness to her starving. If she does not promise to mend in that article, I beg Your Lordship will burn her Barge.—I have a very fair medal worth sixpence, of Edwd 3d I know not whether it be worth putting into Your Series of Engl Kings. Pray My Lord look upon me as the Greek Emperr did upon the Country men who offerd him a very large turnip. You commanded me to enquire into coyns here; and as an ignorant man I may do ignorant things. Your Lordship acted your own part, a Harley part, in your generosity and favor to Mr Whalley, and I had the honor to act on the same principle, when I entreated your Lordship to befriend an honest Oxford Gentleman against the vigor and cruelty of the common law. The loser sends complaints hither, that he was overcome by Party. I wish it were true, for then there would be some hopes of a bett^r world: but I believe the event will shew, that the Loser will be a gainer, and that they will take care to see a most abominable Poet, and a strong party man reimburst by a Bishoprick: Our friend Carteret is gone, and we are in the clouds, apprehending he will not be rewarded according to his merit; which (as I have often told him) is excessively great, according to the best merits of a chief governor here; which are to put on more chains, and to get more money, wherein none of his Predecessors ever equalled him, nor met with more stupid, slavish, complying beasts to manage.[1] Mr Wesley will not be encouraged by the person you mention from the same principle that Buckley was. I most humbly thank your Lordship for the favorable invitation you are pleased to give me. But time and the miseryes I see about me have made me almost as stupid as the people I am among, and altogether disqualifyed me from living with better. I desire to present my most humble respect to my Lady Oxford and Lady Marget. I am with the truest respect | My Lord Your Lordship's most obed^t and most | humble Ser^t | Jon: Swift.

Endorsed: Dean Swift, Dublin | April · 28 · R. May · 8 · | 1730. Dover Street.—

Longleat xiii (Harleian transcripts)

Swift to Alexander Pope

Dublin May 2d. 1730.

I have yours mentioning one Mrs Sykins, whom at her earnest request I ventured to recommend that she might come back full of vanity with the honor of seeing you.[2] It is to be understood that the only women of tast here are three Shopkeepers wives? of The other two, one is both a Scholar and Poet,[3] the other a Poet only, and Mrs Sykins but a good reader and a judge. Mrs Barber who is a Poet only, but not a Scholar, is going to England but I shall give her no letter of recommendation, and you will pardon me for what I did to Mrs Sykings. I must tell you that the Mortal Sin of your painter was praising a *Papist*, for we have no other zeal or merit than what arises from the utter detestation of your Religion.[4] *Ludlow* in his Memoirs

[1] Carteret's retirement appears to have been voluntary. He was offered the post of Lord Steward left vacant by the appointment of the Duke of Dorset as Lord-Lieutenant, but refused any further office under Walpole.

[2] See Swift to Pope, 6 Feb. 1729–30, and note. [3] Mrs. Grierson.

[4] The allusion is to Swift's eulogy of Pope in the *Libel on Doctor Delany*.

mentions one Lord Fitzwilliam with this Character, that he was a civil Person, *though a Papist.*—[1]

The Lawyers say I have absolutely recovered my fortune, for my Creditor has done what you understand not; he hath levyed a fine[2] and suffered a recovery, to sell his Estate, and my money with costs and Interest will be payd me at Michaelmas, and I hope I shall never complain again upon my own affairs (like friend Gay) except I am compelled by Sickness; but the noise will not be loud enough for you to hear it.—As to Virtue, you have more charity than I, who never attempt to seek it, and if I had lost all my money I would disdain to seek relief from Power. The loss would have been more to some wanting friends and to the Publick than my self. Besides, I find that the longer I live I shall be less expensive. It is growing with me as with Sir John Mennis,[3] who when he grew old, boasted of his happiness to a friend, that a groat would make him as drunk, as half a Crown did formerly, and so with me, half a pint of wine will go as far as a pint did some Years ago, and probably I shall soon make up an abstemious Triumvirate with you and Mr Gay. Your Usquebagh is set out by long Sea a fortnight ago.[4] I wish I may be once lucky in my commissions from hence. Some Rascal in London hath *packeted* me as far as two shillings with a Paper writ in favor of Wood the Copperman on a project of his to make Iron with pit-coal.[5] I shall not upon third thoughts trouble your female Courtier with a letter, any more than Lord Burlington. As to the Wine I give it up; for positively I will not go to China till I receive my law money. Nothing could keep me from seeing you but the dread of my deafness returning, although I must tell you that almost three years in my share of life to come make a difference as much as an inch in a man's

[1] Edmund Ludlow, 1617?–1692, the regicide, whose *Memoirs* were first printed in three volumes 1698–9. The Lord Fitzwilliam here mentioned was the second holder of an Irish viscountcy. See *Memoirs of Edmund Ludlow*, ed. Sir Charles Firth.

[2] A legal phrase for the compromise of a suit for the possession of lands.

[3] Sir John Mennes, 1595–1676, actively employed at sea throughout a large part of his life, rose to be an admiral. During the civil war he served with the royalist army. After the restoration he was appointed Comptroller of the Navy. Pepys found him 'most excellent pleasant company' although 'not fit for business'.

[4] Consigned to Lord Bathurst, who on 30 June acknowledged the safe receipt of four bottles, three of which he forwarded to Pope.

[5] The pamphlet sent to Swift was probably *An Account of Mr. Wood's Iron made with pulverized Ore and Pit-Coal.*

nose, yet I hitherto walk as much, and ride oftner than formerly. I intend to make no distant journey this Summer even here, nor be above two nights out of the power of returning to my home.[1] I certainly expect that neither Tyths, nor Lands let to the full value will in a Year or two yield any money at all. All my comfort is, that I have 250. a year which I receive from lands of above three times the value, and that will support me in some sort while there is any remnant of trade or money left among us. And so much for my scurvy Domestick. It is current here that the D. of Dorset will be Lieutenant I have known him from his Youth. But, see the misfortune. There is one Lady Allen whom you employ'd in a commission. Her Lord and she have been some years caressing me in the most friendly manner when the Lord on a sudden without the least provocation rayl'd at me in the Privy Council and the H. of Lords as a Jacobite, and Libeller of the Government &c.[2] He hath been worryed by some well-wisher of mine[3] in a Paper called a Vindication of Lord Carteret &c. and all this is lay'd on me. The libel is that paper of verses where you are mentioned, the other thing is Prose. Now this Lady hath been an old Favorite of the D. of D. and consequently will use all means to put me on a worse foot than my Station requires me to be with a Chief Governor, and who can help it, for I shall not so much as desire Lady Betty Germain to mend the matter,[4] but rather, when the Parliament sits here a year and a half hence I will if my health permits pass that winter between you and London.

I writ to my Lord Oxford t'other day, and told him Sincerely that I had no credit to get one Subscriber for Mr Wesley, except myself.

I am not acquainted with one Lord either Temporal or Spiritual, nor with three Squires, a half dozen middling Clergymen are all the Croneys I have, who never will be worth a Guinea before hand.—I will say nothing to my Lord Boling— here, but write to him inclosed as this is to my debtor.[5] It is the safest way to his Lordship and you, though it may reach you later. There is a knot of little fellows here either in the University or among the Younger Clergy, who deal in verse and sometimes shrewdly enough. These have been pestering

[1] Swift changed his mind. Two months later he paid his last visit to the Achesons—the end of June to the end of Sept. 1730.

[2] See Lord Allen's attack on S. as a Jacobite, p. 374.

[3] The well-wisher was Swift himself.

[4] Swift hoped that Lady Betty Germain would use her influence on behalf of his friends. See her letter to him, 19 Sept. 1730.

[5] Lord Bathurst.

Dr Delany for several Months past, but how they have been provoked I know not, unless by envy at seeing him so very domestick with the Lord Lieut. The Doctor as a man of much strickness in his Life was terribly mortifyed with two or three of the first Squibbs, but now his Gall is broke. He hath a Country House very agreeable within a Mile of this Town, fit to lodge you, in a fine college[1] much more retired than Twickenham. But the Deanery is your habitation. He is a man of the easyest and best conversation I ever met with in this Island, a very good listner, a right reasoner, neither too silent nor talkative, and never positive; but hath too many acquaintance.—I am now told I may drill on five years more without my money. My most humble service to Lord Burlington, Lord Bathurst, Lord Masham, Mr Poulteney, the D.[2] Mr Lewis, and friend Gay. None to Lord Boling— for I will write to him and my particular services to Mrs Pope; and love to Patty Blount and to Mrs Howard if you please, when you see her, and Mrs Howard if she has a mind may present my Duty to the Qu— and by the way is Her M— angry at the Line where your Painter hath named her with relation to you,[3] or hath she by chance heard of it. Pray God bless you and restore and preserve your health.

To Mr. Pope.

Faulkner 1741

Alexander Pope to Swift

[*c.* 19 *June* 1730][4]

My Lord has spoken justly of his Lady: Why not I of my Mother? Yesterday was her birth-day, now entering on the ninety-first year of

[1] Clearly written 'college' in the Harleian transcript. Probably a scribal error for 'country'. Sherburn suggests 'cottage' as a possible reading.

[2] Dr. Arbuthnot.

[3] The allusion is to line 74 in the *Libel on Doctor Delany* alleging that Pope 'Refus'd the Visits of a Queen'.

[4] As Prof. Sherburn points out this letter is clearly a fragment, probably a postscript to a lost letter of Bolingbroke to Swift of June 1730. 'In 1741 Pope transferred it to the end of another Bolingbroke letter to Swift dated by Pope as 29 Mar. (see 20 Mar. 1730–1). The Harleian transcript of Bolingbroke's letter bears in Oxford's hand the date 20 Mar.'—Sherburn. The date here assigned to the letter is based upon the fact that Pope believed his mother's birthday to be 18 June. She was in fact baptised on that day.

her age; her memory much diminished, but her senses very little hurt; her sight and hearing, good; she sleeps not ill, eats moderately, drinks water, says her prayers; this is all she does. I have reason to thank God for continuing so long to me a very good and tender parent, and for allowing me to exercise for some years, those cares which are now as necessary to her, as hers have been to me. An object of this sort daily before one's eyes very much softens the mind, but perhaps may hinder it from the willingness of contracting other tyes of the like domestick nature, when one finds how painful it is even to enjoy the tender pleasures. I have formerly made some strong efforts to get and to deserve a friend: perhaps it were wiser never to attempt it, but live Extempore, and look upon the world only as a place to pass thro', just pay your hosts their due, disperse a little charity, and hurry on. Yet am I just now writing, (or rather planning) a book, to make mankind look upon this life with comfort and pleasure, and put morality in good humour.[1]—And just now too, I am going to see one I love tenderly; and to-morrow to entertain several civil people, whom if we call friends, it is by the Curtesy of England.—*Sic, sic juvat ire sub umbras.*[2] While we do live, we must make the best of life,

> *O Vita! Stulto brevis, sapienti longa!*
> *Cantantes licet suque (minus via laedat) eamus,*[3]

as the shepherd says in Virgil, when the road was long and heavy. I am yours.

Forster copy

Swift to Knightley Chetwode

Dublin, June 24, 1730.

Sir,

I had yours,[4] but it came a little later than usual. You are misinformed; I have neither amused myself with opposing or defending anybody. I live wholly within myself; most people have dropped me, and I have nothing to do, but fence against the evils of age and

[1] The *Essay on Man.* [2] *Aeneid*, iv. 660.
[3] *Eclogues*, ix. 64. The second line only.
[4] An answer to Swift's letter of 12 Feb.

sickness as much as I can, by riding and walking. Neither have I been above six miles out of this town this nine months; except once at the Bishop's visitation in Trim. Neither have I any thought of a villa either near or far off, having neither money, youth, nor inclination for such an achievement. I do not think the country of Ireland a habitable scene without long preparation and great expense. I am glad your trees thrive so well. It is usual when good care is taken, that they will at last settle to the ground.

I cannot imagine how you procure enemies, since one great use of retirement is to lose them, or else a man is no thorough retirer. If I mistake you not, by your sixty friends, you mean enemies. I knew not Webb. As to your information of passages in private life, it is a thing I never did nor shall pursue; nor can envy you or any man for knowledge in it, because it must be liable to great mistakes, and consequently wrong judgements. This I say, though I love the world as little, and think as ill of it as most people; and I would as lief peep three hours a morning into a jail. Mr. Cusack died a week after I left Trim, and is much lamented by all parties.[1] What embroilments you had with him I know not, but I always saw him act the part of a generous, honest, good-natured, reasonable, obliging man. I find you intended to treat of a marriage by proxy in England and the lady is dead. I think you have as ill luck with burying your friends, as good with burying your enemies. I did expect that would be the event when I heard of it first from you. I know not what advertisement you read of any libels or stories against me, for I read no news, nor any man tells me of such things, which is the only way of disappointing such obscure slanderers. About three years ago I was shown an advertisement to some such purpose,[2] but I thought the person who told me had better let it alone. I do not know but they will write Memoirs of my actions in war. These are natural consequences that fall upon people who have writings laid to their charge, whether true or not.

I am just going out of town, to stay nowhere long, but go from

[1] The reference is to one of Swift's neighbours in the county of Meath, Christopher Cusack of Rathaldron, in respect of whose property a grant of administration had been issued on the 13th of that month.—Ball. The Cusacks were among the earliest Anglo-Norman settlers in Ireland. The most distinguished member of the family was Sir Thomas Cusack, 1490–1571, Lord Chancellor of Ireland.

[2] The advertisement of the *Memoirs of a Certain Irish Dean* was still being issued. A Dublin edition, published by R. Dickson, appeared in 1730.

house to house, whether inns or friends, for five or six weeks merely for exercise. I am, Sir, | Your most obedient, &c.

I direct to Maryborough by guess, never remembering whether that or Mountmellick be right.

Endorsed: A serious letter when he was ill and leaving town.

4805

Lord Bathurst to Swift

[30 June 1730]

Dear Dean

I recd a Letter from y^u[1] sometime ago wch gave me infinite pleasure, & I am going to return y^u an answer im̃ediately but when I set down to write I found my thoughts roll'd upon the trifles wch fill the scene of life in that busy sensless place[2] where I then was, & tho' I had nothing to do there, at least nothing worth doing, & time lay upon my hands; I was resolv'd to difere writing to y^u till I cou'd clear my head from that Rubbish wch every one must contract in that Place. I can't but fancy if one of our heads were dissected after passing a winters campaigne ther, it wou'd appear just like a Pampht shop, you'd see a Collection of treaties a bundle of farces, a parcel Encomiums another of Satyrs speeches Novels Sermons Bawdy-songs Addresses Epigrams Proclamations Poems Divinity-lectures Quack-bills Historical acc^ts fables & Godknows-w^t.

The moment I got down here I found my self quite clear from all these affairs, but really the Hurry of business wch came upon me after a state of Idleness for 6 months must excuse me to y^u. here I am absolute Monarch of a circle of above a mile round, at least 100 acres of Ground, w^ch (to speak in the Stile of one of the Country-men) is very populous in Cattle fish & fowl. To enjoy this power, wch I relish extreamly, & regulate this Dominion, wch I prefere to any other, has taken up my time from morning to night. There are Yahoos in the Neighbourhood, but having read in History that the southern part of Britain was long defended ag^st the Picts by a wall, I have fortified my territories all round; that wise People the Chinese yu know did the same thing, to defend y^mselves ag^st the Tarters.

[1] A missing reply to Lord Bathurst's letter of 12 Feb.

[2] Parliament. Bathurst was writing from Cirencester.

Now I think on't as this letter is to be sent to y^u, it will certainly be open'd, & I shall have some observations made upon it because I am within three miles of a certain Castle[1] therefore I doe hereby declare that nothing herein contain'd, shall extend or be construed to extend so far, & furthermore I think my self in Honour bound to acknowledge that under our present just and prudent Ministry I doe not fear the least molestation from that quarter, neither are the fortifications aforemention'd in any wise design'd to keep them out, for I am well satisfied they can break thro' much stronger fences, than these, if they shou'd have a mind to it. Observe how naturally power & Dominion is attended with fear & Precaution when I am in the Herd I have as little of it ab^t me as anybody, but now that I am in the midst of my own Dominions, I think of nothing but preserving them, & grow fearfull lest a certain great man shou'd take a fancy to them & transport them into Norfolk to place them as an Iland in one of his new-made fish-ponds[2] or if y^u take this for too proud a thought I will only suppose it to be hung out under a great Bow-window;[3] in either case I must confess to y^u that I dont like it, In the first place I am not sure his new-made ground may hold good, in the latter case I have some reason to doubt the foundations of his House are not so solid as he may imagine. now therefore I am not so much in the wrong as y^u may conceive to desire that my territory may remain where it is. for tho' I know y^u cou'd urge many arguments to show the advantages I might reap by being so near him Yet I hold it as a maxim that he who is contented with what he has, ought not to risque that, even tho' he sou'd have a chance to augment it in any proportion; I learnt this from our friend Erasmus, & the corrupt notions that money is power, & therefore every man ought to get as much as he can in order to create more power to himself, have no weight with me.

But now to begin my letter to y^u, I have recd 4 Bottles of Usquebagh & sent 3 of them to Mr Pope so that I have detaind only one for my self I don't believe such an instance of Honesty punctuality disinterestedness & self-denial can be giv'n in this Age. the whole

[1] The reference is to Cirencester, represented in the main by Tories. This was one of the 'scot and lot' boroughs, where all the inhabitants paying local taxes had the right to vote, a wide franchise for those days.

[2] The construction of the great mansion at Houghton and the layout of the grounds occupied Walpole from 1722 to 1735.

[3] Evidently a reference to Walpole's lodge in Richmond Park in which a design with bow-windows was adopted.

being in my power I have with held but ¼ part. I expect if ever I come to be a great man y^u will write a vindication of me whether I am aspers'd or not. till then I remain | y^r most faithfull | & most obedient ser^t.

Endorsed by Swift: Ld Bathurst | Jun · 30 · 1730

4805

John Gay to Swift

[4 July 1730]

You tell me that I have put myself out of the way of all my old acquaintance, so that unless I hear from you I can know nothing of you;[1] is it not barbarous then to leave me so long without writing one word to me? If you wont write to me for my sake methinks you might write for your own. How do you know what is become of your money? If you had drawn upon me when I expected it you might have had your money, for I was then in town; but I am now at Amesbury near Salisbury in Wiltshire at the Duke of Queensberry's; the Dutchess sends you her services; I wish you were here, I fancy you would like her, and the Place; you might fancy yourself at home, for we have a Cathedral near us, where you might find a Bishop of the same name.[2] You might ride upon the Downs & write conjectures upon Stonehenge. We are but five & twenty miles from the Bath, and I was told this very Evening by General Dormer[3] who is here that he heard somewhere or other that you had some intentions of coming there the latter Season; I wish any thing would bring us together but your want of health. I have left off wine & writing, for I really think that man must be a bold writer who trusts to Wit without it.

[1] Swift to Gay, 19 Mar. 1729–30.

[2] The famous Dr. Benjamin Hoadly had occupied the see of Salisbury since 1723. His brother, John, was consecrated Bishop of Leighlin and Ferns in 1727; and when a vacancy occurred in the Archbishopric of Dublin by the death of King in July 1729 Boulter wrote to Townshend and Walpole (Boulter, *Letters*, i. 242, 255) warmly commending Hoadly as a successor. In consequence Hoadly was translated to Dublin in 1730. On Boulter's death in Oct. 1742 he became Archbishop of Armagh.

[3] Lieut.-Gen. James Dormer, 1679–1741, who served under Marlborough and in Spain. *D.N.B.*

I took your Advice, & some time ago took to Love, & made some advances to the Lady[1] you sent me to in Soho, but I met no return, so I nave given up all thoughts of it, & now have no pursuit or Amusement. A State of indolence is what I dont like; tis what I would not chuse; I am not thinking of a Court or preferment; for I think the Lady I live with is my friend, so that I am at the height of my ambition. You have often told me, there is a time of life that every one wishes for some settlement of his own; I have frequently that feeling about me; but I fancy it will hardly ever be my Lot; so that I will endeavour to pass away Life as agreeably as I can in the way I am. I often wish to be with you or you with me, & I believe you think I say true. I am determin'd to write to you, though those dirty fellows of the Post Office do read my Letters, for since I saw you I am grown of that consequence to be Obnoxious to the man I despise; so that it is very probable in their hearts they think me an honest man. I have heard from Mr Pope but once since I left London. I was sorry I saw him so seldom but I had business that kept me from him. I often wish we were together again. If you will not write, come. I am, Dear Sir, | Yours most sincerely & | affectionately.

Amesbury, near Salisbury in Wiltshire. July 4. 1730.

Endorsement: Mr Gay. | Jul. 3d. 1730

Longleat xiii (Harleian transcript)

The Earl of Oxford to Swift

Dover Street July 15 1730

Reverend S[r]

M[r] Clayton[2] telling me he was going for Ireland, I could not forbear sending you a few lines by him, thought[3] I may punish you, yet it is so great a pleasure to me to think of you and to converse with you even in this manner that I must expect you will be so good as to forgive the trouble this gives you.

I do not know what notions you entertain of us here I fear and

[1] Mrs. Drelincourt who had arrived in London.

[2] Who acted in a secretarial capacity and frequently carried Oxford's letters to Swift.

[3] Thus in the manuscript for 'though'. The scribe was careless and used little pointing. Some has been judiciously supplied.

believe you are in a very bad way, this is my thought that devoured, we certainly shall be,[1] but this only will be the Difference who shall have that great favour and instance of mercy that we shall have the Honour to follow you and be the last devoured and though this is so plain and that demonstrable yet we have so many unthinking, unaccountable Puppys among us, that to them every thing seems to go well as it should do, and are so pleased with this thought or rather do not think at all that it is in vain to say anything to them, this is a very disagreeable subject and I will therefore leave it.—

My Wife is I thank God pretty well her stomach is rather better than it was, Peggy is very well, both desire you will accept of their humble service, you mention you[r] Law affairs, I know so much of that sort of people called Lawyers, that I pitty most heartily any one that is obliged to be concerned with them, if you are not already I hope you will be soon safe out of their hands.

I suppose Mr Whaley is by this time got safe to his living and enjoying the fruit of his victory peace and quietness,[2] I believe he has had enough of Law, of Lawyers, and of Lords both spiritual and Temporal, I hope he is well if you see him.

I wish you would come over here that we might have the pleasure of seeing you, why should you not pass the Winter here? I should think it would be more agreeable to you than where you are.

Lord Bathurst has had a Fever, but he is now well again, Pope I saw yesterday he is pretty well.

I am with true respect and esteem | Sr | Your most affectionate | humble Servant | Oxford

Endorsed on verso of leaf: July 15 1730 | Copy of a Letter to | Dean Swift

Portland Papers, B.M. Deposit, List 1[3]

Swift to the Earl of Oxford

[From the North parts of Ireland 28 August 1730]

My Lord.

I am the onely man since the first Villars Duke of Buckingham that ever succeeded in favor from a Father to a Son; for I can boast my

[1] The allusion is to Swift's *Modest Proposal.*

[2] See p. 393.

[3] Portland Deposit in the B.M., List 1, Miscellaneous Papers 1725–40, 714 A.

self to have been in the good graces of two Earls of Oxford. But I have one advantage over the Duke that I am in no danger to be stabbed on account of the kindness and distinction you are pleased to show me. Your letter was sent to me by Mr Clayton to a friend's house here in the North,[1] where I have been passing a cool summer these two months, and shall finish the third before I return to Dublin. Neither my present condition of health, or private fortune will suffer me to make larger Journyes. I have had Your Lordships letter near a month, and by the return of an old Disorder, a giddyness in my head, I have wanted spirits to make my acknowledgments for the honer you have done me.—God forgive my revengefull temper if I am not sorry for any mortifications on your side. Your Ministers have ruined this Country, which Your Lordships father from principles of Justice prudence and humanity took care to preserve . . You will forgive me My Lord; for, the zeal of Liberty hath eaten me up, and I have nothing left but ill thoughts, ill words and ill wishes . . of all which I am not sparing, and like roaring in the gout, they give me some imaginary ease.

I hope to recover my little fortune in two or three months, and have no other value for it, than that upon any publick distress, or any strains of power that may affect my conscience, I may have somewhat independent to keep my nag, my self, and a glass of ale in Wales.

What should I do in England, when I find my self entirely ruined at Court, and in utter disgrace with the Minister—if they would pay what they honestly owe me,[2] I would be just their humble servant as much as I am already. If a scribble comes out complaining of our hardships here, it is infallibly layd at my door . . It is well I have the rabble on my side: That hath been very lately told them, and the affect not to believe it . .—There is a fellow here from England one Sawbridge, he was last term indited for a Rape.[3] The Plea he intended was his being drunk when he forced the woman; but he bought her off. He is a Dean and I name him to your Lordship, because I am confident you will hear of his being a Bishop; for in short, he is just the counterpart of Chartres,[4] that continuall favorite of Ministers.

[1] At Market Hill.

[2] The subsidy promised on his installation as Dean of St. Patrick's.

[3] *Poems*, pp. 516–20.

[4] For Col. Charteris see p. 385, n. 4.

I congratulate with My Lord Bathurst for his recovery from a feever. It is the disease of a young man, and foretells a long life, if that be any satisfaction in such a world.

The good account you are pleased to give me of my Lady Oxford's health, hath removed a great load from my shoulders; for I was ever in pain about her Ladyships want of appetite: and could often hardly forbear acting the Physician, by prescribing my onely remedy, which I take twice a day in fair weather, and once in foul; I mean Exercise, which although it be the cheapest of all drugs, yet you great people are seldom rich enough to purchase. Pray God preserve My Lady Margaret and Your Lordship in the health you possess. I must expect that your Lordship will please to present my most humble respects and Services to both their Ladyships . . Your whole family have my constant prayers. | I am with great respect and gratitude for a thousand | favors, | My Lord | Your Lordships most obedient | and most humble Servant | Jonath: Swift

From the North parts | of Ireland | Aug: 28th 1730.

Address: To the most Honorable | the Earle of Oxford in | Dover street | London

Endorsed: R: at Wimpole Sepr 15 · 1730.

4806

Lord Bathurst to Swift

[Cirencester, 9 September 1730]

Dear Sr

You have taken all the precautions wch a prudent man cou'd possibly,[1] to break off an impertinent correspondence, & yet it won't doe. One must be more stupid than a Dutch Burgur Master not to see thro' the design of the last letter[2]—*I show all yr letters to our Irish Wits—One of them is going to write a treatise of English Bulls & Blunders*[3]—and for further security yu add at last *I'm going to take a*

[1] 'take' scrawled out in manuscript.

[2] Bathurst to Swift, 30 June 1730.

[3] Perhaps an allusion to Sheridan's *The Blunderful Blunder of Blunders. Being an answer to the Wonderful Wonder of Wonders* [Dublin, 1721].

Progress God knows where & shall[1] *be back again God knows when.* I have given y^u a reasonable breathing time and now I must att y^u again. I receive so much Pleasure in reading y^r letters that according to the usuall Good nature & justice of Mankind I can dispense with the trouble I give y^u in reading mine. But if y^u grow obstinate & won't answer me I'll plague y^u & Pester y^u & doe all I can to Vex y^u I'll take y^r works to Peices & show y^u that it is all borrow'd or stoln, have not y^u stoln the sweetness of y^r Numbers from Dryden & Waller, have not y^u borrow'd thoughts from Virgil & Horace, at least I am sure I have seen something like them in those Books, & in y^r Prose writings, wch they make such a Noise ab^t, they are only some little improvements upon the Humour y^u have stoln from Miguel de Cervantes & Rabelais. well but the Stile—a great matter indeed for an English man to value himself upon, that he can write English. why I write English too, but 'tis in another stile.

But I won't forget y^r Political tracts y^u may say that y^u have ventur'd y^r Ears at one time & y^r Neck at another for the Good of the Country, why that other People have done in another manner upon less occasions and are not at all Proud of it. you have overturn'd & supported Ministers y^u have sett Kingdoms in a Flame by y^r Pen. Pray w^t is there in that, but having the Nack of hitting the Passions of Mankind, with that alone, & a little knowledge of Ancient & Modern History, & seeing a little further into the inside of things than the Generality of Men, y^u have made this bustle. there is no Wit in any of them, I have read them all over & don't remember any of those pretty flowers those just antitheses, wch one meets with so frequently in the French writers. none of those clever turns upon words nor those apt quotations out of Latin Authors wch the writers of the last Age amongst us abounded in. None of those pretty similes wch some of our Modern Authors adorn their works with that are not only a little like the things they wou'd illustrate but are also like twenty other things. In short as often as I have read any of y^r tracts I have been so tir'd with them that I have never been easy till I got to the End of them. I have found my brain heated my Imagination fir'd just as if I was drunk. a Pretty thing indeed for one of y^r Gown to value Himself upon, that with sitting still an hour in his study he has often made three Kingdoms drunk at once.

I have twenty other points to maul y^u upon if y^u provoke me but

[1] shall] *original manuscript*, shan't *Hawkesworth*, shall not *Ball.* The negative is superfluous.

if y^u^ are civil & Good natur'd & will send me a long, a very long letter in answer to this I will lett y^u^ alone a good while Well Adieu now if I had had a better Pen I can tell y^u^ that I shou'd not have concluded so soon

Cirencester Sepr 9th 1730

Endorsed by Swift: Ld Bathurst—| Sep^t^ 9^d^ 1730

4806

Lady Elizabeth Germain to Swift

London | 19 Sep: 1730

Had I not been retired into the Country yours shoud certainly[1] have been answered long before,[2] as to your Poetess I am her obliged servant and must confess the fact just as you state it, tis very true I was Gaming and upon the dapper youths[3] delivering me a paper, which I just open'd found they were verses so slunk them into my pocket, and there truly they were kept exceeding private for I cannot accuse my self of showing them to a mortal, but let me assure you twas not out of modesty but in great hopes that the Author woud have divulged them, which you know woud have lookt decenter and prityer than trumpeting my own fame but it seems unhappily we were both bitt and judged wrong of each other, however since you desire it you may be very sure she shall not fail of my entreaties to his Grace of Dorset for her, tho you have not yet let me into the Secret of what her request is, so till my Lord Carteret does his part or that I hear from you again it will be but a blind sort of a petition. I have not seen his Grace this great while, and he is now at Windsor, and I choose rather to speak to him upon all accounts having not so fine a talent of writing as that same Lords Lady, And whether just or no, I wont attempt disputing with her Ladyship— but as you are commonly esteemed by those that[4] pretend to know

[1] Hawkesworth, followed by Ball, omits 'certainly'.

[2] Probably Lady Betty had been staying at Drayton, Northamptonshire, one of the most beautiful houses in England, where the room she used as a library is still to be seen. Evidently Swift had appealed to her to use her influence with the Duke of Dorset on behalf of Mrs. Barber.

[3] A dapper youth may have been Mrs. Barber's son, who appears in her verses.

[4] that] who *Hawkesworth*, *Ball*.

you to have a tollerable share of honesty and Brains I do not question your doing what is right by him, nor his paying you all the civility and kindness you can desire, nor will I hope, their influence, ever can make him do otherways tho he has the unfashionable quality of esteeming his old friends, but however partial to them yet not being biased against his own sense and judgment, and the consequence of this I hope will be your coming to England and meeting often with him in Lady Bettys chamber,[1] where the happy Composition[2] shall exert her skill in ordering dinner, and I wont mistake Oyl of Amber for the Spirit of it, but continue as I ever was, Your sincere friend, as well as | faithfull Humble | servant | E. Germain

Address: To | The Revd Mr Dean Swift | at the Deanry of St Patricks | Dublin
Postmark: 19 SE
Endorsed by Swift: Sep^{tr} 9th | L^{dy}] B. Germain | Answd. No^{v}] 10th 1730. *and:* L^{dy}] Elis. Germain. | Sep^{tr} 19th 1730

Forster copy

Swift to Lord Bathurst

[October 1730][3]

My Lord, I had the honor of your letter[4] three days before I returned from the Northern parts of this Kingdom, where I past three months in search of cold weather & exercise; but deferred my Acknowledgments till I returned to town, and am now—from riding three times a week to settle an ill head—resumed my old Cathedral formalityes: Constantly at prayers by nine, and reprimanding my vicars.

[1] Lady Betty appears to be recalling lines in 'The Humble Petition of Frances Harris':

'Lord help me, said *Mary*, I never stirr'd out of this Place!
Nay, said I, I had it in Lady *Betty*'s Chamber, that's a plain Case.'
Poems, i. 70.

[2] Here she calls to mind the early verses 'To Mrs. Biddy Floyd':

'*Jove* mix'd up all, and his best Clay imploy'd;
Then call'd the happy Composition, *Floyd*.'
Poems, i. 118.

[3] A transcript in the Forster Collection (Red Box, F. 44. E. 3) taken from a manuscript among the Croker papers. Undated, but apparently belongs to Oct. 1730.

[4] 9 Sept. 1730.

Your Lordship hath done me an unspeakable injury. I happened to let fall in one of my letters that I showed you to all comers as a boast of my corresponding with you; And yr Lordship in the highest degree of malice hath written to me in such a manner that I cannot communicate the particulars to my nearest friends.

When Sr Wm Temple writ an Essay preferring the Ancient Learning to the Modern,[1] it was said that what he writ showed he was mistaken; because he discovered more learning in that Essay than the ancients could pretend to: But it is none to tell you that I would give the best thing I was ever supposed to publish in exchange to be author of your letters.

I pretend to have been an improver of Irony on the subject of Satyr and praise: but I will surrender up my title to your Lordship. Your injustice extends further. You accuse me of endeavouring to break off all Correspondence with you, & at this same time demonstrate that the accusation is against yourself. You threatened to pester me with letters if I will not write. If I were sure that my silence would force you to one letter in a quarter of a year, I would be wise enough never to write to you as long as I live.

I swear your Lordship is the first person alive that ever made me lean upon my Elbow when I was writing to him, and by Consequence this will be the worst letter I ever writ. I have never been so severely attacked, nor in so tender a point, nor by weapons against which I am so ill able to defend myself, nor by a person from whom I so little deserved so cruel a treatment, and who in his own Conscience is so well convinced of my innocence upon every article. I have endorsed yr name & date, and shall leave it to my Executors to be published at the head of all the libells that have been writ against me, to be printed in five Volumes in folio after my death. And among the rest a very scrub one in verses lately written by myself.

For, having some months ago much & often offended the ruling party, and often worryed by libellers I am at the pains of writing one in their style & manner, & sent it by an unknown hand to a Whig printer who very faithfully published it.[2] I took special care to accuse myself but of one fault of which I am really guilty, and so shall continue as I have done these 16 years till I see cause to reform:[3]—

[1] *Works*, 1720, i. 151–69.

[2] Swift is here referring to *A Panegyric on the Reverend Dean Swift In Answer to the Libel on Dr. Delany, and a certain Great Lord*, written by him Feb.–Mar. 1729–30. See introductory note, *Poems*, ii. 491.

[*For note 3 see opposite.*

but with the rest of the Satyr I chose to abuse myself with the direct reverse of my character or at least in direct opposition to one part of what you are pleased to give me.

I am afraid your Lordship is spending the latter end of a summer par manière d'acquit among you neighbouring squires at Cirencester without My Lady or your olive branches.

What I mentioned in a former letter is true: that a certain Wag, one of my followers, in collecting materials for a tolerable Volume of English Bulls, in revenge of the reproaches you throw on us upon this article. The Author is a great reader of jest books, and in those of poor Robin he hath met with several passages of Mr Abdy, the famous bull-maker of his time.[1] All these are to be gathered, others invented, and many transplanted from here to England. All the Bulls fathered upon names at length, with their places of abode. Your Lordship as an old offender against me shall have half a dozen blunders charged upon your groom & coachman (no matter which). And there must be a long Introduction proving the native Irish rabble to have a better tact for Wit than the English, for which philosophical causes shall be assigned and many instances produced.

I will tell you further that I have another operator: A smart ingenious young fellow: who is employed to collect all the clever things written in verse & prose for four or five years past, such as libels on the publick, complaints of oppression, and the like, under the title of the Dublin Miscellany: and I will put down yr Lordship among a dozen or two more of my friends on your side for subscribers merely to shame you, though we get not one of your Crowns. I mean Mr Pope, Gay, the Doctr, Lords Oxford, Bolingbroke, Dartmouth, Orrery, Mr Pulteney, &c And how will you help your selves? And if you advertize we will re advertize, and reply & rejoyn to the world's end. And a little young poetical parson, who has a

[1] Ball suggests that the reference is to *Poor Robin's Jests or the Compleat Jester*, which was compiled by William Winstanley, 1628?–98. This work was frequently reprinted; but there is no association with the name Abdy. For Winstanley see further *D.N.B.*

---

[3] In *A Panegyric*, ll. 77–79, Swift declares himself deficient in wit:

'You never had commenc'd a *Dean*,
Unless you other Ways had trod
Than those of *Wit*, or Trust in God.'

littler young poetical wife, shall have the whole profit. And take notice that the word littler is no blunder.[1]

And the young parson aforesaid very lately printed his own works, all in verse and some not unpleasant: in one or two of which I have the honor to be celebrated which cost me a guinea and two bottles of wine.[2]

Thus we continue to keep up our spirits in the most miserable country upon Earth, where a man of 1500^{ll} a year cannot command as many shillings, Except he be a Bishop, a Soldier, a Commissioner of the Revenue, or a Vicar choral in my Cathedral who touches more ready money than his Dean. So that if any Kingdom was ever in a right Situation of breeding poets, it is this; whither you & your crew unpardonably sent me 16 years ago, and where I have been ever since, studying as well as preaching revenge, Malice, Envy, and hatred, and all uncharitableness.—And I desire by grace, Lady Bathurst may not be angry, for I do assure her upon the word of a Dean that it is all the pure uncorrupt fruit of a true publick spirit. —I reckon the Season is driving you up to St. James's Square, where this letter will find you, where Mr Pope will tell you that there is an Irish poetess now in London, solliciting the D of Dorset for an Employment though she be but a woollen draper's wife,[3] and that we have another the wife of a bookseller who has lately published a fine edition of Tacitus with a Latin dedication to Ld Carteret.[4] These two will much enrich our Miscellany I nunc et verbis virtutem illuda superbis.[5] I will not this time employ your Lordship as a postman but as a salutigerulus—(read Plautus) to present my humble services to Lord Bol— Mr Pulteney, Lord Masham, the D^{r} &c. I will answer Mr Pope's last letter very soon. My most humble service to my Lady Bathurst, & all my best prayers & wishes for you & your whole family.—I am ever with the truest respect

Your most obed^{t} S^{t}

[1] This is Swift's first mention of the Rev. Matthew Pilkington, the poor and diminutive Irish parson, who in 1729 had married the notorious Laetitia to whose *Memoirs* we owe side-lights on the Dean's later years. Swift took them into his favour and induced John Barber to appoint Pilkington his chaplain during his term of office as Lord Mayor of London, 1732–3. Later Swift grew ashamed of the pair, and even went so far as to erase Pilkington's name from old letters in which mention was made of him.

[2] A Dublin edition of Pilkington's *Poems on Several Occasions* appeared in 1730. This volume was reprinted in London 1731.

[3] Mrs. Barber. [4] Mrs. Grierson. [5] Virg. *Aen.* ix. 634.

4806, ff. 7–9

John Arbuthnot to Swift

[5 November 1730.]

Dear Sir[1]

The passage in Mr popes Letter[2] about your health dos not alarm me, both of us have had this distemper these 30 years. I have found that Steel the warm Gumms & the Bark all do good in it. therefor first take the Vomit A, then every day the quantity of a Nutmeg in a Morning of the Electuary markd B with five spoonfuls of the Tinctur marked D. take the Tinctur; but not the Elect in the afternoon yow may take one of the pills marked C at any time when yow are troubld with it or 30 of the drops markd E in any vehicle evn water. I had a servant of my owne that was cur'd merely with vomiting. Ther is another medicine not mentiond which you may trye the pull Rad [Val] sylvestris[3] about a scruple of it twice a day. how came yow to take it in your head that I was Queens physician, when I am so you shall be a bishop, or any thing yow have a mind to. pope is now the great Reigning poetical Favourite. your Lord Lieutenant[4] has a mind to be well with you. Lady Betty Germain complains yow have not wrote to her, since she wrote to you[5] I have showd as much civility to Mrs Barber as I could, & she likewise to me. My family especially Nanny, gives yow her service. I have no more paper, but what serves to tell yow, that I am, with great sincerity | Your most faithfull humble | servant | Jo: Arbuthnott.

I recommended Dr Helsham to be physician to the Lord Lieutenant I know not what effect it will have. My respects to him and Dr DeLany.

Address: To | The Reverend the | Dean of St Patricks | Dublin
Postmark: 5 NO
Endorsed by Swift: Dr Arbuthnott | Rx Novr 13 · 1730
and: Dr Arbuthnott | with Receits | Nov^r^—1730

[1] Tipped in between leaves 7 and 9 is a slip of paper endorsed by Swift—'Dr Arbuthnots | Receit for Bitters'. On the same side in another hand—'Green stage Court at the Green | Dragon Bishop Gate Street | a Quarter after four'. On the verso of the slip is a receipt for the bitters.

[2] A letter lost or suppressed.

[3] Pulvis radicis valerianae sylvestris.

[4] Duke of Dorset.

[5] Swift's endorsement to Lady Betty Germain's letter of 19 Sept. shows that he replied on 10 Nov.

Enclosure:

A

℞ pulv. rad. ipecacuanhæ ℈s.

B

℞ conserv. flavedin. aurant., absynth. Rom. ana ʒvj. rubigin. Martis in pulverem redact. ʒiij. syrup ☿ succi kermes, q. s.

C

℞ as. fœtid. ʒii. tinctur. castor q. s. m. fiant pilulae xxiv.

D

℞ cortic. Peruviani, elect. rubigin. Martis ana ʒj. digere tepide in vini alb. Gallic. ℔ij per 24 horas: postea fiat colatura.

E

℞ sp. cor. cerv., sp. lavandul., tinctur. castor. ana ʒij. misce.

Take of zedory Root one drachm Galangal
Roman wormwood of each two drachms Orange peel a drachm
Lesser Cardamon seeds two scruples
Infuse all in a Quart of Boyling Spring water for six hours. Strain it off & add to it four ounces of Greater Compound Wormwood water

4806

Gay and the Duchess of Queensberry to Swift

[8 November 1730]

So you are determin'd never to write me again,[1] but for all that you shall not make me hold my tongue, you shall hear from me (the Post office willing) whether you will or no. I see none of the Folks you corespond with, so that I am forc'd to pick up intelligence concerning you as I can, which hath been so very little that I am resolv'd to make my complaints to you as a friend who I know love to relieve the distress'd; and in the circumstances I am in, where should I apply but to my best friend? Mr Pope indeed, upon my frequent enquirys hath told me that the Letters that are directed to him concern me as much as himself, but what you say of yourself, or of me, or to me I know nothing at all. Lord Carteret was here yesterday in his return from the Isle of Wight[2] where he had been a shooting; & left 7 pheasants with us. He went this morning to the Bath to

[1] Swift had apparently not written since 19 Mar. 1729–30. This is the first of a series of joint letters from Gay and the Duchess addressed to Swift.

[2] On Appuldercombe, the property of Sir Robert Worsley, father of his first wife.

Lady Carteret who is perfectly recover'd. He talk'd of you for three hours last night, & told me that you talk of me; I mean that you are prodigiously in his favour, as he says, & I believe that I am in yours; for I know you to be a just & equitable person, and tis but my due. He seem'd to take to me; which I take to proceed from your recommendation; though there is another reason for it, for he is now out of Employment, and my friends have generally been of that sort; for I take them as being naturally inclin'd to those who can do no mischief. Pray, do you come to England this year, he thinks you do, I wish you would, & so does the Dutchess of Queensberry. What would you have more to induce you? Your Money crys come spend me; and your friends cry come see me. I have been treated barbarously by you; if you knew how often I talk of you, how often I think of you, you would now & then direct a Letter to me, & I would allow Mr Pope to have his share in it, in short I dont care to keep any Man's money that serves me so; Love or money I must have, & if you will not let me have the comfort of the one, I think I must endeavour to get a little comfort by spending some of the other. I must beg that you would call at Amesbury in your way to London, for I have many things to say to you, & I can assure you, you will be welcome to a three prong'd fork.[1] I remember your prescription, & I do ride upon the Downs, and at present I have no Asthma; I have kill'd five brace of Partridges, & four Brace & a half of Quails, & I do not Envy either Sir Robert, or Stephen Duck, who is the favorite Poet of the Court.[2] I hear sometimes from Mr Pope, & from scarce any body else; Were I to live here never so long I believe I should never think of London, but I cannot help thinking of you. Were you here, I could talk to you, but I would not, for you shall have all your share of talk which was never allow'd you at Twickenham. You know this was a grievance you often complain'd of, & so in revenge you make me write all, & answer nothing. I beg you my compliments to Dr Delany. I am Dear Sir, | Yours most Affectionately. | JG.

Amesbury near Salisbury in Wiltshire.
Novr. 8. 1730

[1] In his letter to Gay of 19 Mar. 1729–30 Swift had complained of the difficulty of eating with a two-pronged fork.

[2] Stephen Duck, a Wiltshire agricultural labourer, took to writing verses which were brought to the notice of the Queen, who gave him a little house in Richmond Park. His *Poems on Several Subjects*, 1730, ran through many editions. See 'On Stephen Duck', *Poems*, ii. 520.

I ended the Letter as above to go to the Dutchess, & she told me I might go down & come a quarter of an hour hence; I had a design to have asked her to have sign'd the invitation that I have made you as I dont know how much she may have to say to you, I think it will be prudent to leave off that she may not be stinted for want of room. So much I will say, that whether she signs it or no, both the Duke & Dutchess would be very glad you would come to Amesbury; & you must be persuaded that I say this without the least private view; for what is it to me whether you come or no? for I can write to you, you know.

I would fain have you come, I cannot say you'll be welcome—for I don't know you, & perhaps I shall not like you, but if I do not—(unless you are a very vain person) you shall know my thoughts as soon as I do my self.— | C Q

Endorsed by Swift: Mr Gay, and the Dutchess | of Queensberry | Novr 8th 1730

Longleat xiii (Harleian transcript)

Swift to John Gay

Dublin Nov. 10. 1730.[1]

When my Lord Peterborow in the Queen's time went abroad upon his Ambassyes, the Ministry told me, that he was such a vagrant, they were forced to write at him by guess, because they knew not where to write *to* him.[2] This is my case with you, sometimes, in Scotland, sometimes at Ham walks, sometimes God knows where. You are a man of business, and not at leisure for insignificant correspondence. It was I got you the Employment of being my Lord Duke's premier Ministre; for his Grace having heard how good a manager you were of my ⌜Bathurst⌝ revenue, thought you fit to be intrusted with ten talents. I have had twenty times a strong inclination to spend a Summer near Salisbury downs, having rode over them

[1] This letter was published by Pope in 1741. It is here printed from the Harleian (Longleat) transcript, xiii. Half-brackets indicate omissions from all the printed texts of 1740–2.

[2] See 'To the Earl of Peterborow', *Poems*, ii. 396–8:

'A Messenger comes all a-reek,
Mordanto at *Madrid* to seek:
He left the Town above a Week.'

more than once, & with a young son of Salisbury reckoned twice the stones at Stonehenge, which are either 92 or 93: ⌜I thank you for offering me the neighbourhood of another Hoadly; I have enough of one; he lives within 20 yards of me, our gardens joyn,[1] but I never see him except upon business.⌝ I desire to present my most humble acknowledgements to my Lady Dutchess in return of her civility. I hear an ill thing, that she is matre pulchra filia pulchrior.[2] I never saw her since she was a girl, and would be angry she should excell her Mother, who was long my principall Goddess. I desire you will tell her Grace, that the ill management of forks is not to be helpt when they are only bidential, which happens in all poor houses, especially those of Poets, upon which account, a knife was obsolutly necessary at Mr Pope's, where it was morally impossible with a bidential fork to convey a morsel of beef with the incumberance of mustard & turnips into your mouth at once. And her Grace hath cost me 30 pounds to provide tridents for fear of offending her, which Sum I desire she will please to return me.[3]—I am sick enough to go to the Bath, but have not heard, it will be good for my disorder [You remember me giddy sometimes, & very violently; I am now constantly so, but not to so high a degree. I ride often every week, & walk much; but am not better. I thank God the pain is not great, nor does it spoyl my sleep. But I grow listless, & good for nothing.⌝ I have a strong mind to spend my 200ll next Summer in France. I am glad I have it, for there is hardly twice that Summ left in this Kingdom. ⌜I have left of writing, but not wine though I have lost six hogsheads that grew muddy in the bottles, and I have not one family upon whom I can spunge.—⌝ You want no settlement, I call the family where you live, & the foot you are upon, a Settlement, till you increase your fortune to what will support you with ease & plenty, a good horse & a garden; The want of this I much dread in you. For I have often known a she cousen of a good family & small fortune passing months among all her relations, living in plenty, & taking her circles, till she grew an old maid, & every body weary of her. Mr Pope complains of seldom seeing you, but the evil is unavoidable, for different circumstances of life have always separated those whom friendship would joyn, God hath taken care—of that to

[1] A road now divides St. Sepulchre's Palace from the garden of the Deanery

[2] Horace, *Odes*, I. xvi. I.

[3] Swift exaggerates his domestic penury. He was well furnished with silver plate, as Lyon (Forster Collection, no. 579) assures us.

prevent any progress towards real happyness here, which would make life more desirable & death too dreadfull. I hope you have now one advantage, that you allways wanted before, and the want of which made your friend as uneasy as it did yourself. I mean that sollicitude about your own affairs which perpetually filled your thoughts & disturbed your conversation; For if it be true what Mr Pope seriously tells me, ⌜that you are principal manager of the Duke's affairs,⌝ you will have opportunity of saving every groat of the interest you receive, and so, by the time he and you grow weary of each other, you will be able to pass the rest of your wine less life in ease & plenty, ⌜with as good a house & gardens as Mr Pope, and⌝ with the additional triumphial comfort of never having received a penny from a tasteless ungratefull court, from which you deserved so much, and which deserves no better Genius's than those by whom it is celebrated,—so let the Post rascal open this letter, and let Walpole read it.—Mr Ford is with us upon the death of his Mother,[1] who has left him money enough to supply the nole wancyes[2] of rents for 2 years in London. He tells me, that he herd I was out of favour with the—The loss is not great. I made a present, or rather it was begged from me, of about 35ll. The trifle promised me, worth about 15ll was never remembered, & after I had made my present shame would not suffer me to mind them of theirs. If you see Mr Cesar[3] present my humble service to him, & let him know that the Scrubb libel printed against me here, & reprinted in London, for which he shew'd a kind concern to a friend of us both, was written by my self, and sent to a whig printer. It was in the style & Genius of such scoundrels, when the humor of libelling ran in this town, against a friend of mine whom you know.—But my paper is ended. ⌜My most humble service to Lord Peterborow, Bolin.—Masham, Bathurst, Lord Oxford, Mr Pulteney, the Doctor Mr Lewis, Mr Pope, &c.—Ever Yours.⌝

⌜ Lord Burlington never remembers the request made him in a

[1] Edward Ford, father of Charles, married in 1676 Letitia, widow of Phineas Preston of Ardsallagh (*Letters of Swift to Ford*, p. x).

[2] The legal phrase is inserted in Lord Oxford's hand. Elwin and Ball print in its place 'not receiving', which is not what is written in the Harleian transcript. See Sherburn, iii. 149, n 2.

[3] Swift had known Charles Caesar since the days of Queen Anne. He was M.P. for Hertford and took the place of Robert Walpole as Treasurer of the Navy, June 1711. He died in broken circumstances in 1741, and his executors sold the family estate of Benington in Hertfordshire for the payment of his debts. For an account of the family see Clutterbuck's *County of Hertford*, ii. 282–5.

Solemn manner about his ancester's tomb: however he owed in civility an answer to a letter from so considerable a body. he that would not sacrifice twenty acres out of two hundred thousand to the honor of his family may live to see them not return him two hundred thousand pence, towards which I believe he feels enough already.⌝

Deane Swift 1765

Swift to the Earl of Chesterfield

November 10th, 1730.

My Lord,[1]

I was positively advised by a friend,[2] whose opinion hath much weight with me, and who hath a great veneration for your Lordship, to venture a letter of solicitation: And it is the first request of this kind I ever made since the public changes, in times, persons, measures, and opinons, drove me into distance and obscurity.

There is an honest man whose name is Launcelot; he hath been long a servant to my Lord Sussex: He married a relation of mine, a widow, with a tolerable jointure; which, depending upon a lease which the Duke of Grafton suffered to expire about three years ago, sunk half her little fortune. Mr. Launcelot had many promises from the Duke of Dorset, while his Grace held that office which is now in your Lordship, but they all failed, after the usual fate that the bulk of court-suiters must expect.

I am very sensible that I have no manner of claim to the least favour from your Lordship, whom I have hardly the honour to be known to, although you were always pleased to treat me with much humanity, and with more distinction than I could pretend to deserve. I am likewise conscious of that demerit which I have largely shared with all those who concerned themselves in a court and ministry, whose maxims and proceedings have been ever since so much exploded. But your Lordship will grant me leave to say, that, in those times, when any persons of the ejected party came to court, and were

[1] In 1728 Chesterfield had been appointed to the English embassy at The Hague. On May 1730 he was elected a Knight of the Garter, and the next day received the staff of Lord Steward of the Household in the place of the Duke of Dorset. His duties were mainly honorary and he returned to The Hague.

[2] i.e. Pope.

of tolerable consequence, they never failed to succeed in any reasonable request they made for a friend. And, when I sometimes added my poor solicitations, I used to quote to the then ministers a passage in the Gospel, *The poor* (meaning their own dependents) *you have always with you*, &c.

This is the strongest argument I have to entreat your Lordship's favour for Mr. Launcelot, who is a perfect honest man, and as loyal as you could wish. His wife, my near relation, hath been my favourite from her youth, and as deserving as it is possible for one of her level. It is understood, that some little employment about the Court may be often in your Lordship's disposal; and that my Lord Sussex will give Mr. Launcelot the character he deserves: And then let my petition be (to speak in my own trade) a drop in the bucket.

Remember, my Lord, that, although this letter be long, yet what particularly concerns my request is but a few lines.

I shall not congratulate your Lordship upon any of your present great employments, or upon the greatest that can possibly be given to you; because you are one of those very few who do more honour to a Court, than you can possibly receive from it: Which I take to be a greater compliment to any Court than it is to your Lordship. I am, | My Lord, *&c.*

Longleat xiii (Harleian transcript)

Swift to John Gay and the Duchess of Queensberry

Dublin novr 19th 1730.

I writ you a long Letter about a fortnight past[1] concluding you were in London, from whence I understood one of your former was dated; nor did I imagine you were gone back to Aimsbury so late in the year, at which Season I take the Country to be onely a Scene for those who have been ill used by a Court on account of their Virtues; which is a State of Happyness the more valuable, because it is not accompanyed by Envy; although nothing deserves it more. I would gladly sell a Dukedom to lose favour in the Manner their Graces have done. I believe, my Lord Carteret, since he is no longer Lieutenant, may not wish me ill, and I have told him often, that I hated him onely as Lieutenant. I confess he had a genteeler manner of binding the Chains of this Kingdom, than most of his Predecessors;

[1] 10 Nov.

and I confess at the same time that he had six times a regard to my recommendation, by preferring so many of my Friends in the Church, and the two last Acts of his Power was to add to the Dignityes of Dr Delany and Mr Stopfort,[1] the last of whom was by you and Mr Pope put into Mr Pulteney's hands. I told you in my last that a continuance of giddyness, tho' not in a violent degree prevented my thoughts of England at Present. For in my Case a domestick Life is necessary, where I can with the Centurian say to my Servant go and he goeth, and do this and he doth it. I now hate all people whom I cannot command, and consequently a Dutchess is at this time the hatefullest Lady in the World to me, one onely excepted,[2] and I beg her Grace's Pardon for that exception, for in the Way I mean her Grace is ten thousand times more hatefull. I confess I begin to apprehend you will squander my money, because I hope you never less wanted it, and if you go on with Success for two years longer, I fear I shall not have a farthing of it left. The Doctor hath ill informed me, who says that Mr Pope is at present the cheif poeticall favorite, yet Mr Pope himself talks like a Philosopher and one wholly retired. But the vogue of our few honest folks here is that Duck is absolutely to Succeed Eusden in the Lawrell,[3] the contention being between Concannan or Theobald, or some other Hero of the Dunciad. I never charged you for not talking, but the Dubious State of your Affairs in those Days was too much the Subject; and I wish the Dutchess had been the Voucher of your Amendment.

Nothing so much contributed to my ease as the turn of Affairs after the Queen's Death, by which all my hopes being cut off, I could have no Ambition left, unless I would have been a greater Rascal than happened to Suit with my Temper. I therefore sat down quietly at my morsel, adding onely thereto a principle of hatred to all Succeeding Measures and Ministryes, by way of Sauce to relish my meat; and I confess one point of Conduct in My Lady Dutchess's Life hath added much poignance to it. There is a good Irish practical Bull towards the end of your Letter, where you Spend a dozen lines in telling me you must leave off, that you may give my Lady Dutchess room to write, and so you proceed to within three Lines of the bottom, tho' I would have remitted you my 200ll to have left place for as many more.

[1] On 8 June Delany became Chancellor of St. Patrick's Cathedral; and about the same time Stopford was appointed Provost of Tuam.

[2] The exception was the Queen.

[3] Eusden had died on 27 Sept.

To the Dutchess

Madam,—My beginning thus low[1] is meant as a Mark of respect, like receiving your Grace at the bottom of the Stairs. I am glad you know you Duty; for it hath been a known and established rule above twenty years in England that the first advances have been constantly made me by all Ladyes who aspired to My Acquaintance, and the greater their Quality the greater were their advances. Yet, I know not by what Weakness, I have condescended gratiously to dispense with you upon this important Article. Tho' Mr Gay will tell you, that a Nameless person[2] sent me eleven Messages before I would yield to a Visit. I mean a Person to whom he is infinitely obliged for being the Occasion of the happyness he now enjoys under the Protection and favor of my Lord Duke and your Grace. At the same time I cannot forbear telling you, Madam, that you are a little imperio[us] in your Manner of making your advances. You say; perhaps, you shall not like me; I affirm you are mistaken, which I can plainly demonstrate; for I have certain Intelligence, that another Person dislikes me of late, with whose likings yours have not for some time past gone together. However, if I shall once have the Honor to attend your Grace, I will out of fear and Prudence appear as vain as I can that I may not know your thoughts of me. This is your own direction; but it was needless, for Diogenes himself would be vain to have received the Honor of being one Moment of his Life in the thoughts of your Grace.

I am with the greatest | Respect Your Grace's &c.

B.M. Add. MS. 22625

Swift to Mrs. Howard

[Dublin, 21 November 1730]

Madam.

I do not now pity the leisure you have to read a letter from me;[3] and this letter shall be a history . . First therefore, I call you to wit-

[1] In imitation doubtless of the original letter the transcript here printed leaves a wide vacant space between the end of Gay's letter and the bottom of the page where, four lines from the bottom, begins the portion addressed 'To the Duchess'. Deference to rank is thus indicated.—Sherburn.

[2] The Queen.

[3] In his letter to Pope of 26 Feb. 1729–30 Swift refers to Mrs. Howard as

ness that I did not attend on the Queen till I had received her own repeated messages, which of course occasioned my being introduced to you. I never asked any thing till, upon leaving England the first time, I desired from you a present worth a Guinea, and from her Majesty, one worth ten pounds, by way of a memorial. Yours I received;[1] and the Queen, upon my taking my leave of her, made an excuse, that she had intended a medal for me, which not being ready, she would send it to me the Christmas following . . Yet this was never done, nor at all remembered when I went back to England the next year, and by her commands attended her as I had done before . . I must now tell you Madam, that I will receive no medal from Her Majesty, nor any thing less than her picture at half length, drawn by Jervas; and if he takes it from another original; the Queen shall sit at least twice for him to touch it up. I desire you will let Her Majesty know this in plain words, although I have not heard that I am under her displeasure . . But this is a usual thing with Princes, as well as Ministers, upon every false representation and so I took occasion to tell the Queen, upon the quarrel Mr Walpole had with our friend Gay, the first time I ever had the honour to attend her.

Against you I have but one reproach, that when I was last in England, and just after the present Kings accession, I resolved to pass that Summer in France, for which I had then a most lucky opportunity, from which those who seemed to love me well dissuaded me by your advice;[2] and when I sent you a note conjuring you to lay aside the character of a Courtier and a favourite upon that occasion, your answer positively directed me not to go in that juncture; and you said the same thing to my friends who seemed to have power of giving me hints that I might reasonably hope for a Settlement in England; which God knows was no very great ambition, considering the station I should leave here, of greater dignity, and which might have easily been managed to be disposed of as

'our half-discarded friend', a supposition he drew from statements 'in some of the prints'. Rumours had been current as early as 1728 that Mrs. Howard's position at Court was becoming difficult and that she was proposing retirement. In actual fact her ostensible position had undergone no change, and Swift's assumption of her new-found 'leisure' must have been embarrassing.

[1] The ring mentioned in Swift's letter to Mrs. Howard of Oct. 1726.

[2] During his visit to England of 1727 Swift had contemplated crossing to France, but upon the death of George I he was advised against this project. See Bolingbroke to Swift, 17 June 1727.

the Crown pleased. If these hints came from you, I affirm, you then acted too much like a Courtier. But I forgive you, and esteem you as much as ever . . You had your reasons, which I shall not inquire into; because I always believed you had some virtues, besides all the accomplishment of mind and person, that can adorn a Lady. I am angry with the Queen for sacrificing my friend Gay to the mistaken piques of Sr R. Walpole, about a libel writ against him, although he were convinced at the same time of Mr Gay's innocence; and although, as I said before, I told Her Majesty the whole story. Mr Gay deserved better treatment among you, upon all accounts, and particularly for his excellent unregarded Fables, dedicated to Prince William, which I hope His Royal Highness will often read for his instruction. I wish Her Majesty would a little remember what I largely said to her about Ireland, when before a witness she gave me leave and commanded me to tell here what she spoke to me upon that subject, and ordered me, if I lived to see her in her present Station, to send her our Grievances, promising to read my letter, and do all good offices in her power for this miserable and most loyall Kingdom, now at the brink of ruin, and never so near as now. As to my self, I repeat again, that I never asked anything more than a trifle, as a memorial of some distinction which Her Majesty graciously seemed to make between me and every common Clergyman. But that trifle was forgot according to the usual method of Princes, although I was taught to think myself upon a foot of pretending to some little exception.

As to your self, Madam, I most heartily congratulate with you for being delivered from the toyl, the envy, the slavery, and vexation of a favorite, where you could not always answer the good intentions that I hope you had. You will now be less teased with sollicitations, one of the greatest evils in life; You possess an easy employment: with quiet of mind, although it be by no means equal to your merit, and if it shall please God to establish your health, I believe and hope you are too wise to hope for more. Mr Pope hath always been an advocate for your sincerity, and even I in the character I gave you of your self, allowed you as much of that Virtue as could be expected in a Lady, a Courtier and a Favorite. Yet I confess, I never heartily pledged your health as a Toast upon any other regards than Beauty, wit, good sense and an unblemished character. For, as to Friendship, Truth, Sincerity, and other trifles of that kind, I never concerned my self about them, because I knew them to be only parts of the lower morals, which are altogether useless at Courts. I am content that you should tell the Queen all I have said of her, and in my own words, if you please. I could have been a better Prophet in the character I gave you of your self, if it had been good manners, in the Height of your credit to put you in mind of its mortality. For you are not the first by at least three Ladyes[1] whom I have known to undergo the same turn of Fortune. It is allowed that Ladyes are often very good Scaffoldings, and I need not tell you the use that Scaffoldings are put to by all Builders, as well politicall as mechanick. I should have begun this letter by telling you, that I was encouraged to write by my best friend,[2] and one of your great admirers, who told me, that, from something which had passed between you, he thought you would not receive it ill . . After all, I know no person of your Sex, for whom I have so great an esteem, as I do and believe I shall always continue to bear for you; I mean a private Person, for I must except the Queen, and it is not an exception of form, because I have really a very great veneration for her great Qualityes, although I have reason to complain of her conduct to me, which I could not excuse although she had fifty kingdoms to govern . . I have but room to conclude with my sincere professions of being, with true respect | Madam | Your most obedient humble ser^t | JS.

Dublin. Novr 21st 1730.

If you were a Lord or Commoner I would have sent you this in an Envelope.[3]

T. Cottrell-Dormer, Rousham

Swift to Mrs. Caesar

[Dublin, 3 December 1730]

Madam

A Gentleman of your name who lived about eighteen hundred years ago, got severall victoryes by making round marches of great

[1] Croker, *Letters of Henrietta, Countess of Suffolk*, i. 402, suggests that these three were possibly Lady Orkney, King William's favourite, the Duchess of Marlborough, and Lady Masham.

[2] Doubtless Pope.

[3] The letter covered three pages. This last sentence was the only one written on page 4. Ultimately the letter, for safety, was enclosed in an envelope.

circumference, and coming suddenly upon his enemy when he was least expected; thus you have dealt with me; for in your march round by Mrs Barber, you have got the victory, and forced me to own my self overcome . . That Gentlewoman, in a letter she lately writ to a very worthy friend[1] of hers and mine, hath much enlarged upon the very favorable reception you are pleased to give her; and at the same time hath placed it all to my account; wherein she seems to have acted more like a Courtier than is consistent with her many virtues; but,[2] very unskilfully, by leaving me who understand the trade better, an opportunity of betraying her: For you see plainly that by this proceeding she takes half the merit from you and gives it to me, which in conscience I cannot accept,[3] and I think you ought to resent . . However, if notwithstanding this mistake in conduct, you still think she deserves your good grace, I am forced to confess, that you cannot place them better, nor confer a greater obligation upon me, to which I could add the esteem of every person in this wretched kingdom, whose esteem is of any value;

I desire to present my most humble Service to Mr Caesar, and pray God bless your fire side. They are now all grown out of my knowledge. I wish I had an account of them.

I am with true respect | Madam | Your most obedient and | obliged Servant | Jonath Swift.

Dublin | Decbr. 3ᵈ 1730.

Address: To | Mrs Caesar

4806

The Earl of Chesterfield to Swift

Hague Decem: 15ᵗʰ NS. [o.s. 4] 1730

Sʳ

You need not have made any excuses to me for your Sollicitation, on the contrary, I am proud of being the first person, to whom you have thought it worth your while to apply, since those changes, which you say, drove you into distance and obscurity.[4] I very well

[1] Possibly Delany. See Swift to Pope, 20 July 1731.

[2] Four words scrawled out after 'but'.

[3] 'I' and 'accept' written above the line.

[4] Chesterfield is quoting from Swift's letter to him of 10 Nov.

know the person you recommend to me, having lodg'd at his house a whole summer at Richmond. I have always hear'd a very good character of him, which alone would incline me to serve him, but your recommendation I can assure you, will make me impatient to do it. However that he may not again meet with the common fate of Court suitors, nor I lye under the imputation of making court promises, I will exactly explain to you how farr it is likely that I may be able to serve him. When first I had this Office I took the resolution of Turning out no body, so that I shall only have the disposal of those places, that the death of the present possessors will procure me; Some old servants that have serv'd me long and faithfully, have obtain'd the promises of the first four or five vacancys; and the early sollicitations of some of my particular friends have tie'd me down for about as many more; But after having satisfied those engagements, I do assure you Mr Lancelot shall be my first care. I confess his prospect is more remote than I could have wish'd it, but as it is so remote, he won't have the Uneasyness of a disappointment, if he getts nothing, and if he getts something we shall both be pleas'd.

As for his Politicall Principles, I am in no manner of pain about them, were he a Tory, I would venture to serve him, in the Just expectation that, should I ever be charg'd with having preferred a Tory, the Person who was the Author of my Crime, would likewise be the Author of my Vindication. | I am, with reall esteem | Sr | Your most obedient | humble servant | Chesterfield,

4806

John Gay and the Duchess of Queensberry to Swift

Amesbury, 6 December 1730

Dear Sir.

Both your Letters to my great satisfaction I have receiv'd;[1] you were mistaken as to my being in town for I have been here ever since the beginning of May; but the best way is to direct my Letters always to the Duke's house in London; and they are sent hither by his Porter. We shall stay here till after the Holidays; you say we deserve Envy, I think we do, for I envy no man either in town or out of it; We have had some few Visitors and every one of 'em such that one

[1] 10 and 19 Nov.

would desire to visit; the Dutchess is a more severe check upon my finances than even you were and I submit, as I did to you, to comply to my own good; I was a long time before I could prevail with her to let me allow myself a pair of shoes with two heels, for I had lost one, and the shoes were so decayd that they were not worth mending; you see by this that those who are the most generous of their own can be the most covetous for others; I hope you will be so good to me as to use your interest with her, (for whatever she says, you seem to have some) to indulge me with the extravagance suitable to my fortune. The Lady you mention that dislikes you hath no discernment.[1] I really think you may safely venture to Amisbury, though indeed the Lady here likes to have her own way as well as you which may sometimes occasion disputes, and I tell you beforehand that I cannot take your part, I think her so often in the right, that you will have great difficulty to persuade me She is in the wrong; then there is another thing I ought to tell you to deterr you from this place, which is, that the Lady of the house is not given to show civility to those she does not like; she speaks her mind, and loves truth; for the uncommonness of the thing I fancy your curiosity will prevail over your fear & you will like to see such a Woman. but I say no more, till I know whether her Grace will fill up the rest of the Paper.

[*The Duchess*]

write I must, particularly now as I have an opportunity to indulge my predominant passion contradiction, I do in the first place contradict most things Mr Gay says of me—to deterr you from coming here which if you ever do I hereby assure you that unless I like my own way better you shall have y^rs^, & in all disputes you shall convince me if you can. but by what I see of you this is not a misfortune that will allways happen for I find you are a great Mistaker, for example you take prudence for imperiousness tis from [this] first that I determind not to like one who is too gid[dy h][2]eaded for me to be certain whether or no I shall ever be acquainted with [him], I have often known people take great delight in Building Castles in the Air—but I should chuse to Build friends upon a more Solide foundation. I would fain know you—for I often hear more good likeable things than tis possible any one can deserve. pray come that I may find out something wrong, for I, and I believe most women have an inconceivable pleasure to find out any faults—except their own—Mr Cibber is

[1] The Queen. [2] Hole in the paper.

made Poet Laureat.[1] I am S^r as much y^r Hum^ble Servant as I can be to any person I dont know | CQ

Mr Gay is very peevish that I spell & write ill but I dont care for the pen nor I can do no better besides I think you have flatterd me & such people ought to be put to trouble.

[*Gay*]

Now I hope you are pleas'd; and that you will allow for so small a summ as 200^l you have a bumping penniworth.[2]

Amesbury · Dec^br 6 · 1730.

Address: For | The Reverend Dr Swift | Dean of St Patrick's in | Dublin | Ireland | by way of London.
Postmark: 7 DE
Endorsed by Swift: Dec^br 14th 1730 · Mr Gay— | and D^s of Q—y
and: Mr Gay, and | D—S of Q—y Dec^br 6th 1730 | Answered

4806

Lady Elizabeth Germain to Swift

[24 Dec: 1730]

Since you with a modest assurance affirm you understand and practice Good manners better than any other person in either Kingdome, I wish you woud therefore put into very handsome terms my excuse to Dean Swift, that I have not answerd his letter I received before the last,[3] for even Prebend Head asured my Brother Harry[4] that he in all form and justice, took place of a Collonel as being a Major General in the Church, and therefore you need not have called a Councill to know whether you or I were to write last because as being but a Poor Curtezy Lady[5] [I] can pretend to no place but

[1] To succeed Eusden.

[2] In his letter to Gay and the Duchess of 19 Nov. Swift said that he would have given £200 for three lines more from the Duchess in their last letter.

[3] This implies that Swift had written twice to Lady Betty since receiving her letter of 19 Sept.

[4] Henry Head, a canon of Bristol, had previously been Lord Berkeley's vicar in Gloucestershire. The Hon. Henry Berkeley, son of the second Earl and Lady Betty's eldest brother, was a colonel of the Horse Guards. He had served at Blenheim and elsewhere under Marlborough.

[5] The reference is to her title as an Earl's daughter.

what other Peoples Goodness gives me—this being settled, I certainly ought not to have writ again, but however I fear I shou'd have been wrong enough to have desired the correspondence to be kept up but that I have been ill this fortnight, and of course lazy and not in a writing Mood, first as to Mrs. Barber, as I told you before so I tell you the same again that upon your recommendation, I shall be very glad to serve her, tho I never did see her, and as I had not your letter till I went from Tunbridge, she passed unmarkt by me in the croud, nor have I mett with her since,[1] She writ to me to present [Pilkington's][2] Poems to the Duke and Dutchess of Dorset. I answered her letter, and obey'd her commands—and as to her own I shall most willingly subscribe, tho I am of the opinion we ladies are not apt to be good Poets especially if we cant spell; but thats by way of inviolable secret between you and I, so much for this letter,[3] now to your last Epistle for which it seems I am to give you thanks for honouring me with your Commands. Well I do so, because this gets a proof that after so many years acquaintance there is one that will take my word which is a certain sign that I have not often broke it, therefore behold the consequence is this, I have given my word to the Duke of Dorset that you woud not so positively affirm this fact concerning Mr. Fox[4] without knowing the certain truth that there is no deceit in this declaration of trust, and tho it has been recommended to him as you say, he never did give any answer to it nor design it till he was fully satisfied of the truth, and even then I believe woud not have determined to have done it because tis an easy way of securing a place for ever to a family, and were this to be an example be it so many Pence or so many Pounds for the future they woud be inheritances, so now not to show my power with his Grace (in spight of his dependents who may cast their Eyes on 't) for that I dare affirm there never will be need of where Justice or goodnature is necessary, but to show you his dependence on your honour

[1] Mrs. Barber's preface to her *Poems*, 1734, and several poems, pp. 46, 65, 141, 147, 215, show that when in England she was for some time at Tunbridge Wells.

[2] The name has been obliterated. There can be no doubt, however, that the volume intended was Pilkington's recently published *Poems on Several Occasions*. After Swift ceased to recognize Pilkington and his wife he erased the name wherever it occurred in his letter-book.

[3] In the end Lady Betty subscribed for five copies of Mrs. Barber's *Poems* and the Duke of Dorset for ten.

[4] Perhaps William Fox, a member of Swift's choir.

and integrity he gives me leave to tell you it shall certainly be done, nor does this at all oblige you to give the thanks you seem to be so desirous to save, for at any time whensoever you have any business service or request to make to his Grace of Dorset, (whether my proper business or no) till you two are better acquainted with one anothers Merits. I shall be very glad to show how sincerely I am your friend | and faithfull | Humble | servant | E. Germain

Address: To | The Revd Dean Swift | at Dublin | Ireland.
Endorsed by Swift: Rx Ja^r^ 8th 1730 | Lady Betty Germain
and: Jan^r^ 8th 1730–1 | L^dy^] Elis Germain

Deane Swift 1768

Swift to Mrs. Whiteway

Dec. 28th, 1730.

You might give a better reason for restoring my book, that it was not worth keeping.[1] I thought by the superscription that your letter was written by a man; for you have neither the scrawl nor the spelling of your sex. You live so far off, and I believe are so seldom at home, and I am so ill a visitor, that it is no wonder we meet so seldom: but if you know what I say of you to others, you would believe it was not want of inclination: I mean what I say of you as I knew you formerly; for as to what you are now, I know but little. I give you the good wishes of the season; and am, with true esteem and affection, yours, *&c.* | J. Swift.

Deane Swift 1765

Swift to the Earl of Chesterfield

January 5, 1730–1.

My Lord,

I return your Lordship my most humble thanks[2] for the honour and favour of your letter, and desire your justice to believe, that,

[1] Martha Whiteway was the daughter of Swift's uncle Adam by his second wife. She was born in 1690 and twice married; first to the Rev. Theophilus Harrison, and secondly, in 1716, to Edward Whiteway, who was still living at the time this letter was written. Although she lived in Dublin it appears from the letter that for years she and Swift had seen little of each other.

[2] In reply to Chesterfield's letter of 4 Dec. O.S. [N.S. 15 Dec.].

in writing to you a second time, I have no design of giving you a second trouble. My only end at present is to beg your pardon for a fault of ignorance. I ought to have remembered, that the arts of courts are like those of play; where, if the most expert be absent for a few months, the whole system is changed, that he hath no more skill than a new beginner. Yet I cannot but wish, that your Lordship had pleased to forgive one, who hath been an utter stranger to public life above sixteen years. Bussy Rabutin himself, the politest person of his age, when he was recalled to court after a long banishment, appeared ridiculous there: And what could I expect from my antiquated manner, of addressing your Lordship in the prime of your life, in the height of fortune, favour, and merit; so distinguished by your active spirit, and greatness of your genius? I do here repeat to your Lordship, that I lay the fault of my misconduct entirely on a friend whom I exceedingly love and esteem, whom I dare not name, and who is as bad a courtier by nature as I am grown by want of practice. God forbid that your Lordship should continue in an employment, however great and honourable, where you can be an ornament to the Court so long, until you have an opportunity to provide offices for a dozen low people like the poor man whom I took the liberty to mention. And God forbid, that, in one particular branch of the King's family, there should ever be such a mortality, as to take away a dozen of his meaner servants in less than a dozen years.

Give me leave, in further excuse of my weakness, to confess, that, besides some hints from my friends, your Lordship is in a great measure to blame, for your obliging manner of treating me in every place where I had the honour to see you; which I acknowledge to have been a distinction that I had not the least pretence to, and consequently as little to ground upon it the request of a favour.

As I am an utter stranger to the present forms of the world, I have imagined more than once, that your Lordship's proceeding with me may be a refinement introduced by yourself: And that as, in my time, the most solemn and frequent promises of great men usually failed, against all probable appearances, so that single slight one of your Lordship, may, by your generous nature, early succeed against all visible impossibilities. I am, *&c.*

Scott 1814

Swift to Samuel Gerrard

Dublin, Jan · 6, 1730[–1.]

Sir,

It was with great concern that I first heard a dubious, and then a certain account of the death of our common friend Mr. Cusack,[1] whom, in an acquaintance of many years, I never found otherwise than a gentleman of honour, sincerity, candour, and every other good quality that can recommend a man to the friendship and esteem of all worthy persons. He is a great example of the uncertainty of life, for except an aptness he complained of to take cold in his head, I have known few persons likelier to live long. I am but too sensible of his unhappy family's loss in him, and particularly of the condition of his lady, who I hope will not live under the tyranny of that odious old woman.[2] To her poor Mr. Cusack owed that he never passed one happy day at home, while she was under his roof. I must needs condole with you particularly for your loss in so worthy a friend: a thing so scarce in the country of Ireland, where the neighbouring squires are usually the most disagreeable of all human creatures.

You know, Sir, that last year he let me have a little mare, which I have rode ever since. I have often desired him to let me know the value he put on her. He answered, it was a present to him, and should be so to me; I protested I would suffer no such thing; he likewise sent me another young mare, which he was breeding up for me. I hope she will be good when she is cured of her starting; and in the

[1] Scott relates that this letter 'was copied from the original' which was then 'in the possession of Miss Cusack, grand-daughter of the gentleman whose loss he laments. They were a Catholic family. Tradition, which fondly preserves the most minute particulars of Swift's life, has recorded, that one day passing through the town of Navan, with the purpose of dining at Mr Cusack's, he recollected it was fast-day, and therefore purchased a leg of mutton, to secure his own commons. The son of Mr Metye, (grandfather of the Baron) at whose house the mutton had been left while the Dean attended prayers, plunged it by way of jest into a pot which was boiling in the kitchen fire. When the Dean returned and discovered what had happened, his passion was outrageous. He redeemed the half-boiled leg of mutton, however, and carried it with him to Mr Cusack's. Such an anecdote is not worth mentioning, were it not to shew the consequence which the Irish have gratefully and justly attached to the minutest particulars of Swift's life.'

[2] Ball suggests that she may possibly have been Cusack's mother to whom administration was granted for the benefit of his widow and six children.

mean time is very proper for a servant. I desire you will give your judgement what they both are worth; and I will pay the money immediately to the unfortunate widow's order, who may perhaps have occasion for it under her present circumstances. I shall continue for some weeks in town, and then, if my health permits, wander for a month or two in the country to preserve it. I am much obliged to our poor friend for bringing me acquainted with you, and he was a good judge of men, as I find by the character he often gave me of you; and I hope you will never come to this town while I am in it, without doing me the favour of calling on me. I am Sir, with true esteem, | Your most faithful humble servant, | J. Swift.

Address: To Samuel Gerrard, Esq. Navan.

Longleat xiii (Portland Papers)

Swift to Alexander Pope

Dublin Jan. 15. 1730–1

I have just finished a letter to my Lord Bolin— It is one of my many evenings when I have nothing to do, and can do nothing. read at night I dare not for my eyes, and to write any thing but letters, or those to any but a few friends I find all inclination is gone. I awake so indifferent to every thing which may pass either in the world or my own little domestick, that I hardly think it worth my time to rise, and would certainly ly all day a bed if decency and dread of Sickness did not drive me thence. This I ow not so much to years (at least I would hope so) as to the Scene I am in. . . .

I dine tête à tête five times a week with my old Presbyterian Housekeeper,[1] whom I call Sir Robert, and so do all my friends & Neighbours. I am in my Chamber at five, there sit alone till eleven, and then to bed. I write Pamphlets and follys meerly for amusement, and when they are finished, as I grow weary in the middle, I cast them into the fire, partly out of dislike, and chiefly because I know they will signify nothing. I walk much every day and ride once or twice a week and so you have the whole State of my life.[2] What you

[1] Mrs. Brent.

[2] Swift exaggerates the loneliness of his life at this time. He had, for example, spent the preceding Christmas season with the Grattans at Belcamp.

dislike in the letter you saw to a Lady.[1] I ought to also dislike, and shall do so, although my conscience be clear. For I meant only a reproach in a matter long since at an end, for I did ill explain my self, if it was not understood that I talked of Schemes long since at an end; for sure, if I had any the least hopes left, I would not have writ in a manner to render them desperate, as I think I did, and as I am sure, I intended, both in what I related to her & her Mistress; and therefore I intreat when you see her next, to let her know, that from the moment I saw her last, to the moment I writ to her last, and from that moment to this moment, I never had one single imagination, that the least regard would ever be shown for me.

You reproach me very unjustly for my apology in giving you an account of my self and my little affairs; and yet in your letter there is not a Syllable that concerns your health, which I know is always so precarious, and so seldom as it should be. I can walk 8 or ten Miles a day, & ride 30 Irish ones. You cannot ride a mile nor walk two—Will you dare to think that this doth not hang on my Spirits. I am unhappy in Sickly friends. There are my Lord and Lady Bolin—the Doctor You, and Mr Gay, are not able to contribute amongst you to make up one Sturdy healthy person. If I were to begin the World, I would never make an acquaintance with a poor or Sickly Man, with whom there might be any danger of contracting a friendship. For I do not yet find that years have begun to harden me. Therefore I argue that avarice and hardness of heart are the two happiest qualitys a man can acquire who is late in his life, because by living long we must lessen our friends, and may increase our fortunes.—

I have inquired for Mr Brandreth,[2] but cannot hear he is yet landed. I shall be very glad of such an acquaintance if he be but one half of what he is described to you; but I shall probably have more need of his countenance than he of mine. Yet with all his Merits, the D. of D. if I had been his Councellor would have waited till himself came over, at least, it would have been more popular to have bestowed those midling preferments at first, to Persons of this

[1] Pope, whose letter has not been preserved, apparently, and not unnaturally, protested against the tone of Swift's letter (21 Nov. 1730) to Mrs. Howard.

[2] The Rev. John Brandreth had been tutor to the Duke of Dorset's son, and thus gained valuable church preferments. In the following year he became Dean of Armagh.

Kingdom, as well as the first great one;[1] and yet he hath already acted otherwise in both, though he has time enough before him. Lord T[2] in what you write of him acts directly suitable to his Character, he hath treated twenty persons in the like manner. Pray tell me whether your Col. Cleland be a tall Scots Gentleman, walking perpetually in the Mall, and fastning upon every body he meets, as he hath often done upon me? As to his letter before the Dunciad, I know not the Secret, but should not suspect him for it.[3] I must tell you how affairs pass between Lord Chesterfield and me. By your encouragement I writ to him, but named you not. He sent me a long and gracious answer. As to the point, it was that he had five dependars, and as many prior Engagements; after which he would provide for Mr Launcelet. This I took as a jest, but my answer was thankful and serious: that I hoped his Lordship would not continue in any post where he could be only an Ornament to the Court so long till a dozen vacancys should fall and God forbid there should be ever such a Mortality in any one branch of the Kings family, that a Dozen people in low offices should dye in less than a dozen years. So I suppose he finds that we understand each other, and there is an end of the matter. I have writ to Mr Poulteney to congratulate with him on his Son.[4] I wait but an opportunity to supply Sir C. Cotterell's refusal, and when you receive them it will be left entirely to you, provided you will be as severe a judge as becomes so good and dear a Friend.[5] My humble service (I must still name them) to my Lord Bathurst, Oxford Peterborow (how is his health?) Mr Poulteney, the Doctor Mr Lewis and Mr Gay; and particularly Mrs Pope.

[1] The see of Ossory having become vacant the Duke of Dorset appointed to that bishopric a cousin of Archbishop Tenison.

[2] An undoubted reference to Lord Townshend who had retired from ministerial office in June 1730.

[3] The 'Letter to the Publisher' prefixed to *The Dunciad*, *Variorum* was signed by a William Cleland. The letter itself was composed by Pope. The 'Scots Gentleman' was probably the Cleland who served under Lord Rivers in Spain. After the peace he became a commissioner of customs in Scotland; and after 1723 a commissioner of the land tax and house duties in England. See *The Dunciad*, ed. James Sutherland, pp. xxv, 434.

[4] Pulteney's only son who predeceased him.

[5] Pope contemplated a further volume of *Miscellanies* and hoped to obtain some of Elijah Fenton's papers which Sir Clement Cotterel was unwilling to surrender. Swift is offering to supply the deficiency. The volume did not appear till Oct. 1732.

And pray tell Patty Blount, that I am her constant lover and admirer.

I had a letter lately from Mr Budgel,[1] the direction a feign'd hand and inclosed to Mr Tickel. He desires I would write to some of my great friends in England to get him into the H. of Commons there, where he will do wonders what shall I do? I dare not answer him, and fear he will be angry. Can nobody tell him that I have no great friends in England, and dare not write to him.

To Alexander Pope Esq at | Twitenham in Middlesex | By way of London.

Faulkner 1741

Viscount Bolingbroke to Swift

[? 17] Jan. 1730–1.[2]

I begin my letter by telling you that my wife hath been returned from abroad about a month, and that her health, tho' feeble and precarious, is better than it hath been these two years. She is much your servant, and as she hath been her own physician with some success, imagines she could be yours with the same. Would to God you were within her reach. She would I believe prescribe a great deal of the *medicina animi*, without having recourse to the Books of Trismegistus. Pope and I should be her principal apothecaries in the course of the cure; and tho' our best Botanists complain, that few of the herbs and simples which go to the composition of these remedies, are to be found at present in our soil, yet there are more of them here than in Ireland; besides, by the help of a little chymistry the most noxious juices may become salubrious, and rank poison a specifick[3]—Pope is now in my library with me, and writes to the world, to the present and to future ages, whilst I begin this letter which he is to finish

[1] Eustace Budgell's official career in Ireland had been far from successful; his mind had now been failing for some time and he was in serious difficulties. *D.N.B.*

[2] Pope in his editions gives no day of the month, nor does Faulkner, 1741, p. 155. Warton and Bowles dated the letter 17 Jan. In a letter to Richardson, Wednesday, 13 Jan., Pope proposes spending Sunday, the 17th, with him in town. See Sherburn, iii. 160 n.

[3] Thus Pope, 'writing to the world', says that the bee—'From pois'nous herbs extracts the healing dew.' (*Essay on Man*, i. 220).—Sherburn.

to you.[1] What good he will do to mankind I know not, this comfort he may be sure of, he cannot do less than you have done before him. I have sometimes thought that if preachers, hangmen, and moral-writers keep vice at a stand, or so much as retard the progress of it, they do as much as human nature admits: A real reformation is not to be brought about by ordinary means, it requires these extraordinary means which become punishments as well as lessons: National corruption must be purged by national calamities. Let us hear from you. We deserve this attention, because we desire it, and because we believe that you desire to hear from us.

4806

William Pulteney to Swift

[9 February 1730–1]

Dear Sir

Among the many compliments I have receiv'd from my Friends on the birth of my son, I assure none gave me greater pleasure than the kind letter you honoured me with on the occasion.

When you was last in England your stay was so short, that I scarce had time; and very few opportunitys to convince you how great a desire I had to bear some share of your Esteem, but should you return this summer I hope you will continue longer among us. Lord Bolingbrook, Ld Bathurst, Pope, my self & others of your Friends are got togather in a Country neighbourhood, which would be much enliven'd if you would come and live among us. Mrs Pulteney joyns wth me in the Invitation, and is much obliged to you for remembring her. She bid me tell you that she is determin'd to have no more Children unless you will promise to come over and Christen the next. You see how much my happyness in many respects depends upon your promise. I have always desired Pope when he writ to you to remember my Compliments, & I can assure you with the greatest truth, tho' you may have much older acquaintances, that you have not in England a Friend that loves and honours you more than I do, or can be with greater sincerity than | I am | Your most humble and | Obedient servant | Wm Pulteney.

London Feby ye 9th | 1730

[1] Pope's part of this letter, if written, was not printed.

If any of our Pamphletts (with which we abound) are ever sent over to Ireland, and you think them worth reading, you will perceive how low they are reduced in point of argument on one side of the Question. This has drove certain People to that last resort of calling Names; *Villain Traytor Seditious Rascal* and such ingenious appellations have frequently been bestow'd on a couple of Friends of yours. Such usage has made it necessary to return the same polite language, and there has been more Billingsgate stuff utter'd from the Press within these two months than ever was known before. Upon this Dr Ar—t has writ a very humourous Treatise,[1] which he shew'd me this morning, wherein he proves from many learned Instances that this sort of Altercation is Ancient Elegant, and Classical, and that what the world falsly imagines to be Polite, is truly Gothick and Barbarous. He shews how the Gods and Goddesses used one another, *Dog Bitch* and *whore* were pretty common expressions among them. Kings Heroes Embassadors and Orators abused one another much in the same way, and concludes that it is pity this method of objuration should be lost. His Quotations from Homer Demosthenes Æschines and Tully are admirable, & the whole is very humourously conducted. I take it for granted he will send it you him self as soon as it is printed.[2]

Endorsed by Swift: Mr Pulteney Febr 9th 1730–1 | Answrd

Rothschild

Swift to Mrs. Barber[3]

[23 February 1730–1]

I desire that Mrs Britton shou'd be one of your Collectors Mrs Caesar shall be another and you must get somebody to let Lady

[1] *A Brief Account of Mr. John Ginglicutt's Treatise concerning the Altercation or Scolding of the Ancients*, which was published in Feb. 1731. See Aitken's *Arbuthnot*, pp. 382–91, and Lester M. Beattie, p. 299. Pope, writing to Swift 1 Dec. 1731, rated the pamphlet 'of little value'.

[2] The letter carries no address.

[3] The transcript of this letter in a contemporary hand is signed by Swift. The letter, hitherto unprinted, is tipped into a scrap-book of Mrs. Charles Caesar of Benington, Hertfordshire. The scrap-book and the letter are now in Lord Rothschild's Library, nos. 564 and 2292. The date is, without doubt, Feb. 1731, when Swift was occupied in collecting subscriptions for the projected

Catherine Hyde know that I command her to be a third, and her Neice Sharlotte (who refused to read to me) her Assistant if they will not submit by these tokens I shall send circular letters and force them to obedience. you have been very wise in gathering Subscriptions they must be all ready money and twenty Collectors of both sexes would suffice. I believe my name would do to Lord Abingdon, Marsham, Ld and Lady Bathurst Ld Bolingbroke Ld Dartmouth Orrery Burlington Ld and Lady Oxford and daughter Ld Foley Ned Harly and his Son Ld Peterborow Tom: Harly Mr Poulteney Ld Isley D: Argyle D: Hamilton Ld and Lady Orkeney Ld Chesterfield Mrs Howard Mr Doddington D: Leeds D: Chandos Ld Arran I could in time think of more. if the people already named and any others who know me be told that it is by my request and earnest recommendation. I should fancy they will not refuse. I shall write soon to Mr Gay and Mr Pope to befriend you, I will add one thing that of all the verses I have seen of yours there is not one which with a little correction will not give you some credit and show your good sense and to show you and all my friends that I am in earnest I will contrary to my general custom subscribe my name by assureing you that with great esteem for your Virtue, Piety, and Genious above your Sex | I am Madam your most | faithfull humble Servt | Jonath Swift.

Dublin 23 Feb: 1730

P: S

I add to this Catalogue the following persons Sr John Hinde Cotton Ld Bristol Ld and Lady Harvey and so let Mrs Howard know that I recommend you to the Queen and wou'd apply to her in person if I were in England. Colonel Disney Earl of Winchelsea and his Cos: Ld Alesford and Ld Paget Earl of Pembroke D: of Grafton Mr Digby Ld Inchiquin Ld Strafford

volume of poems by Mrs. Barber which appeared as a quarto in 1734 with an imposing list of subscribers. Mrs. Britton and William Britton, Esq., were subscribers. Others named by Swift may be discovered in the index to these volumes. 'Marsham' stands for 'Masham', or 'Massam' as it appears in the list of subscribers. Swift subscribed for ten copies.

4806

Lady Elizabeth Germain to Swift

23 Feb: 1730–1

Now was you in vast hopes you shoud hear no more of me I being slow in my motions, But dont flatter your self you began the correspondence, set my Pen a going and God knows when it will end, for I had it by inheritance from my father ever to please my self when I coud, and tho I dont just take the turn my Mother did of fasting and praying, yet too be sure that was her pleasure too, or else she woud not have been so greedy of it,[1] I dont care to deliver your Messages this great while to Lieutenant Head,[2] he having been dead this two year and tho he had as you say (a Head) I loved very well but however from my Dame Wadkers[3] first impression, have ever had a Natural antipathy to Spirits—I have not acquaintance enough with Mr Pope which I am sorry for, and expect you shoud come to England in order to improve it, if it was the Q. and not the Duke of G: that picked out such a Laureat she deserves his Poetry in her praises.[4] your friend Mrs Barber has been here. I find she has some request, but neither you nor she has yet let it out to me what tis, For certainly you cant mean, that, by subscribing to her Book; if so; I shall be mighty happy to have you call that a favour for surely there is nothing so easy as what one can do ones self nor nothing so heavy as what one must ask other People for; tho I dont mean by this that I shall ever be unwilling when you require it, yet shall be much happier when tis in my own power to show how sincerely I am my old friends | Most faithfull | Humble servant | E Germain.

Mrs Floyd is much yours but Dumber than ever having a Violent Cold.

Address: To the Rev[d] Dean Swift | at Dublin | Ireland
Postmark: 27 FE
Endorsed by Swift: Feb. 23[d] 1730–1 | L[dy]] Betty Germain | Ansd. Ap[r] 3[d] 1731.

[1] The Countess of Berkeley, Lady Betty's mother, was of a pious disposition.

[2] Prebendary Henry Head; *see* p. 429, n. 4.

[3] Dame Wadgar, the old deaf housekeeper of 'Mrs. Harris's Petition' (*Poems*, i. 70).

[4] Cibber's appointment as Laureate was dated 3 Dec. 1730 Grafton was Lord Chamberlain.

Forster copy

Knightley Chetwode to Swift

[February 1730–1]

Sir,

I came to town the 12th of December and leave it the 12th of March, and could never see you but in the street The last time I met you I merrily thought of Horace's ninth satire, and upon it pursued you to your next house though not *prope Caesaris hortos.*[1] I had a desire to catch you by your best ear for half an hour, and something to tell you, which I imagined would surprise and please you, but with the cunning of experienced courtiers, grown old in politics, you put me off with a 'I will send to you,' which probably you never intended.

I am now returning to Woodbrooke from an amour which has proved little profitable to myself. Business here I have none but with women; those pleasures have not with me as yet [lost] their charms. And though when I am at home I do not like my neighbourhood, and shall therefore probably seldom stir beyond the limits of my gardens and plantations, which are full big enough for my purse, or what is even more insatiable my ambition, yet if my amusements there are scanty, my thoughts are unmolested, I see not the asperity of rascals, I hear not the complaints of the worthy, I enjoy the sun and fresh air without paying a fruitless attendance upon his Eminence of St. Patrick, my fruit will bloom, my herbs be fragrant, my flowers smile though the Dean frowns, and looks gloomy. Take this as some sort of return for the greatest neglect of me I have met since my last coming to this town, [together with] many ill offices, and what is far more extraordinary with half a dozen females, who have cleared up the truth of it to a mathematical demonstration.[2] This causes me to reflect upon the Jewish method formerly to make proselytes, which, I think, St. Ambrose well expresses in the following words: *Hi arte immiscent se hominibus, domos penetrant, ingrediuntur praetoria, aures judicum et publica inquietant, et ideo magis praevalent quo magis impudenter.*

I saw you pass last Friday by my window like a lady to take horse,

[1] 'Nil opus est te
Circumagi; quendam volo visere non tibi notum;
Trans Tiberim longe cubat is, prope Caesaris hortos.'

[2] The ungracious, even offensive, tone of this letter marks the approaching end of a long friendship between Chetwode and Swift.

with your handkerchief and whip in your hand together; your petticoats were of the shortest and you wanted a black cap, or I might have thought of Lady Harriott Harley, now Lady Oxford.

Longleat xiii (Harleian transcripts)

Swift to Gay and the Duchess of Queensberry

Dublin, March 13th 1730–1.

[1]⌜Before I go to answer your Letter,[2] I must tell you, that I am perpetually battling against my disorders by riding and walking whether the weather favors or no. I have not for almost two years been rid of a kind of giddyness, which tho' not violent as formerly, keeps me low in Spirits and humor, and makes me a bad Walker whenever it grows towards night: This and some smal returns of deafness have hindred me from Acknowledging yours of above two months old, but that I matter not. What is worse, I have wanted Courage to return my humblest thanks to her Grace the Dutchess of Qu— which I shall leave till I come to her Grace's Part. Mr Pope in all his letters complains he has no Acquaintance with you, and is utterly ignorant of your Affairs.⌝ Your Scituation is an odd one. The Dutchess is your Treasurer, and Mr Pope tells me you are the Duke's. And I had gone ⌜on⌝ a good way in some verses on that Occasion, prescribing Lessons to direct your Conduct, in a negative way, not to do so and so &c like other Treasurers; how to deal with Servants, Tenants and Neighbouring Squires, Which I take to be Courtiers, Parliament and Princes in Alliance, and so the Parallell goes on; but grew too long to please me.

⌜I will copy some Lines.[3]

Let some reward to merit be allow'd;
Nor with your Kindred half the Palace crowd:
Nor think yourself secure in doing wrong,
By telling Noses with a Party strong;
Be rich; but of your Wealth make no parade
At least before your Master's debts are paid.

[1] As first printed by Pope and Faulkner large omissions were made in these letters. The omissions are here enclosed within half-brackets.

[2] Of 6 Dec.

[3] These five words are in Lord Oxford's hand.

Nor in a Palace built with Charge immense
Presume to treat him at his own Expence &c[1]

Then⌉ I prove that Poets are the fittest Persons to be Treasurers and Managers to great Persons, from their Virtue and contempt of money &c—Pray why did not you get a new heel to your Shoe;[2] unless you would make your Court at St James's, by affecting to imitate the Prince of Lilliput—But the rest of your letter being wholly taken up in [a] very bad Character of the Dutchess, I shall say no more to you, but apply myself to her Grace.

Madam,—Since Mr Gay affirms that you love to have your own way, and that I have the same Perfection; I will settle that matter immediately to prevent those ill consequences he apprehends. Your Grace shall have your own way in all Places, except your own house, and the domains about it. There and there onely I expect to have mine. So that you have all the world to reign in, bating onely two or three hundred Acres, and two or three houses in Town and Country. I will likewise out of my *Special grace*, *certain Knowledge*, *and meer Motion*, allow you to be in the right against all human kind, except myself, and to be never in the wrong but when you differ from me. You shall have a greater Priviledge in the third Article, of speaking your Mind, which I shall graciously allow you now and then to do even to myself, and onely rebuke you when it does not please me—

Madam—I am now got as far as your Grace's Letter, which having not read this fortnight (having been out of Town, and not daring to trust myself with the Carriage)[3] the presumptuous manner in which you begin had slipt out of my memory. But I forgive you to the seventeenth line; where you begin to banish me for ever, by demanding me to answer all the Kind Character some partial Friends have given me—Madam, I have lived sixteen years in Ireland, with onely an Intermission of two Summers in England; and consequently am fifty years older than I was at the Queen's Death, and fifty thousand times duller, and fifty million times more peevish perverse and morose; so that under these disadvantages I can onely pretend to excell all your other Acquaintance about some twenty barrs length.

[1] These are lines 57–64 of 'To Mr. Gay on his being Steward to the Duke of Queensberry', first printed by Faulkner in 1735 (*Poems*, ii. 530–6). The poem developed into an attack on Walpole's stewardship of the nation's affairs.

[2] See Gay's letter to Swift of 6 Dec.; and chap. iv of 'A Voyage to Lilliput' for the distinction between the wearers of high heels and low heels.

[3] Carriage) the] carriage of it *Faulkner 1741*, *Pope 1740–2*.

Pray, Madam, have you a clear Voice, and will you let me sit at your left hand, at least within three of you; for of two bad ears, my right is the best. My Groom tells me he likes your Park, but your House is too little. Can the Parson of the Parish play at Backgammon and hold his tongue? Is any one of your Women a good nurse, if I should fancy myself sick for four and twenty hours? How many dayes will you maintain me and my Equipage? When these preliminaries are settled, I must be very poor, very sick, or dead, or to the last degree unfortunate, if I do not attend you at Aimesbury. For I profess you are the first Lady that ever I desired to see since the first of August 1714.[1] And I have forgot the date when that desire grew Strong upon me, but I know I was not then in England, else I would have gone on foot for that happyness as far as to your house in Scotland. But I can Soon recollect the time, by asking Some Ladyes here the Month the day and the hour when I began to endure their company, which however I think was a Sign of my ill judgment; for I do not perceive they mend in anything but envying or admiring your Grace, I dislike nothing in your letter but an affected apology for bad writing bad Spelling and a bad pen; which you pretend Mr Gay found fault with wherein you afrount Mr Gay, you affrount me, and you affrount your self: False Spelling is onely excusable in a chamber-maid for I would not pardon it in any of your waiting women—Pray God preserve your Grace and family and give me leave to expect that you will be So just to number[2] me among those who have the greatest regard for Virtue, goodness, prudence, Courage and generosity; after which you must conclude that I am with the greatest respect and gratitude Madam, your Graces most obedient and most humble Servant &c

—to Mr Gay.

I have just got yours of Feb. 25[3] with a Postscript by Mr Pope. I am in great concern for him, ⌜for I did not know that the Rhumatism was in the number of his disorders. I ow him for a Letter some time ago that I had from Mr Brandrath, who is gone to his preferments that are about 300ll. per ann: if any money is to be got by Lands or Tythes in this most miserable country, God knows I have inducements enough to be with you, besides the uneasiness of beggary and desolation in every Scene and person round me. But that law suit

[1] The day on which Queen Anne died.

[2] number] remember *Faulkner 1741*, *Pope 1740–2*.

[3] Not forthcoming.

of mine, wherein almost my whole fortune depends, is still on foot, for land is to be Sold to pay me, and that is Still delay'd, but I am told will be done in may, I hope from drinking wine by advice, you will arrive to drink it by inclination, else I Shall be a bad companion; for I do it indeed onely by advice, for i love ale better⌝—I find Mr Pope dictated to you the first part ⌜of what he would Say⌝, and with great difficulty Some days after added the rest.[1] I See his weakness by his hand-writing, How much does his Philosophy exceed mine, I could not bear to See him, I will write to him Soone

⌜I received lately a very friendly letter from Mr Pulteney.[2] Adieu, pray God preserve you both. Dr Delany keeps much at his villa. about 2 miles from this town,[3] he will be very happy with Mr Pope's kind remembrance of him, I am not perfectly master how to direct to the Duke's house pray tell me. Ex:⌝

4806

John Gay to Swift

[20 March 1730–1]

I think 'tis above 3 months ago that I wrote to you in partnership with the Dutchess. About a fortnight since I wrote to you from Twickenham for Mr Pope and myself, he was then disabled from writing by a severe rheumatic pain in his arm but is now pretty well again and at present in town. Lord Oxford, Lord Bathurst, He and I din'd yesterday at Barnes with old Jacob Tonson where we drank your Health. I am again by the advice of Physicians grown a moderate Wine drinker after an abstinence of above two years, and I now look upon myself qualified for society as before.

I formerly sent you a state of the Account between us.[4] Lord B[5] this day hath payd me your principal & interest; the interest amounted to twelve pounds; and I want your directions How to dispose of the principal which must lye dead 'till I receive your orders. I had a

[1] Gay wrote to Swift, 20 Mar. 1730–1, 'About a fortnight since I wrote to you from Twickenham, for Mr. Pope and myself. He was then disabled from writing by a severe rheumatic pain in his arm.' The letter of 'a fortnight since' is lost.—Sherburn.

[2] 9 Feb. 1730–1.

[3] Delville.

[4] In his letter of 3 Mar. 1729–30.

[5] Bathurst.

Scheme of buying two Lottery Tickets[1] for you & keeping your principal entire; and as all my good fortune is to come, to show you that I consult your advantage, I will buy two more for myself, and you and I will go halves in the ten thousand pounds. That there will be a Lottery is certain, the Scheme is not yet declar'd, but I hear it will not be the most advantageous one for we are to have but 3 per Cent. I sollicit for no Court favours so that I propose to buy the tickets at the market price when they come out; which will not be these two or three months. If you do not like to have your money thus dispos'd of, or if you like to trust to your own fortune rather than to share in mine Let me have your orders, and at the same time tell me what I shall do with the principal Summ.

I came to town the 7th of January last with the Duke & Dutchess about business for a fortnight, as it depended upon others we could not get it done 'till now. Next week we return to Amesbury in Wiltshire for the rest of the year; But the best way is always to direct to me at the Duke's in Burlington Gardens near Piccadilly. I am order'd by the Dutchess to grow rich in the manner of Sir John Cutler;[2] I have nothing at this present writing but my Frock that was made at Salisbury and a Bob periwig. I persuade myself that it is shilling weather as seldom as possible[3] and have found out that there are few Court visits that are worth a shilling, in short I am very happy in my present independency, I envy no man, but have the due contempt for the voluntary slaves of Birth and fortune. I have such a Spite against you that I wish you may long for my company as I do for yours; though you never write to me you cannot make me forget you, so that if it is out of friendship you write so seldom to me it doth not answer the purpose. Those, who you would like should remember you, do so, whenever I see 'em. I believe they do it upon their own account, for I know few people who are solicitous to please or flatter me. The Dutchess sends you her compliments & so would many more if they knew of my writing to you.

March 20. 1730/1

Address: To | The Revd Dr Swift | Dean of St Patrick's in | Dublin | Ireland

[1] Apparently this was the last year during which Gay continued to serve as a commissioner of the lottery.

[2] For Sir John Cutler, 1608?–93, see Pope's *Epistle to Bathurst*, ll. 315–34. A London merchant, he acquired great wealth; and, at the same time, became a legendary example of mean parsimony. In actual fact he contributed liberally to worthy objects. Pope's account of him is quite unhistorical.

[3] Weather necessitating the hire of a hackney coach.

Longleat xiii (Harleian transcript)

Viscount Bolingbroke and Pope to Swift

march: 20. 1730|1[1]

[Bolingbroke writes:]

I have delayed several posts answering your letter of January last,[2] in hopes of being able to speak to you about a Project which concerns us both, but me the most, since the success of it would bring us together,[3] it has been a good while in my head, and at my heart. if it can be set a going you shall hear more of it. I was ill in the beginning of the Winter for near a Week, but in no danger either from the nature of my distemper or from the attendance of three Physicians. Since that bileous intermitting Fever, I have had, as I had before,—better health than the regard I have payed to health deserves. We are both in the decline of life, my Dear Dean, and have been some years going down the hill, let us make the passage as smooth as we can, let us fence against Physical Evil by care, and the use of those means which Experience must have pointed out to us. Let us fence against moral Evil by Philosophy. I renounce the Alternative you propose. But we may, nay if we follow nature, and do not work up imagination against her plainest Dictates; we shall of course grow every year more indifferent to life, and to the affairs and interests of a System out of which we are soon to go, this is much better than Stupidity. the decay of passion strengthens Philosophy, for passion may decay, and stupidity not Succeed, Passions, says our divine Pope, as you will see one time or other, are the Gales of life,[4] let us not complain that they do not blow a Storm. What hurt does Age do us in Subduing what we toil to Subdue all our lives? It is now, six in the morning. I recal the time, and am glad it is over, when about this hour I used to be going to bed, Surfeited with pleasure, or jaded with business, my head often full of Schemes, and my heart as often full of anxiety. Is it a misfortune, think you, that I rise at this hour; refreshed, Serene, and calm? that the past, & even the present affairs of life

[1] The date in the Harleian transcript is in the hand of Lord Oxford. In Pope's texts (1740–2) it is printed 29 Mar.; so also in Faulkner 1741 and 1762.

[2] Unknown. Swift had written to Pope 15 Jan.

[3] The project for securing Swift an English preferment.

[4] *An Essay on Man*, Ep. ii. 107–8:

On life's vast ocean diversely we sail
Reason the card, but Passion is the gale.

stand like objects at a distance from me, where I can keep [off][1] the disagreeable so as not to be strongly affected by them and from whence I can draw the others nearer to me? Passions in their force would bring all these, nay even future contingencys, about my ears at once, and Reason would but ill defend me in the Scuffle. I leave Pope to speak for himself, but I must tell you how much my Wife is obliged to you. She says she would find strength enough to nurse you, if you was here, and yet God knows She is extreamly weak. The slow Fever works under, and mines the constitution. We keep it off sometimes, but still it returns, and makes new breaches before nature can repair the old ones. I am not ashamed to say to you that I admire her more every hour of my life. Death is not to her the King of Terrors, She beholds him without the least. When She suffers much, she wishes for him as a Deliverer from pain; when life is tollerable, she looks on him with dislike, because He is to separate her from those friends to whom She is more attached than to life it self. You shall not stay for my next, as long as you have for this letter; and in every one Pope shall write something much better than the Scraps of old Philosophers, which were the presents, munuscula, that Stoical Fop Seneca used to send in every Epistle to his Friend Lucilius.

[Pope writes:][2]

⸢My Lord promises too much for me. I can write nothing, not even so much as good Scraps, for I'm become but a Scrap of my self, and quite exhausted by a long Pain and Confinement[.] The Doctor puts me into Asses Milk, and I must neither use Study nor Exercise, I'm too weak. I am to do nothing but Sleep and Eat (if I can) were my Life my own, even without Health, I would come and show you the last of me in Ireland. My Spirits continue good, and Fear is a Stranger to me. Mrs. Barber desires I would correct her Verses, truly I should do it very ill, for I can give no Attention to any thing. Whatever Service I can render her, by speaking well &c. I will. Whatever Friends I can get to Subscribe to her, I will. But you know my Circle is vastly Contracted, as I seldom have been out of the Country[3] these two Years. All your Friends She will have without

[1] The word 'off' omitted in the Harleian transcript.

[2] Pope's portion of this letter was not printed by him. In its place he substituted the postscript properly dated June 1730 (q.v.). So also Faulkner 1741, vii. 159–60. Sherburn suggests that the omission was made because this present letter contains trivial personalities.

[3] Twickenham.

me; and all their Friends. But I'll do all I can. I must in return press you to speak well (as You justly may) of an Abridgment of the Roman History,[1] a Subscription for which is going in Ireland and the Profit of which the Gentleman (who is a very valuable Man and my particular friend) gives to the repairing of St Mary Hall in Oxford. Pray also desire Mr Brandreth from me to promote it what he can.

⌜My hearty Services to Dr Delany. I writ to you the first time I was able, with Mr Gay, about two weeks since. My Mother is yours, and at this present, better than I. I hope your Lawsuit is well ended: how is your health? | Adieu.⌝

Endorsed by Lord Oxford: Ld. B. & Mr Pope to | the Dean of St. Patricks.

4806

John Gay and the Duchess of Queensberry to Swift

[11 April 1731]

Dear Sir.

The fortunes of the person you interest yourself in,[2] amounts to at present (all debts paid) above three thousand four hundred pounds, so that, whatever other people think, I look upon him, as to fortune, to be as happy that is to say an independant creature. I have been in expectation post after post to have receiv'd your directions about the disposal of your money w[ch] L[d] B paid into my hands some time ago: I left that sum with two hundred of my own in M[r] Hoare's hands[3] at my coming out of town. I shall go to town for a few days very soon; if I hear nothing from you, I will do with it as I do with my own. I made you a proposal about purchasing Lottery tickets in partnership with myself, that is to say, four tickets between us; this can be done with overplus with the interest money I have receiv'd; but in this I

[1] Elwin thought this was the project of a young friend of Pope, Walter Harte, who had been at St. Mary Hall; but nothing of the kind was ever published by him. Nathanael Hooke, who was also at St. Mary Hall, where he enjoyed the patronage and friendship of the principal, Dr. William King, issued a *Roman History* in four volumes 1738–71. The last two volumes appeared posthumously. It is more likely that Pope refers to him. *D.N.B.*

[2] Gay himself.

[3] A banker, son of Sir Richard Hoare, Lord Mayor of London, who died in 1718.

will do nothing till I hear from you. I am now got to my residence at Amesbury, getting health & saving money. Since I have got over the impediment to a writer of water-drinking, if I can persuade myself that I have any wit, & find I have inclination I intend to write, though as yet I have another impediment for I have not provided myself with a Scheme. Ten to one but I shall have a propensity to write against Vice, & who can tell how far that may offend? But an Author should consult his genius rather than his interest, if he cannot reconcile 'em. Just before I left London I made a visit to Mrs Barber, I wish I could any ways have contributed to her subscription; I have always found myself of no consequence & am now of less than ever; but I have found out a way in one respect, of making myself of more consequence, wch is by considering other people of less. Those who have given me up, I have given up, & in short I seek after no friendships, but am content with what I have in the house, & they have subscrib'd; I propos'd it before Jo Taylor,[1] who upon hearing she was a friend of yours, offer'd his subscription & desir'd his compliments to you. I believe she hath given you an account that she hath some prospect of success from other recommendations to those I know, and I have not been wanting upon all occasions to put in my good words, which I fear avails but little. Two days ago I receiv'd a letter from Dr Arbuthnot wch gave me but a bad account of Mr Popes health, I have writ to him but have not heard from him since I came into the country. If you knew the pleasure you gave me you would keep your contract of writing more punctually, & especially you would have answer'd my last Letter, as it was about a money affair, & you have to do with a man of business. Your Letter was more to the Dutchess than to me, so I now leave off, to offer her the paper.

[The Duchess writes:]

it was Mr Gay's fault that I did not write sooner, which if I had I hope you would have been here by this time, for I have to tell you that all y^r^ articles are agreed to & that I only love my own way when I meet not with others, whose ways I like better, I am in great hopes, that I shall aprove of yours, for to tell you the truth I am at present a little tir'd of my own. I have not a clear or a distinct voice, except when I am angry but I am a very good Nurse when people do not fancy them selves sick, Mr Gay knows this, & he knows too how to play att Backgammon, whether the Parson of the parish can I know

[1] Clerk of the Bridewell Hospital.

not but if he cannot hold his tongue I can—pray sett out the first fair wind & stay with us as long as ever you please, I cannot name any fixt time that I shall like to maintain you & y^r^ equipage, but if I dont happen to like you I know I can so far govern my temper as to Endure you for about five days. so come away directly for at all hazards you'll be alow'd a good Breathing time. I shall make no sort of respectfull conclusion, for till I know you I cannot tell what | I am to you.

[Gay writes]

The direction is to the Duke of Queensberrys in Burlington Gardens in Piccadilly: now I have told you this you have no excuse from writing but one which is coming. Get over your Lawsuit & receive your money. ⌜he[1] shall not write a word more
Aprile ye 11th 1731

from Amesbury in wiltshire

yr Groom was mistaken for the house is big enough but the Parke is too Little⌝

Address: To | The Revd Dr Swift Dean | of St Patricks in | Dublin | Ireland by London.
London postmark: 12 AP
Endorsed by Swift: Mr Gay and | D—s of Q—y | Rx Apr 20th 1731

Scott 1814

Swift to the Rev. John Blachford

[16 April 1731]

Sr[2]

I begged some mutton of you, and you put me off with a Barrell of ale, these disappointments we must endure. But the main business

[1] The lines within half-brackets are written in the hand of the Duchess.

[2] This letter was first printed by Scott, *Works*, 1814, xvii. 326. The two other letters to Blachford were also first printed by Scott—12 Dec., 17 Dec. 1734, xviii. 299, 301. In the British Museum, however, is an isolated volume used by Scott when preparing his edition of Swift's *Works*. It is made up of two volumes of Nichols's edition bound together. In this book a transcript of the above letter to Blachford is bound in. The transcript has all the appearance of being copied from the original and is used for this text. Blachford, a man of ability and scholarly instincts, who held the prebend of Wicklow, was for more than twelve years a member of Swift's chapter, and Mrs. Tighe, 1772–1810, his granddaughter, won fame with her poem *Psyche, or the Legend of Love*.

is, whether it be your own brewing and here is another silentium. I knew we must not look a gift horse in the mouth, But ale must look into ours.

Here is another point; I would fain know what title you have to send me ale or anything else, when you hardly see the inside of the Deanry, or tast my Bad wine.

I have intentions to drink some of your Wicklow ale upon the place because I fancy it is better where it grows, and in such a Case it will not be improper that the minister should be actually residing.

I shall observe your directions of keeping it, and Mr John Grattan will be delighted with ale strong and stale, or Beer stout and clear.

You are a stranger to these proverbs. I am truly obliged to you for remembering me; although it be the duty of you Country-folks, as it is of us town-folks to forget you, and therefore we have a legal title to your presents.

However for once I will break this rule by assuring you that I have been; am, | and shall be always | Your obedient, and | obliged serv^{t} | J: Swift

Ap^{r} 16th. 1731.

4806

Lord Bathurst to Swift

April 19th 1731

I never design'd to have writ to yu any more because you bantr'd & abus'd me so grossly in y^{r} last.[1] to flatter a man from whom you can get nothing nor expect any thing is doing mischief for mischief sake, & consequently highly imorall. However I wont carry my resentments so far, as to stand by & see yu undone without giving you both notice & advice. Cou'd any man but you think of trusting John Gay with his money; none of his friends wou'd ever trust him with his own whenever they cou'd avoid it. he has call'd in the 200^{ll} I had of y^{rs}, I pay'd him both principal & interest; I suppose by this time he has lost it, I give y^{u} notice y^{u} must look upon it as annihilated. Now as I have consider'd that y^{r} Deanery brings y^{u} in

[1] in his lengthy letter of [October 1730].

little or nothing, & that you keep ser^{ts} & horses, & frequently give little neat dinners wch are more expensive than a few splendid entertainments, besides which y^{u} may be said to water your flock with french wine, wch altogether must consume y^{r} substance in a little while; I have thought of putting y^{u} in a method that y^{u} may retrieve your affairs. In the first place y^{u} must turn off all y^{r} serv^{ts}, and sell y^{r} Horses (I will find exercise for y^{u}) y^{r} whole family must consist of only one sound wholesom wench she will make y^{r} bed & warm it beside washing y^{r} linen and mending it, darning y^{r} stockings &c. but to save all expense in House-keeping y^{u} must contrive some way or other that she shou'd have milk, and I can assure y^{u} it is the opinion of some of the best Phisitians that womans milk is the wholesomest food in the world; Besides this Regimen (take it altogether) it will certainly temper & cool y^{r} blood, y^{u} will not be such a boute-feu as y^{u} have been, and be ready upon every trifling occasion to set a whole Kingdom in a flame; had the Drapier been a milk-sop Poor Wood had not suffer'd so much in his reputation & fortune. It will allay that fervour of blood & quiet that hurry of spirits, wch breaks out every now & then into Poetry & seems to communicate it self to others of the Chapter, y^{u} wou'd not then encourage Delany & Stopfort in their Idleness, but lett them be as grave as most of their order are with us. I am convinc'd they will sooner get preferment than in the way they now are, & I shall not be out of hopes of seeing y^{u} a Bishop in time when y^{u} live in the regular way wch I propose. In short in a few years, y^{u} may lay up money enough to buy even the Bishopric of Durham. for if you keep Cows instead of Horses in that high-walled Orchard and cultivate by your own industry a few Potatoes in y^{r} Garden, the maid will live well & be able to sell more butter & cheese than will answer her wages. you may preach then upon temperance with a better grace than now, that y^{u} are known to consume 7 or 8 hogsheads of wine every year of y^{r} life. you will be mild & meek in your conversation & not frighten Parliament-men & keep even L^{ds} Lieutenant in awe you will then be qualified for that slavery wch the country you live in, and the order y^{u} profess, seem to be design'd for, it will take off that giddiness in y^{r} head which has disturb'd y^{r} self and others; the disputes between Sir Arthur & My Lady,[1] will for the future be confind to Prose, and an old thorn may be cut down in peace, & warm the Parlour chimney, without heating the heads of poor innocent people & turning their

[1] Sir Arthur and Lady Acheson.

brains.[1] you ought to remember what St Austin says Poesis est vinum Daemonum Consider the life y^u now lead you warm all that come near you with y^r wine & conversation; and the rest of the world, with y^r pen dippt deep in St Austins vinum Daemonum.[2] So far for y^r soul's health. now as to the health of y^r Body, I must inform you, that part of what I prescribe to y^u is the same which our great friar Bacon prescribed to the Pope who livd in his days. Read his Cure of old Age and preservation of youth, Cap. 12th,[3] y^u us'd to say that you found benefit from riding; the french, an ingenious people, use the word chevaucher instead of monter a cheval, and they look upon it as the same thing in effect.

Now if y^u will go on after this in y^r old ways, and ruin y^r health y^r fortune & y^r reputation, it is no fault of mine. I have pointed out the road which will lead y^u to riches & preferment, & that you may have no excuse from entering into this new course of life, upon the pretence of doubting whether y^u can get a person properly qualified to feed you and compose y^r new family, I will recommend to you John Gay, who is much better qualified to bring increase from a woman, than from a summ of money. but if he shou'd be lazy (and he is so fat that there is some reason to doubt him) I will without fail supply y^u my self, that you may be under no disappointment. Bracton[4] says, Conjunctio maris et foeminae est jure naturae. Vide Coke upon Littleton Calvins case in volume reports. This I send you from my closet at Ritchings[5] where I am at leisure to attend serious affairs; but when one is in town, there are so many things to laugh at, that it is very difficult to compose ones thoughts even long enough to write a letter of advice to a friend. If I see any man serious in that crowd, I look upon him for a very dull or designing fellow. by the by- I am of opinion, that folly & cunning are nearer allied than people are aware off. if a fool runs out his fortune & is undone we say the Poor man has been outwitted, is it not as reasonable to say of a

[1] The references are to 'Cutting down the Old Thorn at Market Hill' and 'The Grand Question debated' (*Poems*, iii. 847, 863).

[2] *De Civitate Dei*, II. xiv.

[3] Under this title Roger Bacon's *Libellus . . . de retardanis senectutis accidentibus et de sensibus conservandis*, 1590, appeared in an English version, published in 1683 by Richard Browne. The twelfth chapter treats of the incident narrated in 1 Kings I. 1–4.

[4] Henry de Bracton, d. 1268, whose *De Legibus et Consuetudinibus Angliae* was the first attempt to treat the whole extent of English law systematically.

[5] Bathurst's country seat near Colnbrook.

cunning Rascal who has lived miserably & died hated and despised to leave a great fortune behind him, that he has outwitted himself In short to be serious ab[t] those trifles w[ch] the Majority of mankind think of consequence seems to me to denote folly, & to trifle with those things w[ch] they generally treat ludicrously, may denote knavery. I've observed that in Comedy the best Actor plays the part of the Droll, while some scrub-Rogue is made the Hero or fine Gentleman so in this farce of life wise men pass their time in mirth while fools only are serious. Adieu continue to be merry and wise but never turn serious or cunning.

Address: To | The Revd. Dr. Swift Dean of | St Patricks | Dublin
Endorsed by Swift: L[d] Bathurst | Apr. 19th 1731 | Answ. Jul. 1731 (*and*) Tis too late for me to turn serious now

Longleat xiii (Harleian transcript)

Swift to Alexander Pope

Dublin April 20. 1731.

From your own letters as well as one I just had from Mr Gay, I have by no means a good account of your health. The common saying of life being a Farce is true in every sense but the most important one, for it is a ridiculous tragedy, which is the worst kind of composition: I know but one temporal felicity that hath fallen to your share, which is, that you never were a strugler for bread. As to the rest, I mean the esteem of friends, and enemys of your own and other Countrys, your Patience and fortitude, and a long et cetera, they are all Spiritual blessings. The misfortune I most lament is your not being able by exercise to battle with your disorders, as I do by riding and walking, at which however I repine, and would not do it meerly to lengthen life, because it would be ill husbandry, for I should save time by Sitting still, though I should dye seven Years sooner; but the dread of pain and torture makes me toyl to preserve health from hand to mouth as much as a laborer to support life. I am glad you are got into Asses milk. It is a remedy I have a great opinion of, and wish you had taken it sooner. And I wish too you were rich enough to keep a Coach and use it every day you are able; and this you might do if your private Charitys were less extensive, or at least suspended till you were able *nare sine cortice*:[1] I believe you have as good reason as any Christian man to be a Stranger to fear, But I cannot endure the thought that you should live in pain, and I believe when Horace said *Quisquis erit vitæ scribam color*;[2] he understood, that Pain was to be excepted. Mrs Barber acted weakly in desiring you to correct her Verses, I desired her friends here to warn her against every thing of that kind. I do believe there was a great Combat between her modesty and her Ambition. I can learn nothing of this Roman history, you did not tell me the Gentleman's name and I know not where to enquire.[3] Mr Brandreth is gone to his livings and will stay there till the D. of D.'s[4] arrival hither, or at least till towards the end of Summer. Perhaps you may hear that I and my Chapter are erecting a Stone over the body of the old Duke of Schomberg, killed at the Boyn, We had applyed often to the Countess of Holderness, now Lady Fitzwater, for a monument over her Grandfather, and could receive no answer.[5] The Latin inscription hath been printed by the News-writers here, and hath I suppose reached England, and I hear the relations are angry: Let them take it for their pains. I have ordered the Stone to be fixed up. I long to know the Success of your Asss' milk, if it hinders you ftom Study the world will be the chief Sufferer. Descend in the name of God, to some other amusements as common Mortals do. Learn to play at Cards,[6] or Fables, or Bowls, get talking females, who will go on, or stop at your commands, contrive new tramgams in your Garden or in Mrs Howards, or my Lord Bolingbroke's; or when you are able, go down to Aymsbury, and forget your self for a fortnight with our friend Gay and the Dutchess. Sweeten your milk with mirth and motion. For my own part, I

[1] Cf. Horace, *Sat.* I. iv. 120.

[2] *Satires*, II. i. 60.

[3] See Pope to Swift, 20 Mar. Nathanael Hooke's *Roman History*.

[4] Duke of Dorset, whose chaplain Brandreth was.

[5] On 14 Apr. the *Dublin Intelligence* printed an English translation of the 'elegant Latin' of the epitaph to the Duke of Schomberg which Swift and his Chapter had agreed should be deposited in the Cathedral. See Swift's letter to the Countess of Holderness, 22 May 1729, which requested no more than a 'moderate sum' for a 'plain marble monument'. As 'frequent solicitations' met with no response the Dean and Chapter placed a memorial exhibiting how much more the virtues of the Duke weighed with strangers than 'the nearest ties of blood with his own relations'.

[6] This seems to imply that Pope did not play cards. The celebrated game of ombre in *The Rape of the Lock* provides some evidence to the contrary. It may not have been a favourite pastime.

think when a Man is Sick, or Sickly, great Lords and Ladies let them be ever so civil, so familiar and so friendly, are not half so commodious as middling folks, whom one may govern as one pleases, and who will think it an honor and happiness to attend us, to talk or be silent, to laugh or look grave just as they are directed. The old Lord Sunderland was never without one or more of these, Lord Sommers had a humdrum Parson with whom he was used to forget himself for three pence at Backgammon, and our friend Addison had a Young fellow (now of figure in your Court)[1] whom he made to dangle after him, to go where, and to do whatever he was bid. I often thought you wanted two or three of either Sex in such an employment, when you were weary, or Sick, or Solitary, and you have my probatum est; if that be of any value. My old Presbyterian Housekeeper tells me, that if you could bring your Stomach to woman's Milk, it would be far better then Asses. I would have you contrive to get as much of Summer Air as it is possible, of which we have yet had nothing here but a long run of Northeast winds that have almost ruined my fruit, for I suffer peach and Nectarin and pear-weeds to grow in my famous Garden of Naboth's Vineyard, that you have heard me boast of. I protest to you, that nothing so much discourages me from an English journey as the prospect of Domestick casments when I am from home, and at a distance of such a kind that I cannot come back but by the pleasure of Waves and Winds. However if my health and Law will permit me I shall venture once more to see you. For as to my Law, the land of my Creditor is not sold, but after a dozen hopes I have the thirteenth that it will be done in a Month. Yet then I know not what to do with the money; for Mr Gay tells me I can hardly expect even 4 per Cent. besides the trouble of returning it and safely putting it out: and here I hope to have Six on good Security of Land; if land continues to yield any thing at all, for without a Miracle we are just at our last gasp, beyond the imagination of any one who does not live in this Kingdom. And most of my sorry revenues being of the Tyth-kind; I am forced to watch my Agents and farmers constantly; to get nothing. This, and Years, and uncertain health have sunk my Spirits, and I often wish my self a Vicar in Wales. I ride constantly here but cannot afford to support a couple of horses in England.—

Pardon this particular impertinence of relating my difficulties so contrary to my desires. I was just reading one of your letters three

[1] It is doubtful whom Swift had in mind. Tickell or Carey have been suggested.

Months old, wherein you are hard on me for saying you were a Poet in favour at Court:[1] I profess it was writ to me either by Lord Bol. or the Doctor. You know favor is got by two very contrary qualitys, one is by fear, the other by ill taste; as to Cibber if I had any inclination to excuse, the Court I would alledge that the Laureats place is entirely in the Lord Chamberlain's gift; but who makes Lord Chamberlains is another question. I believe if the Court had interceded with D. of Grafton[2] for a fitter Man, it might have prevailed. I am at the end of my Paper, you are in my constant prayers to your health. I hope you will present my humble service to my List Lord Per[3] Lord Oxford Lord Bol. & Lady Lord Bathurst Lord Masham, Mr Poulteney the Dr Mr Lewis Mrs Pope and Patty very heartily. Nothing to Mrs Howard, you drew me in to write to her, and see how she hath served me,[4] for which She is a—

Endorsed by Lord Oxford: April . 20: 1731 | Dean Swift to Mr Pope.

4806

John Gay to Swift

Amesbury, April 27. 1731

Yours without a date[5] I receiv'd two days after my return to this place from London where I stayd only four days, I saw Mr Pope who was much better. I din'd with him at Lord Oxford's who never fails drinking your health & is always very inquisitive after every thing that concerns you. Mr Pulteney had receiv'd your Letter[6] & seem'd very much pleas'd with it, & I thought you very much too in the good graces of the Lady. Sir W Wyndham, who you will by this time have heard hath buried Lady Catherine, was at Dawley in great Affliction.[7] Dr Arbuthnot I found in good health & spirits; His

[1] The allusion is in Arbuthnot's letter of Nov. 1730. In the Longleat transcript the word 'Court' is supplied by Oxford.

[2] He held the office of Lord Chamberlain.

[3] Lord Peterborough. The scribe could not read the name and did not attempt to complete it. Perhaps Swift really wrote 'Pet'. The word 'List' is supplied by Oxford.

[4] By not answering. Words fail Swift, and he ends with a dash.—Sherburn.

[5] Missing.

[6] Probably a reply to Pulteney's letter of 9 Feb.

[7] Sir William Wyndham, Secretary of War in 1712, Chancellor of the

neighbour Mr Lewis was gone to the Bath. Mrs Patty Blount I saw two or three times who will be very much pleas'd when she knows you so kindly remember her; I am afraid Mrs Howard will not be so well satisfied with the compliments you send her. I breakfasted with her twice at Mrs Blounts, & she told me that her indisposition had prevented her answering your Letter, this she desir'd me to tell you & that she would write to you soon and she desires you will accept of her compliments in the mean time by me. You should consider circumstances before you censure;[1] twill be too long for a Letter to make her Apology, but when I see you, I believe I shall convince you that you mistake her. The day before I left London I gave orders for buying two South sea or India Bonds for you which carry four per cent & are as easily turn'd into ready money as Bank Bills; which by this time I suppose is done. I shall go to London again for a few days in about a fortnight or three weeks, and then I will take care of the twelve pound affair with Mrs Lancelot as you direct; or if I hear of Mr Pope's being in town, I will do it sooner by a Letter to him. When I was in town (after a bashfull fit for having writ something like a Love Letter, and in two years not making one visit) I writ to Mrs Drelincourt to Apologize for my behaviour, & receiv'd a civil Answer but had not time to see her; they are naturally very civil so that I am not so sanguine to interpret this as any encouragement. I find by Mrs Barber that she very much interests herself in her Affair, and indeed from every body who knows her she answers the character you first gave me. Whenever you come to England if you will put that confidence in me to give me notice I will meet you at your Landing place & conduct you hither, you have experience of me as a traveller, & I promise you I will not drop you upon the road for any visit whatever. You tell me of thanks that I have not given; I dont know what to say to people who will be perpetually laying one under obligations; my behaviour to you shall convince you that I am very sensible of 'em though I never once mention 'em. I look upon you as my best friend & counsellor. I long for the time when we shall meet & converse together; I will draw you into

Exchequer 1713–14, married in 1708 Catherine, second daughter of Charles Seymour, sixth Duke of Somerset. Twice in the *Journal*, 21 June 1711 and 2 Mar. 1712, Swift mentions her as an acquaintance of Stella. Lady Catherine died on the 9th of the month.

[1] Swift's unkindly letter of 21 Nov. 1730 naturally hurt Mrs. Howard's feelings. To their credit Gay, Pope, and others defend her.

no great company besides those I live with, in short, if you insist upon it I will give up all great company for yours. These are conditions that I can hardly think you will insist upon after your declarations to the Dutchess who is more & more impatient to see you, & all my fear is that you will give up me for her which after my ungallant declaration would be very ungenerous. But we will settle this matter together when you come to Amesbury. After all I find I have been saying nothing, for sp[ea]king of her, I am talking as if I were in my own power. You us'd to blame me for oversolicitude about myself, I am now grown so rich that I don't think myself worth thinking on, so that I will promise you never to mention myself or my own Affairs; but you ow'd it all to the inquisitiveness of your friendship; and ten to one but every now and then you will draw me to talk of myself again. I sent you a gross state of my Fortune already, I have not room to draw it out in particulars. When you come over the Dutchess will state it to you. I have left no room for her to write, so that I will say nothing till my Letter is gone, but she would not forgive me if I did not send her compliments.

Address: To | The Revd Dr Swift | Dean of St Patrick's | in Dublin | Ireland | by way of London
Postmark: 28 AP
Endorsed by Swift: May. 4th[1] 1731 | Mr Gay | Answered Jun. 29th | 1731

Forster copy

Swift to Knightley Chetwode

Dublin, May 8, 1731.

Sir,

Your letter[2] hath lain by me without acknowledging it much longer than I intended, or rather this is my third time of writing to you, but the two former I burned in an hour after I had finished them,[3] because they contained some passages which I apprehended one of your pique might possibly dislike, for I have heard you approve of one principle in your nature, that no man had ever offended you against whom you did not find some opportunity to make him regret it, although perhaps no offence were ever designed. This perhaps, and the other art you are pleased with, of knowing the secrets of

[1] The date of receipt. [2] Written in Feb. 1730–1.
[3] One of these letters escaped the flames, and will be found in Appendix XX.

families, which as you have told me was so wonderful that some people thought you dealt with old Nick, hath made many families so cautious of you.

And to say the truth, your whole scheme of thinking, conversing, and living, differs in every point from mine. I have utterly done with all great names and titles of Princes and Lords and Ladies and Ministers of State, because I conceive they do me not the least honour; wherein I look upon myself to be a prouder man than you, who expect that the people here should think more honourably of you by putting them in mind of your high acquaintance, whereas the spirits of our Irish folks are so low and little and malicious that they seldom believe a syllable of what we say on these occasions, but score it all up to vanity, as I have known by experience, whenever by great chance I blabbed out some great name beyond one or two intimate friends; for which reason I thank God that I am not acquainted with one person of title in this whole kingdom, nor could I tell how to behave myself before persons of such sublime quality. Half a dozen middling clergymen, and one or two middling laymen make up the whole circle of my acquaintance.

That you returned from an amour without profit, I do not wonder, nor that it was more pleasurable, if the lady as I am told be sixty, unless her literal and metaphorical talents are very great; yet I think it impossible for any woman of her age, who is both wise and rich, to think of matrimony in earnest. However I easily believe what you say that women have not yet lost all their charms with you, who could find them in a Sibyl. I am sorry for what you say, that your ambition is unsatiate, because I think there are few men alive so little circumstanced to gratify it. You made one little essay in a desperate cause much to the disadvantage of your fortune, and which would have done you little good if it had succeeded; and I think you have no merit with the present folks, though some affect to believe it to your disadvantage. I cannot allow you my disciple; for you never followed any one rule I gave you. I confess the Queen's death cured all ambition in me, for which I am heartily glad, because I think it little consists either with ease or with conscience.

I cannot imagine what any people can propose by attempts against you, who are a private country gentleman, who can never expect any employment or power. I am wondering how you came acquainted with Horace or St. Ambrose, since neither Latin nor Divinity have been your studies; it seems a miracle to me. I agree with that gentleman, whoever he is, that said to answer letters was a part of good breeding, but he would agree with me, that nothing requires more caution, from the ill uses that have been often made of them, especially of letters without common business. They are a standing witness against a man, which is confirmed by a Latin saying, for words pass but letters remain. You hint, I think, that you intend for England;[1] I shall not enquire into your motives. My correspondence there is but with a few old friends, and of these but one who is in employment, and he hath lately dropped me too, and he is in right; for it is said I am out of favour, at least, what I like as well, I am forgotten, for I know not anyone who thinks it worth the pains to be my enemy; and it is mere charity in those who still continue my friends, of which however not one is in power, nor will ever be during my life. I am ashamed of this long letter, and desire your pardon. I am, Sir, | Your, &c.

Address: To Knightley Chetwode, Esq., at Woodbrooke, near Mountmellick.
Endorsed: A very extraordinary letter designed, I suppose, to mortifie me—within this letter are coppies of some lettrs of mine to him.

Rothschild

Swift to Lady Worsley

[Dublin, 11 May 1731]

Madam.[2]

It is now three years and a half since I had the Honor to see Your Ladyship; and I take it very ill that you have not finished my Box above a Month[3] . . But, this is allways the way that You Ladyes

[1] Swift's memory deceived him, or the passage in Chetwode's letter to which he refers has been lost.

[2] This letter was first printed, *Notes and Queries*, I. iv. 218–19, 27 Sept. 1851, as from the original 'written by Swift'. The copyist was careful, and he seems to have been transcribing from the holograph now in Lord Rothschild's library, 2293. Nevertheless, he dates the letter 'May 1re, 1731' and indicates at the close a few omitted words, with the footnote 'A small portion of the original letter has been lost'; whereas the letter in the Rothschild library is exceptionally neatly written and in perfect condition. Possibly the copyist was using a draft. If so it was extraordinarily close to the autograph from which the letter is here printed.

[3] See Swift's letter to Lady Worsley of 19 Apr. 1730 in which he indicated that he expected a present from her. The 'Box' proved to be an escritoire. It is preserved in St. Patrick's Deanery.

treat Your adorers in their absence . . However, upon Mrs Barber's account I will pardon you, because she tells me it is the handsomest piece of work she ever saw; and because you have accepted the honor to be one of her protectors, and are determined to be one of her principall recommenders and encouragers. I am in some doubt whether envy had not a great share in your work, for you were I suppose informed that my Lady Carteret had made for me with her own hands the finest box in Ireland, upon which you grew jealous and resolved to outdo her by making for me the finest box in England; for so Mrs Barber assures me. In short I am quite overloaden with favors from Your Ladyship and your Daughter, and what is worse those loads will lye upon my Shoulders as long as I live. . But I confess my self a little ungratefull, because I cannot deny Your Ladyship to have been the most constant of all my Goddesses, as I am the most constant of all Your Worshippers. I hope the Carterets and the Worseleyes are all happy and in health, and You are obliged to let Sr Robert Worseley know that I am his most humble Servant, but you need say nothing of my being so long his Rival. I hear my friend Harry is returning from the fiery Zone,[1] I hope with more money than he knows what to do with; but whether his vagabond Spirit will ever fix is a question. I beg your Ladyship will prevayl on Sr Robert Worseley to give me a Vicarage in the Isle of Wight;[2] for I am weary of living at such a distance from you. It need not be above fourty pounds a year.

As to Mrs Barber, I can assure you she is but one of four Poetesses[3] in this toun, and all Citizen's wives but she had the vogue of being the best; yet one of them is a Scholar and hath published a new edition of Tacitus with a Latin dedication to My Lord Carteret.

I require that Your Ladyship shall still preserve me some little corner in your memory, and do not think to put me off onely with a Box, which I can assure you will not contribute in the least to increase My esteem and respect for Your Ladyship, since I have been always and shall ever remain | Madam | Your Ladyship's most | obedient and most | humble Servant | Jonath Swift

Dublin. May 11th | 1731.

[1] Henry Worsley, brother to Sir Robert, was at this time Governor of Barbados.

[2] The Worsleys, as noted before, were landed proprietors in the Isle of Wight.

[3] The four in Swift's mind would be Mrs. Grierson, Mrs. Barber, Mrs. Sican, and Mrs. Pilkington.

Forster copy

Knightley Chetwode to Swift

[May, 1731]

Sir,

Upon my return from a visit I found yours of the 8th. The principle you say I approve in my nature, that no person ever offended me against whom I did not find some opportunity to make him repent it, would be of very little signification, did not the offending parties aid and assist me. Had not Whitshed by corruption taken a servant out of my service into his, I had probably never suspected that servant capable of being corrupted. But as I found he designed him for a Judas to betray his master, and would give but, basely, forty pieces of silver, I thought it justifiable to give one piece more, by which I fixed Whitshed in a lodging at Pall Mall to be cured of a dirty distemper, and had accounts every packet of his progress in the cure, and when he got abroad of his applications to preside in our Chancery, upon his brazen merit in favour of his friend Wood's halfpence. This Brodrick, the Chancellor, told me pinched Whitshed more than Scrogg's censure thrown into his coach, or even two letters to the Right Honourable —, and swore by God, it was the best stratagem imaginable, and that he should love me for it, as long as he lived.[1] Raymond, that uninformed lump of clay, did cruelly disoblige and offend me, which compelled me to bring upon the *tapis* Nanny Neary *cum sociis*, to come at the cause of his mad disorders, and when discovered he, to keep me silent and in his humour, betrayed everybody, and all he knew, saw, heard or believed.[2] I

[1] The Irish chancellorship was resigned in 1725, very unwillingly, by Brodrick, otherwise Lord Midleton, and sought unsuccessfully by Whitshed. The latter is compared by Swift in the sixth Drapier's Letter (*Drapier's Letters*, ed. Davis, pp. 113–14) to Chief Justice Scroggs, and a censure passed by the English House of Commons upon Scroggs for conduct similar to that of Whitshed in dismissing the Grand Jury before the conclusion of their business had been printed and circulated. The letters to the Right Honourable — are those signed with the initials N.N. to which Swift alluded in writing to Chetwode at the time of their publication.—Ball.

[2] Whatever Chetwode may have discovered to Raymond's disadvantage does not appear to have interrupted the friendship between Swift and the rector of Trim. In his will, which is dated 21 Oct. 1725, and was proved 28 May 1726, Raymond, who was then resident in London, refers to his 'very good friend Dr. Swift, Dean of St. Patrick's', and in bequeathing to him a gold ring says that he owes him 'the greatest obligations'.—Ball.

know no family so cautious as you say, but some weak people subject to first impressions, and who though clad in glass doublets, will be throwing of stones.

The objection of great names and titles is a threadbare pretext for abusing me. I am extremely sensible how low, little and malicious a spirit reigns amongst some folks, and am as sensible how difficult it is to live and converse with that difficult and mutable creature man; and yet I have done enough in the two great scenes of my life to convince such, who are not proof against conviction, that it is my way to act according to my reason without being driven to anything contrary to my inclination. I can easily bear to be laughed at, for what I am sure is right; besides I have reason to value myself that a person of honour would condescend to make me a subject of jest, and then I have company for my comfort, for I could tell you another besides, whom honour has rendered ridiculous as well as me. Here is a riddle for you, but you have a key for it, but as matters are circumstanced between you and me you must take care to turn it dexterously, in a distinction of honour in the concrete, and honour in the abstract—a distinction I could not for my blood pass over: I mean my vanity to show you I understand a little logic, as well as Latin and Divinity. You are merry upon my late amour, and allow that women have not lost all their charms with me, who could find any in a Sibyl. But if you could do for me as Maro did by Æneas, and bring Sibylla Cumæa to conduct me to the golden branch,[1] *non solus Cadenus, sed eris mihi magnus Apollo.*

What essays I have made, and what to the disadvantage of my fortune, I know better than any other man living can. Whether I have any merit with the present folks is not of one farthing signification to the world; though I have heard frequently of a set of puppies, who, as you say, affect to believe the first to my dishonour. As to my being employed, I may answer as Lady Anne did to Gloucester in Shakespeare's Richard the Third, it is permitted to all men to hope.[2] I cannot help what you say that you cannot imagine what people can propose by attempts against me, but the present attempt is to represent me as poor that I may the more easily be rendered ridiculous, as well knowing that the loss of an ounce of

[1] *Aeneid*, vi. 205–11.

[2] *Richard III*, ii. 199:

Glouc. But shall I live in hope?
Anne. All men, I hope, live so.

credit is the loss of a pound of power. [As to] what you observe of great names, etc., it has always been my opinion that *principibus placuisse viris non ultima laus est*, and Horace, with whom my becoming acquainted seems so great a miracle to you, says

tamen me
Cum magnis vixisse invita fatebitur usque
Invidia.[1]

Your accounts in some of your latest letters to me, that everybody has dropped you, that you are out of favour, that you are forgotten and the like, minds me of the favourite of Augustus, who was so great a master in the art of declining envy. It is, I think, verily in Dr. Swift the merriest affectation I ever met, that you who were bred under Sir William Temple, and have been much about Court, especially [the] four last years of Queen Anne, should not know, how to behave in presence of Traulus,[2] and other sublime Irish quality. What think you of the Countess of Kerry since her trip to France?[3] As to many things which regard me, I think reason furnishes means sufficient to confound some, who refuse to believe unless they can comprehend, and that they are unwilling to do to my advantage. I meet some who love themselves too much to love a friend, and I have often thought, whether this, and some other conduct, has not been designed to take me off the expectation of friendship.

I did say, as you write, that I intend for England. I cannot guess who the Devil succeeds superannuated Manley[4] in his intelligencer's place of writing everything into England, but it has been writ that I was to be at Chester such a day, and a person came [up for me] in his coach, and writes me a letter filled with kind severity for having disappointed him in what I never promised. I received a letter along with yours from Dulman, the parson,[5] intended I suppose more to disturb than please me, wherein he says he received a letter about me wherein his correspondent tells him that I see, and feel, and hear, imagine, suspect, penetrate, and foresee everything so well that a

[1] *Sat.* II. i. 76.

[2] Lord Allen.

[3] During these latter years Swift seems to have formed a friendly acquaintance with Lady Kerry. Her husband, twenty-first Lord and first Earl of Kerry, lived in great state at Lixnaw, his seat near the mouth of the Shannon, and at Kerry House in Dublin. Lady Kerry seems to have suffered in health; and in her letter to Swift of 4 Mar. 1732–3 she complains of failing eyesight.

[4] Isaac Manley the postmaster.

[5] Ball suggests that the allusion may be to Stopford his brother-in-law.

man would be tempted to believe that every one of my passions was guided by a sort of magic, peculiar to me. I think I have read these very words, or something very like them, somewhere, which this coxcomb would apply to me, but cannot for my blood, recollect where. He adds that he heard me terribly fallen upon, and attacked about so many folks, who had offended me, dying in so short a time. I am, | Your humble servant. | K.C.

W. R. Le Fanu[1]

Swift to the Rev. Philip Chamberlain

[24 May 1731]

Sr[2]

One of the Grattans told me to day that you were so kind to object against some passages in the monument intended over D. Schomberg.[3] The first was, *ut hæredes Ducis* I varyed that expression often, but made it æquivocall whether the heirs or the Chaptr desired such a monument might be made I have changed the word *erigi* for *erigendum* as Mr Grattan sd you desired. *Hunc ipsi*[4] *lapidem* That is to

[1] Swift's autograph was at one time in the possession of J. Sheridan Le Fanu, the well-known novelist, by whom this letter was printed in the *Dublin University Magazine*, xii. 269. The original passed to his nephew, Thomas P. Le Fanu of Abingdon, Bray, co. Wicklow; and is now in the possession of his son, W. R. Le Fanu, librarian to the Royal College of Surgeons, Lincoln's Inn Fields, London.

[2] Fifteen years earlier the question of the preferment of the Rev. Philip Chamberlain, a canon of St. Patrick's, was proving a bone of contention between Swift and Archbishop King. In a letter to Archdeacon Walls, 18 June 1716, Swift described Chamberlain as 'a man of very low parts and understanding, with a very high conceit of himself'. See further Landa, *Swift and the Church of Ireland*, pp. 79–82. It is to be noted that now Swift was ready to listen to Chamberlain.

[3] The following is the inscription:

Hic infra situm est Corpus Frederici | Ducis | De Schomberg | ad Bubindam occisi, A.D. 1690. | Decanus, et Capitulum maximopere | etiam | atque etiam peteriunt, | Ut Heredes Ducis monumentum | In memoriam Parentis erigendum curarent | Sed postquam per epistolas, per amicos, | diu ac saepe orando, nil profecere; Hunc demum lapidem ipsi statuerunt, | Saltem ut scias, hospes, | Utinam terrarum Schombergensis cineres | delitescunt. | Plus potuit fama virtutis apud alienos | Quam sanguinis proximitas apud suos. | A.D. 1731.

[4] A word is scrawled out after 'ipsi', and, as will be seen, 'Hunc demum lapidem' was substituted.

avoyd being equivocal, *ipsi* meaning the chapter. *Quantillâ in cellulâ*,[1] these diminutives I was wrong advised in, because, it was rightly observed by another friend, that the Cell was good enough, it was in Ld Corke's tomb, but the fault was that the ashes lay unhonored and forgotten, and therefore I have changed that passage in the Copy on t'other side

I forgot to mention, that some of the Chapter going with me into the church to day, disliked the place ⌜intended⌝[2] for the Monument, which was a space of white wall between the bottom of the East window, and the Top of the ⌜altar-piece⌝ and therefore another place was resolved on which was over the arched door which carryes you the shortest way from the Chapt[r]-house to the altar, and is three yards distant westward from L[d] Corks tomb. Therefore instead of *Hic infra situm est* I begin *Sub altari situm est*.[3]

The trouble given you is a just punishment for your skill in criticism. It is dangerous writing on marble, where one cannot make errata, or mend in a second Edition. I shewed to many persons what I first writ, and was printed; but, except one friend, no other would find any fault; I am therefore[4] obliged to you; and desire by your skill to save me from the reproach of blunders. I send you the first Copy as it was printed, and the second as I altered some parts; and the third at the back of this, where I altered more. I entreat your judgm[t] and correction, for I shall have all the scandal upon any slip. If you please to send me your opinion to morrow, I shall be much obliged to you.

I am with true esteem s[r] Your most obed[t] | humble Serv[t] | Jonath (*sic*).

Deanry-house | May · 20th 1731

Address: To the Reverend | Mr Chamberlayn at | Grange-Gorman[5]

[1] According to Delany, *Observations*, p. 275, the words with which Swift concluded the epitaph were still stronger, namely: 'Saltem ut scias viator indignabundus, quali in cellula, quanti ductoris cineres deletiscunt.' He claimed to have 'had the felicity to prevail upon the Dean to leave out that sentence.'

[2] The words within half-brackets suffer from injury to the paper.

[3] Lord Cork's vault was under the communion table.

[4] 'therefore' is written above 'rather', which is scrawled out.

[5] Grangegorman is in the northern part of Dublin.

4806

Lady Elizabeth Germain to Swift

[5 June 1731]

I fancy you have comforted your self this long time with the hopes of hearing no more from me, but you may return your thanks to a downright fitt of the Gout in my foot and as painfull a Rheumatism that followed immediately after in my Arm, that bound me to my good behaviour, So you may perceive I shoud make but a sad Nurse to Mr Pope who finds the effects of Age and a Crasy carcase already, however if 'tis true, what I am informed that you are coming here soon, I expect you shoud bring us together and if he will bear me with patience I shall hear him with pleasure, I dont know what number of Chaplains the Duke of Dorset intends to carry over but as yet I have heard of but one that he has sent, & he as worthy honest sensible [a] man as any I know, Mr Brandrethe, who I believe was recommanded to your acquaintance, I have not been in any way of seeing Mrs Barber this great while, but I hear & I hope tis, that she goes on in her Subscription very well, nor has the Lady she so much feared done her any harm, if she endeavoured it, which is more than I know that she did,[1] I believe you will find by my writing that tis not quite easy to me, so I will neither tease you nor trouble my self longer, who am | most sincerely your | faithfull Humble | servant | E Germain

Address: To | The Revd Dr Swift | Dean of St Patricks | Dublin
Postmark: 5 IV
Endorsed by Swift: Rx June 14th · 1731 | Ldy] Betty Germain | answrd[2]

Longleat xiii (Harleian transcript)

Swift to John Gay and the Duchess of Queensberry

Dublin Jun. 29th 1731

Dear Friend,—Ever Since I received your letter,[3] I have been upon a balance about going to England, and landing at Bristol, to pass a

[1] Ball suggests that the allusion may be to a Mrs. Clayton, who was accused of attempting to obstruct Mrs. Barber in her canvass for subscribers. See Swift to Pope, 20 July 1731, and note.

[2] The next letter preserved from Swift to Lady Betty Germain is that of 8 Jan. 1732–3.

[3] Of 27 Apr.

Month at Aimsbury, as the Dutchess hath given me leave. But my[1] difficultyes have interfered; first, I thought I had done with my law-suit, and so did all my Lawyers; but my adversary after being in appearance a Protestant these 20 years, hath declared he was always a Papist, and consequently by the law here cannot buy nor (I think) Sell, So that I am at Sea again for almost all I am worth, But I have Still a worse evil; for the giddyness I was Subject to, instead of coming Seldom, and violent, now constantly attends me, more or less, tho in a more peaceable Manner, yet Such as will not qualify me to live among the young and healthy, and the Dutchess in all her youth Spirit and grandure will make a very ill nurse, and her women not much better. Valitudinarians[2] must live where they can command, and Scold; I must have horses to ride, I must go to bed, and rise when I please, and live where all mortals are Subservient to me. I must talk nonsense when I please; and all who are present must commend it. I must ride thrice a week, and walk three or 4 miles besides every day. I always told you Mrs Howard was good for nothing but to be a rank Courtier, I care not whether She ever writes to me or no, She[3] ⌜has Cheated us all, and may go hang her Self, and so may her—⌝ and you may tell this to the Dutchess, and I hate to See you so Charitable, and Such a Cully, and yet I love you for it, because I am one my Self. A. P— on her for hendring me from going to France where I might have recovered my health,[4] and She did it in a most treacherous manner, when I layd it upon her honor, you are the Sillyest lover in Christendom, If you like Mrs.[5] why do you not command her to take you, if She does not, She is not worth pursuing, you do her too much honor, She hath neither Sense nor taste if She dares to refuse you, though She had ten thous'd pounds. I do not remember to have told you of thanks that you have not given, nor do I understand your meaning, and I am Sure I had never the least thoughts of my Self. If I am your friend it is for my own reputation, and from a principle of Self-love, and I do Sometimes reproach you for not honoring me by letting the world

[1] *Pope 1740–2* prints 'many'.

[2] Not in the hand of the scribe. Apparently not Oxford.

[3] The words in half-brackets were not printed by Pope, by whom this severe reflection upon Mrs. Howard could not be tolerated.

[4] In his letter to Mrs. Howard of 27 July 1731 Swift reproached her for advising him not to cross to France shortly after the King's death. In her letter of 25 Sept. she defends her good counsel.

[5] Drelincourt.

know we are friends: I See very well how Matters go with the Dutchess in regard to me. I heard her Say, ⌜prethee⌝ Mr Gay fill your letter to the Dean that there may be no room for me, The frolick is gone far enough, I have writ thrice I will do no more, if the man hath a mind to come let him come; what a clutter is here? *poliliveles*[1] I will not write a Syllable more, ⌜The jest is grown Stale.⌝ She is an ungratefull Dutchess considering how many adorers I have procured her here over and above the thousands She had before, I cannot allow you rich enough till you are worth 7000ll, which will bring you 300ll per ann. and this will maintain you with the perquisite of Spunging while you are young, and when you are old will afford you a pint of Port at night, two Servants and an old Maid, a little garden, and pen and ink provided you live in the Country, ⌜—you never mentioned whether you were Seriously a manager for my Lord Duke in his estate, which the Doctor and Mr Pope absolutely affirm. And pray what will you do with my 200lls, will it yield nothing in the funds?[2] and what are you doing towards encreasing your fame and your fortune,⌝ have you no Scheam either in verse or prose? The Dutchess Should keep you at hard meat, and by that means force you to write; and So I have done with you.

Madam,—Since I began to grow old I have found all Ladyes become inconstant without any reproach from their consciences.[3] If I wait on you, I declare that one of your women, which ever it is that had designs upon a Chaplain, must be my nurse. if I happen to be Sick or pevish at your house: and in that case you must Suspend your domineering Claim till I recover. your omitting the usuall appendix to Mr Gay's Letters, hath done me infinite mischief here; for while you continued them, you would wonder how civil the Ladyes here were to me, and how much they have altered Since. I dare not confess that I have descended So low as to write to your Grace after the abominable neglect you have been guilty of; for if they but Suspected it, I Should lose them all, one of them who had an inclin of the matter (your Grace will hardly believe it) refused to beg my pardon upon her knees, for once neglecting to make my rice milk—Pray consider this, and do your Duty. or dread the consequences. I promise you Shall have your will Six minutes ⌜in⌝ every hour at Aimsbury,

[1] A gloss in the margin of the Harleian transcript interprets this word as 'positively'.

[2] In his letter of 27 Apr. Gay had told Swift that the bonds were at 4 per cent.

[3] This word is not in the hand of the scribe.

and Seven in London, while I am in health. But ⌜if I happen to be sick, I must govern to a Second. Yet properly speaking⌝[1] there is no man alive with so much truth and respect Your Grace's most obedient and devoted Servant the Dean.

Pray tell Her Grace, that Mr Ford (whose affairs keep him here against his heart) toasts[2] her every day, which is a great matter, for he hath thrown off all except Her Grace and Harrietta Pitt.[3]

Forster transcript[4]

Swift to Lord Bathurst

Dublin, 17 July 1731.

My Lord

[I m]ake your Lordship my humblest Acknowledgments for your letter,[5] and the most excellent advice it contains, which [last] I wish had been given to me when I had first the honor to [se]e you, and had life enough before me.

As to my 200ll I know not by what Authority your Ldship payd it to Mr Gay. I have been at law these ten years and still continue so, and have learnt enough to know that I expect my Money from you, & the constant interest too. Besides cost and damage at *valorm cent libr sterl.* The Aggravation is that you know Mr Gay very well, for his first offer to me, after he received the money, was to throw off the interest at hazard with the Government, till I entreated him he would employ it in paying a debt.

As to the regimen you prescribe, I must complain to your Lordship of the hard cirumstances I lye under. I have an old Presbyterian Tory housekeeper whom the neighbourhood call Sir Robert W—[6] She will not suffer a female in the house who is younger than herself, under pretence that if it were otherwise my men and the maids together would multiply my family too much. Then this same Sir Robert hath a dozen Parsons, and two or three squires, who corrupt her to let them in. She hath made one of the Squires my head butler, and one of the parsons my under butler; And these are all preaching

[1] The words within half-brackets, not in the hand of the scribe, are written on the opposite page to the main text of the letter.

[2] Not in the hand of the scribe.

[3] Lord Chatham's sister.

[4] From the Croker MSS. Transcript in the Forster Collection, F. 44. E. 3.

[5] 19 Apr. 1731.

[6] i.e. Mrs. Brent.

how absolutely necessary wine & company are to my health. S[r] Robert delivers them the keys, and in recompense they send her a glass out of every bottle.[1]— I have sent my men one after another twenty times to buy me a wife in the market; but she privately orders them to come back with false & lyeing storyes that there is not one to be sold; and when I complain of these hardships to these very knaves that drink up my wine, they are all unanimously against me.

One thing I take ill of your Lordship, that you did not begin your pres[cription] with me but with D[r] Delany. I say this because I am confident that the two o[r three] sermons he lately preached against black pudding were owing [to] some directions from —. He will not eat a chicken except its thr[oat] hath been cut: he says the blood of other animals inflames our o[wn] and disposeth us to cruelty. This is your own doctrine to me who[m] you call an inflamer.[2]

I beg, my Lord, you will leave me a little wine, because time hath already reformed me in poetry, and I can bring lawful witnesses that I was lately searching three days for rhyme in vain; that I have not written a libel these six months; and that I kept this summer at home rather than [to] go to S[r] A. Acheson's as to my shame I confess I did for two seasons together,[3] of which some false brother hath maliciously informed you.

I have gotten into your directions about Milk, onely with the addition of a little rice, sugar, and nutmeg, in which I hope you will be so good as to indulge me. [I approve your way of getting preferment; but for some reasons I am a little in hast, and humble[y] propose that I may be allowed to pay the expense annually out of the premises, giving my bond & judgment, and a mortgage if it be required. There is another advantage in this expedient: that by being impatient to go out of debt, I shall grow covetous and busy; have neither time to write verses or pamphlets, nor heart to allow my self better drink than small beer.

[1] Mrs. Pilkington in her *Memoirs*, iii. 152–4, narrates a story of her investiture by the Dean with the duty of serving the company with 'good Malt-Liquor' from a cask of 'fine Ale' in his cellar which had been presented to him by 'Mr. Grattan'.

[2] Delany in his *Revelation examined with Candour*, maintained, among other matters, the duty of Christians to abstain from things strangled and from blood. The first volume of this work appeared in 1732, a second in 1734, and a third in 1763, five years before his death.

[3] If 'two' was a slip for 'three' it provides yet another example of Swift's propensity to mistake times and seasons. Was the word used deliberately?

If you had read the notes upon that passage perhaps in St Austin's, you would have found that *vinum dæmonum* is only to be understood damn wine such as is drunk in hedge Taverns at London. If your *double entente* Quibble in French be the same that Fryar Bacon prescribed to the Pope, I believe I and the Pope would make the same use of it that David did. But the King knew her not; & so much for your *friponnerie*.

Besides; I consult my own reputation, being resolved [to avoid the][1] censure of the world; for what would people say if a [person of my] age & gravity would put on seriousness. But I am not [yet entirely] determined in the article of cunning, because every tradesma[n throughout this] Kingdom is a rogue to a man, but of ten Squires not abov[e one or two in a] hundred allowing a quantum of ignorance & folly th[at are not knaves,] beggars or fools, & sometimes all three, so that I am wel[l surrounded] I saw Ld Orrery to day,[2] he is come over on the knavery of a [steward or agent.] May all Irish absentees have the same fate! he dines with me [here I hope on] Tuesday next. He gives a very indifferent account of af[fairs also on] your side. You stick together like sand & cannot agree i[n any single] point de veüe. God be praised, for the condition you are in [is justly brought] upon you by your tyranny and oppression to this kingdom . . . & I the misery (thank my quondam friends [of lingering till] Death in. And god bless some others that shall be n[ameless which I] say with the meaning of a beggar when you cal[l him good friend and] refuse him a penny.

I desire to present my [respectful compliments to] My Lady Bathurst, and God bless you with [your olive branches which would] better become a Parson than a Peer. I always employ you my correspondent to distribute my services occasionally, for instance to Ld Peterborow, Ld Bolingbroke, Ld Oxford, Ld Masham, Mr Pulteney, Mr Pope, the D^r^, &c &c. Are you acquainted with our old brother Lord Lansdowne? He hath two daughters here, and I take it ill he did not order them to be acquainted with me.

Tell your neighbour Lord Burlington that if he does not repair

[1] The latter part of the paper has been badly torn in the margin. The words enclosed in brackets, though conjectural, are probably not far amiss.

[2] Charles Boyle, fourth Earl of Orrery, and father of Swift's biographer. In 1721 he had been thrown into the Tower for six months on a charge of implication in Layer's plot. His health was failing and on this occasion he stayed only a week or two in Ireland. He died on 28 Aug. 1731, soon after his return to England. See *Orrery Papers*, i. xiv–xvi, 94–95.

his Ancestor's Monument, I will use him worse than I have done Duke Schomberg's grand daughter. | I am with truest respect | Y^r^ L^d^ship's most &

4806

The Duchess of Queensberry and John Gay to Swift

July thee Eighteenth | 1731

[*Duchess:*][1] You are my Dear freind, I am sure, for you are hard to be found; that you are so is certainly owing to some Evil genius, for if you say true this is the very properest place you can repair to, there is not a Head here upon any of our Shoulders that is not at some times worse than yours can possible be att your worst & not one to compare with yours when at best (except your friends are your sworn Lyars) so in one respect at least you'll find things just as they could be wishd tis farther necessary to assure you that the Dutchess is neither young or healthy. She lives in all the Spirits that she can and with as little grandeur as she can possibly, she too as well as you, can scold & command, but she can be silent, & obey, if she pleases—& then for a good Nurse tis out of dispute that she must prove an excelent one, who has been so experienc'd in the infirmitys of others & of her own. as for talking nonsense provided you do it on purpose she has no objection. there 's some sense in nonsense when it does not come by Chance. in short I am very sure that she has set her Heart upon seeing you att this place. here are women enough to attend you, if you should happen not to approve of her. she has not one fine Lady belonging to her, or her house. She is impatient to be govern'd, & is chearfully determin'd that you shall quietly enjoy your own will & pleasure as long as ever you please. [*Gay:*] You shall ride; you shall walk, & She will be glad to follow your example, and this will be doing good at the same time to her & your self.

I had not heard from you so long that I was in fears about you & in the utmost impatience for a Letter. I had flatter'd myself your Law-

[1] The handwriting of the Duchess and Gay bore some similarity. This letter is written continuously, without breaks to indicate which writer was holding the pen. The Amesbury correspondents continued this friendly practice in further letters.

suit was at an end & that your own money was in your own pocket, & about a month ago I was every day expecting a summons to Bristol.[1] Your Money is either getting or losing something for I have plac'd it in the funds, for I am grown so much a man of business, that is to say so covetous, that I cannot bear to let a summ of money lye idle. Your friend Mrs H. is now Countess of Suffolk,[2] I am still so much a dupe that I think you mistake her. Come to Amesbury & you & I will dispute this matter & the Dutchess shall be judge. But I fancy you will object against her, for I will be so fair to you as to own that I think she is of my side. But in short you shall chuse any impartial referee you please. I have heard from her, Mr Pope hath seen her, I [be]g that you would suspend your judgment 'till we talk over this affair together, for I fancy by your Letter you have neither heard from her or seen her, so that you cannot at present be as good a judge as we are. I'll be a Dupe for you any time, therefore I beg it of you that you would let me be a Dupe in quiet.

As you have had several attacks of the giddiness you at present complain of, & that it hath formerly left you, I will hope that at this instant you are perfectly well; though my fears were so very great before I receiv'd your Letter that I may probably flatter myself & think you better than you are.

As for my being a Manager for the Duke you have been misinform'd. Upon the discharge of an unjust Steward, he took the Administration into his own hands. I own I was call'd in to his assistance when the state of affairs was in the greatest confusion; like an Ancient Roman I came, put my helping hand to set Affairs right, and as soon as it was done, I am retir'd again as a private man. [*Duchess:*] What you imagin'd you heard her say was a good deal in her Stile, t'was a thousand to one she had said so, but I must do her the justice to say that she did not either in thought or word; I am sure she wants to be better acquainted with you, for which she has found out ten thousand reasons that we'll tell you if you'll come. [*Gay:*] By your Letter I cannot guess whether we are like to see you or no. Why might not the Amesbury Downs make you better? [*Duchess:*] Dear Sir Mr Gay tells me I must write on upon his line for fear of taking [up] too much room. T'was his fault that I omitted my Duty in his last letter, for he never told me one word of writing to you till he had

[1] To meet Swift, who, for convenience of reaching Amesbury, had proposed landing there (29 June).

[2] Her husband had succeeded his brother on 22 June as ninth Earl of Suffolk.

sent away his letter, however as a mark of my great humility, I shall be ready & glad to aske your pardon upon my knees as soon as ever you come, tho not in fault. I own this is a little mean Spirited, which I hope will not make a bad impression, considering you are the accation. I submit to all your conditions, so pray come, for I have not only promis'd myself, but Mr Gay also the Satisfaction to hear you talk as much nonsense as you can possibly utter. [*Gay:*] You will read in the Gazette of a friend of yours who hath lately had the dignity of being disgrac'd;[1] for he & every body (except five or six) look upon it in the same Light. I know were you here, you would congratulate him upon it. I payd the twelve pounds to Mrs. Lancelot for the uses you directed. I have no Scheme at present either to raise my fame or fortune; I daily reproach myself for my idleness; you know one cannot write when one will; I think and I reject; one day or other perhaps I may think on something that may engage me to write. You and I are alike in one particular, (I wish to be so in many) I mean that we hate to write upon other folk's Hints. I love to have my own Scheme and to treat it in my own way; this perhaps may be taking too much upon myself, & I may make a bad choice, but I find I can always enter into a Scheme of my own with more ease & pleasure than into that of any other Body. I long to see you, I long to hear from you; I wish you health, I wish you happiness; & I [shou]ld be very happy myself to be witness that you [enjoy my wishes].

Address: To | The Reverend Dr Swift | Dean of St Patrick's | In Dublin | Ireland | by way of London.
Postmark: 19 IY
Endorsed by Swift: Rx Jul 25th 1731 | Mr Gay and | Du—s of Qu—

Forster 549

Swift to Alexander Pope

Jul 20—1731.

D^r^ S^r^[2]

I writ y a long lett^r^ not many days ago which therefore did not arrive till aftr y^r^ last that I receivd yesterdy with the inclosd from me

[1] From 1725 onward Pulteney was alienated from Walpole and joined Bolingbroke in attacking him through the medium of *The Craftsman*. In 1731 his name was struck off the list of Privy Councillors; and Swift seized the occasion to attack Walpole in 'On Mr. Pulteney being put out of the Council' (*Poems*, p. 537).

[*For note 2 see opposite.*

to the Qu— You hintd something of this in a formr lett^{r}. I will tell you sincerely how the affair stands. I nevr was at Mrs Bar—s house in my life, except once that I chancd to pass by her shop, was desird to walk in and went no furthr—nor stayd three minutes. Dr Delany hath been long her Protectr, and he being many years my acquaintance, desired my good offices for her, & brought her sevrll times to the Deanry. I knew she was poetically given, & for a woman, had a sort of genius that way, she appeard very modest & pious, and I believe was sincere, and wholly turnd to Poetry. I did conceive her Journey to Engld was on the score of her trade, being a woollen drapr, till Dr Del— sd she had a design of printing her poems by Subscription, and desired I would befriend her; wch I did chiefly by yr means. The D^{r} still urging me on upon whose request I writ to her 2 or 3 times, because she thought that my countenancing of her might be of use. Ld Car^{tr} very much befriended her, and she seems to have made her way not ill. As for those 3 lett^{rs} you mention supposed all to be writt by me to the Qu— on M^{rs} B's account, especially the lett^{r} wch bears my name,[1] I can onely say, that the apprehensions one may be apt to have of a friend doing a foolish thing, is an effect of kindness, and Gd knows who is free from playing the fool sometime or oth^{r}: but, in such degree as to write to the Qu— who hath used me ill without any cause, and to write in such a manner as the lett you sent me, and in such a Style, and to have so much zeal for one almost a Stranger, and to make such a description of a woman as to prefer her before all man kind, and to instance it as one of the greatest grievances of Ireld, that Her M— hath not encouraged M^{rs} B— a woollen-drapers wife, declind in the world, because she hath a knack of versifying, was to suppose or fear a folly so transcendent that no man could be guilty of who was not fit for Bedlam. You know the lett you sent inclosed, is not my hand; and why I should disguise and yet sign my name, should seem unaccountable; especially when

[1] The second letter was 'in abuse' of Queen Caroline's friend, Mrs. Clayton, probably for concealing Mrs. Barber's merits from Her Majesty, and was unsigned (Mrs. Thomson's *Memoirs of Viscountess Sundon*, ii. 71). Of the third letter nothing is known.—Ball.

[2] This draft of a letter in Swift's hand is written with many contractions. It concerns the 'counterfeit' letter of 22 June sent from Dublin to the Queen, which was not in Swift's hand, and the signature, which purports to be his, is a clumsy and manifest forgery. See Appendix XXIII. The draft of the fragmentary letter to Pope (Forster Collection, no. 549, 48. G. 6/2) was used from which to print by Deane Swift in 1765.

I am taught and have reason to believe that I am under the Qu—'s displeasure on many accounts, and one very late, for having fixed a Stone over the burying place of the D. of Schombg in my Cathedrall, which however I was assured by a worthy person, who sollicitd that affair last sumer with some relations of the Duke, Her M, on hearing the matt^{r}, sd they ought to erect a monum^{t}. Yet I am told assurdly, that the K— not long ago on the representation and complaint of the Prussian Envoy, (with a hard name) who hath marryd a granddaughter of the Duke,[1] sd publickly in the drawing room, that I had put up the stone out of malice to raise a quarrell between His M. and the K. of Prussia. This perhaps may be talk, because it is absurd, for I thought it was a Whiggish action to hon^{r} D. Schombug, who was so instrumen^{tl} in the Revolution and was Stadthold^{r} of Prussia, and otherwise in the Service of that Electorate which is now a Kingdom. You will observe the lett^{r} you sent me, concluded Your Majesty's loyall Subject, wch is absolutely absurd, for we are onely Subjects to the K; and so is He^{r} M— her self. I have had the happyness to be known to You above 20 Years; and I appeal whether you have known me to exceed the common indiscretions of man kind, or that when I conceived my self to have been so very ill used by her Majesty, whom I never attended but on her own commands; I should turn solliciter to her for M^{rs} B . . If the Qu had not an inclination to think ill of me, she knows me to well to believe in her own heart, that I should be such a coxcomb. I am pushed on by that unjust Suspicion to give up so much of my discretion, as to write next post to my Ldy Suffolk on this occasion, and to desire she will show what I write to the Qu— though I have as much reason to complain of her as of Her M— upon the score of her pride and negligence—which make her fitt^{r} to be an Irish Ldy than an English one—You told me she complaind that I did not write to her;[2] when I did upon your advise, and a lett that required an answer, she wanted the civility to acquit her self. I shall not be less in the favor of God or the esteem of my friends, for either of their Majesty's hard thoughts, which they onely take up from misrepresentations; The first time I saw the Qu, I took occasion upon the Subject of Mr Gay to complain of that very treatment which innocent persons often receive from Princes and great Minis^{trs}, that they too easily receive bad impressions; yet they will never shake them off. This I sd upon

[1] Lady Holderness's sister married Christoph Martin von Degenfeld.
[2] 21 Nov. 1730.

S[r] R. W's treatment of M[r] Gay about a libel, and the Qu fell entirely in with me; yet now falls into the same error. As to the Lett[1] . . .

Endorsed by Swift: Lett to M[r] Pope | about my pretended | Lett[r] to the Qu—&c

Tickell Papers

Swift to Thomas Tickell[2]

[20 July 1731]

1. For *when*, I would advise *where*
2. I do not well understand this line
3 I see what *this* and *that* refer too, but in the line just before there are two words, *present* and *past* and in the next line above *virtues* and *boast*, which will make some difficulty to a common reader.

S[r] After frequent reading with as much care as I could; I found but the three remarks above mentioned that I could possibly make. Onely I would sink nine of the ten thousand fathom, and call it *A thousand.* I desire you will please to finish it. I have been riding out to day, as well as yesterday, for my health. but find my self much disordered . . If I grow better, I will wait on you to morrow; if not, I will send the Paper by a safe Hand.

Deanry-house
July. 20th 1731

I am S[r]
y[r] &c

I have marked the figures
1st, 2, 3. in your original.

Address: To | M[r] Secretary Tickel.

[1] The end of the second leaf is torn off with the loss of eight or nine lines on the recto. The letter ends at the top of the verso with the words—'of accidents, & out of perfect commiseration &c'.

[2] In *Thomas Tickell*, ed. R. E. Tickell, pp. 156–7, it is erroneously stated that the original of Swift's letter is missing. The autograph does survive among the Tickell papers. The unfinished poem, running to 108 lines, submitted to Swift for criticism, will be found, printed for the first time, on pp. 236–9 of the above volume. The letter was first printed by Scott, 1814, xix. 370–1, whence it was copied by Ball. Under '3' Scott, followed by Ball, misread 'virtues and boast' as 'viscus and leach'. Tickell has a note in his Letter Book, no. 2: 'The following is a copy of the unfinished Poem alluded to in the Letter. A few of the lines in it were afterwards transposed into another Poem published by Mr. T.—ll, and addressed to a Lady on her Marriage.'

B.M. Add. MS. 22625, ff. 22–23

Swift to the Countess of Suffolk

[Dublin, 27 July 1731]

Madam.[1]

I give you joy of your new title, and of the consequences it may have, or hath had, on your rising at Court, whereof I know nothing but by common fame; for You remember how I prophesyed of your behaviour, when you should come to be a great Lady, at the time I drew your Character; and I hope you have kept it. I writ to you some time ago by the advice of Mr Pope. I writ to you civily; but you did not answer my letter, although you were not then a Countess, and if you were, your neglect was so much the worse: For, your title hath not encreased your value with me; and your conduct must be very good if it will not lessen you. Neither should you have heard from me now, if it were not on a particular occasion . . I find from severall instances, that I am under the Queen's displeasure; and, as it is usual among Princes, without any manner of reason. I am told there were three letters sent to Her Majesty in relation to one Mrs Barber; who is now in London, and solliciting for a Subscription to her poems. It seems, the Queen thinks that these letters were written by me; and I scorn to defend my self even to her Majesty; grounding my scorn upon the opinion I had of her justice, her tast, and good sense; especially, when the last of those letters, whereof I have just received the originall from Mr Pope, was signed with my name; and why I should disguise my hand, which you know very well, and yet write my name, is both ridiculous and unaccountable.[2]

[1] There is a draft of this letter, not in Swift's hand, in the Forster Collection (no. 550), dated by Swift 'Jul. 24th 1731'. The draft was also endorsed by him: 'Jul. 24. 1731 | Copy of a Letter to | the Countess of | Suffolk—about the | Counterfeit letters | from me to the Qu—'.

[2] Johnson in his *English Poets*, ed. Birkbeck Hill, iii. 39, harshly charges Swift with the authorship of the counterfeit letter. But see Hill's Appendix I. The accusation may be peremptorily dismissed. In the *Correspondence of Mrs. Delany*, First Series, i. 321, a letter from Dr. Delany to Mrs. Clayton, 27 Feb. [1731], is printed in which he refers to two letters written by Mrs. Barber to the Queen 'one in abuse of you, without a name, and another in praise of herself in the name of Dr. Swift; by the last, she hath to my knowledge, entirely lost his friendship, and by the former all hope of yours'. As we know, however, Swift forgave Mrs. Barber. Mrs. Clayton was Charlotte, daughter of John Dyve. She married William Clayton, M.P. for New Woodstock, and became Woman of the Bedchamber to Princess Caroline, afterwards Queen. In 1735 Clayton was created

Last post I writ my whole Sentiments on the matter to Mr Pope, who tells me, that you and he vindicated me on all the three letters: which indeed, was but bare justice in you both, for he is my old friend, and you are in my debt on account of the esteem I had for you. I desire you would ask the Queen, whether since the time I had the honor to be known to her, I ever did one single action, or said one single word, to disoblige her. I never asked her for any thing; and you well know, that when I had an intention to go to France, about the time the late King dyed, I desired your opinion (not as you were a Courtier) whether I should go or not; and that you absolutely forbid me, as a thing that would look disaffected, and for other reasons, wherein I confess I was your Dupe as well as somebody's else, and, for want of that journey, I fell sick, and was forced to return hither to my unenvyed home. I hear the Queen hath blamed me for putting a Stone, with a Latin inscription, over the D. of Schomberg's burying-place in my Cathedral, and that the King said publickly, I had done it in malice, to create a quarrell between him, and the K. of Prussia. But the publick prints, as well as the thing it self will vindicate me; and the hand the Duke had in the Revolution made him deserve the best monument, neither could the K. of Prussia justly take it ill, who must have heard that the Duke was in the Service of Prussia, and Stadt-holder of it, as I have seen in his Titles. The first time I saw the Queen, I talked to her largely upon the conduct of Princes and great Ministers; (it was on a particular occasion) that, when they receive an ill account of any person, although they afterward have the greatest demonstration of the falshood; yet will they never be reconciled; and although the Queen fell in with me upon the hardship of such a proceeding, yet now she treats me directly in this same manner. I have faults enough, but never was guilty of any either to Her Majesty or to you; and as little to the King, whom I never saw but when I had the honor to kiss his hand. I am sensible that I ow a great deal of this usage to S[r] R. Walpole; whom yet I never offended, although he was pleased to quarrel with me very unjustly, for which I showed not the least resentment, (whatever I might have in my heart) nor was ever partaker with those who have been battelling with him for some years past.[1] I am contented that the Queen should see this letter,

Baron Sundon of Ardagh, co. Longford. She died 1 Jan. 1741–2. On his death in 1752 the peerage became extinct.

[1] Temple Scott, *Prose Works*, vii. 392, believes that Swift was the author of

and would be pleased to consider how severe a censure it is to believe I should write thrice to her, onely to find fault with her Ministry, and recommend Mrs Barber, whom I never knew till she was recommended to me by a worthy friend to help her to subscribers, which, by her writings, I thought she deserved. Her Majesty gave me leave, and even commanded me, above five years ago, if I lived till she was Queen, to write to her on behalf of Ireland for the miseryes of which Kingdom, She appeared then to be much concerned. I desired the friend[1] who introduced me to be a witness of her Majesty's promise. Yet that liberty of writing to her I never took, altho I had too many occasions, and is it not wonderfull, that I should be suspected of writing to her in such a style, in a counterfeit hand, and my name subscribed, upon a perfect trifle, at the same time that I well knew my self to be very much out of Her Majesty's good Graces: I am perhaps not so very much awed with Majesty, as others, having known Courts more or less from my early youth: And I have more than once told the Queen that I did not regard her Station half so much, as the good understanding I heard and found to be in her . . I am a good Whig by thinking it sufficient to be a good subject, with little personal esteem for Princes, further than as their virtues deserve; and upon that score, had a most particul[r] respect for the Queen Your Mistress. One who asks nothing, may talk with freedom; and that is my case. I have not said half that was in my heart; but I will have done: and remembring that you are a Countess, will borrow so much ceremony, as to remain, with great respect | Madam | Your Ladyships | most obedient, and | most humble servant | Jonath Swift.

Dublin July 27th | 1731.

Address: To the Right Honorable, | the Countess of Suffolk, at | Hampton Court | Middx Via London.
First address: S[t] James's house
Postmarks: DUBLIN 2 AV

the *Answer of the Right Hon. William Pulteney, Esq. to the Right Hon. Sir Robert Walpole*. This is improbable (*a*) on the grounds of style; (*b*) of the fact that from June to the end of September Swift was at Market Hill; (*c*) that the *Answer* is dated 15 Oct. 1730.

[1] i.e. Arbuthnot.

4806

Viscount Bolingbroke to Swift

[2 August 1731]

[1]I am indebted to you, my Reverend Dean, for a letter of a very old date.[2] the Expectation of Seeing you from week to week which our friend Gay made me entertain hindered me from writing to you a good while, & I have since deferred it by waiting an opportunity of sending my letter by a safe hand. that opportunity presents itself att last, and Mr Echlin[3] will put this letter into your hands. You will hear from Him and from others of the general State of things in this Country, into which I returned, and where I am confined, for my Sins. if I entertained the notion, which by the way I believe to be much older than Popery, or even than Christianity, of making up an account with Heaven, and demanding the Ballance in Bliss, of paying it by good works & sufferings of my own & by the merits & sufferings of others, I should imagine that I had expiated all the faults of my life, one way or other, since my return into England. one of the circumstances of my Situation which has afflicted me most, and which afflicts me still so, is the absolute inutillity I am of to those whom I should be the best pleased to serve. Success in serving my friends would make me amends for the want of it in disserving my Enemys. it is intollerable to want it in both & yet both go together generally. I have had two or three projects on foot for making such an Establishment here as might tempt you to quit Ireland. one of them would have succeeded, & would have been agreable in every respect, if Engagements to my Lady's[4] Kinsman, who did not I suppose deserve to be your Clarke, had not prevented it. another of them cannot take place without the consent of those who would rather have you a Dean in Ireland than a Parish Priest in England, & who are glad to keep you where your sincere friend[5] my late Lord Oxford sent you. a third was wholy in our power. But when I

[1] Printed only in part by Elwin though published in full and with notes by Hawkesworth in 1766.

[2] Probably a reply, not now forthcoming, to Bolingbroke's letter of 20 Mar. 1731.

[3] Possibly the Rev. John Echlin whose advice Swift sought concerning the choir and music of St. Patrick's

[4] i.e. his first wife.

[5] Written ironically.

enquired exactly into the value, I found it less than I had believed, the Distance from these Parts was great, & besides all this, an unexpected, & groundless Dispute about the right of presentation, but still such a Dispute as the Law must determine, had arisen. you will please to beleive that I mention these things for no other Reason than to show you, how much those friends deserve you should make them a visit att least, who are so desirous to settle you amongst them. I hope their endeavours will not be always unsuccessful.

[1]I received some time ago a letter from Dr Delany, & very lately Mr Pope sent me some sheets which seem to contain the substance of two sermons of that gentlemans.[2] the Philosophia prima is above my reach, and especially when it attempts to prove that God has done or does so and so, by attempting to prove that so and so is essential to his attributes or necessary to his design, and that the not doing so and so would be inconsistent with the former, or repugnant to the latter. I content my self to contemplate what I am sure He has done, & to adore Him for it in humble Silence. I can demonstrate that every cavil which has been brought against the great system of the world, physical and moral, from the Days of Democritus and Epicurus to this day, is absurd. But I dare not pronounce why things are made as they are, state the ends of infinite wisdom, & shew the proportion of the means.

Dr Delany in his letter to me mentioned some errors in the critical part of learning which he hoped he had corrected, by shewing the mistakes, particularly of Sir J: Marsham,[3] on whose authority these errors were built. Whether I can be of use to him even in this part I know not, for having fixed my opinions long ago concerning all ancient History & chronology, by a careful examination into the first principles of them, I have ever since layed that study totally aside. I confest in the letter I writ lately to the Doctor, notwithstanding my great Respect for Sir John Marsham, that his authority is often precarious, because He leans often on other authoritys which are so. But to you I will confess a little more. I think, nay I know, that there is no possibility of making any system of that kind without doing the

[1] Elwin omitted this and the following two paragraphs.

[2] Ball is probably justified in his supposition that these sheets represented a portion of the first volume of Delany's *Revelation examined with Candour*.

[3] Sir John Marsham, 1602–85, who earned a great reputation for wide knowledge of history, chronology, and languages. His work of chief distinction was *Chronicus Canon Ægyptus, Ebraicus, Graecus, et Disquisitiones*, 1672.

same thing, & that the defect is in the Subject not in the writer. I have read the writings of some who differ from him, & of others who undertook particularly to refute him. it seemed plain to me that this was the case. all the materials of this sort of Learning are disjoynted & broken. Time has contributed to render them so, & the unfaithfulness of those who have transmitted them down to us, particularly of that vile fellow Eusebius,[1] has done even more than Time itself by throwing these fragments into a different order, by arbitrary interpretations, & it is often impossible to make any others, without by a few plausible guesses for the connexion & application of them, a man may with tollerable ingenuity prove almost any thing by them. I tryed formerly to prove in a learned dissertation, by the same set of authoritys, that there had been four Assyrian monarchys, that there had been but three, that there had been but two, that there had been but one, & that there never had been any.

I puzzled myself, & a much abler man than myself, the friend to whom I lent the transcript, & who has I beleive kept it. in short I am afraid that I shall not be very useful to Dr Delany in making Remarks on the work he is about. His communication of this work maybe useful, & I am sure it will be agreeable to me. if you and He are still in Ireland, pray give my best services to Him, but say no more than may be proper of all I have writ to you.

I know very well the project you mean, & about which you say that Pope & you have often teazed me.[2] I could convince you, as He is convinced, that a publication of any things of that kind would have been wrong on many accounts, & would be so even now. Besides, call it Pride if you will, I shall never make either to the present Age, or to Posterity, any Apology for the part I acted in the late Queen's Reign. But I will apply myself very seriously to the composition of just and true Relations of the Events of those times, in which both I and my friends & my Enemys, must take the merit or the Blame which an authentick & impartial Deduction of fact will assign to us: I will endeavour to write so, as no man could write, who had not been a Party in those transactions, & as few men would write who had been concerned in them. I beleive I shall go back in considering the political Interests of the principal Powers of Europe as far as the Pyrenæan

[1] Eusebius of Caesarea, born about A.D. 264, commonly known as the father of ecclesiastical history. His broadmindedness should have commended him to Bolingbroke.

[2] The project, which came to nothing, was a history of his time.

treaty.[1] But I shall not begin a thread of History till the Death of Charles the 2d of Spain, & the accession of Q: Anne to the Throne of England. nay even from that time downwards, I shall render my Relation more full, or piu magra, the word is Father Pauls,[2] just as I have or have not a stock of authentick Materials. these shall regulate my work, & I will neither indulge my own vanity, nor other men's curiosity in going one step further than they carry me. You see my Dear Swift that I open a large feild to my self. with what success I shall expatiate in it, I know as little as I know whether I shall live to go thro' so great a work. But I will begin imediately, & will make it one principal Business of the rest of my life. this advantage att least I shall reap from it, and a great advantage it will be. my attention will be diverted from the present scene. I shall greive less att those things which I cannot mend. I shall dignify my Retreat, and shall wind up the labours of my life in serving the cause of truth. you say that you could easily shew by comparing my Letters for twenty years past how the whole system of Philosophy changes by the several gradations of Life. I doubt it. as far as I am able to recollect, my way of thinking has been uniform enough for more than twenty years. true it is, to my shame, that my way of acting has not been always conformable to my way of thinking. my own passions, & the passions & Interests of other men still more, have led me aside. I launched into the Deep before I had loaded Ballast enough. if the ship did not sink, the Cargo was thrown overboard. the storm it self threw me into Port. my own opinion my own Desires would have kept me there. the opinion the desires of others sent me to sea again. I did, and blamed myself for doing, what others, & you among the Rest, would have blamed me if I had not done. I have payed more than I owed to Party, and as much att least as was due to friendship. if I go off the stage of publick life without paying all I owe to my Enemys, & to the Enemys of my Country, I do assure you the Bankrupcy is not fraudulent: I conceal none of my effects.

does Pope talk to you of the noble work which, att my instigation, he has begun, in such a manner that He must be convinced by this time I judged better of his tallents than He did?[3] the first Epistle which considers man, and the Habitation, of man, relatively to the

[1] The treaty of 1659 between France and Spain concerning the throne of the latter country.

[2] Fra Paolo Sarpi, 1552–1623, the historian.

[3] This passage relates to Pope's progress with the *Essay on Man.*

whole system of universal Being, the second which considers Him in his own Habitation, in Himself, & relatively to his particular system, & the third which shews how an universal cause

works to one end, but works by various laws,

how Man, & Beast, & vegetable are linked in a mutual Dependancy, parts necessary to each other & necessary to the whole, how human societys were formed, from what spring true Religion and true Policy are derived, how God has made our greatest interest & our plainest Duty indivisibly the same, these three Epistles I say are finished. the fourth he is now intent upon. 'tis a noble subject. He pleads the cause of God, I use Seneca's Expression, against that famous charge which atheists in all ages have brought, the supposed unequal Dispensations of Providence, a charge which I cannot heartily forgive you Divines for admitting. you admit it indeed for an extream good purpose, and you build on this admission the necessity of a future state of Rewards & punishments. But what if you should find that this future state will not account for Gods justice, in the present state, which you give up, in opposition to the atheist? would it not have been better to defend God's justice in this world against these daring men by irrefragable Reasons, and to have rested the proof of the other point on Revelation? I do not like concessions made against Demonstration, repair or supply them how you will. the Epistles I have mentioned will compose a first Book. the plan of the Second is settled. you will not understand by what I have said that Pope will go so deep into the argument, or carry it so far, as I have hinted. You enquire so kindly after my wife that I must tell you something of her. she has fallen upon a Remedy invented by a surgeon abroad, & which has had great success in cases similar to hers. this Remedy has visibly attacked the original cause of all her complaints, and has abated in some degree by one gentle & uniform effect all the greivous & various symptoms. I hope, & surely with Reason, that she will receive still greater benefit from this method of cure which she will resume as soon as the great heat is over. if she recovers, I shall not for her sake abstract myself from the world more than I do att present in this place. But if she should be taken from me, I should most certainly yeild to that strong desire, which I have long had, of secluding my self totally from the Company & affairs of mankind, of leaving the management even of my private affairs to others, and of securing by these means for the rest of my life an uninterrupted tenor of philosophical Quiet. I suppose you have seen some of those volumes of scurrility which have been thrown into the world against Mr P: and myself,[1] and the Craftsman which gave occasion to them. I think, and it is the sence of all my Friends, that the Person who published the final answer took a right turn in a very nice & very provoking circumstance. to answer all the falsitys, misrepresentations, & Blunders which a club of such scoundrels as Arnold, Concanen,[2] and other Pensioners of the Minister, crowd togather, would have been equally tedious & ridiculous, and must have forced several things to be said neither prudent, nor decent, nor perhaps strictly honourable to be said. to have explained some points, & to have stopped att others, would have given strength to that impertinent suggestion Guilt alone is silent in the Day of Enquiry. it was therefore Right to open no part of the scene of the late Queen's Reign, nor submit the passages of her administration, & the conduct of any of her Ministers, to the examination of so vile a Tribunal. this was still the more Right because upon such points as relate to subsequent transactions and as affect me singly, what the Craftsman had said was justifyed unanswerably, and what the Remarker had advanced was proved to be infamously false. the effect of this paper has answered the Design of it, and, which is not common, all sides agree that the things said ought to have been said, & that more ought not to have been said. the publick writers seems to be getting back from these personal altercations to national affairs, much against the grain of the Minister's faction. what the effects of all this writing will be I know not, But this I know that when all the information which can be given is given, when all the spirit which can be raised is raised, and all to no purpose, it is to no purpose to write any more. even you men of this world have nothing else to do, but to let the ship drive till she is cast away, or till the storm is over. for my own part I am neither an owner, an officer, nor a foremast man. I am but a Passenger, said my Lord Carbury.[3]

it is well for you that I am got to the end of my paper, for you might else have a letter as long again from me. if you answer me by

[1] Bolingbroke's letter of 22 May 1731 in *The Craftsman* provoked many attacks on himself and Pulteney.

[2] Concanen and Arnall both figured in *The Dunciad*.

[3] George Evans, created Baron Carbery of Carbery, co. Cork, 1715; died 1749.

the post, remember whilst you are writing that you write by the post. Adieu my Reverend Friend—

Aug: the 2d | 1731.

Endorsed by Swift: Lord Bolingbroke. | Dated Aug. 2d · 1731 | Rx Octr 10th. 1731 | Answerd Octr 30: 1731

Tickell Papers

Swift to Thomas Tickell

[Deanery House, Tuesday Morning, August 1731]

Sr[1]

As you have been very obliging to me on all occasions, gratitude would not suffer me to be careless in any thing relating to your credit. The last time you were here, you mentioned a foolish Scribble printed in Mr Pilkingtons Poems, When you were gone I immediatly looked into the book, and as I told you, could not find it. I then sent to Mr Pilkington, who brought me an edition printed in London, where I found it at the end of the book, The Story of the thing is thus: When the money was ordered by my Lord Carteret; Pilkington not used to such Sums, told his Patron Doctr Delany all the particulars of his fear Joy, &c, on the matter which so diverted the Doct, that he made the young man to write it down; that Lord Carteret might see it, and when his Lordship went to England, he writ to the Doctor to send him a Copy, which His Lordship having shown to severall persons, was transcribed, and by the impertinence of the Bookseller, printed at the end of the poems, against Pilkington's knowledge, and much to his Vexation;[2] for the character he

[1] This letter was first printed by Scott, 1814, xix. 379, whence it was copied by Ball. Swift's autograph among the Tickell papers, here used, occupies a piece of paper 8¼ in. by 6¼ in., the letter on pp. 1, 2, 3. P. 4 is blank. No address or endorsement. Pilkington's *Poems on Several Occasions* first appeared in Dublin, 1730, supported by a fair list of subscribers, including the Lord-Lieutenant, peers and peeresses, by Swift and Delany. The ode to George II on his birthday is the last poem in the book, and carries a separate title. This ode was, apparently, used on more than one annual occasion. It appears, for example, in the London *Daily Journal*, 9 Nov. 1734, with a statement that it was performed at Dublin Castle on the occasion of His Majesty's birthday. The appearance of the ode in a London newspaper was probably due to the fact that in 1734 Pilkington was in London.

[2] The London edition of Pilkington's *Poems* contained a prose composition

gives himself in it is a very mean one, and must be remembered, much to his disadvantage if ever he rises in the world. As for your part in it I must declare my thoughts that it does not affect you in the least. You are said to be sick, and could not be seen, and the complaint is of the usuall kind, made by all who attend at Courts. The young man was sorry, as he had reason, to see it in print, lest it might possibly offend a Person of your reputation and consequence. He appears to me to be a modest good natured Man; I know but little of him: Doctor Delany brought him to me first, and recommended him as one whom I might safely countenance. He is in the utmost pain at hearing that you imagine that there was the least design to affront you. Since, as it would be the basest thing in it self, so such a treatment would be the surest method to ruin his interests.

I could not forbear telling you this out of perfect pity to the young Man.

I desire to present my humble Service to Mrs Tickell, and am with great esteem | S^r^ | Your most obedient | humble Servant | Jonath: Swift

Deanry-house | Tuesday | morning.

I am just going out of town for a few weeks; but I have ordered that Mrs Tickell shall have her annuall tribute of Peaches and Nectarines which will be ripe in a few days if the sun be favorable, and thieves will spare them

Longleat xiii (Harleian transcript)

Swift to Gay and the Duchess of Queensberry

⌜The Country.⌝[1] Aug. 28. 1731

[2]You and the Dutchess use me very ill, for I profess I cannot distinguish the Style or the handwriting of either. I think Her Grace

entitled 'The Plague of Wealth, or the Poet's Diary, in a Letter to Dr. Delany'. Carteret had authorized a gratuity of £50 to Pilkington for the ode to the King on his birthday. On several occasions Pilkington, calling on Tickell at the Castle for his gratuity, was denied access. Thereupon he composed in prose a jocular account of his rebuffs, which Tickell seems to have taken in bad part when the London printers, according to Pilkington, included it in the London edition of his *Poems*. For part of the skit see Scott, xix. 379–80.

[1] i.e. Powerscourt.

[2] Pope's (1740–2) and Faulkner's (1741, vii. 182) texts of this letter leave sub-

writes more like you than her self, and that you write more like her Grace than yourself. I would swear the begining of your letter ⌜was⌝ writ by the Dutchess, though it is to pass for yours; because there is a cursed lye in it, that she is neither young or healthy, & besides it perfectly resembles the part she owns. I will likewise swear, that what I must suppose is written is your hand, & thus I am puzzled & perplexed between you, but I will go on in the innocency of my own heart. I am got eight miles from our famous Metropolis to a Country Parsons, to whom I lately gave a City living, such as an English chaplain would leap at.[1] I retired hither for the publick good having two great works in hand, one to reduce the whole politeness wit, humor & style of England into a short System for the use of all persons of quality, and particularly the Maids of Honor:[2] The other is of almost equal importance; I may call it the whole duty of servants, in about twenty several Stations from the Steward & waiting woman down to the Scullion & Pantry boy.[3]—I believe no mortal had ever such fair invitations as ⌜I⌝ to be happy in the best company of England. I wish I had liberty to print your letter with my own comments upon it. There was a fellow in Ireland called Conolly,[4] who from a shoe-boy grew to be several times one of the chief Governors, wholly illiterate, & with hardly common sence. a Lord Lieutenant told the first K. George, that Conolly was the greatest subject he had in both Kingdoms, and truly this Character was gotten & preserved by Conolly's never appearing in England, which was the only wise thing he ever did except

stantial omissions, here enclosed within half-brackets. Swift's comments on the handwriting of Gay and the Duchess refer to their letter to him of 18 July 1731.

[1] Swift was at the time visiting the Rev. John Towers, who held the living of Powerscourt, known ecclesiastically as Stagonil. Towers had received the gift of St. Luke's, Dublin, which was in the gift of the Dean and Chapter of St. Patrick's.

[2] *A Complete Collection of Genteel and Ingenious Conversation*, printed for Motte and Bathurst, 1738.

[3] *Directions to Servants in General*, which was published in 1738 by Dodsley in London and Faulkner in Dublin. Several manuscripts of this work seem to have been in circulation. In the Forster Collection there is a fragment of one with some corrections in Swift's hand; and in Lord Rothschild's library there is, no. 2275, a holograph of three chapters.

[4] Swift's characterization of William Conolly must not be taken literally. He was elected Speaker of the Irish House of Commons in 1715 and held that position till the year of his death in 1729. He was a member of the Privy Council and ten times a Lord Justice of Ireland.

purchasing sixteen thousand pounds a year. Why you need not stare: it is easily applyed. I must be absent in order to preserve my credit with her Grace. ⌜One thing I like well enough, that you & the Dutchess absolutely govern the family, for I have not heard one syllable of my Lord Duke, who I take for granted, submits to all your decrees. I writ some time ago to your new lady Suffolk, and old friend; but have received no answer. she will probably be more civil when she comes to be a Dutchess, but I do not think her sincerity worth disputing; nor will disturb you in your Dupery because it is of no consequence, besides my quarrell with her is partly good manners, and she is a good servant who does the office of a skreen[1]⌝. —Lo here comes in the Dutchess again (I know her by her dd's;[2] but am a fool for discovering my Art) to defend her self against my conjectures of what she said. Madam, I will imitate your Grace and write to you upon the same line. I own it is a base un-Romantick Spirit in me, to suspend the honor of waiting at your Graces feet, till I can finish a paultry Law-suit. It concerns indeed almost my whole fortune; it is equal to half Mr Pope's, & two thirds of Mr Gay's, and about six weeks rent of your Grace's. This cursed accident hath drill'd away the whole summer. But Madam, understand one thing, that I take all your Ironicall Civilities in a literal sense, and when ever I have the honor to attend you, shall expect them to be literally performed, though perhaps I shall find it hard to prove your hand writing in a Court of Justice; but that will not be much for your credit. How miserably hath your grace been mistaken in thinking to avoyd envy by running into exil, where it haunts you more than ever it did even at Court: Non te civitas, non Regia domus in exilium miserunt, sed tu utrasque,[3] so says Cicero (as your Grace knows) or so he might have said.

⌜Sir I profess it was in my thoughts to have writ that congratulatory letter[4] you mention; I never saw the Paper which occasioned the disgrace, It was not suffered to be visible here; But I am told there was something wrong in it, that looked like betraying private conversation. Two Ministers may talk with freedom of their master's

[1] skreen] shrew *Elwin* and *Ball.*—Perhaps mistakenly?

[2] The Duchess retaliated for this remark about her dd's in two 'Coptic' lines appended to Gay's and her letter of 1 Nov. 1731.—Sherburn.

[3] You have not been sent into Exile by the City or by the Royal Family; but both City and Royal Family have been banished by you.—Faulkner.

[4] To William Pulteney.

wrong notions, &c. and it would hardly agree with honor to communicate what was spoken, to any third person, much less to the publick; this I say at a venture; for all things are here misrepresented, and I wish my self better informed.⌉ I am told that the Craftsman in one of his papers is offended with the publishers of (I suppose) the last edition of the Dunciad, & I was asked whether you & Mr Pope were as good friends to the new disgraced person[1] as formerly. This I know nothing of, but suppose it the consequence of some Irish mistake. As to writing; I look on you just in the prime of life for it, the very season when Judgement & invention draw together. But Scheams are perfectly accidental; some will appear barren of hints & matter, but prove to be fruitfull; and others the contrary. And what you say is past doubt, that every one can best find hints for himself; though it is possible, that sometimes a friend may give you a lucky one just suited to your own imagination. But all this is almost past with me, my invention & judgement are perpetually at fisty cuffs, till they have quite disabled each other; And the meerest trifles I ever wrote are serious Philosophical lucubrations in comparison to what I now busy my self about; as (to speak in the Authors phrase) the world may one day see.[2] ⌈—I must desire you (raillerie a part) to let my Lady Dutchess know, that no man is or can be more sensible than my self of her Grace's undeserved civility favour and condescention, with my thanks, for all which I could fill this paper & twenty more to the bottom. but an oppertunity just happening to send this letter to town (for I am out of post rodes) I must here conclude.⌉

Mrs. Pilkington's Memoirs

Swift to Mrs. Pilkington

[6 September 1731]

Madam,[3]

I send you a Piece of Plumb-cake, which I did intend should be at your Christening; if you have any Objection to the Plumbs, or do

[1] To Pulteney.

[2] The reference is to the two works in progress already mentioned.

[3] These two letters were printed in the third volume of Mrs. Pilkington's *Memoirs* (1754), pp. 166–7. She tells us that the Dean had promised to stand godfather to the child she was expecting. When the child, a boy, was born Swift was

not like to eat them, you may return them to, | Madam, | your sincere Friend and Servant, | *J. Swift.*

Mrs. Pilkington to Swift

Sir,

I have heard that Ostridges could digest Iron, but you give me a harder Task, when you bid me eat Gold; but suppose I should, like the rich Streams of the *Tagus*, flow potable Gold, the interpretation of which is, that I mean to drink your Health this Minute, in a glass of Sack; and am, with the utmost Respect, Sir, | Your ever devoted Servant, | *L. Pilkington.*

4806

Lady Elizabeth Germain to Swift

Drayton 7 Sep. 1731

to show how strictly I obey your orders I came from the Dutchess of Dorsets Country House[1] to my own, where I have ridd and Walked as often as the Weather permitted me, nor am I very Nice in that, for if you remember I was not bredd up very tenderly nor a fine Lady, for which I acknowledge my self exceedingly obliged to my parents, for had I had that sort of Education I shoud not have been so easy and so happy as I thank God I now am, as to the Gout indeed I believe I do derive it from my Ancestors but I may forgive even that since it waited upon me no sooner, and especially since I see my Elder & two younger Brothers so terribly plagued with it, so that I am now the only wine Drinker in my family, & upon my Word I am not encreasd in that since you first knew me, I am sorry you are involved in Law suits tis the thing upon Earth I most fear, and wish

absent in the country, and in five days the boy died. The fact is confirmed by the register of St. Andrew's Church, Dublin, in which the burial of Jonathan, son of Matthew and Letitia Pilkington, is entered against the date 28 Aug. 1731. Upon his return, and after a brief visit to the Pilkingtons, Swift's servant appeared with 'a Piece of Ginger-bread, in which were stuck four Guineas', together with an accompanying letter. In reply she sent 'a real Piece of Plumb-cake'.

[1] i.e. Knole.

you had mett with as Complaisant an adversary as I did, for My Lord Peterborough plagued Sr John all his Life time, but declared if ever he gave the Estate to me, he woud have done with it, & accordingly has kept his word like an honourable Man,[1] I saw Mrs Barber the day before I came out of town and shoud be mighty glad to serve her, but I cant say so much by her husband whom for her sake I recommended to the Duke of Dorset to buy his Liverys on, the first thing he did was to ask a greater price than any body else and when we were at Whitchurch[2] where I attended their Graces, he was informed he had Cloth near enough in his shop and they feared they would not be ready against he came over, I hope in God I shall soon hear of their safe Landing and I do not question the People of Irelands Likeing them as well as they deserve, I desire no better for them, for if you dont spoil him there, which I think he has too good sense to let happen, he is the most Worthy honest Good natured great Soul'd man that ever was born, as to My Dutchess she is so reserved that perhaps she may not be at first so much admired but upon Knowledge I will defy any body upon Earth with Sense Judgment and good Nature, not only to admire her but must Love and Esteem her as much as I do and every one else that is really acquainted with her, you know him a Little so for his own sake you must like him, and till you are better acquainted with them both I hope you like them for mine,[3] mine & y^r friend Biddy is just the same as she was Laughs sedately & makes a Joke slily, and I am as I ever was and hope I ever shall be | your most Sincere | friend & faithfull | Humble servant | E Germain

[1] On accession to the title Peterborough did not succeed to all the family possessions, a great part of which went to the Duchess of Norfolk, daughter of the second Earl. The lady was divorced from the Duke in 1700, and on his death in 1701 she married Sir John Germain. Peterborough raised a lawsuit for the recovery of the estates including the family home of Drayton. The proceedings, after dragging on, were decided against him. He opened new proceedings from which, however, he withdrew on Germain's death in 1718, when he left the property to his second wife, Lady Betty Germain.

[2] The route through Whitchurch in Shropshire was frequently favoured by travellers to Ireland.

[3] The Duke and Duchess of Dorset landed in Ireland for the first time on 11 Sept.

4806

The Countess of Suffolk to Swift

[Hampton Court, 25 September 1731]

Sir

You seem to think that you have a Natural Right to Abuse me because I am a Woman and a Courtier;[1] I have taken it as a Woman and as a Courtier ought, with great resentment; and a determin'd resolution of Revenge . . The Number of letters that has been sent and thought by many to be yours (thank God they were all Silly ones)[2] has been a fair field to execute it. Think of my Joy to hear you suspected of Folly, think of my pleasure when I enter'd the list for your justification. indeed I was a little disconcerted to find Mr Pope took the same side; for I wou'd have had the Man of Wit, the Dignified Divine, the Irish Drapier have found no friend but the Silly Woman, and the Courtier. cou'd I have preserv'd myself alone in the list, I shou'd not have dispair'd that this Monitor of Princes, this Irish Patriot, this Excelent Man at Speech and Pen, shou'd have closed the Scene under Suspecion of having a violent Passion for Mrs Barber; and Lady M,[3] or Mrs Haywood[4] have writ the Progress of it. now to my Mortification I find every body inclin'd to think you had no hand in writing these letters. but I every day thank Providence that there is an Epitaph in St Patrick's Cathedral that will be a lasting Monument of your imprudence. I cherish this extremely, for say what you can to Justifie it; I am convinced I shall not easily argue the world into the belief of a Courtiers Sencerity, as you (with all your wit and Eloquence) will be able to convince Mankind of the prudence of that Action. I expect to hear if peace shall ensue, or war continue between us, if I know but little of the art of war, yet you see I do not want Courage; and that has made many an ignorant souldier fight successfully; besides I have a numerous Body of light arm'd Troops to bring into the Field; who where

[1] Swift to the Countess of Suffolk, 27 July 1731.

[2] She refers, presumably, to the counterfeit letter to the Queen, the letter in abuse of Mrs. Clayton, and the third unknown letter. Cf. Swift to Pope, 20 July 1731.

[3] Lady Mary Wortley Montagu.

[4] Eliza Haywood, 1693?–1756, the author of scandalous memoirs, responsible for a scurrilous attack on Martha Blount. She was subjected by Pope to merciless, but deserved, satire. See *The Dunciad*, ed. Sutherland, (A) ii. 149–58, (B) ii. 157–66.

single may be as inconsiderable as a Lilliputian, yet ten thousand of them Embarras'd Capt Gulliver. if you send honourable Articles they shall be sign'd. I insist that you own that you have been unjust to me, for I have never forgot you; but made others send my Compliments because I was not able to write my self: if I cannot justifie the advice I gave you from the success of it; yet you know I gave you my reasons for it; and it was y^r business to have judg'd of my Capacity by the Solidity of my Arguments; if the Principle was false you ought not to have acted upon it; so you have only been the Dupe of your own ill Judgment and not to my falshood. am I to send back the Crown and Plad,[1] well pack'd up in my own Character? or am I to follow my own inclination, and continue very truely and very | much your humble | Ser^t | H Suffolk

Hampton Court | Sepr ye 25th

Endorsed by Swift: Countess of Suffolk. | Sepr 25th 1731 | Answr^d Octb^r 20th 1731

B.M. Add. MS. 22625, ff. 24–25

Swift to the Countess of Suffolk

[26 October 1731]

Madam.[2]

Your Ladyship's letter made me a little grave, and in going to answer it, I was in great danger of leaning on my elbow, (I mean my left elbow) to consider what I should write, which posture I never used except when I was under a necessity of writing to Fools, or Lawyers, or Ministers of State, where I am to consider what is to be said. But, as I write to a person whom I esteem, I am in no pain at all. It would be an injury to you or Mr Pope to give thanks to either of you for justifying me about those letters sent to the Queen, because to think me guilty would disgrace your understandings, and as he is my best friend, so Your Ladyship owes me

[1] The trinket and poplin sent to her by Swift in the autumn of 1726.

[2] Croker in his *Letters of Lady Suffolk*, ii. 26, refrains from printing this letter, substituting a note: 'The loss of Lady Suffolk's letter, to which this is an answer, is much to be regretted; it would probably clear up most of the obscurities in the affair of Dean Swift's complaints against her.'

no malice, except that of Raillery; and good Raillery is always sincere. And if Her Majesty were deceived, it would lessen my opinion of her judgment, which would no otherwise affect me, than by making me sorry upon her own account. But what Your Ladyship would have me discover through all your refined civilityes, is my great imprudence in ordering that monument to be fixed in my Cathedrall. I shall not trouble you with a long story. But if ever a numerous venerable body of dignifyed Clergymen had reason to complain of the highest repeated indignity in return of the greatest honor offered by them, to persons they were wholly strangers to, then my Chapter is not to be blamed, nor I who proposed the matter to them, which however I could have done by my own authority, but rather chose it should be the work of us all; and I will confess it was upon their advice that I omitted the onely two passages which had much bitterness in them, and which a Bishop here, one after your own heart, blamed me very much for leaving out, declaring that the treatment given us by the Schomberg family, deserved a great deal worse. Indeed Madam I shall not attempt to convince England of any thing that relates to this Kingdom. The Drapier, whom you mention, could not do it in relation to the halfpence. Neither can the Parl^{mt} here convince you that we ought not to be put in so miserable condition in every article of distress. Why should the Schomberg family be so uneasy at a thing they were so long warned of, and were told they might prevent for fifty pounds. But here I wish Your Ladyship would put the Queen in mind of what passed between her Majesty and me upon the Subject of Ireland, when she appeared so much to pity this distressed Kingdom, and gave me leave to write to her if ever I lived to see her Queen, [said] that she would answer my letters, and promised that in such a case she would use all her credit to relieve us; whereupon I desired Doctor Arbuthnott, who was present, to be witness of what she said, and Her Majesty confirmed it. I will not ask what the event hath been. If any State-scribble writ here should happen to reach London, I entreat your Ladyship would continue to do me the justice of beleiving my innocence. Because I lately assured the D. of Dorset, that I would never have a hand in any such thing: and I gave him my reason before his Secretary;[1] that, looking upon this Kingdom's condition

[1] Walter Carey, chief secretary to the Duke of Dorset, when Lord-Lieutenant of Ireland. He was previously a member of the English Parliament; and Clerk in Ordinary to the Privy Council, 1729. He has been identified with 'Umbra' in

as absolutely desperate, I would not prescribe a dose to the dead. Some parts of your letter I do not understand. Mrs. Barber was recommended to me by Dr Delany, who is now in London, and whom I once presented to you at Marble-hill. She seems to be a Woman of piety, and a poeticall Genius; and though I never visited her in my life, yet was I disposed to do her good offices on the Doctor's account, and her own good character. By Lady M—[1] I cannot guess whom you mean. Mrs Heywood I have heard of as a stupid, infamous, scribbling woman, but have not seen any of her productions. And now Madam I utterly acquit Your Ladyship of all things that may regard me, except your good opinion, and that very little share I can pretend to in your memory, I never knew a Lady who had so many qualityes to beget esteem, but how you act as a friend, is out of my way to judge. As to the Queen, whom I never offended, since it would be presumption to imagine I ever voluntarily came into her thoughts; so it must be a mortification to think, when I happen to be named in her presence, it is usually to my disadvantage. I remember to have once told Her Majesty, how hard a thing it was that when a Prince or great Ministr hath received an ill impression of any person, although from the most false information, although the Prince were demonstrably convinced of the Person's innocence, yet the impression still continued; and Her Majesty readily condemned the Severity of such a proceeding. I had said the same thing before to Sr Robt Walpole, who upon reporting it to others, was pleased to give it a turn that I did not deserve.[2] I remember the Plad but I forget the Crown, and the meaning of it. If you had thought fit to have sent me as much of the Plad as would have made me a morning cap, before it fell to the share of the lowest of your women, I should have been proud that my head should have worn your Livery; but if you are weary of your *Character*, it must lye upon my head, for I know no other whom it will fit. And if your Lady-

the poem of that name printed in the Pope and Swift *Miscellanies. The Last Volume*, 1727, p. 128. It is questionable, however, whether the poem was written by Pope and whether 'Umbra' is to be identified with Carey. The nameless author of *Characters of the Times*, 1728, is responsible both for the attribution and the identification. See Ault, *Minor Poems of Pope*, pp. 140–1. In Swift's *Legion Club* Carey appears as Briareus, who 'Shews a Bribe in all his Hands' (*Poems*, iii. 833).

[1] Lady Mary Wortley Montagu. Cf. the Countess of Suffok to Swift, 25 Sept.

[2] i.e. that Swift was referring to himself, instead of to Gay.

ship will not allow it to be a character, I am sure it may pass for a Prediction. If you should put the same fancy into the Queen's Head, I must send her a much larger character, and in Royal paper, otherwis she will not be able to wrap the bundle in it. I fear so long a letter is beyond your mercy to forgive. But Your Ladyship is sure to be easy till Mr. Pope shall tell me that you are content to receive another. I should be heartily sorry if your increase in honor and Employment hath not been accompanyed with increase of health. Let Mr Pope in all his letters give me a particular account on this head, and pray God I may never have the least motive to pity you. For as a Courtier I forgive your *ame endurcie* (which I once chargd on my Lord Chesterfield and he did not dislike it) And you have not a favorite or flatterer who makes more outward offers of wishes for your ease and happiness than I do prayers from the bottom of my heart, which proceed entirely from that real respect and esteem, wherewith I am, | Madam, | Your Ladyship's most obedient humble Ser^{t}, | Jonath Swift.

Oc^{tr} 26th 1731

Address: To the Right Honorable the | Countess of Suffolk, Groom | of the Stole to Her Majesty,[1] | at St. James's | London
Postmark: 17 NO
Endorsed: Dr Swift | Octbr. ye 26th: 1731

4806

John Gay and the Duke and Duchess of Queensberry to Swift

[1 November 1731]

For about this month or six weeks past I have been rambling from home or have been at what I may not improperly call other homes, at Dawley & at Twickenham; & I really think at every one of my homes you have as good a pretension as myself, for I find 'em all exceedingly disappointed by the Lawsuit that hath kept you this summer from us. Mr Pope told me that Affair was now over, that you have the Estate that was your security, I wish you had your own

[1] A few days after her accession to the title Lady Suffolk was appointed Mistress of the Robes.

money, for I wish you free from every Engagement that keeps us one from another. I think you decypher'd the last Letter we sent you very judiciously. You may make your own conditions at Amesbury where I am at present; you may do the same at Dawley, and Twickenham you know is your own; But if you rather chuse to live with me, (that is to say, if you will give up your right & title) I will purchase the house you & I us'd to dispute about over-against Ham walks on purpose to entertain you. name your day & it shall be done.[1] I have liv'd with you, & I wish to do so again in any place & upon any terms. The Dutchess does not know of my writing, but I promis'd to acquaint the Duke the next time I writ to you, & for aught I know he may tell the Dutchess, & she may tell Sir W. Wyndham, who is now here, & for fear they should all have something to say to you I leave the rest of the paper 'till I see the Duke.

[2]Mr Gay tells me you seem to doubt what authority my Wife & he have to invite a person hither who by agreement is to have the government of the place during his stay, when at the same time it does not appear that the present master of these Demesnes hath been consulted in it. The truth of the matter is this; I did not know whether you might not have suspected me for a sort of a pert coxcomb had I put in my word in the late correspondence between you & my Wife. Ladies (by the Courtesie of the World) enjoy priviledges not allow'd to men & in many cases the same thing is call'd a favour from a Lady which might perhaps be look'd upon as impertinence from a man. Upon this reflection I have hitherto refrain'd from writing to you having never had the pleasure of conversing with you otherways & as that is a thing I most sincerely wish I would not venture to meddle in a negotiation that seem'd to be in so fair a way of producing that desirable end; but our friend John has not done me justice if he has never mention'd to you how much I wish for the pleasure of seeing you here & tho I have not till now avowedly taken any steps towards bringing it about, what has pass'd conducive to it has been all along with my privity & consent & I do now formally ratify all the preliminary articles & conditions agreed to on the part of my Wife & will undertake for the due observance of them. I depend upon my friend John to answer for my sincerity. I was not long at Court & have been a Country gentleman for some time.

[1] Swift's reply of 1 Dec. suggests that the house belonged to the Countess of Suffolk. It seems improbable, however, that the reference can be to Marble Hill.

[2] The rest of the letter, except the two lines of gibberish, are by the Duke.

Poll manu sub linus darque dds[1]
Sive Nig tig gnipite gnaros

Address: To the Revd Doctor Swift | Dean of St Patricks | in Dublin | Ireland
Postmark: 1 NO
Endorsed by Swift: Mr Gay and the | Duke of Queensberry | No date | Rx Novr 8th 1731

4806

Lady Elizabeth Germain to Swift

[4 November 1731]

I believe in my Conscience that tho you had answerd mine before the second was never the less welcome So much for your topscript not Postscript, and in very sincere earnest I heartily thank you for remembring me so often,[2] since I came out of the Country my riding days are over, for I never was for your Highpark Courses, altho My Courage serves me very well at a Hard Gallop in the Country six or seven Mile with one Horseman and a Ragged Lad a Labourers Boy that is to be Cloathed when he can run fast enough to keep up with my horse, who has yet only proved his dexterity by escaping from School, but my Courage fails me for riding in town where I shoud have the happiness to meet with plenty of your very pretty fellows that manage their own horses to show their Art or that think A Postilions Cap with a white frock the most becoming Dress there and their Grooms I am most bitterly afraid on, because you must know if my Complaisant friend your Presbyterian Housekeeper can remember any thing like such days with me thats a very good reason for me to remember that time is past and your fops woud

[1] These two lines evidently—as Swift divines in his answer to the letter—are added by the Duchess, and refer somehow to Swift's reflection on her dd's in his letter of 28 Aug. 1731. The second of the two lines comes from a piece of gibberish . . . in a letter from Lord Percival to his son written in Bath, 12 May 1730, preserved as Add. MS. 47032, pp. 329–30. The item copied into Percival's letter is alleged to be taken from an inscription 'found upon Malcoms Cross', but it is obviously jocose gibberish of a sort Swift might enjoy. The 'inscription' is in rough hexameters, and the second line reads: 'Spalando Spados sive nig fig Knippite gnaros.' Where the inscription was printed or how the Duchess got hold of it is unknown.—Sherburn.

[2] The surviving letters from Swift to Lady Betty Germain are only five in number, all later than this date.

rejoyce to see A Horse throw an antient Gentlewoman, I am sorry to hear you are no wiser in Ireland than we English for our Birthday[1] was as fine as hands coud make us, but I question much whether we all paid Ready Money. I mightily approve of my Dutchessess being dressed in your Manufacture if your Ladies will follow her example in all things they cant do amiss, and I dare say you will soon find that the more you know of them both the better you will like them, or else Ireland has strangely depraved your taste and that my own Vanity wont let me believe since you still flatter me, Why do you tantalise me, let me see you in England again if your dare and choose your Residence Summer or Winter St James Square, or Drayton, I defy you in all Shapes be it Dean of St Patricks Governing England or Ireland, or Politician Draper but my choice shoud be the Parson in Lady Bettys Chamber, make haste then if you have a mind to oblige your ever Sincere and Hearty old friend. | Lady Betty

4 Nov. 1731

Endorsed by Swift: R^d^ Novr 9th 1731 | Ldy E. Germain | Answd

Longleat xiii (Harleian transcript)

Swift to John Gay and the Duke and Duchess of Queensberry

[1 December, 1731][2]

If your ramble was on horseback I am glad of it. on account of your health, but I know your arts of patching up a journy between Stage coaches and friends coaches, for you are as arrant a cockney as any hosier in Cheap-Side, and one clean Shirt with two Cravats and as many Handkerchefs make up your equipage, and as for a night gown, it is clear from Homer, that Agamemnon rose without one I have often had it in my head to put it into yours, that you ought to have Some great work in Schemes, which may take up Seven years to finish; besides two or three underone's, that may add another thousand pounds to your Stock; and then I shall be in less pain about you, I know you can find dinners, but you love twelve penny

[1] George II's birthday on 30 Oct. was celebrated with great splendour in Dublin. See the Duke of Dorset's letter, 9 Nov., to Lady Suffolk (*Letters of Lady Suffolk*, ii. 33–36).

[2] The date subscribed to this letter was added by Lord Oxford. Since this letter is an answer to that of Gay received on 8 Nov. it may be accepted as correct.

coaches too well, without considering that the interest of a whole thousand pounds brings you but half a crown a day. I find a greater longing than ever to come amongst you, and reason good; when I am seised with Dukes and Dutchesses for a visit; all my demands complyed with and all excuses cut off; you remember; O happy Don Quixet, Queens held his horse, and Dutchesses pulled off his armor, Or Something to that purpose. He was a mean Spirited fellow, I can say ten times more O happy &c' *Such* a Dutchess was designed to attend him, and *Such* a Duke invited him to command his Palace Nam istos reges ceteros memorare nolo, hominum mendicabula:[1] go read your Plautus, and observe Strobilius vapering after he had found the pot of gold: I will have nothing to do with ⌜the house over against Ham-walks, or with⌝ the owner of it,[2] I have long hated her on your account, and the more because you are So forgiving as not to hate her. ⌜I writt her a long letter lately,[3] in answer to her last and let her know I would write to her no more, all⌝ though She has, Good qualityes enough to make her esteemed; but not one grain of truth or honour.I onely wish She were ⌜as great⌝ a fool ⌜as She is a knave⌝. I have been severall months writing near five hundred lines on a pleasant Subject, onely to tell what my friends and enemyes will say on me after I am dead.[4] I Shall finish it soon, for I add two lines every week, and blott out four, and alter eight, I have brought in you and my other friends, as well as enemyes and Detractors.

It is a great comfort to See how corruption and ill conduct are instrumental in uniting Virtuous Persons and lovers of their country of all denominations ⌜Lord B— with W. P. Sir W W with the Aimsbury;⌝[5] Whig and Tory high and low Church as Soon as they are left to think freely, all joyning in opinion. If this be disaffection, pray God Send me allways among the disaffected; And I heartily wish you joy of your Scurvy treatment at Court, which hath given you leisure to cultivate both publick and private Virtue, neither of them likely to be Soon met within the Walls of St James's or Westminster,—But I must here dismiss you that I may pay my Acknowledgements to the Duke for the great honor he hath done me.

[1] Plautus, *Aulularia*, IV. viii. 2–3. Translated by Faulkner, 1741, 'I pass by those other Princes, poor Mendicants of Mankind'.

[2] Pope's printed texts 1740–2 read, 'I will have nothing to do with that Lady'.

[3] That of 26 Oct.

[4] *Verses on the Death of Dr. Swift* (*Poems*, ii. 551–72).

[5] Lord Bolingbroke with William Pulteney, and Sir William Wyndham with the Duke and Duchess at Amesbury.

My Lord,—I could have Sworn, that my pride would be always able to preserve me from vanity, of which I have been in great danger to be guilty for some months past., first by the conduct of My Lady Dutchess and now by that of your Grace, which had like to finish the work; And I should have certainly gone about Shewing my letters under the charge of Secrecy to every blab of my acquaintance, if I could have the least hope of privayling on any of them to believe that a man in So obscure a corner quite thrown out of the present world, and within a few Steps of the next, Should receive Such condecending invitations, from two Such persons to whome he is an utter Stranger, and who know no more of him than what they have heard by the partial representations of a friend; But in the mean time, I must desire your Grace, not to flatter your Self, that I waited for your consent, to Accept the invitation. I must be ignorant indeed not to know, that the Dutchess ever Since you met, hath been most politically employd in increasing those forces., and Sharpening those arms with which She Subdued you at first., and to which, the braver and wiser you grow, you will more and more Submit. Thus I know my Self on the Secure Side, and it was a meer piece of ⌜my⌝ good manners to insert that clause, of which you have taken that advantage, But, as I cannot forbear informing Your Grace, that the Dutchess's great Secret in her art of government, hath been to reduce both your wills into one; So I am content in due observance to the forms of the world to return my most humble thanks to your Grace for so great a favor as you are pleased to offer me and which nothing but impossibilityes Shall prevent me from receiving. Since I am with the greatest reason, truth and Respect My Lord Your Graces most obedient &c.

Madam,—I have consulted all the learned in occult Sciences, of my acquaintance, and have Sate up eleven nights to discover the meaning of those two hieroglyphicall lines in your Graces hand at the bottom of the last Aimsbury letter; but all in vain Onely tis agreed, that the language is Coptick, and a very profound Behmist[1] Assures me the Style is poetick containing an Invitation[2] from a very great person of the Femal Sex to a Strange kind of man whom She never Saw, and this [is] all I can find, which after So many former Invitations will ever confirm me in that respect wherewith I am, Madam | Your Grace's most obedient &c. | ex.

Decr 1st 1731

[1] Should be Behmenist.

[2] 'Invitation' in Oxford's hand.

Faulkner 1741

John Gay and Alexander Pope to Swift

December 1, 1731.

You us'd to complain that Mr. Pope and I would not let you speak: you may now be even with me, and take it out in writing. If you don't send to me now and then, the post-office will think me of no consequence, for I have no correspondent but you. You may keep as far from us as you please, you cannot be forgotten by those who ever knew you, and therefore please me by sometimes shewing that I am not forgot by you. I have nothing to take me off from my friendship to you; I seek no new acquaintance, and court no favour; I spend no shillings in coaches or chairs to levees or great visits, and as I don't want the assistance of some that I formerly convers'd with, I will not so much as seem to seek to be a dependant. As to my studies, I have not been entirely idle, though I cannot say that I have yet perfected any thing. What I have done is something in the way of those fables I have already publish'd.[1] All the mony I get is by saving, so that by habit there may be some hopes (if I grow richer) of my becoming a miser. All misers have their excuses; The motive to my parsimony is Independance. If I were to be represented by the Dutchess (she is such a downright niggard for me) this character might not be allow'd me; but I really think I am covetous enough for any who lives at the court-end of the town, and who is as poor as myself: For I don't pretend that I am equally saving with S-lk-k.[2] Mr. Lewis desir'd you might be told that he hath five pounds of yours in his hands which he fancies you may have forgot, for he will hardly allow that a Verse-man can have a just knowledge of his own affairs. When you got rid of your law-suit, I was in hopes you had got your own, and was free from every vexation of the law: but Mr. Pope tells me you are not entirely out of your perplexity, though you have the security now in your own possession; but still your case is not so bad as Captain Gulliver's, who was ruin'd by having a decree for him with costs.[3] I have had an injunction for me against

[1] 'Volume the Second' of the *Fables* was nearing completion; but it was not published till 1738, six years after Gay's death.

[2] Charles Douglas, second Earl of Selkirk, an unpopular character. In Pope's *Epistle to Bathurst*, ll. 93–94, he is satirized as 'Harpax'.

[3] In chapter vi of 'A Voyage to Brobdingnag' Gulliver explains to the King

pyrating-booksellers, which I am sure to get nothing by, and will, I fear, in the end drain me of some money. When I begun this prosecution I fancy'd there would be some end of it, but the law still goes on, and it is probable I shall some time or other see an Attorney's bill as long as the Book. Poor Duke Disney is dead,[1] and hath left what he had among his friends, among whom are Lord Bolingbroke 500 *l.* Sir William Wyndham's youngest son, 500 *l.* Gen Hill, 500 *l.* Lord Massam's son 500 *l.*

You have the good wishes of those I converse with, they know they gratify me when they remember you; but I really think they do it purely for your own sake. I am satisfied with the love and friendship of good men, and envy not the demerits of those who are more conspicuously distinguish'd. Therefore as I set a just value upon your friendship, you cannot please me more than letting me now and then know that you remember me (the only satisfaction of distant friends!)

P.S. Mr. Gay's is a good letter, mine will be a very dull one; and yet what you will think the worst of it is what should be its excuse, that I write in a head-ach that has lasted three days. I am never ill but I think of your ailments, and repine that they mutually hinder our being together: Though in one point I am apt to differ from you, for you shun your friends when you are in those circumstances, and I desire them; your way is the more generous, mine the more tender. Lady —[2] took your letter[3] very kindly, for I had prepared her to expect no answer under a twelve-month; but kindness perhaps is a word not applicable to courtiers. However she is an extraordinary woman there, who will do you common justice. For God's sake why all this scruple about Lord B—'s[4] keeping your horses who has a park, or about my keeping you on a pint of wine a day? We are infinitely richer than you imagine; John Gay shall help me to entertain you, tho' you come like King Lear with fifty Knights[5]—Tho' such prospects as I wish, cannot now be formed for fixing you with us, time may provide better before you part again: the old

how he had 'been previously almost ruined by a long suit in chancery which was decreed for me with costs'.

[1] He died on 21 Nov. 1731 and was buried in the east cloister of Westminster Abbey.

[2] Lady Suffolk.

[3] That of 26 Oct.

[4] Bolingbroke's.

[5] *King Lear*, II. iv. 260.

Lord[1] may die, the benefice may drop,[2] or at worst, you may carry me into Ireland. You will see a word of Lord B—'s and one of mine;[3] which with a just neglect of the present age, consult only posterity; and with a noble scorn of Politicks, aspire to Philosophy. I am glad you resolve to meddle no more with the low concerns and interests of Parties, even of Countries, (for Countries are but larger parties) *Quid verum atque decens, curare, & rogare, nostrum sit.*[4] I am much pleased with your design upon Rochefoucault's maxim, pray finish it.[5] I am happy whenever you join our names together: so would Dr. Arbuthnot be, but at this time can be pleas'd with nothing; for his darling son is dying in all probability, by the melancholy account I received this morning.[6]

The paper you ask me about is of little value.[7] It might have been a seasonable satire upon the scandalous language and passion with which men of condition have stooped to treat one another: surely they sacrifice too much to the people, when they sacrifice their own characters, families, &c. to the diversion of that rabble of readers. I agree with you in my contempt of most popularity, fame, &c. even as a writer I am cool in it, and whenever you see what I am now writing, you'll be convinced I would please but a few, and (if I could) make mankind less Admirers, and greater Reasoners. I study much more to render my own portion of Being easy, and to keep this peevish frame of the human body in good humour. Infirmities have not quite unman'd me, and it will delight you to hear they are not increased, tho' not diminished. I thank God I do not very much want people to attend me, tho' my Mother now cannot. When I am sick I lie down, when I am better I rise up: I am used to the head-ach, &c. If greater pains arrive (such as my late rheumatism) the

[1] Bolingbroke's father, who lived until 1742.

[2] The benefice Bolingbroke hoped to secure for Swift to bring him back to England.

[3] See the 'Essays Addressed to Mr. Pope' in vols. iii and iv of Mallet's edition of Bolingbroke's *Works*; and Pope's *Essay on Man*.

[4] 'We spend our Time in the Search and Enquiry after Truth and Decency.' —Faulkner. Hor. *Ep.* I. i. 11. Adapted.

[5] The maxim of Rochefoucauld, 'Dans l'adversité de nos meilleurs amis nous trouvons quelque chose, qui ne nous desplaist pas'. Translated by Swift both in prose and verse at the beginning of *Verses on the Death of Dr. Swift* (*Poems*, ii. 551, 553).

[6] The Rev. Charles Arbuthnot, second son of the Doctor, died 2 Dec.

[7] Probably Arbuthnot's *Brief Account of Mr. John Ginglicutt's Treatise*. Perhaps it was under consideration for the *Miscellanies* of 1732.

servants bathe and plaster me, or the surgeon scarifies me, and I bear it, because I must. This is the evil of Nature, not of Fortune. I am just now as well as when you was here: I pray God you were no worse. I sincerely wish my life were past near you, and such as it is I would not repine at it.—All you mention remember you, and wish you here.

W. R. Le Fanu

Swift to Mrs. Fenton (?)

Dublin Dec^{br} 28th 1731

Madam[1]

I have received for some time past many accounts of the Scituation your family is in at present

[1] Mr. W. R. Le Fanu has in his possession the autograph manuscript of Swift's pamphlet 'On the Bill for the Clergy's residing on their livings'. On the last page Swift has written the above scrap of a letter. This may be the beginning of a letter addressed to his sister, Mrs. Fenton, to whom it appears that at this time he was paying an annuity. In his letter to Gay of 19 Mar. 1729–30 he writes, 'I pay an Annuity of 15*ll* per Ann: in Surrey, and shall soon send you a direction for part of it'. The pamphlet above mentioned is printed from Swift's autograph in *Prose Works*, ed. H. Davis, xii. 179–86.

PRINTED IN GREAT BRITAIN
AT THE UNIVERSITY PRESS, OXFORD
BY VIVIAN RIDLER
PRINTER TO THE UNIVERSITY